PUBLIC INTEREST LITIGATION IN SOUTH AFRICA

PUBLIC INTEREST LITIGATION IN SOUTH AFRICA

Jason Brickhill

(Contributing Editor)

JUTA

First Published 2018

© Juta and Co (Pty) Ltd First Floor, Sunclare Building, 21 Dreyer Street, Claremont, 7708, Cape Town

ISBN: 978-1-48512-816-8

The mural used on the front cover appears on a building in downtown Johannesburg, and is used with the permission of the artist, Faith XLVII

Set in 11 on 12 Point Times Roman
Cover design by: Matthew Bubear-Craemer
Typesetting by: B Hopking
Printed and bound by:

DEDICATION

For my mother and father, Joan and Jeremy,
who taught me that every struggle depends on love, solidarity and comradeship,
and good music,
and who have always found my choice of law just a little strange.

FOREWORD

Engagement in any struggle for democracy, equality and dignity must involve the pursuit of justice. *Public Interest Litigation in South Africa* has brought together various social activists who write about their own involvement in this struggle and pursuit through the use of courts and the law.

This volume is a collection of reflections that focus on a modest slice of South Africa's history, which has seen political struggle enmeshed with law and constitutionalism for well over a century. It focuses on the period after the 1994 establishment of the constitutional state. Each chapter recognises the courts (including the cases that have not reached the Constitutional Court) as one site of struggle, while simultaneously seeking to relate this to various social actors who use the law as part of their tactics and strategies.

When dealing with a country which has established political freedom but is so lacking in economic justice, this book asks probing questions about the impact—actual and potential—of public interest litigation (PIL) on the objectives of social movements, individuals and organisations involved in activism and resistance; in the quest for justice, economic restructuring and change. As asserted in one of the quotations in the book: 'For many South Africans, the law is not an effective protection against those who have greater political, economic or physical power.'[1]

The PIL sector in South Africa consists of a range of civil society organisations that employ litigation as but one strategy to seek and effect systemic change. In mapping this sector, this volume notes that not all strategic litigation constitutes PIL. There is also a distinction drawn between two forms of organisations: those who provide legal representation (public interest law centres); and activist or campaigning organisations that use litigation as one strategy amongst others for social change (public interest litigants). In addition, given the breadth and complexity of the law and the interconnectedness and overlap of rights, the notion of 'single-issue' public interest organisations is misleading.

Throughout the book there are reflections that range from whether lawyers have a special role in transforming South Africa to questions around the nature of law itself. It is clear that those lawyers who have engaged in this work seek to improve the lives of the poor; bring significant expertise into play; and attempt to advance constitutional rights not only in law but also in practice. They have been pioneers in this complex endeavour. In addition, throughout the book, some thoughts are offered about the effectiveness of collaboration within the social justice sector and some of the current challenges faced by and critiques about the organisations that constitute this sector are raised.

Importantly, this is a book that encompasses both broader, theoretical discussions including the nature, content and definition of PIL, while also including reflections on litigation in substantive areas of South African law. In doing so, it emphasises the importance of empirical grounding in any consideration of PIL.

---

[1] G Budlender 'On practising law' in H Corder (ed) *Essays on Law and Social Practice in South Africa* (1988) 331.

Given the normativity of constitutionalism, part of legal strategy which concerns lawyers throughout the world is the use of litigation to pursue objectives that extend beyond the interests of individual litigants through cases that encompass issues with far-reaching implications for the rule of law. In this book, the development of legal doctrine is considered alongside such possibilities.

The interface between PIL and the range of social actors to achieve meaningful social change is evident throughout these pages. Different strategies and tactics that such interactions may benefit from can be seen in the reflections about actual work—highlighting both opportunities and shortcomings. It is clear that PIL on its own will not eradicate poverty. The question posed by some of the authors is where and how it can and does contribute.

The book attempts to provide a framework for examination of the role and impact of PIL and grapples with the vexed question of attribution: how are we to link social change in complex situations to any tangible contribution of PIL? How do we understand 'impact'—legal, material and political—and how can it be measured over the short, medium and long term? Some ideas are offered and these contribute to a more grounded understanding.

From the detailed references to the care taken to provide the extensive lists of cases and organisations, links and resources—this book is a treasure-trove for those seeking to engage in and learn more about PIL.

JANET LOVE
AUGUST 2018

FOREWORD

Public interest litigation has a rich history in South Africa, although it was only from the late 1970s that it was given that label. The scope and opportunities for public interest litigation of course increased hugely after the adoption of a democratic constitution. The most obvious reason for this is the extensive rights which were recognised by the interim Constitution and then the final Constitution.

But also very important are the procedural advances that have been made—some of them explicitly stated in the Constitution, and others found by the courts. This should not be surprising. The procedural innovations of the courts in post-emergency India opened up the field, and led to opportunities which were previously unimaginable in courts which follow the English procedural tradition.

We have seen the same in South Africa. Enhanced standing to approach the courts has been critical to public interest litigation. It is the result of section 38 of the Constitution, post-apartheid statutes, and a new willingness on the part of the courts to recognise the need to facilitate, and not obstruct, the accountability of government. Also of great importance has been the *Biowatch* judgment and its progeny. This has enabled would-be litigants to seek to enforce the Constitution without undue fear of an adverse costs order. We have not had to invent protective costs orders, which limit the potential costs liability of litigants, though their time may yet come.

Post-1994 public interest litigation has achieved remarkable—even extraordinary—success in a substantial number of fields. That is demonstrated by this volume, if such demonstration is needed. In my view, there are six major challenges that have to be addressed.

First, we have achieved limited success in addressing the very difficult issue of the content and enforcement of the positive obligation to take reasonable measures to achieve the progressive realisation of social and economic rights. There has been mixed success in building on the early promise of *Grootboom*.

Second, we have had limited success in addressing the needs of rural South Africans, and in particular their land rights and their rights against oppressive or unaccountable 'traditional authorities'. This reflects in part the geographic distribution of public interest law organisations and those whom they represent. The urban bias remains real.

The third challenge is related to this. The current ferment about the constitutional property clause reflects the dismal failure of government to give effect to the transformative provisions of subsections (5) to (9) of section 25, which are intended to act as a counter-balance to the protection of existing property rights. Public interest litigants and organisations have not addressed this issue effectively.

Fourth, recent years teach us the truth of what was said by Chris Hansen:[2] the most difficult public interest litigation does not deal with government which is *inattentive* to its obligations, or government which is *intransigent* in giving effect to rights. The most difficult public interest litigation deals with government which is willing but *incompetent* in carrying out its obligations. That was a key lesson of public interest litigation in the USA. It is now a key lesson in South Africa. The litigation around the government's failure to implement the Land Reform (Labour Tenants) Act has demonstrated the difficulties. We need courts to develop innovative procedures and remedies to address this problem. Costs orders against recalcitrant office-bearers are helpful, but they are a blunt instrument.

Fifth, there has thus far been limited major public interest litigation against private actors. The silicosis class action is a notable exception. Private actors have substantial obligations under the Constitution and under post-apartheid legislation.

Sixth, we have not adequately developed the habit and practice of public interest litigation as part of, rather than as a substitute for, democratic process. About 40 years ago an American public interest lawyer, Gary Bellow, said that the worst thing a lawyer can do is take an issue that could be won by political organisation, and win it in the courts. We need to think more about that.

To identify these challenges is not to dispute the power and potential of public interest litigation. This volume demonstrates that it has had major positive impacts on the lives of many millions of South Africans. It would be empty and self-defeating to deny the huge achievements. Public interest litigation has done much to bring a democratic and transformative Constitution to life. But there is much more to be done.

GEOFF BUDLENDER
AUGUST 2018

---

[2] Chris Hansen 'Making it work: Implementation of court orders requiring restructuring of state executive branch agencies' in SR Humm *Child, Parent and State* (1994) 224–233.

PREFACE

The idea for this book was born when I was working at the Legal Resources Centre, in the heart of the public interest sector in South Africa. Across various organisations that use the law as an instrument for social justice, many people work daily on specific court cases and advocacy campaigns. These organisations are sustained, in their fight for social justice, by the dedication and commitment of their front desk receptionists, paralegals, advocacy and communications officers, finance officers, secretaries and administrative staff, candidate attorneys, researchers, cleaners, management, and lawyers.

This is a book about the law, but it is not a legal textbook. The authors in this volume do not purport to offer a dispassionate, 'objective' description of the law or the process of its development. Instead, the book offers grounded accounts—by leaders in the field—of the campaigns, cases, and causes that have defined key areas of public interest litigation in South Africa since the constitutional transition. The authors share their perspectives on the struggles led by people, communities, activists, and civil society organisations to realise the vision of the Constitution. The book shares the legal narratives of those particular struggles in the hope that this will contribute to the broader, ongoing struggle for social justice. Law sustains and reinforces many of the injustices of contemporary South Africa, but it is also simultaneously an instrument of struggle and a tool for empowerment. It is being used every single day, right across the country, to fight for the equality, dignity and freedom that were promised in the Constitution but remain elusive. This book seeks to share more of the stories of what has been achieved in the courts, beyond the well-trodden, landmark appellate decisions, as a contribution to informed and critical engagement.

In 2014, a workshop was convened at the University of the Witwatersrand, Johannesburg, at which ideas for chapters and the beginnings of draft chapters were presented and discussed. Since then, many people have contributed to making this book a reality. Linda van de Vijver of Juta showed sustained faith in the project, patience with its contributors, and commitment to the quality of the product. I also acknowledge the efforts of all those at Juta who contributed to this book, including working on the cover, editing and proof-reading and type-setting. The authors are all engaged in the struggle for social justice in South Africa on a daily basis. They have carved out time and headspace from their work to reflect and to write. Some potential authors did not manage to escape the trenches to write up their work—not for lack of industry, but because their priority is rightly their clients. Those accounts are still to be written. The reviewer—Michael Bishop— provided insightful and valuable suggestions that improved the final product. Many others generously provided comments on draft chapters and they are acknowledged in those chapters. Justice Edwin Cameron agreed to an interview with me and Tshidiso Ramogale at the start of this project, helping to shape it in its formative stages. Former Deputy Chief Justice Dikgang Moseneke provided encouraging comments on the draft manuscript. Janet Love and Geoff Budlender, both of whom have contributed so much to the public interest sector, each generously agreed to write a foreword.

One of the things that I most enjoyed, and from which I drew most strength and inspiration while working in the public interest sector, was working with and learning from the wonderfully talented people entering the legal profession. A quintet of such lawyers—destined to leave their imprint on the profession—worked with me on this project. Tess Peacock worked with me from the start, helping to convene the initial planning workshop in Johannesburg in 2014, communicating with authors and assisting with editing. Meghan Finn, Tshidiso Ramogale, Michael Tsele and Lara Wallis then joined the enterprise, providing editorial assistance and research support for some chapters. Lara helped to prepare the list of organisations and the contributors' biographies and provided research on the public interest sector today. Tshidiso did substantial research on the history of public interest litigation, and Michael unearthed material on judicial appointments and the relationship of the judiciary to the political branches. Meghan co-authored chapter 3 on the ethics and politics of public interest litigation with me. All five of them have provided valuable support at different stages that has enabled me to carry this project to fruition.

Sanya Samtani sustained me through the project. She provided a sounding board, read and improved my writing, and inspired the book's cover. She discovered the artist Faith XLVII's evocative mural in downtown Johannesburg proclaiming the promise of the Freedom Charter. Sanya tracked down Faith XLVII and Faith agreed to the use of the image. A copy of the Freedom Charter hangs in the home that Sanya and I share. It is a reminder—of a vision unrealised, and of the power of ideas in committed hands.

Jason Brickhill
Johannesburg and Oxford, August 2018

CONTENTS

CONTRIBUTORS

CLARE BALLARD is an attorney of the High Court of South Africa. Clare holds a BA and LLB from the University of Cape Town and an LLM from Cornell University. She established LHR's Penal Reform Programme in 2014. Prior to her appointment to LHR, Clare spent several years doing research work in the fields of penology and constitutional law at the Community Law Centre, University of the Western Cape. In addition to her practice, Clare sits on a number of advisory committees and lectures on an ad hoc basis at the University of Cape Town. She is also a former clerk of the Constitutional Court.

SAMANTHA BRENER is an attorney at SECTION27, focusing on the right to basic education. She has an LLB and a BSc Hons from the University of the Witwatersrand. Prior to her time at SECTION27, she spent two years as a researcher in education and children's rights at the Legal Resources Centre. She has had stints as an attorney in a public law team at Cliffe Dekker Hofmeyr, and as a Constitutional Court clerk to Justice Johan Froneman.

JASON BRICKHILL is a practising advocate and academic. He is also Research Director, Oxford Human Rights Hub and an Honorary Research Associate, University of Cape Town. He holds an LLB from the University of Cape Town and an MSt from the University of Oxford. He is currently completing a DPhil at Oxford on strategic litigation in South Africa. He began his career as law clerk to Justice O'Regan at the Constitutional Court. After a stint at Bowman Gilfillan, he worked at the LRC as an attorney and later advocate (2008–2016), and served as Director of its Constitutional Litigation Unit (2014–2016). He has litigated a wide range of matters across all areas of constitutional law and human rights law. Jason has taught constitutional law at the University of the Witwatersrand and human rights law at Oxford. He has published widely and is a co-author of *Constitutional Litigation* (2014) and an editor of the *Constitutional Court Review*.

MAX DU PLESSIS SC is an Associate Fellow, Chatham House; Senior Researcher, Institute for Security Studies; Advocate of the High Court of South Africa; Associate Tenant, Doughty Street Chambers, London; and Honorary Research Fellow, University of KwaZulu-Natal. He holds the degrees BIuris (SA), LLB (Natal), LLM (Cambridge), and PhD (UKZN). Max is an advocate in South Africa and senior counsel. As an advocate in South Africa (and associate tenant, Doughty Street Chambers, London), he has an extensive practice in public law, human rights and international law. As an international criminal lawyer he has advised states and NGOs before the International Criminal Court and has represented NGOs in domestic (complementarity and universal jurisdiction) public interest cases dealing with arrest warrants for senior government officials implicated in international crimes, and litigating and advising on them in South Africa and other countries. He has written widely on constitutional law issues in South

Africa, including as co-author of *Constitutional Litigation* (2014) and *Class Action Litigation in South Africa* (2017).

JACKIE DUGARD is an associate professor at the School of Law, University of the Witwatersrand, where she lectures Property Law and Constitutional Law. Jackie holds a BA (Hons) from the University of Witwatersrand, an MPhil and PhD from Cambridge University, an LLM from the University of Essex and an LLB from the University of the Witwatersrand. Jackie is on the editorial committee of the *South African Journal on Human Rights*. She was a co-founder and first executive director (2010–2012) of the Socio-Economic Rights Institute of South Africa (SERI). Jackie was the founder and first director of the Gender Equity Office (GEO) at the University of the Witwatersrand (2014–2016). While at the Centre for Applied Legal Studies (CALS), Jackie was involved in public interest litigation on water (*Mazibuko*) and electricity (*Joseph*) (2004–2009). She has published widely on the role of law and courts in social change, socio-economic rights, access to courts, protest and social movements, and property.

MEGHAN FINN is a practising advocate and member of the Johannesburg Bar. She holds BSocSci and LLB degrees from the University of Cape Town, and a BCL degree from the University of Oxford. Meghan previously worked as a law clerk at the Constitutional Court of South Africa to Justice van der Westhuizen, and as a researcher at SAIFAC, a centre of the University of Johannesburg. Meghan has published academic papers on administrative law in the *South African Journal on Human Rights* and *Constitutional Court Review* and is a contributing writer on constitutional law for Juta's *Annual Survey of South Africa Law* and *Quarterly Review*. Her areas of practice are constitutional, administrative and public interest law. She has been counsel in matters focused on administrative justice, principles of constitutional accountability and on the rights to equality, health care, social security and children's rights.

GEORGINA JEPHSON is an attorney at Richard Spoor Inc Attorneys. She is the lead attorney in a class action brought against the South African gold mining industry on behalf of mineworkers with silicosis. Georgina is currently completing an LLM by dissertation on class action law. In May 2016, the High Court certified a class of gold mineworkers with silicosis and the dependents of those who have died as a result of silicosis, and ordered that Richard Spoor Inc, together with Abrahams Kiewitz Inc and the Legal Resources Centre, are the legal representatives of the class (*Nkala and Others v Harmony Gold Mining Company Ltd and Others* 2016 (5) SA 240 (GJ)). Before joining Richard Spoor Inc in 2011, Georgina worked as a research clerk at the Constitutional Court for former Deputy Chief Justice Dikgang Moseneke and she completed her articles at the Wits University Law Clinic.

MELANIE JUDGE is Adjunct Associate Professor in the Faculty of Law at the University of Cape Town. Melanie holds a PhD in Women's and Gender Studies and a Masters in Development Studies from the University of the Western Cape, an Honours in Psychology from the University of Cape Town, and a Business Management Diploma. As a prominent activist for queer rights, Melanie has been extensively involved in litigation, advocacy, public education and research both locally and internationally. Her work on LGBT rights is widely published on academic platforms and in the popular media. She is the author of *Blackwashing Homophobia: Violence and the Politics of Gender, Sexuality and Race* and lead editor of *To Have and To Hold: The Making of Same-sex Marriage in South Africa*. Melanie is an executive member of the Sexuality and Gender Division of the Psychological Society of South Africa and a trustee of GALA, the national queer archives.

CAMERON MCCONNACHIE is an attorney and Regional Director of the Legal Resources Centre's Grahamstown office. Cameron completed an MPhil at the University of Cape Town and an LLB at Rhodes University. He was a school teacher for six years before beginning his legal career at the Legal Resources Centre. His practice has focused on litigating the right to basic education and has included matters dealing with mud schools, minimum norms and standards for school infrastructure, furniture, and scholar transport. Cameron co-authored 'Concretising the Right to a Basic Education', published in the *South African Law Journal* in 2012. A second paper, expanding on the jurisprudence set out in that article, is currently being written.

BONITA MEYERSFELD is a human rights lawyer and academic. Bonita obtained her LLB from the University of the Witwatersrand and her LLM and doctorate in law from Yale Law School. She is an associate professor at the School of Law, University of the Witwatersrand and from 2012 to 2017 she was director of the Centre for Applied Legal Studies. She is an editor and chair of the board of the *South African Journal on Human Rights* and the founding member and chair of the board of Lawyers against Abuse. Bonita teaches and publishes in the areas of international law, business and human rights, women's rights and international criminal law. Prior to her time at the University of the Witwatersrand, Bonita worked in human rights law in the House of Lords and has worked at various non-governmental organisations in the United States, the United Kingdom and South Africa. Bonita has presented expert statements to various United Nations fora and was appointed by the Government of Ecuador as part of a five-member expert panel to provide guidance to the Inter-Governmental Working Group on a binding instrument for business and human rights. She is the author of the book, *Domestic Violence and International Law*.

DARIO MILO is a partner at Webber Wentzel attorneys, where he leads a media and information law team. He also lectures in media law, access to information law, and privacy law at the University of the Witwatersrand, where he is an adjunct professor. He holds a BComm, LLB and LLM from the University of Witwatersrand and an LLM and PhD from University College London. He is the author of *Defamation and Freedom of Speech*, published by Oxford University Press in 2008 and co-author of *A Practical Guide to Media Law*. He has acted for the media and NGOs in numerous high profile cases decided by the South African courts. Dario frequently appears for clients in Parliament, the BCCSA, the Press Council, the Films and Publications Board, ICASA, and the ASA. He is ranked as a leading lawyer in the field of media and broadcasting law by the international publication, Chambers Global. Dario tweets on media and information law developments under the handle @dariomilo.

OSMOND MNGOMEZULU is an attorney working at the South African Human Rights Commission (SAHRC). He is currently completing an LLM in Human Rights Law. Prior to joining the SAHRC, Osmond worked for the Centre for Applied Legal Studies, Wits Law Clinic, Socio-economic Rights Institute of South Africa, ProBono.Org and Lawyers for Human Rights. Osmond has extensive experience in public interest litigation. His areas of interest are environmental justice, access to socio-economic rights (housing, health and basic services) and access to justice. He was involved in a number of seminal socio-economic rights cases, including *Occupiers of Saratoga Avenue v City of Johannesburg*; *Occupiers of 51 Olivia Road v City of Johannesburg and Others*; *Pheko and Others v Ekurhuleni Metropolitan Municipality*; and *Mazibuko and Others v City of Johannesburg and Others*.

NOMONDE NYEMBE is an Advocate of the High Court of South Africa and pupil member of the Johannesburg Bar. Before commencing pupillage, she was an attorney in, and head of, the Business and Human Rights Programme at the Centre for Applied Legal Studies. She holds an LLB from the University of the Witwatersrand and an LLM in public interest law and policy with a focus on Gender, Health and Human Rights from the University of California, Los Angeles. Nomonde completed her legal articles at a corporate law firm, before serving as a law clerk to then Justice Mogoeng Mogoeng at the Constitutional Court. Prior to joining CALS, Nomonde was a Policy Advocacy and Development Associate at Sonke Gender Justice.

TESS PEACOCK currently works at Tshikululu as a Social Investment Specialist where she leads the early childhood development and early literacy work for the FirstRand Foundation and FirstRand Empowerment Foundation. She holds a BSocSci and LLB from the University of Cape Town and an LLM from Harvard University. She is an admitted attorney and completed her law articles of clerkship with Webber Wentzel Attorneys before moving to the Legal Resources Centre as their first researcher on a Ford Foundation International Human Rights project. She then clerked at the Constitutional Court with Justice Cameron and with Acting Justices Leeuw and Jappie. After completing her LLM at Harvard Law School, Tess spent a year working for a remote rural NGO, the Bulungula Incubator, as their Innovation Hub Manager, to obtain grassroots health and education experience.

TSHIDISO RAMOGALE is an Advocate of the High Court of South Africa and a pupil member of the Johannesburg Bar. Tshidiso is a graduate of the University of the Witwatersrand and Harvard Law School. He is also a former clerk of the Constitutional Court and a former legal officer at the South African Human Rights Commission. At Harvard, Tshidiso was the Managing Executive Editor of the *Harvard Human Rights Journal*. His main areas of interest are in constitutional, administrative and competition law.

STUART SCOTT is an Advocate of the High Court of South Africa and a member of the Johannesburg Bar and Group 621 Chambers. He balances a commercial practice focusing on competition law, company law, public procurement, and international law with pro bono and strategic public interest cases, including making submissions on South African hate speech laws for a coalition of well-known South African comedians (including Pieter-Dirk Uys, Chester Missing, Zapiro, and Kagiso Lediga); acting for asylum seekers before the Refugee Appeal Board; and participating in an ongoing constitutional challenge to South Africa's surveillance laws. Before joining the Bar, he completed articles at Webber Wentzel and clerked for Justice Sisi Khampepe at the Constitutional Court. He has published widely in the fields of administrative law, constitutional law and freedom of expression, including co-authoring a chapter in the upcoming edition of *A Practical Guide to Media Law*. He was a Researcher for *The Cambridge University Pro Bono Project* contributing to research papers which sought to reform the international supervision of the United Nations Refugee Convention.

AVANI SINGH is a practising attorney of the High Court of South Africa, and director and co-founder of ALT Advisory and Power Singh Incorporated. Avani's work focuses on international and constitutional law, with a particular interest in media law, digital rights and the intersection of law and technology. ALT Advisory, in association with Power Singh Incorporated, works to develop the (private) public interest law model in South Africa by offering legal advisory, research, training and litigation assistance to clients on a range of media and public law matters. Avani holds BComm (Law) and LLB degrees from the University of Pretoria, and is studying towards an MSt in International Human Rights Law at the University of Oxford. She previously practised as an attorney in the Constitutional Litigation Unit at the Legal Resources Centre and the Information Law team at Webber Wentzel. She also clerked for Justice Thembile Skweyiya at the Constitutional Court and Judge Eboe-Osuji at the International Criminal Court.

ANN SKELTON has worked as a children's rights lawyer in South Africa for over 25 years. She holds a BA and LLB degrees from the University of KwaZulu-Natal and an LLD from the University of Pretoria. She played a leading role in child law reform through her involvement with the committees of the South African Law Reform Commission. Ann is currently the Director of the Centre for Child Law and a Law Professor at the University of Pretoria, where she also holds the UNESCO Chair in Education Law. As an advocate, she frequently appears in the superior courts arguing children's rights issues in public interest law matters. She is an internationally recognised researcher and has published widely. In 2012 she received the World's Children's Honorary Award, presented by the Queen of Sweden. In December 2016 she received the Juvenile Justice Without Borders award presented by the International Observatory on Juvenile Justice. Ann is currently a member of the UN Committee on the Rights of the Child, her term of office having started in 2017.

MICHAEL TSELE is an advocate of the High Court of South Africa. Michael holds a BA LLB from Rhodes University. He served articles of clerkship at the Legal Resources Centre. For two years, he was a sessional lecturer of constitutional litigation at Rhodes University's Faculty of Law. He is a member of the executive committee of the Environmental Law Association of South Africa (ELSA). He has published in accredited journals on matters ranging from administrative and constitutional law to child law.

LARA WALLIS is a public interest lawyer. She holds an LLB and an LLM in Human Rights Law, both from the University of Cape Town. Lara is an admitted attorney, having completed her articles through the Legal Resources Centre in Cape Town where she worked across a range of programmes, including refugee rights, environmental law, equality and non-discrimination, land rights and housing rights. Following this, Lara joined the Centre for Environmental Rights as a Researcher in the Corporate Accountability Programme. Lara has written op-eds and research pieces in the field of refugee rights, and she contributed to the CER's 'Full Disclosure' series of reports on the environmental track record of South African companies. From 2017 to 2018, Lara clerked for Justice Mhlantla and Acting Justice Cachalia at the Constitutional Court of South Africa. Lara is currently completing a second LLM through Columbia Law School as a 2018–2019 Columbia Human Rights Fellow.

KERRY WILLIAMS is an advocate of the High Court of South Africa. She was previously an attorney and partner at Webber Wentzel. She holds an LLB from the University of Cape Town, an LLM from the University of London, and an MPA from the John F. Kennedy School of Government at Harvard University. She has run both a commercial public law practice and a pro bono practice dedicated to protecting and promoting LGBTI rights. Her clients have included individuals, organs of state, global and local businesses and non-profit organisations. She has written academically on topics including public procurement, same-sex marriage, hate crimes and pharmaceutical price regulation.

STUART WILSON is a practising advocate, a visiting senior fellow at Wits Law School, a member of the Johannesburg Bar, and the executive director of the Socio-Economic Rights Institute of South Africa (SERI). His public interest litigation work focuses on socio-economic rights, freedom of expression, protest rights and criminal defence. He has particular expertise in land and housing law.

He has written widely on the politics of law and litigation. His publications include 'Litigating Housing Rights in Johannesburg's Inner City: 2004–2008', published in the *South African Journal on Human Rights* and 'Breaking the Tie: Evictions, Homelessness and the New Normality', published in the *South African Law Journal*.

LIST OF ORGANISATIONS

This list includes public interest law centres that conduct litigation, organisations that fund public interest litigation, and organisations that often intervene in public interest matters as *amici curiae*. The acronyms set out in this list are used in the case citations throughout the book and in the Table of Cases to reflect the involvement of these organisations in specific cases.

NAME	ACRONYM	WEBSITE
Abahlali baseMjondolo	Abahlali	www.abahlali.org
ALT Advisory	ALT	www.altadvisory.africa
Bertha Foundation	Bertha	www.berthafoundation.org
Canon Collins Trust	Canon Collins	www.canoncollins.org.uk
Centre for Applied Legal Studies	CALS	www.wits.ac.za/cals
Centre for Child Law	CCL	www.centreforchildlaw.co.za
Centre for Environmental Rights	CER	www.cer.org.za
Centre for Housing Rights and Evictions	COHRE	www.cohre.org
Claude Leon Foundation	Leon Foundation	www.leonfoundation.co.za
Comic Relief		www.comicrelief.com
Community Law and Rural Development Centre (previously Community Law Centre)	CLRDC	www.clrdc.org.za
Constitutionalism Fund		www.constitutionalismfund.co.za
Corruption Watch	CW	www.corruptionwatch.org.za
Council for the Advancement of the South African Constitution	CASAC	www.casac.org.za
ELMA Foundation	ELMA	www.elmaphilanthropies.org
Equal Education	EE	www.equaleducation.org.za
Equal Education Law Centre	EELC	eelawcentre.org.za
Foundation for Human Rights	FHR	www.fhr.org.za
Freedom of Expression Institute	FXI	www.fxi.org.za
Freedom Under Law	FUL	www.freedomunderlaw.org
Helen Suzman Foundation	HSF	www.hsf.org.za
Justice Alliance of South Africa	JASA	www.justicealliance.co.za

NAME	ACRONYM	WEBSITE
Lawyers for Human Rights	LHR	www.lhr.org.za
Legal Aid South Africa	LASA	www.legal-aid.co.za
Legal Resources Centre	LRC	www.lrc.org.za
National Coalition for Gay and Lesbian Equality (later Lesbian and Gay Equality Project)	NCGLE	N/A
Natural Justice	NJ	www.naturaljustice.org
Ndifuna Ukwazi	NU	www.nu.org.za
Open Society Foundation for South Africa	OSF-SA	www.osf.org.za
Power Singh Inc	Power Singh	www.powersingh.africa
ProBono.Org	PB	www.probono.org.za
Raith Foundation	Raith	www.raith.org.za
Scalabrini Centre	Scalabrini	www.scalabrini.org.za
SECTION27	SECTION27	www.section27.org.za
Sigrid Rausing Trust	SRT	www.sigrid-rausing-trust.org
Sonke Gender Justice	Sonke	www.genderjustice.org.za
Socio-Economic Rights Institute of South Africa	SERI	www.seri.org.za
South African Human Rights Commission	SAHRC	www.sahrc.org.za
Treatment Action Campaign	TAC	www.tac.org.za
University of Cape Town Refugee Rights Unit	Refugee Rights Unit	www.refugeerights.uct.ac.za
University of the Witwatersrand Law Clinic	Wits Law Clinic	www.wits.ac.za/lawclinic
Webber Wentzel	WW	www.webberwentzel.com
Women's Legal Centre	WLC	www.wlce.co.za

TABLE OF CASES

[Below each case citation, the involvement of any organisations appearing in the List of Organisations is noted in square brackets, eg '[LHR acted for the applicants; EE was admitted as *amicus curiae*, represented by SERI]'. The full names and websites of the organisations appear in the List of Organisations. These organisations include public interest law centres and organisations that regularly engage in public interest litigation, either as primary litigants or as intervening parties or *amici curiae*.]

SOUTH AFRICA

PART I

GENERAL THEMES

Chapter 1

INTRODUCTION: THE PAST, PRESENT AND PROMISE OF PUBLIC INTEREST LITIGATION IN SOUTH AFRICA

Jason Brickhill[1]

[1] The writing of this chapter has been informed by my experience working at the Legal Resources Centre (LRC) from 2008 to 2016, as an attorney and later counsel and Director of its Constitutional Litigation Unit. I acknowledge the deep influence of the LRC and my colleagues there on this work, as well as colleagues at other public interest organisations with whom I have collaborated and who have also shaped many of the views in this chapter. I am indebted to Allie Wilson, Michael Tsele, Tshidiso Ramogale and Lara Wallis for research assistance. Justice Edwin Cameron kindly agreed to an interview at the start of this project, which helped to shape it. I also received valuable comments on an earlier draft from Nurina Ally, Geoff Budlender, Jackie Dugard, Gilbert Marcus, Kaajal Ramjathan-Keogh, Sanya Samtani, Mandisa Shandu, Ann Skelton, Nikki Stein, Wim Trengove and many of the contributors to the rest of this volume. This chapter has also been influenced by my ongoing doctoral research at the University of Oxford, under the supervision of Prof Kate O'Regan and Prof Sandra Fredman.

1.1 INTRODUCTION

'The People Shall Govern!' declared the first clause of the Freedom Charter, adopted on 25 and 26 June 1955 by the Congress of the People in Kliptown, Johannesburg. This political demand reflected the reality of the day—that the vast majority of South Africans were deprived of the right to self-govern and to vote. The racist legal system of apartheid made any meaningful political participation impossible. Despite the entrenchment of apartheid through law, poor people, communities and activists turned to the courts for redress in what, even then, was called 'public interest litigation'. How could the disenfranchised and oppressed ever hope to secure any relief from the judicial arm of the apartheid state which excluded them from the polity? How could litigation in such courts pursue the 'public interest' at all? But indeed, the courts were one site of struggle. People's continued faith in the role of law in resisting the apartheid state was one of its paradoxes.[2] Though severely constrained by the substantive and procedural legal terrain, public interest litigation (PIL) was possible during apartheid, and yielded outcomes that at the very least mitigated some of the worst excesses of apartheid.

The demand that 'the people' must govern was never limited to formal political representation. Throughout the freedom struggle, it was articulated as a demand for economic equality, realisation of human rights, and fair access to social goods, status, and opportunities. This demand—framed in the language of human rights and constitutionalism—runs like a golden thread through the twentieth century history of resistance in South Africa, at intervals being refined and re-articulated in important written claims instruments.[3] In 1923, African lawyers working through the African National Congress (ANC) prepared the 'African Bill of Rights for South Africa'.[4] Two decades later, at its annual conference in December 1943, the ANC adopted the Africans' Claims in South Africa which set out a proposed Bill

---

[2] Regarding the period of the late nineteenth and early twentieth centuries, see Tembeka Ngcukai-tobi *The Land Is Ours: Black Lawyers and the Birth of Constitutionalism in South Africa* (2018). Regarding the period from 1980–1994, see Richard L Abel *Politics by Other Means: Law in the Struggle against Apartheid, 1980–1994* (1995). See also biographical accounts, such as George Bizos *No One to Blame? In Pursuit of Justice in South Africa* (1998); George Bizos *Odyssey to Freedom* (2007); Edwin Cameron *Justice: A Personal Account* (2014); Dikgang Moseneke *My Own Liberator: A Memoir* (2016).

[3] See Albie Sachs *Oliver Tambo: The Quiet Revolutionary* (2017) 13.

[4] Ngcukaitobi (note 2 above) 89.

of Rights that included, in addition to the abolition of political discrimination, rights in relation to mineral resources and land, education and health care.[5] A little over a decade later, the 1955 Freedom Charter envisioned a democratic state in which the people would share in the country's wealth, the land would be shared among those who work it, there would be work, the doors of learning and culture would be opened, and where there would be houses, security and comfort. As Ngcukaitobi notes, '[constitutionalism] . . . did not emerge as an alternative to political struggle. Instead, constitutionalism is an integral part of South Africa's political struggle'.[6]

Given that apartheid was enforced through the law and that human rights and constitutionalism were central to the political resistance to colonialism and apartheid, it followed that the courts would become an important site of struggle. Though it may not have been described as such, it was as early as the nineteenth century that PIL commenced in South Africa.[7] The constitutional transition established a legal framework that embodied the central tenets of the freedom struggle. PIL did not end with the formal demise of apartheid—individuals, communities, social movements and other civil society actors continued to use it as one strategy to secure largely the same goals as articulated in the Freedom Charter.

This book—except for section 1.2 of this introduction—considers the development and use of PIL in the constitutional era. The Constitution revolutionised the procedural and substantive legal environment.[8] The most significant substantive developments in this respect included the shift from parliamentary to constitutional supremacy; a justiciable Bill of Rights, including socio-economic rights; and a robust doctrine of the rule of law. Procedurally, important constitutional innovations included the broadening of standing rules; greater receptiveness to *amici curiae* and intervening parties; the creation of flexible and extensive remedial powers for courts; and a protective regime relating to costs in constitutional litigation.[9]

In the democratic era, the paradox of pursuing the 'public interest' in the courts of an undemocratic, racist state has fallen away. There is, however, another paradox that remains: in a country with political freedom seemingly won but economic freedom still a distant hope, what does PIL have to contribute? It is this paradox that the mural from downtown Johannesburg on the cover confronts,

---

[5] See the African National Congress website, last accessed from <http://www.anc.org.za/content/africans-claims-south-africa> on 26 May 2018.

[6] Ngcukaitobi (note 2 above) 5.

[7] Tembeka Ngcukaitobi 'The forgotten origins of public interest litigation in South Africa' (2016) 29 *The Advocate* 34.

[8] The interim Constitution introduced the changes to which I refer here, but they were cemented in the Constitution. All further references to the Constitution in this chapter, unless otherwise stated, are to the 1996 Constitution.

[9] See chapter 4, Georgina Jephson & Osmond Mngomezulu 'Constitutional litigation procedure'.

reiterating the demand that 'the people shall govern'—perhaps with irony, perhaps renewed urgency.

PIL is notoriously difficult to define. Other terms are used, such as 'struggle lawyer', 'cause lawyer', 'human rights lawyer' and the practices of 'strategic litigation', 'impact litigation', 'movement lawyering' and 'community lawyering', which overlap with one another, but also have different connotations. In South Africa, 'public interest litigation' has resonance. PIL in this context is best understood as the use of litigation to pursue objectives that extend beyond the interests of individual litigants in a case and that are normatively justifiable. This departs from the Indian context where, for example, PIL is understood as a procedural mechanism for the expansion of standing.[10] In South Africa public interest standing is just one way in which the courts may be approached on matters involving constitutional rights, and much PIL does not employ public interest standing at all. Although South African organisations define the content of those objectives differently, all frame them within the normative system of the Constitution and most associate PIL specifically with human rights, constitutionalism,[11] and the pursuit of social justice.[12]

South Africa has attracted enormous attention in international literature on the judicial enforcement of human rights, with a 'South African obsession' framing contemporary debate about the extent to which it is possible to realise social rights and have a meaningful impact through litigation.[13] This international discourse about the possibilities of contributing to social change through the law typically ranges across the Anglo-American and common-law jurisdictions of the United States, India,[14] Canada, the United Kingdom, to Latin American states[15] such as

---

[10] Anuj Bhuwania *Courting the People: Public Interest Litigation in Post-Emergency India* (2017) 2.

[11] In particular, the concept of transformative constitutionalism has resonance in the public interest sector and human rights literature in South Africa. Karl Klare's article opened up a rich discourse on transformative constitutionalism: Karl Klare 'Legal culture and transformative constitutionalism' (1998) 14 *SAJHR* 146. See also Pius Langa 'Transformative constitutionalism' (2006) 17 *Stell LR* 351. Accepting that there is no single accepted definition of transformative constitutionalism, Justice Langa proposed that, at the very least, transformative constitutionalism includes economic transformation and a change in legal culture. For a recent contribution, see J Brickhill & Y van Leeve 'Transformative constitutionalism—Guiding light or empty slogan?' 2015 *Acta Juridica* 141 (special edition: A Price & M Bishop (eds) *A Transformative Justice: Essays in Honour of Pius Langa*).

[12] For an overview of the 'theories of change' of organisations in the public interest sector, see SPII in a paper commissioned by the Raith Foundation 'Theories of change in social justice initiatives' (2012) *Raith Foundation* 3, last accessed on 6 July 2015 from <www.raith.org.za/resources.html>.

[13] David Landau 'The reality of social rights enforcement' (2012) 53 *Harv Int'l LJ* 189, 196.

[14] For a compelling recent contribution, see A Bhuwania 'Courting the people: The rise of public interest litigation in post-emergency India' (2014) 34 *Comparative Studies of South Asia, Africa and the Middle East* 314.

[15] A useful overview of the literature on strategic litigation in Latin America is provided in Daniel M Brinks & William Forbath 'Social and economic rights in Latin America: Constitutional Courts and the prospects for pro-poor interventions' (2010) 89 *Tex L Rev* 1943.

Brazil,[16] Colombia[17] and Argentina[18] and beyond. Although comparative perspectives are increasingly heavily influenced by South Africa, they have been informed only by a very limited picture. Indeed, some have suggested that not only has the debate increasingly focused almost entirely on a single country, but also on a single court[19] and often even on a single case![20] As significant as some of the jurisprudence of the Constitutional Court has been, including the *Grootboom* decision,[21] this has been a very narrow frame. To properly understand the possible lessons of South African public interest lawyering for other jurisdictions, the lens should be widened to include the many hundreds of cases that may not even have reached the Constitutional Court.

Within South Africa, important academic works on the development of constitutional jurisprudence have examined cases that resulted from PIL and other campaign strategies aimed at the realisation of rights.[22] These works have tended to focus on the development of legal doctrine, and usually prioritised the most well-known decisions of apex courts, especially the Constitutional Court. Most have adopted the perspective of courts (or court-watchers), rather than of the activist-lawyers who ran the cases or of the individuals, communities, social movements, and other clients whom they represented.[23] In other words, court decisions and the law are analysed in great detail, without much attention to the social actors who use the law, their tactics and strategies, and empirical evidence of the impact of their work. More recently, there is an emerging body of work that

---

[16] See eg, Octavio Luiz Motta Ferraz 'Harming the poor through social rights litigation: Lessons from Brazil' (2011) 89 *Tex L Rev* 1643.

[17] See eg, César Rodríguez-Garavito 'Beyond the courtroom: The impact of judicial activism on socioeconomic rights in Latin America' (2010) 89 *Tex L Rev* 1669.

[18] See eg, Paola Bergallo 'Courts and social change: Lessons from the struggle to universalize access to HIV/AIDS treatment in Argentina' (2011) 89 *Tex L Rev* 1611.

[19] Philip Alston 'Foreword' in Malcolm Langford (ed) *Social Rights Jurisprudence: Emerging Trends in International and Comparative Law* (2008) ix.

[20] Landau (note 13 above) 196.

[21] *Government of the Republic of South Africa and Others v Grootboom and Others* [2000] ZACC 19; 2001 (1) SA 46 (CC) [the SAHRC and CLC were admitted as *amici curiae*, represented by the LRC].

[22] See eg, Sandra Liebenberg *Socio-Economic Rights: Adjudication under a Transformative Constitution* (2010); Christopher Mbazira *Litigating Socio-Economic Rights: A Choice between Corrective and Distributive Justice* (2009); David Bilchitz *Poverty and Fundamental Rights: The Justification and Enforcement of Socio-Economic Rights* (2008).

[23] An exception is Malcolm Langford et al (eds) *Socio-Economic Rights in South Africa: Symbols or Substance* (2014).

attempts to map and analyse the value and impact of PIL,[24] including a recent set of research reports supported by long-time funders of this work.[25]

The authors of this volume offer a unique contribution to this debate, both within South Africa and in the international arena, regarding the potential of South African courts to contribute to social justice. They provide a grounded account and analysis by leading public interest lawyers who have actually litigated in the areas in which they write. Their accounts therefore go beyond law reports and academic discourse on landmark cases; they look beyond appellate courts to the breadth of litigation in the lower courts and particularly the High Court, where most PIL is conducted. The contributors to this volume identify the key social actors involved: individuals, communities, social movements, and civil society organisations that employ PIL as a strategy for social change, often in parallel to other strategies and as part of broader campaigns. Each chapter traces the development of PIL in a particular area of law, observing techniques, tactics, doctrines, and approaches that public interest lawyers and their adversaries employed. The authors analyse the impact of PIL in that area and predict the key frontiers of future contestation. Naturally, accounts by lawyers with an interest in presenting a positive picture of the work that they do should be approached critically, acknowledging the risk that lawyers valorise the law and its potential.

Although there is much common ground, the authors and the organisations for which they work differ on many conceptual, methodological, strategic, and ethical issues, amongst other things. This contestation is healthy, and it is valuable that a plurality of voices is included in this volume.[26] In order to set the stage for this to unfold, in the remainder of the introduction, I trace the development of PIL and the PIL sector in South Africa (section 1.2). I then go on to provide a descriptive account of the sector as it now stands (section 1.3). In section 1.4, I engage with some of the current critiques of, and contemporary challenges to, PIL in South Africa and outline how this volume speaks to them. Section 1.5 confronts the issue of impact, and how the effects and value of PIL should be understood. Finally, section 1.6 explains the structure of this volume, and provides an overview of the various contributions that it collates.

---

[24] Jackie Dugard & Malcolm Langford 'Art or science—Synthesising lessons from public interest litigation and the dangers of legal determinism' (2011) 27 *SAJHR* 39; Jason Brickhill 'Public interest alchemy: Combining art and science to litigate for social change' Paper presented at New York Law School's Twenty Years of South African Constitutionalism Symposium (14–16 November 2014); Jason Brickhill 'Public interest alchemy: Combining art and science to litigate for social change' *Social Science Research Network*, last accessed from <https://ssrn.com/abstract=3172855>.

[25] Steven Budlender, Gilbert Marcus & Nick Ferreira *Public Interest Litigation and Social Change in South Africa: Strategies, Tactics and Lessons* (2014); Socio-Economic Rights Institute of South Africa *Public Interest Legal Services in South Africa: Project Report* (2015) (SERI Report); Open Society Justice Initiative *Strategic Litigation Impacts: Equal Access to Quality Education* (2017) (Open Society Justice Initiative).

[26] The views in this introduction should not be attributed to the other contributors to this volume.

1.2 THE DEVELOPMENT OF PUBLIC INTEREST LITIGATION IN SOUTH AFRICA

To understand PIL in South Africa today, one must appreciate how it evolved, what principal areas of contestation attracted PIL and who was driving it at different points. In this section, I provide a brief overview of the evolution of PIL over three periods. The first was the period from the earliest use of the courts to resist colonial dispossession and injustice in the nineteenth century, through to the imposition of apartheid in 1948 and its implementation through the 1950s to 1970s. The second period, beginning at the end of the 1970s, saw the establishment of dedicated public interest organisations, which used the law to resist apartheid. The third period is the constitutional era, which saw new actors emerge in the public interest sector, specialising in discrete areas.

(a) Public interest litigation in the struggle against colonialism and apartheid (nineteenth century–1978)

In the previous section, I highlighted that constitutionalism and human rights were central normative underpinnings of the freedom struggle, as embodied in particular by the ANC. Many of the ANC's early leaders were themselves lawyers, including Pixley kaIsaka Seme, Anton Lembede and Richard Msimang. Along with other lawyers, they turned to the courts for redress over issues of land dispossession, voting rights and racial classifications.[27] This intensified under apartheid, with an increase in defensive PIL in the form of political trials.[28] Political activists were defended by a pool of individual attorneys and advocates from across the country, particularly by small black firms.[29] However, the cost of litigation was mounting. Although there was a coordinated source of funding from 1960 through the South African Defence and Aid Fund (SADAF) and (after it was banned) the International Defence and Aid Fund from 1966,[30] there were no institutions able to run these cases. PIL was prolific, but it was uncoordinated, largely reactive and depended on individual lawyers taking on cases.

In the early period of apartheid, most strategic litigation was conducted as a defensive response to apartheid laws. In particular, a vast number of political trials were conducted. As former Deputy Chief Justice Dikgang Moseneke has explained, these court cases 'became sites not only of mass mobilisation and resistance, but also of political or ideological contests. The accused, and so too, their counsel, claimed the space to display their superior notions of a just society'.[31] The two most famous examples are the Treason Trial and the Rivonia Trial.

---

[27] Ngcukaitobi (note 2 above).

[28] Abel (note 2 above).

[29] Moseneke (note 2 above) 208–12.

[30] Mary McClymont, Stephen Golub & Ford Foundation (eds) *Many Roads to Justice: The Law-Related Work of Ford Foundation Grantees around the World* (2000) 22.

[31] Moseneke (note 2 above) 209.

The Treason Trial of 1956 lasted until 1961 and resulted in the acquittal of the 156 accused, all prominent political or community leaders. Although all were acquitted, the Treason Trial ruined many families, careers, and livelihoods of the trialists and diminished the effectiveness of their political activism.[32] Shulamith Muller was one of the attorneys in the 1956 Treason Trial and her practice was at the forefront of defending black South Africans persecuted by apartheid laws. In 1971, Muller was removed from the roll of attorneys at the behest of the Law Society as she was listed by the apartheid government as a 'communist'. In 2005, she was posthumously re-enrolled.[33]

The Rivonia Trial, officially *S v Mandela and Others*, is a central strand of the history of South African resistance to apartheid through the law. It resulted in the conviction of Nelson Mandela and many of the leadership of the ANC.[34] They were sentenced to either life imprisonment or long periods of detention. Many accounts have been given of the Rivonia Trial, in which the accused were represented by Joel Joffe as attorney, with a counsel team of Bram Fischer, Vernon Berrangé, Arthur Chaskalson and George Bizos. A year after the Rivonia Trial, Bram Fischer himself was convicted for furthering the aims of communism and conspiracy to overthrow the state.[35] He spent the last decade of his life in custody. George Bizos was probably involved in more of the political trials before and after the Rivonia Trial than any other lawyer in South Africa.[36] He went on to work as counsel at the Legal Resources Centre (LRC), which was founded by Arthur Chaskalson. Chaskalson was later appointed by his former client, President Mandela, as the first President of the Constitutional Court of South Africa (later Chief Justice). However, in addition to the iconic political trials such as the Treason Trial and the Rivonia Trial, there were scores of cases in which political activists were hauled before the courts. Many lawyers dedicated much of their careers to defending political activists and I can only provide a limited account here.

There were many lawyers, especially small firms of black attorneys and sole practitioners across the country, who stepped forward to represent political activists throughout apartheid. The most famous of these was Mandela and Tambo Attorneys, which operated from 1952 to 1956.[37] However, other lawyers who took on many of the political trials of the apartheid period included Johannesburg attorneys such as Raymond Tucker, Godfrey Pitje (earlier an articled clerk at

---

[32] Moseneke (note 2 above) 208.

[33] Ruth Nathanya Muller *A Certain Legal Practitioner: Reconstructing the Life of Shulamith Muller* (unpublished LLM thesis, Wits, 2012).

[34] See Joel Joffe *The State vs. Nelson Mandela: The Trial that Changed South Africa* (2007).

[35] Stephen Clingman *Bram Fischer: Afrikaner Revolutionary* (1998).

[36] George Bizos *Odyssey to Freedom* (2007).

[37] Moseneke (note 2 above) 208.

Mandela and Tambo),[38] Shun Chetty and Priscilla Jana; in Pretoria, Maluleke, Seriti and Moseneke; in Durban, Griffiths and Victoria Mxenge; in the Cape, Ahmed Allie, Himie Bernadt, Siraj Desai, Cissie Gool, Essa Moosa, Dullah Omar, Michael Richman and Percy Sonn; in Port Elizabeth, Silas Nkanunu and Herbert Fischat; in Mthatha, Dumisa Ntsebeza; and in East London, Ben Ntonga and Hintsa Siswa.[39] Many of these lawyers were themselves imprisoned for political offences, including Nelson Mandela, Bram Fischer,[40] Dikgang Moseneke,[41] Dumisa Ntsebeza,[42] Gcina Malindi,[43] Albie Sachs[44] and many others. Some, such as Tambo, Sachs, Joe Slovo and Duma Nokwe, South Africa's first black advocate, joined the armed struggle and went into exile. Some, such as the courageous struggle lawyer couple, Griffiths and Victoria Mxenge, were murdered by the regime.

In the absence of formalised institutions to represent accused persons in political trials, it was necessary to secure lawyers in private practice to represent them. This required funds. The Treason Trial Defence Fund was set up to secure representation for the 156 accused in the Treason Trial, which dragged on for five years.[45] In 1960, SADAF was established to fund political trials, and it later supported other civil and criminal litigation opposing apartheid.[46] When SADAF was banned in 1966, the International Defence and Aid Fund was established in London to channel funds surreptitiously to lawyers defending political activists.[47]

Even during apartheid, a conviction in a political trial was not inevitable and accordingly the law was employed to defend political activists with some notable

---

[38] Pitje was himself convicted for refusing a magistrate's instruction to move to a table designated for black lawyers and insisting on sitting at the table designated for whites. The Appellate Division upheld his conviction in *R v Pitje* 1960 (4) SA 709 (A).

[39] Ibid 210–12. Geoff Budlender drew my attention to additional attorneys who did this work apart from those mentioned in Moseneke (note 2 above).

[40] See Clingman (note 35 above).

[41] See Moseneke (note 2 above).

[42] See Dumisa Ntsebeza 'Address by the Incoming Chancellor of the University of Fort Hare, Advocate Dumisa Buhle Ntsebeza SC, on the occasion of his inauguration and investiture' 3 May 2017 10–11, last accessed on 1 June 2018 from <http://www.ufh.ac.za/files/Chancellors%20Address.pdf>. Ntsebeza was imprisoned for four years, during which he completed his law degree. He later served as a commissioner of the Truth and Reconciliation Commission. Recently, he represented the families of the deceased mineworkers in the Marikana Commission of Inquiry.

[43] A key member of the BLA and the National Association of Democratic Lawyers (NADEL). Malindi was one of the accused in the Delmas Trial. He was convicted and spent five years on Robben Island, where he studied law.

[44] See Albie Sachs *The Jail Diary of Albie Sachs* (1990). Sachs, in 1988, survived an assassination attempt in which he lost an arm and the sight of one eye. He went on to serve as a justice on the first bench of the Constitutional Court.

[45] McClymont et al (note 30 above) 22.

[46] Ibid.

[47] Ibid.

acquittals.[48] In addition, some 'losing cases' were understood nevertheless to have significant impact, by providing a platform to articulate resistance to apartheid and to preserve the historical record. The series of inquests into the deaths of detained activists—each absolving the state—provides a powerful example.[49]

(b)   The establishment of dedicated public interest organisations (1978–1994)

As apartheid—and the freedom struggle—intensified into the 1970s, discussions within the legal profession began to develop the idea of establishing organisations to engage in PIL to resist the daily rights violations of apartheid laws and even to seek to attack the legal architecture of apartheid itself. Eventually, in 1978–1979, having secured international seed funding, three organisations were set up. Although today all three organisations employ full-time lawyers and conduct PIL, they were initially structured differently. The LRC was established as a public interest law firm. The Centre for Applied Legal Studies (CALS), based at the University of the Witwatersrand, was initially set up as a legal research institute, but soon also began to take cases of its own. Lawyers for Human Rights (LHR) was initially formed as a membership association for lawyers committed to doing human rights work. In the mid-1980s, it also took on permanent staff and began conducting PIL.

Reflecting on the establishment of these three organisations at an event to mark their founding on their 35th 'birthday', Edwin Cameron explained:

> The founding of CALS in 1978, by Professor John Dugard, and of the LRC in 1979, by Arthur Chaskalson and Felicia Kentridge, with Dugard's backing and assistance, with LHR following just a few years later, therefore represented the triumph of an idea—the belief that lawyers had an especial role and a particular responsibility in the face of gross injustice. That idea was animated by the iniquities of apartheid. But behind it lay a deeper belief about the nature of law itself. These lawyers' opposition to apartheid embodied the insight that law need not only oppress, separate, subordinate and exclude, but could be used and indeed should be used in the fulfilment of a deeper and better ordering of human society: that this was its true role.[50]

---

[48] One significant acquittal was the Pietermaritzburg Treason Trial in 1984, in which 16 leaders from the South African Allied Workers Union, the United Democratic Front and the Transvaal or Natal Indian Congress were tried for treason. See *S v Ramgobin and Others* 1986 (1) SA 68 (N).

[49] George Bizos *No One to Blame* (1998) describes a number of inquests into the deaths in custody of political activists, including Ahmed Timol, Steve Biko, Simon Mndawe, Neil Aggett and the 'Cradock Four' of Matthew Goniwe, Fort Calata, Sparrow Mkhonto and Sicelo Mhlauli. Every inquest discussed by Bizos resulted in a finding that the authorities were not responsible. However, the inquests drew the world's attention to the deaths in custody and secured a historical record of the events. Recently, with the support of Bizos, the 1972 inquest of Ahmed Timol was successfully reopened, and the original decision replaced with a finding of murder by state agents. See *The Re-opened Inquest into the Death of Ahmed Essop Timol* [2017] ZAGPPHC 652 [WW acted for the Timol family; Bizos of the LRC gave evidence].

[50] Edwin Cameron 'Remarks at the celebration of the founding of CALS, the LRC and LHR at the Public Interest Law Gathering' 24 July 2014, last accessed on 1 June 2018 from <http://www.publicinterestlawgathering.com/justice-cameron-speech-pilg-2014-24-july/>.

In section 1.3 below, I return to the founding of CALS, the LRC and LHR and the work that they did during this period and subsequently. But there were many other important role-players.

It was also during this period that the Black Lawyers Association (BLA) was established.[51] Initially set up as the Black Lawyers Discussion Group to address the professional needs of black legal practitioners, the BLA later established the BLA Legal Centre, which ran programmes that provided professional training for black lawyers but also had the power to litigate in the public interest in exceptional circumstances.[52] The BLA ran a number of programmes, including a placement programme that supported young black law graduates in placements with practising attorneys and a successful advocacy programme.[53] Therefore, although the BLA did not conduct much PIL in its own name, it provided substantial support to public interest practice and its members were heavily involved in such cases. Almost all the early members of the BLA went on to become judges in democratic South Africa.[54]

During the 1970s and 1980s, social movements working in collaboration with activist lawyers undertook considerable PIL. Social movements, such as the trade unions, the churches, the United Democratic Front (UDF) and later the Mass Democratic Movement (MDM), identified the need, initiated the litigation and either acted as applicants or found suitable people to do so. They did not have the resources to hire lawyers, in any event not at commercial rates. They accordingly collaborated with CALS or the LRC, or with activist law firms. These law firms charged reduced rates and were subsidised by international funders, sometimes in clandestine fashion. This collaboration between social movements and activist lawyers generated a great deal of significant impact litigation particularly in the 1980s.

The cumulative efforts of these various role-players—CALS, the LRC and LHR, as well as the BLA, Black Sash, social movements, private attorneys and advocates—generated a wide range of PIL with some important results. In addition to political trials and inquests, the period saw significant PIL in the areas of forced removals, pass laws, labour laws, and censorship.

Among the many forced removals cases, notable cases included the drawn-out struggle of the Bakwena ba Mogopa, who won an important victory in the Appellate Division after they had already been removed from their land.[55] The

---

[51] For an overview of the history of the BLA written by one of its founders, see Moseneke (note 2 above) 206–20.

[52] Ibid 216.

[53] Ibid 217.

[54] Ibid 220.

[55] *More v Minister of Co-operation and Development* 1985 ZASCA 89; 1986 (1) SA 102 (A) [CALS acted for the Bakwena ba Mogopa]; Abel (note 2 above) 385–433; Gilbert Marcus 'Section 5 of the Black Administration Act: The case of the Bakwena ba Mogopa' in C Murray & C O'Regan

decision made further forced removals difficult; it energised the community's reoccupation of the land; and it contributed to the apartheid government's settlement of the Mfengu land restitution claim. The dispossession of land was coupled with the enforcement of pass laws to implement geographical apartheid. In respect of the pass laws, two of the most significant cases of the period were the *Komani*[56] and *Rikhoto*[57] cases litigated by the LRC. *Komani* involved a successful challenge to regulations requiring the dependents of black workers to obtain permits to reside in white areas. Following the success in *Komani*, the LRC assisted approximately 200 clients with similar cases the following year, launched proceedings over a dozen times and succeeded in rendering the system of forcing dependents of black workers to obtain permits ineffectual. *Rikhoto* concerned the problem that black workers who were employed in white areas could not acquire urban residence even after ten years' employment with a single employer because the authorities considered annual leave as terminating the employment contract. The court held that annual leave did not interrupt continuous employment.

In 1980, legislative reforms resulted in the recognition for the first time of black trade unions, revolutionising labour relations in South Africa. CALS and the related private firm, Cheadle Thompson & Haysom, entered this new space and secured important victories on behalf of the new trade union sector. Important areas of PIL during this period were the protection of union leadership against victimisation, the acquisition of organisational and bargaining rights and protection of striking workers.[58]

Censorship was a central strategy of apartheid, and also a site of resistance. CALS, in particular, ran a large number of successful cases challenging censorship of material and the banning of particular newspapers or publications.[59] Notable examples included challenges by the UDF to censorship of the Argus and Saan Newspapers,[60] and the unsuccessful attempts to prevent the shut-down of the *New Nation*.[61] The successful appeal before the Publications Appeal Board to unban the

---

(eds) *No Place to Rest: Forced Removals and the Law in South Africa* (1990) 20. Geoff Budlender provided useful comments on the impact of this case.

[56] *Komani NO v Bantu Affairs Administration Board, Peninsula Area* 1980 (4) SA 448 (A) [the LRC acted for the appellant] (*Komani*).

[57] *Oos-Randse Administrasieraad v Rikhoto* 1983 (3) SA 595 (A) [the LRC acted for the respondent] (*Rikhoto*).

[58] Clive Thompson 'Trade Unions Using the Law' in Hugh Corder (ed) *Essays on Law and Social Practice in South Africa* (1988) 340–5.

[59] See Gilbert Marcus 'Reasonable censorship' in Hugh Corder (ed) *Essays on Law and Social Practice in South Africa* (1988).

[60] Abel (note 2 above) 263.

[61] *Catholic Bishops' Publishing Co v State President and Another* 1990 (1) SA 849 (A).

Freedom Charter meant that many of the affiliates of the UDF and the trade unions adopted it as their manifesto.[62]

Across the areas of forced removals, pass laws, labour rights and censorship, the courts were therefore an important site of struggle in which some significant victories were secured. Geoff Budlender, writing in 1988, put the PIL victories of this period in perspective:

> It is important that the famous victories of the past few years should not mislead one into the failure to recognize a depressing reality. For many South Africans, the law is not an effective protection against those who have greater political, economic or physical power. This is perhaps most stark in the transparent failure of the authorities to take effective action to stop or even curb vigilante activities. In some parts of the country, people are afraid even to approach the courts for an interdict against threatened violence, for fear that this will trigger reprisals by people who seem totally confident that their actions will go unpunished.[63]

But through the throes of the dying apartheid system, South Africa made the transition to democracy and the interim Constitution was adopted in 1993. This heralded a new era for PIL.

(c) Growth and specialisation of the sector in the constitutional era (1994–present)

After 1994, South Africa saw continuing growth in the PIL sector. Alongside the three existing generalist PIL organisations, namely CALS, the LRC and LHR, new specialist organisations were established to work in particular substantive areas. The first of these were the Centre for Child Law (CCL) and Women's Legal Centre (WLC) in 1998 and 1999, established shortly after the Constitution came into effect. As the chapters in this volume discussing PIL on children's rights and gender demonstrate, it is misleading to describe these as 'single-issue' organisations, given the breadth and complexity of these areas of law and the interconnectedness and overlap of rights.

The Southern African Litigation Centre (SALC), established in 2005, had a different focus to all the domestic organisations that already existed. It was the first PIL organisation to adopt a regional focus on litigating human rights and rule of law issues in Southern African countries. From 2009, the sector saw the establishment of several more organisations with a focus on socio-economic rights. The Centre for Environmental Rights (CER) and the Socio-Economic Rights Institute of South Africa (SERI) were both established in 2009, with SECTION27—also a socio-economic rights organisation—set up the following year in 2010. Subse-

---

[62] CALS successfully overturned the banning of the Freedom Charter before the Publications Appeal Board in 1983. See interview with Gilbert Marcus, 17, LRC Oral History Project, archived in the Historical Papers Research Archive of the University of the Witwatersrand last accessed from <www.historicalpapers.wits.ac.za> on 1 June 2018.

[63] Geoff Budlender 'On practising law' in Hugh Corder (ed) *Essays on Law and Social Practice in South Africa* (1988) 331.

quently, two organisations that now engage in movement lawyering were launched. Ndifuna Ukwazi (NU), which focuses on urban land and housing, was founded as a non-profit organisation allied to the Reclaim the City campaign in 2011, and later registered as a law clinic in 2015. Equal Education Law Centre (EELC) similarly grew out of a social movement, Equal Education (EE). It was founded in 2012 as a specialist education law centre. In the next section, I describe the PIL sector in more detail, including the other role-players such as clients, funders and other partners.

1.3 THE PUBLIC INTEREST LAW SECTOR TODAY

PIL should *not* be the exclusive preserve of dedicated public interest law organisations or 'educated Constitutional Court watchers'.[64] The Constitution must infuse all law, and every litigant—especially poor people and communities—must have access to the courts. The Constitutional Court recently confirmed that, at least in some cases, the right of access to courts in s 34 of the Constitution may require the state to provide free legal representation in civil matters.[65] But the reality is that Legal Aid South Africa, the statutory entity responsible for discharging the state's legal aid duties, provides legal aid in only very narrow categories of civil matters, to a small proportion of the people who need it.[66] In the absence of state-aided civil legal aid, it is left to law clinics and public interest organisations to fill the gap.[67] PIL is complex, expensive and requires extensive evidence-gathering and legal expertise.

In *Mazibuko*, towards the end of a judgment in which the court rejected a public interest case seeking to enforce the right to water, O'Regan J recognised the important role of public interest organisations in bringing socio-economic rights litigation:

> It is true that litigation of this sort is expensive and requires great expertise. South Africa is fortunate to have a range of non-governmental organisations working in the legal arena seeking improvement in the lives of poor South Africans. Long may that be so. These organisations have developed an expertise in litigating in the interests of the poor to the great benefit of our society. The approach to costs in constitutional matters means that litigation launched in a serious attempt to further constitutional rights, even if unsuccessful, will not result in an adverse costs order. The challenges

---

[64] Tshepo Madlingozi 'The Constitutional Court, court watchers and the commons: A reply to Professor Michelman on constitutional dialogue, "interpretive charity" and the citizenry as Sangomas: Lead essay/response' (2008) 1 *CCR* 63, 74.

[65] *Legal Aid South Africa v Magidiwana and Others* [2015] ZACC 28; 2015 (6) SA 494 (CC) paras 22–7 [SERI acted for the 8th and 9th respondents; LRC acted for the 18th respondent].

[66] Jason Brickhill & Christine Grobler 'The right to civil legal aid in South Africa: *Legal Aid v Magidiwana*' (2016) 8 *CCR* 256–282.

[67] Jason Brickhill 'The right to a fair civil trial: The duties of lawyers and law students to act pro bono' (2005) 21 *SAJHR* 293, 303–7.

posed by social and economic rights litigation are significant, but given the benefits that it can offer, it should be pursued.[68]

The public interest sector today works across all areas of human rights law. The Constitutional Court has recognised its collective impact. In *Biowatch*, Sachs J paused to observe:

> Interventions by public interest groups have led to important decisions concerning the rights of the homeless, refugees, prisoners on death row, prisoners generally, prisoners imprisoned for civil debt and the landless. There has also been pioneering litigation brought by groups concerned with gender equality, the rights of the child, cases concerned with upholding the constitutional rights of gay men and lesbian women, and in relation to freedom of expression.[69]

Today, the public interest sector is increasingly specialised and varied in its approach, but also increasingly cohesive and able to act collectively. Once a year, the sector comes together for the Public Interest Law Gathering (PILG), which has taken place annually since 2011.[70] PILG brings together 'public interest legal practitioners and organisations, law students, paralegals, social movement leaders and legal academics with the aim of serving as a focal point for professionals in the field to share and develop knowledge'. It is organised by a coordinating committee comprising public interest organisations, including CALS, the EELC, LHR, the LRC, ProBono.Org, SALC, SECTION27, SERI, Students for Law and Social Justice (SLSJ), and the School of Law at the University of the Witwatersrand. PILG is just one manifestation of the collaborative approach of the sector. Indeed, as the sector has grown, the collaboration among organisations has deepened.[71] Collaboration is vital for several reasons: advancing claims for social justice on behalf of communities often requires a joint approach, or at least coordination; this can be strategically effective and increase the effectiveness of litigation; it optimises the use of limited resources; and the issues are complex, benefiting from the expertise and insights of different organisations and individuals.[72]

The sector now includes the three public interest law organisations established in the late 1970s as what has been described as a 'three-pronged assault on apartheid'[73]—the LRC, LHR and CALS. It also includes a growing number of

---

[68] *Mazibuko and Others v City of Johannesburg and Others* [2009] ZACC 28; 2010 (4) SA 1 (CC) [CALS/Wits Law Clinic and FXI acted for the applicant; and COHRE was admitted as *amicus curiae*, represented by the LRC].

[69] *Biowatch Trust v Registrar Genetic Resources and Others* [2009] ZACC 14; 2009 (6) SA 232 (CC) [CCL, LHR and CALS were admitted as *amici curiae*] para 19.

[70] See the PILG website, last accessed from <www.publicinterestlawgathering.com> on 27 May 2018.

[71] SERI Report (note 25 above) 64–96.

[72] Ibid 67.

[73] Interview with John Dugard, LRC Oral History Project (note 62 above) 18.

newer organisations focusing on a particular area of law. The newer organisations work in the areas of women's rights and gender,[74] socio-economic rights,[75] children's rights,[76] freedom of expression,[77] environmental justice,[78] and education rights.[79] The newer, specialist public interest organisations all operate from one urban centre and all are based in Johannesburg, Pretoria or Cape Town. The LRC and LHR remain the only organisations that operate nationally. As the public interest sector grew, it also saw a diversification of strategies and an increase in the amount of litigation undertaken by these organisations. University law clinics also provide valuable legal services across the country, including engaging in PIL from time to time. Their focus, however, is on providing advice and assistance to walk-in clients. In addition, some private firms of attorneys and some advocates at the Bar engage in PIL, often on a pro bono basis.

The public interest sector draws its funding primarily from institutional donors, amongst other sources. In the early period, the Carnegie Foundation, the Ford Foundation and the Rockefeller Brothers Fund supported the establishment of the LRC and CALS.[80] The Ford Foundation continues to fund many of the organisations in the sector to this day. The Atlantic Philanthropies provided substantial support to the public interest sector in South Africa for the first two decades of the constitutional era from 1994 to 2013, during which time it invested over US$355 million.[81] Other major institutional donors from the early period and more recently have included the Bertha Foundation,[82] the Canon Collins Trust,[83] the Claude Leon Foundation,[84] Comic Relief,[85] the newly established Constitutionalism Fund,[86] the ELMA Foundation,[87] the Foundation for Human

---

[74] The WLC and Sonke Gender Justice.

[75] The ALP, which was later subsumed in SECTION27; SERI; and NU.

[76] The CCL.

[77] The Freedom of Expression Institute (FXI).

[78] The CER and Natural Justice (NU).

[79] The EELC, which works closely with the social movement, EE.

[80] McClymont et al (note 30 above) 24.

[81] Budlender et al (note 25 above) II. This important study was itself funded by the Atlantic Philanthropies as it ended its grant-making.

[82] See the Bertha Foundation website, last accessed from <www.berthafoundation.org> on 1 June 2018.

[83] See the Canon Collins Trust website, last accessed from <www.canoncollins.org.uk> on 1 June 2018.

[84] See the Claude Leon Foundation website, last accessed from <www.leonfoundation.co.za> on 1 June 2018.

[85] See the Comic Relief website, last accessed from <www.comicrelief.com> on 1 June 2018.

[86] See the Constitutionalism Fund website, last accessed from <www.constitutionalismfund.co.za> on 1 June 2018.

[87] See the ELMA Foundation website, last accessed from <www.elmaphilanthropies.org> on 1 June 2018.

Rights,[88] Legal Aid South Africa,[89] the Open Society Foundation for South Africa,[90] the Raith Foundation,[91] the Sigrid Rausing Trust,[92] and others. Individual donations and donations from South African companies, including lawyers and law firms, are also sources of funding for most public interest organisations. These organisations provide crucial material support to the sector and help facilitate collaboration among organisations and important research projects.[93]

In addition to the dedicated public interest sector, South Africa has also experienced growth in the number of civil society organisations that employ litigation as but one strategy to seek and effect systemic change. Social movements, such as the Treatment Action Campaign (TAC),[94] Abahlali Base Mjondolo,[95] EE,[96] the Right2Know Campaign,[97] Reclaim the City[98] and the Social Justice Coalition have demonstrated the potential of movement lawyering. In addition, non-governmental organisations (NGOs) such as Corruption Watch,[99] the Council for the Advancement of the South African Constitution (CASAC),[100]

---

[88] See the Foundation for Human Rights website, last accessed from <www.fhr.org.za> on 1 June 2018.

[89] See the Legal Aid South Africa website, last accessed from <www.legal-aid.co.za> on 1 June 2018. Legal Aid South Africa supports specific cases under its impact litigation programme.

[90] See the Open Society Foundation for South Africa website, last accessed from <www.osf.org.za> on 1 June 2018.

[91] See the Raith Foundation website, last accessed from <www.raith.org.za> on 1 June 2018. The Raith Foundation also funded the important recent study, SERI Report (note 25 above).

[92] See the Sigrid Rausing Trust website, last accessed from <www.sigrid-rausing-trust.org> on 1 June 2018.

[93] Most notably, Budlender et al (note 25 above); SERI Report (note 25 above); Open Society Justice Initiative (note 25 above); Public Affairs Research Institute & The Raith Foundation *Confrontational, Complementary, Co-Operative or Co-Opted? Social Justice Organisations Working with the State* (2016).

[94] See Mark Heywood 'South Africa's Treatment Action Campaign: Combining law and social mobilization to realize the right to health' (2009) 1 *JHRP* 14–36; *Minister of Health and Others v Treatment Action Campaign and Others (No 2)* [2002] ZACC 15; 2002 (5) SA 721 (CC) [LRC acted for the respondents; and IDASA, CLC and the Cotswolds Baby Sanctuary were admitted as *amici curiae*, represented by Wits Law Clinic] (*Treatment Action Campaign*).

[95] See eg, *Abahlali Basemjondolo Movement SA v Premier of the Province of KwaZulu-Natal and Others* [2009] ZACC 31; 2010 (2) BCLR 99 (CC) [SERI acted for the applicants].

[96] See generally, chapter 11, Cameron McConnachie & Samantha Brener 'Litigating the right to basic education' and see the discussion of the work of the EELC below.

[97] See chapter 13, Dario Milo & Avani Singh 'Access to information'; *Right2Know Campaign and Another v Minister of Police and Another* [2014] ZAGPJHC 343; [2015] 1 All SA 367 (GJ) [M&G Media was admitted as *amicus curiae*].

[98] See the discussion of the work of NU in partnership with Reclaim the City below.

[99] See eg, *Corruption Watch (RF) NPC and Another v President of the Republic of South Africa and Others; Council for the Advancement of the South African Constitution v President of the Republic of South Africa and Others* [2017] ZAGPPHC 743; [2018] 1 All SA 471 (GP) [the LRC acted for CASAC; WW acted for FUL; and HSF was admitted as *amicus curiae*, represented by WW]. The case involved a successful application to set aside a settlement agreement between former President Zuma and former National Director of Public Prosecutions (NDPP).

[100] Ibid.

the Helen Suzman Foundation (HSF),[101] Freedom Under Law (FUL)[102] and Sonke Gender Justice have increasingly not only intervened in PIL but also initiated it. More recently, formal political movements, including opposition political parties, have increased their use of strategic litigation. The opposition political parties, the Democratic Alliance (DA)[103] and the Economic Freedom Fighters (EFF),[104] in particular, have engaged in significant strategic litigation (though it is arguable whether such cases constitute PIL).

Finally, the public interest space has also seen increased activity from conservative actors and those working to preserve white privilege, who have used litigation as a strategy to pursue their objectives.[105] Examples include the litigation by trade union Solidarity in the area of affirmative action;[106] Afriforum in cases involving freedom of expression,[107] language rights[108] and street name

---

[101] See eg, *Helen Suzman Foundation v Judicial Service Commission* [2018] ZACC 8 [WW acted for the applicant; and The Trustees for the Time Being of the Basic Rights Foundation of South Africa were admitted as *amicus curiae*]. The case concerned an application to compel the JSC to disclose the record of its deliberations in a review of a decision regarding judicial appointments.

[102] See eg, *Justice Alliance of South Africa v President of Republic of South Africa and Others, Freedom Under Law v President of Republic of South Africa and Others, Centre for Applied Legal Studies and Another v President of Republic of South Africa and Others* [2011] ZACC 23; 2011 (5) SA 388 (CC) [FUL was an applicant, represented by WW; CALS and CASAC were also applicants in the consolidated matter; and NADEL, BLA and Mario Gaspare Oriane-Ambrosini MP were admitted as *amici curiae*]. The case involved a successful challenge to legislation extending the term of the Chief Justice.

[103] Perhaps most notably, *Democratic Alliance v President of South Africa and Others* [2012] ZACC 24; 2013 (1) SA 248 (CC), in which the DA successfully challenged the appointment of the NDPP and had it set aside.

[104] In a recent line of three cases, the EFF (along with other opposition parties) approached the courts in support of its attempts to impeach former President Zuma. See *Economic Freedom Fighters v Speaker of the National Assembly and Others; Democratic Alliance v Speaker of the National Assembly and Others* [2016] ZACC 11; 2016 (3) SA 580 (CC) [Corruption Watch was admitted as *amicus curiae*], in which the court found a report by the Public Protector recommending that President Zuma pay money back to the state in connection with upgrades to his residence to be binding; and *United Democratic Movement v Speaker of the National Assembly and Others* [2017] ZACC 21; 2017 (5) SA 300 (CC), in which the court set aside a decision of the Speaker not to hold a secret ballot in a vote of no confidence against the President; and *Economic Freedom Fighters and Others v Speaker of the National Assembly and Another* [2017] ZACC 47; 2018 (2) SA 571 (CC) [Corruption Watch was admitted as *amicus curiae*], in which the court ordered Parliament to make rules regulating the removal of a President.

[105] Budlender et al (note 25 above) 15–21.

[106] *Solidarity and Others v Department of Correctional Services and Others* [2016] ZACC 18; 2016 (5) SA 594 (CC) [Police and Prisons Civil Rights Union and SAPS were admitted as *amici curiae*]; *South African Police Service v Solidarity obo Barnard* [2014] ZACC 23; 2014 (6) SA 123 (CC) [Police and Prisons Civil Rights Union was admitted as *amicus curiae*].

[107] *Afri-Forum and Another v Malema and Others* [2011] ZAEQC 2; 2011 (6) SA 240 (EqC) [Vereniging van Regslui vir Afrikaans was admitted as *amici curiae*].

[108] *AfriForum and Another v University of the Free State* [2017] ZACC 48; 2018 (2) SA 185 (CC).

changes;[109] Agri South Africa in relation to land and property rights;[110] and the Justice Alliance of South Africa (JASA) in cases involving advocating for conservative moral positions.[111]

It is not possible to describe the history, structure and work of every organisation that engages in PIL in South Africa in this chapter. However, included in this volume is a list of organisations, broadly construed to include not just those that provide legal representation (public interest law centres),[112] but also those organisations that litigate in their own name, especially by intervening as *amici curiae*, using litigation as one strategy for social change (public interest litigants). The second category—organisations that engage in PIL as client/litigant—is an open-ended section of civil society, but I have attempted to include the most frequent actors. In respect of each organisation in the list, a link to its website is provided where further information can be found. The Table of Cases in this volume includes, in respect of each case, an annotation reflecting the involvement of the listed organisations.

In the remainder of this section, I offer a brief account of the first category—public interest law centres—chronologically by date of establishment. I describe their founding, structure and approaches to their work, focus areas and staffing, as well as mentioning some notable alumni. This is only meant to be a brief overview of the sector. I acknowledge that in the space available I cannot hope to do justice to the histories, work, and people of these organisations.

---

[109] *City of Tshwane Metropolitan Municipality v Afriforum and Another* [2016] ZACC 19; 2016 (6) SA 279 (CC).

[110] *Agri South Africa v Minister for Minerals and Energy* [2013] ZACC 9; 2013 (4) SA 1 (CC) [CALS was admitted as *amicus curiae*, represented by the LRC].

[111] *Print Media South Africa and Another v Minister of Home Affairs and Another* [2012] ZACC 22; 2012 (6) SA 443 (CC) [JASA and Section 16 were admitted as *amici curiae*] (*Teddy Bear Clinic*) concerning a constitutional challenge to a statute giving wide censorship powers, which JASA defended. JASA's objective is described at para 6 as 'to uphold and develop Judeo-Christian and constitutional values by means of litigation and involvement in legislative processes'. See also *Teddy Bear Clinic for Abused Children and Another v Minister of Justice and Constitutional Development and Another* [2013] ZACC 35; 2014 (2) SA 168 (CC) [CCL represented the applicants; JASA, the Women's Legal Centre Trust and Tshwaranang were admitted as *amici curiae*]. The case concerned a constitutional challenge to legislation criminalising consensual sexual behaviour between children under 16. JASA unsuccessfully defended the legislation.

[112] The list also includes one commercial firm, Webber Wentzel. This firm has a pro bono unit that has conducted significant public interest litigation, supported by other lawyers within the firm. It has also acted on a commercial basis for leading media entities in litigation concerning access to information and freedom of expression, as reflected in chapters 12 and 13 by Dario Milo & Avani Singh. Other leading commercial firms, such as Edward Nathan Sonnenbergs, Bowman Gilfillan, Deneys Reitz, Werksmans and Cliffe Dekker Hofmeyr, as well as many others, have also conducted some PIL and provided pro bono services. The leading labour firm Cheadle Thompson Haysom has played a particularly significant role in developing South Africa's statutory labour law framework and developing its jurisprudence to protect the rights of workers and trade unions.

(a) The Centre for Applied Legal Studies

The story of public interest law centres in South Africa begins with CALS. CALS was founded in 1978 by John Dugard.[113] Dugard initially envisaged that '[CALS] would research issues that would then be litigated by the [LRC] and so the two would work very closely together'.[114] Although they have worked collaboratively throughout their existence,[115] the two organisations developed independently. Based at the University of the Witwatersrand in Johannesburg, CALS initially developed its legal research expertise, but later also began to engage in advocacy and impact litigation across its focus areas. At the start, however, the Law Society refused to allow attorneys from CALS to practise. This indirectly led to the creation of another important institution in South African history, when three early CALS' appointees, CALS deputy director Halton Cheadle, Clive Thompson and Fink Haysom, were forced to establish a new law firm in 1983 in order to practise.[116] Although they continued to work for CALS, they founded Cheadle Thompson and Haysom, which became the foremost labour firm in South Africa, acting for the country's leading trade unions.[117]

CALS' focus areas have changed over time, with the times. From its founding until the democratic transition in the early 1990s, CALS' approach was primarily responsive rather than proactive, focusing on challenging apartheid policies on security and policing, education and labour law.[118] CALS' early work included censorship cases, driven by Gilbert Marcus.[119] In the 1990s, its programmes included the AIDS Law Project (ALP),[120] the Gender Research Programme, the Land Rights Research Programme, the Freedom of Expression Project, the Constitutional Programme, and the Labour Programme. In addition to its impact litigation cases, CALS was involved in developing new policy and legislative measures following the dissolution of the apartheid government.

Currently, CALS focuses on research, advocacy, and litigation in five overlapping areas: basic services, business and human rights, environmental justice,

---

[113] See generally, interview with John Dugard, LRC Oral History Project (note 62 above).

[114] Ibid 16.

[115] The LRC's first National Director, Arthur Chaskalson, served on the first Board of Trustees of CALS, along with George Bizos, Denis Kuny and Raymond Tucker. Ibid.

[116] John Dugard interview, LRC Oral History Project (note 62 above) 16–7; Gilbert Marcus interview, LRC Oral History Project (note 62 above) 13.

[117] Gilbert Marcus interview, LRC Oral History Project (note 62 above) 12–13.

[118] Centre for Applied Legal 'Studies Fighting for Justice: The Centre for Applied Legal Studies 1978–1991' last accessed from <http://www.wits.ac.za/files/am6lp_639150001343035773.pdf> on 19 June 2018.

[119] Ibid 21.

[120] See the discussion of SECTION27, which grew out of ALP, below.

gender, and the rule of law.[121] CALS has been involved in a wide range of litigation since its establishment,[122] and has played a particularly influential role in the development of the law in the areas of gender[123] and housing.[124]

CALS now employees 21 people, including 4 attorneys, 4 researchers and 5 candidate attorneys.[125] Its most recent Director was Bonita Meyersfeld. Lisa Chamberlain is currently its Acting Director and Wandisa Phama and Palesa Madi are the Acting Deputy Directors. Among the alumni of CALS are renowned academics, such as its founder, John Dugard, and Theunis Roux;[126] leading practitioners such as Gilbert Marcus SC, the labour trio of Cheadle, Thompson and Haysom, and judges, including David Unterhalter, Raylene Keightley,[127] Dennis Davis,[128] and Edwin Cameron who currently serves on the Constitutional Court. Jackie Dugard and Stuart Wilson, who founded SERI (discussed below) also worked for many years at CALS, litigating socio-economic rights cases on housing, water, and electricity.

(b) The Legal Resources Centre[129]

The LRC, South Africa's largest public interest law firm, was founded in 1979 by Arthur Chaskalson, Felicia and Sydney Kentridge and Geoff Budlender. Arthur Chaskalson was the first National Director.[130] Janet Love, a key figure in the anti-apartheid struggle, currently heads the LRC.[131] It now employs approximately 100

---

[121] See the CALS website, last accessed from <www.wits.ac.za/cals/our-programmes/> on 30 May 2018.

[122] A search of the Southern African Legal Information Institute (SAFLII) databases that cover all the South African courts, reflects that CALS was referred to in 173 cases reported on SAFLII as at 1 June 2018, including 79 Constitutional Court cases. This is only a portion of the actual number, as SAFLII's coverage is limited in time (beginning only in the 1980s and 1990s for most High Courts) and does not include every judgment delivered, but only those judgments furnished to SAFLII. However, the figure is also inflated because it includes later references to cases in which CALS had been a party.

[123] See chapter 6, Bonita Meyersfeld & Nomonde Nyembe, 'Gender and public interest litigation in post-apartheid South Africa: Have systematic motifs of discrimination been addressed?'.

[124] See chapter 5, Stuart Wilson 'Making space for social change: Pro-poor property rights litigation in post-apartheid South Africa'.

[125] CALS website (note 121 above).

[126] Head of the Law and Transformation Programme at CALS from 1999–2003.

[127] Judge of the South Gauteng High Court in Johannesburg, and former head of CALS.

[128] High Court judge who sits on other specialist courts, including the Competition Appeal Court and Labour Appeal Court.

[129] See, generally, the LRC website, last accessed from <www.lrc.org.za> on 30 May 2018 and the LRC Oral History Project (note 62 above). Approximately 200 interviews were conducted, including with the LRC's founders and many staff who have worked for the LRC during different periods.

[130] In addition to Chaskalson, the original advocates at the LRC were Felicia Kentridge and Ramola Naidoo. The original attorneys were Geoff Budlender, Debbie Dison, Charles Nupen and Morris Zimmerman.

[131] Love is due to step down towards the end of 2018 and the LRC has announced that Nersan Govender will succeed her.

staff, including approximately 5 advocates, 17 attorneys, 17 candidate attorneys, 7 paralegals and 5 researchers. It has offices in Johannesburg, Cape Town, Durban and Grahamstown, and satellite offices in smaller towns in Limpopo, KwaZulu-Natal, Mpumalanga and the Eastern Cape. Its work spans urban and rural areas leading it to have the widest national reach of any public interest law centre in South Africa.

The LRC has re-framed its focus areas from time to time over the years, reorganising areas of work under different programmes or themes. Its work spans the full range of rights enshrined in the Constitution, with a roughly equal balance of work in civil and political rights and in socio-economic rights.[132] Because it has the longest history of conducting PIL, the broadest substantive scope of work and the widest national reach, the LRC has litigated more reported cases than any other organisation in South Africa.[133] It has also litigated some of South Africa's most well-known landmark cases, such as *Khomani*[134] and *Rikhoto*[135] challenging the pass laws under apartheid, and subsequently *Makwanyane* abolishing the death penalty,[136] the *Treatment Action Campaign* case on access to antiretrovirals for people infected with HIV-AIDS (working alongside the ALP),[137] and *Grootboom* on housing,[138] among many others. The LRC also operates internationally, in the regional and international human rights law systems. It has observer status at the African Commission on Human and Peoples' Rights and is an active participant in the United Nations human rights system.

For an organisation its size, the LRC has produced approximately 20 judges, all appointed to the bench after 1994. The LRC's first National Director, Arthur Chaskalson, was appointed the first President of the Constitutional Court by his former client, President Nelson Mandela.[139] Other former LRC lawyers have been

---

[132] The LRC is a member of the International Network of Civil Liberties Organisations (INCLO) and ESCR-Net.

[133] A search of the SAFLII databases that cover all the South African courts reflects that the LRC had been involved in 327 cases reported on SAFLII as at 1 June 2018, including 97 Constitutional Court decisions. As described in note 122 above, this is an incomplete counting of LRC's decided cases.

[134] *Komani* (note 56 above). *Komani* was the first case to come to the LRC, as a referral from Black Sash: G Budlender interview, LRC Oral History Project (note 62 above) 7.

[135] *Rikhoto* (note 57 above).

[136] *S v Makwanyane and Another* [1995] ZACC 3; 1995 (3) SA 391 (CC) [the LRC acted for the applicant; LHR, CALS and the Society for the Abolition of the Death Penalty were admitted as *amici curiae*].

[137] *Treatment Action Campaign* (note 94 above).

[138] *Grootboom* (note 21 above).

[139] The most recent judicial appointee is Mahendra Chetty, who was appointed to the KwaZulu-Natal High Court in 2014 after serving as an LRC attorney for over 20 years. See the discussion of his interview for judicial office, and controversial remarks by Deputy Minister Fatima Chohan during the interview, in chapter 3, Jason Brickhill & Meghan Finn 'The ethics and politics of public interest litigation'.

appointed and served leadership roles on the Constitutional Court,[140] Supreme Court of Appeal (SCA),[141] Land Claims Court,[142] High Court[143] and Labour Court.[144] Other LRC alumni include leading advocates Geoff Budlender SC (one of the LRC's founders), Bongani Majola,[145] Tembeka Ngcukaitobi,[146] and Wim Trengove SC.[147] Veteran human rights lawyer, George Bizos SC, one of South Africa's most well-known struggle lawyers, continues to work for the LRC.

(c) Lawyers for Human Rights

LHR was established in 1979 as a membership organisation. It functioned as a group of lawyers contributing pro bono work to what was originally a volunteer association. The first chairman of LHR was Johann Kriegler, later a judge of the Constitutional Court, who was responsible for the name 'Lawyers for Human Rights'.[148] Its original members included Peter Motlhe, Arthur Chaskalson, John Dugard, Johan van der Vijver, George Bizos, and Jules Browde, among others. LHR created its national directorate and appointed its first full-time lawyers in 1986.[149] Its first director was Brian Currin and most recent director was Urmila Bhoola.[150] It now employs just under 50 people and has offices in Upington, Johannesburg, Pretoria, Musina, Cape Town and Durban.

Prior to 1994, LHR focused on the abolition of the death penalty, providing legal assistance to political detainees, and investigating disappearances.[151] After 1994, LHR shifted its focus to a range of projects that included human rights education as well as access to justice. Its programmes from 2006 included security

---

[140] Including former Chief Justice Sandile Ngcobo and Justice Sisi Khampepe.

[141] Including President of the SCA, Lex Mpati, and Justices Mahomed Navsa and Azhar Cachalia.

[142] Including Fikile Bam, who served as Judge President of the Land Claims Court, Alan Dodson and Shenaz Meer, current Acting Judge President.

[143] Including Dunstan Mlambo, Judge President of the North Gauteng High Court, and High Court judges Lee Bozalek, Vincent Saldanha, Chris Nicholson, Chantal Fortuin and Edwin Molahlehi (formerly of the Labour Court), Ellem Francis (formerly of the Labour Court).

[144] Including Urmila Bhoola, who was a fellow at the LRC and later served as National Director of LHR, a judge of the Labour Court and was appointed United Nations Special Rapporteur on Contemporary Forms of Slavery in 2014.

[145] Chairperson of the South African Human Rights Commission and former Assistant Secretary-General of the United Nations International Criminal Tribunal for Rwanda, who served as National Director of the LRC.

[146] Head of the LRC's Constitutional Litigation Unit (CLU) from 2009 to 2013. See interview with Ngcukaitobi, LRC Oral History Project (note 62 above).

[147] A leading senior advocate who led the LRC's CLU from 1995–2000. See interview with Trengove, LRC Oral History Project (note 62 above).

[148] John Dugard interview, LRC Oral History Project (note 62 above) 18.

[149] Lawyers for Human Rights Annual Report 2006', last accessed from <http://www.lhr.org.za/sites/lhr.org.za/files/LHR%20Annual%20Report%202006.pdf> on 1 June 2018.

[150] The Directors of LHR following Currin were Jody Kollapen, Vinod Jaichand, Rudolph Jansen, Jacob van Garderen and Urmila Bhoola.

[151] Lawyers for Human Rights Annual Report 2006 (note 149 above).

of farm workers, HIV/AIDS, gender, refugee and migrant rights, strategic litigation, and legal assistance.[152]

LHR's current programmes and projects include refugee and migrant rights, and statelessness; the Strategic Litigation Unit, which focuses on administrative justice and land; environmental rights; penal reform; security of farmworkers; and the Mozambican Mineworkers Project.[153] LHR has litigated widely across a broad range of issues and in all of South Africa's courts.[154] It has played a leading role in the areas of refugee and migrants' rights[155] and, more recently, penal reform.[156] LHR both operates as a law clinic and conducts strategic litigation. It therefore combines assisting large numbers of people, most notably in the context of refugee and migrant rights, while also contributing to the development of the law.

(d)   The Centre for Child Law

The CCL was founded in 1998. Based at the University of Pretoria, it conducts both academic research and litigation in relation to children's rights. It has litigated many of the most significant cases in this area.[157] The CCL has a relatively small staff complement of seven employees including one advocate and three attorneys. The organisation operates from the Faculty of Law at the University of Pretoria. Prof Ann Skelton and Deputy Director Karabo Ozah head the CCL.[158]

Initially, the CCL engaged primarily in academic work, until its litigation project commenced in 2003.[159] The CCL litigates those matters with the potential to set precedents in the field of children's rights in both criminal and civil matters.[160] The CCL has brought matters in its own name, on behalf of individual children or children's organisations, and in the public interest. The courts have also appointed the organisation or individual CCL lawyers to act as curator *ad litem* for children in several cases. The CCL has also frequently been admitted as

---

[152] Lawyers for Human Rights Annual Report 2006. See note 151 above.

[153] See the LHR website, last accessed from <www.lhr.org.za> on 30 May 2018.

[154] A search of the SAFLII databases that cover all the South African courts reflected that LHR was referred to in 205 cases reported on SAFLII as at 1 June 2018, including 56 Constitutional Court cases. As described in note 122 above, this is an incomplete portion of LHR's decided cases. It is also likely to be inflated by references to cases in which LHR was a named party, as the search will include all later references to those cases.

[155] David Cote & Jacob Van Garderen 'Challenges to public interest litigation in South Africa: External and internal challenges to determining the public interest' (2011) 27 *SAJHR* 167; Roni Amit 'Winning isn't everything: Courts, context, and the barriers to effecting change through public interest litigation' (2011) 27 *SAJHR* 8.

[156] See chapter 14, Clare Ballard & Frances Hobden 'Public interest litigation and prisoners' rights'.

[157] See chapter 10, Ann Skelton 'Children's rights'.

[158] Prof Skelton is also a member of the United Nations Committee on the Rights of the Child.

[159] See the CCL website, last accessed from <http://www.centreforchildlaw.co.za/about-us/about-us>.

[160] See Centre for Child Law *Strategic Impact Cases 2004–2011* (2011).

amicus curiae in matters concerning the rights of the child. The CCL works closely with a network of children's rights organisations, such as Teddy Bear Clinic for Abused Children and Childline, which bring their concerns to the CCL and are often the applicants or *amici* in child law matters.

The CCL aims to hold government to account in areas when it has failed to meet its constitutional and international law obligations regarding the rights of the child. Cases that have been brought by CCL have addressed issues including child justice,[161] child justice and witnesses, family law,[162] child protection, children and the media, educational policy, and other civil law matters.[163] The CCL's most frequently cited case is the matter of *S v M*,[164] in which it was admitted as *amicus curiae*. The case concerned the consideration of 'a child's best interest' in the sentencing of a primary caregiver of children. This judgment set a precedent requiring sentencing courts to give preference to non-custodial sentences when sentencing primary caregivers, but its jurisprudential impact is wider, and has been applied in almost every context where best interests are considered.

The CCL engages in policy and law reform through its work with government departments and at Parliament. It has been effective, together with partners, in ensuring that its legal wins are carried through into legislative change.[165] With respect to academic work, the CCL works within the Faculty of Law at the University of Pretoria, and aims to encourage law students to engage with the subject of child law.[166] The CCL assists in the teaching of an undergraduate course in child law, and also facilitates a postgraduate LLM in child law.

---

[161] See eg, *DPP Transvaal v Minister of Justice and Constitutional Development and Others* [2009] ZACC 8; 2009 (4) SA 222 (CC) [CCL, Childline South Africa, RAPCAN, Children First, Operation Bobbi Bear, POWA and Cape Mental Health Society were admitted as *amici curiae*]. This case challenged the constitutionality of sections in the Criminal Procedure Act 51 of 1977 that concerned the treatment of child victims and witnesses during trial proceedings. The Constitutional Court ordered that the Director-General for the Department of Justice and Constitutional Development would be required to furnish the court with a list of intermediaries available to child victims and witnesses in such proceedings. See also *Teddy Bear Clinic* (note 111 above) where the CCL, as applicant, was successful in challenging provisions of the Sexual Offences Act that criminalised consensual sexual conduct between minors.

[162] See eg *Ex Parte van Niekerk* (2005) JOL 14218 [CCL represented the affected children] (T); *S v J and Another* 2011 (3) SA 126 (SCA).

[163] See, generally, chapter 10, Ann Skelton, 'Children's rights'.

[164] *S v M* [2007] ZACC 18; 2008 (3) SA 232 (CC) [CCL was admitted as *amicus curiae*].

[165] For example, the cases of also *Teddy Bear Clinic* (note 111 above) and *J v National Director of Public Prosecutions and Another* [2014] ZACC 13; 2014 (2) SACR 1 (CC) [LASA acted for the appellant; Childline South Africa, Teddy Bear Clinic and National Institute for Crime Prevention and the Reintegration of Offenders were admitted as *amici curiae*, represented by the CCL] culminated in the Criminal Law (Sexual Offences and Related Matters) Amendment Act 5 of 2015.

[166] Primarily through an annual child law moot at the national university level, and involvement in the national schools' moot.

(e) The Women's Legal Centre

The Women's Legal Centre (WLC) was established in 1999, with Michelle O'Sullivan as its first director.[167] Describing itself as 'an African feminist legal centre', the WLC uses litigation, legislative monitoring, and policy advocacy to promote gender equality. The WLC also provides free legal advice to women who are referred to the WLC by the state, a Chapter 9 institution, a court or another NGO. The WLC has a staff complement of 20, including three attorneys, two candidate attorneys, three legal advisors and a paralegal.

Its focus areas include violence against women,[168] fair access to resources in relationships,[169] access to land/housing,[170] fair labour practices,[171] access to health care,[172] HIV/AIDS and the rights of sex workers.[173] It has litigated many of the most significant cases concerning women's rights and gender issues to have been decided by the South African courts.

Some of the WLC's cases include challenging the discriminatory provisions of laws relating to intestate succession, thus enabling women married in terms of monogamous Islamic marriages,[174] polygynous Islamic marriages,[175] and

---

[167] See the WLC website, last accessed from <www.wlce.co.za> on 30 May 2018. Unless stated otherwise, the material in this section is drawn from WLC's website.

[168] The WLC publishes reports on various aspects of state protection from gender-based violence. Its publications include an analysis of the legal obligations of the state in response to sexual violence, a report on progress in the legislation on sexual and domestic violence, and a report on human rights abuses against sex workers. The WLC participates in litigation on various gender violence issues, including the adequacy of protections given to child complainants in criminal proceedings on sexual abuse and the ability of victims of domestic violence to recover delictual patrimonial damages. The WLC trains NGOs on state obligations with respect to gender-based violence and makes submissions to various government entities with respect to national legislation such as the Protection from Harassment Act 17 of 2011.

[169] The WLC uses litigation and advocacy to ensure that women receive a fair share of resources following the dissolution of relationships. Much of this work has concentrated on the rights of women, in particular second and subsequent wives, under the Recognition of Customary Marriages Act 120 of 1998.

[170] As many women only have access to land and housing through the tenure of a male relative or their husbands, the WLC works to improve security in access to land and housing.

[171] The WLC focuses on preventing sexual violence in the workplace, particularly in the state employment context.

[172] The WLC focuses on women's reproductive health rights and access to health care services. The Centre has brought two cases claiming damages from health care facilities for sterilising two women, one a refugee from the DRC and the other an HIV-positive woman, without their informed consent.

[173] The WLC has also worked with sex workers in cases involving police harassment, failure to keep HIV status confidential, rape of sex workers and the denial of ARVs during detention.

[174] *Daniels v Campbell and Others* [2004] ZACC 14; 2004 (5) SA 331 (CC) [WLC acted for the applicant].

[175] *Hassam v Jacobs NO and Others* [2009] ZACC 19; 2009 (5) SA 572 (CC) [the Muslim Youth Movement of South Africa and the Women's Legal Centre Trust were admitted as *amici curiae*, the former represented by the LRC and the latter by WLC].

Hindu marriages to inherit from their spouses;[176] challenging the African customary law rule of male primogeniture;[177] challenging the interpretation of an 'employee' in the Labour Relations Act 66 of 1995 which prevented sex workers from obtaining labour protections in terms of legislation and the Constitution;[178] challenging the provisions of legislation governing customary marriages that discriminated unfairly between women married before and after the promulgation of that statute, thus extending the remedies available to women married before the Act;[179] and developing the state's duty of care in giving effect to women's rights to be free from violence.[180] The WLC drove an important *amicus curiae* intervention in the narrowly unsuccessful attempt to strike down the criminalisation of sex work.[181]

(f) The Centre for Environmental Rights

The CER was established in 2009 by eight NGOs working in South Africa's environmental and environmental justice sector, in order to provide legal and related support to environmental organisations, community organisations, and communities.[182] The CER's offices are based in Cape Town. Its strategies include facilitating the participation and engagement of NGOs and communities in the environmental decision-making process at a provincial and national level, providing legal advice on rights and remedies associated with s 24 of the Constitution and engaging in research and analysis of legal developments in the area of environmental law. CER employs 21 staff, including 11 attorneys, 2 candidate attorneys and a legal campaigner.

The CER's focus areas include transparency, corporate accountability, mining, biodiversity and conservation, water and pollution, and climate change.[183] In the

---

[176] *Govender v Ragavayah NO and Others* [2008] ZAKZHC 86; 2009 (3) SA 178 (D) [the Women's Legal Centre Trust was admitted as *amicus curiae*, represented by WLC].

[177] *Bhe and Others v Khayelitsha Magistrate and Others* [2004] ZACC 17; 2005 (1) SA 580 (CC) [the WLC acted for the applicant in the first matter; the LRC acted for the SAHRC as applicant in the second matter; the CGE was admitted as *amicus curiae*, represented by LHR].

[178] *Kylie v Commission for Conciliation Mediation and Arbitration and Others* [2010] ZALAC 8; 2010 (4) SA 383 (LAC) [WLC acted for the appellant].

[179] *Gumede (born Shange) v President of the Republic of South Africa and Others* [2008] ZACC 23; 2009 (3) SA 152 (CC) [the LRC represented the applicant; Women's Legal Centre Trust was admitted as *amicus curiae*, represented by WLC].

[180] *K v Minister of Safety and Security* [2005] ZACC 8; 2005 (6) SA 419 (CC) [WLC acted for the applicant].

[181] *S v Jordan* [2002] ZACC 22; 2002 (6) SA 642 (CC) [Sex Workers Education and Advocacy Task Force, CALS and the Reproductive Health Research Unit were admitted as the first to third *amici curiae*, represented by WLC; the Commission for Gender Equality, represented by the LRC, was admitted as the fourth *amicus curiae*].

[182] Unless otherwise stated, the following material is drawn from CER's website, last accessed from <www.cer.org.za> on 1 June 2018.

[183] Ibid.

field of transparency, the CER makes use of requests under the Promotion of Access to Information Act 2 of 2000, in order to gain access to information relating to the environmental consequences of major industries. In the area of mining, the CER has published a review of past litigation on mining and its impact on the environment. The organisation has also published a guide outlining how environmental laws may be used in criminal prosecutions to enforce respect for the right to an environment that is not harmful to one's health and well-being. In the area of biodiversity and conservation, the CER has challenged the grant of prospecting rights in protected areas and submitted comments on the draft Conservation of Agricultural Resources Amendment Bill. With respect to water, the CER has published a report on how civil society can advocate for water governance. They have also submitted regulatory proposals on water governance. They have furthermore challenged mines in operation without lawful water use licences. In the areas of pollution and climate change, the CER has spearheaded advocacy for stricter environmental regulations, including stricter air quality emissions standards. The CER has represented other environmental NGOs in court proceedings to compel the disclosure of requisite environmental permits, compliance documents and environmental records. The CER also recently successfully litigated South Africa's first case centred on climate change.[184]

(g) The Socio-Economic Rights Institute of South Africa

Jackie Dugard, its first executive director, and Stuart Wilson, its current head, founded SERI in 2009. Its office is based in Johannesburg but it is active across the country. SERI works to support the socio-economic struggles of poor communities and low-income households through research, advocacy and litigation. It presently has 22 employees, including 1 advocate (also its Executive Director), 5 attorneys and 3 candidate attorneys. SERI also has a substantial researcher complement: currently 6 researchers at differing levels of seniority. In this respect, SERI has dedicated a substantial proportion of its resources and activities to research, as compared to the other organisations in the sector. SERI provides research and advocacy services, together with legal advice and representation, to its client communities. The idea is that these blended methodologies can be used by poor and vulnerable people to independently articulate and assert their socio-economic rights, and to ensure that those rights are fulfilled in a manner appropriate to the needs that actually exist on the ground.

At its founding, SERI's primary focus areas were access to the basic services enshrined in s 27 of the Constitution, and housing and evictions. They later expanded their focus areas to include 'political space', encompassing the protection of freedom of speech and the right to peacefully assemble and protest. These rights are inextricably linked to socio-economic rights, as they are the means through which communi-

---

[184] *Earthlife Africa Johannesburg v Minister of Environmental Affairs and Others* [2017] ZAGPPHC 58; [2017] 2 All SA 519 (GP) [CER acted for the applicants].

ties can challenge the state's failure to deliver socio-economic rights adequately. As discontent has grown with respect to the failure of the state to deliver on basic services, the significance of these rights has been amplified. SERI now organises its work under three themes—'securing a home', 'making a living' and 'expanding political space'. SERI's approach is based on an understanding of socio-economic rights as political tools for accountability, mobilisation, and empowerment.

SERI has conducted substantial PIL in all three of its focus areas.[185] In respect of access to basic services, SERI has successfully launched applications to compel municipalities to provide basic water and sanitation facilities in several communities.[186]

It is in the area of housing and evictions, however, where SERI has done most to drive the development of the law. Building on the foundation of early jurisprudence established primarily by the LRC and CALS (where SERI's founders worked before launching SERI), SERI has consolidated a strategic sequence of PIL cases concerning the procedural and substantive rights of occupiers facing eviction.[187] SERI has also driven litigation to compel informal settlement upgrading;[188] to establish that the termination of residential lease contracts must be fair in all the circumstances;[189] to enforce dignified, family-friendly living conditions in shelters for the homeless;[190] and to ensure proper notice and dispute resolution procedures before banks are permitted to foreclose against residential property.[191]

In the focus area of political space and its impact on the realisation of socio-economic rights, SERI has published reports and case studies on civil society and the role of protest movements in South Africa.[192] SERI has litigated

---

[185] SERI maintains a list of its cases, including the papers and heads of argument, on its website, last accessed from <http://seri-sa.org/index.php/litigation/cases/12-litigation/cases?layout=blog> on 1 June 2018. A SAFLII search reflects that SERI is referred to in 28 cases included on that database, including nine Constitutional Court decisions. As noted above, SAFLII's records are under-inclusive.

[186] See chapter 7, Jackie Dugard, 'Basic services'.

[187] See chapter 5, Stuart Wilson, 'Making space for change: Pro-poor property rights litigation in post-apartheid South Africa'.

[188] *Melani and Others v Johannesburg City and Others* [2016] ZAGPJHC 55; 2016 (5) SA 67 (GJ) [SERI acted for the applicants].

[189] *Maphango and Others v Aengus Lifestyle Properties (Pty) Ltd* 2012 (3) SA 531 (CC).

[190] *Dladla and Others v City of Johannesburg and Another (Centre for Applied Legal Studies and Another as amici curiae)* 2018 (2) SA 327 (CC).

[191] *Gundwana v Steko Development and Others* [2011] ZACC 42; 2011 (3) SA 608 (CC) [the National Consumer Forum was admitted as *amicus curiae*, represented by the LRC]; *Sebola and Another v Standard Bank of South Africa Ltd and Another (Socio-Economic Rights Institute of South Africa and Others as Amici Curiae)* [2012] ZACC 11; 2012 (5) SA 142 (CC) [SERI was admitted as first *amicus curiae*].

[192] See SERI website, last accessed from <http://www.seri-sa.org/index.php/2013-03-07-10-16-20/political-space>.

cases on the failure of the state to respect the right to assemble,[193] including damages claims against the police for injuries sustained in claims of police intimidation against protestors.[194] SERI played a pivotal role in the Marikana Commission of Inquiry, in which it acted for the families of most of the deceased mineworkers. SERI also led litigation to reverse 'Operation Clean Sweep', which saw the temporary eviction of 8 000 informal traders from the Johannesburg inner city before it was reversed by the Constitutional Court in a rare urgent appeal.[195]

Outside the courts, SERI has set the standard in the sector for rigorous legal and social research across all its focus areas.[196] This has included work on the supply and demand for low cost housing in Johannesburg;[197] the suppression of dissent in informal settlements[198] and university campuses;[199] and the lived reality of informal trade.[200] SERI has also published a useful set of resource guides on housing and sanitation that combine laws, policies, and case studies to provide a tool for Community Based Organisations (CBOs) and NGOs.

(h) Southern African Litigation Centre

SALC was founded in 2005 as a regional NGO that engages in PIL, training, research and advocacy in 12 Southern African countries,[201] including South Africa. Their aim is to realise and advance the rights of marginalised and vulnerable groups and to strengthen the rule of law. SALC was initially set up as a joint initiative of the International Bar Association and Open Society Initiative for Southern Africa (OSISA). SALC has a relatively small, but effective staff complement of 11 employees, including eight lawyers, drawn from several countries in the region. It is based in Johannesburg and is currently headed by Kaajal Ramjathan-Keogh, who succeeded Nicole Fritz.

---

[193] See inter alia *S v Nkosi and 13 Others* unreported decision of Protea Regional Magistrate's Court [SERI acted for the accused]; *S v Moyo, Swetsana and Sisulu* unreported decision of the Germiston Magistrate's Court [SERI acted for the accused].

[194] *Mke and Others v Minister of Safety and Security* (DHC) unreported case 9934/07 of 5 December 2012; *Abahlali baseMjondolo and 52 Others v Minister of Police and Others* (KZNHC) unreported case 9955/2012 of 25 September 2012 [SERI acted for the applicants].

[195] *South African Informal Traders Forum and Others v City of Johannesburg and Others* 2014 ZACC 8; 2014 (4) SA 371 (CC) [SERI acted for the applicants].

[196] Including a valuable recent research report on PIL in South Africa, SERI Report (note 25 above).

[197] Minding the Gap: An Analysis of the Supply of and Demand for Low-Income Rental Accommodation in Inner City Johannesburg (November 2013).

[198] An Anatomy of Dissent and Repression: The Criminal Justice System and the 2011 Thembelihle Protest (June 2014).

[199] Double Harm: Police Misuse of Force and Barriers to Necessary Health Care Services during Student Protest (October 2017).

[200] 'The End of the Street?' Informal Traders' Experiences of Rights and Regulations in Inner City Johannesburg (September 2015).

[201] Angola, Botswana, Democratic Republic of the Congo, Lesotho, Malawi, Mozambique, Namibia, South Africa, Swaziland, Tanzania, Zambia and Zimbabwe. SALC has also conducted ad hoc litigation in Tanzania and Nigeria.

Within its overall regional approach, SALC's focus areas include international criminal justice, business and human rights, women's land and property rights, refugee and migrant rights, freedom of expression, prisoners' rights, health rights, sex worker rights, LGBTI rights, sexual and reproductive rights, disability rights, the rule of law, and children's rights. SALC does not run a high volume of cases,[202] but its matters tend to be cutting-edge, complex, far-reaching and often politically fraught.[203] A prominent example is the 'torture docket case' in which SALC secured an order compelling the South African National Prosecuting Authority to investigate allegations of torture perpetrated upon Zimbabweans in Zimbabwe.[204] Another politically contentious case involved SALC obtaining an order for the arrest of Sudanese President al-Bashir on the strength of a warrant issued by the International Criminal Court.[205] In addition to its litigation, SALC incubated the African Legal Information Institute (AfricanLII) from 2010 to 2013. AfricanLII is a project to support the establishment and operation of independent national legal information institute projects in Africa.

SALC's board and staff have included a rich, international pool of judges, lawyers and activists. Board members have included Sanji Monaheng, former judge of the International Criminal Court, South African writer Sisonke Msimang, Lord Abernethy (Justice Alastair Cameron) of the Botswana Appeal Court, International Bar Association head Mark Ellis, Tawanda Mutasah, renowned Zimbabwean human rights lawyer Beatrice Mtetwa and Justice Malcolm Wallis of the Supreme Court of Appeal of South Africa, an advisory member who supported SALC at its inception.

(i) SECTION27

SECTION27 was established in May 2010 by founding members Mark Heywood,[206] Adila Hassim and Jonathan Berger. SECTION27 grew out of and subsumed the ALP,

---

[202] A search for SALC on SAFLII reflects that it is referred to in nine South African cases and one in Botswana. SALC's modus operandi entails that it supports cases regionally and its name therefore does not appear in the case (unless it litigates in its own name). The full list of cases appears in SALC's ten-year Case Book and more currently on its website, last accessed from <http://www.southernafricalitigationcentre.org/cases/precedent-cases/>.

[203] Several of SALC's cases feature prominently in chapter 2, Max du Plessis & Stuart Scott, 'The world's law and South African domestic courts: The role of international law in public interest litigation'.

[204] *National Commissioner of the South African Police Service v Southern African Human Rights Litigation Centre and Another* [2014] ZACC 30; 2015 (1) SA 315 (CC) [LHR acted for the respondents, SALC and Zimbabwe Exiles Forum; and Tides Centre, Peace and Justice Initiative and CALS were admitted as *amici curiae*, represented by the LRC].

[205] *Minister of Justice and Constitutional Development and Others v Southern African Litigation Centre and Others* [2016] ZASCA 17; 2016 (3) SA 317 (SCA) [SALC was a respondent; and HSF was admitted as *amicus curiae*, represented by WW].

[206] See Mark Heywood *Get up! Stand up! Personal Journeys Towards Social Justice* (2017).

which had been founded by Edwin Cameron in 1993 and spearheaded litigation and advocacy for the rights of people living with HIV.[207] SECTION27 currently has 35 employees, including attorneys, researchers and paralegals. As its name reveals, SECTION27's core mandate concerns the rights protected in s 27 of the Constitution—access to health care services, and the social determinants of health, namely food, water, social security and the right to education in s 29.[208]

In the area of the right of access to health care, SECTION27 plays a leading role in using the law to advance the rights of health care users. It has continued the work of the ALP, which focused on the rights of people living with HIV but has also extended this work to include litigation and advocacy to strengthen and improve the broader health systems on which health care users rely. Focusing on the obligations of both public and private actors, SECTION27 engages in work regarding access to medicines, budgeting for health, quality and affordable health care services and human resources. More recently, SECTION27 has included the right to mental health care services as one of its focus areas and represented 63 families who lost their loved ones during the Life Esidimeni tragedy.

The right to basic education enshrined in s 29 of the Constitution is a further priority area of SECTION27. The organisation views the right to education as a health determinant and a gateway right for the realisation of other constitutional rights, including the rights to equality and dignity. Their work is aimed at ensuring that key elements for quality education such as textbooks, adequate sanitation and infrastructure are present in schools. They also work towards addressing sexual violence in schools and ensuring the rights of disabled learners. SECTION27 instituted the groundbreaking textbooks litigation against the Minister of Basic Education based on the failure of the Limpopo Department of Education,[209] and continues to work to ensure that all learners, including learners with visual impairments, have access to their prescribed learning materials.

SECTION27 introduced the right of access to food as a focus area on the basis that access to food impacts social justice and is a determinant of health. The organisation works towards appropriate regulation of and accountability in the food industry and for the availability of food for all.

With regard to governance and accountability, SECTION27 is focused on advocating for more effective parliamentary oversight over the Executive and a better understanding of the constitutional obligations of the private sector with regard to the rights to health and education.[210] One of the focal points in this area

---

[207] On the history and work of the ALP see Didi Moyle *Speaking Truth to Power: The Story of the AIDS Law Project* (2015).

[208] SECTION27 'Priority work areas', last accessed from <http://section27.org.za/priority-work-areas/> on 1 June 2018 (SECTION27 Priority work areas).

[209] See chapter 11, Cameron McConnachie & Samantha Brener 'Litigating the right to basic education'.

[210] SECTION27 Priority work areas (note 209 above).

is working with partner organisations to tackle corruption, because achieving social justice and realising the rights enshrined in the Constitution are not possible for as long as corruption remains rampant in our society.

(j) Equal Education Law Centre

The EELC was founded in 2012 by a group of activist lawyers who had been involved in the formation of its partner organisation, social movement EE, some years earlier.[211] Arthur Chaskalson was the founding chairperson of EELC's Board of Trustees. Its initial director was Dmitri Holtzman and it is now headed by Nurina Ally. Based in Cape Town, the EELC has 12 staff, including 5 attorneys, 3 candidate attorneys, and researchers.

The EELC conducts strategic litigation and legal advocacy. It runs a specialist law clinic one afternoon every week in which clients from across the country with issues related to education can obtain free legal advice and support. Its litigation has included cases concerning school infrastructure, scholar transport, discrimination against learners on various grounds, language policies in schools, and fee exemptions for single parents, among other issues. Its advocacy work has included making submissions and recommendations to relevant government institutions, conducting legal and policy research, conducting investigations, disseminating information on the inadequacies and inequalities in the education system, and assisting communities to formulate their own policy perspectives. In addition to its 'community lawyering' for other clients such as school communities, the EELC works closely with EE in a model of 'movement lawyering' inspired by the legal work of the TAC. The EELC has represented EE as *amicus curiae* in several important cases dealing with education rights.[212]

The EELC has furthermore brought a number of key cases concerning the right to display religious and cultural traditions at school,[213] the protection of the rights of pregnant learners,[214] the right to fair disciplinary process,[215] the right of

---

[211] See the EELC website, last accessed from <www.eelawcentre.org.za> on 30 May 2018.

[212] For example, *AB and Another v Pridwin Preparatory School and Others* [2017] ZAGPJHC 186 [EE was admitted as *amicus curiae*, represented by EELC] *Federation of Governing Bodies for South African Schools (FEDSAS) v Member of the Executive Council for Education, Gauteng and Another* [2016] ZACC 14; 2016 (4) SA 546 (CC) [EE was admitted as *amicus curiae*, represented by the EELC]; *Head of Department, Department of Education, Free State Province v Welkom High School and Another; Head of Department, Department of Education, Free State Province v Harmony High School and Another* [2013] ZACC 25; 2014 (2) SA 228 (CC) [EE was admitted as first *amicus curiae*, represented by the EELC; CCL was admitted as second *amicus curiae*].

[213] *Radebe and Others v Principal of Leseding Technical School and Others* (1821/2013) ZAFSHC 111 [EELC acted for the applicants].

[214] *Head of Department, Department of Education, Free State Province v Welkom High School* (note 212 above).

[215] *Savage and Others v MEC, Western Cape Education Department and Others* (WCHC) unreported case 18155/13 [EELC acted for the applicants].

indigent learners to fee exemptions in fee-charging public schools,[216] the neglect of the infrastructure and monitoring of schools in rural regions,[217] and safety in schools.[218] The EELC also, in collaboration with EE, assisted in compelling the publication of Minimum Norms and Standards with respect to the resources and facilities necessary to provide learners with a quality education as required by the South African Schools Act 84 of 1996.[219] This litigation ultimately led the Minister to publish final and binding Norms and Standards for School Infrastructure (Norms and Standards). This was a historic victory in South Africa as the Norms and Standards expressly require that all schools must have water, electricity, safe classrooms, security, and sanitation facilities within a set period of time.[220]

(k) Ndifuna Ukwazi

One of South Africa's newest and most dynamic public interest organisations, NU, combines research, political organising, and litigation in campaigns to advance urban land justice in Cape Town. Their primary mission is to expand and protect access to affordable housing and build an inclusive city. Mandisa Shandu[221] heads the NU Law Centre, making it one of the few public interest law firms headed by a Black woman. NU employs 17 staff, including 4 attorneys, 6 'organisers' and 4 researchers. NU began as a campaign organisation in 2011 and registered as a law centre in 2015. It now works closely with Reclaim the City, a campaign launched in Cape Town in February 2016 and originally led by NU. Reclaim the City is a movement of tenants and working-class people living in the inner city and surrounds of Cape Town who campaign against evictions and displacement. NU's approach to lawyering is thus firmly rooted in activism and movement-building.

The NU Law Centre uses movement lawyering and other strategies to disrupt the reproduction of spatial apartheid, advance equitable access to urban land and housing, and mitigate the effects of displacement following an eviction. NU recently formed part of the NGO complainant coalition that participated in the Commission of Inquiry into policing in Khayelitsha,[222] and which defended the

---

[216] *Dean Carelse v MEC, Western Cape Education Department and Others* [WCHC] unreported case 21602/2012 [EELC acted for the applicants].

[217] *Manyokole and Others v District Director, Maluti District, Western Cape Department of Basic Education and Others* (ECHC) unreported case 603/2012 [EELC acted for the applicants].

[218] *Manenberg Teachers' Steering Committee and Others v Western Cape Education Department and Another* (WCHC) unreported case 3054/2011 [EELC acted for the applicants].

[219] *Equal Education and Others v Minister of Basic Education and Others* (ECBHC) unreported case 81/2012 [the LRC acted for acted for the applicants, supported by the EELC].

[220] See the discussion in chapter 11, Cameron McConnachie & Samantha Brener, 'Litigating the right to basic education'.

[221] Shandu heads the law centre and co-directs the umbrella body of NU with Jared Rossouw.

[222] See 'Towards a safer Khayelitsha: Report of the Commission of Inquiry into allegations of police inefficiency and a breakdown in relations between SAPS and the community of Khayelitsha', last accessed from <http://www.saflii.org/khayelitshacommissionreport.pdf> on 1 June 2018.

establishment of the Commission when it was challenged in the courts.[223] One of NU's pending cases is *Adonisi*,[224] in which they seek to review a decision of the City of Cape Town to sell strategically located public land in Cape Town while also challenging the failure to make land available on an equitable basis in terms of s 25(5) of the Constitution. This is the first case to tackle this issue. The case is allied to a public campaign—#StopTheSale[225]—by Reclaim the City.

The PIL sector therefore consists of a range of organisations. Three are generalist public interest centres, while the others specialise in substantive areas of law. The organisations also vary in their structure, positionality, and approaches to PIL. While some organisations, such as SECTION27, the EELC and NU adopt an avowedly 'activist' approach, others such as the LRC and LHR operate more in the mode of law firms representing clients.[226] In the next section, I engage with some of the challenges that the PIL sector faces and the critiques to which it has been subjected.

1.5 CRITIQUES AND CHALLENGES

The development of PIL in South Africa, both as a strategy for social change and as a civil society sector, has not gone without criticism. The sector also faces several operational challenges today. The critiques and challenges are intertwined. As I will go on to describe, academic critiques have focused on the capacity of PIL (or the courts and the law more generally) to produce meaningful social change. Other critiques, including those within the sector, have pointed to its failure adequately to transform its racial composition and its failure to put in place adequate systems to address incidents of sexual harassment. These criticisms are interrelated, as they speak to the role of public interest organisations within a deeply unequal society still characterised by structures of racism and patriarchy.

In relation to the challenges that the sector faces, a research report commissioned by the Atlantic Philanthropies drawing on a wide range of interviews, identified three major challenges, namely a lack of funding, lack of experienced, skilled staff, and the attitude of government.[227] Antagonism from some quarters in government, in the context of specific cases, complicates the conduct of PIL.[228]

---

[223] *Minister of Police and Others v Premier of the Western Cape and Others* [2013] ZACC 33; 2014 (1) SA 1 (CC) [WLC was the 8th respondent, acting on behalf of the SJC, TAC, EE, Free Gender, Triangle Project and NU; the SJC was the 9th respondent, represented by the LRC].

[224] *Adonisi and Others v Minister for Transport and Others* (WCHC) unreported case 7908/17 [NU acts for the applicants].

[225] See 'A just vision of Tafelberg', last accessed from <www.stopthesale.net/a-just-vision-for-tafelberg> on 1 June 2018.

[226] See the discussion of the ethical dimensions of these differences in chapter 3, Jason Brickhill & Meghan Finn, 'The ethics and politics of public interest litigation'.

[227] Budlender et al (note 25 above) 9–11.

[228] See chapter 3, Jason Brickhill & Meghan Finn, 'The ethics and politics of public interest litigation'.

There is fortunately, however, no impending threat to the independent existence and operations of PIL organisations. Funding and the related ability to attract and retain skilled staff present more immediate challenges to their operations. The subsequent SERI Report again highlighted that the sector struggles to train and retain skilled practitioners.[229] PIL organisations do have some ways to mitigate the cumulative difficulties of funding and staffing, including the use of in-house and pro bono counsel, briefing counsel on contingency or reduced fee arrangements, and having attorneys exercise rights of appearance.[230] Funding and staffing have an added dimension—the imperative to transform the PIL sector and the pool of counsel briefed in PIL. I return to transformation below. The operational challenges of funding and staffing arise in a context in which the PIL sector faces criticism regarding its mission and its operations.

Academic commentators, recognising that South Africa remains a deeply unequal society characterised by high levels of unemployment and poverty, have launched a range of critiques of the law,[231] the Constitution,[232] human rights,[233] the Constitutional Court[234] and PIL.[235] At the heart of the most far-reaching of these critiques is the claim that meaningful social change, which should be directed ultimately at the eradication of poverty, cannot be achieved by these means. Joel Modiri has asserted that the law and rights are insufficient 'as a means of serious social change',[236] and later that '[w]hen realised in their most progressive and effective form, [rights] can only improve and minimally relieve the position and condition of impoverished people without transforming that position or abolishing that condition'.[237] Some of the more generalised academic critiques are weakened by their over-reliance on American literature[238] and their failure to

---

[229] SERI Report (note 25 above) 138.

[230] Discussed in chapter 3, Jason Brickhill & Meghan Finn, 'The ethics and politics of public interest litigation'; and SERI Report (note 25 above) 102–26.

[231] See eg, Anton Kok 'Is law able to transform society?' (2010) 127 *SALJ* 59.

[232] Tshepo Madlingozi 'Social justice in a time of neo-apartheid constitutionalism: Critiquing the anti-black economy of recognition, incorporation and distribution' (2017) 28 *Stell LR* 123.

[233] Joel Modiri 'Law's poverty' (2015) 18 *PER/PELJ* 224, 258; Joel M Modiri 'The colour of law, power and knowledge: Introducing Critical Race Theory in (post-)apartheid South Africa' (2012) 28 *SAJHR* 405.

[234] Madlingozi (note 64 above).

[235] Madlingozi (note 232 above).

[236] Modiri (2012) (note 233 above) n 129.

[237] Modiri (2015) (note 233 above) 258.

[238] There are several significant differences between the South African and American systems that require any comparisons to be cautiously made. These include the inclusion in the South African Constitution of justiciable socio-economic rights, a substantive conception of equality that supports the use of affirmative action and other restitutionary measures, and procedural features including wide-standing provisions, flexible remedial powers and a protective costs regime.

conduct any meaningful empirical research.[239] Despite these limitations, they ask legitimate questions that PIL lawyers must confront in their work and in their writing.

In a scathing critique targeting the 'social justice project' and the sector more directly, Tshepo Madlingozi characterises South Africa as being in a state of 'neo-apartheid constitutionalism'.[240] He argues that in this time of neo-apartheid the contemporary discourse of social justice, which is 'transformative constitutionalism's master frame for social emancipation', is 'actually complicit in the continuation of the anti-black bifurcated societal structure'.[241] Madlingozi's critique rejects also what he considers the ANC's unacceptable compromise and the Constitution itself. In addition, he condemns the public interest sector not merely for championing what he sees as the fatally flawed constitutional project but also for its own practices and representivity.

The academic questioning of the value of PIL—of which Madlingozi forms the sharpest end of the spear—is speculative, as it generally does not include empirical research. It poses hard challenges and vital questions to the public interest sector and society as a whole about the utility of PIL as a strategy to achieve social change. However, the discourse needs to extend beyond theoretical discussions of the nature of rights and high-level analyses of well-worn Constitutional Court decisions. It needs empirical grounding. In section 1.5 below, I offer a working analytical frame which I am developing to analyse the impact and value of PIL.

There is a second level to the criticism of PIL, which focuses on the composition and practices of the PIL sector. Public interest organisations are not insulated from the racist, patriarchal society within which they operate. Although these organisations exist to combat these ills, they have also been afflicted. The public interest sector has been challenged for its failure adequately to transform to be more racially representative of the South African society. Critics such as Madlingozi have noted that the executive directors of the most influential public interest organisations are white, that five white male senior counsel dominate social justice litigation before the Constitutional Court and that white people dominate the production of social justice knowledge in academia.[242] These criticisms are well founded, although some progress has since been made. In relation to leadership, several PIL organisations have undergone succession and others are in the process of doing so.[243] It is likely that the majority of PIL organisations will soon be headed by black directors.[244]

---

[239] In particular, Kok (note 231 above) and Modiri (2015) (note 233 above).

[240] Madlingozi (note 232 above).

[241] Ibid 125.

[242] Ibid 144.

[243] The heads of SALC, LHR, CALS have all stepped down. SECTION27 and LRC are in the process of succession from their current directors.

[244] At present, the EELC, NU and SALC have black directors.

There has also been some progress in relation to the briefing of counsel by the PIL sector, with the dominance of established white male senior counsel receding.[245] The briefing patterns of the public interest sector, and legal profession more broadly, came into sharp focus during the hearing of the landmark silicosis class action litigation. The mammoth case highlighted in one graphic instance that white advocates continue to be briefed disproportionately, especially in high-profile and lucrative cases. The case also included PIL organisations that attracted criticism for their briefing practices. The public outcry prompted reform at the Johannesburg Bar, which modified its rules, thus making it a disciplinary offence for lead counsel to accept a brief or remain on brief where there is a team of three or more counsel on brief in a matter, and no member of the team is a black person.[246]

Subsequently, a group of young employees within the public interest sector formed an association, which they later named the 'Black Workers Forum', to take up transformation issues within the sector. At the Public Interest Law Gathering in August 2016, they asserted several demands of the sector, relating in particular to racial transformation of the sector, succession and development of Black lawyers.[247] These demands tapped into strong political currents in contemporary South Africa regarding the need to accelerate transformation, especially racial and gender justice, and including the growing urgency of effective land reform.[248]

The latest challenge to confront the PIL sector, and civil society more generally, concerns allegations of sexual harassment by senior male employees at organisa-

---

[245] See the discussion of transformation in chapter 3, Jason Brickhill & Meghan Finn, 'The ethics and politics of public interest litigation'.

[246] Resolution adopted at the Annual General Meeting of the Johannesburg Society of Advocates on 29 October 2015.

[247] Demands of Public Interest Gathering Young Professionals on 31 August 2016, available on the website of PILG, last accessed from <http://www.publicinterestlawgathering.com/wp-content/uploads/2016/09/Transformation-in-Public-Interest-Law_List-of-Demands-31082016.pdf> on 1 June 2018. The demands included that the organisations in the sector must adopt transformation plans, succession plans, transparency in salaries and pay scales, briefing policies to promote the briefing of black advocates, plans on how black lawyers will be groomed, mentored and supported to do pupillage, cultural and gender sensitivity training, including through follow up on reported incidents, commitments to recruit people living with disabilities, gender empowerment policies and to adopt hiring policies that accommodate graduates from other African countries who study in South Africa. One of the demands, very interestingly, was 'land reclamation and redistribution, there must be proactive fully funded programs designed to address this'.

[248] At its 2017 national conference, the ruling ANC resolved to 'pursue land expropriation without compensation as a matter of policy'. See ANC website, last accessed from <http://anc.org.za/sites/default/files/54th_National_Conference_Report.pdf> on 1 June 2018. There has since been debate in Parliament concerning whether it is necessary to amend the property clause in s 25 of the Constitution to facilitate land expropriation without compensation. In 2018, an important book on land and constitutionalism was published by an advocate who previously worked in the sector and is frequently involved in public interest litigation, which further ignited debate: Ngcukaitobi (note 2 above).

tions in the sector.[249] These allegations have prompted a conversation within the PIL sector concerning patterns of sexual harassment and institutional weaknesses in addressing it.[250] Concerns about how the sector deals with sexual harassment reflect not only pervasive societal structures of patriarchy and misogyny, but also the institutional weaknesses of PIL organisations. Having good policies, systems and people in place is a prerequisite to address sexual harassment and transformation. This makes it all the more important that PIL organisations are able to attract and retain skilled staff, especially in management and human resources, and secure sufficient funding to enable them to lead the profession in addressing transformation and sexual harassment.

1.6 THE IMPACT AND VALUE OF PUBLIC INTEREST LITIGATION IN SOUTH AFRICA

One of the aims of this volume is to analyse and share accounts of PIL in South Africa, to enable a richer and fuller assessment of what it has achieved, and what that means for the future of PIL. These contributions set the stage for a more informed discussion on the role of PIL in achieving the constitutional vision of social justice, as well as reflecting on the strategies and tactics that are likely to be effective in the future. The determination of this role leaves us with an important question: how are we to attribute down-the-line effects of social change to PIL, in complex situations with multiple moving parts? In other words, how do we determine the real, actual impact of 'successful' PIL?

(a) Causation and contribution

The first challenge in assessing impact is the causal question of the attribution of on-the-ground social change, amongst other effects, to litigation.[251] This arises because litigation is only one of the possible strategies to seek social change and advance claims to secure social justice. The counter-factual—what would have happened without the PIL—is often impossible to determine. My view, in these circumstances, is that the best approach is not to eliminate all other possible causes of social change, or to attempt to create a counter-factual, but to ask whether PIL has in any way *materially contributed* to such change. Whether PIL has materially contributed to particular impacts can be inferred from a range of sources, including the judgment or order itself, government and policy documents, parliamentary proceedings, speeches of officials, newspaper reports, interviews with affected

---

[249] The allegations that first drew public attention to the issue concerned senior employees of the social movement, EE. Later, reports emerged of a senior attorney at the LRC who resigned after being found guilty of sexual harassment.

[250] See Nicolette Naylor 'Social justice organisations are not squeaky clean, and we must do better' *Mail & Guardian* 23 May 2018, last accessed from <https://mg.co.za/article/2018-05-23-social-justice-organisations-are-not-squeaky-clean-and-we-must-do-better> on 1 June 2018.

[251] Open Society Justice Initiative (note 25 above) 74; Gerald N Rosenberg, *The Hollow Hope: Can Courts Bring About Social Change?* (2008) 108.

individuals and communities and opinion polls. Other attributive indicators may include secondary literature, comparing the timing of key events, statements by claimants and key actors in the policy-making process about whether they were influenced by court decisions, or explicit references to court actions in the policy-making process. One can then move on to analyse the dimensions and directness of that impact, including its type, temporal considerations and its reach.

(b) A typology of impact—legal, material and political

To determine the causality of impact, we must first understand exactly what kinds of effects we are looking for. In other words, how do we understand impact? Two broad approaches emerge from the literature.[252] First, the 'materialist' or 'neorealist' approach to impact tends to focus on the direct and tangible effects of litigation.[253] This is contrasted with a 'social mobilisation' or 'constructivist' approach to impact, which emphasises the political and politicising effects of PIL.[254] The first approach is illustrated in the international literature by Gerald Rosenberg's *The Hollow Hope*,[255] while the second is most clearly employed in Michael McCann's *Rights at Work*.[256] In the South African literature, the study conducted by the Atlantic Philanthropies has been characterised as taking a materialist/neorealist view. It understands impact to mean 'tangible and sustainable impact on the ground for those who ought to benefit from [rights]'.[257] Later contributions have sought to extend the understanding of impact to include the broader effects, attentive to the mobilising and politicising role of PIL, moving closer to the second approach.[258]

PIL may have a range of different effects. To assess all of these effects, I propose a working typology of impact that includes three analytical categories: the *legal*, *material* and *political* effects of PIL.[259] Legal effects are defined to include changes to law or policy. Material effects include the provision of social goods or services, the payment of compensation or damages, and compelling or prohibiting specific conduct. In my view, this is a significant distinction.[260] There is an

---

[252] Langford et al (note 23 above) 21–3.

[253] Rodríguez-Garavito (note 17 above) 1687.

[254] Ibid 1688.

[255] Rosenberg (note 251 above).

[256] Michael W McCann *Rights at Work: Pay Equity Reform and the Politics of Legal Mobilization* (1994).

[257] Budlender et al (note 25 above) 96.

[258] Dugard & Malcolm Langford (note 24 above) 55–6; SERI Report (note 25 above) 10–4.

[259] For other proposed typologies of the type of impact of litigation, see: Rodríguez-Garavito (note 17 above) ('material' and 'symbolic' effects); Dugard & Langford (note 24 above) ('enabling' and 'material' impact); Langford et al (note 23 above) 22–3 ('material', 'political' and 'symbolic/recognition' impacts).

[260] Some approaches include legal impacts as part of material impact, eg, Langford et al (note 23 above) 23; Dugard & Langford (note 24 above) 57.

important analytical difference between changing the law on paper, for example by establishing that the right to basic education includes textbooks, and realising that law in action—when learners actually receive textbooks. The legal/material distinction ensures that one is alive to the potential for PIL victories on paper that do not necessarily translate into tangible change. The third category of political impacts concerns effects on power relations, discourse and shifts in the narrative or 'agenda' in relation to a particular set of issues. Analysing impact through this lens can unlock the potential of PIL as a tool for social justice, reflected so powerfully in the chapters of this volume that cover substantive areas of law.

(c) Temporality and the 'reach' of impact

These sets of questions include the temporal dimension and the reach or extent of impact. As to the temporality of impact, one may take a longer or shorter view. It is possible to begin with a baseline and focus on the immediate effects in the aftermath of a court order; medium-term effects in the subsequent years following that order; or long-term, even inter-generational effects of the change that PIL brings. These approaches may offer various insights into the value and effectiveness of PIL.

As to 'reach', the effects of a case may be narrowed or broadened by the scope of the order granted by the court. A case concerning access to a social good, such as housing or water, might result in an order granting relief to identified individual claimants. It might also go further, extending to all similarly situated persons. The order might strike down a law or policy, or an exclusion from a law or policy so as to extend a benefit to a class of persons, as in the case of legalising same-sex marriage. Reach may also be geographical, in that it might apply to a single province, such as the Limpopo textbooks litigation.

The chapters in this volume do not expressly apply this framework of impact. They may very reasonably assume causation or attribution, without interrogating it. Some chapters focus primarily on legal and material impact,[261] while others pay more attention to political impact.[262] However, the framework of *legal, material* and *political* impact provides an overarching frame through which to view these contributions, and hints at the broader questions that this volume seeks to pose.

1.7 STRUCTURE OF THE BOOK

This volume is divided into two parts. **PART I** addresses a set of topics that relate to PIL generally and that span questions of law, history, political science, philosophy and sociology. **PART II** of the book turns to the actual conduct of PIL in ten

---

[261] For example, chapter 11, Cameron McConnachie & Samantha Brener, 'Litigating the right to basic education'.

[262] For example, chapter 6, Bonita Meyersfeld & Nomonde Nyembe, 'Gender and public interest litigation in post-apartheid South Africa: Have 'Systematic Motifs of Discrimination' been addressed?' and chapter 9, Kerry Williams & Melanie Judge "Happy (N)ever after: Public interest litigation for LGBTI equality'.

important substantive areas of South African law—property and housing; gender; basic services; health care; LGBTI rights; children's rights; education; access to information; freedom of expression; and criminal justice and prisoners' rights. This section of the book therefore traces PIL across civil and political rights and socio-economic rights. Each chapter identifies the key drivers of PIL in the particular area, the most significant issues and cases, and identifies features, strategies and challenges that may be distinctive about PIL in that area.

PART I begins on the international plane. Max du Plessis and Stuart Scott explore the relationship between international law and PIL in South Africa in **chapter 2**, 'The world's law and South African domestic courts: The role of international law in public interest litigation'. Du Plessis and Scott outline how the courts have grappled with international law's place in the South African domestic system and when the courts have been receptive to international law arguments, identifying important areas of PIL that have been heavily influenced by international law, especially international human rights law.

In **chapter 3** on 'The ethics and politics of public interest litigation', Meghan Finn and I address some of the implications of PIL relating to the formal *Political* process, its *political* implications for the exercise of power in society, and some of the questions of professional and moral ethics that arise. These include exploring the values and objectives that animate PIL; how public interest organisations should relate to government, big business and other social actors; the imperative to transform the public interest sector and contribute to the transformation of the profession; the tensions between individual *clients* and broader *causes*; and financial considerations including costs, fees and funding.

In **chapter 4** on 'Constitutional litigation procedure', Georgina Jephson and Osmond Mngomezulu map out the procedural landscape within which PIL is conducted. They focus on the particular procedural rules that have facilitated PIL under the Constitution—jurisdiction, standing, *amici curiae*, constitutional remedies and costs.

This concludes PART I. The litigation discussed in PART II often (but not always) forms part of broader campaigns by social movements, communities and other civil society actors. These ten chapters each situate their account of the cases in the particular socio-political context. They do not merely provide a neutral, black-letter account of an area of constitutional law but adopt the grounded perspective of those engaged in the struggles to realise rights. Notably, the contributors have all been personally involved in driving PIL in the areas that they cover.

In **chapter 5**, Stuart Wilson identifies property rights as a key site of struggle in post-apartheid South Africa, in many ways paradigmatic of the double-edged threat and promise that the law offers poor people. This chapter covers a range of areas of law that fall under property rights. Just as property rights determine the physical spaces that people may occupy, the law defines the spaces within which agency is possible. And within the paradox of the law as a 'structurant of social practice' lies the paradox of property rights. Property law, Wilson observes, expresses class relationships that structure some of the most fundamental forms of social and economic equality in present day South Africa. But if property law can be reshaped, then so can these class relationships. He argues that the traditional common-law ownership model has been challenged in the areas of unlawful occupation of land, landlord and tenant law, and the law governing debtors and creditors. Legal innovations have developed, often as limitations on the rights of a common-law 'insider' to dispossess an 'outsider'.

In **chapter 6** on 'Gender and public interest litigation in post-apartheid South Africa: Have systematic motifs of discrimination been addressed?', Bonita Meyersfeld and Nomonde Nyembe consider how PIL has been used to achieve gender equality. They take an intersectional approach, considering the relationships of gender, race and class with one another. They consider PIL in the areas of equality, gender-based violence, labour in the form of sex-work, caregiving, culture and religion, and domestic partnerships. This chapter goes on to describe how women's rights organisations have brought a powerful intersectional analysis into cases, often by way of *amicus curiae* interventions. The Constitutional Court has seldom demonstrated sensitivity to these concerns, although minority judgments have often taken them into account and these have sometimes led to legislative reform.

In **chapter 7** on 'Basic services', Jackie Dugard explores the relatively limited PIL so far undertaken in relation to basic services, including water, sanitation and electricity systems. Dugard speculates that the lack of coherence in the jurisprudence may point to inadequate coordination in the PIL sector in this area of work. Taken as a whole, despite the overall incoherence of the jurisprudence and some significant disappointments, there have been important gains in particular in relation to water quality standards, administrative justice-based claims for electricity supply, and the affirmation of the use of positive discrimination to redress historical disadvantage in relation to basic services in black areas.

Chapter 8 on 'Health care' by Nikki Stein traces the important PIL that has already been conducted regarding health care services, including most famously the *TAC* case regarding access to antiretroviral drugs to prevent mother-to-child transmission of HIV. Stein explores PIL concerning both positive and negative obligations—the obligation to direct resources towards improving health care services, and the obligation not to take away existing access. While much of the initial PIL on health care focused on the positive obligations of the state, the focus is increasingly shifting to include state cut-backs threatening the negative obligation. Stein also considers the role of private actors in the advancement of access to quality health care services.

In **chapter 9**, 'Happy (n)ever after: Public interest litigation for LGBTI equality', Kerry Williams and Melanie Judge juxtapose the remarkable set of PIL victories formally developing equality law for LGBTI people with ongoing institutionalised violence, inequality and discrimination experienced by LGBTI people. They argue that the social impact of PIL on LGBTI rights has generally been over-estimated as the law still falls short of enabling contextualised under-standings of the lived experiences of social discrimination and exclusion. The chapter analyses the multiple forms of violence to which LGBTI people are subjected, including physical, psychological and state violence, suggesting how lawyers and activists can adjust their tactics and approaches to respond to these forms of violence.

Chapter 10 on 'Children's rights' by Ann Skelton traces the rapid growth, variety and complexity of PIL on the rights of children, which has accelerated in the last decade. The jurisprudence recognises the protection and autonomy of children and has largely upheld their dignity and other rights. Skelton introduces the South African children's rights movement and traces the PIL in respect of children's socio-economic rights, the best interests of the child principle and criminal matters. She reveals some of the strategic considerations that informed this litigation and discusses some of the unexpected sites of litigation on children's rights, systemic challenges, the importance of networking in the sector and the use of international law to support this work. Looking ahead, Skelton foresees PIL on children's socio-economic rights, the registration of births, and the rights of migrant children.

Cameron McConnachie and Samantha Brener trace the groundbreaking recent streams of PIL on education rights in **chapter 11**, 'Litigating the right to basic education'. Noting that—unlike other socio-economic rights—the right to a basic education is immediately realisable and not subject to resource availability, McConnachie and Brener explain how, after a slow start, education PIL has accelerated. The main focus of the chapter is on cases to secure education infrastructure and resources, including the 'Mud Schools' litigation, litigation to secure norms and standards for school infrastructure, textbooks, school furniture, teachers and scholar transport. The authors describe how much of this PIL unfolded alongside the use of other strategies by communities and social move-ments, especially EE. One stream of cases concerned struggles for power between school authorities and government over language, pregnancy, and admissions. Important lessons in education PIL have included the use of innovative remedies and techniques to secure systemic relief. The authors suggest that future PIL is likely to focus on further monitoring and enforcement of existing orders, procure-ment and tender processes, the role of private schools and religion in schools.

Dario Milo and Avani Singh contribute a pair of companion chapters, **chapter 12** on 'Freedom of expression' and **chapter 13** on 'Access to information'. In both areas, PIL has particularly been driven by the print media and NGOs such as the Right2Know Campaign, committed to building openness and transparency. In relation to freedom of expression, South Africa has seen litigation on a range of restrictions to expression, including civil and criminal defamation and statutory restrictions on reporting. The courts have had to grapple with the balance between expression and privacy, both constitutional rights. The authors also deal with protest as a form of expression, including the right to record during protests. The right to open justice has developed as an important principle governing judicial proceedings. The digital age has presented new challenges, including the regulation of social media. The authors share some of the strategies developed to litigate effectively in this field.

In their second chapter, Milo and Singh describe how PIL to secure access to information has been lengthy and time-consuming, costly, and often futile where the information sought is time-sensitive in nature. They argue that there is a serious and urgent need to review whether the existing mechanisms give meaningful effect to the right of access to information.

The final chapter in the volume, **chapter 14** by Clare Ballard and Frances Hobden, discusses 'Public interest litigation and prisoners' rights'. They trace the constitutional protection of prisoners' rights and examine PIL on prison conditions, including in relation to accommodation, amenities and sanitation; health and medical treatment; and education. They then turn to discuss other rights of prisoners not related to conditions of detention, including voting, privacy, just administrative action and parole. PIL on prisoners' rights presents a particular set of obstacles, including logistical challenges in securing evidence, the lack of a dedicated lobby in civil society, and a weak legal framework. Priority areas for future PIL include overcrowding and the violation of rights of inmates, especially relating to assault.

Although the authors have situated their accounts within broader campaigns for social justice led by communities, social movements and other civil society actors, this volume has focused on PIL and paid particular attention to dedicated PIL organisations. Even within that narrow frame, there are important areas of PIL that this volume does not cover. It is hoped that future work will explore these areas, including in particular PIL on the rights of refugees and migrants, customary law, environmental justice, and struggles for access to land[263] and natural resources. The space continues to shift, with the emergence of new organisations and areas, including most recently in relation to new technologies, media and privacy.[264] This volume only tells part of the story so far.

---

[263] Wilson covers land to some extent in chapter 5 on property rights but it is a complex area that lies at the heart of the struggle for social justice.

[264] A new advisory firm, ALT Advisory (Applied Law and Technology) was established in 2017 by two former LRC attorneys, Avani Singh and Michael Power, to work in this area. See ALT Advisory website, last accessed from <www.altadvisory.africa> on 1 June 2018.

Chapter 2

THE WORLD'S LAW AND SOUTH AFRICAN DOMESTIC COURTS: THE ROLE OF INTERNATIONAL LAW IN PUBLIC INTEREST LITIGATION

Max du Plessis & Stuart Scott

2.1 INTRODUCTION

The scope of international law today is ever expanding. Viewing international law as law that is exclusively argued by international lawyers representing nations before international courts and tribunals does not adequately capture the current state of play. International law is increasingly being invoked before domestic courts and by individuals, corporations and organisations. Certainly, international law remains by and large about the affairs of states, but it is also, and increasingly so, aimed at non-state entities and individuals—whether because of international human rights norms, environmental norms, or international criminal law norms, to name but three new departures from the traditional state-centred approach.

This reality provides an opportunity for international law to operate as a powerful legal tool supporting public interest litigation (PIL) in South African domestic courts. In particular, international law arguments can be used to press the development of the law in scenarios where domestic legal avenues have been exhausted. Indeed, in recent years South African courts have seen a proliferation of domestic cases involving international law arguments. The courts have generally been receptive to international law arguments. This is particularly so since the Constitution entrenches its role. Section 39(1)(b) provides that when interpreting the Bill of Rights, a court, tribunal or forum "must consider international law".

The reaction that international law arguments has received centred on the courts' concerns about two principal issues. The first is the question of international law's proper place in domestic law. That is, the extent to which counsel is correct in invoking international law as an argument in the first place. And to the extent that international law was correctly invoked in the case at hand, the second issue becomes relevant, namely, whether other considerations preclude the court from ruling in favour of the international law arguments raised. The second issue might be described as being one of justiciability and involves concerns about judicial restraint.

In this chapter, we seek to outline how the courts have grappled with these two questions to explain, in a practical way, the manner in which international law arguments may be employed before South African courts in order to bolster public interest cases.

We outline five methods of employing international law before domestic courts, with examples from the jurisprudence. The first is where South Africa has undertaken obligations at the international level and has subsequently incorporated those obligations into domestic law. Second, we consider reliance on customary international law, which under our Constitution is automatically law unless it conflicts with an Act of Parliament. Third, there are situations where South Africa has undertaken the obligations at the international level and these international obligations are used to interpret the provisions of the Constitution or legislation. Fourth, we look at where international norms are used as guide for the exercise of official discretion. Fifth, we consider the cases where international law is used as a basis to press the development of the common law. In order to do so we draw on several key cases, such as *Glenister II*[1] and *Fick*,[2] in which international law arguments were of crucial significance to the outcome of the case.

In our view, in South African law today, a proper grasp of international law principles and how these may be raised in our courts are essential components in the public interest lawyer's tool kit. As Budlender, Marcus and Ferreira explain:

> [L]egal research is essential if public interest litigation is to be given a proper theoretical foundation. It involves a particular emphasis on making use of foreign law and international law which is often not easily accessible, but which can play a pivotal role.[3]

In this chapter, we provide an account of the kinds of international law arguments that can be employed: those that have previously been successful, and those that have not. In addition, we seek to explain the circumstances in which the courts may be more hesitant to embrace the position followed in international law. While we engage critically with the reasoning of the courts in the cases under discussion, the primary role of this chapter is descriptive and pedagogical rather than providing a detailed normative analysis of the particular holdings of the courts.

This chapter is divided into three main parts: we first set out some fundamental international law concepts with particular reference to South African law; next, we turn to the manner in which international law arguments may be invoked in South African courts; and, finally we outline the issue of justiciability and how it can best be navigated to increase the prospects of success of raising international law arguments.

2.2 KEY CONCEPTS AND THE SOURCES OF INTERNATIONAL LAW

When examining the place that international law occupies within the South Africa domestic legal system, it should be appreciated that international law, as law made principally by and between states, does not generally provide norms that can automatically be pleaded before South African domestic courts. Litigants in South African courts must first negotiate their way around various principles before they can safely call international treaties or customary international law into service in domestic cases.

The principles discussed below are nuanced and complex, and we do not and could not hope to give a full précis of them in this chapter. Various other texts have

---

[1] *Glenister v President of the Republic of South Africa and Others* [2011] ZACC 6; 2011 (3) SA 347 (CC) [the HSF, represented by WW, was admitted as *amicus curiae*] (*Glenister II*).

[2] *Government of the Republic of Zimbabwe v Fick and Others* [2013] ZACC 22; 2013 (5) SA 325 (CC).

[3] Steven Budlender, Gilbert Marcus & Nick Ferreira *Public Interest Litigation and Social Change in South Africa: Strategies, Tactics and Lessons* (2014) 121.

been dedicated to that task.[4] Rather, we highlight some of the key theoretical concepts that underpin the remainder of the chapter and which will require further investigation in order for those involved in PIL to raise an international law argument successfully in a domestic court.

(a) The sources of international law

Like law in the domestic sphere, international law needs to be ascertained by having regard to several sources. However, discerning the rules of international law is often a more complex process than determining the law in the domestic sphere because there is 'no single body able to create laws internationally binding on everyone, nor a proper system of courts with comprehensive and compulsory jurisdiction to interpret and extend the law'.[5]

Article 38 of the Statute of the International Court of Justice (the ICJ Statute)[6] is widely regarded as the 'most authoritative and complete statement' of the sources of international law.[7] Article 38 provides that:

> 1. The Court, whose function is to decide in accordance with international law such disputes as are submitted to it, shall apply:
> *(a)* international conventions, whether general or particular, establishing rules expressly recognized by the contesting States;
> *(b)* international custom, as evidence of a general practice accepted as law;
> *(c)* the general principles of law recognized by civilized nations;
> *(d)* subject to the provisions of Article 59,[8] judicial decisions and the teachings of the most highly qualified publicists of the various nations, as subsidiary means for the determination of rules of law.

An issue, which has been the subject of much academic attention, is the extent to which para 1 of art 38 creates a hierarchy of sources.[9] It should be noted that in classical international law all norms and rules enjoyed equal ranking. Dugard notes that '[a]lthough no provision is made for a hierarchy of sources, in most instances treaties, which take the place of legislation in the domestic sphere, are viewed as the primary source, while custom is the secondary source'.[10] Some commentators argue with much force that art 38 no longer 'accurately reflects all

---

[4] Malcolm N Shaw QC *International Law* 8 ed (2017); James Crawford *Brownlie's Principles of Public International Law* 8 ed (2012); John Dugard *International Law: A South African Perspective* 4 ed (2011); Antonio Cassese *International Law* 2 ed (2005); James Crawford & Martti Koskenniemi (eds) *The Cambridge Companion to International Law* (2012).

[5] Shaw (note 4 above) 51.

[6] 'Statute of the International Court of Justice', last accessed from <http://www.icj-cij.org/en/statute>.

[7] Shaw (note 4 above) 51; see also Crawford (note 4 above) 5.

[8] Article 59 provides: 'the decision of the Court has no binding force except between the parties and in respect of that particular case'.

[9] Crawford (note 4 above) 5.

[10] Dugard (note 4 above) 27.

the materials and forms of state practice that comprise today's sources of international law'.[11]

(i) *Treaties*

The most frequent method of creating international rules is by concluding agreements known as treaties.[12] Article 2(1)*(a)* of the Vienna Convention on the Law of Treaties (VCLT) defines a treaty as '[a]n international agreement concluded between states in written form and governed by international law, whether embodied in a single instrument or in two or more related instruments and whatever its particular designation'.[13]

This definition points to several important features of treaties. First, treaties are agreements concluded between states. Second, treaties must be written. Third, treaties may be embodied in a single instrument or in several related instruments.

Treaties may be either bilateral or multilateral. A bilateral treaty is a treaty between two states, whereas a multilateral treaty is one between more than two states. Examples of bilateral treaties include the bilateral investment treaties (BITs) discussed below, in respect of which South Africa has seen PIL activity. In this regard, the Rome Statute of the International Criminal Court (the Rome Statute) is a good example of a multilateral treaty.

In the context of multilateral treaties, where a state finds that some of the clauses are too onerous but still wishes to enter into the treaty, it may make reservations, that is, 'unilateral statements intended to either *(a)* exclude the application of one or more provisions, or *(b)* place a certain interpretation on them'.[14]

Article 31 of the VCLT provides that 'a treaty shall be interpreted in good faith in accordance with the ordinary meaning to be given to the terms of the treaty in their *context and in the light of its object and purpose'*. Three interpretive principles may be derived from this (which are similar to South African law):[15] first, words should be given their ordinary meaning; second, the purpose of the treaty is a significant and helpful indicator in discerning the meaning of the words used in the treaty; third, the intention of the parties (as reflected in *travaux*

---

[11] Dugard (n 4 above) 27.

[12] Cassese (note 4 above) 171.

[13] Vienna Convention on the Law of Treaties, 1155 UNTS 331, entered into force 27 January 1980. The VCLT regulates all the main features of international treaties. In 1986, the Vienna Convention on the Law of Treaties between States and International Organizations, an extension to the VCLT, was concluded, which supplements and clarifies the operation of treaties between states and international organisations like the UN.

[14] Cassese (note 4 above) 173.

[15] In this regard see *Natal Joint Municipal Pension Fund v Endumeni Municipality* [2012] ZASCA 13; 2012 (4) SA 593 (SCA) paras 17–19 where the SCA neatly summarises the key principles of interpretation of statutes and contracts under South African law.

preparatoires) may be used in order to discern the proper meaning of the particular clause. In this regard, art 32 of the VCLT provides:

> Recourse may be had to supplementary means of interpretation, including the preparatory work of the treaty and the circumstances of its conclusion, in order to confirm the meaning resulting from the application of article 31, or to determine the meaning when the interpretation according to article 31:
> *(a)* leaves the meaning ambiguous or obscure; or
> *(b)* leads to a result which is manifestly absurd or unreasonable.

In the context of PIL, the most significant international treaties include the nine core UN human rights treaties.[16] South Africa is a party to all of these treaties, although surprisingly it only ratified the Covenant on Economic, Social and Cultural Rights (CESCR) in 2015. The non-binding Universal Declaration of Human Rights (UDHR),[17] and the binding International Covenant on Economic, Social and Cultural Rights (ICESCR) and International Covenant on Civil and Political Rights (ICCPR) (and its two Optional Protocols) are commonly regarded as constituting the International Bill of Human Rights. At the regional level, South Africa is a party to the African Charter on Human and Peoples' Rights (Banjul Charter) (1987), which is also frequently relied upon in public interest cases.

(ii) *Custom (customary international law)*

Article 38*(b)* of the ICJ Statute defines 'international custom, as evidence of a general practice accepted as law' as a source of international customary law. International custom occupies a very significant place in international law. Unlike a treaty where states give express consent to be bound by the particular rules, consent to international custom is inferred from the conduct of states.[18]

Article 38 provides that custom must be 'evidence of a general practice accepted as law'. From this exposition two main requirements for a customary rule to come into existence may be discerned. First, the conduct must be settled practice amongst states (*usus*) and, second, there must be acceptance of an obligation to be bound (*opinio juris sive necessitates*).

---

[16] The International Covenant on the Elimination of All Forms of Racial Discrimination, 660 UNTS 195, entered into force 4 January1965; the International Covenant on Civil and Political Rights, 999 UNTS 171, entered into force 3 January 1976; the International Covenant on Economic, Social and Cultural Rights, 993 UNTS 3, entered into force 23 March 1976; the Convention on the Elimination of All Forms of Discrimination against Women, 1249 UNTS 13, entered into force 3 September 1981; the Convention against Torture and Other Cruel, Inhuman or Degrading Treatment or Punishment, 1465 UNTS 85, entered into force 26 June 1987; the Convention on the Rights of the Child, 1577 UNTS 3, entered into force 2 September 1990; the International Convention on the Protection of the Rights of All Migrant Workers and Members of Their Families, 2220 UNTS 3, entered into force 1 July 2003 (1990); the International Convention for the Protection of All Persons from Enforced Disappearance, 2716 UNTS 3, entered into force 23 December 2010; and the Convention on the Rights of Persons with Disabilities, 2515 UNTS 3, entered into force 3 May 2008.

[17] Adopted by General Assembly Resolution 217 A (III) of 10 December 1948.

[18] Dugard (note 4 above) 29.

Custom should not be confused with 'usage'. Usage is a general practice that does not reflect a legal obligation, for example the practice of exempting diplomatic vehicles from parking prohibitions.[19] Notably, customary rules usually bind 'all members of the world community', while treaties only bind states that ratify or adhere to them.[20] Acceptance of an international obligation by most states, with a corresponding acceptance by such states of the obligation to be bound, can therefore be said to constitute a customary international law norm. In many states, customary international law is generally regarded—*automatically*—as forming part of domestic law. Crawford helpfully explains this principle as follows:

> The dominant principle, normally characterized as the doctrine of incorporation, is that customary rules are to be considered part of the law of the land and enforced as such, with the qualification that they are incorporated only so far as is not inconsistent with Acts of Parliament or prior judicial decisions of final authority.[21]

As we set out in more detail below, South Africa also follows this model.

(iii)   *General principles of law recognised by civilised nations*
In situations where no rules from treaties or customary law are applicable, international tribunals may draw on general principles of law recognised by civilised nations.[22] This means that the tribunals 'turn to common principles of law found in municipal systems—in so far as they are capable of application to relations between states—in order to fill the gaps in international law'.[23] This exercise is not peculiar to international law and similar situations often arise in the domestic context when there are gaps in the law. As Shaw notes, '[i]n such instances the judge will proceed to deduce a rule that will be relevant, by analogy from already existing rules or directly from the general principles that guide the legal system, whether they be referred to as emanating from justice, equity or considerations of public policy'.[24]

Thus, 'it is important to appreciate that while there may not always be an immediate and obvious rule applicable to every international situation, "every international situation is capable of being determined as a matter of law"'.[25] One controversial aspect of the general principles of law is that, unlike treaties and custom, they do not have a consensual basis.[26] Some theorists reject this source of law since it lacks the consent of states.[27] While reliance on this source of law is not

---

[19] Crawford (note 4 above) 6.

[20] Cassese (note 4 above) 157.

[21] Crawford (note 4 above) 41.

[22] Notably, as Shaw explains, the phrase 'recognized by civilized nations' is now generally regarded as redundant; see Shaw (note 4 above) 95.

[23] Dugard (note 4 above) 38.

[24] Shaw (note 4 above) 72–3.

[25] Ibid.

[26] Dugard (note 4 above) 39.

[27] Ibid.

as prevalent as treaties or custom, international courts have occasionally had regard to various general principles. As Dugard notes, the list of principles invoked include: unjust enrichment, reparation for breach of an undertaking, *res judicata*, the limited liability of corporations, estoppel, and the rule against bias (*nemo judex in re sua*).[28]

(iv) *The works of prominent commentators and additional sources*

Article 38(1)(*d*) of the ICJ Statute provides that the following are sources of international law: 'judicial decisions and the teachings of the most highly qualified publicists of the various nations'. Interestingly, while these are listed as 'subsidiary means for the determination of rules of law' the works of prominent international law commentators have often been one of the primary sources of establishing international customary law. That is so because courts do not call for evidence regarding the content of international law. As Crawford notes:

> Once a court has ascertained that there are no bars within its own legal system to applying the rules of international law or provisions of a treaty, the rules are accepted as rules of law and are not required to be established by evidence, as in the case of matters of fact and foreign law.

Unlike foreign law, however, in the case of international law there are difficulties associated with this treatment. As Crawford correctly explains, 'there is a serious problem involved in finding reliable information of international law, especially customary law, in the absence of formal proof and resort to expert witnesses.'[29] Because of these difficulties, the courts—worldwide—have tended to rely to a large extent on academic commentaries.[30] Thus, in our view, it is no longer apt to describe prominent academic commentators as a secondary source (since at times they may actually 'espouse' customary international law, or at least be regarded by the domestic judge as doing so).

Other secondary sources include 'soft law' instruments, for instance, General Comments. Various human rights treaty bodies publish interpretive statements known as 'General Comments'. These statements are not per se binding. However, these comments 'serve to clarify the application of specific provisions and issues relating to the Covenants, and as such are of significant normative value within the human rights system'.[31] South African courts, on various occasions, have had regard to General Comments when considering international-law principles. For instance, in *Mazibuko and Others v City of Johannesburg and Others*,[32] the Constitutional Court cited General Comment No. 3 by the United Nations

---

[28] Dugard (n 4 above) 38.

[29] Crawford (note 4 above) 56.

[30] Ibid.

[31] Ibid 640.

[32] *Mazibuko and Others v City of Johannesburg and Others* [2009] ZACC 28; 2010 (4) SA 1 (CC) [CALS/Wits Law Clinic and the FXI acted for the applicants; the Centre on Housing Rights and Evictions, represented by the LRC, was admitted as *amicus curiae*]. See also *Government of the*

Committee on Economic, Social and Cultural Rights[33] when interpreting the notion of 'progressive realisation' in the Constitution:

> This formulation of the positive obligation applies to most of the social and economic rights entrenched in our Constitution and is consistent with the principles of international law (para 40)—General Comment 3, 'General Comment 3: The nature of States Parties' obligations (art 2(1))' Fifth Session, 1990, U.N. Doc E/1991/23 at para 9 where the concept of 'progressive realisation' is helpfully explained as follows:
>
> > 'The concept of progressive realisation constitutes a recognition of the fact that full realisation of all economic, social and cultural rights will generally not be able to be achieved in a short period of time ... Nevertheless, the fact that the realisation over time, or in other words progressively, is foreseen under the Covenant should not be misinterpreted as depriving the obligation of all meaningful content. It is on the one hand a necessary flexibility device, reflecting the realities of the real world and the difficulties involved for any country in ensuring full realisation of economic, social and cultural rights. On the other hand, the phrase must be read in the light of the overall objective, indeed the raison d'être, of the Covenant which is to establish clear obligations for States Parties in respect of the full realisation of the rights in question. It thus imposes an obligation to move as expeditiously and effectively as possible towards that goal. Moreover, any deliberately retrogressive measures in that regard would require the most careful consideration and would need to be fully justified by reference to the totality of the rights provided for in the Covenant and in the context of the full use of the maximum available resources.'

(b) Bilateral investment treaties

The conclusion of agreements between the particular states regulate foreign investment. These agreements are known as BITs. The practice of concluding BITs began 'in Europe in the 1950s and became generalised a quarter-century later'.[34] According to the United Nations Conference on Trade and Development, by 2006 there were more than 2 400 BITs in force.[35] South Africa is a party to approximately 40 BITs that it has concluded since 1994, which typically include dispute resolution clauses providing for investor–state arbitration before international tribunals, including under the International Centre for the Settlement of Investment Disputes (ICSID).[36] The ICSID is an arbitral institution that operates under the auspices of the World Bank. BITs typically establish various principles that are

---

Republic of South Africa and Others v Grootboom and Others [2000] ZACC 19; 2001 (1) SA 46 (CC) paras 29–31 [the SAHRC and CLC, represented by the LRC, were admitted as *amici curiae*].

[33] UN Committee on Economic, Social and Cultural Rights (CESCR) General Comment No. 3: 'The Nature of States Parties' Obligations (Art. 2, Para. 1, of the Covenant), 14 December 1990, E/1991/23.

[34] Crawford & Koskenniemi (note 4 above) 367.

[35] Ibid 405.

[36] Jason Brickhill & Max du Plessis 'Two's company, three's a crowd: Public interest intervention in investor–state arbitration (*Piero Foresti v South Africa*)' (2011) 27 *SAJHR* 155.

intended to give businesses clarity and notional confidence about investing in another state. For instance, they establish:

> [T]he principle of fair and equitable treatment for investors, protection from expro-
> priation (in contrast to the sovereign right to nationalise resources asserted in the
> 'public' sphere), free transfer of capital and full protection and security of invest-
> ment. They also establish dispute resolution procedures that dramatically restrict the
> jurisdiction of national courts.[37]

A prominent debate regarding the use of BITs is their impact on human rights in the developing world.[38] The main concern is that BITs stifle the regulatory space available to developing states, in particular in relation to environmental protection and providing equitable access to natural resources for the poor. A significant recent development in the use of BITs is increased engagement by public interest organisations. Public interest organisations can intervene in an investment dispute by participating as a Non-Disputing Party (NDP). This role is very much akin to the role played by an *amicus curiae* before South African courts.[39] However, the role that NDPs could play in investment disputes has traditionally been far more limited and the mere participation in the dispute did not provide an effective platform for proper participation (because the nature of the information and documents provided to an NDP was, at best, limited or, at worst, non-existent).

The dispute in *Piero Foresti, Laura De Carli v Republic of South Africa*[40] has widened the scope for NDPs. *Piero Foresti* concerned a claim instituted against South Africa by a group of investors in the ICSID. A coalition, consisting of two South African human rights organisations,[41] intervened in *Piero Foresti* focusing on two issues: first, the various procedural challenges that NDPs faced when participating in investment arbitrations; second, the extent to which human rights arguments could be advanced in the international investment law context. In this piece, we focus on the first of these issues.

The claimants in the dispute alleged that South Africa was in breach of the relevant BITs' prohibitions on expropriation (art 5 of both BITs) in two respects. First, by the Mineral and Petroleum Resources Development Act 28 of 2002 (the MPRDA) becoming operational (which took effect on 1 May 2004), it extinguished certain putative old order mineral rights allegedly held by the

---

[37] Crawford & Koskenniemi (note 4 above) 405–6.

[38] See in this regard Brickhill & Du Plessis (note 36 above).

[39] See ch 4 'Constitutional Litigation Procedure' by Georgina Jephson and Osmond Mngomezulu, on the role of *amici curiae*.

[40] *Piero Foresti, Laura De Carli v Republic of South Africa* ICSID case no ARB(AF)07/01.

[41] The Legal Resources Centre (LRC) and the Centre for Applied Legal Studies (CALS). They were joined in the coalition by two international organisations, the International Centre for the Protection of Human Rights (INTERIGHTS) and the Centre for International Environmental Law (CIEL).

claimants. Second, the coming into effect of the MPRDA, combined with the Mining Charter dated 13 August 2004, introduced compulsory equity divestiture requirements with respect to the claimants' shares in their operating companies.

The NDPs requested that the Tribunal grant them three types of relief: first, leave to file written submissions concerning matters within the scope of the dispute; second, access to specific arbitral documents identified by the petitioners, for the purpose of enabling them to make 'useful, unique, and well-informed submissions'; and, third, absent any objection by the parties, permission to attend and present the NDPs' key submissions at the oral hearings when they took place, or in the alternative, to attend and observe the oral hearings.[42]

The NDPs successfully argued that the present state of regional and international human rights law on access to information combined with the constitutional and legislative guarantees in South Africa demonstrate that transparency must be the starting point and default position in the conduct of any proceeding involving the state.[43] They submitted that investment arbitration is no exception and that permissible restrictions can only be justified in exceptional circumstances. The NDPs had requested disclosure of discrete categories of documents in the proceedings to enable them to participate meaningfully in the arbitration and effectively argued that a lack of transparency undermines the integrity of investor–state arbitrations no less than in court proceedings.

The Tribunal concluded that the parties needed to agree on and disclose certain redacted documents to the NDPs.[44] The Tribunal explained in its award that it had ordered the parties to provide the NDPs with certain redacted documents because it had taken the view that the NDPs must be allowed access to those papers submitted to the Tribunal by the parties that were necessary to enable the NDPs to focus their submissions upon the issues arising in the case and to see what positions the parties had taken on those issues.[45] It added that it had set the calendar for the NDP submissions and the parties' responses to ensure that the NDPs be given adequate opportunity to prepare and deliver their submissions in sufficient time before the hearing for the parties to be able to respond to those submissions.[46]

---

[42] *Piero Foresti* (note 40 above) para 8.1.

[43] Ibid para 6.11.

[44] In its decision regarding the NDP petitions, the Tribunal noted that its decision was animated by two basic principles: (1) that NDP participation is intended to enable NDPs to give useful information and accompanying submissions to the Tribunal, but is not intended to be a mechanism for enabling NDPs to obtain information from the parties; and (2) where there is NDP participation, the Tribunal must ensure that it is both effective and compatible with the rights of the parties and the fairness and efficiency of the arbitral process. The Tribunal made an initial decision on 11 September 2009, for which it provided reasons on 25 September (see para 28).

[45] *Piero Foresti* (note 40 above) para 28.

[46] Ibid.

The NDPs' application was regrettably, however, less successful as regards its request to make oral submissions or, alternatively, to be permitted to attend and observe the hearing. While the Tribunal was—prima facie—leaning towards not granting the request, it noted that it would only make a final decision later in the proceedings. Ultimately, however, the hearing only proceeded on the question of costs (rather than the merits of the dispute)—and thus the Tribunal did not finally resolve this question. In any event, *Piero Foresti* was the first occasion—of which we are aware—where an NDP has been granted access to the arbitral documents and, where the claimants had expressly objected to access being provided. This leaves much more scope for the future participation of public interest organisations to participate effectively as NDPs in investment disputes that fall within their mandate.

2.3 THE MANNER IN WHICH INTERNATIONAL LAW ARGUMENTS MAY BE INVOKED IN SOUTH AFRICAN COURTS

As Crawford notes, questions of how international law relates to domestic law and how it may be employed involve questions of a 'constitutional character'.[47] Below we discuss five of the most common ways in which international law arguments can be utilised before South African domestic courts. These are:

(a) relying on international law treaties and conventions that have been incorporated domestically;

(b) raising international law arguments premised on customary international law;

(c) relying on an international treaty that has not been domestically incorporated to operate as a tool to interpret the Constitution or legislation;

(d) using international law as a guide for the exercise of official discretion; and

(e) arguing that a treaty that is binding at the international level should motivate a development of the common law.

(a) Relying on international law treaties and conventions that have been incorporated domestically

As set out above, s 231 of the Constitution deals with international agreements. It provides:

International agreements
231. (1) The negotiating and signing of all international agreements is the responsibility of the national executive.

(2) An international agreement binds the Republic only after it has been approved by resolution in both the National Assembly and the National Council of Provinces, unless it is an agreement referred to in subsection (3).

(3) An international agreement of a technical, administrative or executive nature, or an agreement which does not require either ratification or accession, entered into by the national executive, binds the Republic without approval by the National

---

[47] Crawford (note 4 above) 55.

Assembly and the National Council of Provinces, but must be tabled in the Assembly and the Council within a reasonable time.

(4) Any international agreement becomes law in the Republic when it is enacted into law by national legislation; but a self-executing provision of an agreement that has been approved by Parliament is law in the Republic unless it is inconsistent with the Constitution or an Act of Parliament.

(5) The Republic is bound by international agreements which were binding on the Republic when this Constitution took effect.

The public interest lawyer's first port of call is, thus, to investigate whether South Africa is party to any applicable international treaties germane to the case at hand. If so, the next step is to check whether there is any domestic legislation that has incorporated those obligations into the domestic realm through an Act of Parliament. This method does not, in truth, deal with the application of international law at all—it is simply the application of domestic South African law. While a specific statutory instrument may directly domesticate the treaty, or its relevant provisions, it is the specific statutory instrument, the Act, which courts thereafter give effect to.[48] In *Glenister II* the majority of the Constitutional Court neatly explained the scheme of s 231 as follows:

> In our view the main force of s 231(2) is directed at the Republic's legal obligations under international law, rather than transforming the rights and obligations contained in international agreements into home-grown constitutional rights and obligations. Even though the section provides that the agreement binds the Republic, and Parliament exercises the Republic's legislative power, which it must do in accordance with and within the limits of the Constitution, the provision must be read in conjunction with the other provisions within s 231. Here, s 231(4) is of particular significance. It provides that an international agreement becomes law in the Republic when it is enacted into law by national legislation. The fact that s 231(4) expressly creates a path for the domestication of international agreements may be an indication that s 231(2) cannot, without more, have the effect of giving binding internal constitutional force to agreements merely because Parliament has approved them. It follows that the incorporation of an international agreement creates ordinary domestic statutory obligations.[49]

Similarly, the minority judgment of Ngcobo CJ set out the principles as follows. While the minority and majority took polar judicial approaches to many issues in the case, there was consensus in relation to the explanation of s 231.[50] Ngcobo CJ stated:

---

[48] See also the statement of Lord Hoffmann in *R v Lyons and Others* [2002] UKHL 44 para 27, discussed below: '[I]t is firmly established that international treaties do not form part of English law and the English courts have no jurisdiction to interpret or apply them . . . Parliament may pass a law which mirrors the terms of the treaty and in this sense incorporates the treaty into English law. But even then, the metaphor of incorporation may be misleading. It is not the treaty but the statute which forms part of English law.'

[49] *Glenister II* (note 1 above) para 181.

[50] Ibid paras 89–90.

The constitutional scheme of section 231 is deeply rooted in the separation of powers, in particular the checks and balances between the executive and the legislature. It contemplates three legal steps that may be taken in relation to an international agreement, with each step producing different legal consequences. First, it assigns to the national executive the authority to negotiate and sign international agreements. But an international agreement signed by the executive does not automatically bind the Republic unless it is an agreement of a technical, administrative or executive nature. To produce that result, it requires, second, the approval by resolution of Parliament.

The approval of an agreement by Parliament does not, however, make it law in the Republic, unless it is a self-executing agreement that has been approved by Parliament, which becomes law in the Republic upon such approval, unless it is inconsistent with the Constitution or an Act of Parliament. Otherwise, and third, an international agreement becomes law in the Republic when it is enacted into law by national legislation.

Thus, while entering into treaties at the international plane rests in the province of the executive (under s 231(1) of the Constitution), s 231(2) and (4) fetter that power and 'enjoin the national executive to engage Parliament'.[51] Our courts have held that 'once Parliament approves the agreement, internationally the *country* becomes bound by that agreement' and, at the domestic level, 'the process is completed by Parliament enacting such international agreement as national law in terms of s 231(4)'.[52]

Various recent important international law public interest cases have centred on the Rome Statute, which has been domesticated in accordance with s 231 of the Constitution. The court explained the background to the Rome Statute in *DA v Minister of International Relations and Cooperation and Others*:[53]

The Rome Statute was adopted and signed on 17 July 1998 by a majority of states attending the Rome Conference, including South Africa. This paved the way for the establishment of the ICC. South Africa ratified the Rome Statute on 27 November 2000. It was the obligation of state parties, which signed and ratified the Rome Statute, to domesticate the provisions of the statute into their national law to ensure that domestic law was compatible with the statute. South Africa accordingly passed the Implementation Act on 16 August 2002. The preamble of the Act reads:

'[T]he Republic of South Africa is committed to—bringing persons who commit such atrocities to justice, either in a court of law of the Republic in terms of its domestic laws where possible, pursuant to its international obligation to do so when the Republic became party to the Rome Statute of the International Criminal

---

[51] *Democratic Alliance v Minister of International Relations and Cooperation and Others (Council for the Advancement of the South African Constitution Intervening)* [2017] ZAGPPHC 53; 2017 (3) SA 212 (GP) [SALC, Amnesty International, Peace and Justice Initiative, CHR and HSF were respondents; and CASAC was admitted as *amicus curiae*] para 34 (*DA v Minister of International Relations*).

[52] Ibid para 34.

[53] Ibid.

Court, or in the event of the national prosecuting authority of the Republic declining or being unable to do so, in line with the principle of complementarity as contemplated in the Statute, in the International Criminal Court, created by and functioning in terms of the said Statute; . . . .'

Schedule 1 of the Implementation Act creates a structure for the national prosecution of the international crimes of genocide, war crimes, and crimes against humanity, which includes the crime of apartheid. The overall purpose of the Implementation Act is to bring the perpetrators of serious international crimes to justice, in domestic courts or in the ICC. The Implementation Act also creates the domestic legal framework for South Africa's cooperation with the ICC. Section 3(a) of the Implementation Act provides for the creation of a framework to ensure that the Rome Statute is effectively implemented in the country.[54]

We discuss three important cases that demonstrate that even after international law has been expressly domesticated, there still may well be contested areas and tricky terrain that must be navigated. These decisions helpfully explain, inter alia: the reach of South Africa's international obligations, how they relate to regional law obligations, as well as the procedure that the country needs to follow if it wishes to withdraw from an international instrument.

In *National Commissioner of the South African Police Service v Southern African Human Rights Litigation Centre and Another*,[55] the central question was the extent to which the South African Police Service (SAPS) had domestic and international law powers and obligations to investigate alleged crimes against humanity, including torture, committed by foreign nationals in a foreign territory (in that case, by allegations of torture committed *by* Zimbabweans *against* Zimbabweans *in* Zimbabwe). We note that the prohibition on torture is a *jus cogens* norm of international law: that is, it is 'accepted and recognized by the international community of States as a whole as [a norm] from which no derogation is permitted'.[56]

In 2007, the Zimbabwean police detained and allegedly tortured approximately one hundred Zimbabwean nationals. The alleged torture was apparently part of a widespread and systematic attack by the ruling party, ZANU-PF (the Zimbabwe African National Union—Patriotic Front), on officials and supporters of the largest

---

[54] *Democratic Alliance* case supra paras 9–10.

[55] *National Commissioner of the South African Police Service v Southern African Human Rights Litigation Centre and Another* [2014] ZACC 30; 2015 (1) SA 315 (CC) [LHR acted for the respondents, SALC and Zimbabwe Exiles Forum; and Tides Centre, Peace and Justice Initiative and CALS were admitted as *amici curiae*, represented by the LRC] (*National Commissioner of SAPS v SALC*).

[56] Crawford (note 4 above) 596. This may be contrasted with an obligation *erga omnes*, which means an obligation that is 'valid against "all the world" ie all other legal persons, irrespective of specific consent on the part of those thus affected'. See Crawford (note 4 above) lxxviii. We note that, while certain norms, for example, the prohibition against torture may well amount to an obligation that is both *jus cogens* as well as *erga omnes*, the two concepts are distinct. For instance, some norms may well amount to customary international law rules—and thus take an *erga omnes* character—even though they have not reached the threshold of being a norm that is, *jus cogens* (for instance, if the norm may be departed from in certain instances).

opposition party, the Movement for Democratic Change, in the build-up to the national elections.[57] The Southern African Litigation Centre (SALC)—a non-governmental organisation based in Johannesburg which provides support to human rights and PIL within Southern Africa—collected and collated evidence of the allegations of torture into a dossier (the torture docket). SALC hand-delivered the torture docket to the Priority Crimes Litigation Unit (the PCLU) of the National Prosecuting Authority in South Africa (NPA) and requested that the NPA consider the evidence and investigate the matter further. SALC feared that the Zimbabwean courts might not hold the perpetrators accountable. SALC submitted that the allegations, if true, amounted to a crime against humanity under the Implementation of the Rome Statute of the International Criminal Court Act 27 of 2002 (the ICC Act). In June 2009, however, the NPA advised SALC that the SAPS had declined to investigate the matter.

SALC and the Zimbabwe Exiles' Forum (ZEF) applied to the High Court to review and set aside the SAPS's decision. The applicants were successful in both the High Court as well as the Supreme Court of Appeal (SCA). The National Commissioner thereafter appealed to the Constitutional Court. There were essentially three key issues before the Constitutional Court.

The first issue was whether the suspected perpetrator of an alleged international crime—committed outside of South Africa—needed to be *present* in South Africa in order to create jurisdiction under the ICC Act for the SAPS to investigate the crime. The court noted that the answer to that question depends on the proper construction of s 4(3) of the ICC Act which reads:

> In order to secure the jurisdiction of a South African court for purposes of this Chapter, any person who commits a crime contemplated in subsection (1)[58] outside the territory of the Republic, is deemed to have committed that crime in the territory of the Republic if—
>
> *(a)* that person is a South African citizen; or
>
> *(b)* that person is not a South African citizen but is ordinarily resident in the Republic; or
>
> *(c)* that person, after the commission of the crime, is present in the territory of the Republic; or
>
> *(d)* that person has committed the said crime against a South African citizen or against a person who is ordinarily resident in the Republic.

The SAPS sought to rely on international scholars to suggest that presence was required before any investigation could take place, since the allegations dealt with Zimbabweans torturing other Zimbabweans *in Zimbabwe, not South Africa.* The

---

[57] *National Commissioner of SAPS v SALC* (note 55 above) para 9.

[58] Section 4(1) provides:
Despite anything to the contrary in any other law of the Republic, any person who commits a crime, is guilty of an offence and is liable on conviction to a fine or imprisonment, including imprisonment for life, or such imprisonment without the option of a fine, or both a fine and such imprisonment.

court rejected this argument holding that there was 'no unanimity amongst international-law scholars on whether presence [was] a requirement for investigation'. The court referred to the informative examination of foreign and international law undertaken by the SCA and held that it appeared that 'the predominant international position' was that presence of a suspect was only required at a more advanced stage: when the prosecution has begun, after the investigation has been conducted.[59] The Constitutional Court held that, while the presence of the suspect in the country was required in order to prosecute the suspect there was no analogous presence requirement for investigation under international or South African law.[60] The presence of the suspect was merely one factor, among various factors, that the SAPS needed to balance in determining the practicability and reasonableness of conducting an investigation into the allegations.

The second issue was whether the police had the power or a duty to investigate allegations of torture in a foreign country. The SCA held that the SAPS had the power to investigate. The Constitutional Court went even further,[61] holding that there was not simply a power to investigate but a duty to do so. That duty arose from the applicable legislative and constitutional scheme 'understood in the light of international customary law and other international obligations'.[62] This scheme included s 205(3) of the Constitution as interpreted by the court in *Glenister II*,[63] read with s 4(1) of the ICC Act as well as s 17D(1)(*a*) of the South African Police Service Act 68 of 1995.[64]

The third question was whether there were limits on the police investigating international crimes committed outside of South Africa by and against foreign nationals. The court held that the universal jurisdiction to investigate international crimes was not absolute and was subject to at least two limitations.[65] First, South Africa may not investigate or prosecute international crimes 'in breach of considerations of complementarity and subsidiarity':[66] an investigation was only

---

[59] *National Commissioner of SAPS v SALC* (note 55 above) para 47.

[60] Ibid paras 46–8.

[61] Ibid para 55.

[62] Ibid para 61.

[63] *Glenister II* (note 1 above).

[64] Section 17D(1)(*a*) of that Act provides that the functions of the Hawks 'are to prevent, combat and investigate national priority offences, which in the opinion of the National Head of the Directorate need to be addressed by the Directorate'.

[65] *National Commissioner of SAPS v SALC* (note 55 above) para 61.

[66] Ibid para 61. The principle of subsidiarity 'requires that ordinarily there must be a substantial and true connection between the subject-matter and the source of the jurisdiction' (at para 61); and the principle of non-intervention in the affairs of another country demanded that 'investigating international crimes committed abroad is permissible only if the country with jurisdiction is unwilling or unable to prosecute and only if the investigation is confined to the territory of the investigating state. See, further, the Court's explanation of the principle of subsidiarity, citing *National Commissioner of SAPS v SALC* (note 55 above), in *My Vote Counts NPC v Speaker of the National Assembly and Others* [2015] ZACC 31 para 48 [WW acted for the applicant]:

permissible if the foreign state was unwilling or unable to prosecute, and the investigation was confined to the territory of South Africa.[67] The second limiting principle was whether it was reasonable and practicable for the police to investigate in the circumstances of each particular case.[68] The court set out some of the relevant considerations to be considered:

> Foremost amongst these considerations are whether the investigation is likely to lead to a prosecution and accordingly whether the alleged perpetrators are likely to be present in South Africa on their own or through an extradition request; the geographical proximity of South Africa to the place of the crime and the likelihood of the suspects being arrested for the purpose of prosecution; the prospects of gathering evidence which is needed to satisfy the elements of a crime; and the nature and the extent of the resources required for an effective investigation. In some instances a preliminary investigation to test the reasonableness of undertaking a full-blown investigation may be necessary. In each case the ultimate enquiry is whether, all relevant considerations weighed, the SAPS acted reasonably in declining to investigate crimes against humanity committed in another country.[69]

On the facts, the Constitutional Court found that the High Court and the SCA correctly set aside the SAPS's decision not to investigate. An investigation was justified based on a variety of considerations, namely: *(a)* South Africa had a substantial connection to the crime; *(b)* an investigation within South Africa would not infringe the principle of non-intervention; and *(c)* there was no indication that Zimbabwe had instituted an investigation (or would ever institute one, given the time that had already elapsed) and it sufficed 'that it was very unlikely that the Zimbabwean police would have pursued the investigation with the necessary zeal in view of the high profile personalities to be investigated' (this was particularly so since six Cabinet Ministers and Directors General of the ruling party were allegedly implicated).[70] The court found that the SAPS's decision not to investigate was wrong in law and ordered the police to do so.[71] In concluding, the Constitutional Court sounded a cautionary word about the importance of the

---

In international law, subsidiarity is employed to resolve a clash of jurisdictions. It determines which state should act when multiple states have jurisdiction over the same events constituting an international crime. Under our Constitution, it signifies that the duty of the South African Police Service to investigate international crimes, including crimes against humanity, is subsidiary to that of the foreign state in which the crimes were committed.

[67] *National Commissioner of SAPS v SALC* (note 55 above) paras 61–2.

[68] Ibid para 63.

[69] Ibid para 64.

[70] Ibid para 62.

[71] Ibid paras 77–80. The court found that the Promotion of Administrative Justice Act 3 of 2000 applied to SAPS's decision. The court thereafter, in essence, ordered a substitution of the administrator's decision—though it did not traverse the ordinary requirements for a substitution. The court's reasoning was that '[a] remittal to the High Court would serve no purpose and would merely add further delay' (para 82).

country honouring its obligations under the ICC Act in the context of the serious offences in the Rome Statute:

> Our country's international and domestic law commitments must be honoured. We cannot be seen to be tolerant of impunity for alleged torturers. We must take up our rightful place in the community of nations with its concomitant obligations. *We dare not be a safe haven for those who commit crimes against humanity.*[72] [Emphasis added]

As it turns out, the court's cautionary note amounted to a striking premonition in relation to the executive's next failure to follow its international law obligations, which forms the subject of the second important case involving the Rome Statute.

In June 2015, President Omar al-Bashir attended the African Union (AU) summit in Johannesburg. The Pre-Trial Chamber of the International Criminal Court had already issued two international warrants for his arrest. President al-Bashir was charged with war crimes, crimes against humanity, as well as genocide. All of the charges related to events in the Darfur region of Sudan. The ICC sent copies of the warrants to all member states, including South Africa, requesting member states to cooperate under the Rome Statute and cause President al-Bashir to be arrested and surrendered to the ICC. We note that the South African government had previously sent invitations to al-Bashir to attend events in South Africa. However, while the hosts were polite enough to send the invitation, al-Bashir had been careful enough to follow South Africa's additional request that he not attend. This time, however, al-Bashir actually arrived in South Africa. As signatories to the Rome Statute, South Africa had an obligation to arrest him when he entered the country, but did not. Instead, the government cited its obligations under the AU and customary international law, to respect al-Bashir's immunity as a head of state as reasons for why it refused to arrest al-Bashir when he attended the AU summit. According to the South African executive, the circumstances gave rise to a collision between regional and international law obligations. This argument stems from the premise that AU member states that are also States Parties to the Rome Statute have to manage and navigate two conflicting legal obligations: the duty to honour the ICC's arrest warrant requests, and 'the binding obligations imposed by the decisions of the AU not to cooperate with the ICC in respect of requests to arrest African heads of states'.[73]

SALC brought an urgent application to the High Court for an interdict ordering the government to arrest al-Bashir while he was in the country.[74] The government gave the High Court an interim undertaking that al-Bashir would not be permitted to leave the country until after the court had handed down its decision. The High

---

[72] *National Commissioner of SAPS v SALC* (note 55 above) para 80.

[73] Max du Plessis 'The Omar Al-Bashir case: Exploring efforts to resolve the tension between the African Union and the International Criminal Court' in Maluwa et al (eds) *The Pursuit of a Brave New World in International Law: Essays in Honour of John Dugard* (2017) 434.

[74] *Southern Africa Litigation Centre v Minister of Justice and Constitutional Development and Others* [2015] ZAGPPHC 402; 2015 (5) SA 1 (GP) (*al-Bashir*).

Court dismissed the government's arguments and held that South Africa was indeed obliged to arrest the sitting president of Sudan. However, by the time it had done so, notwithstanding assurances from his legal team during the hearing that he was still in the country, President al-Bashir's plane—Sudan 1—had already taken off from the Waterkloof military airbase. The High Court concluded its judgment with cutting remarks regarding the executive's apparent failure to comply with its order to keep al-Bashir in the country pending the outcome of the case.[75] The South African government appealed to the SCA where the majority of the SCA held that the hosting agreement did not cover heads of state or representatives of states attending AU meetings; hence neither the hosting agreement nor the ministerial proclamation immunised al-Bashir from arrest.[76]

The SCA held that South Africa was bound by its obligations under the Rome Statute and the ICC Act to cooperate with the ICC and to arrest and surrender persons in respect of whom the ICC had issued warrants.[77] While a head of state enjoyed immunity as a matter of customary international law,[78] the ICC Act removed all forms of immunity (including those under s 4(1) of the Immunities Act) that al-Bashir might otherwise have enjoyed.[79] Ponnan JA penned a separate concurring judgment, in which Lewis JA concurred, holding that the purported clash between the Immunities Act and the ICC Act was non-existent. Section 10(9) of the ICC Act made it clear that the immunity conferred by s 4(1)(*a*) could be invoked only if it was not in conflict with the ICC Act, thus negating any head-of-state immunity claimed by al-Bashir.[80]

The government then instituted a further appeal with the Constitutional Court, which was set down to be heard on 22 November 2016. But subsequently, after heads of argument had already been filed, and only a few weeks before the appeal was set to be heard, the government changed tack. It withdrew the appeal from the Constitutional Court and instead sought a political solution: it purported to the steps to withdraw from the Rome Statute altogether. Instead of inviting the Constitutional Court to cure the findings of unlawfulness by the High Court and SCA, the executive instead sought to immunise itself against future non-compliance.

---

[75] The court held as follows at para 37.2:

> A democratic State based on the rule of law cannot exist or function, if the government ignores its constitutional obligations and fails to abide by court orders. A court is the guardian of justice, the corner-stone of a democratic system based on the rule of law. If the State, an organ of State or State official does not abide by court orders, the democratic edifice will crumble stone-by-stone until it collapses and chaos ensues.

[76] *Minister of Justice and Constitutional Development and Others v Southern African Litigation Centre and Others* [2016] ZASCA 17; 2016 (3) SA 317 (SCA) [SALC was a respondent; and HSF was admitted as *amicus curiae*, represented by WW] paras 40–8 (*al-Bashir* SCA).

[77] Ibid para 61.

[78] Ibid paras 66–84.

[79] Ibid para 86–103.

[80] Ibid para 123.

Consequently, on 19 October 2016, the national executive took a decision to withdraw from the Rome Statute. The Minister of International Relations signed a notice of withdrawal to give effect to that decision and it was deposited with the Secretary-General of the United Nations (UN). This withdrawal became the subject of the case in *Democratic Alliance v Minister of International Relations* (the Withdrawal Case).

The Withdrawal Case is an important decision for international law scholars as it clarifies that, where South Africa wishes to withdraw from a treaty, parliamentary approval is required before the executive seeks to give effect to that decision.

The primary questions in the case were whether the national executive's power to conclude international treaties under s 231 of the Constitution included the implied power to give notice of withdrawal from international treaties *without parliamentary approval*; and, whether it was constitutionally permissible for the national executive to deliver a notice of withdrawal from an international treaty without first repealing the domestic law giving effect to that treaty.

Various other public interest organisations participated in the proceedings as supporting respondents (respondents who were cited by the Democratic Alliance (DA) because of their interest in the al-Bashir matter that was due to be heard in the Constitutional Court prior to the state withdrawing its appeal). Though cited as respondents, the organisations in fact supported the relief sought by the applicants. Several public interest groups joined as intervening parties—these were the Council for the Advancement of the South African Constitution (CASAC), the SALC, the Centre for Human Rights; and the Helen Suzman Foundation.[81]

The DA challenged the withdrawal on four grounds:[82] first, prior parliamentary approval was required before the notice of withdrawal was delivered to the UN; second, prior repeal of the ICC Act was required before the notice of withdrawal was delivered to the UN; third, the delivery of the notice of withdrawal without prior consultation with Parliament was procedurally irrational; and fourthly, the withdrawal from the Rome Statute breaches the state's obligations in terms of s 7(2) of the Constitution.

The government argued that prior parliamentary approval was not required for the notice of withdrawal to be given because s 231 does not contain any provision setting out such a requirement.[83] The government argued, amongst other things, that treaty-making lay in the heartland of the national executive[84] and that a construction of the Constitution according to which parliamentary approval was required prior to a withdrawal should not be preferred because it is at odds with

---

[81] Professors John Dugard and Guenael Mettraux and Amnesty International Ltd—who were cited as respondents to the proceedings—all filed notices to abide by the decision of the court.

[82] *DA v Minister of International Relations* (note 51 above) para 30.

[83] Ibid para 37.

[84] Ibid para 38.

international law. The government argued that 'in international law a notice of withdrawal from an international agreement does not require approval. In this regard, counsel pointed out that Article 56 of the Vienna Convention on the Law of Treaties, 1969, on which Article 127 of the Rome Statute is based, contemplates only a notice of withdrawal signed by the head of state, head of government or minister of foreign affairs or other representative of the state concerned, with no parliamentary approval, ratification or confirmation required'. Following this construction would thus, according to the government, be at odds with the constitutional requirement to interpret the Constitution and South African law in compliance with international law.[85]

In any event, said the government, parliamentary approval was in the process of being obtained and accordingly the issue of whether parliamentary approval was required did not arise on the facts of the case.[86]

The court rejected the construction proffered by the government and held that:

> A notice of withdrawal, on a proper construction of s 231, is the equivalent of ratification, which requires prior parliamentary approval in terms of s 231(2). As correctly argued on behalf of the DA, the act of signing a treaty and the act of delivering a notice of withdrawal are different in their effect. The former has no direct legal consequences, while, by contrast, the delivery of a notice of withdrawal has concrete legal effects in international law, as it terminates treaty obligations, albeit on a deferred basis in the present case.

The court emphasised that, while the withdrawal would only take effect after a year, the notice still constituted—at the international level—'a binding, unconditional and final decision of withdrawal from the Rome Statute'.[87]

The court further rejected the government's argument that prior parliamentary approval was at odds with international law—premised on art 56 of the VCLT. The court held that art 56 of the VCLT 'has nothing to do with who has the authority to make a decision to withdraw', rather, it concerns 'the designated government official who signs and delivers the notice to the United Nations after a competent authority (either the national executive or the legislature) had taken a decision to withdraw'. By contrast, the court held that whether prior parliamentary approval was required was a domestic issue determined by South African law rather than a question of international law.[88] The court emphasised as follows:

> [I]t is trite that, where a constitutional or statutory provision confers a power to do something, that provision necessarily confers the power to undo it as well. In the context of this case, the power to bind the country to the Rome Statute is expressly conferred on Parliament. It must therefore, perforce, be Parliament which has the power to decide whether an international agreement ceases to bind the country. The

---

[85] *DA v Minister of International Relations* (note 51 above) para 40.

[86] Ibid para 42.

[87] Ibid para 47.

[88] Ibid para 50.

conclusion is therefore that, on a textual construction of s 231(2), South Africa can withdraw from the Rome Statute only on approval of Parliament and after the repeal of the Implementation Act.[89]

In essence, the court found—correctly—that if it is Parliament which determines whether an international agreement binds the country, then it is constitutionally untenable that the national executive could unilaterally terminate such an agreement.[90] It also followed that South Africa could only withdraw from the Rome Statute after prior approval of Parliament *and* after the repeal of the ICC Act[91] so the attempt to do so 'violated s 231(2) of the Constitution, and breached the separation of powers doctrine enshrined in that section.'[92]

As regards the question of *ex post facto* approval—the court held that this was of no assistance for two reasons. First, the important constitutional principle of separation of powers had already been implicated. Because the national executive had purported to exercise a power it constitutionally did not have, its conduct was invalid and had no effect in law.[93] Whatever Parliament did about the national executive's subsequent request to it, to approve the notice of withdrawal, would not cure its invalidity.[94] Second, although the notice of withdrawal did not take effect immediately, this did not mean its delivery had no consequences until the effective date. The ICC and member states to the Rome Statute would begin preparing for existence without South Africa.[95]

The court also found that the notice was procedurally irrational, because of the failure to consult Parliament prior to filing the notice of withdrawal, particularly since the success of the withdrawal turned on the ICC Act having been repealed by October 2017.[96] However, even if that were notionally possible (though Parliament should not 'be dictated to by the national executive to rush through the repeal bill in order to meet the national executive-created deadlines'), Parliament might decide not to repeal the Bill or there could be a constitutional challenge. The court accordingly declared the notice of withdrawal to be invalid and ordered the government to withdraw the notice.[97]

---

[89] *DA v Minister of International Relations* (note 51 above) para 53.

[90] Ibid para 51.

[91] Ibid para 53.

[92] Ibid para 57.

[93] Ibid para 59.

[94] Ibid para 59.

[95] Ibid para 60.

[96] Ibid paras 64–70.

[97] Ibid paras 83–4.

(b) An argument premised on customary international law

As Crawford notes:

> The dominant principle, normally characterized as the doctrine of incorporation, is that customary rules are to be considered part of the law of the land and enforced as such, with the qualification that they are incorporated only so far as is not inconsistent with Acts of Parliament or prior judicial decisions of final authority.[98]

Section 232 of the Constitution provides that '[c]ustomary international law is law in the Republic unless it is inconsistent with the Constitution or an Act of Parliament'. Section 232 codifies the South African common-law position and proceeds from the premise that customary international law is *automatically* part of South African municipal law without the need for the procedure of ratification set out in the Constitution being followed.

Accordingly, if customary international law is not inconsistent with the Constitution or an Act of Parliament, s 232 provides lawyers with a powerful hook on which to hang their public international law arguments.[99]

Of course, the evolving nature of customary international law and the associated difficulties of proof simultaneously provide an opening and a risk. As set out above, courts do not consider evidence regarding the content of international law and there are various challenges in attempting to ascertain international law, in general, and international customary law, in particular, without regard to expert witnesses being involved in a case. Courts have accordingly been inclined to rely on academic commentaries regarding what amounts to international customary law. Public interest lawyers are thus provided with an opening to be creative in making arguments involving customary international law. But in the background is the attendant risk that the court will not endorse that creativity since it may not be willing to go where no other court has gone before.

Kaunda and Others v President of the Republic of South Africa[100] is one example. The applicants were 69 South African citizens who were being held in Zimbabwe. During March 2004, 15 men were arrested in Equatorial Guinea and were accused of plotting a coup against the President of Equatorial Guinea. The applicants feared that they might be extradited from Zimbabwe to Equatorial Guinea and put on trial. The applicants argued that if this were so, then they would not get a fair trial and, similarly, if convicted they ran the risk of being sentenced to death. The relief sought by the applicants amongst other things, required the South African government to take steps at the diplomatic level to ensure that the relevant governments would respect the applicants' constitutional rights. The

---

[98] Crawford (note 4 above) 41.

[99] See Sam Wordsworth 'Public international law in the English courts' *Oxford Law Society*, last accessed from <www.oxfordlawsoc.com/files/verdict/MT03/Sam%20Wordsworth%20Art.doc> on 23 March 2018.

[100] *Kaunda and Others v President of the Republic of South Africa* [2004] ZACC 5; 2005 (4) SA 235 (CC) [Society for the Abolition of the Death Penalty was admitted as *amicus curiae*] (*Kaunda*).

applicants pinned one of their arguments to international customary law, arguing that South Africa was obliged to exercise diplomatic protection in favour of the South African nationals abroad. However, the Constitutional Court was not persuaded that the norm pressed amounted to general state practice. The court held:

> It appears from the ILC report that although there was some support for this development, and some recent national constitutions made provision for such an obligation, presently this is not the general practice of states. Currently the prevailing view is that diplomatic protection is not recognised by international law as a human right and cannot be enforced as such. To do so may give rise to more problems than it would solve. Diplomatic protection remains the prerogative of the state to be exercised at its discretion. It must be accepted, therefore, that the applicants cannot base their claims on customary international law. No contention to the contrary was addressed to us in argument.[101]

It is accordingly important to give the court comfort that the customary international law norm is settled. In *Koyabe*,[102] for example, the Constitutional Court was encouraged to circumvent the difficult exercise of examining state practice by relying on the decision of the ICJ in the *Interhandel* case[103] as authority for the proposition that the duty to exhaust available domestic remedies before approaching an international tribunal forms part of customary international law.[104] This is a sensible approach.

Similarly, if counsel is able to stress for the court that a number of well-respected international authors agree that a particular rule forms part of customary international law, the court will more likely be comforted about the proof of that rule without having to consider or confirm actual state practice. For instance, in *National Commissioner of SAPS v SALC*,[105] counsel encouraged the Constitutional Court to accept that South Africa, in terms of customary international law, is required, where appropriate, to exercise universal jurisdiction in relation to international crimes like torture. The court accepted the argument, referring to the writings of leading international authors and decisions of foreign courts to reinforce its view about the existence of the customary international law rule:

> Torture, even if not committed on the scale of crimes against humanity, is regarded as a crime which threatens 'the good order not only of particular states but of the international community as a whole'. Coupled with treaty obligations, the ban on torture has the customary international law status of a peremptory norm from which no derogation is permitted.

---

[101] Kaunda (n 100 above) para 29.

[102] *Koyabe and Others v Minister of Home Affairs and Others* [2009] ZACC 23; 2010 (4) SA 327 (CC) [LHR was admitted as *amicus curiae*].

[103] *Interhandel Case (Switzerland v United States)* Preliminary Objections, 1959 ICJ Reports 6 at 27. The ICJ described the duty to exhaust local remedies as 'a well-established rule of customary international law'.

[104] *Koyabe* (note 102 above) para 41.

[105] *National Commissioner of SAPS v SALC* (note 55 above).

As a result of the absolute ban on torture, 'the torturer has become, like the pirate or the slave trader before him, *hostis humani generis*, an enemy of all [hu]mankind'. This statement, albeit in a civil case, applies equally to criminal cases. Torture attracts universal condemnation and all nations have an interest in its prevention, regardless of the nationality of the perpetrator or of the place where it has occurred. The Court in *Filártiga* held further that 'an act of torture committed by a state official against one held in detention violates established norms of the international law of human rights, and hence the law of nations'.

Along with torture, the international crimes of piracy, slave-trading, war crimes, crimes against humanity, genocide and apartheid require states, even in the absence of binding international treaty law, to suppress such conduct because 'all states have an interest as they violate values that constitute the foundation of the world public order'. Torture, whether on the scale of crimes against humanity or not, is a crime in South Africa in terms of section 232 of the Constitution because the customary international law prohibition against torture has the status of a peremptory norm.[106]

Having given that rendition of customary international law, the court was then moved to conclude that '[b]ecause of the international nature of the crime of torture, South Africa ... is required, where appropriate, to exercise universal jurisdiction in relation to these crimes as they offend against the human conscience and our international and domestic law obligations'.[107]

(c) Using an international treaty that has not been domestically incorporated as an interpretive tool

There is very little room to draw upon an unincorporated treaty in a domestic case. Very little room, however, does not mean no room at all. As long as a statute does not clearly trump the application of international law, there are certain situations where an undomesticated treaty may still find its use in an advocate's legal arsenal, mostly through its 'indirect' effect in domestic law. There are two primary methods by which to do so. First, s 39(1)(*b*) of the Constitution provides that '[w]hen interpreting the Bill of Rights' a court, tribunal or forum: 'must consider international law'. Second, s 233 of the Constitution provides that '[w]hen interpreting any legislation, every court must prefer any reasonable interpretation of the legislation that is consistent with international law over any alternative interpretation that is inconsistent with international law'.

A South African court is accordingly entitled to consider the provisions of a treaty to which South Africa is not party, to gain insight into the proper interpretation of the Bill of Rights, or as a trump card when deciding between competing constructions of a statute. This allows courts to have regard to unincorporated

---

[106] *National Commissioner of SAPS v SALC* (note 55 above) paras 35–7.
[107] Ibid para 38.

treaties, including 'international case law arising under them' as long as the court does not purport to enforce the treaty obligation.[108]

Both of these techniques have been used widely and successfully in public interest cases. In essence, a party or an *amicus curiae* will refer the court to a relevant international instrument as well as any decisions interpreting those provisions. Relevant treaties include those arising from the UN system at the international plane. In addition, regional instruments such as the African Charter provide a further, strong platform for the public interest lawyer. South Africa signed the African Charter in 1995 and ratified it in 1996 and it has been frequently relied upon in PIL throughout the constitutional era.[109]

A good example of a matter in which international law was invoked to interpret a statutory provision is *S v Baloyi*,[110] which dealt with a constitutional challenge to s 3(5) of the Prevention of Family Violence Act 133 of 1993 (the predecessor to the Domestic Violence Act 116 of 1998) (Prevention of Family Violence Act). The question was whether the impugned provision imposed a reverse onus on an accused who was required to attend an enquiry in terms of the Prevention of Family Violence Act for breaching the terms of an interim interdict, while the accused was still awaiting a criminal trial. In the course of balancing the competing rights and ultimately finding that the statute survived constitutional scrutiny, the court referred to numerous international instruments including the UDHR, the Declaration on the Elimination of Violence Against Women[111] and the Convention on the Elimination of All Forms of Discrimination Against Women, commonly known by the acronym 'CEDAW'. The Constitutional Court also referred to regional instruments in the form of art 18 of the Banjul Charter, which obliges signatory states to ensure the elimination of discrimination against women. The court held that these injunctions were directly relevant to the matter because, in terms of s 233 of the Constitution, 'when interpreting the Act, the Court must prefer any reasonable interpretation that is consistent with international law over interpreted that is inconsistent with it'. The court ultimately interpreted the provision as not imposing a reverse onus and therefore not unconstitutional.

See too, more recently, the decision of the Constitutional Court in *S v Okah*.[112] Here the court had to confront the correct interpretation of s 15(1) of the Protec-

---

[108] R Higgins 'The role of domestic courts in the enforcement of international human rights: The United Kingdom' in B Conforti & F Francioni (eds) *Enforcing International Human Rights in Domestic Courts* (1997) 41.

[109] See eg, *National Commissioner of the SAPS v SALC* (note 55 above) para 39 and fn 45.

[110] *S v Baloyi and Others* [1999] ZACC 19; 2000 (2) SA 425 (CC) [the CGE was admitted as first intervening party, represented by CTH].

[111] General Assembly Resolution 48/104 of 1993.

[112] *S v Okah* [2018] ZACC 3; 2018 (4) BCLR 456 (CC) [SALC and the Institute for Security Studies were admitted as *amici curiae*—with the Court having issued a directive specifically calling upon parties with an expertise in international law to intervene in the case to assist with the international law questions—see para 15].

tion of Constitutional Democracy against Terrorist and Related Activities Act 33 of 2004. The central question was whether the section conferred extra territorial jurisdiction on South African courts to try terrorist acts committed abroad, beyond the financing of terrorism.

In coming to its decision, the court used the international law instruments in question to insist that it was obliged to accept a particular interpretation of the Act over the one that the SCA had incorrectly adopted. Cameron J's judgment in this regard highlights the powerful confirmatory role that international law often plays in deciding the proper meaning of a domestic statute, and which the Constitution obliges a court to adopt:

> The statute fulfils a number of international instruments. These establish that South Africa is under both a general duty to combat terrorism and a specific duty to bring to trial perpetrators of terrorism, wherever perpetrated, whom it does not extradite. The international instruments establishing these twin duties include conventions, protocols and UN Security Council resolutions.
>
> [37] The general duty to combat terrorism is broad. It commands a reading of the Act that enables South Africa to participate, as a member of the international community, in the fight against an international and transnational phenomenon. The conspicuous consequence of the contested interpretation is that it would pull the Act's teeth, rendering futile its expressed endeavour to give bite to this duty.
>
> [38] The specific duty to prosecute or extradite provides a yet stronger imperative to overturn that interpretation. Even if one were to assume that interpretation were reasonable, which a textual analysis shows it is not, section 233 of the Constitution requires this Court to interpret the Act in line with international law. Here, there is a clear obligation that South Africa prosecute or extradite persons like Mr Okah. The interpretation in this judgment gives effect to that obligation, whereas the Supreme Court of Appeal's interpretation does not.[113]

In addition to the African Charter, our courts have also frequently relied on other key regional human rights instruments such as the European Convention on Human Rights[114] and the American Convention on Human Rights of 1969,[115] as well as significant decisions by the European Court of Human Rights,[116] the

---

[113] *S v Okah* (note 112 above) paras 36–8.

[114] *S v Makwanyane and Another* [1995] ZACC 3; 1995 (3) SA 391 (CC) para 50 [the LRC acted for the applicant/accused; LHR, CALS and the Society for the Abolition of the Death Penalty were admitted as *amici curiae*]; *S v Williams and Others* [1995] ZACC 6; 1995 (3) SA 632 (CC) para 27 [the LRC acted for the accused]; *De Lange v Smuts NO* [1998] ZACC 6; 1998 (3) SA 785 (CC) para 45; *Mohamed and Another v President of the Republic of South Africa and Others* [2001] ZACC 18; 2001 (3) SA 893 (CC) paras 45–60 [the Society for the Abolition of the Death Penalty and the Human Rights Committee Trust were admitted as *amici curiae*, represented by the LRC].

[115] *Certification of the Constitution of the Republic of South Africa, 1996* [1996] ZACC 26 [LRC, CALS and the CLC made submission]; 1996 (4) SA 744 (CC) para 50 fn 46; *Motsepe v S* [2014] ZAGPPHC 1016; 2015 (5) SA 126 (GP) para 34 [WW acted for the appellant].

[116] *AD and Another v DW and Others* [2007] ZACC 27 para 36 fn 18 [CCL was admitted as *amicus curiae*]; *The Citizen 1978 (Pty) Ltd and Others v McBride* [2011] ZACC 11; 2011 (4) SA 191 (CC) para 95; *Minister of Home Affairs and Others v Tsebe and Others, Minister of Justice and*

Inter-American Commission on Human Rights[117] and the Inter-American Court of Human Rights.[118]

A particularly creative manifestation of this approach is found in *Glenister II,*[119] which concerned the government's controversial decision to disband the Directorate of Special Operations (commonly known as 'the Scorpions') and instead to establish the Directorate for Priority Crimes Investigation (DPCI) (commonly known as 'the Hawks').

Two questions arose in the case. The first was whether the Constitution imposed an obligation on the state to establish and maintain an independent body to combat corruption and organised crime (such as the Scorpions).[120] Second, if so, did the Hawks satisfy the requirement of being sufficiently independent?[121] The interesting international law question was that the United Nations Convention against Corruption[122] had been signed and ratified by the national executive, *but not domesticated.*

As regards the first question, the majority of the court held 'unequivocally' that, while the relevant treaty had not been domesticated, 'the Constitution itself imposes that obligation on the state'.[123] The majority found that 'on a common-sense approach, our law demands a body outside executive control to deal effectively with corruption'.[124] It went on to emphasise that this body could not hope to carry out its mandate, or be reasonably perceived by the public to be effectively carrying out its mandate, without fear, favour, or prejudice, without proper independence from political influence and interference. Instead of relying on an undomesticated treaty, the majority found that the independence of the DPCI was an implicit constitutional requirement.[125] The majority found the implied requirement using an expansive and creative construction of the Constitution. The Constitution required an independent corruption-fighting unit for the protection of several of the rights in the Bill of Rights (moreover, s 7(2) of the Constitution,

---

Constitutional Development and Another v Tsebe and Others [2012] ZACC 16; 2012 (5) SA 467 (CC) para 43 [Society for the Abolition of the Death Penalty was a respondent, represented by the LRC; Amnesty International was admitted as *amicus curiae*]; *Mlungwana and Others v S and Another* [2018] ZAWCHC 3; 2018 2 All SA 183 (WCC) para 73.

[117] *S v Makwanyane* (note 114 above) para 50; *Koyabe* (note 102 above) para 43; *Minister of Home Affairs v Rahim and Others* [2016] ZACC 3; 2016 (3) SA 218 (CC) para 10; *Mlungwana* (note 116 above) para 72.

[118] *Makwanyane* (note 114 above) 35.

[119] *Glenister II* (note 1 above).

[120] Ibid para 163.

[121] Ibid.

[122] United Nations Convention against Corruption, 2349 UNTS 41, entered into force 14 December 2005.

[123] Glenister II (note 1 above) para 163.

[124] Ibid para 200.

[125] See the majority judgment of Moseneke DCJ and Cameron J in *Glenister II* (note 1 above) paras 175–202.

obliges the state to respect, protect, promote and fulfil the rights in the Bill of Rights), particularly when interpreted in the light of South Africa's international law obligations and commitments. The majority reasoned as follows:

> Now plainly there are many ways in which the State can fulfil its duty to take positive measures to respect, protect, promote and fulfil the rights in the Bill of Rights. This court will not be prescriptive as to what measures the State takes, as long as they fall within the range of possible conduct that a reasonable decision-maker in the circumstances may adopt. A range of possible measures is therefore open to the State, all of which will accord with the duty the Constitution imposes, so long as the measures taken are reasonable.
>
> And it is here where the courts' obligation to consider international law when interpreting the Bill of Rights is of pivotal importance. Section 39(1)(b) states that when interpreting the Bill of Rights a court 'must consider international law'. The impact of this provision in the present case is clear, and direct. What reasonable measures does our Constitution require the State to take in order to protect and fulfil the rights in the Bill of Rights? That question must be answered in part by considering international law. And international law, through the inter-locking grid of conventions, agreements and protocols we set out earlier, unequivocally obliges South Africa to establish an anti-corruption entity with the necessary independence.
>
> That is a duty this country itself undertook when it acceded to these international agreements. And it is an obligation that became binding on the Republic, in the international sphere, when the National Assembly and the NCOP by resolution adopted them, more especially the UN Convention.
>
> That the Republic is bound under international law to create an anti-corruption unit with appropriate independence is of the foremost interpretive significance in determining whether the state has fulfilled its duty to respect, protect, promote and fulfil the rights in the Bill of Rights, as section 7(2) requires. Section 7(2) implicitly demands that the steps the state takes must be reasonable. To create an anti-corruption unit that is not adequately independent would not constitute a reasonable step. In reaching this conclusion, the fact that section 231(2) provides that an international agreement that Parliament ratifies 'binds the Republic' is of prime significance. It makes it unreasonable for the state, in fulfilling its obligations under section 7(2), to create an anti-corruption entity that lacks sufficient independence.
>
> This is not to incorporate international agreements into our Constitution. It is to be faithful to the Constitution itself, and to give meaning to the ambit of the duties it creates in accordance with its own clear interpretive injunctions.[126]

We note that there is no express obligation in the Constitution for Parliament to incorporate treaties domestically. There is, however, a general duty on South Africa to align its national laws with its obligations at the international level.[127] It is for South Africa's organs of state to determine the appropriate method of

---

[126] *Glenister II* (note 1 above) paras 191–5.

[127] Article 26 of the VCLT: 'treaties in force are binding upon the parties to them and must be performed by them in good faith.'

achieving this.[128] An international agreement binding at the international level also imposes a domestic obligation upon the South African government and its organs, to act in good faith domestically[129] and to refrain from acts that would defeat the object and purpose of the treaty until the legislative branch has made its intention clear as regards how to fulfil South Africa's international obligation.[130]

The public interest lawyer may thus ably employ international law, even if not domesticated. Moreover, as *Glenister II* demonstrates, if carefully executed the courts may be willing to indulge a profoundly purposive construction of the Constitution that goes fairly far beyond what is contained in the words of the text.

Equally, however, the public interest lawyer must heed the caution sounded by the Constitutional Court in *Glenister II*, where the court emphasised that while international law sources would be instructive, ultimately what was required was to interpret *our* Constitution and to discern the particular 'native' notion of independence it demanded.[131]

An example of the Constitutional Court drawing a distinction between what is required at international law and under our Constitution is the *Mazibuko* case.[132] *Mazibuko* concerned the proper construction of s 27(1)*(b)* of the Constitution, which provides that everyone has the right to have access to 'sufficient water'. The dispute arose out of the implementation of a pilot project in Phiri in Soweto by the City of Johannesburg and its water service company, Johannesburg Water. The project involved relaying water pipes to improve water supply and reduce water losses and the introduction of a free basic water allowance, as well as pre-paid meters for any water used in excess of the free water allowance. The project was introduced because of the acute water shortages experienced in Soweto coupled with the fact that the City was not recovering payment for water in the area.[133]

In *Mazibuko*, the applicants argued that the Constitutional Court should determine the content of the right in s 27(1)*(b)* by quantifying the amount of water *sufficient* for a dignified life.[134] The applicants urged the court to find that the appropriate amount was 50 litres per person per day. The applicants further contended that the court should then determine whether the state acted reasonably in seeking to achieve the progressive realisation of this right.

The Constitutional Court held that s 27(1)*(b)* (the right of access to sufficient water) coupled with s 27(2) do not require the state, upon demand, to provide every person with 'sufficient water'. Instead, the sections require the state to 'take

---

[128] P Malanczuk *Akehurst's Modern Introduction to International Law* (1997) 64.

[129] Article 18 of the VCLT.

[130] E de Wet 'South Africa' in D Shelton (ed) *International Law and Domestic Legal Systems: Incorporation, Transformation and Persuasion* (2011) 567, 578.

[131] *Glenister II* (note 1 above) para 211.

[132] *Mazibuko* (note 32 above).

[133] Ibid para 166.

[134] Ibid para 50.

reasonable legislative and other measures progressively to realise the achievement of the right of access to sufficient water, within available resources'.[135]

Interestingly, the Constitutional Court—while denouncing any international law association with minimum core—noted that the notion of 'progressive realisation' is consistent with principles of international law. While the applicants in *Mazibuko* had ably sought to distinguish what was being sought from the 'minimum core' approach, the Constitutional Court rejected the argument, finding that it was akin to the minimum core approaches that had been advanced in earlier cases.

The court held that the applicants' argument was, in effect, not only similar to a minimum core argument—it was actually 'more extensive because it goes beyond the minimum'.[136] The court held that the argument must fail for the same reasons that the minimum core argument failed in *Grootboom*[137] and *Treatment Action Campaign No 2*.[138] In our view, the court conflated two separate enquiries since giving some form of quantification to the term 'sufficient water' in no way means that the obligation becomes immediately realisable or deprives the enquiry of context. However, the case is instructive because it demonstrates that the public interest lawyer should be particularly careful when relying on international human rights standards to persuade the courts that these standards apply with equal force, under the text and framework of our particular Constitution.

(d) Using international law as a guide in the exercise of official discretion

Another means of using international law arguments, even where the particular principles have not been expressly incorporated into South African law, is as a guide in the exercise of official discretion. Courts throughout the Commonwealth have accepted that the values reflected in unincorporated human rights treaties ought to inform the exercise of official discretion.

For instance, in *Baker v Minister of Citizenship and Immigration; Canadian Council of Churches et al., Interveners,*[139] the Supreme Court of Canada held that an immigration decision was unreasonable because it failed to give sufficient weight to the best interests of the child (a principle derived from the Convention on the Rights of the Child, which had been *ratified* by Canada but *not directly incorporated* into Canadian law). The court referred to the principle that 'the values reflected in international human rights law may help inform the contextual approach to statutory interpretation and judicial review'. The court then concluded as follows:

---

[135] *Mazibuko* (note 32 above) para 50.

[136] Ibid para 55.

[137] *Grootboom* (note 32 above).

[138] *Minister of Health and Others v Treatment Action Campaign and Others (No 2)* [2002] ZACC 15; 2002 (5) SA 721 (CC) [LRC acted for the respondents; IDASA, CLC and Cotlands Baby Sanctuary were admitted as *amici curiae*).

[139] 174 DLR (4th) 1999.

> The principles of the Convention and other international instruments place special importance on protections for children and childhood, and on particular consideration of their interests, needs and rights. They help show the values that are central in determining whether this decision was a reasonable exercise of . . . power.[140]

The English courts have taken a similar approach. In *R v Secretary of State for the Home Department Ex parte Ahmed*,[141] Lord Woolf stated as follows:

> I will accept that entering into a Treaty by the Secretary of State could give rise to a legitimate expectation on which the public in general are entitled to rely. Subject to any indication to the contrary, it could be a representation that the Secretary of State would act in accordance with any obligations which he accepted under the Treaty.[142]

Again, in *R v Uxbridge Magistrates' Court exp. Adimi,* Simon Brown LJ approved the statements by Lord Woolf in *Ahmed* and accepted that the UK's ratification of a treaty could create a legitimate expectation that its provisions would be followed. Similar approaches have been followed in New Zealand[143] and Australia.[144]

The same principle has begun to find application in South African law. This flows from the well-established requirement to interpret legislation in a manner that complies with international law.[145] The South African SCA has ruled in *Progress Office Machines*:[146]

> Not only is a court bound to 'prefer any reasonable interpretation of the legislation that is consistent with international law over any alternative interpretation that is inconsistent with international law' but subordinate legislation such as the notice by the Minister of Finance imposing the anti-dumping duty must be reasonable. Dugard submits that a court may 'insist on compliance with a State's international obligations as a requisite for the validity of subordinate legislation'. The duration of the anti-dumping duty imposed beyond the period allowed by the Anti-Dumping Agreement would not only be a breach of the Republic's international obligations and an unreasonable interpretation of the notice but also unreasonable and to that extent invalid.

The simple point is that an international law treaty, even if not domestically incorporated, is a relevant consideration that any decision-maker would have to

---

[140] *Baker* (note 139 above) para 71.

[141] *R v Secretary of State for the Home Department Ex parte Ahmed* [1998] INLR 570.

[142] Ibid 583. See also *R v Uxbridge Magistrates' Court, Ex Parte Adimi* (DC) 3 WLR [2000] 451.

[143] *Ashby v Minister of Immigration* [1981] 1 NZLR 222 (CA); *Tavita v Minister of Immigration* [1994] 2 NZLR 257 (CA).

[144] *Minister for Immigration and Ethnic Affairs v Teoh* (1995) 183 CLR 273.

[145] As Devenish writes in GE Devenish *Interpretation of Statutes* (1992) 212:
> The Courts endeavour to construe a statute in conformity with International Law and not in conflict with it. There is a presumption that Parliament in enacting statutes did not intend to derogate from, or legislate in conflict with the principles of International Law.

[146] *Progress Office Machines CC v South African Revenue Service and Others* [2007] ZASCA 118; 2008 (2) SA 13 (SCA) para 11.

weigh in the balance. And if he or she failed to do so, then that would be a ground for review based on a failure to apply his or her mind.

(e) An argument that a treaty, binding at the international level, should motivate a development of the South African common law

The fifth kind of argument that may be raised is premised on the Constitutional Court's decision in *Government of the Republic of Zimbabwe v Fick and Others*.[147] That is, using international obligations as a catalyst for developing the common law.[148]

Fick extended the common law to provide for the execution of judgments of international tribunals. The respondents were three farmers whose farms were expropriated in Zimbabwe without compensation. Zimbabwe had ousted the jurisdiction of the courts to determine disputes relating to expropriation. Aggrieved parties, according to the Constitutional Court, 'literally had no forum to take their cases to in Zimbabwe'.[149]

The farmers took their case to the Southern African Development Community (SADC) Tribunal for adjudication. While Zimbabwe participated in the proceedings before the SADC Tribunal, it later refused to carry out the Tribunal's order. The farmers went back to the SADC Tribunal for further relief. The matter was subsequently referred to the Summit—the SADC's supreme policy-making body that comprised the Heads of State or Government of the SADC member states[150]—whereafter the SADC Tribunal imposed costs orders against Zimbabwe. Zimbabwe also failed to pay these costs orders. The respondents then took a novel step. They approached the courts in South Africa for recognition and registration of the Tribunal's order as a prelude to the execution of those orders.

Zimbabwe's principal challenge to the application was premised on its sovereign immunity against suits in South African courts in terms of the Foreign States Immunities Act 87 of 1981 (the Immunities Act). It also contended that the South African Parliament had not approved the SADC Treaty and Tribunal Protocol and accordingly our courts had no power to enforce the Tribunal's costs orders, as there had not been compliance with s 231 of the Constitution.[151]

The farmers were successful in both the High Court and the SCA. The SCA held that the common-law rule applicable to domestic foreign judgments should also be extended to apply to orders of international tribunals:

---

[147] *Fick* (note 2 above).

[148] See also, *Carmichele v Minister of Safety and Security* [2001] ZACC 22; 2001 (4) SA 938 (CC) [CALS was admitted as *amicus curiae*] para 61 where the Constitutional Court had regard to various articles of CEDAW (see para 62 fn 5 for the court's description of CALS).

[149] Ibid para 80.

[150] Ibid para 9.

[151] Ibid para 18.

While the authorities referred to in that passage from the judgment are directed at the enforcement of a judgment of the domestic courts of a foreign country I see no reason to disagree with Patel J that they are applicable as well to an order of an international tribunal whose legitimacy has been accepted. There is also no question that the order now sought to be enforced satisfies all the requirements of paras (ii)-(vi) tabulated in the extract from the judgment in *Jones v Krok* [1995 (1) SA 677 (A)] that is cited in the passage above.[152]

The case ultimately reached the Constitutional Court where the central question was whether South African courts had jurisdiction to register the enforcement of the costs order made by the SADC Tribunal against Zimbabwe—like the courts would in relation to a foreign judgment.[153]

Zimbabwe argued that it was immune from the jurisdiction of our courts as a foreign state and South Africa's alleged non-compliance with its own constitutional requirements in relation to giving binding effect to international agreements.[154] The general position is that a foreign state enjoys immunity from the jurisdiction of the South African courts under s 2(1) of the Immunities Act. There are, however, some exceptions. For instance, s 3(1) provides that immunity is forfeited in relation to proceedings in which the state expressly waived its immunity.[155] Mogoeng CJ, for the majority of the court, found that Zimbabwe had waived its immunity because of its agreement to be bound by the Tribunal Protocol, including article 32 which imposed an obligation on Member States 'to take all steps necessary to facilitate the enforcement of judgments and orders of the Tribunal'.[156]

One of the key anterior questions was whether the Amended Treaty, which incorporated the Tribunal Protocol, was binding on South Africa.[157] Zimbabwe argued, that Parliament did not approve the Treaty in terms of s 231 of the Constitution and that non-compliance was an absolute bar to the enforcement of the costs order in South Africa.[158] The Constitutional Court dispensed with this argument on the basis that Parliament had approved the Treaty in 1995 and that '[t]his accession was approved by the Senate and National Assembly on 13 and 14 September 1995 respectively'.[159] The court observed that '[t]he Treaty and the Amended Treaty [were] thus binding on South Africa, at least on the international plane'.

---

[152] *Government of the Republic of Zimbabwe v Fick and Others* [2012] ZASCA 122 (*Fick SCA*) para 29.
[153] *Fick* (note 2 above) para 23.
[154] Ibid para 22.
[155] Ibid para 32.
[156] Ibid paras 33–5.
[157] Ibid para 23.
[158] Ibid para 29.
[159] Ibid para 30 fn 42.

Moreover, art 32(2) of the Tribunal Protocol 'imposes a legal obligation on South Africa to take all legal steps necessary to facilitate the execution of the decisions of the Tribunal created in terms of the Treaty that our Parliament has approved'.[160]

The next significant question was whether the High Court had jurisdiction under the common law to enforce the costs order against Zimbabwe.[161] One of the common-law requirements for the enforcement of a judgment of a foreign court is that the foreign court must have had jurisdiction.[162] Zimbabwe argued that the Tribunal itself did not have jurisdiction over Zimbabwe. The Constitutional Court held:

> No ratification was required for the Amended Treaty, and by extension the Tribunal Protocol, to bind Member States. Since the Treaty had already been ratified by the prescribed majority, including Zimbabwe, acceded to by South Africa and duly approved by our Parliament, the Tribunal Protocol that was subsumed under it, became immediately operational upon adoption by the requisite majority. The Tribunal therefore had jurisdictional competence over Zimbabwe at all times material hereto. When the matter that gave rise to the costs order was filed by the farmers in 2007 and the costs order was later made, the Tribunal Protocol had already been operational for about six years.[163]

The court held that a suite of provisions made clear that 'both Zimbabwe and South Africa effectively agreed that domestic courts in the SADC countries would have the jurisdiction to enforce orders of the Tribunal made against them'.[164]

The court held that in terms of South Africa's common law, a foreign court or tribunal was 'clothed with jurisdiction if that party submits to the jurisdiction of that forum'.[165] As Zimbabwe had 'recognised and accepted the Tribunal's jurisdiction but for the alleged absence of standards on human rights or agrarian reform' Zimbabwe had submitted to the Tribunal's jurisdiction.[166] The court held that this was sufficient in order to satisfy the first common-law jurisdictional requirement. The question that remained was whether the common law that applied to foreign courts also applied to international courts or tribunals.

The Constitutional Court found that the common law on the enforcement of foreign civil judgments, as it stood, only provided for the execution of judgments made by domestic courts of a foreign state.[167] The court held that it was necessary to develop the common law 'in order to pave the way for the enforcement of

---

[160] *Fick* (note 2 above) para 31.

[161] Ibid para 38.

[162] Ibid para 40.

[163] Ibid para 47.

[164] Ibid para 48.

[165] Ibid para 49.

[166] Ibid para 49.

[167] Ibid para 53.

judgments or orders made by the Tribunal'.[168] The court emphasised that this development 'extends to the enforcement of judgments and orders of international courts or tribunals, based on international agreements that are binding on South Africa' at the international level.[169]

For present purposes, what is particularly relevant is that the Constitutional Court underscored that a significant factor pointing to the need to develop the common law was that 'certain provisions of the Constitution facilitate the alignment of our law with foreign and international law'. What is novel is that the Constitutional Court used the obligations that were binding on South Africa at the international level as a basis to develop the common law. The court held:

> Article 32 of the Tribunal Protocol is an offshoot of the Amended Treaty that binds South Africa. It is foundational to the development of the common law on enforcement in this matter and provides that States 'shall take forthwith all measures necessary to ensure execution of decisions of the Tribunal.' It also provides that the 'law and rules of civil procedure for the registration and enforcement of foreign judgments in force in the territory of the State in which the judgment is to be enforced shall govern enforcement' of the Tribunal's decisions. Since the Enforcement Act does not apply to this matter, the only other applicable foreign judgment enforcement mechanism is the common law. We must, therefore, turn to the South African common law. Based on article 32(1), the common law must be developed in a way that would empower South Africa's domestic courts to register and facilitate the enforcement of the Tribunal's decisions.

> Article 32 imposes a duty upon Member States, including South Africa, to take all execution-facilitating measures, such as the development of the common law principles on the enforcement of foreign judgments, to 'ensure execution of decisions of the Tribunal.' It also gives binding force to the decisions of the Tribunal on the parties including the affected Member States, paves the way and provides for the enforceability of the Tribunal's decisions within the territories of Member States. South Africa has essentially bound itself to do whatever is legally permissible to deal with any attempt by any Member State to undermine and subvert the authority of the Tribunal and its decisions as well as the obligations under the Amended Treaty. Added to this, are our own constitutional obligations to honour our international agreements and give practical expression to them, particularly when the rights provided for in those agreements, such as the Amended Treaty, similar to those provided for in our Bill of Rights, are sought to be vindicated. We are also enjoined by our Constitution to develop the common law in line with the spirit, purport and objects of the Bill of Rights.[170]

The Constitutional Court found that it was enjoined not only by article 32 of the Tribunal Protocol but also by various provisions of the Constitution to develop the common law. The court emphasised that when courts are obliged to develop the

---

[168] *Fick* (note 2 above) para 53.

[169] Ibid para 53.

[170] Ibid paras 58–9 (original footnotes omitted).

common law or promote access to courts, they must remember that their 'obligation to consider international law when interpreting the Bill of Rights is of pivotal importance'. The Constitutional Court found:

> A construction of the Amended Treaty as well as the right of access to courts, with due regard to the constitutional values of the rule of law, human rights, accountability, responsiveness and openness, enjoins our courts to be inclined to recognise the right of access to our courts to register and enforce the Tribunal's decision. This will, as indicated above, be achieved by extending the meaning of 'foreign court' to the Tribunal.[171]

Moreover, the court referred to the effect of s 233 of the Constitution which enjoined a court to prefer any reasonable interpretation of legislation that is consistent with international law to one that is not.[172] The Amended Treaty, incorporating the Tribunal Protocol, said the court, placed an 'international law obligation on South Africa to ensure that its citizens have access to the Tribunal and that its decisions are enforced'. It followed that:

> Section 34 of the Constitution must therefore be interpreted, and the common law developed, so as to grant the right of access to our courts to facilitate the enforcement of the decisions of the Tribunal in this country. This, as said, will be achieved by regarding the Tribunal as a foreign court, in terms of our common law.[173]

We note that when this question has arisen in other jurisdictions,[174] classifying international bodies and tribunals as 'foreign courts' has been found to be an unsatisfactory route.[175] Indeed, a recent analysis shows the enforcement model in *Fick* is largely unprecedented.[176] Critics may say that when the courts develop the common law where Parliament has expressly decided not to domesticate international law norms, this gives rise to counter-majoritarian concerns. However, what cannot be denied is that the judgment in *Fick* creates a distinct and powerful additional tool for international law to be relied upon to press the development of the law in public interest cases.

2.4 JUSTICIABILITY

(a) The limits on relying on international law before domestic courts
Above, we have outlined five of the main methods available to the public interest lawyer seeking to rely upon international law before South African courts. A

---

[171] *Fick* (note 2 above) paras 68.
[172] Ibid para 69.
[173] Ibid para 69.
[174] *Gathuna v African Orthodox Church of Kenya* CA 4/1982; *Gauthier v Canada* Communication No 633/1995, UN Doc CCPR/C/65/D/633/1995 (5 May 1999).
[175] RF Oppong & LC Niro 'Enforcing judgments of international courts in national courts' 2014 *Journal of International Dispute Settlement* 1–28.
[176] Ibid.

separate, but no less important an issue confronting that lawyer is the question of justiciability. That is, even if international law was correctly invoked in the case at hand, other considerations might preclude the court from ruling on the questions that the international law arguments raised. Put differently, a court 'confronted with an intricate issue of international law, may simply conclude that it is beyond its capacity to decide [the issue], that it, is non-justiciable'.[177] This principle exists in England as well as other common-law jurisdictions.[178]

South African courts accept that issues in relation to the actions of foreign states may not be justiciable in domestic South African courts or should not be adjudicated. The key principles are sometimes referred to as the act of state doctrine or judicial restraint, or as the principle of non-justiciability. The label is not what matters. What is important is that South African courts, like other domestic courts, recognise that they must be astute not to violate foundational principles of sovereignty and equality of states by sitting in judgment on the actions of a foreign state.[179]

In the seminal case of *Swissborough*,[180] Joffe J, after considering the development of the principles of the act of state doctrine and judicial restraint in the (US) and the (UK), held that:

> The basis of the application of the act of State doctrine or that of judicial restraint is just as applicable to South Africa as it is to the USA and England. The comity of nations is just as applicable to South Africa as it is to other sovereign States. The judicial branch of government ought to be astute in not venturing into areas where it would be in a judicial no-man's land. It would appear that in an appropriate case, as an exercise of the Court's inherent jurisdiction to regulate its own procedure, the Court could determine to exercise judicial restraint and refuse to entertain a matter, notwithstanding it having jurisdiction to do so, in view of the involvement of foreign States therein.
>
> In the present matter it is apparent that decisions have to be made in regard to the alleged unlawful conduct of GOL [the Government of the Kingdom of Lesotho] in Lesotho and the control of GOL and its relationship with the RSA. As far as the latter is concerned there can be little doubt that this is not an area for the judicial branch of government. It belongs to international law. As was held in Buttes Gas (supra), the Court would be in judicial no-man's land. It would have no judicial or manageable standards by which to judge the issue. It clearly is a matter in respect of which this Court should exercise judicial restraint. As far as the former is concerned the matter appears to be even more complex.[181]

---

[177] Crawford (note 4 above) 59.

[178] Ibid 59.

[179] See generally Shaw (note 4 above) 143–4.

[180] *Swissborough Diamond Mines (Pty) Ltd v Government of the Republic of South Africa* 1999 (2) SA 279 (T).

[181] Ibid 334.

Our courts have consistently referred to and approved *Swissborough*. In particular, using *Swissborough* as authority, the SCA held that 'Courts should act with restraint when dealing with allegations of unlawful conduct ascribed to sovereign States'.[182]

As made clear in *Swissborough*, the principle of the act of state doctrine is predicated on comity (which is itself predicated on the principle of state sovereignty and equality of states). For instance, in the *Campaign for Nuclear Disarmament* decision, the UK Court held that '[t]he general rule is that, in the interests of comity, domestic courts do not rule on questions of international law which affect foreign sovereign states'.[183]

Similarly, in the Constitutional Court decision of *Kaunda*,[184] Ngcobo J (as he then was), pointed out that 'comity compels States to respect the sovereignty of one another; no State wants to interfere in the domestic affairs of another'.[185] In the same case, Chaskalson CJ also emphasised the recognition of state sovereignty in limiting the territorial scope of South African laws, holding that: '[f]or South Africa to assume an obligation that entitles its nationals to demand, and obliges it to take action to ensure, that laws and conduct of a foreign State and its officials meet not only the requirements of the foreign State's own laws, but the rights that our nationals have under our Constitution, *would be inconsistent with the principle of State sovereignty*'.[186] [our emphasis]

In *Kolbatschenko*,[187] the Cape High Court (comprising Thring J and Van Heerden J) made several broad findings in relation to when certain matters are non-justiciable and recognised the basis for this being the equality of sovereign states (relying on inter alia *Swissborough*). The court held:

> South African Courts have refused to evaluate decisions or actions in the realm of foreign relations involving issues of a 'high executive nature'. Thus, for example, matters such as the recognition by the South African Government of a foreign State or of a foreign government, or of the status of diplomatic representatives of a foreign State, have generally been regarded as non-justiciable (see, for example, *Inter-Science Research and Development Services (Pty) Ltd v Republica Popular de Moçambique* 1980 (2) SA 111 (T) at 117D–G). Such decisions usually involve the relationship between the South African state and the foreign State concerned, directly affecting the interests of such States *as States*, and are often so 'political' in nature that the Courts have 'no judicial or manageable standards' by which to judge them (*per* Joffe J in *Swissborough Diamond Mines (Pty) Ltd and Others v Government of*

---

[182] *Van Zyl and Others v Government of the Republic of South Africa* [2007] ZASCA 109; 2008 (3) SA (SCA) 294 para 5.

[183] *The Campaign for Nuclear Disarmament v The Prime Minister of the United Kingdom and Others* [2002] EWHC 2759 (QB) para 38 (*CND*).

[184] *Kaunda* (note 100 above).

[185] Ibid para 172.

[186] Ibid para 44.

[187] *Kolbatschenko v King NO and Another* 2001 (4) SA 336 (C).

the Republic of South Africa and Others (supra at 334F–G), citing the judgment of
Lord Wilberforce in *Buttes Gas and Oil Co v J Hammer and Another (Nos 2 and 3)*;
*Occidental Petroleum Corpn and Another v Buttes Gas and Oil Co and Another
(Nos 1* A *and 2)* [1981] 3 All ER 616 (HL) at 633a–f)[188] (our emphasis).

(b) Navigating the non-justiciability difficulty

In understanding the scope and application of the principles of non-justiciability, it
is important to recognise that where there is evident tension between the relevant
principles of international law and policy considerations relied upon by the
executive, the courts *may be* more reluctant to entertain international law arguments.

Accordingly, it is important to be aware of the limited exceptions to the usual
rule that domestic courts are reluctant to traverse issues of foreign relations
implicated in international law cases. The *Kuwait Airways*[189] case, an English
decision, is a good example. It involved a tort claim in relation to the claimant's
aircraft seized by Iraq in its invasion of Kuwait. While the House of Lords
declined to give effect to the Iraqi resolution purporting to validate the seizure, this
was specifically since the UN Security Council had formally and bindingly
determined that the relevant actions by Iraq were in breach of international peace
and security. As Lord Steyn summarised the position:

> On 2 August 1990 the United Nations Security Council adopted Resolution 660
> which condemned the invasion of Kuwait as a breach of international peace and
> security. This was followed by a series of supplementary Security Council resolu-
> tions which decreed that the annexation of Kuwait was null and void; called on
> member states to give no recognition directly or indirectly to any aspect of the
> annexation; and required all states to impose sanctions on Iraq. These measures were
> duly taken under Ch VII of the United Nations Charter.[190]

Hence, the House of Lords found that act of state doctrine and issues of justiciability did not present an obstacle to the court deciding the case. The UN Security
Council resolutions issued under Chapter VII of the UN Charter, which were
binding on all UN member states, including Kuwait, Iraq and the UK, required
non-recognition of any indirect aspects of Iraqi annexation of Kuwait (which
included the seizure of the aircrafts), including by the UK courts.

The most recent UK Supreme Court decision to consider issues of act of state
doctrine and state immunity is *Belhaj*[191] and it too sets out important exceptions.
In *Belhaj* the claimants sought to bring claims in tort against the UK government

---

[188] *Kolbatschenko* (note 187 above) 356H—357C.
[189] *Kuwait Airways Corporation v Iraq Airways Co. (Nos. 4 and 5)* [2002] UKHL 19; [2002] 2 AC
883 (this is a later iteration—technically, *Kuwait (No 3)*—of an earlier decision *Kuwait (No 1)*).
[190] Ibid para 107.
[191] *Belhaj and Another v Straw and Others; Rahmatullah v Minister of Defence and Others* [2017]
UKSC 3 (17 January 2017).

and certain officials for alleged complicity in their rendition and mistreatment at the hands of foreign states. It was that 'domestic foothold'[192] which allowed for the exception's application.

In its judgment, the Supreme Court recognised that in English law there were three grounds of act of state. It held, first, that a UK court would normally treat a foreign state's legislation as valid insofar as it affects movable or immovable property within the foreign state's jurisdiction, and second, a UK court would not normally question the validity of a foreign governmental act in respect of property within the foreign state's jurisdiction. It was the scope of the third type of foreign act of state that was principally in issue, and which is of importance for our purposes. This is the rule of non-justiciability or judicial abstention whereby a domestic court will not adjudicate upon sovereign acts committed by a foreign state abroad, which our courts have recognised from *Swissborough* onwards (as discussed earlier) and which Lord Sumption styled as an '*international act of state*'.[193] Such a situation may arise, inter alia, where: a court cannot properly hear a claim due to a lack of judicial or manageable standards, or as a function of the separation of powers, where a court considers that it should not hear a claim since it is outside the proper bounds of its constitutional functions, particularly where the question arising is the lawfulness of a state's acts in its dealings with other states and their subjects.

According to the UK Supreme Court, those foreign relations brakes on its competence were not present in *Belhaj*. *Belhaj* was brought not in relation to any foreign property interests or territorial title, nor, as the Supreme Court found were any foreign states' legal interests affected. Rather the case was squarely focused on the lawfulness of the UK government's and its officials' actions. In any event, ruled the UK Supreme Court, it was permissible for the court to deal with the issues raised—even assuming that foreign relations implications arose—on the basis of a public policy exception to the act of state doctrine. In deciding whether an issue is non-justiciable, the Court held that English law will have regard to the extent to which the fundamental rights (in that case, of liberty, access to justice and freedom from torture) are engaged by the issues raised.[194]

One of the cases relied on by the UK Supreme Court in *Belhaj* regarding when public policy might limit the scope of the act of state doctrine, is the House of Lords decision in *Oppenheimer v Cattermole*.[195] In this case, one of the issues was whether an English court should recognise a Nazi decree of 1941 (made in the middle of World War II) which deprived Jews of their German nationality and property. Importantly, the issue (and others) arose in a clearly domestic context: whether Mr Oppenheimer (a British national) subject to UK income tax laws, was

---

[192] *Belhaj* (note 191 above) para 226 as per Lord Sumption.

[193] Ibid paras 234 onwards.

[194] Ibid paras 37, 98 and 101.

[195] *Oppenheimer v Cattermole (Inspector of Taxes)* [1975] 1 All ER 538 (HL).

entitled to an exemption in relation to his German pension. Relevant to the exemption was whether Mr Oppenheimer was a German national at certain relevant times. In the House of Lords, Lord Cross, with whom Lords Hodson and Salmon agreed, held that, although the case was decided on other grounds, had the point arisen, the Nazi decree would have been disregarded. Lord Cross's view was based on the fact that 'a law of this sort constitutes so grave an infringement of human rights that the courts of this country ought to refuse to recognise it as a law at all'.[196]

These exceptions then, while limited, are availing in the right cases. What is significant for present purposes is how the public interest lawyer can—alive to the problems of justiciability in cases that trigger foreign relations concerns—better increase the prospects of success of his or her argument. What tools are available to the public interest lawyer in this regard?

In the first place, it is important for a lawyer seeking to navigate this tension to be aware of and to frame his or her case within the exceptions to the principles discussed above. One exception would be where the matter, while potentially entailing consideration of international acts of state and treaties, is carefully tailored to ensure that a domestic court is asked to focus its energy on the domestic aspects of those international acts or treaties. A good example is the *Earthlife* decision of the High Court, dealing with the government's decision to enter into a cooperation treaty with Russia for the supply of nuclear energy, and where the matter potentially involved the conduct of foreign sovereign states. In *Earthlife*,[197] the court was called upon to determine whether the Minister of Energy's tabling of an intergovernmental agreement with Russia (the Russian IGA) before Parliament in terms of s 231(3) of the Constitution (which did not require Parliamentary approval), instead of s 231(2) (which did require such approval), was unconstitutional. The government argued that the Russian IGA was non-justiciable with reference to *Swissborough* as it involved determining the true agreement between two states. The court set out the principles of *Swissborough* (as discussed above), with clear approval, but accepted the applicants' arguments that these did not apply in the case before it, which related to the domestic lawfulness of the South Africa Minister's actions in tabling the Russian IGA.[198]

The challenge brought by the applicants in *Earthlife* was brought against a domestic government respondent (the Minister of Energy) who had failed to comply with a domestic constitutional requirement (to table the Russian IGA before the South African Parliament under a specific section, which would have required Parliament's approval to make the agreement binding). If the Russian IGA had been tabled under the incorrect provision of the Constitution, s 172(1)(*a*)

---

[196] *Oppenheimer* (note 195 above) 567.

[197] *Earthlife Africa Johannesburg and Another v Minister of Energy and Others* [2017] ZAWCHC 50; 2017 (5) SA 227 (WCC).

[198] Ibid paras 101–5.

of the Constitution required the court to declare this unconstitutional. The applicants furthermore made it clear that the court was *not being asked to consider the lawfulness or actions of Russia*. It was simply being enjoined to consider whether the domestic actions of the South African government complied with the procedural requirements of s 231 of the Constitution, for tabling international agreements. Indeed, the court made clear that it had 'not been asked to determine whether the IGAs [with Russia, South Korea and the US] are valid as a matter of international law at the international level', and it was in fact only due to this (that the validity of the international agreements was not being determined) that the court found that the foreign states had no legal interest in the matter.[199]

Accordingly, it is important how one frames a case: while the *Earthlife* matter implicated the Russian/South African international treaty, and issues of (non)justiciability potentially loomed large, the applicants had focused their efforts on the *domestic* legal steps and mistakes made by the government in relation to that treaty—matters that are essentially domestic and within the province of a domestic court applying principles of administrative and constitutional law with which all domestic judges are well acquainted.

Another tool available to the public interest lawyer is to keep in mind that a court may be more likely to accept an appeal to international law where the argument is directed at showing that the international rule actually reflects or is consistent with government policy. That is the force of international law even where it has not been domesticated, because where a country, like South Africa, has entered into a treaty at the international level, that could be said to evince government policy, even if the treaty has not (yet) been domesticated into our law. *Kuwait Airways* is a good example, in English Law.[200] Lord Steyn in that case was willing to have recourse to the unincorporated UN Charter's prohibition on the use of force and the relevant Security Council Resolutions. The House of Lords was able to embrace international law in this way, safe in the knowledge that its decision would accord with the policy considerations of the Executive. One of those considerations, as expressed by Sir Franklin Berman (then FCO Legal Adviser) in a letter before the court, was that the UK considered itself bound by the Security Council Resolutions, which condemned the invasion of Kuwait as a

---

[199] *Earthlife* (note 197 above) para 90.

[200] In the South African context, we highlight *Glenister II* again (note 1 above) para 193 where the majority of the Constitutional Court invoked this mode of reasoning in aid of its conclusion:

> That is a duty this country itself undertook when it acceded to these international agreements. And it is an obligation that became binding on the Republic, in the international sphere, when the National Assembly and the NCOP by resolution adopted them, more especially the UN Convention . . . That the Republic is bound under international law to create an anti-corruption unit with appropriate independence is of the foremost interpretive significance in determining whether the state has fulfilled its duty to respect, protect, promote and fulfil the rights in the Bill of Rights, as section 7(2) requires.

breach of international peace and security.[201] Resultantly, the Executive's policy considerations were consistent with the international law arguments pleaded before the court—and hence, it presented Lord Steyn with no difficulty to take on board the unincorporated UN Charter and Security Council Resolutions.

The lesson is clear: as persuasive as international law might be, litigants need to be especially careful to characterise their international law arguments in light of the particular provisions of our Constitution, and (as much as possible) as being consistent with government policy that has been approved by Parliament (where there is, for instance, a treaty binding at the international, even if not the national, plane).

2.5 CONCLUSION

Whatever the position might be in other states, in South African law it is beyond debate that international law offers a number of powerful techniques to bolster domestic law arguments. Arguments based on international human rights law have particular significance in PIL, with the UN universal human rights treaties and the African Charter frequently invoked, either by principal parties or as complementary arguments advanced by *amici curiae*. We have traversed five of the main techniques. In addition, we have sought to demonstrate that international law arguments may sometimes present their own form of justiciability problems, and simply relying on international legal principles may not be enough to persuade a court to adopt a particular international law rule. It may even be a basis for a judge to refuse to decide the case on the basis that the case raises a foreign relations issue that is beyond the remit of a domestic court.

That being said, the cases discussed in this chapter illustrate the exciting nature of litigation for the public interest lawyer raising international law issues in South African courts. They also illustrate the importance of the issues at stake—and the imperative of framing the cases correctly, alive to the potential and pitfalls of international law litigation before domestic courts.

---

[201] See *Kuwait Airways* (note 190 above) para 114.

Chapter 3

THE ETHICS AND POLITICS OF PUBLIC INTEREST LITIGATION

Jason Brickhill and Meghan Finn[1]

---

[1] In respect of Jason Brickhill, some of the ideas in this chapter were developed during the course of doctoral studies at the University of Oxford, under the supervision of Prof Kate O'Regan and Prof Sandra Fredman. I have also drawn from my experience working at the LRC from 2008 to 2016. We are very grateful for wonderfully helpful comments on drafts of this chapter received from Sanya Samtani, Tess Peacock and participants in Prof Sandra Fredman's research group at the University of Oxford. Michael Tsele provided useful research.

3.1 INTRODUCTION

In this chapter, we grapple with some of the ethical and political dimensions of public interest litigation (PIL). The ethical questions include issues of professional ethics—such as attorney-client relationships—and broader moral questions—such as what values or objectives should animate PIL. On the politics of PIL, we consider both the political, related to power and power structures in society, and the 'Political,' concerning the formal processes and institutions of government and the state. We identify the various approaches taken by public interest organisations in South Africa to these questions and tease out some of their implications for the clients, for the cause and for the legal system more generally.

PIL is notoriously difficult to define. In South Africa, PIL is best understood as the use of litigation as a means to pursue strategic objectives extending beyond the interests of individual litigants in a case. This departs from the Indian context where, for example, PIL is understood as a procedural mechanism, for the expansion of standing in the 'public interest.'[2] In South Africa, the procedural device of public interest standing is just one way in which the courts may be approached on matters involving constitutional rights. It is only one type of PIL, which is understood in South Africa to include certain substantive objectives. Although South African organisations define the content of those objectives differently, most associate PIL with human rights, constitutionalism,[3] and the pursuit of social justice.[4] We return to some of these high-level objectives below, when we discuss the normative commitments of public interest lawyers and organisations in South Africa.

Since PIL involves using law to pursue broad strategic objectives related to social justice and human rights, its value surely cannot lie simply in winning or pursuing cases in court.[5] The public interest work of many organisations in South Africa extends beyond 'litigation'; it encompasses legal research, advice and

---

[2] Anuj Bhuwania *Courting the People: Public Interest Litigation in Post-Emergency India* (2017) 2.

[3] In particular, the concept of transformative constitutionalism has resonance in the public interest sector and human rights literature in South Africa. Karl Klare's seminal article opened up a rich discourse on transformative constitutionalism: Karl Klare 'Legal culture and transformative constitutionalism' (1998) 14 *SAJHR* 146. See also Pius Langa 'Transformative constitutionalism' (2006) 17 *Stell LR* 351. Accepting that there is no single accepted definition of transformative constitutionalism, Justice Langa proposed that, at the very least, transformative constitutionalism includes economic transformation and a change in legal culture. For a recent contribution, see J Brickhill & Y van Leeve 'Transformative constitutionalism—Guiding light or empty slogan?' 2015 *Acta Juridica* 141 (special volume: A Price & M Bishop (eds) *A Transformative Justice: Essays in Honour of Pius Langa*).

[4] For an overview of the 'theories of change' of organisations in the public interest sector, see SPII in a paper commissioned by the 'Theories of change in social justice initiatives' (2012) *Raith Foundation* 3, last accessed on 6 July 2015 from <www.raith.org.za/resources.html> (SPII Raith Theories of Change).

[5] Roni Amit 'Winning isn't everything: Courts, context, and the barriers to effecting change through public interest litigation' (2011) 27 *SAJHR* 8.

advocacy work in respect of legislation and policy in the pursuit of various normative commitments. How should we determine the value of PIL and other strategies? Should we measure tangible and material rights impacts? Shifts in social structures? Richer opportunities for participatory democracy? In our view, all these types of impacts must be assessed together. We propose an analytical typology of impact that includes the legal, material, and political effects of PIL.[6] Legal effects include changes to law or policy. Material effects include providing social goods or services, paying compensation or damages, and compelling or prohibiting specific conduct. Political impacts concern effects on power relations, discourse, and shifts in the narrative or 'agenda' in relation to a particular set of issues. Analysing impact through this lens can reveal the full potential of PIL, as reflected in the chapters of this volume covering substantive areas of law. This also enables public interest organisations and lawyers to better appreciate and address the full ethical and political implications of their work.

As Abel powerfully captured in the title of his important work on PIL under apartheid, *Politics by other Means*,[7] public interest lawyering is a political activity as much as a legal one if one understands the political realm as one where people, ideas and institutions gain or lose power. This recognition is reflected in some of the other terms that have been used to describe this kind of work in South Africa, including 'struggle lawyering',[8] 'cause lawyering'[9] and 'movement lawyering'.[10]

If public interest lawyering is necessarily *political* and *Political*—in that it concerns power, and often affects formal political actors and processes—what implications does this have for the relationships between public interest organisations and government? More specifically, how can public interest organisations determine their own internal values and structure, balance their aims of securing concrete relief or precedent, and reconcile the interests of their client against the cause? These are some of the questions explored in the remainder of this chapter,

---

[6] For other proposed typologies of the type of impact of litigation, see: C Rodriguez-Garavito 'Beyond the courtroom: The impact of judicial activism on social and economic rights in Latin America' (2011) 89 *Tex L Rev* ('material' and 'symbolic' effects); J Dugard & M Langford 'Art or science? Synthesising lessons from public interest litigation and the dangers of legal determinism' (2011) 27 *SAJHR* 37 ('enabling' and 'material' impact); M Langford et al *Socio-Economic Rights in South Africa: Symbols or Substance?* (2014) 22–3 ('material', 'political' and 'symbolic/recognition' impacts).

[7] Richard L Abel *Politics by other Means: Law in the Struggle against Apartheid 1980–1994* (1995); G Bizos *No One to Blame: In Pursuit of Justice in South Africa* (1998).

[8] This term refers to those lawyers who took on cases resisting the apartheid regime, especially the political trials of activists.

[9] This term is less commonly used in South Africa but captures the idea of a lawyer or law firm that is itself committed to a substantive goal, such as advancing LGBTI rights.

[10] 'Movement lawyering' is exemplified by the legal campaign of the TAC, working with the LRC and AIDS Law Project; and, more recently, by the partnership between the social movement, Equal Education, and the public interest law clinic, Equal Education Law Centre. It refers to a form of lawyering that builds upon a campaign led by a social movement.

which concludes by considering the financial aspects of public interest practice such as funding, legal fees, and costs. We begin by considering how public interest organisations relate to government and other key social actors, including big business.

3.2 RELATIONSHIP TO GOVERNMENT AND OTHER SOCIAL ACTORS

Public interest lawyering does not take place in a vacuum. Politics and socio-economic context underpin it. Individuals, communities, and organisations engaged in PIL must necessarily interact with the government, and other powerful social actors. In this section, we examine the normative considerations that inform these relationships. We begin by discussing when public interest organisations should adopt a more adversarial or collaborative approach when dealing with the state. Thereafter, we consider a related enquiry, namely the political and social conditions that are significant for certain core PIL goals. We then turn to a brief examination of the relationships of public interest organisations to social movements and other societal actors, including big business.

(a) Public interest litigation and the state

The constitutional culture of any system will shape how public interest law is litigated.[11] A constitution that is based on participatory democracy and premised on the idea that the courts can—and should—exercise important powers of review is likely to foster active PIL. Conversely, a regime that only allows for limited judicial review, and concentrates power in the legislature and executive to determine the public interest, restricts the use of courts for public interest groups. Examining approaches to PIL across jurisdictions, David Feldman observes that the constitutional theory underpinning a jurisdiction influences (and is in turn influenced by) the forms of litigation open to public interest organisations.

The legal framework of a state, including both the substantive and procedural law, certainly plays a significant role in determining what social aims litigation can pursue.[12] Apartheid South Africa serves as a clear example of this. While PIL during that time was subversive and robust, it was largely confined to issues of criminal and administrative justice and freedom of movement and association. Litigation directly responded to the laws that propped up apartheid's oppressive and restrictive legal system. Civil society generally played a vital role during apartheid, often 'providing a state [substitute] to people whom the State refused to

---

[11] David Feldman 'Public interest litigation and constitutional theory in comparative perspective' (1992) 51 *The Modern Law Review* 44.

[12] Georgina Jephson and Osmond Mngomezulu discuss the procedural framework governing PIL in South Africa in ch 4 'Constitutional litigation procedure'.

provide for'[13] and vigorously opposed the state through litigious and other means.[14]

Things shifted in the early years of the constitutional era. The PIL sector saw an attrition of individuals who had been active in the apartheid era, but then left non-governmental organisations, often to work for government.[15] Public interest organisations, at least in the initial constitutional years, re-orientated themselves. Instead of viewing the government as a force to be opposed in all circumstances, many held the view that the democratic state would 'do the right thing' and needed to be given the space to do it rather than being antagonised.[16] Public interest organisations focused on bolstering governmental efforts, contributing to drafting legislation, developing policy, and assisting with implementing these new legal frameworks. The view that government is itself an agent for necessary social change and so should be strengthened rather than opposed was reinforced by those who had remained in the public interest sector seeing former colleagues in positions of governmental power.[17] Litigation against the state came to be viewed by some as not just a last-resort strategy, but even as unpatriotic; a betrayal of the new constitutional dispensation.[18]

Things shifted again, particularly in respect of securing socio-economic rights. Thabo Mbeki's AIDS denialism forced civil society's hand, and resort to the courts was necessary to vindicate the rights of HIV-positive pregnant women to access health care services to prevent mother-to-child transmission of HIV.[19] The orientation of public interest organisations—and of political parties—to the state (and its ruling party) veered even more dramatically in the Zuma era. Indeed, in the final

---

[13] SPII Raith Theories of Change (note 4 above) 3.

[14] *Rikhoto v East Rand Administration Board* 1983 (4) 278 SA (AD) [the LRC acted for the appellant], which challenged the pass laws, is one pivotal example. See ch 1 on the history of public interest litigation in South Africa.

[15] Steven Budlender, Gilbert Marcus SC & Nick Ferreira *Public Interest Litigation and Social Change in South Africa: Strategies, Tactics and Lessons* 2 ed (2014) 8 (Atlantic Report).

[16] Budlender et al (note 15 above) 8. See also Geoff Budlender 'People's power and the courts' (2011) *Bram Fisher Memorial Lecture*, last accessed on 20 February 2015 from <www.constitution-allyspeaing.co.za/geoff-budlender-bram-fisher-memorial-lecture/>.

[17] David Cote & Jacob van Garderen 'Challenges to public interest litigation in South Africa: External and internal challenges to determining the public interest' (2011) 27 *SAJHR* 167 at 169. For example, Geoff Budlender, one of the founders of the LRC, served as Director-General of Land Affairs from 1996 to 2000. Janet Love, the current National Director of the LRC, served as a member of Parliament for the African National Congress in the first democratic Parliament and worked at the South African Reserve Bank, she later served as a Commissioner of the Human Rights Commission and a Commissioner of the Independent Electoral Commission.

[18] Mark Heywood 'Preventing mother-to-child HIV transmission in South Africa: Background, strategies and outcomes of the Treatment Action Campaign case against the Minister of Health' (2003) 19 *SAJHR* 278 at 300.

[19] *Minister of Health and Others v Treatment Action Campaign and Others (No 2)* [2002] ZACC 15; 2002 (5) SA 721 [TAC as first respondent; Children's Rights Centre as third respondent; IDASA, CLC and Cotlands Baby Sanctuary were admitted as *amici curiae*] (*Treatment Action Campaign*).

years of the Zuma presidency, some of the most notable litigation was trenchantly politicised, and often brought by opposition political parties appealing to the courts to hold the line.[20] Political parties and civil society's turn to the courts has thrown into relief some central concerns regarding the role of the judiciary, and the extent to which litigation alone can secure lasting change.[21] In sum, the vicissitudes of Politics, politics and political players—and the public service culture that often follows—equally affect PIL.

We note that the relationship between PIL and the state is not limited to the highest echelons of state power. Whether to give government and its officials room to 'do the right thing' remains an important question. How should public interest organisations decide when to cooperate with the state, bolstering its efforts, and when instead to adopt an adversarial approach, holding the state to account for dereliction of its duties? A recent study, commissioned by the Raith Foundation and written by SERI, explores the complex dynamics that are at play when deciding how to engage the government.[22] Some stories are positive: ongoing relationships with governmental officials mean that information is shared, resources are allocated, and material impacts are felt. In these cases, litigation risks not only being a blunt tool but also a destructive one, at least if it damages existing constructive relationships. But of course this is not always so; public interest organisations report that some sympathetic officials, whose efforts are obstructed by political will, welcome litigation because it supports their efforts to implement progressive developments within government.[23] The state is not monolithic, and the relationship that the sector providing public interest legal services has with different components of the state—including the executive and legislative braches in the national, provincial, and local spheres of government—is crucial.[24]

Importantly, public interest organisations are not necessarily opposed to state action. There have been some significant instances in which public interest organisations have entered litigation in support of the state and against private interests. For example, when South Africa was sued in an investor–state arbitration following the implementation of the Mineral and Petroleum Resources Development Act 28 of 2002 (MPRDA) before the International Centre for the Settlement of Investment Disputes (ICSID), a coalition of NGOs that included the LRC and CALS applied to intervene in the proceedings as a non-disputing party in support

---

[20] See, eg, *Democratic Alliance v Speaker of the National Assembly* [2016] ZACC 8; 2016 (3) SA 487 (CC); *Economic Freedom Fighters v Speaker of the National Assembly* [2016] ZACC 11; 2016 (3) SA 580 (CC); *United Democratic Movement v Speaker of the National Assembly* [2017] ZACC 21; 2017 (5) SA 300 (CC).

[21] For while this litigation was often successful in the narrow sense, in that parties frequently were awarded the relief they sought, it did not and could not act as a stand-in for political will.

[22] SERI 'Public interest legal services in South Africa' (2015) 34–8, last accessed from <http://www.seri-sa.org/images/Seri_Pils_report_Final.pdf> on 4 June 2018 (Raith SERI Report).

[23] Ibid 91.

[24] For space considerations, we do not address litigation involving Chapter 9 institutions.

of the government.[25] The provisions of the MPRDA in issue are aimed at the equitable redistribution of the country's mineral resources. In addition, when a compensation claim was brought in the South African courts that also threatened the implementation of the MPRDA, CALS (represented by the LRC) intervened as *amicus curiae*, advancing arguments that again supported the state's position.[26] Finally, in the same period, CALS and the LRC participated in a process in which the Department of Trade and Industry was reviewing the state's policy on bilateral investment treaties in the light of the ICSID claim and other developments. Accordingly, this area of activity saw the sustained involvement of public interest organisations both in litigation and in policy formulation with the objective of supporting a government policy that was considered to promote constitutional rights.

Even when public interest organisations adopt positions that do not directly support the state, litigation can be a democratising force (even though, as we discuss later, if conducted in ways that do not engage with clients' realities, it can also be disempowering).[27] This is true not only regarding its democratising effects for the public, whose voices can be heard and interests vindicated, but also for the state itself, especially if it emboldens or impels officials better to fulfil their mandates and remain accountable to the people.

It is true that officials who fall short of their mandate are not always, or even predominantly, motivated by bad faith. Roach and Budlender note that government officials do not comply with constitutional standards largely due to inattentiveness, incompetence and intransigence.[28] Nevertheless, under the Zuma era, the state showed increased hostility to public interest organisations.[29] There has been heightened unwillingness in some parts of government to engage with, and even antagonism towards, public interest organisations. In mid-2015, this reached fever-pitch levels when SALC brought proceedings seeking the arrest of Omar Al-Bashir, the president of Sudan who is wanted by the International Criminal Court for charges of crimes against humanity (and was present in South Africa for a meeting of the African Union). Although SALC was successful in securing a high court order interdicting Al-Bashir from leaving the country,[30] the government

---

[25] *Piero Foresti, Laura de Carli and Others v The Republic of South Africa* ICSID case no ARB(AF)/07/01. For an account of the litigation and the civil society intervention in it, see J Brickhill & M du Plessis 'Two's company. Three's a crowd in investor–state arbitration (*Piero v South Africa*)' (2011) 27 *SAJHR* 152.

[26] *Agri South Africa v Minister for Minerals and Energy* [2013] ZACC 9; 2013 (4) SA 1 (CC) [CALS was admitted as *amicus curiae*, represented by the LRC].

[27] G Budlender (note 16 above).

[28] Kent Roach & Geoff Budlender 'Mandatory relief and supervisory jurisdiction: When is it appropriate, just and equitable?' (2005) 5 *SALJ* 325 at 345.

[29] Raith SERI Report (note 22 above) 35. See also S Budlender et al (note 15 above) 21–3.

[30] *Southern African Litigation Centre v Minister of Justice and Constitutional Development and Others* [2015] ZAGPPHC 402; 2015 (5) SA 1 (GP).

did not comply with the order. In the aftermath, SALC and other public interest organisations were castigated for having brought the litigation and accused of furthering foreign agendas. This formed part of a worrying trend where government was increasingly antagonistic towards civil society and used this charged rhetoric in an attempt to delegitimise their work in the eyes of the public.[31]

An even more alarming incident took place in March 2016, when the offices of the Helen Suzman Foundation were broken into and computers were removed. This came at a time when the organisation had instituted litigation challenging the appointment of Berning Ntlemeza to head the Hawks, the country's specialist corruption-fighting unit, fuelling speculation that the break-in was related to the litigation.[32]

A possible shift in attitude towards the PIL sector and human rights lawyers has also been perceived in relation to judicial appointments. In the initial period after 1994, a career as a public interest lawyer was favourably considered by the Judicial Service Commission and a large number of judges were appointed from the ranks of the PIL sector, including Chief Justice Arthur Chaskalson. Following recent decisions of the JSC not to appoint certain career human rights lawyers to the bench or to elevate them to the appeal courts, commentators criticised the JSC and questioned its stance towards such candidates.[33] Some indications of this stance emerged during the interview of Mahendra Chetty, an experienced attorney and regional director at the LRC. During his JSC interview, Deputy Minister and JSC member, Fatima Chohan, told Chetty that she had 'slight discomfort' with would-be judges that had an activist background as human rights lawyers.'"[34] Chohan added that '[Chetty's] track record in representing the country's poor and marginalised "worried" her because it meant his subjectivity could be swayed in

---

[31] There were several earlier incidents in different contexts. We provide just two examples. In 2012, Edna Molewa, Minister for Water Affairs, saying that the LRC and LHR were 'waging a war against the state' after they launched litigation, discussed in ch 8, to secure safe drinking water for residents of Carolina in Mpumalanga. See S Blaine 'Water law suit is war against the state' *Business Day* 8 August 2012, available at <http://www.bdlive.co.za/articles/2012/07/11/water-lawsuit-is-war-against-the-state>. In 2013, in response to the campaign (including PIL) to secure norms and standards for school infrastructure, Minister for Basic Education, Angie Motshekga, claimed that EE was 'a group of white adults organising black children with half-truths' and branded EE 'opportunistic, patronizing and simply dishonest'. See V John 'Basic Education lashes out at Equal Education's White adults' Mail & Guardian 19 June 2013, available at <http://mg.co.za/article/2013-06-19-basic-education-lashes-out-at-equal-educations-white-adults>.

[32] See 'Helen Suzman Foundation says break-in not "ordinary"' *Mail & Guardian online* 21 March 2016, last accessed on 16 July 2016 from <www.mg.co.za>.

[33] Prominent examples include Geoff Budlender, one of the LRC's founders, who was overlooked for appointment four times by the JSC, and Clive Plasket, another former LRC lawyer, who was not elevated to the SCA.

[34] F Rabkin 'Few magistrates make the grade' *Business Day* 10 April 2014, last accessed on 1 June 2018 at <http://www.bdlive.co.za/national/law/2014/04/10/few-magistrates-make-the-grade-with-jsc>.

that direction'.[35] Chohan said while she had respect for lawyers whose career was focused on fighting cases on behalf of the indigent, she wanted reassurance that he would deal impartially in cases where indigent people took on the state.[36] Chohan went to on to say she found it 'a bit disturbing' that some candidates sought appointment 'while espousing very fervent human rights activist tendencies'.[37] The views revealed by Chohan may not be shared by other JSC members, and certainly do not reflect the constitutional criteria for judicial appointment, but they are nonetheless worrying.

In the context of the complex and shifting relations among PIL organisations, the courts and government officials, lawyers and activists need to carefully consider how best to relate to other actors. Whether a collaborative or adversarial stance towards government is best suited to the circumstances is not limited to deciding to initiate litigation or not. It can also affect what relief is sought, and how it is enforced.

An important trend is the use of structural interdicts by courts, requiring parties to take mandatory steps to meet their obligations, and relying on courts' supervisory jurisdiction to monitor compliance with their orders.[38] Most vivid in recent times has been the extensive structural interdict imposed by the Constitutional Court on SASSA, in an attempt to ensure the effective and timeous administration of social grants payments and, strikingly, the court's resumption of its supervisory jurisdiction when SASSA yet again failed to meet its constitutional mandate.[39] This, too, is an indication of 'the times': the courts in the Mandela and Mbeki eras were far more reticent to impose such interdicts on government, trusting the state to comply with its orders.

Relatedly, the Constitutional Court has come to rely more upon ordering that parties meaningfully engage with one another to find solutions to the dispute.[40] In

---

[35] N Tolsi 'JSC eases separation anxieties' *Mail and Guardian* 31 October 2014 & last accessed on 1 June 2018, at <http://mg.co.za/article/2014-10-31-00-jsc-eases-separation-anxieties>.

[36] F Rabkin 'Few magistrates make the grade with JSC' *Business Day* 10 April 2014 (last accessed on 12 July 2018 at <http://www.bdlive.co.za/national/law/2014/04/10/few-magistrates-makethe-grade-with-jsc).

[37] Ibid.

[38] Christopher Mbazira *Litigating Socio-Economic Rights in South Africa: A Choice between Corrective and Distributive Justice* (2009) 173; *Nyathi v Member of the Executive Council for the Department of Health Gauteng and Another* [2008] ZACC 8; 2008 (5) SA 94 (CC) [Centre for Constitutional Rights was admitted as *amicus curiae*] is one Constitutional Court example. And this is not limited to the Constitutional Court; if anything, high courts have been leading this trend, as Mbazira argues.

[39] *Black Sash Trust v Minister of Social Development and Others (Freedom under Law NPC Intervening)* [2017] ZACC 8; 2017 (3) SA 335 (CC) [Corruption Watch and SAPO were admitted as *amici curiae*].

[40] See, in particular, *Occupiers of 51 Olivia Road, Berea Township and 197 Main Street Johannesburg v City of Johannesburg and Other* [2008] ZACC 1; 2008 (3) SA 208 (CC) (*51 Olivia Road*) and, more recently, *Head of Department, Department of Education, Free State Province v Welkom High*

51 Olivia Road, the court noted that '[e]ngagement has the potential to contribute towards the resolution of disputes and to increased understanding and sympathetic care if both sides are willing to participate in the process'.[41] The concept of meaningful engagement can strengthen the South African model of separation of powers, because the judiciary exerts its authority to determine the constitutionality of law and conduct, while carving out a space for the executive or legislature to perform their own functions.[42] As Van Leeve argues in the context of recent education rights litigation, '[p]ut into action, meaningful engagement may be the most appropriate remedy to deal with systemic challenges'.[43] However, the effectiveness of meaningful engagement orders may depend on whether there is trust among the parties, or strictures on the negotiating process.[44] For this reason, judicial orders directing meaningful engagement and consultation are sometimes criticised for prioritising procedure over substance.[45] At the very least, the increasing frequency of structural orders has important ramifications for the public interest organisations that often litigate the cases subject to these orders. Even after an order has been won through the litigation process, these organisations might be required to engage directly with governmental officials in shaping how that order is fulfilled. Especially for repeat players in the field, this may change the contours of their relationships with officials. It can begin to build trust and a healthy rapport or, if the engagement sours, it can entrench antagonistic attitudes.

Organisations also need to weigh up the advantages of an oppositional approach over a cooperative one when deciding whether to bring contempt of court proceedings when officials fail to comply with court orders. In theory, contempt of court proceedings, which can attract fines or imprisonment, deter officials from flouting court orders. In practice, showing that the failure was wilful or in bad faith, which is required to prove contempt of court, is difficult and risks ratcheting up tensions. SECTION27's litigation on the delivery of textbooks to schools in Limpopo is just one example of this. After securing a court order directing the Department of Education to deliver textbooks, the organisation had to decide whether to litigate again to ensure compliance with the order when the Department failed to fulfil its terms, or instead to adopt a less aggressive approach and

---

School and Another; Head of Department, Department of Education, Free State Province v Harmony High School and Another [2013] ZACC 25; 2014 (2) SA 228 (CC) [EE and CCL were admitted as *amici curiae*].

[41] *51 Olivia Road* (note 40 above) para 15.

[42] A Pillay 'Toward effective social and economic rights adjudication: The role of meaningful engagement' (2012) 10 *Int'l J Const L* 732.

[43] Yana van Leeve 'Executive heavy handedness and the right to basic education: A reply to Sandra Fredman' (2015) 6 *CCR* 199 at 215.

[44] Stu Woolman *The Selfless Constitution* (2013) 331.

[45] Sandra Fredman 'Procedure or principle: The role of adjudication in achieving the right to education' (2015) 6 *CCR* 165.

negotiate with the Department.[46] Even though the organisation initially opted to re-enter negotiations, it later found it necessary to bring follow-up proceedings to address continued violations of rights. In another example, the LRC attached motor vehicles used by the Minister of Basic Education and her Director General following their failure to comply with an order requiring the state to pay approximately R28 million in unpaid salaries to teachers in the Eastern Cape.[47] The attachment of the motor vehicles resulted in the prompt payment of the unpaid teacher salaries. Although a measure of last resort, the attachment was an effective method of securing compliance in that particular case.

A final significant development is the burgeoning role of commissions of inquiry, including the Marikana Commission of Inquiry, the provincial commission into policing in Khayelitsha and the commission of inquiry into the funding of higher education. In these contexts, public interest organisations assume a very different role; in theory, the state and public interest organisations are on the same side, in pursuit of 'the truth'. While commissions have vindicated some important ends—not least, the promotion of transparency and accountability—some have also been subject to criticism for being too easily manipulable—partly, to depoliticise tense situations by engaging in long, drawn-out processes—or exorbitant.[48]

There are no hard and fast rules for when collaboration, rather than opposition, is likely to be appropriate or effective. This will depend on contextual factors such as the nature of the issue, the legal framework, the relevant stakeholders and their relationships, the history of contestation or collaboration and the objects sought to be achieved. Respondents in the Raith study rightly note that 'there should be a willingness to try to engage with the government where possible and a willingness to confront where necessary'.[49]

(b)   Other social actors

Public interest law organisations interact with powerful social actors other than government, including political parties, trade unions, religious bodies, media bodies, and corporations. In this section, we outline three main sites of interaction: first, when PIL is embedded within a social movement or community-based organisation, and so the collaboration between those litigating and the clients is

---

[46] Faranaaz Veriava, in a study commissioned by SECTION27 *The 2012 Limpopo Textbook Crisis* (2013); Budlender et al (note 15 above) 85–6.

[47] See Setumo Stone & Karl Gernetzky 'Motshekga's car seized over teachers' pay' *BDlive* 1 October 2014, last accessed on 16 July 2016 from <www.bdlive.co.za>. The attachment followed the successful class action litigation by the LRC in *Linkside and Others v Minister of Basic Education and Others* [2015] ZAECGHC 36.

[48] For a comprehensive discussion, see Michael Bishop 'An accidental good: The role of commissions of inquiry in South African Democracy' 2014 *NYLS Law Review*, last accessed on 4 June 2018 from <http://www.nylslawreview.com/wp-content/uploads/sites/16/2014/11/Bishop.pdf>.

[49] Raith SERI Report (note 22 above).

close; second, when public interest law organisations work alongside other social actors whose mandates may be slightly different, but who have a common interest in litigation or a particular aspect of law; and third, when PIL targets a social actor other than the state, and so the interaction between the two is adversarial. The contestation between public interest organisations and the business sector, in particular 'big business', is especially significant and charged.

PIL is just one way to agitate for meaningful social change, and 'cannot be a substitute for the organisation of the power, development of community self-reliance and establishment of effective organizational structures'.[50] Bratton Blom notes that lawyering for social movements is distinguished, in part, by lawyers' connections to a network of people committed to a specific cause, including the possibility to collaborate with those who have accumulated expertise on particular issues.[51] PIL often—though not always[52]—occurs in the context of broader community organising. Thus, sensitivity to the ways in which litigation should be supportive, rather than disruptive, of the broader social movement is important; 'the lawyer is not the protagonist'.[53] The Atlantic Report points out that PIL that is primarily lawyer-driven risks being dislocated from clients' realities.[54] As we argue below, communities and clients, rather than lawyers, should determine the ultimate objectives that litigation seeks to secure.

There are several important South African examples of collaboration between public interest law organisations, social movements, and other social actors. The model of movement lawyering is exemplified by Equal Education Law Centre, which operates as a public interest law clinic in partnership with the social movement, Equal Education. For most other organisations, these relationships arise in specific cases. The most well-known example is probably the campaign of the Treatment Action Campaign (TAC) for the supply of anti-retroviral drugs, which included litigation culminating in the landmark *TAC* decision.[55] Nevertheless, there are many other examples across different areas and with various models of relationship between lawyers, communities, social movements and other sections of civil society. In litigating for the recognition of Muslim marriages and their legal consequences, for example, the Women's Legal Trust has laboured

---

[50] PN Bhawati, quoted in J Cooper 'Public interest law revisited' (1999) 25 *Commonwealth Law Bulletin* 140.

[51] B Bratton Blom 'Cause lawyering and social movements: Can solo and small firm practitioners anchor social movements?' (2006) 39 *Studies in Law, Politics and Society* 119 at 130.

[52] *National Coalition for Gay and Lesbian Equality and Another v Minister of Justice and Others* [1998] ZACC 15; 1999 (1) SA 6 (CC) [CALS was admitted as *amicus curiae*] is cited by Budlender et al (note 15 above) 34 as an example.

[53] J Gordon 'Concluding essay: The lawyer is not the protagonist: Community campaigns, law, and social change' (2007) 95 *Cal L Rev* 2142.

[54] Budlender et al (note 15 above) 114.

[55] Heywood (note 18 above).

alongside religious organisations, only some of which have supported its stance.[56] In other instances, public interest law organisations will act as *amicus curiae*, offering information and expertise to the courts even though the main action was not brought by the organisations themselves.[57] Litigation is not the only tool in this context. The Marikana Commission of Inquiry into the police killing of 34 striking mineworkers in August 2012 is one example where many public law organisations were parties to the enquiry, as were trade unions (SERI served as AMCU's attorneys, for example).

Finally, the Constitution imposes duties on both the state and private actors.[58] While historically, the bulk of public interest legal work concentrates on the state's duties, private and corporate actors wield extensive power, and are often the targets of PIL. Litigation brought by civil society organisations and consumers against bread producers for price fixing is one clear example. Earthlife Africa has also successfully taken on big business in litigation on climate change.[59] Further, business interests rightly yielded to social justice imperatives in litigation that put an end to the staggering abuse of emolument attachment orders.[60] The unprecedented silicosis litigation, undertaken as an enormous class action on behalf of mineworkers against dozens of mining companies, is another vital example.[61]

This litigation illustrates the moral and legal necessity of challenging untrammelled corporate power through PIL. This is not least because of the devastating role that businesses have played in perpetuating socio-economic inequality, and

---

[56] *Women's Legal Centre Trust v President of the Republic of South Africa and Others* [2009] ZACC 20; 2009 (6) SA 94 (CC) [United Ulama Council of South Africa, Women's Cultural Group, Association of Muslim Lawyers and Accountants, Islamic Unity Convention and Coalition of Muslim Women were admitted as *amici curiae*]; Hoodah Abrahams-Fayker 'South African engagement with Muslim personal law: The Women's Legal Centre, Cape Town and women in Muslim marriages' (2011) 15 *Feminist Africa* 39.

[57] See, eg, the Centre for Child Law's *amicus* interventions in *KwaZulu-Natal Joint Liaison Committee v Member of the Executive Council Department of Education, KwaZulu-Natal and Others* [2013] ZACC 10; 2013 (4) SA 262 (CC) [CCL was admitted as *amicus curiae*].

[58] Section 8(2) of the Constitution; N Friedman 'The South Africa common law and the Constitution: Revisiting horizontality' (2014) 30 *SAJHR* 63 and DM Chirwa 'In search of philosophical justifications and suitable models for the horizontal application of human rights' (2008) 8 *AHRLJ* 294.

[59] *Earthlife Africa Johannesburg v Minister of Environmental Affairs and Others* [2017] ZAGPPHC 58; [2017] 2 All SA 519 (GP).

[60] *University of Stellenbosch Legal Aid Clinic and Others v Minister of Justice and Correctional Services and Others; Association of Debt Recovery Agents NPC v University of Stellenbosch Legal Aid Clinic and Others; Mavava Trading 279 (Pty) Ltd and Others v University of Stellenbosch Legal Aid Clinic and Others* [2016] ZACC 32; 2016 (6) SA 596 (CC) [The South African Human Rights Commission was admitted as *amicus curiae*, represented by the LRC].

[61] *Nkala and Others v Harmony Gold Mining Company Ltd and Others* [2016] ZAGPJHC 97; 2016 (5) SA 240 (GJ); 2016 (5) SA 240 (GJ) [LRC acted for the class representatives, along with Richard Spoor Inc and Abrahams Kievitz Inc and SECTION27 acted for the *amici curiae* TAC and Sonke] (*Nkala*).

complicity in political corruption. Pro-bono departments of private law firms that litigate in the public interest may find their public interest work directly limited by corporate or business interests, as there might be a conflict of interests[62] between the potential pro bono clients, and the big business target of that litigation, such as a bank or a mining company, which might be a client of the firm.[63]

Additionally, there is important work to be done to prompt the state to better regulate the private sector. In these instances, the state is the direct subject of legal efforts; after all, its obligations to protect rights encompass the duty to ensure that private entities do not infringe others' rights.[64]

3.3 THE POLITICS OF THE PUBLIC INTEREST SECTOR ITSELF

In the previous section, we discussed the relationship between organisations and the state, and organisations and other social actors. However, the politics of PIL is not confined to organisations' interactions with other entities. Indeed, the sector itself confronts urgent moral and political questions. In this section, we discuss the politics of the public interest sector itself, including how organisations operate in relation to political issues, the imperative to transform the sector itself, and the normative commitments of public interest organisations, given that the public interest sector sees itself as a broad church that encompasses a diversity of ideological positions.

(a) The different structures and approaches of organisations

The introduction to this volume describes the evolution of the public interest sector in South Africa, including the substantive focus areas of these public interest organisations. In this chapter, we confine ourselves to observing some differences in the way the organisations structure themselves and the approach that they take to the politics of public interest lawyering.

Different organisations take divergent approaches on their political/Political role in two important areas. The first concerns the extent to which organisations act in their own name, rather than in a representative capacity on behalf of clients, and conduct campaign activities outside litigation. The second is the extent to which organisations act in cases and on issues that are close to the formal Political processes. In respect of both issues, the differences are matters of degree.

In respect of the first issue, at one end of the spectrum are public interest organisations that seldom litigate in their own name and confine themselves predominantly to litigating on behalf of clients. These organisations may conduct

---

[62] A commercial, if not necessarily ethical, conflict.

[63] Raith SERI Report (note 22 above) 120.

[64] Danie Brand 'Introduction to socio-economic rights in the South African Constitution' in Danie Brand & Christof H Heyns (eds) *Socio-economic Rights in South Africa* (2005) 10.

amici curiae interventions, but they generally do so on behalf of other organisations or communities, and not in their own name. The LRC is an example of such an organisation. Only rarely has the LRC intervened in litigation in its own name, and usually these instances have come at the request of the court or in cases that implicate the legal profession. By contrast, other organisations such as LHR, SALC, CALS, CCL and SECTION27 more frequently act as primary litigants or at least as *amici curiae* in their own name and not only on behalf of clients. Underlying this divergence are different attitudes regarding the extent to which the organisation should actively pursue particular causes or objectives—given the legal or political space they purport to occupy—as opposed to providing legal services to poor people and vulnerable communities to enable them to do so. There is a related variance relating to use of the media and social media. While some organisations have very active media and social media presences, issuing statements in their own names that take strong positions on contentious issues, other organisations have a more constrained approach, limiting media statements to more descriptive accounts of the outcomes of judgments or other significant events. However, in general and in line with global trends, the organisations in the sector have built up their communications functions over the last decade and are all more active in this space. This has proved necessary to counter some of the antagonistic rhetoric levelled at the sector by the state and has provided an additional tool to help shape a political narrative that is more conducive to, or supportive of, the outcomes sought by these organisations. It is still possible to discern differences in approach to the use of 'voice' by public interest organisations, which tends to track the extent to which these organisations are willing to litigate in their own name.

The first issue of modes of activity is related to the second, which concerns the extent to which organisations act on issues and in cases that relate closely to the formal Political process. This includes issues relating to political succession, contestation among political parties and attempts to remove incumbents from office through litigation. Again, the differences in approach are merely a matter of degree. In general, the public interest sector is engaged and concerned with these questions whenever they threaten constitutional rights or the rule of law. Some organisations take a more restrained approach, leaving it to other civil society organisations to take the lead on more overtly political questions. One indication of the differences in approach is the recent example of the Save South Africa campaign.[65] The campaign was launched in late 2016 to confront the allegations of corruption and state capture relating to former President Zuma and the Gupta family. The campaign called for the removal and prosecution of Zuma and those implicated. Undoubtedly, the campaign confronted one of the largest crises to hit South Africa since 1994, but it also went to the heart of the political contestation

---

[65] See generally the Save South Africa website, last accessed from <savesouthafrica.org> on 4 June 2018 .

within the ruling party and country as a whole. The campaign itself faced some criticism regarding the concerns it articulated and the interests it represented, particularly that the protest sought to protect elite—and predominantly white—economic interests.[66] SECTION27, and its Executive Director Mark Heywood in particular, played a leading role in building the Save South Africa campaign. Subsequently, another campaign with similar concerns was formed under the name #UniteBehind.[67] Its campaigns include 'state capture', fixing the public rail system, 'safety, policing and justice' and 'land, housing and the environment'. As with #SaveSA, these are all substantive areas that resonate strongly with the focus areas and objectives of most, if not all, the public interest organisations in South Africa. However, while some organisations have joined #UniteBehind as formal affiliates,[68] others have not participated in this way in their own names even if they have acted in litigation relevant to the campaign. In our view, these differences in approach reflect variance in tactics and strategy rather than values or vision.

(b) Transformation of the legal profession and public interest sector

The legal profession and the public interest sector, as with every sector of the South African economy, face an urgent need for transformation, so that they are more representative of the South African population. The consequences of vastly unequal provision for education for black students, and barriers to entry into the legal profession as well as networks of privilege and influence within the profession meant that at the advent of democracy, white men dominated the legal profession. Transformation of the legal profession still has a staggeringly long way to go.[69] Intersectional disadvantage is particularly in need of redress, with the persistence of numerous barriers impeding the progression of black women in the legal profession. The position of people with disabilities has also received scant attention.

The early public interest organisations were established specifically to resist the injustices and discriminatory laws of apartheid. The LRC, LHR and CALS, all of

---

[66] See, eg, Rufaro Samango 'Why I couldn't march in today's anti-Zuma protest' *OkayAfrica* 7 April 2017, last accessed on 4 June 2018 from <http://www.okayafrica.com/couldnt-march-todays-anti-zuma-protest/>. Some of this criticism must be understood against the backdrop of a deliberate public relations campaign by Bell Pottinger to stir racial tensions—Andrew Cave 'Deal that undid Bell Pottinger: Inside story of the South Africa scandal' *The Guardian* 5 September 2017, last accessed on 4 June 2018 from <https://www.theguardian.com/media/2017/sep/05/bell-pottingersouth-africa-pr-firm>.

[67] See the website of the #UniteBehind campaign, last accessed from <www.unitebehind.org> on 12 April 2018.

[68] According to the campaign website, CER, EE, Ndifuna Ukwazi, SECTION27 and the WLC are all affiliates.

[69] CALS 'Transformation of the legal profession' last accessed from <https://www.wits.ac.za/media/wits-university/faculties-and-schools/commerce-law-and-management/research-entities/cals/documents/programmes/gender/Transformation%20of%20the%20Legal%20Profession.pdf> on 4 June 2018.

which were established between 1979 and 1980, employed black lawyers, while many white commercial law firms refused to do. However, the barriers to transformation also affected them, and the public interest sector in a democratic South Africa today has been criticised for transforming too slowly. Madlingozi, in a broad critique of the social justice sector, observed that the executive directors of all the leading public interest law firms in South Africa are white and that a disproportionate number of their cases are argued by a group of five white male senior counsel.[70] While the staff of these organisations were predominantly black, the most public voices and leadership of the organisations were overwhelmingly white.[71]

Frustration within public interest organisations with the slow rate of transformation, prompted a group of approximately 45 young black professionals to form the Black Workers' Forum (BWF) in 2016.[72] The BWF has since engaged with the organisations in the sector to press for transformation on a range of issues, including leadership, briefing of counsel and the development of black staff.[73]

At the time that Madlingozi wrote, the heads of almost all public interest organisations in South Africa were white. However, that is slowly shifting. The public interest sector is transforming and becoming more representative of the South African population. Since 2016, the executive directors of the leading public interest organisations have either all stepped down or their organisations have commenced the process of replacing them.[74] Black lawyers have also taken up leadership positions at new public interest law firms.[75]

In respect of the briefing of counsel, there has also been some direly needed progress. Skewed briefing patterns, which favour white and male advocates, have long bedevilled the legal fraternity. Matters came to a head in 2015 in the silicosis class action[76] where, of the approximately 40 advocates involved, only two were black.[77]

---

[70] Tshepo Madlingozi 'Social justice in a time of neo-apartheid constitutionalism: Critiquing the anti-black economy of recognition, incorporation and distribution' (2017) 28 *Stell LR* 123 at 143.

[71] Raith SERI Report (note 22 above)126–9.

[72] Madlingozi (note 70 above) fn 95.

[73] Palesa Madi 'Birth of the Black Workers Forum' *Bertha Foundation* 21 July 2017, last accessed on 4 June 2018 from <http://berthafoundation.org/birth-black-workers-forum/>.

[74] The Director of Lawyers for Human Rights, Jacob van Garderen, stepped down in 2017. The Director of CALS, Bonita Meyersfeld, and the LRC's National Director, Janet Love, stepped down in 2018 and has been succeeded by Nersan Govender. We understand that the Directors of SECTION27 and the CCL are also due to step down soon.

[75] The EELC was initially headed by Dmitri Holtzman and later by Nurina Ally. Ndifuna Ukwazi is led by Mandisa Shandu. SALC is headed by Kaajal Ramjathan-Keogh.

[76] *Nkala* (note 61 above).

[77] Nine counsel acted for the mineworkers' class representatives, all white. (Jason Brickhill was one of the counsel for the class representatives, as in-house counsel for the LRC.) Three counsel appeared for the *amici curiae*, of whom only one was black. The remaining 26 counsel appeared for different mining companies. All but one were white according to the appearances recorded in the reported judgment.

When confronted on this, one of the attorneys[78] involved in running the litigation initially commented that only exceptional counsel with an avowed commitment to public interest law would be briefed, and that the 'number of black counsel who meet both these criteria is really small'.[79] This prompted a powerful and unprecedented protest from a group of black advocates,[80] and ultimately galvanised the Johannesburg Society of Advocates to put in place the 'three-counsel rule' that mandates that in a team of three or more advocates, at least one advocate must be black.[81] The three-counsel rule is very welcome but should only be the beginning, not least because the advocates' profession remains hostile to women on a number of fronts. Addressing intersectional disadvantage—in particular, the interests of black women—must be prioritised.

Some public interest organisations, such as the LRC and SECTION27, have throughout their time appointed black advocates to positions as in-house counsel, but these positions are few and even these organisations rely heavily on briefing externally. In relation to the briefing of external counsel among advocates at the Bar, some progress has also been made. The five white male senior counsel referred to by Madlingozi, no longer enjoy a monopoly over briefs, with prominent black counsel emerging as leaders in the profession and counsel of choice for public interest firms. Some public interest law firms have adopted briefing policies to ensure that they brief black and female advocates.[82] Initiatives such as the LRC's Arthur Chaskalson Pupillage Fellowship now provide financial support to enable several black candidates to undertake pupillage, working with LRC in-house counsel as their pupil-mentors.[83]

---

[78] The silicosis class action litigation was run for the mineworkers by the LRC, Richard Spoor Inc and Abrahams Kievitz Inc, the latter two being private firms of attorneys acting on contingency. The statement was made by Richard Spoor. The LRC immediately issued a statement distancing itself from Spoor's comments and apologised.

[79] Sabelo Skiti & Sibongakonke Shoba 'Lawyer's charity jibe sparks race standoff' *Sunday Times* 18 October 2015, last accessed on 4 June 2018 from <https://www.pressreader.com/south-africa/sunday-times/20151018/281496455127869>. See also Dewald van Rensburg 'Inside the big silicosis war' *News24* 18 October 2015, last accessed on 4 June 2018 from <https://city-press.news24.com/Business/Inside-the-big-silicosis-war-20151018>. These comments were subsequently retracted.

[80] See 'Black advocates tell court they object to "racist sting"' *Ground Up* 23 October 2015, last accessed on 4 June 2018 from <https://www.groundup.org.za/article/black-advocates-object-racist-sting-court_3430/>.

[81] Kameel Premhid 'Transformation of the legal profession: Briefing patterns in the spotlight (Quotas)' *Helen Suzman Foundation* undated, last accessed on 4 June 2018 from <https://hsf.org.za/publications/hsf-briefs/transformation-of-the-legal-profession-briefing-patterns-in-the-spotlight-quotas>.

[82] Raith SERI Report (note 22 above) 126–9. As one example, the LRC adopted a briefing policy in terms of which, in any case in which more than one counsel is briefed, the counsel team must include at least one black advocate. The policy also sets numerical targets to brief black counsel in the majority of cases by number and monetary value.

[83] See the LRC website, last accessed from <www.lrc.org.za/lrcarchive/lrc-vacancies> on 12 April 2018.

After lagging behind on matters of transformation, especially in relation to race and gender—and crucially their intersection—it appears that the public interest sector is beginning to make some progress. It is imperative for the viability and credibility of the sector that public interest organisations should live their values and be seen to represent the breadth of South African society. This must also involve some difficult but vitally necessary processes, particularly in scrubbing out discrimination based on gender and sex, especially as it manifests in sexual harassment in the workplace. At the time of publication, the PIL sector in South Africa was shaken by serious, allegations of sexual harassment in significant organisations.[84] The sector urgently needs to change, both so that this conduct (and the conditions that enable it) are quashed but also so that the mechanisms of accountability are accessible, and are sensitive to the immense difficulties inherent in reporting conduct. A number of black female lawyers in the sector wrote publicly to

> call on our sector to interrogate the 'beyond reproach' disposition and to disabuse themselves of the notion that our sector is somehow immune to sexual harassment, racism and other abuses of power. . . [I]t is the hypocrisy of this sector that makes the covering up of sexual harassment cases even more appalling. Not to excuse toxic and corrupt behaviour elsewhere, but ours is a sector that will use loudspeakers to call out the toxicity of others with no consciousness to confront demons from within. It is a sector full of people who do social justice work for fulfilment, power or even public affirmation and want to be thanked with our bodies and at the expense of our skins. It is actually reprehensible that the social justice sector has very little culture of accountability for the ills within the sector.[85]

Organisations must embody a commitment to social justice that is not only outwards-looking, but introspective too. This means holding accountable those who wield power—both politically outside the sector but also within the sector. While the public interest sector employs only a small proportion of the legal profession, it has the potential and the obligation to set an example and lead the legal profession on transformation.

(c) Normative commitments

Is PIL in South Africa dependent on a commitment to a particular political philosophy? Those who litigate in the public interest may be animated by a diverse set of normative motivations. Historically, PIL in South Africa emerged through the freedom struggle and, with the apartheid regime as its adversary, strong normative agreement on certain foundational principles was established.[86] PIL

---

[84] To date, the media has reported on investigations into certain leaders of Equal Education and a senior attorney formerly employed by the LRC.

[85] Basetsana Koitsioe et al 'Wolves in sheep's clothing: Sexual harassment in the public interest sector' last accessed from <//www.dailymaverick.co.za/article/2018-05-28-wolves-in-sheeps-clothing-sexual-harassment-in-the-public-interest-sector/#.WyE2AUiWQ2w> (on 13 June 2018).

[86] See generally Abel (note 7 above).

organisations, and individual lawyers, spanned the political spectrum, embracing diverse belief systems and faiths.

The sector today is not uniformly progressive, although socially progressive movements have generally been at the forefront of the most significant PIL in South Africa. The Atlantic Report observes that, increasingly, conservative public interest law movements in South Africa (such as Afriforum, which typically represents white minority interests) enlist litigation to further their ideological aims.[87] This effect has also been noted across jurisdictions: '[o]ther constitutional democracies that have experienced thriving phases of progressive public interest litigation have found that a backlash or conservative resistance often follows'.[88] In the United States, for example, the wave of PIL brought by left-wing movements in the 1960s was followed by a surge of litigation, also ostensibly in the public interest, initiated by conservative forces.[89] Conservative law firms recruited the litigation strategies shaped by progressive litigants to advance their own normative agendas.[90] And while some left-wing American scholars have expressed circumspection about the ability of legal victories alone to effect social change, conservative groups have drawn on impact litigation as a key strategy.[91] Similarly, in India, PIL models that have been lauded for expanding access to justice today frequently raise middle-class interests and in some instances have 'become positively anti-poor'.[92] Key recent South African cases brought by conservative organisations include litigation by the trade union Solidarity, opposing the implementation of affirmative action measures in the public sector,[93] and the Justice

---

[87] Budlender et al (note 15 above) 13–21. The report cites, as key cases instantiating this trend, *Afri-Forum and Another v Malema and Others* [2011] ZAEQC 2; 2011 (6) SA 240 (EqC) [Vereniging van Regslui in Afrikaans was admitted as *amicus curiae*]; *Agri South Africa v Minister of Minerals and Energy* [2011] ZAGPPHC 62; 2012 (1) SA 171 (GNP) [CALS was admitted as *amicus curiae*]; *Print Media South Africa and Another v Minister of Home Affairs and Another* [2012] ZACC 22; 2012 (6) SA 443 (CC) [JASA and Section 16 were admitted as *amici curiae*] and *Teddy Bear Clinic for Abused Children and Another v Minister of Justice and Constitutional Development and Another* [2013] ZACC 35; 2014 (2) SA 168 (CC) [CCL acted for the applicants; Justice Alliance of South Africa, Women's Legal Centre Trust and Tshwaranang Legal Advocacy Centre were admitted as *amici curiae*] (*Teddy Bear Clinic*).

[88] Budlender et al (note 15 above) 14.

[89] Brian Z Tamanaha *Law as a Means to an End: Threat to the Rule of Law* (2006) 158–62.

[90] SL Cummings 'The future of public interest law' (2011) 33 *UALR Law Review* 355 at 369.

[91] Ibid 370. This difference, however, may be accounted for partially by the fact that the United States courts themselves are fairly conservative, and that much right-wing litigation seeks to preserve the status quo, which obviously does not require on-the-ground changes after litigious success—Gerald Rosenberg 'Courting disaster: Looking for change in all the wrong places' (2005) 54 *Drake L* 796.

[92] James Fowkes 'How to open the doors of the court—Lessons on access to justice from Indian PIL' (2011) 27 *SAJHR* 434 at 454; Bhuwania (note 2 above).

[93] *South African Police Service v Solidarity obo Barnard* [2014] ZACC 23; 2014 (6) SA 123 (CC) [Police and Civil Rights Union was admitted as *amicus curiae*].

Alliance of South Africa, arguing that the criminalisation of consensual sexual behaviour between children was constitutionally justified.[94]

In this section, we argue first, that transformative constitutionalism provides a basic open normative framework that various public interest organisations and lawyers can agree on.[95] This is notwithstanding the increasing use of PIL by conservative as well as progressive social movements. Second, this basic normative framework does not mean that transformative constitutionalism demands unanimity on all ideological commitments. On the contrary, a plurality of beliefs is not only compatible with transformative constitutionalism but is actively welcome.

Transformative constitutionalism in South Africa includes requiring that individuals and groups have scope to pursue their own conceptions of the good.[96] The Constitution does not set up a maximalist system that dictates to people exactly what is valuable in their lives or how they should go about achieving those values. But just because the Constitution does not outline a 'thick' theory of rights does not render the idea of transformative constitutionalism without content.

On the contrary, as Bilchitz proposes, we can arrive at a 'thin' theory of rights that sets out two thresholds.[97] The first is any individual's interest in having resources and capabilities she needs to be free from threats to her survival, including goods and resources (justifying, for example, justiciable socio-economic rights). The second threshold is an individual's interest in having the resources and capabilities she needs to form and realise her purposes.

Both are fundamentally important. Without material resources and support (including food and water, housing, and healthcare services) an individual is not free from threats to her survival. But she also needs other legal guarantees (including civil and political rights, and the right to equality) to be able to pursue her own conception of the good.[98] So, the Constitution is not normatively empty. It provides, as Woolman argues, a minimal framework for flourishing,[99] within which any law organisation or lawyer must litigate.

---

[94] *Teddy Bear Clinic* (note 87 above).

[95] Jason Brickhill 'Public interest alchemy: Combining art and science to litigate for social science', paper presented at New York Law School's Twenty Years of South African Constitutionalism Symposium, 14–16 November 2014, accessed from <http://www.nylslawreview.com/wp-content/uploads/sites/16/2014/11/Brickhill.pdf> on 2 May 2018.

[96] *Ferreira v Levin NO and Others; Vryenhoek and Others v Powell NO and Others* [1995] ZACC 13; 1996 (1) SA 984 (CC) para 50.

[97] D Bilchitz *Poverty and Fundamental Rights* (2007) 646. See also Brickhill (note 95 above) 11-3 and Theunis Roux 'Transformative constitutionalism and the best interpretation of the South African Constitution: Distinction without a difference' (2009) 20 *Stell LR* 258.

[98] Amartya Sen *Development as Freedom* (1999); Woolman (note 44 above) 24–5.

[99] Woolman ibid.

But it also leaves room for lawyers to contest what is permitted and required by law. As Wilson reflects:

> For practitioners of rights (whether or not they are formally qualified lawyers), the lesson is not to see law, rights and the institutions that enforce them as complete normative systems, which describe the proper and immutable distribution of obligations between states, corporations and citizens. Rather, they should be evaluated as partially developed and rather half-hearted gestures at regulating behavior in a more or less predictable way in line with dimly perceived conceptions of the good. Rights and law are *always* contingent and incomplete. Their importance in a strategy for change depends not just on their normative content—which is in any case indeterminate at best—but also on the position of the actor deploying them, his linkages with other individuals and groups in the social system in which he is embedded and his capacity to form alliances across a range of social groups and institutions.[100]

The contingent content of rights—and so, too, of litigation—can be partially accounted for by two connected, but distinct, ideas. Rawls, the renowned political philosopher, set out the idea that any society with plural, and potentially conflicting, views may try to establish 'overlapping consensus' on core political principles.[101] Even though people may reasonably disagree about the specifics of an idea or normative commitment, they can agree about overarching abstract principles. This allows conflicting normative understandings to converge on abstract constitutional essentials. In South Africa's context, these overlapping abstract principles are to a certain extent reflected in the Constitution. Two people may, for instance, reasonably disagree about whether a song is a legitimate form of free expression, but still agree on the more abstract principle that the Constitution protects freedom of speech, save for, for example, advocacy of hatred that incites harm.

And, in a pivotal paper in the late 1990s, Sunstein put forward the notion of 'incompletely theorized agreements'.[102] Within well-functioning legal systems that navigate plural views, participants can reach accord by agreeing on particular results without agreeing on the reasons for those results. As one of us has argued elsewhere, transformative constitutionalism is an incompletely theorised agreement.[103] It does not purport to provide a complete account of what is good and valuable for individuals, or, conversely, the government's duties to realise this.

The point is that organisations litigating in the public interest legal sector—and judges adjudicating public interest claims—need not have homogenous normative commitments. Diversity of views about normative commitments can also be a good thing, for intrinsic and instrumental reasons. Earlier, we discussed that the

---

[100] Stuart Wilson 'Litigating housing rights in Johannesburg's inner city: 2004–2008' (2011) 27 *SAJHR* 127 at 151.

[101] John Rawls 'The idea of an overlapping consensus' (1987) 7 *OJLS* 1.

[102] Cass R Sunstein 'Incompletely theorized agreements' (1995) 108 *Harv L Rev* 1733.

[103] Brickhill (note 95 above) 12.

transformative constitutional system that South Africa has embraced allows individuals to pursue their own understandings of the good, with entitlements to the resources and capabilities they need to be free from threats to survival, and to form and enact these understandings. The commitment to individuals seeking out their own vision of what is valuable means that different views should not only be recognised but also celebrated by those committed to constitutionalism.[104] This is exactly because their existence informs people's abilities to adjudicate for themselves what is worthwhile. There may therefore be a range of views about both the substantive issues at stake and about the appropriate role of courts in pursuing social change. Why public organisations litigate—and why, in some cases, they choose not to litigate—is frequently an instantiation of these views.

A diversity of views can also be instrumentally valuable. It prompts those who are engaging with public interest law to make arguments, and form strategies, that are more robust. This holds for differences in views among progressive organisations,[105] and also with organisations that do not share progressive aims.

But the Constitution does articulate minimal normative premises and so there are some views, or litigation purportedly brought in the public interest, which are outside its proper bounds. Some of the recent litigation undertaken by Afriforum, purportedly brought in the public interest, demonstrates this point: while the Constitution provides a somewhat open normative framework, constitutional principles still set some limits. Litigation that seeks to entrench historically and current privileged positions—in terms of both race and socio-economic status— falls outside those limits. The public interest organisations whose work this book in large part considers, generally act in the interests of poor and black clients, whose interests will far more readily fall within the bounds of the normative premises of the Constitution. Ultimately, the test of this is often in the litigation process itself, with the judiciary adjudicating whether litigation, purportedly in the public interest, is constitutionally sustainable.[106]

3.4 SETTING PRECEDENT OR SECURING RELIEF?

Litigation can trigger 'trajectories of change'[107] for social struggles and reform and enrich participatory politics. In turn, litigation's success is often contingent on

---

[104] Woolman (note 44 above) 113.

[105] See, eg, the Raith SERI Report's discussion of divergent approaches adopted by two public interest organisations that both acted as *amici* in *Mail and Guardian Media Ltd and Others v Chipu NO and Others* [2013] ZACC 32; 2013 (6) SA 367 (CC) [SALC and LHR were admitted as *amici curiae*].

[106] See, eg, *City of Tshwane Metropolitan Municipality v Afriforum and Another* [2016] ZACC 19; 2016 (6) SA 279 (CC) and *Afriforum and Another v University of the Free State* [2017] ZACC 48; 2018 (2) SA 185 (CC).

[107] S Liebenberg 'Rights, needs and transformation: Adjudicating social rights' (2006) 17 *Stell LR* 5–36.

underlying political, social and moral ideas. Lauded as the 'Rolls Royce'[108] of PIL, the *Treatment Action Campaign* strategy model perhaps best exemplifies this idea. By the time the matter reached the Constitutional Court, there was widespread consensus that the government was obliged to plan and implement a programme to prevent the mother-to-child transmission of HIV. This was due to the extensive social mobilisation that the organisation undertook before the matter was litigated at the Constitutional Court.[109] Background political and social conditions, then, can be essential for achieving public interest goals.

Not least, this is because rights are not self-implementing, and litigation alone is insufficient for social reform. The United States legal academy has wrestled with this question: can litigation secure social change, or is that idea a 'hollow hope'? In 1991, Rosenberg published *The Hollow Hope*, in which he argues that the impact of PIL is seriously overstated.[110] He posits, first, that, absent political support, judgments cannot produce social change. Those who turn to the courts for reform are 'looking for change in all the wrong places'.[111] Second, litigation can sometimes actively hamper change, because it diverts necessary human and financial resources away from political organising, and because it can fortify movements that are opposed to change.[112] This point is most devastatingly made in the *Brown v Board of Education* matter, argues Rosenberg. Despite the Supreme Court of the United States ordering that schools be desegregated, not only was this order insufficient for achieving that goal, but the litigation set off a conservative counter-movement that aggressively opposed change, making desegregation even more difficult.[113]

In response, McCann argues that the success of public interest legal action should not principally be measured by the success of any single lawsuit. Rather, litigation is instrumental for its ability to effect legal mobilisation and a 'jurisprudence from below', in which people engaged in a social struggle, can internalise, define and claim entitlement to rights.[114]

Cummings and Rhode suggest a middle ground: PIL is an 'imperfect but indispensable strategy of social change'.[115] Litigation is neither panacea nor

---

[108] Dugard & Langford (note 6 above) 61.

[109] Heywood (note 18 above).

[110] Gerald Rosenberg *The Hollow Hope* (1991).

[111] GN Rosenberg 'Courting disaster: Looking for change in all the wrong places' (2005) 54 *Drake L Rev* 765. In a South African context see, eg, Amit (note 5 above) 15–6.

[112] Ibid 810.

[113] GN Rosenberg 'Tilting at windmills: *Brown II* and the hopeless quest to resolve deep-seated social conflict through litigation' (2006) 24 *Law and Inequality* 31.

[114] MW McCann *Rights at Work: Pay Equity and the Politics of Legal Mobilisation* (1994). See also Wilson (note 100 above) 127.

[115] Scott L Cummings & Deborah L Rhode 'Public interest litigation: Insights from theory and practice' (2009) 36 *Fordham Urb LJ* 603 at 604.

placebo. Instead, it complements other political struggles. Its achievements should be assessed in light of the other available alternatives, and the social, economic and political backdrop in which the litigation is brought.

This debate has played out in the South African context, informing how practitioners and academics track the success of PIL.[116] The Atlantic Report adopts a materialist model of social change, measuring the practical impact on the ground.[117] And, echoing Rosenberg's point, Amit argues that, notwithstanding some in-principle successes, lack of political and legal support has impeded the enforcement of refugees' and asylum seekers' rights.[118] The same point can be made in many other contexts, particularly concerning the enforcement of socio-economic rights. Other writers, such as Dugard and Langford, draw on McCann's position. They emphasise that PIL's worth is not only to be measured by the material success of any single case, but also by its enabling effects on 'the climate of ideas'.[119]

The discussion between those advocating for, as the Raith Report frames it,[120] a materialist position on the one hand, and those for a legal mobilisation position on the other, continues. But the extent of the differences between the two positions should not be exaggerated.

First, in the South African context no one engaged in this debate has assumed a stance as sceptical as Rosenberg's or, for that matter, as naïvely optimistic as the position he sets himself against. In large part, this is because of fundamental features of the South African constitutional order. It is uncontentious that the Constitution—and not Parliament—is supreme and that courts are the arbiters of whether law and conduct withstand constitutional scrutiny. Compared to the United States, there is thus less weight placed on the notion that only change resulting directly from legislative will is legitimate or useful. It is also apparent that, given South Africa's dire poverty and gaping inequality, few would make the mistake of confusing symbols for substance,[121] thinking that victory in court automatically or immediately translates into changed lived realities.

Second, as one of us has argued elsewhere,[122] a good deal of the apparent disagreement between the camps is resolved if one understands the two as

---

[116] Raith SERI report (note 22 above) 42–4.

[117] Budlender et al (note 15 above).

[118] Amit (note 5 above) 31.

[119] Dugard & Langford (note 6 above) 64. See also C Rodríguez-Garavito 'Beyond the courtroom: The impact of judicial activism on socioeconomic rights in Latin America' (2010) 89 *Texas L Rev* 1669.

[120] Raith SERI report (note 22 above) 42–4.

[121] We draw this phrase from Malcolm Langford et al (eds) *Socio-Economic Rights in South Africa: Symbols or Substance?* (2013).

[122] Brickhill (note 95 above) 4–7.

engaging with distinct enquiries: *how* should PIL be conducted to optimise the prospect of success for a particular litigant; and *why* is PIL valuable?

Finally, even when there are disagreements about other aspects of the PIL project, South African lawyers accept two fundamental premises: that concrete gains matter; and that Politics/politics influences the extent to which litigation ultimately contributes to achieving social justice.

Securing precedent should not, then, be conflated with effecting social change. Not all worthwhile public interest lawyering is high-impact, precedent-setting strategic litigation. This is not to understate the importance of strategic constitutional litigation, which has been vital in our constitutional order, and—in conjunction with supportive measures—has effected real change. There is, however, a danger that public interest organisations overly prioritise litigation to establish doctrine, usually at the highest level, to the detriment of ensuring broader access to justice (including where the relevant law is not debatable).[123] Jansen and Achiume argue that there needs to be more concerted effort in prison litigation, for example. Here, there is no pressing need to establish pioneering doctrines; instead, what is needed is 'mainstream, *bread and butter* litigation'.[124] So, too, when it comes to gender-based violence, the underlying law is, for the most part, uncontroversial but there remains a dire undersupply of legal services.[125]

Outside a litigation context, constitutional literacy, too, should be prioritised: a 2014 report by the Foundation for Human Rights found that only 46% of people surveyed had heard of either the Constitution or the Bill of Rights, and less than 10% had read these documents or had them read to them.[126] A number of campaigns and initiatives are animated by the importance of advancing constitutional literacy, but there is far more to be done.[127] This gives traction to the idea that public interest legal work is not an event, but must be part of an ongoing struggle.[128]

---

[123] SPII Raith Theories of Change (note 4 above).

[124] Rudolph Jansen & Emily Tendayi Achiume 'Prison conditions in South Africa and the role of public interest litigation since 1994' (2011) 27 *SAJHR* 183 at 191 (emphasis in text).

[125] Raith SERI report (note 22 above) 22. Cote & Van Garderen (note 17 above) 169 also make the point that:

> Although [specialist public law organisations] have done tremendous work in their particular fields (such as gender, refugee and migrants rights, and HIV/AIDS), it has led to a decrease in giving general legal advice, such as wills and testaments, housing and tenant issues, unfair labour practices and delict (tort) actions.

[126] Report of the AJPCR Baseline Survey on awareness of attitude and access to constitutional rights (2014) Foundation for Human Rights; Tim Fish Hodgson 'Bridging the gap between people and the law' 2015 *Acta Juridica* 189.

[127] See, eg, the Know Your Constitution Campaign (a coalition of civil society organisations); LAWCO (a student-run initiative at the University of Cape Town); Constitution Hill school programmes and the historic bastion, Street Law.

[128] Raith SERI report (note 22 above) 49.

3.5 CASE VERSUS CAUSE: CLIENT'S INTEREST AND THE PUBLIC INTEREST

One of the most challenging tensions—ethically, tactically and in terms of the allocation of resources within public interest organisations—is the balance between the interests of clients and the public interest. Put differently, this is the need to reconcile the specific case and the larger cause. By definition, PIL implicates interests beyond those of the immediate parties. A range of models of PIL is used in South Africa, including test cases, defensive litigation,[129] class actions and a 'sausage factory'[130] approach in which repeat cases are brought to tackle a pattern of rights violations, such as unlawful detentions of foreign nationals. In addition, several public interest organisations operate as law clinics, assisting walk-in clients with the problems that they face. The LRC and LHR are examples of large, national public interest law firms that combine law clinic services with strategic litigation. Common to all these different models of public interest lawyering is that they involve the interests of individual clients and broader interests.

In many situations, no tension arises between case and cause. They are perfectly aligned, as it is possible to seek relief that vindicates a client's rights and interests while at the same time pursuing a broader strategic objective, such as changing the law for all similarly situated people. The landmark decision of the Constitutional Court in *S v Makwanyane* abolishing the death penalty is a powerful example. The case concerned two individual litigants who had been sentenced to death; but many others were also on death row. Ultimately, the Constitutional Court struck down the law providing for capital punishment, prohibited the state from executing any person and ordered that the sentences of the two individual litigants and all others sentenced to death be reviewed and replaced with lawful punishments.[131]

In other situations, there may be a tension between the client's preferences or interests and the broader public interest or strategic objective of litigation. The tension between the interests of individual clients and the broader cause of setting precedent or benefiting the whole class of affected persons is brought into sharp focus by offers of settlement. The effect of a settlement of the claims of individual litigants may have the effect of thwarting precedent-setting litigation.[132] On some occasions, this is the very strategy of defendants, including government and big

---

[129] For example, to respond to unlawful evictions or illegal detentions.

[130] Steven Budlender used this metaphor in a presentation discussing the approach to this book in Johannesburg in 2015. For an account of the work of LHR in bringing almost weekly urgent applications challenging the legality of individual detentions and deportations, see Amit (note 5 above) 15–6.

[131] *S v Makwanyane* [1995] ZACC 3; 1995 (3) SA 391 (CC) para 151 [the LRC acted for the applicants; LHR, CALS and the Society for the Abolition of the Death Penalty were admitted as *amici curiae*].

[132] Budlender et al (note 15 above) 40–1.

business. This certainly appears to have been the strategy of government respondents in serial litigation on two important sets of issues, immigration detention and education infrastructure provision in the Eastern Cape.

In relation to immigration detention, Lawyers for Human Rights has for many years conducted strategic litigation aimed at addressing a range of rights violations, including in relation to the legality, length and conditions of immigration detention. Many of these cases are brought as urgent applications to secure the release, prevent the deportation, or change the conditions of detention of specific individual applicants; but they are also brought with the broader strategic aim of ensuring that other people do not face the same violations. Van Garderen and Cote of LHR describe how the resultant ethical challenges were tackled:

> [O]nce an attorney has agreed to represent the client, the client must give instructions and the lawyer has an obligation (with the obvious exceptions) to follow those instructions, for example if a settlement is offered. But the client must be made aware from the beginning that his or her case forms part of a litigation strategy and that decisions and advice by the lawyer will be guided by that strategy. In the end, however, the strategy may not prejudice a client. If a settlement is offered which does not assist the strategy but will result in further detention, clear instructions from the client must be obtained. The client should have been advised from the beginning of the strategy and encouraged to proceed in his or her best interests as well as that of the strategy. If, however, he or she refuses, it will be necessary to follow the client's instructions. Refusing to do so may have professional consequences for the lawyer and his or her organisation, not to mention lowering the organisation's esteem in the field.[133]

This account emphasises that ultimately, if a tension arises between client interests and strategic objectives, the client's instructions are decisive. This can mean that substantial and scarce resources are exhausted on individual cases without extending relief to others facing the same rights violations. One way of mitigating this risk is to advise individual clients in advance of the broader objectives of the case, such as challenging a law authorising extended detention of foreign nationals, to try to secure the individual clients' commitment to those objectives. Other ways of addressing this tension relate to how the litigation is structured, which is well illustrated by the second set of examples in education rights cases.

In relation to the litigation conducted by the LRC to secure education infrastructure provision in the Eastern Cape, a large proportion of the cases were settled, in whole or in part, in particular on the question whether the right to a basic education required a particular input, such as classrooms or school furniture. McConnachie and McConnachie describe how two early cases, the 'Mud Schools' case and the *Amasango* case concerning the infrastructure of a special needs school, resulted in substantial settlements. However, they observe that '[h]ad either case produced a judgment this would have marked an important milestone

---

[133] Cote & Van Garderen (note 17 above) 180.

in the development of South Africa's nascent education rights jurisprudence'.[134] Writing later, one of the current authors and Van Leeve observed that this trend had continued, with a striking frequency of settlements in the subsequent education cases concerning furniture, teachers, textbooks and scholar transport.[135] By using a combination of individual and institutional litigants, however, and conducting serialised or multi-stage litigation, it was still possible to secure broader relief despite the settlements:

> The effect of conducting the litigation in stages was to enable the litigants to establish the content of the right and the obligations of the state in principle; to secure a basic order requiring provision of the necessary resource; to create a supervisory framework for the implementation of the order and to refine that framework to secure compliance; and thereby to 'scale up' the relief, moving from individual schools in the first stage to an entire province by the end.[136]

A third example illustrates how big business has also employed tactical settlements. Over a period of almost a decade, the LRC litigated a set of test case claims on behalf of underground mineworkers who had contracted silicosis (an incurable lung disease) on mines controlled by Anglo American South Africa Ltd (Anglo). Shortly before the test cases claims were to be arbitrated, Anglo settled the test case claims on terms that are confidential, but which included the payment of money to the test case claimants. As a result, the test cases never proceeded to trial. Following this development, the LRC joined with other lawyers in launching class action litigation that would ensure that all mineworkers would secure relief. Class representatives then took on the role in the knowledge that they also acted in the interests of the entire class. Settlement could no longer bar determination of the case.

At least in class actions, the courts have now taken on a role in balancing the interests of individual class representatives against those of the broader class in the context of settlements. In the silicosis class action proceedings that followed the LRC's litigation described above, the High Court held that any settlement agreement reached after certification of a class action must be approved by the certifying court to ensure that it is 'fair, reasonable, adequate and that it protects the interests of the class.[137] The silicosis class action has since been settled and a hearing to approve the settlement is pending'.

Of course, we should not be understood to suggest that settlements of the individual disputes that underlie public interest cases are always deleterious to the broader cause. Skelton has identified how strategic litigation on the right to

---

[134] Cameron McConnachie & Chris McConnachie 'Concretising the right to a basic education' (2012) 129 *SAJHR* 554, 556.

[135] J Brickhill & Y van Leeve 'From the classroom to the courtroom: Litigating education rights in South Africa' in Sandra Fredman, Meghan Campbell & Helen Taylor (eds) *Human Rights and Equality in Education* (2018).

[136] Ibid 162–3.

[137] *Nkala* (note 61 above) para 39.

education in South Africa led to increased dialogue through settlement talks.[138] Skelton concluded that these led to a better understanding of the difficulties that the government faces in delivering services, although the adversarial nature of the process meant that the dialogue generated has not always been productive.[139]

Ultimately, the tension between assisting individual clients and pursuing a broader strategic objective, such as law reform or relief for all similarly affected people, requires careful balancing by public interest lawyers. At the level of resources, organisations need to decide how to manage the allocation of lawyers and other resources between walk-in clients and proactively planned test cases. Sometimes, a walk-in client's claim becomes a precedent-setting case. This means that, if broader interests are at stake, this should be explained to the client up front. Difficult conflicts can be avoided by including institutional litigants alongside individual claimants, so that a settlement of individual claims will not bring an end to the case.

3.6 FEES, FUNDING AND COSTS

'The law is a scarce resource in South Africa',[140] noted the Supreme Court of Appeal (SCA), not least because of the exorbitant baseline cost of legal services. In this section, we discuss the ethical ramifications of fees, funding and costs for PIL. We touch briefly on some ethical concerns: How do fee arrangements, and funders' requirements, constrain public interest organisations? What are the ethical implications, including the obligations to existing clients, of funding constraints? And are there funding models—or even judicial solutions—that can mitigate these constraints?

(a) Funding sources and their consequences

The right of access to courts is instrumental for the realisation of other rights, but access is so often contingent on litigants' financial means.[141] In the PIL context, the strategic direction available to public interest law organisations is affected by the availability or absence of funding for particular kinds of work.[142] Economic ebbs and flows in turn affect the availability of funding. In South Africa, institutional donors primarily fund the public interest legal sector, with comparatively

---

[138] Open Society Justice Initiative *Strategic Litigation Impacts: Equal Access to Quality Education* (2017) 73.

[139] Ibid.

[140] *Permanent Secretary Department of Welfare, Eastern Cape Provincial Government and Another v Ngxuza and Others* [2001] ZASCA 85; 2001 (4) SA 1184 (SCA) para 1 [LRC acted for the respondents}.

[141] Jason Brickhill & Adrian Friedman 'Access to courts' in Stuart Woolman et al (eds) *Constitutional Law of South Africa* 2 ed (Revision Service 4-05) 59-55.

[142] Cummings (note 90 above) 361.

little individual and local giving.[143] Moreover, funding can be insecure;[144] one of the biggest donors, the Atlantic Philanthropies, recently drew its grant-making programme to an end.[145] The lack of local funding is not because there is insufficient local money to invest.[146] One of the most commonly cited reasons for business not investing in the sector is that it is 'politically risky'. Securing increased local funding must remain a priority for public interest organisations as this will make the sector more secure as well as less vulnerable to the critique that organisations are furthering 'foreign agendas'.

The state is another source of funding for litigation. In criminal matters and civil proceedings, which affect children, it is uncontentious that anyone who is detained, an accused and a child have the right to legal representation at state expense, if substantial injustice would otherwise arise.[147] Less clear until recently was whether the state is obliged to fund legal representation in civil cases beyond those affecting children. The question was raised directly when the victims of the Marikana massacre and their families litigated to secure state-funded legal representation for the Marikana Commission of Inquiry. The High Court held that the right to a fair hearing in s 34 of the Constitution, which guarantees access to courts, includes a right to legal representation at state expense at least in some circumstances.[148] The Constitutional Court ultimately dismissed an appeal against this decision on the basis of mootness, but approved this general principle.[149] The Constitution therefore does confer a right to legal aid, not only in criminal matters and matters affecting children, but also in those civil matters where a failure to

---

[143] Lauren Stuart 'The South African nonprofit sector: Struggling to survive, needing to thrive' (2013) *NGO Pulse* 9 April 2013, last accessed on 13 July 2015 from <www.ngopulse.org/article/south-african-nonprofit-sector-struggling-survive-needing-thrive>.

[144] Ivor Chipkin & Sarah Meny-Gibert *Understanding the Social Justice Sector in South Africa* (2013) 25 note that the social justice sector in South Africa has felt the adverse effects of the funding crisis keenly: a third of the organisations they sampled could not cover their organisational expenses in the previous financial year, and the study does not capture the many organisations who were forced to close shop.

[145] Budlender et al (note 15 above) III.

[146] South African CSI expenditure has expanded from R1.5 billion in 1998 to R9.1 billion in 2017. See http://trialogue.co.za/sa-companies-invest-r9-billion-csi/ (last accessed 21 May 2018). However, almost none of that money is spent on public interest litigation organisations. In October 2017 Mark Heywood of SECTION 27 wrote a letter to more than 20 of South Africa's top CEOs and business leaders trying to get more financial support to public interest organisations, but we are not aware of any change, last accessed from <http://www.702.co.za/articles/275812/business-leaders-be-brave-mark-heywood-section27> on 21 May 2018.

[147] Sections 12(1)(*h*), 35(2)(*c*) and 35(3)(*g*) of the Constitution.

[148] *Magidiwana and Another v President of the Republic of South Africa and Others* [2013] ZAGPPHC 292; [2014] 1 All SA 76 (GP) [SERI acted for most of the families of the deceased mineworkers; LRC acted for the Ledingoane family].

[149] *Legal Aid South Africa v Magidiwana and Others* [2015] ZACC 28; 2015 (6) SA 494 (CC) para 22.

provide it would deprive parties of a fair hearing under s 34.[150] However, the recognition of a right to civil legal aid in principle has not brought with it the immediate delivery of civil legal aid. Legal Aid South Africa (LASA), the statutory body responsible for meeting the state's constitutional obligations, makes very limited provision for assistance in civil matters. To expand this, it will be necessary to challenge the constitutionality of the limitations and exclusions that LASA applies in civil matters.

When it comes to institutional funders, public interest organisations are subject to financial pressures that can have knock-on effects on the kind of work they do. The Raith SERI Report conveys the reflections of respondents in the public interest law sector on funding. They stress a number of important considerations. Donors may view the collaboration between public interest law organisations as ideal, especially when organisations have overlapping fields of expertise. But this should not be forced; 'effective coordination and collaboration has to be voluntary and organic'.[151] Other respondents noted that donors should avoid fuelling competition among organisations in the sector. Funding constraints can affect not only prospective work but also ongoing work, for example, when an organisation has already taken on clients, but funding has become limited. Here, the organisation has a principal obligation to its existing clients, notwithstanding changes in its funding situation, because it has undertaken to represent the clients who have come to rely on the organisation to vindicate their interests.

Financial considerations affect not only the public interest organisations running litigation, but also clients whose pecuniary interests may, for example, favour settling a matter before it reaches court, rather than waiting for an uncertain result. This is so even if that result could potentially set beneficial precedent,[152] as discussed earlier. Public interest organisations serving clients' best interests generally have an ethical obligation to advise their clients to settle where the agreement is more extensive than a court order would grant, even at the expense of securing doctrinal change or relief for all similarly affected people.[153] This is not to draw a false dichotomy between the client's financial interests and the goals of PIL; organisations can manage some of this difficulty, as described above, by taking on a basket of clients or representing organisations so that the litigation can continue, even if individual clients settle.[154]

---

[150] See J Brickhill & C Grobler 'The right to civil legal aid in South Africa: *Legal Aid South Africa v Magidiwana*' (2016) 7 *CCR* 36-61.

[151] Raith SERI Report (note 22 above) 64.

[152] Budlender et al (note 15 above) 76–7 and, discussing this in a United States context, see Nicole T Chapin 'Regulation of public interest law firms by the IRS and the bar: Making it hard to serve the public good' (1993) 7 *Geo J Legal Ethics* 437.

[153] Budlender et al (note 15 above) 94.

[154] Ibid.

One potential concern is that public interest organisations may feel principally accountable to their funders rather than their clients, simply because funders, and not clients, wield financial pressure.[155] In the private legal sector, market forces play a role in ensuring that the client drives the litigation, and is satisfied with how it is conducted. This is not to say that there are no mechanisms to vindicate clients' interests in the litigation process, or that public interest organisations operate without concern for clients' preferences;[156] only that thoughtful consideration is particularly important in the public interest legal sector, where levers of accountability are not always as obvious.

Finally, it is worth gesturing more generally to the role that courts could play in broadening access to justice, given how expensive legal services are in South Africa. Dugard has argued that the Constitutional Court, for example, should overhaul its procedural rules to allow for direct access not just in exceptional circumstances.[157] This, however, risks eroding the important appellate function that the Constitutional Court plays, and overstating its importance to broaden access to justice in all cases. More compelling is Fowkes' modest suggestion that formal procedures remain as the default, but judges, especially at high court level, take on managerial roles that explore more informal or inquisitorial steps to resolving disputes.[158] Because this area of civil procedure is still so nascent, even within the academy, we only mention it here as one possible site of development.

(b) Fee arrangements

Public interest legal organisations do not litigate for profit or expect to benefit financially from the matters that they run. Nonetheless, they incur expenses and must develop working methods to meet them. The two single largest overall expenses for public interest organisations in any given year are almost invariably the salaries paid to their legal staff (predominantly attorneys) and fees paid to external counsel (members of the Bar briefed to argue cases). In this section, we consider the fee arrangements open to public interest law organisations to meet their costs; after all, 'public policy and the right of access to justice requires a relaxation of other restrictions that previously limited the range of fee arrangements that could be concluded between clients and legal practitioners'.[159]

---

[155] SPII Raith Theories of Change (note 4 above) and Cummings & Rhode (note 115 above) 645.

[156] HC Becker 'In defense of an embattled mode of advocacy: An analysis and justification of public interest practice' (1981) 90 *Yale LJ* 1436 at 1456.

[157] J Dugard 'Court of first instance? Towards a pro-poor jurisdiction for the South African Constitutional Court' (2006) 22 *SAJHR* 261; Jackie Dugard 'Closing the doors of justice: An examination of the Constitutional Court's approach to direct access, 1995–2013' (2015) 31 *SAJHR* 112.

[158] James Fowkes 'Managerial adjudication, constitutional civil procedure and *Maphango v Aengus Lifestyle Properties*' (2013) 5 *CCR* 308–30.

[159] *Thusi v Minister of Home Affairs and Others* [2010] ZAKZPHC 87; 2011 (2) SA 561 (KZP) para 108.

Legal services in South Africa are notoriously expensive. This is particularly acute in respect of the fees of litigating counsel, so much so that the Constitutional Court was moved to fulminate against overcharging in *Camps Bay Ratepayers:*

> We feel obliged to express our disquiet at how counsel's fees have burgeoned in recent years. To say that they have skyrocketed in no loose metaphor. No matter the complexity of the issues, we can find no justification, in a country where disparities are gross and poverty is rife, to countenance appellate advocates charging hundreds of thousands of rands to argue an appeal.[160]

Commentators within practice echo this criticism,[161] noting that the highest earners exert upward pressure on counsel costs across the profession. This is notwithstanding the General Council of the Bar's Uniform Rules of Ethics which set out that fees must be reasonable and should neither overestimate nor under-value the value of legal advice and services.[162] When determining fees 'it should never be forgotten that the profession is a branch of the administration of justice and not a mere money-getting trade'. Even if a client can pay more, the General Council of the Bar directs, overcharging is not justified. The converse is obviously not true; a client's lack of means may require a lower or no charge. But these rules have failed to change the prohibitive costs of litigation, and the concomitant effect on access to courts.

The Legal Practice Act 28 of 2014 (Legal Practice Act) (enacted but not yet in operation) may change some of this, at least in theory. One of the purposes of the Act is to put in place a mechanism to determine fees chargeable by lawyers, so that access to justice is broadened. Section 35 of the Legal Practice Act governs fees for legal services. Section 35(4) directs the South Africa Law Reform Commission (SALRC) to investigate and report back to the Minister of Justice and Constitutional Development with recommendations on the problems associated with legal fees and possible interventions, including whether a tariff should be introduced.

The Legal Practice Act also attempts to smooth out information asymmetry and advance clients' 'consumer' interests, by requiring legal practitioners to provide extensive information, in writing and verbally, about the envisaged costs of legal services to instructing clients. Non-compliance constitutes misconduct, and the client will not be required to pay legal costs until the Legal Practice Council, a body set up by the Act, has reviewed the matter, and set the amounts to be paid.

The Act also provides for community service by legal practitioners, either as a part of practical vocational training for candidate attorneys or pupils, or as a minimum period of repeated community service (as required prior to the Act). If a broad-scale community service programme is put in place for new professionals, it

---

[160] *Camps Bay Ratepayers and Residents Association and Another v Harrison and Another* [2012] ZACC 17; 2012 (11) BCLR 1143 para 10.

[161] See, for example, Owen Rogers 'High fees and questionable practices' 2012 *Advocate* 40.

[162] General Council of the Bar's Uniform Rules 7 (Uniform Rules).

will have massive effects on the provision of access to justice.[163] Indeed, given that even reduced legal fees would be out of reach for the majority of South Africans, the provision of community service and increases to the very limited civil legal aid available are more important steps in promoting access to justice.

But the Legal Practice Act, with its proposed measures to control legal costs and advance access to legal services, remains theoretical. Finally, there has been resistance to the Act from within the profession; already, many of its more far-reaching provisions were cut back in the drafting process, and it seems possible that it will face legal challenges once its implementation begins.[164] What this means is that, for the time being, the fees of legal practitioners remain governed by the same rules as those preceding the enactment of the Legal Practice Act, and in accordance with the tariffs made by the Rules Board, although any legal service user continues to be able to agree to pay fees in excess of those tariffs.

We now turn to consider other fee arrangements that public interest law organisations can consider, guided by the discussion reflected in the Raith SERI Report.

(i)   *Fee caps and fee guidelines*
The International Defence and Aid Fund (IDAF), which set out the rates that public interest lawyers should be paid, funded much of PIL during apartheid.[165] Lawyers informally agreed to these tariffs, effectively capping the fees payable to public interest legal practitioners.

One of the proposals to address soaring legal fees made in the Raith SERI Report is that public interest law organisations form a joint strategy on counsel fees, and that donors develop fee guidelines that are flexible, in consultation with organisations.[166]

In part, this draws on Legal Aid South Africa Judicare Model for fee payment to external legal practitioners. Some respondents in the Raith SERI Report advocated for this model, although Legal Aid South Africa reported in mid-2015 that the model has proven to be unsustainable, both financially and in terms of monitoring the services provided by external practitioners.[167] The organisation is thus moving away from the model, instead focusing on recruiting in-house lawyers.

However, fee guidelines may not pass muster under competition law. In 2011, the Competition Commission rejected an application by the Law Society of South

---

[163] See J Brickhill 'The right to a fair civil trial: The duties of lawyers and law students to act pro bono' (2005) 21 *SAJHR* 293–322; Brickhill & Grobler (note 150 above).

[164] Izak Smuts SC 'The case against the Legal Practice Bill' *PoliticsWeb* 12 February 2013, last accessed on 13 July 2015 from <www.politicsweb.co.za/politics/the-case-against-the-legal-practice-bill>.

[165] Raith SERI Report (note 22 above) 105.

[166] Ibid 134–5.

[167] Legal Aid South Africa *Country Report: ILAG Conference* (2015) 10, last accessed 10 July 2015 from <www.legal-aid.co.za/wp-content/uploads/2015/05/ILAG-Report-2015-Final.pdf>.

Africa, finding that the tariff rule imposed on professional fees amounted to price fixing, and inhibited competition.[168] Moreover, any fee capping or guidelines are likely to be met with resistance by counsel. The Raith SERI Report remains optimistic that the Commission, which may also choose to apply different standards to advocates' professional rules, might treat a price ceiling differently.

It is true, also, that flexible fee guidelines should not be conflated with rigid fee caps. A flexible fee guideline is one 'softer' intervention on counsel's fees that may help drive down exorbitant costs. Finally, especially because advocates' fees are not always transparent, the process of sketching out the guidelines itself may be useful and prompt a recalibration of what is considered to be a reasonable charge.

(ii)   *In-house counsel*

One of the most important means of pooling expertise while curbing costs is for public interest law organisations to employ in-house counsel. The LRC employed this strategy since its establishment in 1979, and it has come to be used by other public interest organisations, including LHR, SERI, SECTION 27, the CCL and CALS. It is also used by Legal Aid South Africa, which employs counsel at its Justice Centres. The idea has, however, been questioned on the basis that in-house counsel may become partisan, 'seduced by their own propaganda',[169] and that the 'rational distance' that a lawyer should maintain from her client will be eroded.[170] The criticism is predicated on viewing lawyers as impartial or neutral, mere 'hired guns',[171] or unable to determine when to call on external opinions to make assessments.[172] This assumption grossly underestimates lawyers' ability—even when acting in-house—to assess carefully their clients' claims and the best way of litigating them.

There are clear benefits to in-house counsel. It is cost-effective, and allows legal practitioners to build up expertise, particularly helpful for public interest organisations that are 'repeat players' in bringing matters to court. This means that advocates can assist in developing a long-term strategy over a body of work and are familiar with the on-the-ground realities.[173]

The LRC's Arthur Chaskalson Pupillage Fellowship mentioned above takes the idea of in-house counsel further, linking it to the need to transform the legal profession and the public interest sector. Over time, this initiative and others like it

---

[168] Competition Commission 'Media Release: Commission Rejects Law Society of South Africa Application for Exemption' *Competition Commission* 14 March 2011, last accessed on 13 July 2015 from <www.compcom.co.za/2011-media-releases/>.

[169] Ibid 102, quoting a respondent.

[170] J Krishnan 'Lawyering for a cause and experiences from abroad' (2006) 94 *Cal L Rev* 575 at 581–2.

[171] Stuart A Scheingold 'Essay for the in-print symposium on *The Myth of Moral Justice*' (2006) 4 *Cardozo Public Law, Policy and Ethics Journal* 47 at 52.

[172] Raith SERI Report (note 22 above) 103.

[173] Ibid 101.

will continue to build the pool of counsel with expertise in PIL, while contributing to transforming that group of advocates.

(iii) *Contingency fee agreements*

Under a contingency fee agreement, a lawyer or law organisation will only be paid a fee if the matter is successfully litigated or settled: it is a 'no win, no fee' arrangement. Historically under the common law, contingency fee arrangements were not permitted. But the SALRC issued a report in 1996, recommending that contingency fee agreements be recognised as lawful.[174] The Contingency Fees Act 66 of 1997 (Contingency Fees Act) regulates these agreements. It provides for lawyers to charge fees calculated as a percentage of the proceeds their clients may be awarded in litigation.

This is not to say that contingency fee agreements do not raise ethical considerations. First, the agreements should be appropriately regulated, and must be in line with the Act. The Constitutional Court refused leave to appeal against a High Court judgment that found that it was impermissible for practitioners to charge above the percentages set by the Contingency Fees Act, as certain law societies allowed.[175] The Constitutional Court's judgment noted that the ethical duties that lawyers owe to their clients may conflict with their own financial interest in litigation subject to contingency fee agreements.[176] Second, junior counsel may not easily use contingency fee agreements, as these arrangements are predicated on counsel having reliable cash flows from diverse work.[177] This compounds existing financial barriers for junior counsel, and the impact this may have on transformation within the legal profession is worth considering.

One area of PIL in which contingency fee agreements are increasingly common is class actions. The ethical questions around these arrangements are exacerbated by the increasing interest of foreign law firms in partnering local firms in large class actions. The silicosis class action is the most significant example to date. American attorneys worked with local private attorneys acting for the class representatives and sought to recover large contingency fees.[178] The High Court hearing the certification application carefully examined, and ultimately approved, these contingency fee arrangements.[179] (This arrangement also constituted a champertous agreement, which was separately challenged. We discuss this aspect

---

[174] South African Law Reform Commission *Speculative and Contingency Fees* (Project 93) (1996).

[175] *Ronald Bobroff & Partners Inc v De La Guerre; South African Association of Personal Injury Lawyers v Minister of Justice and Constitutional Development* [2014] ZACC 2; 2014 (3) SA 134 (CC).

[176] Ibid para 10.

[177] Raith SERI Report (note 22 above) 116–7.

[178] American firms Motley Rice and Hausfeld were engaged as consultants to local attorneys Richard Spoor Attorneys and Abrahams Kiewitz Inc. respectively, all acting for the plaintiff class representatives. The LRC also acted for the class, but without seeking to recover any contingency fee.

[179] *Nkala* (note 61 above) paras 147–66.

further below.) Contingency fee agreements are a valuable mechanism to enable poor litigants to secure high-quality legal representation without requiring financially constrained public interest organisations to bear the costs of the litigation. However, such arrangements—and the conduct of lawyers working under them—do require careful appraisal to ensure that ethical concerns do not arise.

(iv) *Pro bono and reduced rates*

It goes without saying that there is scope for legal practitioners, especially counsel, to take on matters at reduced rates or pro bono. The General Council of the Bar's Uniform Rules of Ethics sets out that local bar councils shall require members to take on pro bono work, and members have a duty to represent clients in *pro deo* and legal aid matters if the bar council directs them to do so.[180] But, while lawyers have mandatory minimum pro bono requirements, this simply does not touch sides with the extensive need for legal services in South Africa, in part because obligations are minimal and there are weak mechanisms to monitor professional compliance with them.[181]

And when lawyers undertake pro bono work in private law firms, several difficulties may need to be navigated. First, lawyers might be faced with conflicts of interests between pro bono clients and other clients of the firm. Second, when pro bono work is piecemeal (rather than, for example, carried out by a designated team or department) there is a real risk that lawyers will not have marshalled substantive expertise needed to best vindicate clients' interests.[182] Respondents to the Raith SERI Report emphasise how important it is to be able to aggregate pro bono hours within a firm and equip a dedicated pro bono unit for the accumulation of experience and so that pro bono units can take on matters strategically.[183]

(v) *Champerty and litigation funding*

Champerty involves direct funding of 'frivolous' legal proceedings by a third party that has no other connection to the litigation. In return, if the case is successful the funder is entitled to a share of the proceeds. Historically, champertous agreements were frowned on as they were viewed as interfering with the integrity of the legal process.[184] An exception to this was where a good-faith party assisted an indigent litigant for a financial interest in the legal proceedings. Other jurisdictions, however, started to extensively explore litigation funding models where a third party effectively 'invests' in the outcome of the proceedings.[185] Arguments in favour of permitting champertous agreements include that they alter the balance of

---

[180] Uniform Rules (note 162 above) 5.12.4.

[181] Raith SERI Report (note 22 above) 120.

[182] Cummings & Rhode (note 115 above) 623.

[183] Raith SERI Report (note 22 above) 121.

[184] Feldman (note 11 above) 47–8.

[185] M Steinitz 'Whose claim is this anyway? Third party litigation funding' (2011) 95 *Minn L Rev* 1268.

power, facilitating access to justice and pairing plaintiffs who would not otherwise be able to litigate with powerful funders who are experienced in litigation.[186]

In *PriceWaterhouseCoopers Inc*,[187] the SCA relaxed the rules on litigation funding agreements. It held that public policy regarding litigation has shifted, with more flexible fee arrangements provided for by, for example, the enactment of the Contingency Fees Act. The court found that litigation funding is not generally unlawful; although there may be instances where a champertous agreement might amount to an abuse of process, such agreements have the potential to open access to courts.[188] Recently, the Gauteng Local Division of the High Court crucially affirmed the litigation funding agreement concluded to finance a class action on behalf of mineworkers, claiming damages for the silicosis that they contracted in their employment on mines.[189] The court found that the agreement facilitated access to justice, and that there was no risk that the third party funder was controlling the litigation but hiding behind the formally cited plaintiffs.

This is a prime risk of litigation funding: that the third party exercises undue influence over the course of the litigation or uses the plaintiffs as a mechanism only to further its own ends. There is also the risk that rules of attorney–client confidentiality are weakened, because of the independent relationships between the law organisation and the clients, and the clients and the funder.[190] So, the development of litigation funding in South Africa should be welcomed, but with caution.

(c) Costs

South Africa's regime on costs for constitutional litigation is protective.[191] Historically, costs fell within courts' discretion, with the default rule being that the loser pays. In its *Biowatch* judgment, the Constitutional Court carved out a different baseline position.[192] The *Biowatch* principles recognise the importance of fostering constitutional litigation—both for particular litigants who seek to access

---

[186] *Steinitz* (note 185 above) 1271.

[187] *Price Waterhouse Coopers Inc and Others v National Potato Co-operative Ltd* [2004] ZASCA 64; 2004 (6) SA 66 (SCA).

[188] Ibid para 50.

[189] *Gold Fields Limited and Others v Motley Rice LLC, In re: Nkala v Harmony Gold Mining Company Limited and Others* [2015] ZAGPJHC 62; 2015 (4) SA 299 (GJ).

[190] Steinitz (note 185 above) 1272.

[191] Max du Plessis, Glenn Penfold & Jason Brickhill *Constitutional Litigation* (2013) ch 8 'Costs'; Michael Bishop 'Costs' in S Woolman & M Bishop (eds) *Constitutional Law of South Africa* 2 ed (Revision Service 4-05) 6 and Meghan Finn 'Footing the bill of rights: *Tebeila Institute v Limpopo College of Nursing* [2015] ZACC 4' *African Legal Centre*, last accessed on 13 July 2015 from <africanlegalcentre.org/meghan-finn-footing-the-bill-of-rights-tebeila-institute-v-limpopo-college-of-nursing-2015-zacc-4/>.

[192] *Biowatch Trust v Registrar Genetic Resources and Others* [2009] ZACC 14; 2009 (6) SA 232 (CC). See also the recent *Tebeila Institute of Leadership, Education, Governance and Training v Limpopo College of Nursing and Another* [2015] ZACC 4; 2015 (4) BCLR 396 (CC).

justice but also for the benefit of the legal system at large. The court set out that, when a private party litigates against the state and the state loses, the state should pay the costs of the private party. But if the state wins, each party should bear its own costs. The private party is therefore not called on to foot the bill of the state's litigation, unless the proceedings are frivolous, vexatious, or otherwise manifestly inappropriate.

The reasons for eschewing the historical default rule include that it insulates against the chilling effect cost orders have on pursuing cases. If it is easier for private parties to litigate against the state without fearing that they will bear its costs, claims that are more meritorious may be pursued. Moreover, because the state bears the primary obligations of ensuring that the rights in the Constitution are realised, it is correct for it to shoulder more of the cost burden. This gives effect to 'the commitment to constitutionalism that must animate our whole legal order, including the approach to cost orders'.[193] It also clearly assists the work of public interest law organisations, which would otherwise have to factor in the real possibility of being burdened with the state's costs if litigation is unsuccessful.

The Attorneys Act 53 of 1979 (Attorneys Act), in s 79A, allows for a law clinic to recover costs in its own name, when it has provided legal services to clients. Because the Attorneys Act defines a law clinic as either a centre for practical legal education of law students at a university, or a law centre which is, or is controlled by, a non-profit organisation, this applies to PIL organisations. Costs of counsel, including in-house counsel, are also recoverable. Section 92 of the Legal Practice Act, which will, in due course, replace the Attorneys Act, replicates these provisions.

Finally, many public interest law organisations act as *amici curiae*. In this capacity, they put forward information and argument that bears on the matter and voice interests that have not been articulated by the parties to the litigation. The *Biowatch* principles do not apply to *amici*. Instead, because *amici* are not party to the case and so can neither win nor lose, they are generally not entitled to costs awards.[194] This approach can be criticised for deterring some organisations from litigating and failing to recognise the important guidance *amici* often provide to courts. However, if *amici* are awarded costs, this may open up the dangerous possibility that they will also have costs awarded against them. In practice *amici* interventions typically are not costly and, unlike private litigants who are party to the matter, *amici* will not face the invidious decision to either litigate or suffer ongoing violations to their rights.

---

[193] Finn (note 191 above).

[194] *Hoffmann v South African Airways* [2000] ZACC 17; 2001 (1) SA 1 (CC) para 63 [the LRC acted for the appellant; ALP was admitted as *amicus curiae*, represented by CALS].

3.7 CONCLUSION

In this chapter, we have canvassed some of the core debates animating the ethics of PIL. How should PIL organisations relate to government? To what extent is litigation confronting big business, the new front of PIL? What duties do PIL organisations bear within the sector itself, especially in respect of accommodating and advancing the interests of black and female professionals, and persons with disabilities, and how can these organisations better advance the transformation of the legal profession more broadly? How should litigation navigate tensions between what best serves an individual client and what best serves a broader cause, when these tensions arise? And to what extent can organisations attenuate the pressure that fees and funding exert on the provision of legal services?

In the chapter's first section, we explored the relationship between organisations and government, arguing that whether a more confrontational or collaborative approach is apt is conditioned by context. Litigious approaches will necessarily be adversarial, but even so, the courtroom is not the end of the line, for court orders require enforcement, which in turn requires that the state not be intransigent. In any event, litigation is but one means of public interest lawyering. While public interest organisations are frequently pitted against the state, adversarial relations are not inevitable; at times, bolstering state efforts and securing the enforcement of court orders requires cooperation, and building ongoing relationships. In any event, we argued that the state is not the only important political actor. Increasingly, public interest organisations contest the power wielded by big business. Often, this involves supporting state action or policy.

In the second section, we examined the politics of the public interest sector itself. We recognise that the public interest sector is a broad church, with different organisations structuring themselves and approaching their work in different ways. While strategic litigation alone may not be sufficient for securing large-scale social change, it can and must be a significant tool in the struggle for social justice. Strategic litigation is rarely only about litigation—it is also about movements, media, voice, and representation. But politics are at play not only in how the sector employs, and challenges, the levers of social power, but also within the sector itself, where there are difficult moral and political questions. Public interest lawyers themselves frequently occupy positions as powerful social actors. This places an imperative on PIL organisations to interrogate their own politics and positioning constantly, and to take seriously concerns of transformation and voice (particularly in terms of the difficulty of translating lived experiences into legally enforceable rights).

In the following section, we engaged with the debate on the extent to which litigation secures social change. We argued that in a South African context, the apparent disagreement between camps as to the success of PIL is often overstated. Few would conflate court victory with social change: setting precedent is but one component of the struggle for social justice. The extent of the contribution to social change is a contextual, empirical question. The chapters in Part II of this volume contribute to answering that question in their particular fields.

Next, we tracked the tension that can arise between case and cause, particularly in instances where litigation is settled. We posited that when such tension arises, the client's instructions and interests must be decisive. We identified some of the ways in which PIL may be structured to mitigate the risk of a clash between client and cause, including advising clients up-front of the broader objectives of a case and including institutional litigants that can continue with the public interest aspects of a case if individual claims are settled.

Finally, we examined fees, funding and costs, and how these exert pressure on the provision of public interest legal services. We suggested that the employment of in-house counsel is particularly beneficial in ameliorating some of these pressures.

The debates discussed in this chapter are complex, and public interest organisations sit all along the spectrum between a traditional law-firm model of representation to movement lawyering where lawyers act hand-in-glove with a social movement, and a range of approaches in between. Each approach presents diverse ethical challenges and positions the organisation differently in the political realm. These manifold differences within the South African public interest sector—of political and Political positioning, organisational structure, and strategies and tactics—nevertheless rest on a bedrock shared normative commitment to using the law as an instrument of social justice.

Chapter 4

CONSTITUTIONAL LITIGATION PROCEDURE

Georgina Jephson and Osmond Mngomezulu

4.1 INTRODUCTION

The other chapters in this part of the book provide accounts of developments in substantive areas of law that have resulted from public interest litigation (PIL). As those chapters collectively reflect, South Africa has seen PIL on a significant scale since the adoption of the Constitution, with meaningful outcomes. All of these cases, however, have to be pursued under the rules of procedure governing the South African courts. We do not attempt in this chapter to cover all aspects of constitutional litigation procedure, which are the subject of an entire book, *Constitutional Litigation*.[1] Instead, we concentrate on those features of constitutional litigation procedure that have had the greatest impact on PIL. The Constitution introduced particular changes to procedural rules that have enabled and facilitated PIL. This chapter traces those developments, focusing on jurisdiction, standing, *amici curiae*, constitutional remedies and costs.

---

[1] M du Plessis, G Penfold & J Brickhill *Constitutional Litigation* (2013).

4.2 JURISDICTION

At the commencement of the Constitution, it appeared that jurisdiction would be a significant factor in PIL, in particular the distinction between constitutional matters and other matters. Given this initial distinction, some expected that jurisdiction might have impeded some PIL that did not fall clearly within the category of 'constitutional matters'. However, not only did this not happen under the initial provisions on jurisdiction because 'constitutional matter' was broadly interpreted, but a recent constitutional amendment has now given the Constitutional Court jurisdiction even in non-constitutional matters.

Section 167 of the Constitution governs the Constitutional Court's jurisdiction. Prior to the enactment of the Constitution Seventeenth Amendment Act of 2012 (Seventeenth Amendment Act) in August 2013, the Constitutional Court's jurisdiction was limited to constitutional matters and issues connected to decisions on constitutional matters.[2] Section 167(7) broadly defines a constitutional matter as one that 'includes any issue involving the interpretation, protection and enforcement of the Constitution'.

The Seventeenth Amendment Act, however, has extended the Constitutional Court's jurisdiction to non-constitutional matters. This has made it the highest court of the Republic with regard to both constitutional and non-constitutional issues. Section 167(3) as amended provides:

> (3) The Constitutional Court—
> *(a)*   is the highest court of the Republic; and
> *(b)*   may decide—
> > (i) constitutional matters; and
> > (ii) any other matter, if the Constitutional Court grants leave to appeal on the grounds that the matter raises an arguable point of law of general public importance which ought to be considered by that Court; and
> *(c)*   makes the final decision whether a matter is within its jurisdiction.

Before this amendment came into effect, the question whether a matter raised a constitutional issue was the initial jurisdictional hurdle to clear before parties gained access to the Constitutional Court. Section 174 of the Constitution lists matters that are within the court's exclusive jurisdiction[3] and s 167(5) provides

---

[2] Prior to the enactment of the Seventeenth Amendment Act, s 167(3) provided:
    The Constitutional Court
    (a)   Is the highest court in all constitutional matters;
    (b)   may decide only constitutional matters, and issues connected with decisions on constitutional matters; and
    (c)   makes the final decision whether a matter is a constitutional matter or whether an issue is connected with a decision on a constitutional matter.

[3] Section 174(4) provides that:
    Only the constitutional Court may—
    (a)   decide disputes between organs of state in the national or provincial sphere concerning the constitutional status, powers or functions of any of those organs of state;

that the Constitutional Court must confirm any order of constitutional validity or invalidity[4] made by other courts before the order can be enforced. As the jurisprudence developed, the Constitutional Court found that a broad range of issues fell within its formerly limited 'constitutional' jurisdiction, including:

- the judicial review of the exercise of *all* public power;[5]
- the review of administrative action as defined in the Promotion of Access to Information Act 3 of 2000;[6]
- the interpretation of legislation that seeks to give effect to a fundamental right in the Constitution;[7]
- disputes relating to a right in the Bill of Rights;[8] and
- the interpretation of legislation that may extinguish a common-law right of action that gives effect to a constitutional right.[9]

The Seventeenth Amendment Act put an end to what had become a fairly insignificant jurisdictional filter for 'constitutional' matters, enabling the court to hear any matter that raises an arguable point of law that is 'of general public importance'. This expansion of jurisdiction has the potential to enhance access to justice by broadening the types of disputes that the court may adjudicate; however, it does not give the Constitutional Court unfettered jurisdiction to hear non-constitutional matters. It has jurisdiction only if three criteria are met: the matter must raise an arguable point of law, it must be of general public importance and it must be a matter that the court ought to consider.[10]

(b) decide on the constitutionality of any parliamentary or provincial Bill, but may do so only in the circumstances anticipated in section 79 or 121;

(c) decide applications envisaged in section 80 or 122;

(d) decide on the constitutionality of any amendment to the Constitution;

(e) decide that Parliament or the President has failed to fulfil a constitutional obligation; or

(f) certify a provincial constitution in terms of section 144.

[4] Section 167(5) provides:
The Constitutional Court makes the final decision whether an Act of Parliament, a provincial Act or conduct of the President is constitutional, and must confirm any order of invalidity made by the Supreme Court of Appeal, the High Court of South Africa, or a court of similar status, before that order has any force.

[5] *Pharmaceutical Manufacturers Association of South Africa and Another: In re Ex Parte President of the Republic of South Africa and Others* [2000] ZACC 1; 2000 (2) SA 674 para 51.

[6] *Bato Star Fishing (Pty) Ltd v Minister of Environmental Affairs and Others* [2004] ZACC 15; 2004 (4) SA 490 para 25.

[7] *National Education Health and Allied Workers Union v University of Cape Town and Others* [2002] ZACC 27; 2003 (3) SA 1 (CC) paras 13–17 and *National Union of Public Service and Allied Workers obo Mani and Others v National Lotteries Board* [2014] ZACC 10; 2014 (3) SA 544 (CC) para 44.

[8] *Machele and Others v Mailula and Others* [2009] ZACC 7; 2010 (2) SA 257 (CC) para 26.

[9] *Mankayi v AngloGold Ashanti Ltd* [2011] ZACC 3; 2011 (3) SA 237 (CC) para 19.

[10] See *Food and Allied Workers Union v Ngcobo NO and Another* [2013] ZACC 36; 2014 (1) SA 32 (CC) para 44 and *Dengetenge Holdings (Pty) Ltd v Southern Sphere Mining & Development Co Ltd and Others* [2013] ZACC 48; 2014 (5) SA 138 (CC) para 43.

In an early line of cases following the Seventeenth Amendment Act, the Constitutional Court avoided deciding whether a matter falls within its broader jurisdiction.[11] However, in *Paulsen*,[12] the court did address the requirements for its expanded jurisdiction. Madlanga J confirmed the criteria mentioned above in that the amended provision establishes three requirements for jurisdiction: first, the matter must raise an arguable point of law; second, the point must be of general public importance; and, third, the point must be one that ought to be considered by the court.[13] Madlanga J held that it is possible that a point of law may be arguable and of general pubic importance, but that there may still be factors that militate against the granting of leave, including the factors that are relevant to the interests of justice enquiry in constitutional matters.[14]

The first requirement is that the matter must raise an arguable point of law. This excludes points of fact, consistent with the court's earlier jurisprudence[15] on leave to appeal in constitutional matters.[16] Madlanga J had no difficulty in finding that the matter raised points of law.[17] Regarding the second part of the first requirement—that the point of law be 'arguable'—Madlanga J held that it does not suffice that the applicant advances a legal argument on the point 'which, at first blush, may appear convincing' but is 'totally unmeritorious' on closer inspection.[18] The main judgment's approach here suggests that 'arguable' will be equated with having prospects of success and that, in a matter in which several issues are raised, it will suffice for the granting of leave that some of them bear prospects of success.[19]

Regarding the second requirement, that the matter be of general public importance, Madlanga J considered foreign law, in particular Kenyan and English jurisprudence.[20] The main judgment summed up the meaning of this requirement as follows:

> In sum, for a matter to be of general public importance, it must transcend the narrow interests of the litigants and implicate the interest of a significant part of the general

---

[11] *Ferris and Another v Firstrand Bank Ltd*; 2014 (3) SA 39 (CC) paras 7–8, *Loureiro and Others v Imvula Quality Protection (Pty) Ltd* [2014] ZACC 4; 2014 (3) SA 394 (CC) paras 31–6, *Cool Ideas 1186 CC v Hubbard and Another* [2014] ZACC 16; 2014 (4) SA 474 (CC) paras 24–5, and *Dengetenge* (note 10 above) paras 43–4.

[12] *Paulsen and Another v Slip Knot Investments 777 (Pty) Ltd* [2015] ZACC 5; 2015 (3) SA 479 (CC). See discussion in M Bishop & J Brickhill 'Constitutional law' (2015) 3 *Juta's Quarterly Review* 2.2.1.

[13] *Paulsen* (note 12 above) para 16.

[14] Ibid para 17, citing Du Plessis, Penfold & Brickhill (note 1 above) 33–4.

[15] See *S v Boesak* [2000] ZACC 25; 2001 (1) SA 912 (CC) para 15 and the other cases cited in fn 31 of *Paulsen* (note 12 above).

[16] *Boesak* (note 15 above) para 20.

[17] Ibid para 20.

[18] Ibid para 21.

[19] Bishop & Brickhill (note 12 above) 2.2.1.

[20] *Boesak* (note 15 above) paras 25–6.

public. It will serve a litigant well to identify in clear language what it is that makes the point of law one of general public importance.[21] (original footnotes omitted)

Madlanga J addressed the final requirement—that the matter is one that the court 'ought to consider'—under the heading 'interests of justice' and expressly confirmed that the interests of justice is applicable, holding that that court will 'borrow from the Court's existing jurisprudence on interests of justice' when exercising its non-constitutional appellate jurisdiction.[22]

The court's jurisdiction, even when ostensibly limited to 'constitutional' matters, did not act as a substantial barrier to PIL. Following the expansion of its jurisdiction, the Constitutional Court will enjoy even more generous jurisdiction. Of course, most PIL takes place in the high courts, which have inherent jurisdiction. Nevertheless, the expansion of the court's jurisdiction does mean that jurisdiction should not be a bar to PIL matters ending up in the Constitutional Court.

4.3 STANDING

(a) Introduction

In the pre-constitutional dispensation and in terms of the common law, only persons who had a personal interest in a matter and who had been adversely affected by an alleged wrong had standing to approach a court for relief.[23] This restricted the opportunities to seek redress from the courts for groups of people, which limited access to justice. Section 38 of the Constitution has significantly broadened the common-law rules of standing. It provides:

> Anyone listed in this section has the right to approach a competent court, alleging that a right in the Bill of Rights has been infringed or threatened, and the court may grant appropriate relief, including a declaration of rights. The persons who may approach a court are—
> *(a)* anyone acting in their own interest;
> *(b)* anyone acting on behalf of another person who cannot act in their own name;
> *(c)* anyone acting as a member of, or in the interests of, a group or class of persons;
> *(d)* anyone acting in the public interest; and
> *(e)* an association acting in the interest of its members.

Accordingly, s 38 has extended the common-law notion of standing to the four additional categories listed above and, as a result, has enhanced access to justice. In *Ferreira*,[24] the Constitutional Court found that the standing provisions in s 38 of the Constitution should be given a broad interpretation in order 'to ensure that

---

[21] *Boesak* (note 15 above) para 26.

[22] Ibid para 30.

[23] Du Plessis, Penfold & Brickhill (note 1 above); C Loots 'Standing, ripeness and mootness' in S Woolman & M Bishop (eds) *Constitutional Law of South Africa* 2 ed (2004) 7-1.

[24] *Ferreira v Levin No and Others; Vryenhoek and Others v Powell NO and Others* 1996 (1) SA 984 (CC).

constitutional rights enjoy the full measure of the protection to which they are entitled'.[25]

Whilst s 38 broadens the common-law rules of standing, the common-law rules governing litigants approaching a court on the basis of own-interest standing have been preserved. Such litigants have standing only if they show that the law or the conduct sought to be challenged directly affected their rights or interests.[26]

The two categories of standing that are most relevant to constitutional litigation in South Africa are those listed in s 38*(c)* and 38*(d)* above, namely anyone acting in the interests of a group or class of persons and anyone acting in the public interest. Both of these categories can be used to ensure the realisation of a constitutional right for a group of people, but they operate differently.

(b) Section 38*(d)*: Litigation in the public interest

Litigation brought in the public interest under s 38*(d)* of the Constitution is brought by a representative in the interest of the public generally, but not necessarily in the representative's interest. For instance, a non-governmental organisation might act as representative applicant in the public interest. An order of court made in such a matter is not binding on the persons in whose interest the litigation is brought (and who are not parties to the proceedings).

Whether a person or organisation is permitted to approach a court in the public interest in terms of s 38*(d)* will depend on the facts and circumstances of each case.[27] The primary consideration is whether the party is genuinely acting in the public interest,[28] taking into account the relevant factors, including:

(a) whether there is another effective manner in which the challenge may be brought;
(b) the nature of the relief sought;
(c) whether the relief sought has general and prospective application;
(d) the range of persons potentially affected directly or indirectly by a court order;
(e) whether such persons have the opportunity to make a case before the court;[29]
(f) the degree of vulnerability of people affected;
(g) the nature of the right said to be infringed; and

---

[25] *Ferreira* (note 24 above) para 165.

[26] *Giant Concerts CC v Rinaldo Investments (Pty) Ltd and Others* [2012] ZACC 28; 2013 (3) BCLR 251 (CC) paras 41 and 43.

[27] Separate judgment of O'Regan J in *Ferreira* (note 24 above) para 234. The majority of the Constitutional Court endorsed O'Regan J's judgment in *Lawyers for Human Rights and Another v Minister of Home Affairs and Another* [2004] ZACC 12; 2004 (4) SA 125 (CC) para 17 [LRH was first applicant].

[28] *Lawyers for Human Rights* (note 27 above) para 18 and *Ferreira* (note 24 above) para 234.

[29] Separate judgment of O'Regan J in *Ferreira* (note 24 above) para 234. The majority of the Constitutional Court endorsed O'Regan J's judgment in *Lawyers for Human Rights* (note 27 above) para 17.

(h)   the consequences of the infringement of the right.[30]

The right to litigate in the public interest has been used widely in South Africa.[31] Invoking the right in s 38*(d)* of the Constitution is a powerful tool in the enforcement of rights. Although court orders in such matters do not bind persons who are not a party to the dispute, the application of such orders can impact large groups of persons.

(c)   Section 38*(c)*: Class action litigation

The class action is a procedural mechanism whereby a large number of individual claims are litigated against one or more defendants in one action.[32] The mechanism operates by allowing a class representative to institute action on behalf of a class of persons who have suffered the same alleged harm as the class representative. The class members' claims must share common issues of law or fact with the class representative's claim.[33] Accordingly, the use of the class action mechanism is appropriate only when the relief sought and the issues involved are substantially similar in respect of all members of the class.

In addition to issues of commonality amongst class members' claims, it is appropriate to invoke the right to institute a class action where there are numerous people who fall within the class. The numerosity requirement is satisfied if the class representative can show that the large number of potential class members makes it impractical to join all of them to the action.[34] This means that the identity of all of the class members is often unknown at the time of instituting the action. Accordingly, class members are not party to the action, however, they are all bound by decisions on the common issues in the action.[35] As a result of the application of *res judicata*, should a class action ultimately fail, class members will be precluded from instituting individual actions based on the same cause of action.[36] It is in this sense that the primary distinguishing feature between litigation in the public interest and class action litigation is revealed: court orders in litigation in the public interest bind only the parties.

The right to place disputes before a court as a member of or in the interests of a class in terms of s 38*(c)* has not been exercised extensively, although this is changing. The laws and procedures governing the use of the class action mecha-

---

[30] *Lawyers for Human Rights* (note 27 above) para 18.

[31] Du Plessis, Penfold & Brickhill (note 1 above) 129–30.

[32] R Mulheron *The Class Action in Common Law Legal Systems* (2004) 3. See also *Trustees for the time being of Children's Resource Centre Trust and Others v Pioneer Food (Pty) Ltd and Others* [2012] ZASCA 182; 2013 (2) SA 213 (SCA) para 16 [LRC was admitted as *amicus curiae*], where the SCA approved Mulheron's definition of a class action.

[33] Mulheron (note 32 above) 3.

[34] Ibid 115–6.

[35] Loots (note 23 above) 7-7.

[36] Ibid.

nism are still in the early stages of development. The South African Law Commission has encouraged the promulgation of legislation to govern class actions,[37] but the courts continue to develop the law of class actions. Although the courts have only recently developed rules to govern class actions, class actions have become a prominent and increasingly attractive form of PIL.[38]

The High Court and Supreme Court of Appeal (SCA) have considered class action litigation,[39] but the Constitutional Court's decision in *Mukaddam*[40] has settled some aspects of class action procedure in South Africa. Prior to *Mukaddam*, it was uncertain whether s 38*(c)* extends to non-constitutional class actions, where there is no alleged infringement of a constitutional right. Second, it was not clear whether prior certification is a requirement in our procedure. Finally, if the courts were to adopt prior certification as a requirement, there was a need for Constitutional Court authority on the test for certification.

Prior certification is a preliminary procedural step where parties seeking to institute a class action must obtain a court's permission to do so, before they can bring the action.[41] In the context of the enforcement of rights, class actions have two primary advantages: they enhance access to justice and they promote judicial economy.[42] However, class action litigation can be complex, time consuming and expensive. Further, and as has been discussed, class actions are dispositive of class members' rights without their knowledge of, or participation in, the action.[43] Prior certification provides the opportunity for a court to sanction the use of the class action mechanism before parties and courts become embroiled in matters not suited to be litigated on a class basis.[44]

Section 38 of the Constitution (set out in full in *(a)* above) governs the enforcement of rights where there is an alleged threat to or breach of a constitutional right. On its face, it only allows for constitutional class actions involving

---

[37] See generally, South African Law Commission *Report on the Recognition of Class Actions and Public Interest Actions in South African Law* (Project 88) (1998).

[38] See generally M du Plessis et al *Class Action Litigation in South Africa* (2017).

[39] See generally *Ngxuza and Others v Permanent Secretary, Department of Welfare, Eastern Cape Provincial Government and Another* 2001 (2) SA 609 (E) [the LRC acted for the applicants], *Permanent Secretary, Department of Welfare, Eastern Cape and Another v Ngxuza and Others* [2001] ZASCA 85; 2001 (4) SA 1184 (SCA) [the LRC acted for the respondents], *The Trustees for the Time Being for the Children's Resource Centre Trust and Others v Pioneer Foods (Pty) Ltd and Others, Mukaddam and Others v Pioneer Foods (Pty) Ltd and Others* [2011] ZAWCHC 102, *Children's Resource Centre Trust* (note 32 above), *Mukaddam and Others v Pioneer Food (Pty) Ltd and Others* [2012] ZASCA 183; 2013 (2) SA 254 (SCA) (*Mukaddam SCA*).

[40] *Mukaddam v Pioneer Food (Pty) Ltd and Others* [2013] ZACC 23; 2013 (5) SA 89 (CC); [LRC was admitted as *amicus curiae*] (*Mukaddam CC*).

[41] Mulheron (note 32 above) 23.

[42] Ibid 52 and 57–8.

[43] Ibid 24.

[44] Ibid.

infringements of constitutional rights, which raised the issue whether class actions could be instituted for breaches of common-law rights.

In *Mukaddam*, the Constitutional Court confirmed that prior certification is a requirement in non-constitutional class actions. The court also confirmed that the test for certification is whether it would be in the interests of justice for the class in question to be certified.[45] The court held that the factors which are relevant to the enquiry into whether it is in the interests of justice to certify a class are whether:[46]

(a)　there is an identifiable class of persons;

(b)　a cause of action is disclosed;

(c)　there are issues of fact or law which are common to the class;

(d)　a suitable representative is available;

(e)　the interests of justice so require; and

(f)　the class action is the appropriate method of proceeding with the action.[47]

The certifying court is not required to determine liability of the defendant(s). Its role is purely to decide whether the class action should proceed. Class actions are an important procedural mechanism for two reasons. First, they enhance access to justice by providing the opportunity for large 'David and Goliath' type disputes to be resolved where the inequality of arms between the parties might otherwise have precluded such cases. Second, they promote judicial economy by dispensing with the need for members of a class to bring multiple individual cases.[48] Courts should therefore not be hasty to close the door to class actions.[49] In our view, the interests of justice test for class certification is appropriately flexible, with its relatively low threshold.

One question still to be finally decided by the Constitutional Court is whether certification is required as a first step in all class actions. Jafta J suggested in *Mukaddam* that certification may not be necessary for class actions based on rights

---

[45] *Mukaddam CC* (note 40 above) paras 34–41. The court left open the question whether prior certification is a requirement in matters involving the horizontal application of the Bill of Rights.

[46] The court reasoned that it would be contrary to the unlimited right of access to justice (s 34 of the Constitution), the right to approach a court on behalf of a class (s 38*(c)* and the court's inherent power to regulate its process (s 173) if the factors were made strict requirements for certification. *Mukaddam CC* (note 40 above) paras 34–7.

[47] The list of requirements originated from the recommendations made by the South African Law Commission (note 37 above) and Wallis JA listed them as requirements for class certification in *Children's Resource Centre Trust* (note 32 above) 228B–H and 229A–E. In his judgment in *Mukaddam SCA* (note 39 above), Nugent JA joined Wallis JA's judgment and adopted the same list as requirements for certification.

[48] *Nkala and Others v Harmony Gold Mining Company Ltd and Others* [2016] ZAGPJHC 97; 2016 (5) SA 240 (GJ) [Richard Spoor Attorneys acted for the first to 30th applicants; Abrahams Kiewitz Inc acted for the 31st to 39th applicants; LRC acted for the 40th to the 52nd applicants and the TAC and Sonke Gender Justice were admitted as *amici curiae*, represented by SECTION27]. The court noted at para 34 that class actions protect the defendant from 'facing a multiplicity of actions resulting in it having to recast or regurgitate its case against each and every individual plaintiff'.

[49] As the court observed in *Mukaddam CC* (note 40 above) para 38.

in the Bill of Rights. On this issue, the view of Mhlantla AJ (as she then was) in her separate concurring judgment in *Mukkadam* is to be preferred. Mhlantla AJ took the view that prior certification should be a requirement in all class actions, regardless of the basis of the claim.[50] Prior certification ensures that only class actions that are in the interests of justice are permitted. Further, the certification process allows all potential class members to be notified of their rights in relation to the class action, affording them the opportunity to include or exclude themselves from a binding order.[51]

More recently, in *Nkala*,[52] the High Court considered an application for certification of a class action relating to the contraction of silicosis and tuberculosis as a result of working underground on the South African gold mines. In certifying the silicosis and tuberculosis classes, the court affirmed the decision in *Mukaddam*.[53] The court also found that, in the case of a class action, which is ultimately settled after a class been certified, the settlement agreement must be approved by the court in order to be valid.[54] The silicosis class action has since been settled and a hearing to consider the settlement is pending.

There are still many aspects of class action litigation which need to be tested in and adjudicated by the courts: when it may be appropriate to invoke the class action mechanism as opposed to PIL, the effect of the institution of certification proceedings on the prescription of the class members' claims, and further the practical application of the interests of justice test to determine what types of classes should be certified. As litigants increasingly invoke the right to approach courts on behalf of or in the interests of a class of persons, the laws and procedures governing the mechanism will be further developed and clarified.

4.4 *AMICI CURIAE*

The rules of all the courts of South Africa now permit the admission of *amici curiae* or 'friends of the court'.[55] This mechanism has been widely used by civil society organisations, in particular, to enable them to participate in litigation launched by other parties. The chapters in part II of this book provide rich examples of some of the most effective *amicus curiae* interventions across different areas of law and in courts at different levels. Although the most common form of *amicus curiae* intervention is in a civil matter before the High Court or in

---

[50] Ibid para 58.

[51] Jason Brickhill & Janice Bleazard 'Bill of Rights class actions' in Du Plessis (note 38 above) 71–5, taking the view that the distinction between Bill of Rights class actions and non-Bill of Rights claims is not sustainable and that certification should be required in all class actions.

[52] *Nkala* (note 48 above).

[53] Ibid para 32.

[54] Ibid para 82.

[55] The relevant rules of all the courts that provide for *amici curiae* are set out in an appendix to Du Plessis, Penfold & Brickhill (note 1 above).

an appeal before the SCA or Constitutional Court, South Africa has also seen *amici curiae* admitted in civil trials,[56] criminal matters[57] and before the lower courts[58] and specialist courts,[59] such as the Labour Court, the Equality Court and the Land Claims Court.

It goes beyond the scope of this chapter to trace the requirements and process for admission as *amicus curiae* in all the different courts. We confine ourselves to commenting on the approach in the Constitutional Court, and focus on two aspects—the rules for admission and the possibility of an *amicus curiae* introducing new evidence.

Rule 10 of the Constitutional Court Rules makes provision for the admission of interested persons as *amici curiae* to a matter before the court. Admission as an *amicus* is a two-stage process: a person or organisation seeking to be admitted as an *amicus* is required to request the consent of all other parties to the proceedings to be admitted as an *amicus*; and they must apply to the court for admission as an *amicus*.[60] The High Court,[61] being the court where most PIL is initiated, and the SCA[62] have their own rules and procedures governing the admission of interested persons as *amici curiae*.

Whether the parties to the matter consent to the admission of the *amicus curiae* does not remove the court's discretion to grant (or refuse) the person or organisation's application to be admitted as an *amicus curiae*. The parties' consent (or non-consent) to the admission of the *amicus* is a factor to be taken into account by the court in

---

[56] *Agri South Africa v Minister of Minerals and Energy* [2011] ZAGPPHC 62; 2012 (1) SA 171 (GNP) [CALS was admitted as *amicus curiae*, represented by the LRC].

[57] See J Brickhill 'The intervention of amici curiae in criminal matters: *S v Zuma* and *S v Basson* considered' (2006) 123 *SALJ* 391; T Thabane ' "Stacking the odds against the accused": Appraising the curial attitude towards amici participation in criminal matters' 2011 *SACJ* 19.

[58] *S v Madubaduba and 2 Others* (GRC) unreported case B385/08 of 9 December 2011 [OUT LGBT Wellbeing was admitted as *amicus curiae*, represented by WW].

[59] See Du Plessis, Penfold & Brickhill (note 1 above) 55.

[60] Rule 10 of the Constitutional Court Rules provides:
  (1) Subject to these rules, any person interested in any matter before the Court may, with the written consent of all the parties in the matter before the Court, given not later than the time specified in subrule (5), be admitted therein as an amicus curiae upon such terms and conditions and with such rights and privileges as may be agreed upon in writing with all the parties before the Court or as may be directed by the Chief Justice in terms of subrule (3).
  . . .
  (4) If the written consent referred to in subrule (1) has not been secured, any person who has an interest in any matter before the Court may apply to the Chief Justice to be admitted therein as an amicus curiae, and the Chief Justice may grant such application upon such terms and conditions and with such rights and privileges as he or she may determine.

[61] Rule 16A of the Uniform Rules of Court makes provision for the admission of interested persons as *amici curiae* to a matter before the High Court.

[62] Rule 16 of the Rules of the Supreme Court of Appeal, 1998 (as amended) regulates the admission of interested persons as *amici curiae* to a matter before the High Court.

deciding the application for admission as *amicus*.[63] When exercising its discretion to grant an application for admission as *amicus curiae* in terms of rule 10(4), the court will consider whether the *amicus* intends to make submissions that are relevant to the matter before it, whether the submissions will be useful to the court and whether they are different from those made by the parties already before the court.[64]

Rule 31 of the Constitutional Court Rules allows an *amicus* to present factual material that is relevant to the determination of the issues before the court, provided that it is either common cause or expert evidence. In this regard, the Constitutional Court has found that the role of an *amicus curiae* is

> to draw the attention of the Court to relevant matters of law and fact to which attention would not otherwise be drawn. In return for the privilege of participating in the proceedings without having to qualify as a party, an *amicus* has a special duty to the Court. That duty is to provide cogent and helpful submissions that assist the Court. The *amicus* must not repeat arguments already made but must raise new contentions; and generally these new contentions must be raised on the data already before the Court. Ordinarily it is inappropriate for an *amicus* to try to introduce new contentions based on fresh evidence.[65]

In *Children's Institute*,[66] the Constitutional Court considered rule 16A of the Uniform Rules of Court.[67] The issue before the court was whether, in the absence of an express provision in rule 16A, *amici* are entitled to lead new evidence in the High Court. The court held that rule 16A does indeed allow *amici* to lead new evidence when it is in the interests of justice to do so.[68] The court reasoned that *amici curiae* play a crucial role in the promotion and protection of constitutional rights. It held that, in the particular context of PIL, which often involves disputes relating to the constitutional rights of vulnerable and marginalised people, the courts (particularly the lower courts) should be slow to prevent an *amicus* from adducing new (and relevant) evidence, which will assist the court in arriving at an informed and just decision.[69] The court noted that allowing an *amicus* to admit new evidence also enhances access to the courts. It allows an interested non-party

---

[63] *Ex Parte Institute for Security Studies: In Re S v Basson* [2005] ZACC 4; 2006 (6) SA 195 (CC) paras 7–9.

[64] Rule 10(7) of the Constitutional Court Rules provides that *amici curiae* are entitled to lodge written submissions in a matter, 'provided that such written argument does not repeat any matter set forth in the argument of the other parties and raises new contentions which may be useful to the court.' *Basson* (note 63 above) para 7.

[65] *In re Certain Amicus Curiae Applications: Minister of Health and Others v Treatment Action Campaign and Others* [2002] ZACC 13; 2002 (5) SA 713 (CC) para 5 [IDASA, CLC and Cotlands Baby Clinic were the *amici curiae*, the last represented by Wits Law Clinic].

[66] *Children's Institute v Presiding Officer of the Children's Court, District of Krugersdorp and Others* [2012] ZACC 25; 2013 (2) SA 620 (CC) [LRC acted for the applicant].

[67] Rule 16A of the Uniform Rules of Court allows for the admission of *amici curiae* in High Court matters.

[68] *Children's Institute* (note 66 above) para 34.

[69] Ibid para 33.

with certain information, experience, and expertise to provide insight on important constitutional and public interest matters.[70]

The judgment and reasoning of the Constitutional Court in *Children's Institute* are to be supported. It is appropriate that courts of first instance faced with complex matters are allowed to consider new evidence from an appropriately qualified *amicus*, especially where the rights of vulnerable members of society are at issue. Allowing *amici* to admit new evidence at the High Court level enhances their role as friends of the court. It broadens the scope for their involvement in PIL and, crucially, promotes better informed judicial decisions. There are relatively few instances of *amici curiae* adducing evidence, but this practice is increasing. Courts are growing more accustomed to managing the introduction of evidence by *amici* in ways that ensure fairness to all parties.

Amici curiae are a powerful vehicle for organisations to engage in PIL that they have not initiated. This allows civil society organisations to bring additional perspectives, policy concerns, law, and even factual material to the attention of the court. The practice is widely used in South Africa and the courts are familiar with dealing with *amici curiae*, which often have a vital impact on cases.

4.5 CONSTITUTIONAL REMEDIES

The next aspect of constitutional litigation that we consider is remedies.[71] The issue of what constitutes appropriate relief in constitutional litigation is complex.[72] In instances where a dispute relates to a policy-laden or polycentric decision, the court's remedy may involve an unconstitutional violation of the separation of powers,[73] and appeal courts are frequently asked to overturn a lower court's remedy on the basis that the relief intrudes on the terrain of the executive. In *National Treasury*[74] and *International Trade Administration Commission*,[75] the Constitutional Court set aside interdicts granted by the High Court on the basis that they improperly breached the doctrine of separation of powers.

To give effect to the supremacy of the Constitution,[76] s 172(1) of the Constitution provides:

---

[70] *Children's Institute* (note 68 above) paras 25–7 and 34.

[71] See generally Du Plessis, Penfold & Brickhill (note 1 above) ch 7 'Remedies'.

[72] *Bhe and Others v Khayelitsha Magistrate and Others; Shibi v Sithole and Others* [2004] ZACC 17; 2005 (1) SA 580 (CC) [LRC and WLC acted for the applicants; LHR acted for the *amicus curiae*, the Commission for Gender Equality]. See para 101 where the Constitutional Court stated that 'perhaps the most difficult aspect of this composite case is the issue of remedy'.

[73] *Mkhize v Umvoti Municipality and* Others [2011] ZASCA 184; 2012 (1) SA 1 (SCA) para 12: The court stated that 'the dominant inquiry, . . ., is whether the chosen remedy is an unconstitutional intrusion in the domain of the legislature'.

[74] *National Treasury and Others v Opposition to Urban Tolling Alliance and Others* [2012] ZACC 18; 2012 (6) SA 223 (CC).

[75] *International Trade Administration Commission v SCAW South Africa (Pty) Ltd* [2010] ZACC 6; 2012 (4) SA 618 (CC).

[76] Section 2 of the Constitution provides:

When deciding a constitutional matter within its power, a court—

(a) must declare that any law or conduct that is inconsistent with the Constitution is invalid to the extent of its inconsistency; and

(b) may make any order that is just and equitable, including—

(i) an order limiting the retrospective effect of the declaration of invalidity; and

(ii) an order suspending the declaration of invalidity for any period and on any conditions, to allow the competent authority to correct the defect.

Section 172(1)*(a)* mandates the courts to declare law or conduct which is inconsistent with the Constitution to be invalid,[77] and s 172(1)*(b)* gives courts a discretion to grant appropriate relief, or to make an order that is just and equitable.[78]

South African courts have developed an innovative and flexible approach to remedies using the constitutional framework. Where there has been a constitutional violation, the Constitutional Court has formulated two primary principles to apply when deciding an appropriate remedy. First, the remedy should provide the relief sought by the litigants. Second, the remedy should ensure that constitutional rights are protected and enforced, thereby affording relief to all other persons in the same situation as the applicant litigants. These principles were established early in the development of our constitutional jurisprudence. Some of the key cases in which these principles have been expressed are detailed below. The court in *S v Bhulwana; S v Gwadiso*[79] noted that:

[C]entral to a consideration of the interests of justice in a particular case is that successful litigants should obtain the relief they seek. . . . In principle, too, the litigants before the Court should not be singled out for the grant of relief, but relief should be afforded to all people who are in the same situation as the litigants.

In *Fose*,[80] Ackermann J stressed that the object in remedying a violation of the Constitution should be to vindicate the Constitution and to deter further infringements. Ackermann J stated that:

[A]ppropriate relief will in essence be relief that is required to protect and enforce the Constitution. Depending on the circumstances of each particular case the relief may be a declaration of rights, an interdict, a mandamus or such other relief as may be

---

This Constitution is the supreme law of the Republic; law or conduct inconsistent with it is invalid, and the obligations imposed by it must be fulfilled.

[77] The use of the word 'must' in this provision indicates that courts have no discretion in relation to declaring law or conduct invalid because of its inconsistency with the Constitution. Du Plessis, Penfold & Brickhill (note 1 above) 109 argue that this mandatory remedy is consistent with the supremacy clause of the Constitution, which proclaims that the Constitution is the supreme law of the Republic; law or conduct inconsistent with it is invalid, and the obligations imposed by it must be fulfilled.

[78] The use of the word 'may' indicates that courts have discretion to grant appropriate relief or to make an order that is just and equitable.

[79] *S v Bhulwana; S v Gwadiso* [1995] ZACC 11; 1996 (1) SA 388 (CC) para 32.

[80] *Fose v Minister of Safety and Security* [1997] ZACC 6; 1997 (3) SA 786 (CC) [Wits Law Clinic acted for the applicant] para 19.

required to ensure that the rights enshrined in the Constitution are protected and enforced. If it is necessary to do so, the courts may even have to fashion new remedies to secure the protection and enforcement of these all-important rights.

In *Steenkamp*,[81] Moseneke DCJ (as he then was), held that:

> In each case the remedy must fit the injury. The remedy must be fair to those affected by it and yet vindicate effectively the right violated. It must be just and equitable in the light of the facts, the implicated constitutional principles, if any, and the controlling law.

South African courts have wide remedial powers to ensure that their orders grant effective relief for a breach of a constitutional right.[82] Such remedies include reading down,[83] reading in,[84] notional severance,[85] actual severance,[86] the limiting of retrospective effect of the declaration of invalidity,[87] suspension of the declaration of invalidity of the impugned provisions for a specified period,[88] an interdict,[89] and the development of the unconstitutional law in accordance with the 'spirit, purport and objects of the Bill of Rights'.[90]

In *Pheko No 2*,[91] the court remarked on the difficulties inherent in compelling recalcitrant state parties to comply with court orders. In line with their responsibil-

---

[81] *Steenkamp NO v Provincial Tender Board of the Eastern Cape* [2006] ZACC 16; 2007 (3) SA 121 (CC).

[82] *Allpay Consolidated Investment Holdings (Pty) Ltd and Others v Chief Executive Officer of the South African Social Security Agency and Others (No 2)* [2014] ZACC 12; 2014 (4) SA 179 (CC) [CCL was admitted as *amicus curiae*, represented by the LRC] para 71 (*Allpay 2*).

[83] Where a court affords a narrower meaning to a statutory provision to avoid unconstitutionality.

[84] Reading in means adding a word to the legislation after a court has concluded that the legislation is constitutionally invalid. I Currie & J de Waal *The Bill of Rights Handbook* 5 ed (2005) 204 state that reading in is predominantly used when the invalidity is caused by an omission, and it is necessary to add words to cure it of such invalidity. The Constitutional Court granted a reading in remedy in *National Coalition for Gay and Lesbian Equality and Another v Minister of Justice and Others* [1998] ZACC 15; 1999 (1) SA 6 (CC) [CALS was admitted as *amicus curiae*] para 97.

[85] That focuses on the words 'to the extent that' and rather than eliminating specific words in a provision, narrows the scope of the provision by indicating circumstances to which the provision is not applicable.

[86] Actual severance involves excising words or provisions from a statute so as so render it constitutionally compliant.

[87] Section 172(1)(*b*)(i) of the Constitution.

[88] Ibid s 172(1)(*b*)(ii); *Allpay Consolidated Investment Holdings (Pty) Ltd and Others v Chief Executive Officer of the South African Social Security Agency and Others* [2013] ZACC 42; 2014 (1) SA 604 (CC) [CCL was admitted as *amicus curiae* represented by the LRC] para 98 (*Allpay 1*).

[89] *Allpay 2* (note 82 above) para 71, *Pheko and Others v Ekurhuleni Metropolitan Municipality* [2015] ZACC 10; 2012 (2) SA 598 (CC) [SERI was admitted as *amicus curiae*] para 53 (*Pheko No 1*).

[90] Section 39(2) of the Constitution.

[91] *Pheko and Others v Ekurhuleni Metropolitan Municipality (No 2)* [2015] ZACC 10; 2015 (5) SA 600 (CC) [SERI was admitted as *amicus curiae*] para 25 (*Pheko No 2*).

ity to shape innovative remedies,[92] courts are increasingly making use of structural interdicts as a remedy to secure the protection and enforcement of constitutional rights in appropriate circumstances.[93] A structural interdict, or supervisory order, is an order where the court exercises supervisory jurisdiction over the relevant organ of state to ensure its order is properly implemented.[94] More recently, in *Minister of Home Affairs v Somali Association*,[95] the SCA emphasised that a structural interdict allows the court to be informed about the progress being made in the implementation of its order. It is no surprise that public interest litigants, who in recent years have litigated against the state more and more frequently, are increasingly asking the courts to grant structural interdicts to secure compliance with court orders. Supervisory orders are increasingly commonly granted and in increasingly sophisticated forms. Two recent developments have been the appointment by courts of third parties with supervisory roles: most notably, the Land Claims Court appointed a special master to process the claims of labour tenants in *Mwelase*,[96] and the appointment by the Constitutional Court of a committee of independent experts to evaluate the implementation of payment of social grants in *Black Sash*.[97]

Early on there were instances where the Constitutional Court and the SCA refused to make an order for a structural interdict. These courts noted that a structural interdict should not be granted unless it is necessary to do so,[98] because a structural interdict may blur the distinction between the executive and the judiciary, which in turn may affect the separation of powers.[99] While the courts

---

[92] In *Fose* (note 80 above) para 69 Ackermann J stated that 'court have a responsibility to ". . . forge new tools" and shape innovative remedies'.

[93] *Sibiya and Others v Director of Public Prosecutions, Johannesburg and Others* [2006] ZACC 22; 2005 (5) SA 315 (CC) para 64; *Nyathi v MEC for Department of Health, Gauteng and Another* [2008] ZACC 8; 2008 (5) SA 94 (CC) para 92 [Centre for Constitutional Rights was admitted as *amicus curiae*]; *Residents of Joe Slovo Community, Western Cape v Thubelisha Homes and Others* [2009] ZACC 16; 2010 (3) SA 454 (CC) [LRC acted for the applicants and Centre on Housing Rights and Evictions and CLC were admitted as *amici curiae*] para 7; *Occupiers of Portion R25 of the Farm Mooiplaats 355 JR v Golden Thread Ltd and Others* [2011] ZACC 35; 2012 (2) SA 337 (CC) [LHR acted for the applicants] para 21; *Pheko No 1* (note 89 above) para 53; *Minister of Home Affairs and Others v Somali Association of South Africa Eastern Cape (SASA EC) and Another* [2015] ZASCA 35; 2015 (1) SA 151 (CC) para 39.

[94] *Modderfontein Squatters, Greater Benoni v Modderklip Boerdery (Pty) Ltd; President of the Republic of South Africa and Others v Modderklip Boerdery (Pty) Ltd* [2005] ZACC 5; 2004 (6) SA 40 (CC) [LRC acted for the second, third and fourth *amici curiae*] para 39.

[95] *Minister of Home Affairs v Somali Association* (note 93 above) para 39.

[96] *Mwelase and Others v Director-General for the Department of Rural Development and Land Reform and Others* [2016] ZALCC 23; 2017 (4) SA 422 (LCC) [the LRC acted for the applicants].

[97] *Black Sash Trust v Minister of Social Development and Others (Freedom Under Law NPC Intervening)* 2017 ZACC 8; 2017 (3) SA 335 (CC) [CALS acted for the applicant; FUL intervened; Corruption Watch was admitted as first *amicus curiae*].

[98] *Minister of Health and Others v Treatment Action Campaign and Others (No 2)* [2002] ZACC 15; 2002 (5) SA 721 (CC) para 129 (*TAC No 2*).

[99] *Modderfontein Squatters* (note 94 above) para 39.

may have established this line early on, the recent practice has reflected a greater judicial willingness not only to grant simple structural interdicts, but also to incorporate innovative mechanisms to secure implementation of orders.

Constitutional damages are a further potential just and equitable remedy for the breach of a constitutional right.[100] The award of constitutional damages however remains an underdeveloped remedy. In *Fose*, the court held that there is no reason in principle why 'appropriate relief' should not include an award of damages,[101] but it refused to grant constitutional damages in that matter. Save for two cases, *Modderfontein Squatters*[102] and *Kate*,[103] South African courts have been reluctant to award constitutional damages.[104]

It is evident from *Fose*[105] and *Law Society of South Africa*[106] that the Constitutional Court prefers that common-law remedies and statutory remedies, if available, be used to protect and enforce the constitutional right breached. In March 2018, the Chairperson of the Life Esidimeni Arbitration, former Deputy Chief Justice Moseneke, awarded constitutional damages to claimants,[107] for the government's 'unjustifiable and reckless breach of various provisions of the Constitution'.[108] Although not a judicial decision, this arbitration award is a significant instance of an award of constitutional damages and may reflect a greater willingness to grant such a remedy.

It remains uncertain whether the courts will develop the law and broaden the circumstances under which the award of constitutional damages is an appropriate remedy for the breach of a constitutional right once all other remedies have been exhausted. However, while constitutional damages may have been rarely granted, the courts have widely used the range of remedial options available to them in

---

[100] *Minister of Police v Mboweni and Another* [2014] ZASCA 107; 2014 (6) SA 256 (SCA) para 4.

[101] *Fose* (note 80 above) para 60.

[102] *Modderfontein Squatters* (note 94 above).

[103] *MEC for the Department of Welfare v Kate* [2006] ZASCA 49; SA 478 (SCA) para 33.

[104] *Mboweni* (note 100 above) the SCA upheld an appeal against an order of the High Court granting the plaintiffs the right to claim for constitutional damages on behalf of the minor children of their deceased father. See the recent decision in *Komape and Others v Minister of Basic Education* [2018] ZALMPPHC 18 [SECTION27 acted for the plaintiffs; EE was admitted as second *amicus curiae*, represented by EELC]. The case involving a claim for constitutional damages for grief on behalf of a young boy who drowned when he fell into a pit toilet at his school. The claim for constitutional damages was dismissed but is under appeal.

[105] *Fose* (note 80 above).

[106] *Law Society of South Africa and Others v Minister for Transport and Another* [2010] ZACC 25; 2011 (1) SA 400 (CC) para 74. The court held that '[i]t seems obvious that the delictual remedy resorted to must be capable of protecting and enforcing the constitutional right breached'.

[107] The claimants comprise families of the affected mental health care users who died or survived after being removed from the Life Esidimeni facility following the termination of the contract between the government and Life Esidimeni. See the discussion of this arbitration in ch 8 of this volume: Nikki Stein 'Health Care'.

[108] Families of mental health care users affected by the *Gauteng Mental Marathon Project v National Minister of Health of the Republic of South Africa and Others* (19 March 2018) para 226.

constitutional matters. The breadth and flexibility of the remedial powers of the courts are a powerful advantage for those engaging in PIL.

4.6 COSTS

(a) Introduction

The final procedural aspect that we consider is costs.[109] The issue of legal costs is an important factor to consider when deciding whether to initiate or intervene in litigation as a public interest litigant. The possibility of an adverse costs award has major ramifications for a litigant's ability to represent the public interest in court proceedings. Alive to the potential chilling effect of adverse costs orders on individuals or organisations acting in the public interest, the Constitutional Court has developed a special costs regime to facilitate constitutional litigation.[110] Further, the Constitutional Court has recognised that the participation of public interest groups is vital to the development of the Constitutional Court's jurisprudence.[111] In *Biowatch*,[112] Sachs J stated that:

> Interventions by public interests groups have led to important decisions concerning the rights of the homeless, refugees, prisoners on death row, prisoners generally, prisoners imprisoned for civil debt and the landless. There has also been pioneering litigation brought by groups concerned with gender equality, the rights of the child, cases concerned with upholding the constitutional rights of gay men and lesbian women, and in relation to freedom of expression. (Footnote omitted).

In the pre-constitutional era, South African courts observed two general principles in respect of costs: first, that the court of first instance has judicial discretion to award costs; and second, that the unsuccessful party should generally be ordered to pay the costs of the successful party.[113] As discussed earlier in this chapter,[114] the advent of our constitutional democracy brought about the possibility of initiating litigation in the public interest. Public interest litigants (and their legal representatives) are generally non-governmental organisations or other non-profit organisations, dependant on external funding for their work. Strict adherence to the principle that the losing party must pay the winning party's legal costs would have deleterious effects on the capacity of public interest litigants to litigate in

---

[109] See generally Du Plessis, Penfold & Brickhill (note 1 above) ch 8 'Costs'.

[110] Steven Budlender, Gilbert Marcus & Nick Ferreira *Public Interest Litigation and Social Change in South Africa: Strategies, Tactics and Lessons* (2014) 147 term this a 'protective costs regime'.

[111] *Mazibuko and Others v City of Johannesburg and Others*; 2010 (4) SA 1 (CC) para 165 [CALS and LRC were admitted as *amici curiae*].

[112] *Biowatch Trust v Registrar Genetic Resources and Others* [2009] ZACC 14; 2009 (6) SA 232 (CC) [CCL, LHR and CALS were admitted as *amici curiae*] para 19.

[113] These general principles were emphasised by Lord De Villiers CJ in *Fripp v Gibbon* 1913 AD 354, 357.

[114] See section 4.3 on Standing.

defence of constitutional rights, as adverse costs orders against such litigants could result in bankruptcy.[115]

In order to prevent litigants from being deterred from bringing constitutional challenges, the second general principle of costs has been relaxed. In *Ferreira*,[116] Ackermann J stated that the general principle is subject to a large number of exceptions where the successful party may be deprived of a costs order in his or her favour, depending on the circumstances of the case, including, amongst others, the nature of the litigants and the nature of the proceedings.[117]

The special regime for costs applies in all constitutional litigation, not only PIL. Constitutional litigation can arise out of a dispute between three different categories of persons: either between a private party and the state, between private parties, or between private litigants where the state is sued for a failure to fulfil its responsibilities to regulate competing claims between private parties. The Constitutional Court has developed a flexible costs regime in constitutional litigation, depending on the parties to the litigation.

(b) Costs in disputes between private parties and the state
In the context of constitutional litigation between a private party and the state, the Constitutional Court in *Affordable Medicines* laid down the principle that, as a general rule in constitutional litigation, an unsuccessful litigant ought not to be ordered to pay costs unless the litigation is vexatious, frivolous, professionally unbecoming or in any other way abusive of the processes of the court.[118] In *Biowatch*,[119] the Constitutional Court held that the rationale for the general rule for costs in constitutional litigation between a private party and the state is three-fold:

> In the first place, it diminishes the chilling effect that adverse costs orders would have on parties seeking to assert constitutional rights . . . Secondly, constitutional litigation, whatever the outcome, might ordinarily bear not only on the interests of the particular litigants involved, but on the rights of all those in similar situations. Indeed, each constitutional case that is heard enriches the general body of constitutional jurisprudence and adds texture to what it means to be living in a constitutional democracy. Thirdly, it is the state that bears primary responsibility for ensuring that both the law and state conduct are consistent with the Constitution. If there should be a genuine, non-frivolous challenge to the constitutionality of a law or of state conduct, it is appropriate that the state should bear the costs if the challenge is good,

---

[115] Budlender, Marcus & Ferreira (note 110 above) 134; see also the *amici curiae's* submissions on the deleterious effect that negative costs orders would have on the capacity of public interest law bodies to initiate litigation in defence of constitutional rights in *Biowatch* (note 112 above) para 5.

[116] *Ferreira* (note 24 above).

[117] Ibid para 3.

[118] *Affordable Medicines Trust and Others v Minister of Health and Another* [2005] ZACC 3; 2006 (3) SA 247 (CC) para 138. See also *Biowatch* (note 112 above) paras 18 and 21.

[119] *Biowatch* (note 112 above).

but if it is not, then the losing non-state litigant should be shielded from the costs consequences of failure.[120]

The Constitutional Court in *Biowatch* cautioned that the rule on costs in constitutional litigation is not inflexible and it emphasised that there are circumstances that justify a departure from the rule.[121] For example, in *Motsepe*,[122] Ackermann J warned that the cautious approach to the award of costs in constitutional litigation between a private party and the state should not be allowed to develop into an inflexible rule which may induce litigants into believing that they are free to challenge the constitutionality of statutory provisions where there is little merit in doing so.[123]

Despite the Constitutional Court's flexible approach to costs in constitutional litigation, in *Roberts*,[124] Mavundla J made an adverse costs order against indigent litigants who sought to vindicate their constitutional rights to equality and social assistance and to challenge the constitutionality of the provisions of s 10 of the Social Assistance Act 13 of 2004. An adverse costs order was also made against the *amici curiae*, on the basis that they had 'ganged up' with the applicants against the respondents.[125] Evidently, Mavundla J misdirected himself by omitting to take account of the constitutional dimension of the case. In *Biowatch* the Constitutional Court deemed it a serious misdirection to omit to take account of the constitutional dimension of a case when deciding what costs award to make.[126] Undoubtedly, bearing in mind the established principles in respect of costs in constitutional matters, an appeal court would have overturned this adverse costs order, had an appeal been pursued. In *Tebeila*, the Constitutional Court set aside a costs order of the High Court.[127] In that matter, the High Court granted a private litigant the substantive order it sought but did not make an adverse costs order against the state respondents. The High Court therefore departed from the principle laid down in *Biowatch*, which is that in constitutional litigation between a private party and the state, if the private party is successful, it should have its costs paid by the state, while, if unsuccessful, each party should pay its own costs.[128] The Constitutional Court further stated that *Tebeila* serves as a reminder to judicial officers handing down costs orders of the general principle in constitutional litigation laid down in *Biowatch*.

---

[120] *Biowatch* (note 112 above). para 23.

[121] Ibid para 138.

[122] *Motsepe v Commissioner for Inland Revenue* [1997] ZACC 3; 1997 (2) SA 897.

[123] Ibid para 30.

[124] *Roberts and Others v Minister of Social Development and Others* (TPD) unreported case 32838/05 of 1 March 2010.

[125] Ibid para 41.

[126] *Biowatch* (note 112 above) para 42.

[127] *Tebeila Institute of Leadership Education, Governance and Training v Limpopo College of Nursing and Another* [2015] ZACC 4; 2015 (4) BCLR 396 (CC).

[128] *Biowatch* (note 112 above) para 43.

In a recent matter, the Constitutional Court itself departed from the *Biowatch* rule by upholding an award of costs against LHR.[129] The court worryingly suggested that costs might be awarded, even against a public interest organisation, simply on the basis that proceedings had been brought in a way that is 'manifestly inappropriate' (here, as an urgent application),[130] even if the litigant had not acted frivolously or vexatiously. More recently, however, the Constitutional Court has reasserted the *Biowatch* rule and clarified that the exception to it applies to frivolous and vexatious litigation.[131]

(c) Costs in disputes between private parties

Where litigation between private parties raises constitutional issues, which will affect the interests of the public,[132] the award of costs falls within the discretion of the court considering the issue.[133] The Constitutional Court refused to make an award for costs against the unsuccessful party in *Campus Law Clinic*,[134] on the basis that it had sought to raise constitutional issues in the public interest.

Constitutional litigation involving a dispute between private litigants may also arise in suits where the state is required to perform a regulating role, in the public interest, between competing private parties.[135] In constitutional litigation of this nature, the Constitutional Court has ordered the state to pay the costs of the private parties involved.[136] For example, in *Bengwenyama*,[137] the dispute before the court concerned the granting of a prospecting right by the state to a company on the land of another private party. The private party in question was a community which had been deprived of ownership of its land by racially discriminatory laws. The Constitutional Court ordered the company and a state respondent to pay the community's costs jointly and severally.[138]

Although the risk of costs had the potential to operate as a significant deterrent to PIL, the special costs regime developed in constitutional matters mitigated this

---

[129] *Lawyers for Human Rights v Minister in the Presidency* [2016] ZACC 45; 2017 (1) SA 645 (CC).

[130] Ibid para 23.

[131] *Harrielall v University of KwaZulu-Natal* [2017] ZACC 38; 2018 (1) BCLR 12 (CC).

[132] In *Barkhuizen v Napier* [2007] ZACC 5; 2007 (5) SA 323 (CC) para 90, the Constitutional Court considered the nature and importance of the constitutional issues raised in the matter and that the determination of the issues would be beneficial to all those involved in contractual relationships.

[133] *Bothma v Els and Others* [2009] ZACC 27; 2010 (2) SA 622 (CC) para 91.

[134] *Campus Law Clinic (University of KZN Durban) v Standard Bank of SA Ltd and Another* [2006] ZACC 5; 2006 (6) SA 103 (CC) para 28.

[135] *Biowatch* (note 112 above) para 28.

[136] *City of Johannesburg Metropolitan Municipality v Blue Moonlight Properties 39 (Pty) Ltd and Another* [2011] ZACC 33; 2012 (2) SA 104 (CC) [Wits Law Clinic acted for the second respondent; LHR was admitted as *amicus curiae*] para 103.

[137] *Bengwenyama Minerals (Pty) Ltd and Others v Genorah Resources (Pty) Ltd and Others* [2010] ZACC 26; 2011 (4) SA 113 (CC).

[138] Ibid para 89.

risk. A party engaging in constitutional litigation against the state, even if unsuccessful, will generally not be mulcted in costs if the litigation is not frivolous or vexatious. This is a powerful factor facilitating PIL.

4.7 CONCLUSION

The Constitution heralded major changes to South African law, not limited to the substantive developments discussed in the other chapters of this volume, but also to the procedural rules that govern constitutional litigation. In this chapter, we have focused on the changes to jurisdiction, standing, the role of *amici curiae*, remedies, and costs. In each of these areas, the law has opened up greater scope for PIL. The Constitutional Court's generous approach to what constitutes a 'constitutional matter' meant that jurisdiction did not operate as a barrier to PIL. The recent Seventeenth Amendment Act, which gave the court plenary appellate jurisdiction in all matters, means that PIL can now often be expected to end up in the Constitutional Court. The courts have developed a generous approach to standing, applying the Constitution's provisions that now enable public interest standing and class actions. Class action proceedings, under rules developed by the courts, are now introducing significant new possibilities to conduct large-scale PIL benefiting many claimants. *Amici curiae* are a common feature in cases with a public interest character. Courts are increasingly receptive to their arguments, and occasionally even to *amici curiae* introducing new evidence. In respect of remedies, the South African courts have used their broad and flexible remedial powers to develop a powerful range of remedies, including structural interdicts and constitutional damages. Finally, the *Biowatch* rule on costs protects litigants engaging in PIL from the risk of an adverse costs order in litigation against the state. All of these procedural features combine to create a legal environment that greatly facilitates PIL.

PART 2

PUBLIC INTEREST LITIGATION
IN KEY AREAS OF THE LAW

Chapter 5

MAKING SPACE FOR SOCIAL CHANGE: PRO-POOR PROPERTY RIGHTS LITIGATION IN POST-APARTHEID SOUTH AFRICA

Stuart Wilson

5.1 INTRODUCTION

It is common to locate a paradox at the heart of the law: 'We use the law though we are terrified of it, contemptuous of its Janus face'. We ask the law for 'what we need, hoping [it] will not kill us before we have finished stating our claims'.[1] The law promises emancipation, yet requires obedience. It insists on its own equal application, but can seldom be engaged except by those with the resources necessary to deploy lawyers, their expertise and the money to pay for it. It promises justice, but its institutions, processes and ideology everywhere sustain injustice, in the form of the wrongful deprivation of liberty, the infliction of state and corporate violence and the dispossession of the poor and vulnerable.

This chapter considers the efforts made to address that paradox through pro-poor property rights litigation since the end of apartheid. The paradox is at its most acute when we consider the recognition and protection of property rights. Property law—and the 'ownership model'[2] on which it is based—shapes the terms on which ordinary people access the basic resources which are essential not only to

---

[1] Eddie Bruce Jones 'Black lives and the state of distraction' *Los Angeles Review of Books* 21 September 2015, last accessed on 4 March 2016 from <https://lareviewofbooks.org/essay/black-lives-and-the-state-of-distraction>.

[2] Joseph William Singer *Entitlement: The Paradoxes of Property* (2000) 3.

their survival and material comfort, but also to the terms on which they interact socially. In practice, though, the protection of one person's property rights often means the extinction of another's. At the same time as it seeks to guarantee one of the most important conditions of freedom—access to the resources that enable the exercise of meaningful agency—law often drives the processes of dispossession that constrain or destroy individuals' capacity to act autonomously.

Nonetheless, using the law as a means of securing progressive social change remains attractive. We celebrate when the law exonerates the innocent, when it curbs the overweening state and corporate power, and when it compensates those who have been wronged. Over the past 50 years, since at least the birth of the civil rights movement in the United States, we have praised litigants, and their lawyers, as they have sought redress through the legal system—often against terrible odds—even where they have ultimately failed. And, except in perhaps the most particular of circumstances, failure has been the easiest interpretation of what has happened when litigants have pressed for broad social change through the law. The civil rights movement substantially desegregated the US in law, but failed to address the manifold social consequences of structural racism, especially insofar as those consequences mapped on to economic disadvantage.[3] In South Africa, the adoption and enforcement of socio-economic rights may have coincided with greater income inequality.[4] Across the world, even as human rights protections have been enhanced, global poverty and inequality remains overwhelming. In addition, governments and courts have curtailed civil liberties in the name of security against terrorism.

And yet, at least in South Africa, faith remains in seeking change through creating and enforcing legal rights. Our Constitutional Court is celebrated for its decisions on the rights of access to adequate housing,[5] healthcare,[6] freedom of expression,[7] children's rights,[8] and a slew of criminal procedure rights.[9] Political disputes between parliamentary factions regularly end up in court.[10] The courts

---

[3] Howard Zinn *A People's History of the United States* (1980) 466–77.

[4] Jeremy Seekings & Nicoli Natrass *Class, Race, and Inequality in South Africa* (2005) 3–4.

[5] *Government of the Republic of South Africa v Grootboom and Others* [2000] ZACC 19; 2001 (1) SA 46 (CC) [LRC was admitted as *amicus curiae*].

[6] *Minister of Health and Others v Treatment Action Campaign and Others* [2002] ZACC 15; 2002 (5) SA 721 (CC) [LRC acted for the respondents and the WLC].

[7] *Laugh It Off Promotions CC v South African Breweries International (Finance) BV t/a Sabmark International and Another* [2005] ZACC 7; 2006 (1) SA 144 (CC).

[8] *Christian Education South Africa v Minister of Education* [2000] ZACC 11; 2000 (4) SA 757 (CC).

[9] *S v Zuma* [1995] ZACC 1; 1995 (2) SA 642 (CC) and *S v Makwanyane and Another* [1995] ZACC 3; 1995 (3) SA 391 (CC) [LRC acted for the applicant and BAFO, LHR, CALS and SADPSA were admitted as *amici curiae*].

[10] *Democratic Alliance v Speaker of the National Assembly and Others* [2015] ZAWCHC 60; 2015 (4) SA 351 (WCC).

themselves are perceived as a key arena of dissent in our dominant-party democracy.[11] Social movements, such as *Abahlali baseMjondolo*, the Anti-Privatisation Forum and the Treatment Action Campaign, together with labour unions, regularly turn to the courts to advance and defend their interests—as do thousands of other individual and group litigants where they can marshal the resources necessary to do so.[12]

Why is this? Are we caught up in a fantasy? Are we profoundly mistaken about the law and its capacity to achieve social change? Or, can struggles about the law, in some non-trivial sense, actually drive social change? In this chapter I want to suggest that we are not mistaken in assigning value to law as an agent of change, but that the available theories of law's role in social change are not adequate to account for what happens when people—whether organised political groups or ordinary men and women—turn to the law and lawyers to advance their social interests.

The standard accounts of the role of law in social change either reduce law to an epiphenomenon of the balance of political and social forces, or, at best, an instrumentality through which social change is effected by people who have the specialist knowledge necessary to integrate it into an effective political strategy. The 'law as epiphenomenon' account simply misconstrues the nature of law and the role it plays in social practice. The 'law as instrumentality' account correctly assumes that law is at least partially autonomous from the power relationships to which it can be applied, but fails to ask why this is so, and what flows from law's status as a structurant of social practice.

Something beyond the standard accounts is required. In this chapter, I offer an account of law as a social structurant that shapes the spaces within which agency is possible. Law constitutes a fundamental form of social practice. It is woven into the background attitudes and constraints within which ordinary people negotiate the terms of their interactions with one another: 'Inherited legal conventions shape the very terms of citizen understanding, aspiration and interaction with others'.[13] Law also helps shape the contours of possible action. It often places 'effective inhibitions on power',[14] whether by direct coercion or by moulding an agent's perceptions of what is permissible action, and therefore what is possible. Law

---

[11] *Economic Freedom Fighters v Speaker of the National Assembly and Others; Democratic Alliance v Speaker of the National Assembly and Others* [2016] ZACC 11; 2016 (3) SA 580 (CC).

[12] Julian Brown & Stuart Wilson 'A presumed equality: State and citizen in post-apartheid South Africa' (2013) 72 *African Studies* 86 at 86–106 and Julian Brown *South Africa's Insurgent Citizens: On Dissent and the Possibility of Politics* (2015) 127–47.

[13] Michael McCann *Rights at Work: Pay Equity and the Politics of Legal Mobilisation* (1994) 6.

[14] EP Thompson *Whigs and Hunters: The Origins of the Black Act* (1975) 266. The distinction between 'property outsiders' and 'property insiders' that follows was inspired by, but differs from, the distinction drawn between property 'outlaws' and 'property alt-laws' in Eduardo Penalver & Sonia Katyal *Property Outlaws: How Squatters, Pirates, and Protesters Improve the Law* (2010).

accordingly plays an important part in defining the spaces within which agency is possible.

But law is also malleable, subject to interpretation and change, and the validity and application of particular laws can be challenged and reshaped in particular circumstances. Law, besides being a key structurant of the spaces within which agency is possible, is also a tool with which it is possible to refashion those spaces.

To illustrate this, I return to the paradox of property rights. I offer an account of the development of South African property law since the end of apartheid. Property law expresses class relationships that structure some of the most fundamental forms of social and economic inequality in present day South Africa. If property law can be reshaped, then so, in a non-trivial sense, can the class relationships which sustain ongoing inequality.

In this chapter, I argue that this is precisely what is happening in key areas of property law. Litigants, courts, the state and Parliament have embarked on a sustained process of re-imagining the nature and purposes of South African property law. The ownership model has been repeatedly challenged as a way of structuring property relationships, and groups of people traditionally denied rights in the South African property regime have been granted a degree of legal recognition. This recognition has created and expanded the spaces within which it is possible for these 'property outsiders'—those who lack existing property rights, or whose property rights are subordinated to the will of those who hold stronger property rights—to reshape the terms on which property is distributed. Through everyday practices of negotiation and challenge, property outsiders have begun to interfere with the legal processes of dispossession, which sustain inequality.

The particular areas in which this reshaping has taken place are the law applicable to unlawful occupation of land, landlord and tenant law and debtor/creditor law. In each of these areas, the processes of dispossession which give effect to the rights and expectations of 'property insiders'—owners, or those whose property rights give them a dominant position in legal relationships about property—have been limited, qualified or challenged by reference to the social needs of the property outsiders who are at risk of dispossession. Evictions that lead to homelessness have been declared generally unlawful.[15] Landlords seeking to terminate residential leases have been required to show that the termination is fair.[16] Creditors seeking to execute against defaulting debtors must now show that

---

[15] *The Occupiers, Shulana Court, 11 Hendon Road, Yeoville, Johannesburg v Steele* [2010] ZASCA 28; 2010 (9) BCLR 911 (SCA) para 16; *Occupiers, Berea v De Wet NO and Another* [2017] ZACC 18; 2017 (5) SA 346 (CC) para 57 [SERI acted for the applicants; the LRC acted for the *amicus curiae*, the Poor Flat Dwellers Association].

[16] *Maphango and Others v Aengus Lifestyle Properties (Pty) Ltd* [2012] ZACC 2; 2012 (3) SA 531 (CC) [SERI acted for the applicants and Inner City Resource Centre was admitted as *amicus curiae*].

alternatives to execution have been offered[17] and, where execution would lead to loss of the debtor's home, that execution is a proportionate response to the default.[18] These legal innovations have often been developed as limitations on a property insider's ordinary common-law rights to dispossess an outsider. It is within the spaces created by these limitations that everyday challenges to economic power can begin to effect powerful social change.

5.2 THE STANDARD ACCOUNTS

Before developing the argument set out above, it is necessary to consider the standard accounts of law and social change, and their limitations.

There are, it seems to me, two broad traditions in which to locate a theory of law and social change. The first, grounded in a Marxist analysis of law, asserts that legal rules are the super-structural epiphenomena of base economic and political interests. The enforcement of legal rules is made possible by the strength of those base interests.[19] In other words, law, in itself, is incapable of forcing social change, because it is merely reflective of the interests that exercise it. Legal rules change because the balance of political and economic forces requires it. Law has no autonomy. There is accordingly little point in seeking social change through the deployment of legal resources—for example, lawyers seeking remedies that will advantage relatively unempowered litigants—because legal victories are unenforceable without pre-existing political power.[20] And since the acquisition of political power, usually through gaining control of the state, or through revolution, is sufficient to achieve political and economic goals, there is no point in using the law at all. Law reflects rather than animates political change. To be meaningful, political struggle must take place outside the institutions of the law and state power, in direct challenge to them.

This position is normally defended by eliding the distinction between law as a general social form, and the specific role that law plays in a capitalist system of commodity exchange. Pashukanis, the foremost Soviet legal theorist, posited that law emerges out of particular relationships established during commercial exchanges that take place between owners of private property.[21] Legal ideas of freedom, equality and autonomy are therefore only meaningful insofar as they protect the freedom, equality and autonomy of the owners of private property in a system of commodity exchange. Legal concepts and relationships are therefore

---

[17] *Sebola and Another v Standard Bank of South Africa Ltd and Another* [2012] ZACC 11; 2012 (5) SA 142 (CC) [SERI was admitted as *amicus curiae*].

[18] *Jaftha v Schoeman and Others, Van Rooyen v Stoltz and Others* [2004] ZACC 25; 2005 (2) SA 140 (CC) [LRC acted for the appellants].

[19] Karl Marx *Critique of the Gotha Programme* (1938).

[20] Gerald N Rosenberg *Hollow Hope: Can Courts Bring About Social Change?* (2008).

[21] Bob Fine *Democracy and the Rule of Law: Marx's Critique of the Legal Form* (2002) 158 and Evgeny Pashukanis *Law and Marxism: A General Theory* (1987) 85.

firmly tethered to, and reflective of, economic relationships which can only be transformed, if at all, through state capture or revolution. Pashukanis himself advocated a purely 'technical' role for law, as a regulatory instrument necessary to implement the transition from market relationships to an economy based on centrally planned production and distribution.[22] This social role for law in a Soviet planned economy was perhaps imagined as the mirror image of the role Pashukanis thought it played in capitalist society—a form of regulation purely subordinate to the economic forms it was needed to implement.

More recently, Rosenberg critiqued the use of law to achieve social change by denying that court judgments can ever be effectively implemented without popular political support, and that the very act of seeking change through legal reform or litigation automatically disempowers ordinary men and women who would otherwise organise to implement strategies of collective action to bring about social change. Here, too, Rosenberg insists that law is merely reflective of motive forces of social change produced elsewhere, rather than constitutive of those forces.[23]

The problem with this approach is that it adopts too narrow a conception of what the law actually is. Few people would now accept, as Pashukanis suggested, that law serves a purely regulatory purpose. In addition to a means of regulating behaviour, law is, broadly speaking, a set of ideas which constitutes dimly perceived conceptions of the social good and which provides a mechanism for resolving disputes between differently situated groups and individuals. It is the role of law as a source of normative claims, and as a means of resolving conflict, that gives it a degree of autonomy and efficacy in bringing about social change. Rosenberg, too, seems to assume that a particular legal regulation is simply the outcome of a particular social struggle, the success of which is dependent on *not* deploying law and lawyers because these necessarily disempower grassroots community action. But this ignores the ways in which legal ideas and processes can constitute and empower political claims. If equality and freedom are not just the equality and freedom of commodity exchange, then the forms of equality and freedom that the law offers are matters of debate and contestation which cannot simply be foregone because of the particular ways in which lawyers, as a professional class, might interact negatively with social movements seeking change.

The second tradition, grounded in liberal politics, recognises this. It sees more potential for the law to act as a potentially powerful political resource when used in concert with a range of other strategies, such as community organising, civil disobedience, public advocacy and, occasionally, strategic engagement with electoral politics. While accepting that legal rules are not simply the product of the

---

[22] Fine (note 21 above) 163 and Pashukanis (note 21 above) 131.

[23] Gerald Rosenberg 'Saul Alinsky and the campaign to win the right to same-sex marriage' (2009) 42 *John Marshall Law Rev* 643.

balance of economic forces, and that they offer potentially powerful symbolic and normative advantages in a programme for change, this tradition sees the bite of legal rules as particularly weak without the backing of, say, a social movement or an organised political campaign.[24] It follows that the success of change-oriented litigation, and other forms of legal campaigning, require careful political planning and coordination, in order to ensure that symbolically powerful but practically fragile legal victories can be made 'real' by further political action.[25]

This account of the use of law in implementing social change strategies is the dominant account of law and social change in South Africa. Law becomes a tool in the hands of relatively elite political activists, and indisputably elite lawyers, who plot out carefully planned strategies for change. This approach is evident in much of the recent South African writing on law and social change. Marcus, Budlender and Ferreira seek to plot out the necessary preconditions for the exercise of a successful change-oriented litigation strategy, arguing that deploying law as an instrument of social change requires careful judgment by specialist legal activists, by reference to a preset list of a-contextual criteria.[26] Heywood argues that the South African left should reorient itself completely towards the Constitution as a 'unifying vision' for social change, which will form the basis of a coordinated and apparently centrally directed struggle for 'the full gamut of constitutionally-enshrined human rights which, as they are realised, will create a more socially-just and politically empowered society'.[27] Elsewhere, I have myself perhaps over-celebrated the role of the public interest lawyer as: 'Something of a game-player, particularly skilled in the law, but keenly aware of its limitations and the social conditions necessary for its effective deployment.'[28]

This account reduces the law to instrumentality rather than epiphenomenon. It overlooks the manifold ways in which everyday struggles about the forms and content of the law, in and of itself, trigger valuable motive forces with transformative potential. Law need not only be a tool in the hands of elite actors. It constitutes forms of social action at the grassroots. It opens, forecloses, and shapes everyday opportunities for social action. To reduce law to an instrument in the hands of political activists ignores a whole range of struggles about and within the forms and content of law at the level of everyday practice.

---

[24] Mark Heywood 'Shaping, making and breaking the law in the campaign for a national HIV/AIDS treatment plan' in Peris Jones & Kristian Stokke (eds) *Democratising Development: The Politics of Socio-Economic Rights in South Africa* (2005).

[25] Steven Budlender, Gilbert Marcus & Nick Ferreira *Public Interest Litigation in South Africa: Strategies, Tactics and Lessons* (2014).

[26] Ibid 110.

[27] Mark Heywood 'Seize power! The role of the Constitution in unifying social justice struggles in South Africa' in Vishwas Sagtar (ed) *Capitalism's Crises: Class Struggles in South Africa and the World* (2015) 270.

[28] Stuart Wilson 'Litigating housing rights in Johannesburg's inner city: 2004–2008' (2011) 27 *SAJHR* 127–151.

The argument is not that politics do not matter. It is that progressive and radical political projects have underestimated the extent to which law and legal remedies can trigger meaningful social change. No doubt, where amplified by coordinated political action, these changes can be made more powerfully, durably or effectively. But, individual litigants, without a consciously political project, can have profoundly political effects because they shape the content of legal rules. By shaping the content of legal rules, they change social practices, and by changing social practices, they affect the distribution of social power.

5.3 TOWARDS A NEW ACCOUNT

Forty years ago, in a now-famous dissent from the standard Marxist analysis, EP Thompson observed that 'the rhetoric and rules of society are something a great deal more than sham'.[29] In his path-breaking study of the implementation of the Black Act—a piece of legislation which sought to protect the property rights of a prosperous commercial elite against petty crime and civil disobedience, by rapidly and substantially enlarging the use of the death penalty—Thompson suggested that, in clothing the enforcement of their interests in the rule of law, the commercial class had to accept significant limitations on the exercise of what would otherwise have been irresistible force. Although the English propertied class of the early eighteenth century was 'a political oligarchy inventing callous and oppressive laws to serve its own interests' it cannot be concluded that 'the rule of law itself was humbug'. He went on to argue that 'the rule of law itself, the imposing of effective inhibitions upon power and the defence of the citizen from power's all-intrusive claims, seems to me to be an unqualified human good'. To overlook this 'is to throw away a whole inheritance of struggle *about* law, and within the forms of law, whose continuity can never be fractured without bringing men and women into immediate danger'.[30]

Thompson's observations about the law's ability to structure the exercise of power were made in the context of a statute that was designed to facilitate the execution of petty criminals. His point was that the law exercised a protective force. Fewer people were sentenced to death, and fewer executions were carried out, because the forms of law restrained the exercise of power.

Thompson's observations about the way in which legal forms curb the exercise of power in wicked legal systems were absorbed in South Africa under apartheid as a way of explaining the participation of lawyers and judges in the apartheid legal system. Apartheid was presented as a legally regulated and sanctioned system of social ordering that was implemented in a fair and predictable manner. Ideas of fairness, freedom and equality embedded in the law could accordingly be turned against the system to ameliorate some of its most pernicious effects in

---

[29] Thompson (note 14 above) 265.
[30] Ibid 266.

specific contexts, and, perhaps more importantly, to expose apartheid as a system of government which was anything but fair, predictable and law-governed.[31]

However, Thompson's suggestive remarks on the role of law in unjust societies can be pushed further. For Thompson, law was able to limit and direct power because, at least in modern capitalist societies, law is imbricated in every important social and economic relationship. It exists at multiple levels and is embedded in a range of different social contexts. There is no meaningful separation, for example, between 'law' and 'economics', because economics can only be studied as a set of predefined normative relationships between people, resources, capital, commodity and labour. In other words, social power relationships are 'simultaneously economic, social and moral'.[32] Law plays a vital role in structuring these relationships precisely because it is a set of normative claims about the right forms of social order that is backed up by authority.

If law structures social relationships in the way Thompson suggests it does, then it also shapes the opportunities for action available to ordinary men and women in everyday contexts. Based on Thompson's insight, I want to suggest that the power of law as an agent of social change lies in its ability to create or destroy spaces in which socially subordinate groups—the poor, racial minorities, women, sexual minorities and indigenous populations—can think and act to give effect to their plans and aspirations.

Conceiving of the law in this way requires us first to recognise the inherent limitations of using the law as a political strategy. If law creates, expands, and contracts opportunities for action, then its role in bringing about social change is at best secondary. It is the agents that act within the spaces law carves out that actually change things. However, without the space in which to act, the changes that can follow on an effective legal strategy are not themselves possible. It seems to me that this way of understanding legal strategies for change makes sense of, but places appropriate limits on, the critiques of the law's capacity to bring about change. It suggests that it is not enough to make the simple (and often irrefutable) observation that changes in the law following legislative reform or progressive court victories have not always been commensurate with changes in practice. That is true of almost all social change lawyering. Judgments and statutes do not magically produce change (although they are often no more or less effective than a range of other more traditional political strategies). At the same time, however, real social change is seldom possible without an alteration in the rules people create to govern their everyday behaviour. Accordingly, while it is correct to point out, for example, that the civil rights movement has hardly succeeded in desegregating the US, it is equally unlikely that such desegregation that has taken place would have been possible without the legal victories of the civil rights movement.

---

[31] Richard Abel *Politics by other Means: Law in the Struggle against Apartheid 1980–1994* (1995).

[32] EP Thompson *Poverty of Theory and other Essays* (1978) 289.

The civil rights struggle and its use of law have fundamentally shaped more modern challenges to racial injustice in the US, such as #BlackLivesMatter.

The second advantage of thinking about the space-creating, agency-enhancing potentials of legal strategies for social change is that it honours our common-sense intuitions about in whose hands social agency actually lies. It does not lie primarily in the hands of lawyers and judges—or even legislators—exercising their legally endowed powers. Law shapes the terms on which agents act, form relationships and adopt social practices. But it does not in itself constitute the changes in behaviour and social practice that it sometimes brings about. This observation is a particularly important antidote to the liberal tradition of social change lawyering, which tends to privilege lawyers, elite activists and their specialist capacities to 'strategise' about the law and persuade judges and legislators to adopt particular dispositions. Too much of the writing in that tradition discusses the formulation and execution of elite strategy and stops when a change in the law has been achieved. Little is said, or thought, about how the way in which lawyers and litigants frame their arguments promotes or retards the spaces in which ordinary people will subsequently act, once the law has been changed. However, if we are serious about drawing convincing links between law and social change, we cannot avoid placing this relationship at the centre of our enquiry.

A third advantage of this way of conceiving of law and social change is that it accords with powerful accounts of the conceptual foundations of legal rights. James Griffin's account of human rights helps illustrate the point. Griffin locates the philosophical justification of rights in their capacity to protect the conditions necessary for the exercise of agency.[33] Rights, in other words, create spaces in which humans can act to pursue their goals, to realise themselves and forge a path through life. If, as Griffin urges, rights protect and enhance human agency, then we cannot ignore the extent to which particular laws—through which general rights are protected, limited or realised in particular contexts—constrain or expand the spaces in which ordinary men and women think and act.

It is against this background that we should, in my view, be considering the relationship between law and social change in contemporary South Africa. Law can neither be reduced to the handmaiden of base economic and social interests nor to an instrument in the hands of the savvy activist. Law is embedded in the fabric of everyday social practices. It shapes perceptions, expectations, moral world-views, and concrete action—not just on the operatic terrain of political struggle, but in the mundane interactions that constitute everyday life. Changes in the law shape these everyday practices by helping to define the boundaries of the possible.

---

[33] James Griffin *On Human Rights* (2008) 33.

5.4 PROPERTY LAW AND SOCIAL PRACTICE

Nowhere is this account of the relationship between law and social change more obviously illustrated than in the rules and practices of property law. Property law defines the scope of access to material goods. It embodies 'how we, as a society have chosen to reward the claims of some people to finite and critical goods, and to deny the claims to the same goods by others'.[34] It not only shapes important terms of social participation; it affects the ways in which men and women exist in space. The rules of land tenure define where ordinary people may live and the terms on which they can stay there. The rules applicable to consumer credit define the extent of the monetary resources they can deploy to meet their material wants and needs. The rules of consumer credit also provide for the forfeit of homes, cars and other goods which are necessary to chart a course through everyday life.

In short, the rules of property law form part of the social fabric. They are deeply immersed in the background noise of everyday life. Often without conscious thought, they shape basic social expectations and behaviour. For that reason, the rules of property law are often thought to be static. But they are not.

We live in the grip of a pervasive 'ownership' model of property.[35] This model posits property as tangible goods or incorporeal rights over which individuals or corporations have exclusive control. The world is carved up into domains of ownership—exclusive control of a right or an object, and freedom to do with it as one wishes. We have lived with this ownership model since at least the late Roman Republic.[36] And, although we accept that an owner's complete freedom to use his property entirely as he wishes is a fiction (ownership of a shotgun does not entitle its owner to use it to kill people), social claims on ownership interests have been carved out as exceptions to a general rule: that property is something controlled, dominated, and from which other social claims are excluded in favour of the personal use and enjoyment of its owner. To be sure, an owner can enter into various contracts alienating one of the incidents of his ownership. He can lease his property to a tenant. He can encumber it as security for a debt. He can sell it. He can even lay waste to it on a whim. But these limitations on ownership rights are granted by the consent of the owner, and are usually revocable, on notice, more or less at the owner's will.

Redistributive claims, concerns about inequality, poverty and social needs have always been located outside property law. It has seldom been accepted that the structure of property rights itself is affected by concerns about inequality. Rather, it is the distribution of property rights on the ownership model that has traditionally been the concern of the state, not the nature of those property rights. Welfare states

---

[34] Laura S Underkuffler-Freund 'Property: A special right' (1996) 71 *Notre Dame L Rev* 1033 at 1046.

[35] Singer (note 2 above) 2–3.

[36] David Graeber *Debt: The First 5,000 Years* (2011) 200.

have generally aimed to enhance the capacity of individual men and women to purchase property rights on the open market through welfare payments, or to provide goods to individual men and women by establishing relationships modelled on traditional property law categories. For example, the state may provide housing by paying out a rent voucher, renting out its own public housing, or transferring ownership of land and a house to an individual. In each case, the ownership model of property rights is reinforced, or at least left unchallenged.

5.5 CONTEMPORARY STRUGGLES OVER PROPERTY RIGHTS IN SOUTH AFRICA

What if that changed? I want to argue that, at least in South Africa, some of the most basic structures of property law have undergone substantial alteration since the end of apartheid, and that these alterations have created spaces in which ordinary people started to reshape the terms on which they access land, tenure, credit and commercial urban space.

At the end of apartheid, South African property law was a substantially unreformed artefact of the law of the Province of Holland in seventeenth-century Netherlands. Legal concepts and principles dating back as far as the late Roman Republic heavily influenced the property regime inherited from seventeenth-century Holland. Apart from planning law, land administration and statutes providing for expropriation[37] and limitations on prescription,[38] this Roman-Dutch common law of property was largely free from statutory interference. This 'common law' of property is a system of largely inflexible rules which created a hierarchy of rights in property. At the top of the hierarchy sits ownership—complete control or 'dominium' over a thing, defined as the freedom to deal in one's property entirely as one wishes. Without limiting the generality of the concept of dominium, common-law writers have sought to develop the concept of ownership as a 'bundle' of rights and powers over a thing.[39] The usual list includes the right to use, enjoy the fruits of, consume, possess, dispose of, vindicate and defend the owned property.[40]

Although the common law does place some internal limitations on the rights of owners, for example through the law of nuisance (governing the circumstances under which a landowner can be interdicted from using his land to the prejudice of his neighbours) and the law of estoppel (which potentially limits an owner's right to vindicate property he has negligently represented as in fact the property of another), these limits are relatively negligible and highly specific. In particular, except to the extent that an owner chooses to limit or sell one or more of his

---

[37] Prescription Act 68 of 1969.

[38] Expropriation Act 63 of 1975.

[39] AM Honoré 'Ownership' in Anthony Gordon Guest (ed) *Oxford Essays in Jurisprudence: A Collaborative Work* (1961) 370.

[40] Francois du Bois et al (eds) *Wille's Principles of South African Law* 9 ed (2007) 470.

ownership rights, the common law does not limit ownership rights to achieve redistributive ends, or to meet perhaps urgent and pressing social needs of non-owners. So, for example, the *rei vindicatio*, which is the common-law action through which an owner recovers possession of his property from another, does not recognise the social consequences of dispossessing a holder of an owner's property as a possible reason not to permit the owner to repossess it. Potential homelessness, for example, would never have been recognised as a reason not to allow a property owner to repossess his land from a person living on it. Only the existence of a counter-veiling common-law right is sufficient to defeat an owner's vindicatory action.[41]

The common law accordingly parcels the world off into a series of (almost) absolute domains within which, in the absence of his agreement to limit his rights (for example by leasing his property or putting it up as security for a debt), an owner has exclusive rights to possess and deal in his property as he sees fit, without regard for the economic needs or well-being of others.

The common-law regime accordingly lends itself to the creation of at least two classes of person. First, there is the 'property insider'. A property insider is a holder of a recognised common-law right in property. The ultimate property insider is a common-law owner, with his virtually unfettered rights to possess and use his property as he sees fit. But property insiders are also lessees, mortgagees, holders of servitudes, usufructuaries and so on: people who hold rights against the owner of a thing because the owner has chosen to encumber his property by creating a subordinate right in it. These subordinate rights can sometimes be quite extensive. Leases can be very long. A mortgagee can have extensive rights to sell an owner's property in execution of a debt. A usufructuary has a lifetime right to use and take the fruits of the relevant property. However, these rights are all conceptualised as a 'subtraction from the dominium'[42] of the owner. In other words, subordinate common-law rights are held from the owner, are always temporary, and will revert to the owner once the conditions necessary for their termination are satisfied.

A 'property outsider' is someone who uses property without any common-law rights to do so. Although the common law acknowledges the existence of property outsiders by, for example, recognising precarious occupation,[43] and the possibility that prescription may turn an ostensibly unlawful possessor of property into an owner after 30 years,[44] it assigns them no substantive rights. The *mandament van spolie* accords thin procedural protection to a possessor—even an unlawful

---

[41] *Chetty v Naidoo* 1974 (3) SA 13 (A).

[42] *Ex Parte Geldenhuys* 1926 OPD 155.

[43] *Malan v Nabygelegen Estates* 1946 AD 562, 573.

[44] Section 6 of the Prescription Act. This is a codification of the law.

possessor—who is dispossessed of property without due process of law.[45] Before the advent of the Constitution, however, even this protection was fairly easy to oust by statute.[46] Fundamentally, a property outsider is, at best, tolerated, and at worst, subject to prompt dispossession, more or less at the will of the property owner. Property outsiders include people who once had common-law rights, but who no longer do so—for example tenants who are holding over and debtors whose loans have been called up. They are outsiders because the common law provides no protection for them from the moment their common-law rights have been terminated at the will of the owner—whether by the exercise of what has been called a landlord's 'bare power'[47] to terminate a lease on notice, or because of the consequences that follow on a debtor's default on a credit agreement. The common law affords property outsiders no positive right to acquire property, and tacitly assumes that property outsiders will have sufficient resource endowments to acquire some form of property right and become an 'insider' again.

However, in the conditions of extreme inequality that characterise the South African economy, this assumption simply cannot be made. A large proportion of the South African population is unemployed, unable to access credit and effectively locked out of urban rental land and housing markets.[48] In these circumstances, neither the common law of property itself nor the economy provides an easy route from property outsider to property insider status.

Accordingly, models of property law that address the rights and obligations of owners and holders of lesser common-law rights have begun to look increasingly anachronistic. Traditional legal analysis tends to be focused on the relationships between owners, holders of other common-law rights and, where relevant, the state. What contemporary property law writing has all but ignored is how the law deals with people who have no common-law rights at all. How to regulate the relationships between people with and without common-law property rights is one of the most contentious political debates in contemporary South Africa. Yet this debate is not a mainstream concern of property law.

It clearly should be. The study of a system of law that does not ask questions about the interests that system tends to exclude, or subordinate is, at best, incomplete and at worst, unjust. More fundamentally, however, it is important to recognise that, in the last 20 years, there have been many constitutional, statutory and jurisprudential developments that have attempted to address the needs of

---

[45] As Voet famously put it, even a thief can bring a spoliation application: see Voet 41.2.16; endorsed by the Constitutional Court in *Ngqukumba v Minister of Safety and Security* [2014] ZACC 14; 2014 (5) SA 112 (CC) para 21.

[46] Prevention of Illegal Squatting Amendment Act 42 of 1975.

[47] *Maphango* (note 16 above) para 10.

[48] Minding the gap: An analysis of the supply of and demand for low-income rental accommodation in inner city Johannesburg' *Socio-Economic Rights Institute* November 2013, last accessed on 24 April 2018 from <http://www.seri-sa.org/images/Minding_the_Gap.pdf>.

property outsiders. In doing so, these developments have not only punctured the ownership model of property law, but they have begun to carve out spaces in which the processes of dispossession that help sustain rampant economic inequality can be challenged.

It is to an outline of these developments that I now turn.

(a) The rights of unlawful occupiers

The most dramatic post-apartheid reform of property law has perhaps been the way in which s 26(3) of the Constitution and the Prevention of Illegal Eviction from and Unlawful Occupation of Land Act 19 of 1998 (the PIE Act) have sought to re-balance the relationship between landowners and unlawful occupiers.

The regime in force before the advent of the Constitution accorded virtually no rights to unlawful occupiers. In 1975, an amendment to the Prevention of Illegal Squatting Act 52 of 1951 had taken away even the most elementary common-law protection against eviction without due process of law from occupiers who had never had the landowner's consent or another legal right of occupation. The situation was not much better for those who once had the consent of the landowner or another right in law to occupy land, or whose right of occupation was unclear. In *Chetty v Naidoo*[49] the Appellate Division (as it then was) (AD) had cast the onus on defendants in eviction proceedings to prove their rights of occupation, unless the landowner had acknowledged upfront that some right of occupation had previously existed. Even then, if there was a dispute, the defendant still bore the full onus of proving the nature of the right and the fact that it had not been validly terminated.

The interaction between apartheid 'anti-squatting' legislation and the common law placed landowners in a position of overwhelming dominance. Most of the time, all the owner had to prove was his ownership and the fact of occupation by the defendant. From those two facts, it was generally presumed that, in the absence of counter-veiling evidence, an eviction order would follow. Few poor people of dubious title who faced eviction from land would have been able to afford a lawyer to challenge their eviction in court by providing that evidence (if it existed). Even those fortunate enough to get into court had almost no substantive rights. The displacement of countless poor black people—almost certainly several million people over the 46 years between 1948 and 1994—has been documented in at least two book-length studies on the subject.[50] It is, however, unlikely that we will ever be able to quantify the human cost of these evictions.

Towards the end of apartheid, there were attempts to ameliorate the worst aspects of the statutory regime. In *Komani NO v Bantu Affairs Administration*

---

[49] *Chetty v Naidoo* (note 41 above).

[50] Christina Murray & Catherine O'Regan *No Place to Rest: Forced Removals and the Law in South Africa* (1990) and Cherryl Walker & Laurine Platzky *The Surplus People: Forced Removals in South Africa* (1985).

Board, Peninsula Area,[51] the AD declared invalid an influx control measure which precluded a man from living together with his wife in a 'white' urban area. In *S v Govender*,[52] the Transvaal Supreme Court ruled that eviction in terms of s 42(2) of the Group Areas Act 36 of 1966 did not automatically follow upon conviction for the offence of living in a group area designated for another racial group without a permit. In that matter, Govender, an Indian, was convicted of residing in a white group area without a permit. Govender was sentenced to 15 days imprisonment or a fine of R50, suspended for three years on condition that she was not convicted of the same offence again. Without being asked to do so, the presiding magistrate also ordered her ejectment from her home. On appeal, Goldstone J held that an order for ejectment need not necessarily follow upon conviction for contravening s 42(2). Whether to order ejectment was a matter of wide discretion. An ejectment order should only be made after 'the fullest enquiry' involving 'many considerations', including the hardship which would follow upon ejectment, had been conducted.[53] In short, an order for ejectment may only be made after considering all the relevant circumstances.

Despite these exceptions (which attempted to blunt the force of apartheid legislation rather than the common law), for most people, dispossession, even if preceded by some legal process, was likely to have been swift, brutal and final.

Section 26(3) of the final, post-apartheid Constitution was an attempt to level the playing field and unseat landowners from their dominant position in eviction proceedings. It provides that 'no one may be evicted from their home, or have their home demolished, without an order of court made after considering all the relevant circumstances. No legislation may permit arbitrary evictions'. Its implications, though not immediately accepted by the post-apartheid courts, were far-reaching. Instead of casting the onus to resist an eviction order on the defendant, s 26(3) places a duty on a court to consider all the relevant circumstances.

At common law, only the existence and relative strengths of the parties' common-law rights were relevant, and the onus to prove the existence of a common-law right usually lay with the occupier. On its face, s 26(3) of the Constitution now accorded a court an open discretion and required the court to consider what 'circumstances' were relevant to the exercise of that discretion. On a plain reading of the section, a court has a wide discretion to measure the social impact of an eviction and decide what is fair in the circumstances.

There was predictable resistance to this generous interpretation of the way in which s 26(3) of the Constitution changed the relationship between owner and

---

[51] *Komani NO v Bantu Affairs Administration Board, Peninsula Area* 1980 (4) SA 448 (A) [LRC acted for the appellant].

[52] *S v Govender* 1986 (3) 969 (T).

[53] Ibid 971B-J.

occupier. In *Brisley v Drotsky*[54] the Supreme Court of Appeal (SCA) held that s 26(3) of the Constitution requires a court to consider only circumstances that are 'legally relevant'[55] to the exercise of its discretion. If the discretion to refuse an eviction order was not specifically conferred on a court by the common law or a statute, the Constitution itself does not authorise a court to decline to order an eviction to which a landowner would otherwise be legally entitled—s 26(3) did not allow a court to decide what was fair in the circumstances.

But, the decision in *Brisley*, while never formally overruled, has effectively been ignored by the Constitutional Court. Just two years later, a unanimous Constitutional Court held that s 26(3) of the Constitution:

> imposes new obligations on the courts concerning rights relating to property not previously recognised by the common law. It counterposes to the normal ownership rights of possession, use and occupation, a new and equally relevant right not arbitrarily to be deprived of a home . . . . The judicial function in these circumstances is not to establish a hierarchical arrangement between the different interests involved, privileging in an abstract and mechanical way the rights of ownership over the right not to be dispossessed of a home, or vice versa. Rather it is to balance out and reconcile the opposed claims in as just a manner as possible taking account of all the interests involved and the specific factors relevant in each particular case.[56]

Ultimately, however, the debate about what the direct application of s 26(3) of the Constitution might mean for unlawful occupiers has been rendered academic by the broad application that has been given to the PIE Act. The PIE Act, which came into effect in 1998, set two conditions for the eviction of unlawful occupiers. First, unlawful occupiers must be given 'written and effective notice'[57] of any proceedings for their eviction. Failure to provide effective notice vitiates eviction proceedings.[58] Second, no unlawful occupier can be evicted unless it is 'just and equitable' to do so.[59] In other words, unlawful occupiers stay where they are unless they are informed of proceedings for their eviction, and their eviction would be substantively fair.

Early decisions grappling with what 'justice and equity' meant as between owner and occupier resorted to the common law. What was fair, so some of the earlier decisions held, was that the owner be restored to exclusive possession of his property.[60] But that attempt to cling on to the common law did not last long. In a series of decisions, starting with *Grootboom* in 2000, the Constitutional Court

---

[54] *Brisley v Drotsky* [2002] ZASCA 35; 2002 (4) SA 1 (SCA).

[55] Ibid para 42.

[56] *Port Elizabeth Municipality v Various Occupiers* [2004] ZACC 7; 2005 (1) SA 217 (CC) para 23.

[57] Section 4(2) of the PIE Act.

[58] *Cape Killarney Property Investments (Pty) Ltd v Mahamba and Others* [2001] ZASCA 87; 2001 (4) SA 1222 (SCA) [LRC acted for the respondents].

[59] Sections 4(6), 4(7) and 6(1) of the PIE Act.

[60] *Betta Eiendomme (Pty) Ltd v Ekple-Epoh* 2000 (4) SA 468 (W) para 8.2.

and the SCA developed a careful, structured account of what justice and equity required in relation to both the scope and content of a court's enquiry, and the substantive result that had to be achieved in eviction proceedings.

The overriding principle, now firmly established, is that evictions of unlawful occupiers should not lead to homelessness.[61] Where it appears that an eviction might lead to homelessness, a court is required to conduct the necessary enquiries to decide whether and to what extent homelessness would result from an eviction, and to seek input from the state, usually the local authority, on what steps are to be taken to ensure that the unlawful occupiers concerned will have access to alternative accommodation if they are evicted.[62] In rare cases, a court will refuse an eviction order outright.[63] More often, though, a court will make a structured eviction order, obliging the local authority to provide accommodation to the unlawful occupiers before the date on which the unlawful occupiers may be evicted, and specifying the nature and location of the alternative accommodation to which the unlawful occupiers are to be relocated.[64]

The state's response to the new duties imposed on it has been sluggish.[65] Eviction applications have, in some cases, taken several years to finalise.[66] Depending on the size of the community involved, and the logistical difficulties with providing alternative accommodation, large communities can establish de facto rights of occupation in the years it takes to obtain an eviction order. In *Modderklip*, the unlawful occupiers were simply left where they were, the state bought the land they had occupied, and a low-cost housing development was eventually constructed on it.[67] In the *Ratanang informal settlement* case,[68] the local authority entered into a court-sanctioned 36-month lease with the owner of the property on behalf of the occupiers—effectively, if only temporarily, giving

---

[61] *PE Municipality* (note 56 above) para 28; *Shulana Court* (note 15 above) para 16 and *Mathale v Linda* [2015] ZACC 38; 2016 (2) SA 461 (CC) para 50. *Occupiers, Berea* (note 15 above).

[62] *City of Johannesburg v Changing Tides 74 (Pty) Ltd and Others* [2012] ZASCA 116; 2012 (6) SA 294 (SCA) para 40 [LRC acted for the second to 97th respondents and SERI was admitted as *amicus curiae*].

[63] *Ekurhuleni Metropolitan Municipality and Another v Various Occupiers, Eden Park Extension 5* [2013] ZASCA 162; 2014 (3) SA 23 (SCA) [LRC acted for the respondents] and *All Builders And Cleaning Services CC v Matlaila and Others* [2015] ZAGPJHC 2 [SERI acted for the first, second and third respondents].

[64] *Hlophe and Others v City of Johannesburg and Others* [2013] ZAGPJHC 98; 2013 (4) SA 212 (GSJ) [SERI acted for the applicants].

[65] *City of Johannesburg Metropolitan Municipality and Others v Hlophe and Others* [2015] ZASCA 16; 2015 (2) All SA 251 (SCA) [SERI acted for the first to 182nd respondents].

[66] Ibid.

[67] Kate Tissington 'Demolishing development at Gabon informal settlement: Public interest litigation beyond Modderklip?' (2011) 27 *SAJHR* 192–205.

[68] *De Clerq and Others v Occupiers of Plot 38 Meringspark, Klerksdorp and Others* [SERI is acting for the first respondent]. Case pending at the time of writing. Papers available at <http://www.seri-sa.org/index.php/19-litigation/case-entries/188-de-clerq-and-others-v-the-occupiers-of-plot-38-meringspark-klerksdorp-and-others-ratanang>, last accessed on 4 March 2016.

legal recognition to the informal setters' rights of occupation. In the *Joe Slovo informal settlement* case,[69] the conditions placed by the Constitutional Court on the state's right to evict and relocate the occupiers of the informal settlement proved so onerous that the eviction order could not be carried out, and was ultimately discharged.[70] The unlawful occupiers in that case are now negotiating the terms on which the Joe Slovo informal settlement will be upgraded *in situ.*

Even where the unlawful occupiers ultimately have to move, this has had significant knock-on effects for urban planning. A series of eviction cases in the Johannesburg inner city has resulted in the creation of a small, but growing, public housing stock created to accommodate unlawful occupiers evicted from buildings in the course of inner-city regeneration initiatives.[71] The terms on which that accommodation is provided have opened up a new front in unlawful occupiers' struggles to retain access to the city. The courts have directed local authorities to provide accommodation within a reasonable distance of the land from which the unlawful occupiers have been removed.[72] They have also directed that family accommodation be provided and struck down restrictive rules and conditions placed on residence in the housing stock the state provides.[73]

Restrictions have also been placed on the legal steps private owners and the state can take to prevent the urban poor from moving onto vacant land. The courts have rejected attempts to obtain land occupation interdicts which permit eviction without a court order where unlawful occupiers have moved onto land for a relatively short period—often because they have been evicted from elsewhere.[74] The Constitutional Court, in particular, has disapproved of coercive responses to new land occupations, emphasising the need to engage with homeless people moving on to land for the first time, and to deal with their needs on a case-by-case basis.[75]

---

[69] *Residents of Joe Slovo Community, Western Cape v Thubelisha Homes and Others* [2009] ZACC 16; 2010 (3) SA 454 (CC) [LRC acted for the applicants represented by the Task Team; the WLC acted for the *amici curiae*, the COHRE and CLC].

[70] *Residents of Joe Slovo Community, Western Cape v Thebelisha Homes and Others* [2011] ZACC 8; 2011 (7) BCLR 723 (CC) [LRC acted for the applicants represented by the Task Team and the WLC acted for the *amici curiae*, the COHRE and CLC].

[71] Wilson (note 28 above) 127–51.

[72] *City of Johannesburg Metropolitan Municipality v Blue Moonlight Properties 39 (Pty) Ltd and Another* [2011] ZACC 33; 2012 (2) SA 104 (CC) para 104 [Wits Law Clinic acted for the second respondent and LHR was admitted as *amicus curiae*].

[73] *Dladla and Others v City of Johannesburg* [2017] ZACC 42 [SERI acted for the applicants; CALS was admitted as first *amicus curiae*, represented by the LRC and the CCL was admitted as second *amicus curiae*].

[74] *Zulu and Others v eThekwini Municipality and Others* [2014] ZACC 17; 2014 (4) SA 590 (CC) [LRC acted for the appellants and SERI acted for the *amicus curiae*, Abahlali baseMjondolo Movement South Africa].

[75] *Grootboom* (note 5 above).

In practice, this new scheme for the adjudication of eviction cases, the execution of eviction orders and the management of unlawful land occupation has opened up a fairly wide space within which unlawful occupiers can shape the terms of their access to land. The apartheid legal regime, buttressed by the overwhelming power that common-law eviction proceedings assigned to land-owners, produced a vast number of eviction orders, which were granted and executed irrespective of the social consequences of suddenly making large numbers of very poor people homeless. The post-apartheid constitutional and statutory scheme for the management of eviction proceedings has instead sought to create a space in which the competing social claims of landowners and unlawful occupiers can be balanced and reconciled, and in which poor people can negotiate the terms of their residence in urban areas. This has led to resettlement of significant tracts of urban land by poor people, and changes in government policy and practice, increasing the availability of public rental housing stock, and the frequency with which informal settlement upgrades take place.

(b) The rights of residential tenants

The imbalance of power between landlords and tenants is another example of the way in which the common law of property creates insiders and outsiders. At common law, a landlord is entitled to terminate a residential lease on notice 'with no let or hindrance'.[76] This 'bare power of termination'[77] is an incident of several features of a lease (whether residential or not) that the common-law writers have identified. Unless otherwise specified in the contract, a lease is generally at the will of the landlord, inherently temporary in nature, and terminable on reasonable notice whatever the landlord's reasons for doing so.[78] In other words, unless otherwise agreed, a tenant's right to occupy his or her home can be terminated at the will of the landlord for any purpose whatsoever. The scarcity of residential accommodation, especially in urban areas, creates an inequality of bargaining power that makes it virtually impossible for a tenant to negotiate extensive lease-based protections for himself.

Common-law leases are therefore remarkably easy to form and terminate. This makes some commercial sense where one assumes a plentiful supply of property, reasonable rental prices, and tenants who can pay those prices—in other words, where market conditions are near-perfect. The trouble is that housing markets, especially urban housing markets, are, across the world, often grossly unequal. Left to operate on its own, the residential housing market would exclude a sizeable portion of those in need of accommodation and create abnormally high rents and profits for landlords.

---

[76] *Maphango* (note 16 above) para 29.

[77] Ibid.

[78] Johannes Voet *The Selective Voet, being the Commentary on the Pandects* (1880) 3 413.

These imperfections in residential housing markets have long been recognised. Statutory rent control regimes are still a common feature of most advanced urban economies. In South Africa, the Rents Act 13 of 1920 (Rents Act) provided that a lessee could not be evicted from residential property unless he committed a breach of the lease, caused damage to property or a nuisance to his neighbours, or the landlord needed the rented property for his own personal occupation or the occupation of an employee.[79] The Rents Act also provided for statutory rent boards—which had wide-ranging powers—to fix what it considered to be reasonable rents, and even to reduce rents otherwise agreed upon between landlord and tenant.[80]

These extensive powers to interfere with the landlord–tenant relationship endured, with some amendment, from 1920 until rent control was finally abolished in 1999.[81] At that point, the Rent Control Act 80 of 1976 (the successor statute to the Rents Act), was repealed in its entirety, and replaced with the Rental Housing Act 50 of 1999 (Rental Housing Act). The Rental Housing Act did not replicate specific prohibitions on the right to terminate a residential lease. Nor did it preserve the explicit power of rent boards to reduce rent on application by a tenant. However, the Rental Housing Act does impose one general limitation on the landlord's rights to terminate a residential lease: a lease cannot be terminated on 'grounds which constitute an unfair practice'.[82] An unfair practice is behaviour which is proscribed by the Minister of Housing, or which is in breach of the Act itself.[83] Any landlord or tenant can complain of an unfair practice to a Rental Housing Tribunal, which is empowered to make any order to discontinue an unfair practice by providing a just and fair remedy.[84] This power expressly includes the power to determine rents between the parties.[85]

While the state's powers to interfere with the landlord and tenant relationship have been significantly watered down in the Rental Housing Act, the core power to refuse to allow the landlord to terminate a lease and to set exorbitant rents remains in the hands of a statutory tribunal. That the Rental Housing Tribunal has these powers was finally confirmed by the Constitutional Court in *Maphango v Aengus Lifestyle Properties*.[86] In that case, a property developer purchased a rundown building in the centre of Johannesburg. The tenants in the building at the time were paying rent in terms of leases that guaranteed them significantly lower rents than

---

[79] WE Cooper *The Rent Control Act: A Supplement to the South African Law of Landlord and Tenant* (1977) 2.

[80] Sections 2 and 6 of the Rents Act.

[81] *The Law of South Africa* (2 ed) 3 para 163.

[82] Section 4(5)*(c)* of the Rental Housing Act.

[83] Section 1.

[84] Section 13(4)*(c)*.

[85] Section 13(5).

[86] *Maphango* (note 16 above).

the property developer could secure on the open market. The property developer therefore offered the tenants a choice: their leases would be terminated, and they would have to vacate, or they could elect to pay up to twice their current rent to stay in the property. Not surprisingly, the tenants rejected both options and lodged a complaint with the Rental Housing Tribunal about what they said was an unfair rent. In order to avoid the Tribunal's jurisdiction, the property developer brought an application for eviction in the High Court. The eviction order was granted in the High Court and upheld in the SCA.[87] Both courts held that they had no power to interfere with a commercial decision to terminate a lease. The SCA also held that, even if it did have such a power, it saw nothing wrong with a property owner terminating a tenant's lease in order to secure a higher rent.[88]

The Constitutional Court disagreed. It held that the Rental Housing Act 'super-imposes its unfair practice regime on the contractual arrangement that the individual parties negotiate'.[89] This superimposition means that the Tribunal, and presumably courts as well in appropriate cases, have the power to disallow the termination of a residential lease, and to set rents between the parties.

Because Rental Housing Tribunals are easily accessible, without legal representation, and without any of the fees and formalities imposed on litigants by courts, they constitute a vital space in which tenants can shape the terms of their relationships with landlords. Rental Housing Tribunals have acted as a source of equitable rules for the landlord and tenant relationship, and as an informal dispute resolution space within which landlords and tenants meet on more or less equal terms. One of the most important contributions to the law of landlord and tenant to emanate from the Rental Housing Tribunals is the decision of the Gauteng Rental Housing Tribunal to outlaw the practice of landlords levying service charges on tenants' consumption of electricity and water in residential buildings.[90]

(c) Debtors

Moneylenders have long been able to rely on courts to recover debts, and interest owing on them, promptly, and to take the property of debtors who cannot afford to pay. Most moneylending agreements contain some sort of acceleration clause, which entitles the moneylender, when the debtor defaults, even if only on a single repayment, to recover the entire amount lent, plus interest, or the equivalent value in the debtor's property. The South African common law has long favoured the rights of moneylenders, and the courts have ruthlessly enforced the strict terms of

---

[87] *Maphango (Mgidlana) and Others v Aengus Lifestyle Properties (Pty) Ltd* [2011] ZASCA 100; [2011] 3 All SA 535 (SCA).

[88] Ibid para 34.

[89] *Maphango* (note 16 above) para 51.

[90] *Young Ming Shan CC v Chagan NO and Others* [2015] ZAGPJHC 25; 2015 (3) SA 227 (GJ) [SERI acted for the second respondent].

credit agreements, with few exceptions.[91] Execution of a debt against a person's property was long seen as a purely administrative exercise, in which the moneylender had to show little more than the debtor's default and the right to accelerate.[92]

However, post-apartheid legal reform has intervened extensively in the relationship between debtor and creditor. The general effect of these interventions has been to make the debt recovery process more disputatious, and to provide debtors with a wider range of options to stave off acceleration of their debts, and execution against their property. The two main sources of these interventions are the National Credit Act 34 of 2005 (National Credit Act), and a line of cases in which the courts have imported a constitutional principle of proportionality into the enquiry to be conducted before authorising a creditor to execute an unpaid debt against a debtor's home.

Some of the most extensive interferences with creditors' rights to call up a debt are set out in s 129 of the National Credit Act. Section 129 specifies a range of procedures that a moneylender[93] must follow in order to enforce repayment of a debt, or execution against property on which a debt is secured, through the courts. Section 129(1) of the National Credit Act requires a moneylender to draw a debtor's[94] attention to a range of options, such as debt counselling, restructuring, or alternative dispute resolution, to which a debtor may divert a moneylender seeking execution against his property, or a judgment on the debt. Section 129(3) of the Act provides a debtor with an even more drastic remedy: the right to reinstate a credit agreement simply by repaying all outstanding arrears, together with the costs the moneylender incurred trying to collect the debt up to the point the arrears were repaid. At common law, only the repayment of the entire debt plus interest could stay enforcement proceedings. But s 129(3) of the National Credit Act allows the debtor to reinstate the moneylending agreement merely by bringing his repayments up to date.[95]

Arguably, greater interferences in a moneylender's rights spring from the principle of constitutional proportionality, first developed and applied by the Constitutional Court in *Jaftha v Schoeman*.[96] In that case, the Constitutional Court decided that the execution of a debt against a person's home constitutes an infringement of the right of access to adequate housing in s 26(1) of the Constitu-

---

[91] See the Usury Act 73 of 1968.

[92] *Ledlie v ERF 2235 Somerset West (Pty) Ltd* 1992 (4) SA 600 (C).

[93] In the Act's terminology a 'credit provider'.

[94] The Act defines debtors as 'consumers' of credit. The steps required to draw the attention of a 'reasonable' consumer to these options are set out in *Sebola* (note 18 above) and *Kubyana v Standard Bank of South Africa Ltd* 2014 (3) SA 56 (CC) [SERI was admitted as *amicus curiae*].

[95] *Nkata v Firstrand Bank Limited and Others* [2016] ZACC 12; 2016 (4) SA 257 (CC) [SERI was admitted as *amicus curiae*].

[96] *Jaftha* (note 18 above).

tion. Although the Constitution might permit an infringement in terms of its limitations clause,[97] the infringement always has to be justified. An infringement of the right of access to adequate housing to recover a debt secured against a home is only justified when it is 'proportional'. In other words, the moneylender taking and selling a debtor's house to recover the debt must be a proportionate response to the debtor's default. This principle is generally parsed to mean that alternatives to execution, if they exist, must be explored before the sale of a debtor's home is authorised, and that execution will not be permitted for 'trifling' or relatively small arrears.[98]

Taken together, s 129 of the National Credit Act and the constitutional principle of proportionality open up important spaces in which debtors can challenge unfair lending practices and even blunt a moneylender's rights to execute against their homes where—a debtor's failure to repay notwithstanding—it would be disproportionate to do so. Section 129 and the proportionality principle differ from other ways of monitoring corporate compliance with the law because, unlike 'watchdog' agencies or media shaming, they link a moneylender's right to recover or execute on a debt in every case to the debtor's option to seek alternative dispute resolution, to make good on his arrears, and to the overall fairness of executing against a person's home.

5.6 CONCLUSION

Law does not, in itself, produce or constitute social change. Its role is more complex than that. It shapes the spaces in which ordinary people act. It does so not only by regulating the circumstances under which one person may coerce another, but also by shaping what differently situated social actors consider to be the courses of action open to them, and being one constituent, through its ideological power, of the normative limits of social action.

Changes in the law adjust the boundaries of human agency. They therefore, albeit indirectly, lead to social change, whether or not anyone immediately changes his or her behaviour. It is enough that spaces of possible action are opened up or closed down. Over time, new spaces will be occupied and acted in, and old spaces will be abandoned, either as a result of coercion, or voluntarily, as individuals and groups adjust their behaviour in light of what the law says about the boundaries of socially acceptable action.

Property law is one of the most important sources from which spaces of social action are constructed and reshaped. It sets the terms on which people may access and exploit material goods. Through reforms to property law, South Africa has embarked on a fundamental reimagining of those terms. Unlawful occupiers of

---

[97] Section 36 of the Constitution.
[98] *Jaftha* (note 18 above) para 57. See also *Gundwana v Steko Development and Others* 2011 (3) SA 608 (CC) [LRC acted for the *amicus curiae*, National Consumer Forum].

land have gained temporary, limited and circumscribed rights to remain where they have no common-law entitlement to be. Tenants can insist that their landlords act fairly, even where their leases specify otherwise; and can hold out against a landlord who wants to repossess his property by arguing that the landlord has acted unfairly. Debtors who have failed to repay their debts can stave off debt recovery, restructure their obligations, and even prevent some forms of execution altogether, even though they have borrowed money that they have not given back.

These important amendments to South African property law are reshaping social and economic relationships across a wide range of geographical and social contexts. They are driving social change. But the change that is being wrought is subtle, complex, contingent and takes time to reveal itself. It is also taking place against the background of deeply entrenched social and political norms that are fundamentally hostile to it. Changes in legal rules do not automatically lead to revision of the moral and political value systems in which the law is embedded. Still less do they have any immediate impact on the structures of economic power to which they are addressed, or may inadvertently alter over time. It is only when legal rules are acted upon by the state, or, more importantly, by ordinary men and women who make millions of decisions every day about the way in which they relate, for example, to banks, landlords, or landowners, that the content of a legal rule passes into the social world.

The mechanism through which this occurs is the way in which changes in legal rules influence individual and group behaviour. But this influence is seldom straightforward. For example, an unlawful occupier may simply be unaware that he cannot lawfully be evicted if his eviction would lead to homelessness. If he does know this, he may or may not act on that knowledge by resisting his eviction. Many unlawful occupiers do not act on that information because they lack the legal resources necessary to contest a court application; because they are afraid of violent reprisal by the landowner or the state; because they are isolated, and unable to draw on the solidarity of a broader community in resisting eviction; or because they genuinely believe that the landowner ought to be able to remove them from his property, even if that means they will be left homeless, and the law affords them the right to remain in occupation, at least until alternative accommodation becomes available to them. Other unlawful occupiers may use the knowledge of the content of legal rules, not to resist eviction, but enhance their bargaining position in a negotiation for more time, or for some other benefit, such as money, to be given to them before they vacate.

Conversely, the principle that evictions should not lead to homelessness may drive, and has often driven, widespread community-based legal resistance to eviction. If every community under threat of homelessness by eviction responded in this way, there can be little doubt that property relations in South Africa would be transformed overnight. Not every community responds to a threat of eviction in this way. However, to detect and begin to describe a relationship between law and social change, it is enough that some communities do respond in this way, and that the law creates, expands or helps protect the space in which this is possible.

All of this is to underscore the common sense, but often overlooked, notion that the intent of a law does not translate neatly into practice, and why a theory for the relationship between law and social change cannot hope to draw a straight line between the intent, or even the plain language, of a legal rule and its social impact. Laws shape the conditions under which people act, but they do not determine that action. That is why it is best, as this chapter argues, to theorise the relationship between law and social change as the creation or destruction of spaces in which ordinary men and women can act for themselves. Property rights litigation in South Africa is doing just that.

Chapter 6

GENDER AND PUBLIC INTEREST LITIGATION IN POST-APARTHEID SOUTH AFRICA: HAVE 'SYSTEMATIC MOTIFS OF DISCRIMINATION' BEEN ADDRESSED?

Bonita Meyersfeld and Nomonde Nyembe

6.1 INTRODUCTION

During apartheid, many parts of the women's movement in South Africa assumed a homogenous woman and a homogenous woman's experience. Because many women's rights activists were white and middle-class, a white and middle-class outlook informed their advocacy and interventions. While not universally true of all white-led women's rights organisations, the failure by some to address the intersectionality between race, gender and poverty has contributed to the current status quo where there are more advances for white women, while women of colour continued—and continue—to experience gender-*and* race-based discrimination.

The essentialist nature of women's rights activism, however, began to shift as the political climate of apartheid began to change. In the 1990s, various women's organisations saw the need for democratic mechanisms to remedy 'patterns of discrimination' while others called for an interpretation of human rights and democracy that 'encompass[es] women's diverse experiences'.[1]

Following various interventions by women's groups, gender equality and women's rights were incorporated into the drafting of the Constitution, which was enacted in 1996. The Constitution advances the cause of gender equality in three overarching ways: s 1 provides that South Africa is a democracy founded on non-sexism; s 9(2) prohibits unfair discrimination on the grounds of both sex and gender; and ss 181(1)*(d)* and 187 establish the Commission for Gender Equality, tasked with ensuring equality for women. In addition to prohibiting unfair discrimination based on gender and sex, the Constitution acknowledges that discrimination may be committed on more than one ground, thus incorporating the intersectional nature of discrimination.

In this chapter, we analyse the extent to which civil society organisations have used the courts and constitutional aspirations to achieve gender equality, not only in form, but also in substance, with a particular focus on intersectionality. We therefore question whether the 'systematic motifs' of discrimination have been addressed.[2] We further examine the areas of equality, gender-based violence (GBV), labour in the form of sex-work, caregiving, culture and religion, and domestic partnerships.

Overall, it is clear that women's rights organisations and institutions often bring an intersectional analysis to their interventions. However, the Constitutional Court has seldom demonstrated sensitivity to, or an understanding of, the multiplicity of ways in which black women in particular experience discrimination in post-apartheid South Africa. However, the *minority* judgments often take gender-based and intersectional *amici* arguments on this basis into account, which arguments are on occasion later reflected in legislative reform. In this way, an *amicus* intervention may have an impact that extends beyond the four corners of the judgment itself.

6.2 EQUALITY

Post-apartheid society has not prioritised or condemned gender-based discrimination as much as racial discrimination. This has resulted in deep patterns of disadvantage, particularly for black women, who experience overwhelming hard-

---

[1] Sheila Meintjes 'The women's struggle for equality during South Africa's transition to democracy' (1996) 30 *Transformation* 47 at 58 and Women's National Coalition *Women's Charter for Effective Equality: Working Document Adopted in Principle at the National Convention Convened by the Women's National Coalition, 25–27 February, 1994* (1994).

[2] *Brink v Kitshoff* [1996] ZACC 9; 1996 (4) SA 197 (CC) para 41 [CALS was admitted as *amicus curiae*].

ship as a result of race, sex and economic status.[3] Has post-apartheid jurisprudence addressed these entrenched patterns of inequality? In addition to considering jurisprudence, we also look at social, legislative and policy advances. We conclude this section with a brief assessment of the pursuit of gender equality as an overarching concept through the courts and state.

(a) Jurisprudence

Cases brought to the courts alleging unfair discrimination based on gender have laid the foundation for the courts' jurisprudence on equality generally.[4] These cases reveal instances where the courts demonstrate cognisance of intersectional discrimination.

The first case to appear before the Constitutional Court regarding gender discrimination was *Brink*.[5] This case concerned s 44 of the Insurance Act 27 of 1943, which deprived married women, in certain circumstances, of some or all of the benefits of life insurance policies ceded to them by their husbands. The court held that this section unfairly and unjustifiably discriminated against married women, on the basis of two intersecting characteristics, namely, sex and marital status, taking into account South Africa's history of 'the most visible and most vicious pattern of discrimination'.[6]

The Centre for Applied Legal Studies (CALS), a public interest litigation (PIL) and research entity at the University of the Witwatersrand, intervened as *amicus*, arguing that 'the context of an alleged rights violation . . . should be understood to include these intersecting social and economic inequalities—the particular complexity of women's lives'.[7] The court noted that this intervention 'presented detailed and helpful argument as to the manner in which s 8 [the right to equality under the interim Constitution] should be interpreted'.[8]

O'Regan J, writing for the majority, stated that South Africa's history of systematic discrimination should be used to interpret the equality clause and that discrimination was based not only on race but other 'systematic motifs of discrimination',[9] which included the intersectional discrimination with regard to marital status, sex and race.[10] She noted further that 'these patterns of disadvan-

---

[3] Ibid para 44.

[4] Section 9(2) of the Constitution and generally *Minister of Justice v Van Heerden* [2004] ZACC 3; 2004 (6) SA 121 (CC) para 30 and *President of the Republic of South Africa v Hugo* [1997] ZACC 4; 1997 (4) SA 1 (CC) para 41.

[5] *Brink* (note 2 above).

[6] Ibid para 41.

[7] Catherine Albertyn 'Gendered transformation in South African jurisprudence: Poor women and the Constitutional Court' (2011) 22 *Stell LR* 591 at 600.

[8] *Brink* (note 2 above) para 32.

[9] Ibid paras 41–51.

[10] Ibid para 44.

tage are particularly acute in the case of black women, as race and gender discrimination overlap'.[11]

The decision in *Harksen*[12] is often lauded for the unfair discrimination test developed in Goldstone J's judgment.[13] While the majority of the court ultimately found that unfair discrimination had not occurred,[14] the minority, in a judgment penned by O'Regan J, found that there had been unfair discrimination.[15] O'Regan J noted that discrimination on the basis of marital status is often tied to gender and 'an assumption that women were primarily responsible for the maintenance of a household, and the rearing of children, while men's responsibilities lay outside the household'.[16] Sachs J, in his own dissent, said that the impugned provisions reinforce stereotypical and archaic notions of marriage, which were demeaning to spouses in the constitutional era.[17]

The *amicus* intervention in this case was not by a typical social justice public interest law organisation. Rather, the Council of South African Banks lodged an intervention that the Court described as 'most helpful'.[18] It is arguable that this intervention, which submitted that the provisions in question were *not* unconstitutional, did influence the majority decision.[19]

This analysis leads to two important conclusions regarding the Constitutional Court's approach to gender and equality. The first is that, at this stage of the Constitutional Court's jurisprudence, an *amicus* intervention was seminal in leading the court to specific conclusions, one way or another. The second is that in cases where there was no social justice intervention, there was a gap: such an *amicus* may have influenced an alternative finding. This underscores the importance of both *the amicus* in a case and *the type* of *amicus* intervention.

(b) Social, legislative and political change

Between 1994 and 2013, a number of Acts were passed with the aim of ensuring gender equality, including the Promotion of Equality and Prevention of Unfair Discrimination Act 4 of 2000 and the Employment Equity Act 55 of 1998.[20] In

---

[11] Ibid.

[12] *Harksen v Lane NO and Others* [1997] ZACC 12; 1998 (1) SA 300 (CC).

[13] Ibid para 54(*b*). The SCA in *Minister of Basic Education v Basic Education for All* [2015] ZASCA 198; 2016 (4) SA 63 (SCA) para 47 [SECTION27 acted for the first to 23rd respondents and the SAHRC acted for the 24th respondent] applied this enquiry.

[14] *Brink* (note 2 above) para 68.

[15] Ibid para 102.

[16] *Harksen* (note 12 above) para 95.

[17] Ibid paras 119 and 121.

[18] Ibid para 3.

[19] Ibid para 100.

[20] Others include the Commission for Gender Equality Act 39 of 1996 and the Traditional Leadership and Governance Framework Act 41 of 2003.

2014, women's organisations, collectively and individually, engaged in policy advocacy around the Women Empowerment and Gender Equality Bill (B50-2013) (WEGE Bill).[21] The WEGE Bill was designed to 'establish a legislative framework for the empowerment of women'.[22] The idea of the WEGE Bill was welcomed by many women's organisations, but the means by which it hoped to achieve its objectives were not.[23] While the WEGE Bill did speak to the elimination of gender discrimination and empowerment, it did not address the immediate effects of gender discrimination. In particular, it did not speak to the needs of sexual minorities, and social, cultural and religious norms that perpetuate gender inequality.[24] Although the National Assembly passed the WEGE Bill, it lapsed before the National Council of Provinces and was ultimately not made law.[25] This is due in no small part to the role of civil society.

(c) An assessment of equality jurisprudence
The two-part test for a violation of the equality provisions of the Constitution as developed in *Harksen* is one of the most important outcomes in respect of PIL around gender equality. According to the court, civil society's interventions were a powerful contribution to its decisions. There were, however, some missed opportunities. In our view, this is in part due to the fact that only specialised women's rights organisation intervened in gender-specific cases. Non-gender specific civil society organisations did not usually incorporate a gendered perspective into their interventions. In this regard, there is a marked difference in PIL today. Many 'mainstream' non-gender specific organisations will either include a gendered analysis in their submissions or request that specialised organisations or units intervene in a matter in a synchronised and aligned manner.[26]

---

[21] Women Empowerment and Gender Equality Bill B50-2013 *GG* 37005 of 6 November 2013.

[22] Ibid.

[23] Comments on Women Empowerment and Gender Equality Bill *GG* 35637 of 29 August 2012 4 and Sonke Gender Justice 'Submission on the Women Empowerment and Gender Equality Bill' 2, last accessed from <http://pmg-assets.s3-website-eu-west-1.amazonaws.com/140129sonke.pdf> on 11 January 2018.

[24] See generally Sonke Gender Justice *Submission to the Department of Women, Children and People with Disabilities on the Women Empowerment and Gender Equality Bill* and Centre for Applied Legal Studies and Centre for the Study of Violence *Comments on the Women's Empowerment and Gender Equality Bill* [B50—2013].

[25] See 'Women Empowerment and Gender Equality Bill [B50-2013]: adoption, in presence of Minister', last accessed from <https://pmg.org.za/committee-meeting/16980/> on 13 July 2016.

[26] For instance, in *Nkala and Others v Harmony Gold Mining Company Ltd and Others* [2016] ZAGPJHC 97; 2016 (5) SA 240 (GJ) [Richard Spoor Inc Attorneys acted for the first to 30th applicants and LRC acted for the 40th to 52nd applicants. Sonke and TAC were admitted as *amici curiae*], Sonke intervened as *amicus* to introduce a gendered perspective and CALS intervened to do the same in *Dladla and Another v City of Johannesburg and Others* [2017] ZACC 42; 2018 (2) BCLR 119 (CC) [CALS was admitted as *amicus curiae*, represented by the LRC].

6.3 GENDER-BASED VIOLENCE

GBV was one of the first gender-specific issues to be addressed in South Africa's transition. Legislative changes were brought about to improve the safety and positioning of women in domestic relationships and to reduce the incidence of GBV.[27] These developments, however, were not mindful of the intersectional experience of GBV for women of colour. The Matrimonial Property Act 88 of 1984, for example, served the needs of women married under civil law to the exclusion of women of colour married under religious or cultural laws.[28] This remains a major problem today.

Unlike the other topics discussed herein, the GBV jurisprudence tends not to address the intersection of race and sex. What is the role, if any, of civil society in this failure?

Despite a Constitution that guarantees the right to physical integrity and the right to be free from all forms of public and private violence,[29] South Africa has among the world's highest rates of rape.[30] Public interest lawyers have used the *amicus* apparatus to: (i) alert the courts to South Africa's international law obligations regarding GBV, and (ii) provide courts with a context of the gendered nature and gendered impact of violent crime.

The Supreme Court of Appeal (SCA) set the groundwork for understanding sexual and GBV in *Chapman*.[31] The SCA held that '[r]ape is a serious offence, constituting . . . a humiliating, degrading and brutal invasion of the privacy, the dignity and the person of the victim'.[32] The Constitutional Court has confirmed this with regard to domestic violence. In *Baloyi*, the court rejected a complaint that domestic violence legislation placed a reverse onus on a defendant to prove an absence of guilt. The Constitutional Court noted the pervasive, gender-specific and patriarchal nature of GBV,[33] holding that 'a non-sexist society promised in the foundational clauses of the Constitution, and the right to equality and non-discrimination guaranteed by section 9 are undermined when spouse-beaters enjoy impunity'.[34] The Commission for Gender Equality (CGE) intervened as *amicus*, noting South Africa's international obligations to eliminate violence against

---

[27] For example, the Prevention of Family Violence Act 133 of 1993.

[28] Section 11 of the Matrimonial Property Act abolished matrimonial power but s 11(3)*(b)* of the Black Administration Act 38 of 1927 continued to relegate black women married under customary law to the status of legal minors under their husbands' authority.

[29] Sections 12(2) and (1)*(c)* of the Constitution.

[30] M Heiskanen 'Trends in police recorded crimes' in S Harrendorf, M Heiskanen & S Malby (eds) *International Statistics on Crime and Justice* (2010) 25.

[31] *S v Chapman* [1997] ZASCA 45; 1997 (3) SA 341 (SCA).

[32] Ibid paras 344I/J–345A.

[33] *S v Baloyi and Others* [1999] ZACC 19; 2000 (2) 425 (CC) para 12.

[34] Ibid para 12.

women and to put in place preventative measures to that end.[35] The court ultimately supported the interpretation espoused by the CGE.[36]

In *Carmichele*, handed down two years after *Baloyi*, the Constitutional Court further demonstrated the influence of interventions by public interest law organisations. As *amicus*, CALS presented the court with arguments concerning the state's positive obligation to prevent GBV.[37] CALS argued that the court should develop the common law to acknowledge the state's positive duty to prevent GBV.[38] Goldstone J accepted these arguments in *Carmichele* and directly quoted CALS saying '[s]exual violence and the threat of sexual violence goes to the core of women's subordination in society. It is the single greatest threat to the self-determination of South African women'.[39]

A year after *Carmichele*, the SCA, in *Van Eeden*, found that s 12(1) of the Constitution contains positive and negative obligations in respect of GBV; the one requires the state to refrain from invading the right itself and the other requires the state to take active steps to prevent a violation of the right.[40] The Women's Legal Centre (WLC) intervened, presenting arguments regarding the gendered character of violent crime and the way in which the Constitutional Court had addressed GBV.[41] Arguably influenced by the *amicus* intervention, the SCA referenced the state's obligations under international law to protect women against violent crime, acknowledging that violent crime is indeed gendered.[42] In a later case also initiated by the WLC, *K v Minister of Safety and Security*, the Constitutional Court extended the vicarious liability of the state in a case involving rape and assault by uniformed and on-duty police officers.[43] O'Regan J held that the police have a duty to protect community members and that this requires that reasonable trust be placed in them.[44]

---

[35] Commission for Gender Equality: Heads of Argument in *Baloyi v S* paras 4.6–4.9. See also Amanda Spies *Amicus Curiae Participation, Gender Equality and the South African Constitutional Court* (unpublished PhD thesis, University of the Witwatersrand, 2014) 57.

[36] *Baloyi* (note 33 above) paras 13 and 26.

[37] *Carmichele v Minister of Safety and Security* [2001] ZACC 22; 2001 (4) SA 938 [CALS was admitted as *amicus curiae*] para 62 and Centre for Applied Legal Studies: Heads of Argument in *Carmichele v Minister of Safety and Security and Another* paras 16–8 and Centre for Applied Legal Studies: Founding Affidavit in *Carmichele v Minister of Safety and Security* para 3.1.

[38] Heads of Argument in *Carmichele* (note 37 above) paras 18 and 21.

[39] *Carmichele* (note 37 above) para 62 and Heads of Argument in *Carmichele* (note 37 above) para 15.

[40] *Van Eeden v Minister of Safety and Security* [2002] ZASCA 132; 2003 (1) SA 389 (SCA) para 13 [Women's Legal Centre Trust was admitted as *amicus curiae*].

[41] Spies (note 35 above) 70.

[42] *Van Eeden* (note 40 above) para 42.

[43] *K v Minister of Safety and Security* [2005] ZACC 8; 2005 (6) SA 419 (CC) [WLC acted for the applicant].

[44] Ibid para 51.

The WLC continued its efforts to influence the Constitutional Court's GBV jurisprudence by intervening as *amicus curiae* in the *Van der Merwe*[45] matter. The WLC presented arguments to the effect that women are often the victims of domestic violence and have greater exposure to economic vulnerability and abuse.[46] Moseneke DCJ, writing for the majority, ultimately did not make a finding based on these arguments but did state that they had 'much cogency'.[47]

Mindful of the fact that sexual violence would also have to be reconceptualised in the democratic era, 18 civil society entities under the banner of the National Working Group on the Sexual Offences Bill (SOA Working Group)[48] mobilised to fast track the enactment of the Sexual Offences Bill.[49]

During the four-year wait for the Sexual Offences Bill to be enacted, the Constitutional Court heard *Masiya*, a case in which CALS and Tshwaranang Legal Advocacy Centre were admitted as *amici*.[50] In this case, the Court was asked to expand the common-law definition of rape to include non-consensual anal penetration of a woman. The *amici* provided a historical explanation for the motivation behind rape and the inconsistency between the common-law definition of rape and the Constitution.[51] Most importantly, the *amici* facilitated the court's analysis of the case as a gendered problem, and not one relating only to women, leading to important *obiter* comments[52] (although the court did not expand the definition of rape to include the non-consensual anal penetration of men).[53] Mindful of Parliament's delay in enacting the Sexual Offences Bill, the Court held that the fact that the Bill was before Parliament did not prevent the court from extending the definition, if doing so was in the interests of justice.[54] The common-law definition

---

[45] *Van der Merwe v Road Accident Fund and Another* [2006] ZACC 4; 2006 (4) SA 230 (CC) [Women's Legal Centre Trust was admitted as *amicus curiae*].

[46] Women's Legal Centre: Heads of Argument in *Van der Merwe v Road Accident Trust* paras 23, 29 and 52.

[47] *Van der Merwe* (note 45 above) para 67.

[48] National Working Group on the Sexual Offences Bill 'Submission to the Parliamentary Joint Ad-Hoc Committee on Socio-Economic Development', last accessed from <http://section27.org.za/wp-content/uploads/2010/04/Sexual-Offences-Bill-2005-WG-on-Sexual-Offences-Bill.pdf> on 11 January 2018.

[49] National Working Group on Sexual Offences Bill 'Factsheet on the National Working Group on Sexual Offences Bill', last accessed from <http://rapecrisis.org.za/downloads/national-working-group-on-sexual-offences.pdf> on 7 July 2016.

[50] *Masiya v Director of Public Prosecutions, Pretoria and Another* [2007] ZACC 9; 2007 (5) SA 30 (CC) [CALS and Tshwaranang Legal Advocacy Centre were admitted as *amici curiae*].

[51] Centre for Applied Legal Studies and Tshwaranang Legal Advocacy Centre: Heads of Argument in *Masiya v Director of Public Prosecutions* paras 28–37; 41–4 and 45–51.

[52] *Masiya* (note 50 above) paras 29–31.

[53] Ibid para 46.

[54] Ibid para 44.

of rape was then extended to include non-consensual penetration by a penis of the anus of a female.[55]

While *Masiya* was limited in its application, Langa CJ's dissenting judgment was borne out in Parliament's inclusion of the rape of men in the definition of rape under the Sexual Offences Act 32 of 2007 (2007 Sexual Offences Act) seven months later.[56]

In a remarkable decision regarding sexual violence, the Equality Court found that Julius Malema's statement that 'real' rape survivors act in a specific and homogenous way (not staying the night for example) constituted hate speech and harassment.[57] Sonke Gender Justice (Sonke), an NGO working towards the realisation of gender equality, presented expert evidence highlighting the link between the objectification and essentialising of women's experiences and the high levels of rape in the country.[58] The Equality Court found in favour of Sonke, concluding that the statement could reasonably be construed as hurtful, harmful, and demeaning to women and thus qualified as hate speech.[59]

Despite some progress, the process for removing discriminatory and harmful provisions from the statute books in law remains slow and mostly occurs on a case-by-case basis. One such case is *Frankel*,[60] which concerned the provisions of s 18 of the Criminal Procedure Act 51 of 1977. This section created a prescription period of 20 years for the prosecution of sexual offences other than rape, compelled rape and using a child or a person with a mental disability for pornographic purposes. While all the parties agreed that the provision was unconstitutional, only the *amici*, WLC, the Teddy Bear Clinic represented by CALS, and Lawyers for Human Rights, took the view that the constitutional invalidity should not be confined to children.[61] The *amici* argued that all forms of sexual violence at any age should be free of prescription because of the traumatic nature of the crime and the way in which survivors are unable to find help through the legal and psychosocial systems. Having been presented with expert evidence by the *amici*, the court found that the distinction between rape, compelled rape and other sexual offences was irrational as the response thereto by the survivors is nuanced and varied.[62] It further ordered that the age at which the offence occurred was irrelevant for purposes of prescription. The court therefore held that there is no

---

[55] Section 74(5) of the Sexual Offences Act.

[56] Ibid s 3.

[57] *Sonke Gender Justice Network v Malema* [2010] ZAEQC 2; 2010 (7) BCLR 729 (EqC) para 17(*b*)(i).

[58] Ibid para 17(*b*)(iii) and (vi).

[59] Ibid para 17(*b*)(x) and (xi).

[60] *L and Others v Frankel and Others* [2017] ZAGPJHC 140; 2017 (2) SACR 257 (GJ) [Women's Legal Centre Trust, Teddy Bear Clinic and LHR were admitted as *amici curiae*].

[61] Ibid paras 8 and 9.

[62] Ibid paras 55–7.

rational basis for a distinction between rape and other forms of sexual violence and equally that there is no rational basis for prescription to apply when the victim is hurt below or above the legal age of 18 years old. It therefore declared the provision inconsistent with the Constitution, gave the legislature a period of 18 months to remedy the defect and ordered that s 18 of the Criminal Procedure Act be read to include all sexual offences under common law and statute, thus doing away with prescription for some sexual offences irrespective of the age of the survivor.[63] At the time of writing this chapter, the Constitutional Court had heard, but not yet decided the application for confirmation of the declaration of invalidity from the High Court.

While positive gains have been made through the courts on GBV, this does not appear to have reduced the level of GBV in the country. This, in our view, speaks more to the limitations of law than to the important role played by public interest law interventions and is a phenomenon that requires social, economic, and criminal enforcement in order for the jurisprudence to curb the extent of the violence.

6.4 THE CRIMINALISATION OF SEX WORK

The Sexual Offences Act 23 of 1957 (1957 Sexual Offences Act) prohibited the sale of sex.[64] It did, not however, prohibit the purchase of sex. Post apartheid, several women's organisations engaged with the South African Law Reform Commission (SALRC) to reform the criminalisation of sex workers, who were mostly women. During this time, the *Jordan*[65] case worked its way through the courts.[66] The Sex Workers Education and Advocacy Taskforce (SWEAT), CALS and the Reproductive Health Research Unit (RHRU) intervened as *amici*. The *amici* argued that the criminalisation of sex work undermined the constitutional rights of sex workers to equality, dignity and safety.[67] The CGE also intervened, arguing that the criminalisation of the sale—and not the purchase—of sex, was discriminatory on the grounds of gender.[68]

The majority in *Jordan* rejected the *amici* argument regarding the gendered nature of the commercial sex work industry, and thus the discriminatory nature of the legislative provision that criminalised only the selling of sex and not the

---

[63] *Frankel* (note 60 above) order.

[64] Sections 2 and 20(1A) of the 1957 Sexual Offences Act.

[65] *S v Jordan and Others* [2002] ZACC 22; 2002 (6) SA 642 (CC) para 118 [SWEAT, CALS, RHRU and CGE were admitted as *amici curiae*].

[66] See South African Law Commission *Sexual Offences: Adult Prostitution* (Project 107) (2002).

[67] The Sex Workers Education and Advocacy Taskforce, Centre for Applied Legal Studies and the Reproductive Health Research Unit: Heads of Argument in *S v Jordan and Others* paras 1.17.6 and 1.17.7. See also *Jordan* (note 65 above) para 118.

[68] *Jordan* (note 65 above) paras 63–5.

purchasing of it.[69] It also rejected the argument that the one-sided criminalisation of the sex worker made the sex worker more vulnerable.[70] The court did not use the opportunity to embrace the multiple, intersecting ways in which the criminalisation of sex work violated the rights of predominantly poor, black women.

Despite the loss, it seems that the arguments of the *amici* found resonance in O'Regan and Sachs JJ's minority judgment, where the justices poignantly noted the societal norms that distinguish between female and male sexuality as follows:

> The female prostitute has been the social outcast, the male patron has been accepted or ignored. She is visible and denounced, her existence tainted by her activity. He is faceless, a mere ingredient in her offence rather than a criminal in his own right, who returns to respectability after the encounter . . . The difference in social stigma tracks a pattern of applying different standards to the sexuality of men and women.[71]

It is conceivable that the points made by the minority influenced the legislature ultimately to criminalise both the sale and purchase of sex in the 2007 Sexual Offences Act.[72] Arguably, this has not altered the societal stigma attached to selling sex and the concomitant relative acceptance of those who purchase it. As with GBV, jurisprudence or legislative reform will not always or necessarily attenuate the social structures that uphold levels of prejudice and this once again shows the limitations of law as an instrument for reform, rather than the limitation of the impact of civil society in advancing constitutional law reform.

In a later High Court decision, SWEAT obtained some protection against unlawful arrest of sex workers, securing an interdict against arrest for any purpose other than prosecution.[73] However, this did not affect the criminalisation of sex work. While sex work remains criminal, the governing party, the African National Congress, took a decision at its elective conference of 2017 to decriminalise sex work.[74] While some laud this decision, what remains to be seen is the speed and form with which decriminalisation will take place, both of which having the potential to perpetuate the violations experienced by sex workers.

Despite these challenges, some degree of labour law protection has been afforded to sex workers, albeit not through the Constitutional Court but a lower court. The WLC, on behalf of a sex worker, brought the case of *Kylie*[75] to the Labour Appeal Court. The court relied on the minority decision in *Jordan* and held

---

[69] *Jordan* (note 65 above) paras 9–14.

[70] Ibid para 16.

[71] Ibid para 64.

[72] Section 11 of the Sexual Offences Act.

[73] *The Sex Worker and Advocacy Taskforce v Minister of Safety and Security and Others* [2009] ZAWCHC 64; 2009 (6) SA 513 (WCC) [the LRC acted for the applicant].

[74] See Masego Rahlaga 'ANC's decision to fully decriminalise sex work welcomed' *Eyewitness News* 9 December 2017, last accessed on 11 January 2018 from <http://ewn.co.za/2017/12/21/anc-s-decision-to-fully-decriminalise-sex-work-welcomed>.

[75] *Kylie v CCMA and Others* [2010] ZALAC 8; 2010 (4) SA 383 (LAC) [WLC acted for the appellant].

that sex workers are entitled to dignity and may not be stripped of their right to fair labour practices, even where the labour itself is unlawful.[76] It supported the argument presented by the WLC that the illegality of the contract, which resulted in its non-recognition, did not detract from the right of the sex worker to fair labour practices in terms of s 23 of the Constitution and the Labour Relations Act 66 of 1995.

By all accounts, the rights of sex workers continue to be violated daily. The courts have not been able to reconcile society's moral antagonism towards sex work with the lived reality of sex workers. This is also due in part to civil society's own grappling with whether sex work is by its very definition violent or whether this should be treated as labour with all the protections involved.

6.5 CAREGIVING

(a) Child caregiving by male parents

Caregiving is deeply gendered. Women are more likely to be caregivers of children, the elderly and ill persons in the home, than men. The Constitutional Court has noted the gendered nature of child caregiving, identifying it as one of the reasons for women's unequal participation and remuneration in the formal economy.[77] Trying to protect women's rights in the context of childcare has had the unintended consequence of entrenching the domestic role of women, essentially denying fathers a legally protected opportunity to undertake caregiving responsibilities themselves. The Constitutional Court has considered two cases on this point: *Fraser*[78] and *Hugo*.[79]

Fraser concerned a challenge to the constitutionality of s 18(4)*(d)* of the Child Care Act 74 of 1983 in that it did not require the consent of a father for the adoption of a child born to unmarried heterosexual parents.[80] CALS intervened, advancing arguments asserting unfair discrimination and suggested that the issue be referred to the legislature for remediation.[81] The court appeared to agree with the *amicus* and noted that the impugned provision unfairly and unjustifiably discriminated against the father of the child on the basis of gender and marital status.[82] The court suspended the declaration of invalidity for two years to allow the legislature to remedy the unconstitutionality.[83] Within nine months of the

---

[76] *Kylie* (note 75 above) para 26.

[77] *Hugo* (note 4 above) paras 37, 38, 80, 93, and 110.

[78] *Fraser v Children's Court, Pretoria North and Others* [1997] ZACC 1; 1997 (2) SA 261 (CC) paras 1–4 [CALS and LHR were admitted as *amici curiae*].

[79] *Hugo* (note 4 above).

[80] *Fraser* (note 78 above) paras 1–4.

[81] Catherine Albertyn 'Defending and securing rights through law: Feminism, law and the courts in South Africa' (2005) 32 *Politikon: South African Journal of Political Studies* 217 at 223.

[82] *Fraser* (note 78 above) paras 24–5.

[83] Ibid para 52.

court's decision, the legislature enacted the Natural Fathers of Children Born out of Wedlock Act 86 of 1997. In addition, the rights of fathers not married to the mothers of their children continue to be protected in terms of s 21 of the Children's Act 38 of 2005.

Months after the *Fraser* decision, the court handed down a split decision in *Hugo*, which similarly concerned the caregiving rights and responsibilities of a father. The court was asked to assess the constitutionality of the presidential pardon for imprisoned mothers, but not fathers, of children 12 years and younger. The majority found that the pardon was discriminatory but not unfair on the basis that it did not qualify as an affront to the dignity and sense of worth of fathers.[84] While no public interest organisations intervened in this case, Mokgoro J did note in her dissenting opinion the concern that the decision reached in *Hugo* retreated from the principles laid down in *Fraser* (a case, as discussed above, that was influenced by intervention from feminist organisations).[85]

In 2010, the Constitutional Court was once again faced with a case relating to child caregiving by a male parent. In *MS*,[86] the court was asked to reconsider the sentence of a mother of young children, on the basis that this would be in the best interests of the children. The majority refused to review the sentence on the ground that the mother was not the sole caregiver of the children. The court was of the view that the father was co-resident in the family home and would be able to look after the children.[87] Khampepe J dissented, taking note of the Centre for Child Law's submission[88] that just because the mother was married to the children's father did not mean that the father had in the past provided, and would in future provide, adequate care.[89]

These decisions reveal a grappling by the courts with the issue of child care and simultaneously not wanting to reify the gendered nature of childcare.[90] It is arguable that this is a nuance that civil society may also be trying to reconcile.

(b) The economic value of caregiving

In May 2016, the Johannesburg High Court handed down a judgment in the case of *Nkala* on the certification application made by former gold mine workers who had contracted TB and/or silicosis while working in South African gold mines.

---

[84] *Hugo* (note 4 above) para 47.

[85] Ibid para 93.

[86] *MS v S* [2011] ZACC 7; 2011 (2) SACR 88 (CC) [CCL was admitted as *amicus curiae*].

[87] Ibid para 63.

[88] Centre for Child Law: Heads of Argument in *MS v S* paras 32–4.

[89] *MS* (note 86 above) paras 47–8.

[90] For another recent case grappling with issues of parenthood, see *AB and Another v Minister of Social Development* [2016] ZACC 43; 2017 (3) SA 570 (CC) [the CCL was admitted as *amicus curiae*]. The majority of the Constitutional Court declined to confirm an order of invalidity in relation to a statutory provision requiring a genetic link for surrogacy arrangements.

While the judgment is lauded for developing South Africa's common law on the certification of class actions, it deserves the same degree of praise for recognising the role women and girls played in giving care to miners who have been rendered ill due to their work on the mine. This finding is directly attributable to Sonke and the Treatment Action Campaign (TAC) intervening as *amici*.

Sonke and the TAC presented evidence indicating that mineworkers, rendered seriously ill due to silicosis, are often dependant on home and community-based care, which women predominantly provided on an unpaid basis.[91] Their evidence further showed that home-based care disproportionately burdened women and exacerbated existing gender inequalities.[92] For these reasons, Sonke and the TAC argued that deceased mineworkers' claims for general damages (ie pain and suffering, loss of amenities of life, disfigurement, loss of expectation of life) should be transmissible to the deceased mineworkers' estates prior to close of pleadings.[93] The court quoted the evidence provided by Sonke and the TAC with approval.[94] The court, through the *amicus* intervention, made a decision that allows women caregivers to claim the general damages due to men in their care where those men have died after the lodgement of the certification application.[95]

This case has imported into the South African jurisprudence a notion of the economic value of caregiving. This is a seminal development towards an under-standing of the unremunerated work done by women and the need to address this burden.

6.6 CULTURE AND RELIGION

(a) Recognition of customary marriages

The Constitution acknowledges the place of customary law in South Africa's pluralist legal system,[96] mandating courts to develop customary law in line with the Bill of Rights.[97] In 1998, the Recognition of Customary Marriages Act 120 of 1998 was enacted, codifying the recognition of customary marriages and departing from the apartheid notions of customary marriages.[98]

---

[91] Peacock affidavit para 17 in *Nkala* (note 26 above).

[92] Ibid para 21.

[93] Ibid paras 30–1.

[94] Ibid paras 214, 222, and 241–3.

[95] Ibid para 222. The majority and minority were, however, in disagreement about whether this development should apply to non-class action cases. The majority were of the view that general damages should be transmissible in all cases after the claim has been lodged (para 217) and the minority was of the view that general damages should only be transmissible after the certification application has been lodged in a class action (para 234).

[96] Sections 15, 30, 31 and 39(3) of the Constitution.

[97] Ibid s 39(3) and (2).

[98] *Gumede v President of the Republic of South Africa* [2008] ZACC 23; 2009 (3) SA 152 (CC) paras 16, 17 and 32 [LRC acted for the applicant and Women's Legal Centre Trust was admitted as *amicus curiae*]. See also s 7 of the Recognition of Customary Marriages Act.

Following its enactment, the Constitutional Court considered the constitutionality of a provision of the Act that precluded a wife from owning a share in the matrimonial estate if married under customary law before 15 November 2000. In the case of *Gumede*,[99] the WLC intervened as *amicus*, supporting the declaration of invalidity on the basis of its inconsistency with not only the Constitution but also with international and regional law.[100] The WLC presented arguments to the court detailing the vulnerability and position of women affected by the provision of the Act, ie older women who are probably black and poor.[101] The court adopted these arguments to varying degrees,[102] ultimately finding the provision to discriminate unfairly and unjustifiably on the basis of gender.[103]

In 2013, the court handed down the *MM*[104] decision that concerned a dispute regarding the validity of a Xitsonga man's second marriage.[105] The WLC, CGE and Rural Women's Movement intervened,[106] questioning the extent to which the court had the necessary knowledge of Xitsonga law to develop the customary law relating to whether a man must obtain his wife's *consent* to a subsequent marriage, or whether *consultation* with her would suffice.[107] The court elected to develop Xitsonga customary law to include the requirement of consent of the first wife, as opposed to the weaker standard of consultation.[108] The judgment is clear about the value of the *amici*:

> The amici have provided invaluable submissions throughout the proceedings before this Court. In particular, the amici's submissions in response to this Court's request for further information regarding Xitsonga customary law have been crucial to the outcome of this case.[109]

This case advances the cause for first wives' agency, human dignity and equality. There is a deficiency in the judgment, which is silent on the question of whether a man needs to request the consent of his first and subsequent wives for further marriages. As pointed out by Jafta J's minority, the case does not make clear what

---

[99] *Gumede* (note 98 above) para 11.

[100] Women's Legal Centre: Heads of Argument in *Gumede v President of the Republic of South Africa* paras 21–34.

[101] Ibid para 35.

[102] *Gumede* (note 98 above) paras 5, 14 and 55.

[103] Ibid paras 34 and 49.

[104] *MM v MN and Another* [2013] ZACC 14; 2013 (4) SA 415 (CC) [Women's Legal Centre Trust, CGE, and Rural Women's Movement were admitted as *amici curiae*, with the LRC representing the latter two].

[105] Ibid para 3.

[106] Ibid paras 94 and 110.

[107] Rural Women's Movement (RWM) and Commission for Gender Equality: Heads of Argument in *MM v MN* paras 35 and 43.1. RWM and CGE also presented evidence on the requirement of consent, see *MM* (note 104 above) para 137.

[108] *MM* (note 104 above) paras 73 and 75.

[109] Ibid para 18.

level of consent or disclosure is required for third, fourth and subsequent marriages.[110] Is the first wife's consent only required for the second marriage and not marriages entered subsequently? And, if there are more than two customary marriages, is consent required from all previous wives for validity or only that of the first wife? The majority of the court left these questions open.[111]

In a recent decision, the Constitutional Court confirmed an order of constitutional invalidity in respect of s 7(1) of the Recognition of Customary Marriages Act, which provided that the proprietary consequences of customary marriages entered into before the commencement of the Act continued to be governed by customary law.[112] The Court struck down the provision, allowing Parliament two years to remedy it, and ordered in the meantime that wives and husbands in polygamous customary marriages will have equal rights over marital property.

(b) Customary succession

The SCA initially upheld the customary law principle of male primogeniture (that the estate of a deceased male goes to the eldest living male descendant or father)[113] as constitutional in the case of *Mthembu*.[114] However, the *Mthembu* decision was overturned in *Bhe*,[115] where the Constitutional Court declared male primogeniture unjustifiably and unfairly discriminatory on the grounds of sex, gender and birth.[116] Public interest law organisations acted in *Bhe* as legal representatives of both the parties and the *amicus* (the CGE). The South African Human Rights Commission and WLC brought a direct access application that expanded the relief sought beyond the declaration of constitutional invalidity of a subsection that permitted primogeniture, to one related to the entire section based on its overt racism.[117] The majority granted the extended order.[118] Without the intervention of these public interest organisations, the extended order may not have been granted. The majority also noted that the provisions supporting male primogeniture

---

[110] *MM* (note 104 above) para 144.

[111] Ibid para 84.

[112] *Ramuhovhi and Others v President of the Republic of South Africa and Others* [2017] ZACC 41; 2018 (2) SA 1 (CC) [the LRC acted for the intervening party; the Women's Legal Centre Trust was admitted as *amicus curiae*, represented by the WLC].

[113] *Bhe and Others v Khayelitsha Magistrate and Others* [2004] ZACC 17; 2005 (1) SA 580 (CC) para 77 [Women's Legal Centre Trust as fourth applicant, the LRC and the WLC acted for the applicants, and CGE was admitted as *amicus curiae*, represented by LHR].

[114] *Mtembu v Letsela and Another* [2000] ZASCA 181; 2000 (3) SA 867 (SCA) para 8 and *Bhe* (note 113 above).

[115] Ibid *Bhe* (note 113 above).

[116] *Bhe* (note 113 above) paras 91–4, 98 and 100.

[117] Women's Legal Centre and South African Human Rights Commission: Heads of Argument in *Bhe v Magistrate, Khayelitsha* paras 75–7.

[118] *Bhe* (note 113 above) paras 31 and 136.2.

affected African women and children in particular, who are regarded as the most vulnerable in society.[119]

(c) Traditional leadership

In 1997, the Valoyi royal family, tribal authority and royal council, chose a woman, Tinyiko Lwandhlamuni Philla Nwamitwa Shilubana, to succeed the chieftainship of the community. They did this on the basis that 'in terms of the new Republic of South African Constitution it is now permissible that a female child be heir since she is also equal to a male child . . . [t]he matter of chieftainship and regency would be conducted according to the Constitution of the Republic of South Africa'.[120]

Nevertheless, a male expectant to the chieftainship disputed Ms Shilubana's accession and was successful in both the High Court and the SCA. On appeal, in an atypical move, the Constitutional Court invited the CGE, National Movement for Rural Women (NMRW) and the Congress for Traditional Leaders in South Africa (Contralesa) to intervene as *amici*, and in so doing signalled the important role played by *amici*. Contralesa was of the view that traditional leadership fairly discriminates on the basis of gender and requested that the court dismiss Ms Shilubana's appeal.[121] The CGE argued that courts should recognise traditional communities' attempts to develop customary law in accordance with the Constitution.[122] The NMRW noted the flexible and living nature of customary law and considered the community's choice of Ms Shilubana a demonstration of living customary law.[123] The court held that the resolution of the community to restore the chieftainship to Ms Shilubana was compelling and decisive.[124] Based on the arguments of the *amici*, the court unanimously held that traditional authorities have the power to develop customary law and practice in line with the Constitution.[125]

(d) Recognition of religious marriages

The non-recognition of Muslim marriages in the constitutional dispensation was interrogated in 1999, when the Minister of Justice mandated the SALRC to present a solution to this question.[126]

---

[119] *Bhe* (note 113 above) para 32.

[120] *Shilubana and Others v Nwamitwa* [2008] ZACC 9; 2009 (2) SA 66 (CC) para 4 [CGE and National Movement of Rural Women were admitted as *amici curiae*, represented by the LRC].

[121] Congress of Traditional Leaders of South Africa: Heads of Argument in *Shilubana v Nwamitwa* paras 41 and 45; *Shilubana* (note 120 above) para 40.

[122] Commission for Gender Equality *Heads of Argument: Shilubana v Nwamitwa* para 55; *Shilubana* (note 120 above) para 33.

[123] National Movement for Rural Women: Heads of Argument in *Shilubana and Others v Nwamitwa* para 6.2; *Shilubana* (note 120 above) para 35.

[124] *Shilubana* (note 120 above) para 77.

[125] Ibid para 75.

[126] South African Law Reform Commission *Islamic Marriages and Related Matters* (Project 29) (2003) para 1.4.

As was the case with regard to anal rape, the SALRC report and draft bill on Muslim marriages did not speed up government's response to non-recognition. Concerned by this, the WLC lodged a direct access application to the Constitutional Court, to compel the legislature to remedy this.[127] The court dismissed the application on procedural grounds regarding jurisdiction rather than for substantive reasons.[128]

The decision of the court effectively slowed down any movement on the recognition of Muslim marriages. This decision has not, however, deterred public interest organisations from pursuing the recognition of marriages conducted in terms of Islamic rites: the Cape Town division of the High Court heard an application of this nature, supported by the WLC, in August 2017 but a judgment had not been handed down at the time of finalising this chapter.[129] However, in the period between the promulgation of the Constitution and December 2017, a series of judicial decisions extended recognition incrementally. In *Amod*, in which the CGE intervened as *amicus*, the SCA expanded the common law to include support for the surviving spouse of a monogamous Muslim marriage on the basis of a contractual duty between the surviving spouse and the deceased.[130] According to Mohamed CJ, this was in line with the *boni mores* of society and the new ethos of tolerance, pluralism and religious freedom that came into effect even prior to the interim Constitution.[131]

Subsequently, in 2004 the Constitutional Court handed down *Daniels*,[132] which dealt with the exclusion of women married under Islamic law from the ambit of the Intestate Succession Act 81 of 1987 (ISA). The WLC played a critical role in advancing an argument to the court which in turn led to a substantive and definitive form of justice. The court interpreted the word 'spouse' in the ISA, to include spouses married in terms of Islamic rites. The court aligned the spirit of the Constitution with the objectives of the ISA to protect the maintenance of surviving spouses.[133]

---

[127] *Women's Legal Centre Trust v President of the Republic of South Africa and Others* [2009] ZACC 20; 2009 (6) SA 94 (CC).

[128] Ibid paras 3 and 24.

[129] See Jana Breytenbach 'Muslim marriages must be declared legally valid, court hears' *News24* 29 August 2017, last accessed on 11 January 2018 from <https://www.news24.com/SouthAfrica/News/muslim-marriages-must-be-declared-legally-valid-court-hears-20170829>.

[130] *Amod v Multilateral Motor Vehicle Accident Fund (Commission for Gender Equality Intervening)* [1999] ZASCA 76; 1999 (4) SA 1319 (SCA) para 25 [CGE was admitted as *amicus curiae*].

[131] Ibid para 20.

[132] *Daniels v Campbell NO and Others* [2004] ZACC 14; 2004 (5) SA 331 (CC) para 1 [WLC acted for the applicant].

[133] Ibid paras 23, 25 and 37.

In 2009 Nkabinde J wrote for a unanimous court in *Hassam*[134] where she held that the ISA's non-application to Muslim polygynous wives is unconstitutional on the ground of unfair and unjustifiable discrimination.[135] The WLC and Muslim Youth Movement of South Africa intervened,[136] providing the court with 'helpful submissions' that 'supported the confirmation of the declaration of constitutional invalidity.'[137] The *amici* significantly informed the finding of intersectional discrimination based on gender, religion and marital status.[138]

In another matter concerning succession under Islamic law—*Moosa*—the Cape High Court in 2017 invalidated the limitation of the phrase 'surviving spouse' in the Wills Act 7 of 1953 (Wills Act) to monogamous spouses married under civil law.[139] The deceased in his will stipulated that his estate should devolve in terms of Islamic law. The executor then sought to distribute his estate to both of his spouses, one of whom was married to the deceased in terms of both civil and Islamic law and the other only in terms of Islamic law. The registrar of deeds took the view that only his wife in terms of civil law was a 'surviving spouse'. The WLC intervened as *amicus curiae* and contended that women affected by the non-recognition of Muslim marriages were especially vulnerable and marginalised.[140] In its judgment, the court found that the exclusion of surviving spouses in polygamous marriages conducted in terms of Islamic rites from the ambit of the Wills Act was unfairly discriminatory in nature and effect on the basis of religion and marital status and was an unjustified infringement of the right to equality.[141] As at the finalisation of this chapter, the declaration of constitutional invalidity had been lodged with the Constitutional Court for confirmation.

In *Khan*, the High Court also recognised spousal maintenance for spouses in polygamous marriages in terms of Islamic rites.[142] This court adopted a different approach from that commonly seen in litigation of this nature: instead of declaring the Maintenance Act 9 of 1998 (Maintenance Act) unconstitutional for failing to include within its ambit spouses in polygamous marriages married in terms of

---

[134] *Daniels* (note 132 above) and *Hassam v Jacobs NO and Others* [2009] ZACC 19; 2009 (5) SA 572 (CC) [the Muslim Youth Movement of South Africa, represented by the LRC, and the Women's Legal Centre Trust were admitted as *amici curiae*].

[135] *Hassam* (note 134 above) para 42.

[136] Ibid para 4.

[137] Ibid para 3.

[138] Ibid para 34.

[139] *Moosa NO and Others v Harnaker and Others* [2017] ZAWCHC 97; 2017 (6) SA 425 (WCC) [WLC was admitted as *amicus curiae*]. The order of invalidity was confirmed by the Constitutional Court in *Moosa NO and Others v Minister of Justice and Correctional Services and Others* [2018] ZACC 19 [the Women's Legal Centre Trust was admitted as *amicus curiae*, represented by the WLC].

[140] Ibid para 19.

[141] Ibid paras 31 and 32 and 35 respectively.

[142] *Khan v Khan* 2005 (2) SA 272 (T).

Islamic law, it chose to interpret the Maintenance Act in conformity with the Constitution and found that 'the purpose of the Act would be frustrated rather than furthered if partners to a polygamous marriage were to be excluded from the protection the Act offers'.[143] Other principles in law have been used by women married in terms of Islamic law to protect their rights to accommodation, for instance: the Prevention of Illegal Eviction from and Unlawful Occupation of Land Act 19 of 1998 was used in *Arendse*;[144] and the common law on long leases was used in *Ismail*.[145]

Case-by-case development is useful in that it serves to create precedent from which to build the comprehensive common-law protection of women married in accordance with Islamic rites. However, few people have the means by which to ensure protection through the courts and attempting to obtain relief through these means does not guarantee protection. The *lacuna* in the law, due to the non-recognition of Muslim marriages, therefore leaves women at the intersection of gender, poverty, and religion, susceptible to ongoing discrimination.

(e) Social movements

The advocacy around the Traditional Courts Bill (B15-2008)[146] serves as a profound example of successful advocacy by organised civil society. This Bill, introduced to Parliament for the first time in 2008[147] was regressive in that it inter alia centralised power in traditional leaders who are mostly men; gave traditional leaders authority to settle civil and criminal disputes with no clear limits of jurisdiction or outcome; and prohibited legal representation before such tribunals.[148] It was introduced in 2008, withdrawn in 2011 and then reintroduced in 2012. Advocacy efforts highlighted the unconstitutional nature of the Bill, and it ultimately lapsed.[149]

---

[143] *Khan* (note 142 above) para 11.12.

[144] *Arendse v Arendse and Others* [2012] ZAWCHC 156; 2013 (3) SA 347 (WCC) [LRC was admitted as *amicus curiae*].

[145] *Ismail v Ismail and Others* [2007] ZAECHC 3; 2007 (4) SA 557 (E).

[146] Traditional Courts Bill B15-2008 *GG* 30902 of 27 March 2008.

[147] Aninka Classens 'What's wrong with the Traditional Courts Bill' *Mail and Guardian* 2 June 2008, last accessed on 11 January 2018 from <http://mg.co.za/article/2008-06-02-whats-wrong-with-the-traditional-courts-bill>.

[148] Sections 4, 5, 6 and 9 of the Traditional Courts Bill.

[149] Parliamentary Monitoring Group 'Traditional Courts Bill B15 of 2008', last accessed from <http://pmg-assets.s3-website-eu-west-1.amazonaws.com/bills/080410b15-08.pdf> on 11 January 2018. Parliamentary Monitoring Group 'Traditional Courts Bill B1 of 2012', last accessed from <http://pmg.org.za/files/bills/120125b1-12.pdf> on 11 January 2018. See also Parliamentary Monitoring Group 'Traditional Courts Bill (B15-2008)', last accessed from <https://pmg.org.za/bill/409/> on 11 January 2018 and Parliamentary Monitoring Group 'Traditional Courts Bill (B1-2012)', last accessed from <https://pmg.org.za/bill/159/> on 11 January 2018.

Through the twin efforts of litigation and advocacy, public interest organisations have had a seminal role in advancing both the right to equality for women and men and an intersectional understanding of discrimination, especially in the context of customary and religious marriage.

6.7 DOMESTIC PARTNERSHIPS

Despite the work of the SALRC and the drafting of a bill, domestic partnerships remain unregulated and unrecognised.[150] In 2004 in *Volks*,[151] the Constitutional Court was faced with a challenge to the Maintenance of Surviving Spouses Act 27 of 1990, arguing that it discriminated against surviving intimate partners on the ground of marital status. CALS intervened, presenting socio-legal evidence of the economic vulnerability of women in domestic relationships and the fact that women often have very little choice about whether or not to marry.[152]

The court rejected this submission on the basis that the evidence was not sufficiently far reaching or 'incontrovertible',[153] therefore holding that it is not unfair for the legislation to distinguish between married and unmarried survivors.[154] The minority judgments, however, acknowledged the discriminatory impact of unrecognised domestic partnerships on women, particularly women living in poverty, a point that CALS raised.[155] Sachs J was mindful of the impact of South Africa's migrant labour system on familial structures. He recognised the multi-layered dimension of discrimination revealed by the evidence presented by CALS.[156]

The SCA revisited the issue in *Volks* in the *Butters* case.[157] In this case, the majority opened the door to a claim for a portion of the profit made during an intimate partnership by means of a tacit universal partnership, thus seeing the continued positive impact of the CALS submissions.[158] Subsequently in *Laubscher N.O v Duplan and Another*, concerning the entitlement of permanent

---

[150] Draft Domestic Partnerships Bill, 2008: For comments (GN 36 in *GG* 30663 of 14 January 2008).

[151] *Volks NO v Robinson and Others* [2005] ZACC 2; 2009 JDR 1018 (CC) [Women's Legal Centre Trust as second respondent and CALS as *amicus curiae*].

[152] Ibid para 30. Catherine Albertyn 'Judicial diversity' in C Hoexter & M Olivier (eds) *The Judiciary in South Africa* (2014) 245, 105. See also Bonita Meyersfeld 'If you can see, look: Domestic partnerships and the law' 2010 *CCR* 271, 274.

[153] *Volks* (note 151 above) para 33.

[154] Ibid para 60.

[155] Ibid paras 110, 121 and 199 respectively. Centre for Applied Legal Studies: Heads of Argument in *Volks v Robinson* paras 1.7, 21.8 and 29. The impugned provisions were found to unfairly discriminate in both minority decisions.

[156] *Volks* (note 151 above) paras 133, 163–6 and 227.

[157] *Butters v Mncora* [2012] ZASCA 29; 2012 (4) SA 1 (SCA).

[158] Ibid paras 11, 19, 22 and 31.

same-sex partners to inherit intestate, the majority of the Constitutional Court declined to reconsider *Volks*.[159]

6.8 CONCLUSION

It would be a task beyond the parameters of this chapter to discuss every social, political and legal advocacy strategy to advance the rights of women in South Africa in the last 20 years. This chapter, in brief form, seeks merely to describe a few of the seminal cases, laws and advocacy strategies directed at decision makers. We attempt to highlight the important role played by civil society organisations generally and public interest law organisations in particular, in securing the constitutional right to equality.

A theme that emerges from these cases is the impact that these organisations have in peeling away at the assumptions of a homogenous South African woman and thus, in some ways, though not always successfully, undoing essentialist remediation. Public interest law organisations have used various means of intervention including *amicus* interventions, direct access and traditional legal representation to contextualise the reality of women's lives and thus unveil the multiplicity of ways in which law impacts the lives of women and the way in which that varies based on race, occupation, caregiving responsibilities, culture and religion. However, often the gendered dimensions of cases are not obvious and the scope for public interest lawyering is vast. One hopes that such intervention will expand in the decades to come.

---

[159] *Laubscher N.O v Duplan and Another* [2016] ZACC 44; 2017 (2) SA 264 (CC) [the CGE was admitted as *amicus curiae*, represented by the LRC] para 53. But see the concurring judgment of Froneman J paras 84–6, which would have overturned *Volks*.

Chapter 7

BASIC SERVICES

Jackie Dugard[1]

7.1   INTRODUCTION

Within South Africa's cooperative governance system, the municipal sphere provides services such as electricity, gas and water reticulation, along with domestic waste-water and sewage disposal systems to households. The Municipal Systems Act 32 of 2000 (Municipal Systems Act), which was enacted 'to enable municipalities to move progressively towards the social and economic uplifting of local communities, and ensure universal access to essential services that are affordable to all', defines a *basic* municipal service as a 'municipal service that is necessary to ensure an acceptable and reasonable quality of life and, if not provided, would endanger public health or safety or the environment'.[2] Although the Municipal Systems Act does not provide a list of which municipal services are regarded as falling into this definition of a basic service, the municipal services

---

[1] It should be noted that I was involved in the *Mazibuko* and *Joseph* PIL cases discussed in this chapter. In this chapter, I therefore rely on independent critique of these judgments. Thanks go to the Research Council of Norway for its contribution to this research as part of the 'Elevating water rights to human rights' project.

[2] Section 1 of the Municipal Systems Act.

that are commonly understood to be basic services are water, sanitation (domestic waste-water and sewage disposal systems) and electricity services.

Interestingly, there has been relatively little public interest litigation (PIL) on basic services, especially compared to the amount of PIL on the right of access to adequate housing. This reality is all the more curious given the high degree of discontent with municipal services as is evident from the significant levels of community protest related to inadequate municipal services.[3] As explored below, this may point to a need for greater reflection and strategising among PIL actors. Nonetheless, and despite some worrying inconsistencies and incoherence in the existing jurisprudence analysed in this chapter, there have been some key PIL cases that have in some instances advanced access to basic services and in others clarified the boundaries of basic services-related goods.

7.2 OVERVIEW OF LAW AND POLICY

Among basic services, water is governed by the most fully developed legal and policy frameworks, and electricity the least, with sanitation falling in between— arguably the regulation is an accurate reflection of the spectrum of human need pertaining to each of these services. The only basic service explicitly protected in the Constitution is water—s 27(1)*(b)* guarantees everyone the right to have access to sufficient water. However, other sections of the Constitution are directly relevant to water, sanitation and electricity services. For example, s 9, the equality clause, requires that there be no unfair discrimination in the provision of services. Section 33, the right to just administrative action, along with the Promotion of Administrative Justice Act 3 of 2000 (PAJA),[4] creates the framework for proce-dural fairness in basic services. This framework embraces the rights to reasonable notice of a decision, and the opportunity to make representation regarding your circumstances, before a decision adversely affecting your rights (such as a discon-nection of your services), is taken. In addition, s 152(1)*(e)* of the Constitution requires that municipalities 'encourage the involvement of communities and community organisations in the matters of local government'. The promotion of the participation of local communities in municipal matters is strengthened by PAJA, which in s 4 mandates consultation and public participation in certain circumstances, including where an administrative decision could adversely affect

---

[3] For an analysis of the mushrooming local community protests see for example Peter Alexander 'Rebellion of the poor: South Africa's service delivery protests—A preliminary analysis' (2010) 37 *Review of African Political Economy* 25. As highlighted in research undertaken by the Community Law Centre at the University of the Western Cape, after access to housing (36.33%), basic service delivery was the highest expressed concern among community members engaging in protests— specifically: access to water (18.36%); access to electricity (18.16%); poor service delivery in general (15.62%); and sanitation (13%) (Hirsh Jain 'Community protests in South Africa: Trends, analysis and explanations' Local Government Working Paper Series no. 1, Community Law Centre, University of the Western Cape (2010) 29–30.)

[4] PAJA was passed to give effect to the s 33 right.

the enjoyment of a right. Moreover, s 10 of the Constitution provides that everyone is entitled to have their inherent dignity respected and promoted, which may be negatively impacted where basic services are denied or inadequate. Finally, there are specific policy and legal requirements governing the availability/ quantity, as well as the quality of basic services.

These six human rights-related dimensions (non-discrimination, just administrative action, dignity, participation, availability/quantity and quality) form the basis for the analytical frame used to examine basic services-related PIL in section 7.3 below. This section furthermore sets out the relevant legal and policy parameters for each basic service (water, sanitation and electricity), as forming the basis for the PIL claims.

(a) Water

Section 3 of the Water Services Act 108 of 1997 (Water Services Act) provides that 'everyone has the right of access to basic water supply'. Section 1 of the Water Services Act defines basic water supply as 'the prescribed minimum standard of water supply services necessary for the reliable supply of a sufficient quantity and quality of water to households, including informal households, to support life and personal hygiene'. The prescribed minimum standard of water, in turn, is found in the Regulations Relating to Compulsory National Standards and Measures to Conserve Water (Compulsory National Standards).[5] Regulation 3 of the Compulsory National Standards clarifies that the minimum standard for basic water supply is a minimum quantity of 25 litres of potable water per person per day, or 6 kilolitres per household per month available within 200 metres of such household.

Giving further effect to these legal iterations, and in recognition that physical access to water is meaningless if water remains unaffordable, the national Department of Water Affairs and Forestry (as it then was) (DWAF)[6] formulated a Free Basic Water (FBW) policy in 2002 to provide—for free—at least 6 kilolitres of basic water per household per month, to be implemented by municipalities.[7] In further advancing the goal to make water affordable, on 11 June 2001, DWAF published the Norms and Standards in Respect of Tariffs for Water Services (Norms and Standards).[8] Section 6(2) of the Norms and Standards requires that all domestic water supply tariffs must have a rising block tariff structure that includes

---

[5] Regulations Relating to Compulsory National Standards and Measures to Conserve Water promulgated in terms of section 9(1) and 73(1)(*j*) of the Water Services Act (GN 509 *GG* 22355 of 8 June 2001).

[6] In May 2009, DWAF became the Department of Water Affairs (DWA), and in May 2014 it became the Department of Water Affairs and Sanitation (DWAS). For ease of reference it is referred to as DWAF throughout this chapter.

[7] DWAF 'Free Basic Water Implementation Strategy' 2 August 2002, last accessed on 15 January 2015 from <www.dwaf.gov.za/Documents/FBW/FBWImplementationStrategyAug2002.pdf>.

[8] Norms and Standards in Respect of Tariffs for Water Services in terms of section 10(1) of the Water Services Act (GN 652 *GG* 22472 of 20 July 2001).

at least three rising blocks, with the tariff increasing for higher consumption blocks (ie luxury water users pay more per kilolitre than basic users) and the first tariff block should be 'set at the lowest amount, including a zero amount' (ie the FBW concept). Finally, echoing the provisions of PAJA, the Water Services Act requires that procedures 'for the limitation or discontinuation of water services' must be 'fair and equitable', 'provide for reasonable notice of intention to limit or discontinue water services and for an opportunity to make representations' and 'not result in a person being denied access to basic water services for non-payment, where that person proves, to the satisfaction of the relevant water services authority, that he or she is unable to pay for basic services'.[9]

(b) Sanitation

The Constitution is silent on sanitation. However, the Water Services Act provides the basis for a rights-based claim to (waterborne) sanitation by referring to 'the right to basic sanitation . . . necessary to secure . . . an environment not harmful to human health or well-being'.[10] The Water Services Act defines basic sanitation as 'the prescribed minimum standards of services necessary for the safe, hygienic and adequate collection, removal, disposal or purification of human excreta, domestic waste-water and sewage from households, including informal house-holds'.[11] Further clarifying these standards, the Compulsory National Standards provides that the minimum standard for basic sanitation includes 'a toilet which is safe, reliable, environmentally sound, easy to keep clean, provides privacy and protection against the weather, well ventilated, keeps smells to a minimum and prevents the entry and exit of flies and other disease-carrying pests'.[12] In terms of pricing, the Norms and Standards requires water services institutions to differenti-ate between sanitation services to households and discharge of industrial effluent to a sewage treatment plant,[13] and also requires water services institutions to consider the right of access to basic sanitation when determining which water services tariffs are to be subsidised.[14]

Moreover, in March 2009, DWAF published a Free Basic Sanitation Implemen-tation Strategy (FBSan), which acknowledges that there is 'a right of access to a basic level of sanitation service', and that municipalities have an obligation to ensure that poor households are not denied access to basic services due to their inability to pay for such services.[15] The FBSan policy is deliberately vague, stating

---

[9] Section 4(3) of the Water Services Act.

[10] Section 2*(a)*.

[11] Section 1.

[12] Regulation 2 of the Compulsory National Standards.

[13] Section 4(1) of the Norms and Standards.

[14] Section 3(2).

[15] DWAF 'Free Basic Sanitation Implementation Strategy' 20 April 2009, last accessed on 15 Janu-ary 2015 from <www.dwaf.gov.za/dir_ws/wspd/policyinfo.aspx?filen=556>.

that free basic sanitation is a controversial issue over which there is no universal agreement. It therefore affords maximum discretion to municipalities to decide what free sanitation services to provide and even whether to implement the strategy. The FBSan policy accordingly skirts the issue of acceptable types of non-waterborne and communal toilets,[16] as well as the question of what constitutes acceptable distances between homes and communal toilets. To the extent that it provides concrete indicators, the FBSan policy recommends that where there is waterborne sanitation, an additional amount of FBW—of between three and four additional kilolitres per household per month or 15 additional litres per person per day—should be allocated to poor households over and above the mandated FBW amount. The provision of sanitation services (as well as water services) to informal settlements, should be undertaken on the basis that such interim services constitute the first phase of permanent services.[17]

(c) Electricity

There is no explicit constitutional right to electricity (or energy). However, this right can arguably be inferred from, inter alia, the right of access to adequate housing, found in s 26 of the Constitution. Internationally, the United Nations Committee on Economic, Social and Cultural Rights has determined that the right to housing can entail a right to electricity.[18] Domestically, the Constitutional Court found in *Grootboom* that 'the state's obligation to provide adequate housing depends on context, and may differ from province to province, from city to city, from rural to urban areas and from person to person', and although 'some may need access to land and no more [,] . . . some may need access to services such as water, sewage, electricity, and roads.'[19] In terms of legislation, since the Electricity Regulation Act 4 of 2006 repealed the Electricity Act 41 of 1987, municipal by-laws mainly govern electricity services. Most municipal by-laws stress equity and procedural fairness considerations.

7.3 RIGHTS-BASED ANALYSIS OF BASIC SERVICES-RELATED PUBLIC INTEREST LITIGATION[20]

The laws and policies relating to basic services outlined above reflect the following six human rights-related dimensions, which have provided the bases for the PIL cases discussed below:

---

[16] These include Ventilated Improved Pit Latrines (VIPs) and chemical toilets.

[17] Upgrading of Informal Settlements Programme (UISP) instituted in terms of s 3(4)(*g*) of the Housing Act 107 of 1997 as contained in ch 13 of the National Housing Code (National Department of Housing, 2000) (referred to as UISP in this chapter).

[18] CESCR General Comment 4 'The right to adequate housing', E/1992/23, annex III at 14, sixth session General Comment 4, The right to adequate housing, Sixth session 1991.

[19] *Government of the Republic of South Africa and Others v Grootboom and Others* [2000] ZACC 19; 2001 (1) SA 46 (CC) para 37 [LRC was admitted as *amicus curiae*].

[20] In this section, where I discuss more than one judgment (whether from the High Court, SCA or Constitutional Court) for a case, I refer to the case generically by its shortened name and cite the specific judgments in full as relevant.

- non-discrimination;
- just administrative action;
- dignity;
- participation;
- availability/quantity; and
- quality.

PIL in respect of basic services has taken up most, though not all, of these parameters, with varying judicial outcomes.[21]

(a) Non-discrimination

The first basic services-related case to come before the Constitutional Court was *Walker*.[22] *Walker* has largely gone under the radar but, although not a PIL case in that it was brought by a private litigant seeking to challenge transformative policies and practices by Pretoria municipality, it established an important principle regarding 'positive' discrimination in municipal services.

Mr Walker, a private resident of a formerly white suburb of Pretoria, asserted that his non-payment of charges for municipal services should be condoned. His argument was that Pretoria City Council's differential tariffs for water and electricity, depending on whether one lived in a formerly white or formerly black area, amounted to unfair discrimination based on race, which contravened s 8 of the interim Constitution.[23] The Constitutional Court judges disagreed, finding that, to the extent that the differential rates disadvantaged formerly white areas, this was an acceptable form of cross-subsidisation. Further, applying the test for unfair discrimination established by the court in *Harksen*,[24] the differential rates did not constitute unfair discrimination as they were implemented in line with a legitimate government purpose to cross-subsidise from historically privileged to historically disadvantaged residents (on the basis of race).

The second major case that attempted, albeit unsuccessfully, to ground a basic services-related claim in unfair racial discrimination, was the PIL battle in *Mazibuko*.[25] In this case, five desperately poor residents of Phiri (Soweto), backed by the social movement the Anti-Privatisation Forum (APF), challenged (on

---

[21] The question what (if any) broader, non-judicial, outcomes there are from litigation even where cases are 'lost' in court is receiving increasing attention in South Africa. See, for example, Jackie Dugard & Malcolm Langford 'Art or science? Synthesising lessons from public interest litigation and the dangers of legal determinism' (2011) 27 *SAJHR* 37. Some of this analysis on broader impact is reproduced below.

[22] *City Council of Pretoria v Walker* [1998] ZACC 1; 1998 (2) SA 363 (CC).

[23] Section 8 of the interim Constitution was similar to s 9 of the final Constitution.

[24] *Harksen v Lane NO and Others* [1997] ZACC 12; 1998 (1) SA 300 (CC).

[25] *Mazibuko and Others v City of Johannesburg and Others* [2008] ZAGPHC 491; [2008] 4 All SA 471 (W) (*Mazibuko* High Court); *City of Johannesburg and Others v Mazibuko and Others* [2009] ZASCA 20; 2009 (3) SA 592 (SCA) (*Mazibuko* SCA); *Mazibuko and Others v City of Johannesburg and Others* [2009] ZACC 28; 2010 (4) SA 1 (CC) (*Mazibuko* CC) [CALS and Wits Law Clinic acted

behalf of themselves and all persons similarly affected), the City of Johannesburg's (the City) water supply in Phiri on a number of grounds (many of these are discussed below[26] One of the grounds was that the imposition of prepaid water meters (PPMs) only in poor black residential areas, despite the common cause evidence of poor creditworthiness across the City, amounted to unfair discrimination based on race as prohibited by s 9 of the Constitution.

The South Gauteng High Court agreed with the residents on this (and all other grounds). The judgment of Tsoka J found the imposition of PPMs in Phiri to amount to unfair discrimination based on race and therefore unconstitutional in that:

> [t]he prepayment meters discriminate between the applicants and other residents . . . If the residents of Sandton, a wealthy and formerly white area, served by the respondents, fell into arrears with their water bills, they are entitled to notices . . . before their water supply is cut off. Moreover, they are given the opportunity to make arrangements with the respondents to settle their arrears . . . The applicants, the residents of Phiri, a poor and predominantly Black area, are denied this right. This is not only unreasonable, unfair and inequitable, it is discriminatory solely on the basis of colour.[27]

> To argue, as the respondents do, that the applicants will not be able to afford water on credit and therefore it is 'good' for the applicants to go on prepayment meters is patronising. That patronization sustained apartheid. . . . This is subtle discrimination solely on the basis of colour. Discrimination based on colour is impermissible in terms of the Constitution. . . . The underlying basis for the introduction of the prepayment meters seems to me, to be credit control. If this is true, I am unable to understand why this credit control measure is only suitable in the historically poor black areas and not the historically rich white areas. Bad payers cannot be described in terms of colour or geographical areas. . . . Bad debt is a human problem not a racial problem.[28]

The *Mazibuko* High Court judgment also raised, mainly through the sensitive judgment of Tsoka J, the issue of unfair discrimination based on gender. (The litigants did not specifically raise gender discrimination; however, the fact that four of the five applicants were women clearly struck a chord with the judge.) In ruling that PPMs were unlawful, Tsoka J commented that in a patriarchal society such as South Africa 'many chores are performed by women' and in this context it

---

for the applicants in all three courts and the Centre on Housing Rights and Evictions, represented by the LRC, was admitted as *amicus curiae* in the SCA and Constitutional Court.]

[26] I have not engaged with all grounds here due to space constraints. For an analysis of all the grounds, as well as a comprehensive critique of the Constitutional Court decision, see Sandra Liebenberg *Socio-Economic Rights: Adjudication under a Transformative Constitution* (2010) 466–80.

[27] *Mazibuko* High Court (note 25 above) para 94.

[28] Ibid paras 153–4.

appears that, by virtue of exacerbating women's struggles to access sufficient water, PPMs 'discriminate against women unfairly because of their sex'.[29]

Regrettably, these findings, that the installation of PPMs in only poor black residential areas amounted to unfair discrimination, did not survive either the Supreme Court of Appeal (SCA) or Constitutional Court appeals. The SCA declined to deal with this argument and the Constitutional Court dismissed it largely through its finding that PPMs did not disadvantage Phiri residents.[30]

(b) Just administrative action

The *Mazibuko* applicants' main challenge to PPMs was that PPMs were unlawful because—in contravention of, inter alia, s 4(3) of the Water Services Act's procedural protections—PPMs disconnected their water supply without either reasonable notice or the opportunity to make representation. This resulted in them being denied access to basic water for days and even weeks at a time for not being able to afford the normal water tariffs.[31] In the High Court this argument found traction with Tsoka J, who ruled that the automatic shutting off of the PPM water supply amounted to 'nothing but [a] limitation, discontinuation or cut off, of water supply'.[32] As such, in the absence of the reasonable notice and opportunity to make representation requirements, Tsoka J found PPMs to be unlawful and ordered the City to provide the applicants and other similarly placed residents of Phiri with the option of a conventional metered water supply installed at the City's expense.[33]

On appeal, the SCA, too, agreed that the PPM's cut-off 'clearly amounts to a discontinuation of the services' which, without notice and an opportunity to make representation, was unlawful.[34] However, despite finding PPMs unlawful on this ground, the SCA suspended the order of invalidity for two years to 'enable' the City 'to legalise the use of prepayment meters in so far as it may be possible to do so'.[35]

Concerned about the prospect of the City making only minor changes to PPMs possibly to comply with this part of the SCA's order, the *Mazibuko* applicants appealed the SCA decision to the Constitutional Court (and the City, along with the other respondents, cross-appealed). Contrary to the High Court and SCA's finding that PPM shut-offs amounted to a discontinuation of the water supply

---

[29] *Mazibuko* High Court (note 25 above) para 159.

[30] *Mazibuko* CC (note 25 above) para 154.

[31] The applicants could also have relied on PAJA's almost identical procedural protections but grounded their claim in the Water Services Act to avoid any arguments about whether a PPM shut off (ie by a machine) is administrative action.

[32] *Mazibuko* High Court (note 25 above) para 84.

[33] Ibid para 183.5.

[34] *Mazibuko* SCA (note 25 above) paras 55 and 56.

[35] Ibid para 62.

(therefore requiring reasonable notice and the opportunity to make representation prior to the disconnection), the Constitutional Court came to the following conclusion on the meaning of the word 'discontinuation':

> The ordinary meaning of 'discontinuation' is that something is made to cease to exist. The water supply does not cease to exist when a pre-paid meter temporarily stops the supply of water. It is suspended until either the customer purchases further credit or the new month commences with a new monthly basic water supply whereupon the water supply recommences. It is better understood as a temporary suspension in supply, not a discontinuation.[36]

This interpretation and, with it, the Constitutional Court's ruling that PPMs were lawful, have been convincingly criticised by leading academic commentators including Geo Quinot,[37] Sandra Liebenberg[38] and Pierre de Vos, the latter noting:

> To reach this conclusion, the Court had to ignore the fact that the Act also includes the word 'limit', which could surely not mean anything but the 'temporary suspension in supply'. In effect this aspect of the judgment ignores the express words of the legislature ('limit') in order to justify its endorsement of the neo-liberal water policies of the City of Johannesburg.[39]

Indeed, as the SCA judgment noted in response to the City's argument that the cut-off of the water supply by PPMs did not 'amount to a discontinuation of water services because the water services are still available against payment': 'On that basis one can argue that water services are not discontinued to a consumer to whom water is provided on credit when the water supply is cut-off due to non-payment.'[40] The Constitutional Court's logic, which allows residents with conventional meters to enjoy procedural protection prior to water shut-offs while denying this to PPM water users, seems to contradict its finding that PPMs do not amount to unfair discrimination.

More generally, the Constitutional Court's dismissal of the *Mazibuko* applicants' claim for procedural protection appears at odds with the approach in two other judgments that highlighted the importance of procedural requirements, one prior to *Mazibuko* from the South Gauteng High Court—*Bon Vista Mansions*[41]— and one the day after *Mazibuko* from the Constitutional Court itself—*Joseph*.[42]

---

[36] *Mazibuko* CC (note 25 above) para 120.

[37] Geo Quinot 'Substantive reasoning in administrative-law adjudication' (2010) 3 *Constitutional Court Review* 111.

[38] Liebenberg (note 26 above) 473–4.

[39] Pierre de Vos 'Water is life (but life is cheap)' *Constitutionally Speaking* 13 October 2009, last accessed on 16 January 2015 from <www.constitutionalyspeaking.co.za/water-is-life-but-life-is-cheap/>.

[40] *Mazibuko* SCA (note 25 above) para 55.

[41] *Residents of Bon Vista Mansions v Southern Metropolitan Local Council* [2002] JOL 9513 (W); 2002 (6) BCLR 625 (W).

[42] *Joseph and Others v City of Johannesburg and Others* [2009] ZACC 30; 2010 (4) SA 55 (CC) [CALS/Wits Law Clinic acted for the applicants].

In *Bon Vista Mansions*, Budlender AJ was faced with undefended applicants whose water supply in a block of flats in Hillbrow had been disconnected following a 'standard notice' from the applicable Johannesburg local council of the time. In ruling that any such disconnection is a *prima facie* violation of the right to water, Budlender AJ granted an interim order for the city council to restore the water supply pending further inquiry, noting:

> A genuine opportunity to make representations is particularly important in the light of the provision that water supply may not be discontinued if it results in a person being denied access to basic water services for non-payment, where that person proves, to the satisfaction of the relevant water services authority, that he or she is unable to pay for basic services.[43]

Echoing this judicial concern over the disconnection of basic service supply, in *Joseph* the Constitutional Court tackled the issue of disconnecting the electricity supply of low-income residents in Johannesburg without notice. Here, in compliance with their rental agreements, the tenants had been paying their landlord for electricity services as part of their monthly rent and were up to date on their payments. However, the landlord, who controlled the building's electricity account with the City and whose responsibility it was to pay all electricity-related charges for the building to the City, had not been passing on the electricity-related payments to the City and had allowed substantial arrears to run up on the municipal account. The City's electricity service provider, City Power, accordingly disconnected the electricity supply after receiving no response to various notices to the landlord regarding the municipal arrears. Relying on the City's electricity by-laws,[44] which allowed disconnecting a tenant's supply without notice, neither the City nor the landlord had notified the tenants of the looming electricity disconnection.

Without an explicit right to electricity in the Constitution or legislation, the applicants' instructing attorneys (the Centre for Applied Legal Studies) considered this a more risky case than *Mazibuko*.[45] To found the PAJA claim aimed at the need for notice to the tenants prior to disconnecting their electricity supply (PAJA requires that a right must be adversely affected), the applicants argued that there was an implicit right to electricity in the right to adequate housing (s 26 of the Constitution). Although not accepting this interpretation, the Constitutional Court ruled in favour of the applicants, finding that they had a 'public law right' to electricity services based on, inter alia, s 73 of the Municipal Systems Act, which provides that municipalities must ensure that 'all members of the local community

---

[43] *Bon Vista Mansions* (note 41 above) para 26.

[44] By-law 14(1) of the Greater Johannesburg Metropolitan Council: Standardisation of Electricity By-laws (GN 1610 *GG* 16 of 17 March 1999) published in terms of s 101 of the Local Government Ordinance 17 of 1939 (Johannesburg's electricity by-laws).

[45] See the comparison of these two cases in Dugard & Langford (note 21 above) 37.

have access to at least the minimum level of basic municipal services' (an argument not raised by the applicants).

On this basis the Constitutional Court found that the applicants could rely on PAJA's procedural protections including the right to be notified before having their electricity supply disconnected and ordered the City to sever the words 'without notice' from their electricity by-laws.

(c) Dignity

The dignity-related implications of inadequate access to basic services have most sharply surfaced in two cases concerning sanitation—*Nokotyana*[46] and *Beja*.[47] These cases resulted in conflicting decisions on the issue, with the Constitutional Court in *Nokotyana* taking a more dismissive approach towards the indignity of inadequate toilets than the Western Cape High Court's subsequent, more sensitive, approach in *Beja*.

Nokotyana concerned an application by the residents of Harry Gwala informal settlement in Ekurhuleni Municipality for, inter alia, the provision of temporary basic sanitation facilities pending the province's decision to upgrade the informal settlement—a decision that has been pending for many years, during which the residents had to use makeshift pit latrines they had dug themselves. Skirting the issue of dignity (by stating that it was not 'most appropriate' to rely on the 'general right to human dignity'[48]), as well as the adequacy of the sanitation facilities— including the municipality's offer on the eve of the Constitutional Court hearing to provide one chemical toilet for every ten households (see section *(e)* below)—the Constitutional Court instead focused on the province's delay in taking a decision to upgrade the settlement, finding the delay of over three years to be 'unjustified and unacceptable' and ordering Gauteng Province to 'take a final decision' on the municipality's application to upgrade the settlement within 14 months.[49]

The Constitutional Court's disappointing approach towards the sanitation/dignity nexus contrasts sharply with that of the Western Cape High Court in *Beja*. In this case, the residents of Makhaza informal settlement in Khayelitsha, Cape Town, asked the court to declare the 1 316 unenclosed toilets that the municipality had constructed as part of an upgrading project undertaken in terms of the UISP unconstitutional. The municipality referred to the toilets as 'loos with a view' and argued that the toilets had been constructed pursuant to an agreement with the community that, instead of the one toilet per five households the municipality was

---

[46] *Nokotyana and Others v Ekurhuleni Metropolitan Municipality and Others* [2009] ZACC 33; 2010 (4) BCLR 312 (CC) [Webber Wentzel's pro bono department acted for the applicants].

[47] *Beja and Others v Premier of the Western Cape and Others* [2011] ZAWCHC 97; [2011] 3 All SA 401 (WCC).

[48] *Nokotyana* (note 46 above) para 49.

[49] Ibid paras 54 and 61. At the time of writing this chapter, over five years after the date of the order, there was still no clear plan about whether or how to upgrade the settlement.

obliged to provide (see sections *(d)* and *(e)* below), it would provide one toilet per household and the residents would enclose the toilets. Having undertaken an inspection *in loco*, Erasmus J found the unenclosed toilets to be 'reprehensible' and that they failed to 'afford any regard to the dignity of poor people'.[50] Having found that the unenclosed toilets violated the residents' s 10 right to human dignity, he ordered the municipality to enclose the 1 316 toilets.[51]

(d) Participation

An implicit underpinning of South Africa's legal and administrative order is the concept of participation. Although there is no stand-alone constitutional right to public participation, the requirement for consultation, engagement, or participation is hardwired into many laws and processes and has been regularly emphasised by the Constitutional Court and other courts as an intrinsic democratic requirement.[52] Yet, in dealing with the question whether the City had properly consulted with residents prior to the installation of PPMs in the *Mazibuko* case, the Constitutional Court opted for a deferential approach that, again, contrasted with the subsequent High Court judgment in *Beja* on the issue of what constitutes adequate consultation.

In *Mazibuko*, the Phiri residents argued that they were not properly consulted prior to the installation of PPMs. To counter this allegation, the City pointed to the notice it had given residents, headed 'Notice: Individual house connection finalization', which advised residents that Johannesburg Water (Pty) Ltd (JW) was giving notice that:

> you will be provided with a Level of Service 3 [PPM] . . . Should you refuse to be metered JW will be obliged to provide you wish [sic] a Level of Service 2 consisting of an unmetered water connection pipe with a flow restriction device linked to a yard standpipe . . . Furthermore, for a Level of Service 2 no plumbing fixtures on the property shall be connected to the water connection pipe or yard standpipe by JW and any such connections by you shall be deemed illegal . . . Should you choose to change to Level of Service 3 at a later stage, after installation of a Level of Service 2 yard standpipe, a connection charge of R650,00 will be later payable by you to JW. Should JW not hear from you within seven (7) calendar days of receipt of this notice, JW will assume that you have opted to [sic] a Level Service 3.[53]

---

[50] *Beja* (note 47 above) para 19.

[51] Ibid para 192.

[52] See for example the commentary on the requirement for meaningful engagement with residents in the context of applications for eviction in *Occupiers of 51 Olivia Road, Berea Township and 197 Main Street Johannesburg v City of Johannesburg* [2008] ZACC 1; 2008 (3) SA 208 (CC) [Wits Law Clinic acted for the applicants and LRC for the Centre on Housing Rights and Evictions and Community Law Centre were admitted as *amici curiae*].

[53] *Mazibuko* High Court (note 25 above) para 108.

In the High Court, Tsoka J found this notice to be misleading, intimidating and unreasonable.[54] From the contents of the handful of other similar notices provided to the residents, he found that 'it is obvious' that the PPMs 'were approved for and not by the residents of Phiri' in that 'the terms of the notices do convey' PPMs as 'a fait accompli'. Tsoka J held that:

> The purpose of the notices was merely to sell an accomplished fact to the residents of Phiri. It is on this basis that, I understand Mr Trengove's argument that, the actions of the respondents were not consultative but a publicity drive for the prepayment measuring systems.[55]

The Constitutional Court, in contrast, glossed over the issue of prior consultation (largely on the basis that it found that the decision to install PPMs did not amount to administrative action[56]), satisfying itself that 'there was extensive consultation with communities about what the project would entail and how it would be implemented' and that, according to a survey by the City, 'the vast majority of residents had accepted pre-paid water meters'.[57] Interestingly, faced with similar modes of 'consultation' undertaken by the City of Cape Town regarding the 'agreement' for residents to enclose their own toilets in *Beja*, Erasmus J stressed the importance of proper consultation with communities. The court ruled that the City of Cape Town's argument of having held some meetings at which sanitation was discussed and having 'collected "happy letters" from the majority of the community ... with only one negative comment', was 'simply not good enough'.[58]

(e) Availability/quantity

There have been four relevant decisions regarding the availability/quantity of basic services. Two cases dealt with water—*Manqele*[59] and *Mazibuko*. The other two cases concerned sanitation—*Nokotyana* and *Beja*. Of these, *Beja* is the only one in which the court agreed that the applicants had a right to a higher level of service than that provided.

In *Manqele*, which was handed down just before the Compulsory National Standards (discussed above) were promulgated, the Durban and Coast Local Division of the High Court ruled that the disconnection of the water supply of Mrs Manqele, an unemployed, desperately poor woman, could not be found to be a violation of the Water Services Act. Moreover, the court ruled that because Mrs Manqele's attorneys had not raised a s 27(1)(b) constitutional challenge at the

---

[54] *Mazibuko* High Court (note 29 above) para 110.

[55] Ibid para 122.

[56] For a critique of this finding see Liebenberg (note 30 above) 474–75.

[57] *Mazibuko* CC (note 25 above) para 167.

[58] *Beja* (note 47 above) paras 93–4.

[59] *Manqele v Durban Transitional Metropolitan Council* 2002 (6) SA 423 (D).

outset of the case, Mrs Manqele was not entitled 'to simply turn her case into an application under the Constitution'.[60]

In *Mazibuko*, both the High Court and the SCA agreed with the Phiri residents that the City's FBW was insufficient to meet their needs (which included water-borne sanitation and the basic water-related needs of multi-dwelling households in an urban setting) and therefore found the policy to be unreasonable. However, despite the common cause fact that households were left without water for days and even weeks at a time, the Constitutional Court ruled that the City's FBW policy was reasonable, largely on the basis that it had improved in the course of the litigation.[61]

Regarding sanitation services, in *Nokotyana* the applicants rejected the municipality's post-high court offer to provide the residents with one chemical toilet per ten households, asking the Constitutional Court to order the municipality to provide one ventilated improved pit latrine per household. Sidestepping the question of the quantity/availability of the sanitation services offered, the Constitutional Court rejected this plea largely on the grounds that the National Housing Code (particularly the UISP) did not oblige municipalities to provide any interim services in informal settlements where no decision had yet been taken regarding the upgrading of such informal settlements.[62] This interpretation of the National Housing Code and UISP has been criticised for being too narrow an interpretation of the state's basic services-related obligations under the National Housing Code.[63]

Unlike the Constitutional Court in *Nokotyana*, in *Beja* the High Court took up the issue of the ratio of toilets to households. Whereas the City of Cape Town had offered one toilet for every five households, purportedly on the basis of the National Housing Code/UISP, Erasmus J found that this ratio was applicable only to emergency housing situations of a temporary nature and that the 'standards that are applicable for emergency housing will be lower than those required for projects designed to be of a longer duration and that can be implemented after considered planning' such as the Makhaza settlement.[64] As such, he ruled that the City could not 'rely on the 1:5 ratio to justify, with reference to any legislative framework, the installation of unenclosed toilets as it did'.[65]

---

[60] *Manqele* (note 59 above) para 427.

[61] *Mazibuko* CC (note 25 above) paras 94–7. For a critique of this finding see Liebenberg (note 26 above) 467–72 and Lucy Williams 'The role of courts in the quantitative-implementation of social and economic rights: A comparative study' (2010) 3 *Constitutional Court Review* 141.

[62] *Nokotyana* (note 46 above) paras 36–43.

[63] Marie Huchzermeyer 'Chapter Nine, A challenge to the state's avoidance to upgrade the Harry Gwala informal settlement' in *Cities with 'Slums': From Informal Settlement Eradication to a Right to the City* (2011) 236–7.

[64] *Beja* (note 47 above) para 114.

[65] Ibid para 117.

(f) Quality

Somewhat surprisingly, there have been few PIL cases thus far dealing with the quality of basic services. It is possible that some of these cases might have been approached from an environmental law angle (which falls outside the scope of this chapter) rather than a basic services angle. One case that stands out for tackling the quality of water services is *FSE*.[66] In this case, in the context of their water supply having been contaminated by acid mine water, the residents of Silobela on the outskirts of Carolina in Mpumalanga brought an urgent application before the North Gauteng High Court for the government (the respondents ranged from national through provincial to municipal spheres) to provide them with access to potable water as prescribed by reg 3*(b)* of the Compulsory National Standards. Relying mainly on the Compulsory National Standards, Mavundla J ordered the acting executive mayor and municipal manager of the Gert Sibanda District Municipality to provide the residents of Silobela with temporary potable water in line with reg 3*(b)* of the Compulsory National Standards.[67]

7.4 CONCLUSION

Undoubtedly, the raft of progressive law and policy frameworks outlined in s 7.2 has provided a solid basis for both community mobilisation (not discussed here[68]) and, to a lesser extent, PIL. That there has not been more PIL might be explained by several factors ranging from the counter-veiling high level of protest over basic services (ie dissatisfied communities have chosen to protest rather than litigate, which is perhaps a more effective form of challenge over these specific services) to the relative incoherence of basic services-related jurisprudence. It is possible that the relative incoherence of basic services-related jurisprudence is itself a consequence of less coordinated PIL mobilisation/organisation[69] in this sector compared, specifically, to the housing PIL sector, which has been able to build a coherent and strategic litigation trajectory beginning with negative rights violations and advancing the frontiers of the right step by step.

Without more comparative research across the various thematic PIL sectors, it is not possible to draw any conclusions regarding the latter point. Whatever the reasons—which might just as well relate to judicial incoherence regarding basic

---

[66] *The Federation for Sustainable Environment and Others v The Minister of Water Affairs and Others* (GPPHC) unreported case 35672/12 of 10 July 2012 [LHR acted for the first applicant and LRC acted for the second applicant].

[67] Ibid para 25.

[68] For a discussion of basic services-related mobilised protest see Jackie Dugard 'Urban basic services: Rights, reality and resistance' in Malcolm Langford et al (eds) *Socio-Economic Rights in South Africa: Symbols or Substance?* (2014) 275.

[69] It is striking and possibly significant that the attorneys/legal teams were different in almost every case, and that in one (*Bon Vista*) there were no attorneys involved and in another it was a private attorney as opposed to a litigating NGO (*Manqele*). There are only two cases that share the same instructing attorneys—*Mazibuko* and *Joseph* (CALS/Wits Law Clinic).

services as to any lack of strategy or coordination among PIL actors—it is worth critically reflecting on the jurisprudence in terms of the gains, gaps, disappointments and contradictions.

Taken as a whole, the *Manqele*, *Mazibuko* and *Nokotyana* judgments have been overwhelmingly disappointing, while the *Bon Vista* judgment profoundly affirmed socio-economic rights. On an issue-based analysis, the clearest legal gain has been regarding the quality of water, as regulated in the Compulsory National Standards and reflected in the unambiguous decision in the *FSE* case, albeit not from an appeal court. In addition, through the *Joseph* judgment, the Constitutional Court has provided a basis for administrative justice-related claims for basic services that are not explicitly referred to in the Constitution such as electricity and refuse removal. And *Beja* stands as a beacon of sensitively progressive law-making, but the conflicting decisions of the Constitutional Court in *Mazibuko* (participation) and *Nokotyana* (dignity and availability/quantity) limit its resonance.

There have been other important gains from the Constitutional Court's affirmation in *Walker* that positive discrimination to redress the historical disadvantage of basic services in black residential areas is not a violation of s 9 of the Constitution. However, the positive impact of *Walker* has been somewhat offset by the disappointment of *Mazibuko* in which the Constitutional Court failed to find that PPMs amounted to unfair discrimination based on either race or gender. As such, *Walker* remains the only socio-economic rights case of the Constitutional Court to have made a finding of unfair discrimination based on race. To date, no socio-economic rights case has definitively ruled on unfair discrimination based on gender (and the only other socio-economic rights case to have a definitive ruling on unfair discrimination is *Khosa*,[70] which found the exclusion of permanent residents from social security benefits to amount to impermissible unfair discrimination based on citizenship).

There also remains a gap—access, whether economic or physical. There has not yet been any basic services-related PIL on this issue. This is surprising given the clearly defined standards for access particularly to water services. And the clearest peer-level contradiction has been the different approach by the Constitutional Court to the issue of the disconnection of basic services found in the *Mazibuko* and *Joseph* judgments. Geo Quinot, among others, has pointed out the contradiction from an administrative justice perspective of the dismissive approach taken by the Constitutional Court to the issue of notice prior to disconnection in *Mazibuko*, compared with the concern to defend it in *Joseph*.[71]

---

[70] *Khosa and Others v Minister of Social Development* [2004] ZACC 11; 2004 (6) SA 505 (CC).
[71] Quinot (note 37 above).

Chapter 8

HEALTH CARE

Nikki Stein

8.1 INTRODUCTION

The introduction of the new Constitution, heralding the advent of democracy and entrenching a progressive Bill of Rights, brought with it a justiciable right of access to health care services. Section 27 of the Constitution provides that:

(1) Everyone has the right to have access to—
(a) health care services, including reproductive health care;
(b) sufficient food and water; and
(c) social security, including, if they are unable to support themselves and their dependants, appropriate social assistance.
(2) The state must take reasonable legislative and other measures, within its available resources, to achieve the progressive realisation of each of these rights.
(3) No one may be refused emergency medical treatment.

Unfortunately, this is not a silver bullet that, on its own, will cause or catalyse the achievement of access to quality health care services. The right to health is complex, and the multi-faceted obligations that arise from it are imposed on various actors. In this chapter, against the background of health rights litigation undertaken so far, I focus on two themes that should inform strategic litigation on the right of access to health care services in an effort to secure maximum impact.

The first is the distinction between positive and negative obligations: the obligation to direct resources at the incremental improvement in health care services, and the obligation not to take away from the existing enjoyment of the right. As I discuss below, there has been an increase in negative breaches of the right to health. This, alongside direct violations of the right to health, undermines any progressive measures to advance the achievement of the right.

The second theme focuses on the obligations of private actors in realising the right to health. As I discuss below, the nature of the right to health is such that it imposes obligations on several actors in both the public and private sectors. Although in early litigation on the right to health the focus was primarily on the role of the state, there is an increasing recognition that the health care system as a whole requires the reasonable exercise of power by both the state and private entities involved in health care services. Litigation and advocacy on the right to health therefore entail challenging both public and private power and supporting the actions of public and private actors who advance the realisation of the right.

After a discussion of these aspects of the right to health, I conclude with a few thoughts on litigating on the right to health in future.

8.2 POSITIVE AND NEGATIVE OBLIGATIONS ARISING FROM THE RIGHT TO HEALTH

The socio-economic rights in our Constitution are framed in such a way that they impose two types of obligations:

- 'positive' obligations, which require reasonable legislative and other measures within available resources to achieve the progressive realisation of rights; and
- so-called 'negative' obligations, which prohibit conduct that limits or diminishes the current enjoyment of the right.

This distinction is reflected in s 7(2) of the Constitution, which requires the state to '*respect, protect, promote* and *fulfil* the rights in the Bill of Rights'. While the obligation to 'respect' is understood to entail the negative obligation not to interfere with existing rights, the duties to 'protect, promote and fulfil' cover a range of positive obligations of the state. The positive obligations arising from the right to health require deliberate, and often resource-intensive steps, to build on access to and quality of health care services so that patients are in a better position than they were previously. This would include, for example, purchasing suitable patient transport vehicles to provide transport services to patients who previously did not have this assistance in accessing health care facilities. It would also include the creation and filling of posts for staff in under-staffed clinics, to ensure that patients relying on these clinics can access the services that they offer.

Where the state takes a decision to close a health care facility with no suitable alternatives for the patients who rely on the services of that facility, it is in breach of its negative obligation to respect the right to health. Similarly, where there is a sharp increase in the price of medicines to the point that they become unaffordable, and patients who could previously access these medicines can no longer do so, their enjoyment of the right to health diminishes.

(a) Legal interventions on the positive obligations falling on the state arising from the right to health

Much litigation on the right to health, particularly in the earlier years of the constitutional dispensation, has focused on the positive obligations arising from the right to health. For example, in *Soobramoney*,[1] the first case before the Constitutional Court involving the right to health, Mr Soobramoney, sought an order compelling the state to provide him with dialysis treatment for chronic renal failure. He was denied this treatment because of the limited resources available for this treatment, and the fact that the dialysis may prolong his life but would not offer a cure. In other words, the case highlighted the difficult but necessary prioritisation of health care services within the context of limited resources.

In analysing the obligations imposed on the state by s 27 of the Constitution, Chaskalson P, in writing for the court, held as follows:

> What is apparent from these provisions is that the obligations imposed on the state by sections 26 and 27 in regard to access to housing, health care, food, water and social security are dependent upon the resources available for such purposes, and that the corresponding rights themselves are limited by reason of the lack of resources. Given this lack of resources and the significant demands on them that have already been referred to, an unqualified obligation to meet these needs would not presently be capable of being fulfilled.[2]

Thus, the question became how the resources available could best be used to provide the greatest benefit. In other words, given the resources available at the time, the court declined to extend the scope of the right to health to include an entitlement to dialysis treatment to treat chronic illness. It recognised the right of the state to triage its resources, and the reality that the state had no choice but to do so.

The Constitutional Court faced a very different situation in one of South Africa's most renowned judicial decisions, the *Treatment Action Campaign* case.[3] In that case, the court adjudicated a challenge by the Treatment Action Campaign (TAC) to a programme for the provision of an antiretroviral drug called nevirapine to prevent mother-to-child transmission of HIV. A single dose of nevirapine, administered to both mother and child, could protect the child from becoming infected with HIV. It was therefore effective—from a cost perspective and a therapeutic perspective—in limiting the number of new HIV infections, in the context of a growing HIV epidemic in South Africa.

At the heart of the TAC's challenge was that the medicine was made available in the public health sector only in a limited number of pilot sites, and mothers giving

---

[1] *Soobramoney v Minister of Health (KwaZulu-Natal)* [1997] ZACC 17; 1998 (1) SA 765 (CC).

[2] Ibid para 11.

[3] *Minister of Health and Others v Treatment Action Campaign and Others (No 2)* 2002 (5) SA 721 (CC) [LRC acted for the respondents; IDASA, Community Law Centre and Cotlands Baby Sanctuary were admitted as *amici curiae*, the last represented by Wits Law Clinic] (*Treatment Action Campaign*).

birth elsewhere would not have access to it. The government's reasoning behind limiting access was that it wanted to ensure the safety and efficacy of the medicine and mitigate any risks of resistance that may arise before providing nevirapine more widely.

A critical distinction between this case and the *Soobramoney* case was that making nevirapine available to all mothers where it was medically necessary would not involve substantial expenditure of resources; the medicine was at that stage being provided to the state free of charge. As such, the TAC argued that the decision not to make nevirapine more widely available was not a 'reasonable measure' in order to achieve the progressive realisation of the right to health, and that the state was therefore in breach of its positive obligations.

The Constitutional Court was therefore called upon to consider whether the state's decision to limit access to nevirapine was reasonable. The court endorsed its previous approach in *Grootboom*[4] that a programme for the realisation of socio-economic rights must:

> be balanced and flexible and make appropriate provision for attention to . . . crises and to short, medium and long term needs. A programme that excludes a significant segment of society cannot be said to be reasonable.[5]

The court found that the policy of the state was unreasonable for the following reasons:

> Government policy was an inflexible one that denied mothers and their newborn children at public hospitals and clinics outside the research and training sites the opportunity of receiving a single dose of nevirapine at the time of the birth of the child. A potentially lifesaving drug was on offer and where testing and counselling facilities were available it could have been administered within the available resources of the state without any known harm to mother or child.[6]

The court also held that, although there was a legitimate government interest in continuing ongoing research into safety, efficacy and resistance to nevirapine, and developing the necessary infrastructure according to its findings, expectant mothers and their children should not be denied access to this medicine until this was all put in place.[7]

Building on the court's decision, and using research, advocacy, education and litigation, the TAC continued to fight for a comprehensive programme for antiretroviral therapy to be provided to people living with HIV. The TAC has therefore used the *Treatment Action Campaign* case as a platform to fight for, and achieve, incremental improvements in access to medicines used in the treatment and

---

[4] *Government of the Republic of South Africa v Grootboom* [2000] ZACC 19; 2001 (1) SA 46 (CC) [LRC was admitted as *amicus curiae*] (*Grootboom*).

[5] Ibid para 43; *Treatment Action Campaign* (note 3 above) para 68.

[6] *Treatment Action Campaign* (note 3 above) para 80.

[7] Ibid para 68.

prevention of HIV.[8] In 2003, a national antiretroviral treatment (ARV) programme was launched in terms of which antiretrovirals became available free of charge in the public sector through a government-funded programme.[9] In 2017, approximately 3.5 million people benefited from this programme,[10] the world's largest antiretroviral programme.

The continued availability and efficacy of this programme is dependent on well-functioning health systems to support it, and so it is essential that work on the right to health going forward takes account of the underlying systems on which the ARV programme depends.

This was one of the reasons that the AIDS Law Project decided in 2010 to close its doors and reconstitute itself as SECTION27. The AIDS Law Project had worked closely with the TAC in securing access to this treatment through litigation, legal research and advocacy. SECTION27, like the AIDS Law Project, is a public interest law centre, but with a broader focus on health systems and the social determinants of health, including the rights to basic education and food.

Following the *Treatment Action Campaign* judgment, therefore, the TAC, the AIDS Law Project[11] and, later, its successor SECTION27, and many of their partner organisations have been involved in advocacy, litigation and other forms of legal challenge that have had a bearing on the right to health.[12] These interventions have mostly followed the trend of the focus on the positive obligations arising from the right to health.

(b) Litigation interventions on the negative obligations arising out of the right to health

More recently, however, litigation and other legal interventions on the right to health have had to focus on regressive measures that diminish the current enjoyment of the right. While this does not exclude or reduce work on the positive obligations arising from the right to health, it is essential to focus on the negative obligations as well to ensure that progress made in access to quality health care services to date does not collapse.

---

[8] See Mark Heywood 'South Africa's Treatment Action Campaign: Combining law and social mobilization to realize the right to health' (2009) 1 *Journal of Human Rights Practice* 14–36.

[9] Ushma Mehta et al 'Pharmacovigilance: A public health priority for South Africa' 2017 *South African Health Review* 125 at 126.

[10] Peter Barron & Ashnie Padarath 'Twenty years of the South African Health Review' 2017 *South African Health Review* 1 at 5.

[11] See Didi Moyle *Speaking Truth to Power: The Story of the AIDS Law Project* (2015).

[12] See generally Jonathan Berger 'Litigating for social justice in post-apartheid South Africa: A focus on health and education' in Varun Gauri & Daniel Brinks (eds) *Courting Social Justice: Judicial Enforcement of Social and Economic Rights in the Developing World* (2008) 38–99.

A startling example of this can be found in the events leading up to and including the Life Esidimeni arbitration.[13] The case found its origin in a decision of the Gauteng Department of Health (GDoH) in October 2015 to terminate its contract with Life Esidimeni (Pty) Ltd (Life Esidimeni). For more than 30 years, Life Esidimeni had been providing highly specialised chronic mental health care services to more than 1 700 mental health care users in the Gauteng province in terms of a public private partnership with the GDoH. At the time that they terminated the contract, the GDoH cited budgetary constraints as the primary reason for the decision. Its plan was to transfer the mental health care users to non-governmental organisations (NGOs) in Gauteng, or to discharge them to the care of their families.

The decision to terminate the contract was met with widespread opposition. It went against advice from medical professionals, including psychiatrists. Family members of the mental health care users scheduled to be discharged also voiced their objections to their loved ones being discharged from Life Esidimeni and transferred to other facilities. At the heart of this opposition lay the concern that mental health care users, who were receiving adequate mental health care services at Life Esidimeni, would experience a lower standard of care and that NGOs or home care by their families would not adequately meet their specific needs.

The decline in the standard of care that ultimately materialised was severe. Mental health care users were transferred to newly established NGOs that did not have the necessary skills, experience, or resources to provide the required levels of care. Reports later emerged that mental health care users were becoming dangerously ill, and many were losing their lives. The causes of death included starvation, dehydration, septic bedsores and overdosing on medication.

To make matters worse, the families of these mental health care users did not even know where their loved ones had been transferred to. Many of them spent weeks or months trying to locate them. Some of these family members only found their loved ones after they had lost their lives. Families persisted in their quest for information that was essential to protect the rights and interests of the mental health care users, but the GDoH persisted in their refusal to engage meaningfully with the families.[14]

The initial broad statement of 'budgetary constraints', together with assertions of the benefits of deinstitutionalisation of mental health care users, remained as the

---

[13] A full discussion of the background to and circumstances of this matter is set out in Malegapuru Makgoba 'The report into the circumstances surrounding the deaths of mentally ill patients: Gauteng Province; No guns: 94+ silent deaths and still counting', *SECTION27* 1 February 2017, last accessed on 19 January 2018 from <http://section27.org.za/wp-content/uploads/2016/04/Life-Esidimeni-FINALREPORT.pdf> (Ombud Report).

[14] The obligation to consult arises from s 25(2)(g) of the National Health Act 61 of 2003 and, among other cases, *Bel Porto School Governing Body v Premier, Western Cape* [2002] ZACC 2; 2002 (3) SA 265 (CC) para 238.

stock explanation from the GDoH for its decision to discharge more than 1 700 mental health care users from specialised facilities to newly established NGOs that lacked the skills and resources to meet even their most basic needs.

The families participated in an arbitration before Moseneke DCJ (retired) from September 2017 until February 2018 to determine equitable redress for those affected by the tragedy. The arbitration resulted from a recommendation by the health ombudsman, who was appointed by the Minister of Health in 2016 to investigate the circumstances of these deaths.[15] In addition to the determination of equitable redress, the process was used to compel the disclosure of information and an explanation of the events leading up to and surrounding the termination of the contract with Life Esidimeni and the discharge of mental health care users.

The arbitration was complex, and a full discussion of the process is not possible in this chapter. One of the clearest threads that emerged through the evidence, however, is that the decision to terminate the contract with Life Esidimeni could not have been motivated by resource constraints. The events that followed the discharge of mental health care users have in fact cost the GDoH far more money than what they would have paid had they not terminated the contract.

The arbitration award was announced on 19 March 2018. Moseneke DCJ (retired) described the project as a 'harrowing account of death, torture and disappearance of utterly vulnerable mental health care users in the care of an admittedly delinquent provincial government'. He stated that the project was a serious violation of the constitutionally entrenched rights to human dignity, family life and access to quality health care services, and that the treatment of mental health care users amounted to torture. In addition, he found that the project offended the constitutional principles governing public administration. He stated that the project entailed 'irregular expenditure, mismanagement, incompetence and possible fraud in the Gauteng Department of Health'.[16]

In his order, Moseneke DCJ (retired) accepted an agreement between the parties for common-law damages amounting to R200 000 for the family of each deceased mental health care user. These included common-law damages for emotional shock and funeral expenses. He also awarded R1 million to each of the families as constitutional damages, arising from the severe breaches of the constitutional rights of the mental health care users and their families.[17] The award of constitutional damages is itself noteworthy. The courts have only awarded constitutional

---

[15] Ombud Report (note 10 above) 55.

[16] SECTION27 welcomes the Life Esidimeni arbitration award', last accessed from <http://section27.org.za/2018/03/section27-welcomes-life-esidimeni-arbitration-award/> on 29 March 2018. The full text of the award is available at: <https://www.timeslive.co.za/news/south-africa/2018-03-20-in-full–life-esidimeni-arbitration-handed-down-by-moseneke/>.

[17] Ibid.

damages in two cases to date,[18] and it is a remedy that is being cautiously developed.[19]

The regressive measures that severely diminished the mental health care users' access to quality health care services ultimately could not be explained or justified. This project is an example of a clear and serious violation of the state's negative obligations arising from the right to health. The project resulted in the death of 144 mental health care users and the pain, suffering and torture of 1 418 surviving mental health care users and their families.[20]

Even if, as alleged by the state in this case, there were budgetary constraints, these do not automatically and entirely absolve the state of its obligations. We know from decisions of our courts on other rights that a mere assertion of budgetary constraints is not sufficient to defend successfully an argument of breach of positive obligations. While a lack of resources is of course relevant, it is incumbent on the state to show that the measures it has taken to advance the right are reasonable, which includes that they are based on a proper understanding of the nature and scope of the right and their concomitant obligations.[21]

The level of scrutiny is even higher in the case of breaches of negative obligations. The Constitutional Court in *Grootboom* discussed the interaction between progressive realisation of socio-economic rights and regressive measures that undermine the realisation of these rights.[22] The court made clear that:

- the goal of the Constitution is to meet the basic rights of members of our society effectively and further that the state must take progressive steps to achieve this goal;
- these progressive steps must demonstrate that the state is acting as expeditiously and effectively as possible towards that goal; and
- that '[a]ny deliberately retrogressive measures in that regard would require the most careful consideration and would need to be fully justified by reference to the totality of the rights' in our Constitution.[23]

---

[18] *Modderfontein Squatters, Greater Benoni v Modderklip Boerdery (Pty) Ltd; President of the Republic of South Africa and Others v Modderklip Boerdery (Pty) Ltd* [2005] ZACC 5; 2004 (6) SA 40 SCA [Agri SA, Nkuzi Development Association, CLC and Programme for Land and Agrarian Studies were admitted as *amici curiae*, the LRC representing the latter three] para 65; *MEC for the Department of Welfare v Kate* [2006] ZASCA 49; SA 478 (SCA) para 33.

[19] See the discussion by Georgina Jephson and Osmond Mngomezulu in ch 4, 'Constitutional Litigation Procedure' in section 4.4.

[20] Ibid.

[21] *City of Johannesburg Metropolitan Municipality v Blue Moonlight Properties 39 (Pty) Ltd* 2012 (2) SA 104 (CC) paras 68–74 [Wits Law Clinic acted for the second respondent and LHR was admitted as *amicus curiae*].

[22] *Grootboom* (note 4 above) para 45.

[23] Although this quotation relates to retrogressive measures in relation to the provisions of the International Covenant on Economic, Social and Cultural Rights, the Court noted that it bears the same meaning in the Constitution in the South African context.

The concept of progressive realisation involves incremental improvements in the advancement of a right, building on what has already been put in place. Where there are breaches of negative obligations, such as withdrawing or reducing resources, personnel or infrastructure, this not only affects the negative aspects of the right, but it frustrates the progressive realisation of the positive obligations as well. It destabilises the foundation that is necessary for incremental improvements in access to quality health care services.

I anticipate that, in the near future, our courts will build on this jurisprudence. A major contributing factor is the ever-increasing fiscal pressure in general, and in relation to the right to health specifically. Unfortunately, there has been a levelling off at best and, more likely, a decrease in real terms in per capita expenditure in the public health sector.[24] With less money to spend on quality health care services, it is probable that there will be an erosion of the services currently available through the public sector, and a consequent breach of the state's negative obligations.

The proposed introduction of National Health Insurance (NHI) seeks to achieve more equitable spending on health care services and, through that, universal health coverage. An NHI Fund will procure health care services from both the public and private sectors. The success of NHI depends on a stable system that can sustain these changes. It will, however, likely require the injection of substantial resources to ensure that everyone has access to quality health care services as envisaged. This is addressed in further detail below.

8.3 PRIVATE POWER AND THE RIGHT TO HEALTH

We know from the early jurisprudence of the Constitutional Court—as well as the text of the Constitution itself—that the rights in the Bill of Rights do not exclusively regulate the relationship between the state and the bearers of rights.[25] Section 8(2) of the Constitution makes clear that 'a provision of the Bill of Rights binds a natural or a juristic person if, and to the extent that, it is applicable, taking into account the nature of the right and the nature of any duty imposed by the right'.

South Africa faces massive inequality in the bifurcated health system, with the wealthiest 16% of people making use of the private for-profit health sector, and the remaining 84% of people relying on the public health care sector for their health care services.[26] While the challenges that arise in the public and private sectors are quite different, they are both subject to the Constitution and therefore carry obligations in respect of health care users.

---

[24] See Mark Blecher et al 'Health spending at a time of low economic growth and fiscal constraint' 2017 *South African Health Review* 25.

[25] See, eg, *Du Plessis v De Klerk* [1996] ZACC 10; 1996 (3) SA 850 (CC).

[26] Shivani Ranchod et al 'South Africa's hospital sector: Old divisions and new developments' 2017 *South African Health Review* 101 at 102.

The private sector can play a role in protecting and promoting the right of access to health care services in several respects. This includes research and development of medicines and medical devices, delivery of quality health care services to those reliant on the private sector (and to ease the burden on the public health sector) and coverage of the costs of private health care through medical schemes.

The state must, however, regulate this power to ensure that the relevant actors in the private sector exercise it in a manner that promotes the right to health, rather than undermining it. In doing this, the state requires the support of civil society in holding private actors accountable where they act in breach of their obligations. This often requires a multi-pronged approach, focused first on compliance with existing law and policy; and second on ensuring that any future developments in law and policy and the manner in which private power is regulated are consistent with the s 27 rights.

Moreover, a homogenous concept of 'private power' fails to take account of the numerous actors within the private sector and their related, but distinct, roles in advancing the right to health. For example, excessive prices in private health care charged by health care service providers will necessarily affect medical schemes, who may then see fit to charge higher premiums to members of the public, and/or decrease the benefits available, to make up for this. A medical scheme that charges inaccessible premiums, or that does not provide an appropriate suite of benefits, may well increase the burden on the public health care sector. This is because health care users become unable to afford medical scheme membership and rely on the public sector as a result.

Thus, the excessive prices of private health care services affect members of the public directly through higher costs of accessing private health care, and indirectly through a more onerous burden on the public health care system and narrower medical scheme coverage.

On 8 March 2013, the President proclaimed the operation of certain provisions of the Competition Act 89 of 1998 that empowered the Competition Commission to conduct formal inquiries into the state of competition in any market where it appears that features of that market may prevent, distort or restrict competition.[27] One of the first markets in which the Competition Commission exercised these powers was the private health care sector, and the excessive pricing of health care services in that sector. In this regard, the terms of reference for this market inquiry noted that the prices of health care services are far higher than what most people can afford, and that they continue to increase at rates beyond inflation.[28]

---

[27] Proclamation R5 in *GG* 36221 of 8 March 2013. These powers are now contained in s 6 of the Competition Act 89 of 1998.

[28] 'Terms of reference for market inquiry into the private healthcare sector' (GN 1166 in *GG* 37062 of 29 November 2013).

These investigations included a public participation process, during which health care professionals, patient groups, regulatory bodies, hospital groups and civil society made submissions that included the following issues:[29]

- *Constitutional obligations, the public interest and social welfare perspective.* Submissions highlighted the right in s 27 of the Constitution of access to quality health care services.
- *The role of prescribed minimum benefits (PMBs)[30] in the rising cost of health care services.* The regulatory provisions governing these benefits oblige medical schemes to provide full cover for certain conditions, regardless of the terms of an individual's membership of a medical scheme. An increasing set of PMBs will therefore increase the liabilities of the medical schemes concerned.
- *The deteriorating quality of services in the public health care sector.* This resulted in an increased demand for health care services from the private sector.
- *Factors that drive health care costs, including developments in health technology and a rise in life expectancy, also increasing the demand for health care services.*
- *The current gaps in the regulation of health care services including the cost and pricing of these services.*

The Competition Commission released its provisional report, containing preliminary findings and recommendations, on 5 July 2018. The provisional report highlights the features of the private health care sector that prevent, restrict or distort competition and drive up costs of private health care.

Against these findings, the package of recommendations is aimed at improving transparency, accountability and the alignment of interests of consumers and funders. The recommendations also seek to achieve better management of supply and demand, address concentrations in the market and develop means to measure the value of health care services, to facilitate value-based purchasing.

It is hoped that this process will catalyse an improvement in the affordability and accessibility of health care services. It is critical that the implementation of the recommendations arising from the inquiry give sufficient priority to the entitlements contained in s 27 of the Constitution, and particularly universal health coverage, rather than relying purely on principles relating to market forces.

---

[29] The submissions are summarised in Umunyana Rugege, Janneke Saltner & Tim Fish-Hodgson 'The market inquiry into the private health care sector' *SECTION27* undated, last accessed on 19 January 2018 from <https://www.health-e.org.za/wp-content/uploads/2014/08/Summarised-inputs-on-statement-of-issues-and-participation-guideslines.pdf>.

[30] PMBs are a core set of benefits to which members of medical schemes are entitled, regardless of the medical scheme plan they have selected. These benefits are aimed at ensuring that there is a minimum basket of services available to them, to allow for affordability of health care services and to prevent any interruptions in care that could prejudice the patients concerned.

There is also a wide range of other areas in which private power must be kept in check to guard against the abuse of this power. While this chapter does not allow for an in-depth analysis of each, some important examples bear mentioning:

- The Fix the Patent Law Coalition includes a number of civil society groups such as the TAC, SECTION 27, Médecins sans Frontières and several patient groups. The coalition has challenged the inflexibility of patent laws and the way that their application drives up the cost of medicines to the point that life-saving medicines become inaccessible to those that need them. The coalition is advocating for a degree of flexibility that would be consistent with the constitutional right of access to health care services. The advocacy work on patent laws must find a balance between incentivising research into and development of safe, high quality and effective medicines and allowing sufficient flexibility so that those requiring these medicines can afford them. This requires continued advocacy and engagement with the Department of Trade and Industry and the Department of Health, as well as the pharmaceutical companies that manufacture the medicines.

- It is necessary, too, to work with the Medicines Control Council (MCC) and its imminent successor, the South African Health Products Regulatory Authority. These bodies are responsible for the registration of medicines and continued monitoring to ensure that access to these medicines is in the public interest. In other words, these bodies ensure that medicines comply with the requirements of safety, quality and therapeutic efficacy. This often requires effective navigation of the power balance between the regulatory agencies and private pharmaceutical companies, focusing on what would be in the public interest.[31]

- There is also a high demand for direct legal services in challenging the conduct of medical schemes, who may seek to escape their obligations arising from the Medical Schemes Act 131 of 1998 (Medical Schemes Act) and other legislation. For example, in 2017, SECTION 27 represented a person living with HIV whose medical scheme refused to cover the costs of her antiretroviral treatment if she obtained this treatment in the private sector. This was despite an earlier judgment of the Supreme Court of Appeal against that medical scheme confirming their obligation to provide full cover for PMBs.[32] Antiretroviral treatment is a PMB in terms of the General Regulations to the Medical Schemes Act. The medical scheme must therefore cover the cost of antiretroviral treatment in full, unless it designates a service provider through which members must obtain their PMBs and the member voluntarily obtains this treatment from elsewhere. In this case, the medical

---

[31] For an example of these competing interests, see *Medicines Control Council v Adcock Ingram Ltd* (NGHC) unreported case 57976/11 of 15 November 2011.

[32] See *Council for Medical Schemes v Genesis Medical Scheme* [2015] ZASCA 161; 2016 (1) SA 429 (SCA).

scheme persisted in its refusal to cover the costs of its member's ARVs, despite not having appointed a designated service provider. SECTION 27 successfully challenged the scheme's conduct, securing an order that it pay for the ARVs in full (including a refund to the patient of the amounts it should have paid since its refusal to cover the costs of her treatment in 2011).

- Finally, individuals and organisations such as the TAC have turned to the Advertising Standards Authority of South Africa in an effort to challenge so-called 'quackery'.[33] This includes the advertisement of supplements or substances with claims as to their efficacy in treatment of certain diseases, where these supplements or substances have not been registered with the Medicines Control Council. Again, it is necessary to launch these challenges in the public interest, so that health care users are not misled into using ineffective and possibly harmful substances to treat disease.

When it uses its powers and market position appropriately, the private sector has the potential to advance the right of access to health care services. However, it also has the potential to frustrate the advancement of the right.

Since 2001, government policy has envisaged a system of national health insurance (NHI), intended to provide universal access to quality health care services, regardless of socio-economic status. After several delays, the National Health Insurance Bill (NHI Bill) was released for public comment on 21 June 2018. The NHI Bill envisages the creation of an NHI Fund, which will procure a basket of health care services from both public and private health care service providers on behalf of the state.

It is not yet known how revenue for the NHI Fund will be raised. We also do not know which health care services will be covered by the NHI, and which services will require direct payment from health care users. Although it appears that health care users will not be prohibited from belonging to medical schemes for benefits that fall outside of those covered by the NHI, they may not be able to afford to do this and so it is likely that some health care services will become inaccessible, potentially undermining the objective of universal health coverage.

There is therefore much debate as to whether successful implementation of the NHI will be possible, particularly in the light of the strength in the private health care sector and the corresponding crisis in the public health care sector. Successful implementation of the NHI, and genuine universal health coverage, will require interventions to strengthen the current provision of health care services, and is dependent on buy-in from all sectors to ensure its success.

The introduction of NHI will bring with it changes to the manner in which medical schemes operate, and to address this the Medical Schemes Amendment Bill, which seeks to amend the Medical Schemes Act 131 of 1998, has also been

---

[33] See, eg a complaint laid by the TAC against a print advertisement: *Immunadue/TAC/4978*, available at <http://www.asasa.org.za/rulings/Immunadue-TAC-4978>.

released for public comment. One of its key objectives is to ensure better access to private health care services for members of medical schemes. A significant amendment is the proposed abolition of co-payments and PMBs, and their replacement with an obligation on medical schemes to provide full cover for a defined suite of benefits. These benefits are expected to include primary health care services, and will be covered at a rate negotiated between medical schemes and health care service providers.

These important amendments will change the way that health care services are accessed and provided in South Africa. They will change the way that the public and private health care sectors will work together to provide universal health coverage. It is likely that these changes will give rise to litigation by several actors who may seek to challenge the proposed overhaul of the health system. What is important is that the rights of health care users remain paramount in navigating the way forward.

8.4 HEALTH RIGHTS LITIGATION GOING FORWARD

Litigation on the right to health has shed some light on both positive and negative obligations arising from the right, as well as the various duty-bearers who must discharge their obligations in order to facilitate the full realisation of the right. While these are essential principles to build on in future advocacy and litigation, they cannot be applied without acknowledgement of the current context.

The difficult reality is that South Africa is in an economic recession, and realisation of the right to health requires a substantial investment of public resources. Difficult questions regarding the allocation of resources are bound to arise in a challenging fiscal climate. Moseneke DCJ (retired) states this eloquently:

> When the Constitution was negotiated, the parties skirted around the need for social change. The negotiators did not stare in the eye the historical structural inequality in the economy. There was no pact on how to achieve the equality and social justice the constitution promised. Instead, the constitution imposed qualified duties on the state to facilitate access to social goods such as health, housing, water, education and social grants. But these socio-economic entitlements were premised on and limited to state transfers as and when funds were available. On the face of it, the protections were praiseworthy, and they promised a state-sponsored reduction of poverty, but in practice socio-economic rights did not speak to how to restructure the economy in a way that rendered it more productive and inclusive.[34]

This may be amplified by the introduction of NHI, which is intended to expand health care services to provide universal health coverage.

This does not mean that we should resign ourselves to a weak health system for the foreseeable future. What it does mean, however, is that we may need to look at our strategies and identify how we can mitigate the impact of structural inequality, exacerbated by an economic recession, on the realisation of the right to health.

---

[34] Dikgang Moseneke *My Own Liberator: A Memoir* (2016) 352–3.

The fact that the right to health is resource-intensive does not mean that the money does not exist. It is not a licence to cut back on the delivery of health care services without the need to account. On the contrary, it highlights the obligation on the duty bearers to conduct themselves in line with the principles of openness, accountability, transparency and responsiveness. These principles, together with the requirement of need-based policy-making, are enshrined in s 195 of the Constitution.[35]

For this reason, litigation and legal advocacy around the right to health cannot be separated from the need to tackle corruption. Not only do corrupt activities direct resources away from the delivery of quality health care services, but they also cause a distortion in the priorities in the delivery of health care services. Corruption can have a devastating impact on the enjoyment of the right to health and rooting out this corruption is a prerequisite to the full enjoyment of the right.

Heywood has drawn a direct link between corruption and the right to health, referencing a research report commissioned by SECTION27 and its partner organisation Corruption Watch in 2011. The report concluded that R20 billion per year is being lost to corruption in the public and private health care sectors. The effect of this will be to inflate health care costs, limit access to health care services and negatively impact on the quality of care.[36] He continues:

> Rispel et al attempt to quantify the cost of corruption in health by studying levels of 'irregular expenditure' that are recorded in reports of the Auditor General. Irregular expenditure is money that is spent without proper authorisation and outside of the legal framework. It is not automatically corrupt—but a very large part of it is. They found, for example, that in four financial years between 2009 and 2013, the total amount of irregular expenditure within provincial health departments was over R24 billion. This is a huge amount of money! It is the equivalent of the annual budget of the HIV conditional grant, or twice the amount currently spent on Emergency Medical Services (which we know to be woefully inadequate).[37]

For this reason, a litigation strategy on the right to health must be alive to the issue of corruption and how it affects the delivery of health care services. It may be appropriate for public interest organisations to intervene in matters such as tender disputes in order to maintain the centrality of the right to health care services in decisions resolving these disputes. It may be important for these organisations to deal with arguments around remedies to ensure that tender disputes do not cause undue interruptions in the delivery of health care services.

---

[35] Nikki Stein (2018) 'A better life for all: using socio-economic rights litigation to enforce the principles governing public administration' SAJHR 34:1, 91–111.

[36] Mark Heywood 'State capture threatens the right to health' *Spotlight* 30 November 2017, last accessed on 7 February 2018 from <*https://www.spotlightnsp.co.za/2017/11/30/state-capture-threatens-right-health/*>.

[37] Ibid.

8.5 CONCLUSION

South Africa is facing profound questions that will have an impact on the delivery of health care and other services. There is a lack of urgency in relation to the continued delivery of these. And many fear that both access to and quality of health care services will continue to deteriorate as the economic climate becomes more volatile and more difficult.

It is likely that there will be an increasing number of violations of the negative aspects of the right to health. This will have a knock-on effect on programmes that have been put in place to achieve incremental improvements in health care service delivery. In other words, both the building blocks of progressive realisation of the right to health, and the foundation on which they are built, may well become more unstable.

In addition to an economic recession, the current political climate brings with it a level of uncertainty. It highlights cases of erosion of accountability, respect for the rule of law and good governance. We see this conduct in decisions regarding the availability of health care services, in the award of tenders for the delivery of these services, and in the failure to hold to account those who act in breach of their obligations. In addition to violating the foundation on which our Constitution is built, these cases will affect the day-to-day living of millions of people.

As such, legal strategies to advance the right of access to health care services are not just about those health care services. It will likely not be enough to focus on progressive realisation of the right to health. It will also likely not suffice to address the positive and negative obligations arising from the right to health without addressing closely related issues such as corruption and financial mis-management. Finally, it is necessary to hold all forms of power to account, in the public and private sectors, to ensure that health care users' rights come first.

Litigation on the realisation of the right to health care services therefore appears to be entering a different phase. The road towards access to quality health care services is a long one and will require sustained and concerted efforts to make health rights a reality.

Chapter 9

HAPPY (N)EVER AFTER?
PUBLIC INTEREST LITIGATION FOR LGBTI EQUALITY

Kerry Williams and Melanie Judge[1]

9.1 INTRODUCTION

The Constitution of the Republic of South Africa, promulgated in 1996, was the first in the world to entrench lesbian, gay, bisexual, transgender and intersex (LGBTI) equality through prohibiting unfair discrimination on the grounds of sexual orientation.[2] This prompted almost a decade of legal victories and the incremental development of equality law for LGBTI people in post-apartheid South Africa, including the legalisation of same-sex marriage.[3] On paper, the

---

[1] Melanie Judge acknowledges the support of the National Research Foundation's South African Research Chairs Initiative (SARCHI) Chair in Security and Justice, in the Faculty of Law at the University of Cape Town. The authors extend thanks to Kate Hofmeyr for her thoughtful comments on the chapter.

[2] Section 9(3) of the Constitution, commonly referred to as the equality clause, provides: 'The state may not unfairly discriminate directly or indirectly against anyone on one or more grounds, including race, gender, sex, pregnancy, marital status, ethnic or social origin, colour, sexual orientation, age, disability, religion, conscience, belief, culture, language and birth.' Section 9(4) of the Constitution provides: 'No person may unfairly discriminate directly or indirectly against anyone on one or more grounds in terms of subsection (3). National legislation must be enacted to prevent or prohibit unfair discrimination.'

[3] *National Coalition for Gay and Lesbian Equality and Another v Minister of Justice and Others* [1998] ZACC 15; 1999 (1) SA 6 (CC) [NCGLE was the first applicant and CALS was admitted as *amicus curiae*, represented by Wits Law Clinic] (*National Coalition I*); *Langemaat v Minister of Safety and Security* 1998 (3) SA 312 (T); *National Coalition for Gay and Lesbian Equality and Others v Minister of Home Affairs and Others* [1999] ZACC 17; 2000 (2) SA 1 (CC) [LRC acted for the applicant] (*National Coalition II*); *Satchwell v The President of the Republic of South Africa and Another* [2003] ZACC 2; 2003 (4) SA 266 (CC); *Du Toit and Another v Minister of Welfare and Population Development and Others* [2002] ZACC 20; 2003 (2) SA 198 (CC) [Wits Law Clinic acted for the applicants and for Lesbian and Gay Equality Project, which was admitted as *amicus curiae*]; *J and Another v Director General, Department of Home Affairs and Others* [2003] ZACC 3;

equal treatment of LGBTI people is affirmed, including their right to human dignity. However, over the last decade LGBTI public interest litigation (PIL) has confronted forms of institutionalised violence, inequality and discrimination that are difficult to address using the jurisprudence that developed out of the Constitution's protection and promotion of equality and dignity. PIL concerning LGBTI peoples' rights after the legalisation of same-sex marriage in South Africa has been primarily concerned with bringing seemingly intractable patterns of violence and exclusion before the courts. This approach, which seeks to bring the lived, embodied experiences of LGBTI people to the fore, has faced numerous socio-legal challenges. In trying to apply the law to the social spheres where pernicious forms of stigmatisation, prejudice and othering continue—despite legal protections against these—there has been an attempt, through LGBTI PIL, to prevent normalised forms of exclusion and discrimination that are often left undisturbed in the law's formal conferral of the right to dignity and equality.

This chapter will focus on PIL in the period after the legalisation of same-sex marriage, the social impact of which, we argue, was somewhat overestimated[4] despite the significant contribution of prior strategic litigation to expanding equality jurisprudence in South Africa.[5] The reasons for this overestimation are complex but include the following: (i) the achievement of marriage rights came to symbolise a consummation of sorts between the right to equality and LGBTI rights, (ii) as a legal gain, it came at the end of a period of (over) optimism about

---

2003 (5) SA 621 (CC) [LRC acted for the applicants]; *Minister of Home Affairs and Another v Fourie and Another* [2005] ZACC 19; 2006 (1) SA 524 (CC); *Lesbian and Gay Equality Project and Eighteen Others v Minister of Home Affairs* [2005] ZACC 20; 2006 (1) SA 524 (CC) [Lesbian and Gay Equality Project as an applicant and Doctors for Life International was admitted as first *amicus curiae*]. Also see, Jonathan Berger 'Getting to the Constitutional Court on time: A litigation history of same-sex marriage' in Melanie Judge, Anthony Manion & Shaun de Waal (eds) *To Have and to Hold: The Making of Same-sex Marriage in South Africa* (2008) 17–28; Steven Budlender, Gilbert Marcus SC & Nick Ferreira 'Public interest litigation and social change in South Africa: Strategies, tactics and lessons' *The Atlantic Philanthropies* (2014), last accessed on 24 October 2017 from <http://www.atlanticphilanthropies.org/app/uploads/2015/12/Public-interest-litigation-and-social-change-in-South-Africa.pdf>.

[4] This is by no means intended to underestimate the importance of the legalisation of same-sex marriage, including that equal marriage rights enable same-sex couples to access the same benefits and protections as married heterosexuals; that the right to marry is a civil right and therefore an entitlement of citizenship; and that the symbolic significance of extending marriage to same-sex couples has a positive impact on democratic inclusivity. For more on debates around marriage, see David Bilchitz & Melanie Judge 'For whom does the bell toll? The challenges and possibilities of the Civil Union Act for family law in South Africa' (2007) 23 *SAJHR: Sexuality and the Law: Special Issue* 466-99; Kerry Williams ' "I do" or "We won't": Legalizing same-sex marriage in South Africa' (2004) 20 *SAJHR* 32–63.

[5] Former Deputy Chief Justice Moseneke puts it thus: 'I think I should just pay tribute to gay and lesbian structures that actually helped wittingly and unwittingly in the development of equality jurisprudence in this country. All those struggles around rights of gay and lesbian people have in many ways allowed the [Constitutional] Court and allowed our Constitution and many other people to be able to express themselves around issues of equality.' Dikgang Moseneke 'Opening of the 13th Out in Africa Gay and Lesbian Film Festival' *[Audio file] Cape Town, South Africa* 1 March 2007.

the extent of South Africa's transition from apartheid to democracy; and (iii) it relied on an assumption that formal legal advances constitute social advances for all LGBTI people in equal measure. Representing the 'grand prize'[6] of the strategic litigation process towards LGBTI formal equality, the marriage victory had tempted a happily-ever-after fate. Yet, after this point, LGBTI PIL became increasingly difficult as attention turned to the persistence of social discrimination and exclusion[7] facing LGBTI communities as *social* problems, rather than as formal legal problems (such as the unfair discriminations that are a product of unjust laws). So, while the law overall acknowledges the dignity of LGBTI people and no longer formally discriminates (or is no longer permitted to formally discriminate) against LGBTI people, it still falls short of enabling contextual understandings of the experiences of social discrimination and exclusion to be fully articulated through law.[8]

This failure partly has to do with the difficulty of framing forms of social discrimination and exclusion as breaches of the right to equality or dignity. It also points to how, amongst other reasons, the law as a social institution continues to reinforce LGBTI inferiorisation. The law at once opens space for marginalised groups to contest oppressive hegemonies, yet, in the same moment, the law reproduces the very relations of power on which such hegemonies turn. This violent side of law,[9] and in particular its implications for justice in the context of LGBTI identity politics,[10] has not been adequately considered in strategic litigation efforts. This is significant precisely because the continuities of colonialism and apartheid, and how these play out in present-day interpretations and practices of law,[11] form part and parcel of the contemporary realities that shape sexual and gendered realities.

---

[6] Berger (note 3 above).

[7] 'Social discrimination and exclusion' include reference to the structural and institutionalised modes through which LGBTI people are denied full access to, and expression of, social, economic and political life, frequently through various forms of violence. We are referring here to something different to direct discrimination in South African equality jurisprudence. Forms of social discrimination were evident in the three cases that are discussed in this chapter. Social discrimination involves forms of violence and exclusion that are *not* rooted in formal unequal or differential treatment of LGBTI people. Instead, social discrimination is about the experience of violence, exclusion, and oppression which is at the centre of the lived experience of inequality.

[8] South African equality jurisprudence (first set out in *Harksen v Lane NO and Others* [1997] ZACC 12; 1998 (1) SA 300 (CC) para 53) requires the isolation of differential treatment and then a determination as to whether such differential treatment amounts to unfair discrimination. If the differential treatment is on a ground listed in s 9(3) of the Constitution, then discrimination is established. Once discrimination is established it becomes necessary to embark upon a contextual analysis underpinning the discriminatory treatment to finally determine if the differential treatment is prohibited *unfair* discrimination. This contextual analysis looks at the impact on the complainant and others in the same situation.

[9] Walter Benjamin 'Critique of violence' in *One-way Street and Other Writings* (1978) 132–54; Robert M Cover 'Violence and the word' (1986) 95 *Yale LJ* 1601.

[10] Chandan Reddy *Freedom with Violence: Race, Sexuality and the US State* (2011).

[11] On this point, Cover (note 10 above) argues that 'legal interpretation takes place in a field of pain and death' in which the violent side of the law is implicated.

Consequently, there are multiple forms of violence directed at LGBTI communities, some of which are the focus of the PIL discussed in this chapter.[12] In sum, LGBTI people continue to experience severe physical violence, psychological violence and state violence.[13] Physical violence is usually criminal and involves LGBTI people being targeted because of their sexuality or gender. Psychological violence concerns the mental health of LGBTI individuals, and the negative impact of inferiorisation, stigmatisation and pathologisation on their well-being.[14] State violence is meted out through the systemic exclusion or marginalisation of LGBTI people within and through the various systems and apparatuses of state governance. By way of example, when LGBTI people encounter state machinery, they might face the denial of the full entitlements of citizenship by homophobic or transphobic officials who use bureaucratic and state-sanctioned power to stymie access to resources, recognition and rights. The experience of these forms of violence, as instrumental to how social discrimination and exclusion take effect, does not easily lend itself to framing a legal complaint as a formal breach of the right to either equality or dignity.

9.2 CRITICAL LITIGATION AND LITIGATING CRITICALLY

Between 1996 and 2005 there were numerous cases litigated in the name of LGBTI equality.[15] A number of these were spearheaded by the National Coalition for Gay and Lesbian Equality which later became the Lesbian and Gay Equality Project. With the benefit of hindsight this course of legal action has been presented as a conscious and strategic approach to litigating LGBTI equality.[16] The result of these cases was almost full formal legal equality,[17] yet the so-called strategic

---

[12] Vulnerabilities to violence are affected by race, class and gender differentials such that black and gender non-conforming LGBTI people are rendered disproportionately vulnerable.

[13] Juan Nel & Melanie Judge 'Exploring homophobic victimisation in Gauteng, South Africa: Issues, impacts and responses' (2008) 21 *Acta Criminologica* 19–36; Graeme Reid & Teresa Dirsuweit 'Understanding systemic violence: Homophobic attacks in Johannesburg and its surrounds' (2002) 13 *Urban Forum* 99–126; Helen Wells *Overall research findings on levels of empowerment among LGBT people in KwaZulu-Natal* (unpublished report, OUT LGBT Well-being, 2006).

[14] Juan Nel 'South African psychology can and should provide leadership in advancing understanding of sexual and gender diversity on the African continent: Editorial' (2014) 44 *S Afr J Psychol* 145 at 145–8; Juan Nel & Duncan Breen 'Victims of hate crime' in Robert Peacock (ed) *Victimology in South Africa* 2 ed (2013).

[15] Note 3 above.

[16] It has been described as a 'well-developed litigation strategy' purposefully designed around a 'shopping list' of law reform goals (See, Berger (note 3 above) 18), largely influenced by Cameron's application of constitutional rights to sexual orientation (Edwin Cameron 'Sexual orientation and the Constitution: A test case for human rights' (1993) 110 *SALJ* 450–72.

[17] The Civil Union Act 17 of 2006, in having introduced a separate piece of legislation that grants the same rights and obligations as the Marriage Act 25 of 1961, probably constitutes a constitutional infringement in establishing a 'separate but equal' legal marriage regime for same-sex couples who remain excluded from the Marriage Act.

LGBTI litigation has also been the subject of significant critique, in particular for not having adequately considered the interests of black and poor LGBTI people.[18] Since 2005 the focus of legal activism has shifted from challenging unequal laws to grappling with forms of violence that continue to delimit the possibilities of LGBTI people leading lives of equal value and worth in both private and public spheres. This has been challenging for PIL, raising a host of issues at the interface of law and society.

In exploring these challenges, we draw on three cases which have been litigated by Webber Wentzel on behalf of various parties,[19] and which all concern forms of physical, psychological and/or state violence directed at LGBTI people. We refer to these cases as *Mazibuko*, *Qwelane* and *Semugoma*, respectively. In summary, *Mazibuko* concerned a hate crime, in the form of assault with intent to do grievous bodily harm, against a young gay man, Deric Mazibuko, at a 'tavern' in a suburb on the East Rand of Gauteng. Mazibuko survived the attack by three men. Mazibuko was determined that the perpetrators be brought to justice, and approached OUT LGBT Well-being (OUT)[20] for assistance, which then in turn approached Webber Wentzel. *Qwelane* involved the publication of an article by Jon Qwelane, a journalist and political figure, in the *Sunday Sun* newspaper in which he expressed support for Robert Mugabe's views on gays;[21] Mugabe had said that being gay was unnatural and compared same-sex marriage to people marrying animals. In his article, Qwelane argued that gay and lesbian equality rights should be removed from the Constitution, prompting the South African Human Rights Commission (SAHRC) to seek an apology from him. The SAHRC instituted a claim against Qwelane, arguing that his words amounted to hate speech and harassment as defined in the Promotion of Equality and Prevention of Unfair Discrimination Act, 2000 (the Equality Act). The Psychological Society of

---

[18] See Mary Hames 'Lesbians and the Civil Union Act: A critical reflection' in Melanie Judge, Anthony Manion & Shaun de Waal (eds) *To Have and to Hold: The Making of Same-sex Marriage in South Africa* (2008) 258–67; Natalie Oswin 'Producing homonormativity in neoliberal South Africa: Recognition, redistribution, and the Equality Project' (2007) 32 *Signs* 649–69.

[19] The co-authors of this chapter have variously been involved in the cases discussed in this chapter. Kerry Williams (together with Nurina Ally) was the attorney responsible for *Qwelane* and *Mazibuko*. Melanie Judge has been integrally involved in the *Mazibuko* and *Qwelane* matters on behalf of OUT and PsySSA, respectively. Tshego Phala, a partner at Webber Wentzel, was the attorney responsible for *Semugoma*. The chapter does not consider or examine other LGBTI PIL cases which may have been litigated in the period post 2005.

[20] OUT is a non-governmental organisation that provides health services for LGBTI people and communities.

[21] In his article, Qwelane wrote that 'there could be a few things I could take issue with Zimbabwean President Robert Mugabe, but his unflinching and unapologetic stance over homosexuals is definitely not among those'. Mugabe's views on homosexuality include referring to it as 'inhumane', and stating that 'gays have no human rights' and are 'worse than dogs and pigs'. See. Michael K Lavers 'Zimbabwe president describes homosexuality as "inhuman"' *Washington Blade* 28 March 2014, last accessed on 9 November 2016 from <http://www.washingtonblade.com/2014/03/28/zimbabwe-president-describes-homosexuality-inhuman/>.

South Africa (PsySSA)[22] was concerned with the effects that Qwelane's words had had on the psychological well-being of LGBTI people. The organisation believed it was important that the psychological impact should be the focus of the case brought by the SAHRC against Qwelane in the Equality Court. PsySSA accordingly approached Webber Wentzel to pursue an *amicus* application on their behalf. *Semugoma* involved the unlawful detention and threatened deportation by the Department of Home Affairs (DHA) of Paul Semugoma, a Ugandan national, to Uganda on his re-entry into South Africa. At the time Uganda was poised to pass the Anti-Homosexuality Bill and so there was a legitimate concern that Semugoma would be prosecuted as an openly gay man. Several South African non-profit organisations, together with Semugoma's partner, approached Webber Wentzel to act on his behalf. Each of these cases featured forms of physical, psychological and/or state violence, and their constructions as strategic legal interventions, as well as the course each took, offer valuable insights into what it means to conduct LGBTI PIL in South Africa at this time.

(a) Constructing the cases

Although LGBTI equality and dignity were at the centre of all these cases, an allegation that there was a breach of the right to equality or dignity was not. In *Mazibuko*, given that the trial was criminal in character, the room to raise breaches of Mazibuko's rights to equality and dignity was limited. The perpetrators were clearly deeply homophobic and targeted Mazibuko because he was gay. In choosing the most appropriate cause of action, it was apparent that the criminal conduct of the accused could not easily be framed in litigation as breaching Mazibuko's rights.[23] For this reason, it made strategic sense to allow the prosecutor to attain the criminal conviction and to then introduce the effects of the homophobic component of the crime in the sentencing phase of the trial.[24] It was

---

[22] PsySSA is a non-profit organisation that represents psychology professionals in South Africa.

[23] It also would not have been possible to construct a case around developing the criminal law (which is common law) to accord with the protections the rights to equality and dignity offer, as the elements required to establish a crime do not call for such development. It is arguable that an appropriate development may be that the onus of proof should shift to the accused if it is alleged that a crime is accompanied by hate speech. However, this is where the formal offerings of constitutional law and the reality of practicing law and protecting the interests of clients, part ways: for Mazibuko to feel a sense of justice he wanted the accused to be punished for their conduct, which hurt him both physically and emotionally, rather than having the onus shifted. Interestingly, at a point in the litigation when the criminal trial was being delayed, he considered instituting a civil claim in delict for damages arising out of the assault, which would have more directly implicated the rights to dignity and equality. If pursued, this could have led to the development of the common law in ways which may accord with the protections the right to equality and dignity offer.

[24] These effects included: (i) the psychological impact of a hate crime on the victim: such victims are at risk of developing mental health problems including depression, anxiety and post-traumatic stress disorder; (ii) the secondary victimisation which follows a hate crime when the victim turns to service providers, such as the criminal justice officials or health care service providers, for support; (iii) that where a person is victimised as a result of his or her sexual orientation, the incident acts as a

believed (perhaps naively) that criminal law could ameliorate the way in which the crime undermined equality and thereby promote equality, albeit indirectly. The decision to intervene in the sentencing phase was intended to forefront the context in which the crime was perpetrated and give prominence to the lived experience of LGBTI people, including Mazibuko, so as to ensure that they and he were not left unseen nor unaccounted for in the criminal justice process despite its focus being on the acts of the accused.

In *Qwelane*, the emphasis was on the Equality Act, promulgated to, inter alia, prevent hate speech and harassment and give effect to the rights to equality and dignity. Although the claim instituted by the SAHRC did not directly involve an assertion that Qwelane had infringed LGBTI peoples' rights, it is clear that the Equality Act's prohibition of hate speech and harassment is intended to protect and promote equality and dignity through an acknowledgement that such conduct undermines equality and dignity. When the SAHRC instituted its claim, it was evident that its approach did not articulate the full nature of the harm caused by hate speech and harassment on LGBTI embodied experiences in a context where LGBTI people are already vulnerable to various forms of violence. As a result, PsySSA believed it imperative that this experience and context be placed before the court. This became all the more pressing when Qwelane challenged the constitutionality of the hate-speech provisions of the Equality Act, suggesting (incorrectly) that they infringed the right to freedom of expression and were vague and overbroad. With this came the risk that the case would centre on Qwelane's rights to express harmful words rather than their harmful effects. It appeared to PsySSA that without a court being fully apprised of the psychological and social effects of homophobic hate speech, it would not make a just decision in relation to the breach of the provisions nor their constitutionality.[25]

---

reminder that it is not safe to make his or her sexual orientation known, which may lead to internalised homophobia; (iv) the trauma of the victimisation on the basis of prejudice and stigmatisation has a significant impact on the victim's relationship with his or her family, including that the victim's family may fear for their own safety; (v) that hate crimes as message crimes have an effect on the community to which the victim belongs, including that other LGBTI people in the community understand that the crime sends a message that they too are unwelcome and unsafe in that community, which contributes to a climate of stress and fear.

[25] PsySSA's intervention was therefore aimed at placing evidence before the court on the harm caused by Qwelane's article. The harms included evidence that hate speech directed at LGBTI people makes them significantly more vulnerable to a range of psychological harms such as depression, suicidal ideation (thoughts about suicide) and internalised homophobia Homophobic hate speech also affects the immediate community in that other LGBTI people in the community experience a lowered self-esteem and high levels of fear (which in turn creates a vulnerability to depression and anxiety) as a result of the hate speech. Finally, homophobic hate speech, like other forms of hate speech, has a detrimental impact on society at large as it actively polarises communities by reinforcing prejudice and existing divisions with the risk that it translates into animosity and sometimes even violence. PsySSA further argued that the Equality Act's prohibition of hate speech was a justifiable limitation on the right to freedom of expression as it was intended to protect the dignity and psychological integrity of those who had experienced historical disadvantage.

In the context of LGBTI PIL since the legalisation of same-sex marriage, it is not surprising that the strategies adopted for the cases relied neither on conventional breaches of the right to equality or dignity nor on the Equality Act's prohibition of unfair discrimination.

The wake of optimism left by the legalisation of same-sex marriage momentarily blinded LGBTI strategic litigators to the possibility of the Constitution, and laws developed by the Constitution, having limitations for the LGBTI community. Relying on criminal law and the Equality Act, and tangentially invoking the right to dignity,[26] were strategies intended to assist in addressing forms of social discrimination and exclusion. The hope was that criminal law and the Equality Act would do the work of LGBTI equality. With the benefit of hindsight, it appears that these legal mechanisms fall short for LGBTI people, demonstrating the difficulty of law[27] per se to address these forms of violence.

(b) Litigating from the margins

In both *Mazibuko* and *Qwelane* the key public interest litigants were *amici curiae*. In *Mazibuko*, one of the early challenges was to create new law to allow an *amicus* to intervene in a criminal trial in the Magistrates Court.[28] OUT intervened as an *amicus* in the sentencing phase of the criminal trial to place evidence before the court on the effects of homophobic hate crimes on the victim, the community and society at large, the purpose of which was to influence the court's assessment of an appropriate sentence for the accused. In *Qwelane*, PsySSA applied successfully to intervene as an *amicus* as the organisation was well-placed to put evidence before the court about the deleterious impact of homophobic hate speech on psychosocial well-being. In both these cases, conducting PIL as an *amicus* had significant implications for the experience of the litigants and the degree to which LGBTI interests could be centred in the trial proceedings. In *Mazibuko* there was a persistent anxiety about overstepping the 'proper role' of an *amicus*, conscious that in an adversarial system (as opposed to an inquisitorial system) criminal procedure is premised on the state's prosecution of those accused of crimes. The legitimacy of this system depends on the balance struck between the accused (the bearer of certain protective criminal justice rights) and the state (the bearer of inordinate power intended to protect the public through prosecution of criminals). Consequently, there was a clear intention not to upset this balance both in respecting the system and in recognising that any such upset might limit the ability

---

[26] In *Qwelane*, PsySSA's evidence showed the impact of homophobic hate speech including the impact that such speech has on self-worth (which implicitly suggested that homophobic hate speech infringes LGBTI peoples' right to dignity). Additionally, PsySSA argued that the prohibition of hate speech in the Equality Act was constitutionally justified as it gives effect to the right to dignity.

[27] Here we refer to law in its broadest sense and to include the rules, systems, structures and practices of law in society.

[28] The magistrate admitted OUT as an *amicus curiae* in the criminal matter on the basis that rule 28 of the Magistrates' Courts Rules allows such admission.

of *amici* interventions in future cases. However, this required an exceptional degree of patience in *Mazibuko,* as it took just over four years for the accused to be brought to trial and convicted. At great cost, in both time and resources, OUT conducted a watching brief throughout this period, and then only when the accused were convicted did the organisation apply to intervene as an *amicus.*[29] This created further anxiety about whether this was an effective and efficient use of PIL resources. In *Qwelane,* PsySSA initially conducted itself like a conventional *amicus.* Having been admitted to give particular evidence before the court, the organisation followed the lead of the SAHRC as it conducted the litigation. However, following this lead became increasingly difficult over the years as the SAHRC failed to pursue the case with any urgency and Qwelane used procedural devices to effect inordinate and justice-denying delays. Eight years after having initiated legal proceedings, the SAHRC finally obtained a court date. However, on the eve of the commencement of the trial Qwelane brought an application to postpone his day in court on the basis of alleged ill-health. It was PsySSA's view that this application was effectively *not* for a postponement, but rather for a permanent stay as according to the evidence available to the Court, Qwelane's condition was presented as chronic and degenerative and therefore unlikely to improve.[30] Judge Moshidi granted Qwelane's postponement application without granting PsySSA or the SAHRC the opportunity to answer the application and put up evidence demonstrating that Qwelane was unlikely to recover. Had they been allowed to present this evidence, it would have shown that Qwelane's deteriorating medical condition was not a reason to postpone the trial but, rather, to start it with haste. PsySSA, as a result, decided to approach the Constitutional Court with an application for leave to appeal the High Court's postponement. The Constitutional Court declined to hear the appeal but in doing so issued a judgment which

---

[29] The trial took over a year to commence, as initially the prosecuting authority decided not to prosecute the accused, arguing it was 'just a tavern fight'. OUT accordingly applied to the National Director of Public Prosecutions to internally review the decision not to prosecute in terms of s 179(5)(*d*) of the Constitution and s 22(2) of the National Prosecuting Authority Act 32 of 1998. The application was successful. Thereafter OUT conducted a watching brief from the moment the accused made their first appearance to the date of their conviction, in the hope that the court would act diligently as a result of being reminded of the LGBTI interests at stake.

[30] Qwelane's treating physician, Dr Seedat, indicated that Qwelane was hypoxaemic and chronically required oxygen. He also had a combination of Chronic Obstructive Pulmonary Disease (COPD) and pulmonary fibrosis with right heart failure. PsySSA's expert physician, Dr Richards, who considered Qwelane's medical report, indicated that his professional view was that Qwelane's condition 'will not improve' and 'his long term prognosis is also very poor ... For hypoxaemix COPD alone, less than 70% of sufferers survive more than a year, and less that 20 to 40% survive up to 5 years ... Dr Seedat's report however indicates that Mr Qwelane suffers not only from hypoxaemic COPD, but also pulmonary fibrosis and right heart failure and a co-existent vascular disease. These additional conditions make Mr Qwelane's prognosis of survival even lower'. (para 15 of PsySSA's application for leave to appeal, the order of the High Court postponing the trial, to the Constitutional Court, case no 226/16).

supported the matter finally proceeding in the High Court in March 2017.[31] The
court further pointed out that postponements were '*not merely for the taking*'[32] and
had to be properly justified and that it was a denial of fair process when the High
Court refused to hear PsySSA's evidence and granted the postponement.[33]

In both *Mazibuko* and *Qwelane*, the law taking its course had effectively
marginalised the defence of LGBTI interests. An *amicus* plays a different role to
an applicant and is by no means *dominus litis*. Much of the preoccupation of the
amici parties in these cases was in grappling with how to enable LGBTI interests
to be wholly considered, while litigating from the margins. This is undesirable as
the LGBTI experience itself is frequently marginalised, and it is thus problematic
when litigation against such marginality begins to mirror, rather than contradict,
that positioning. In this sense the cases reflect somewhat of a double-margin: the
amicus interventions were launched on behalf of a marginalised community
appealing to the law for recourse against prejudice; at the same time these appeals
are made from the margins in that *amici* occupy a relatively de-centred position
from which to shape the interpretation and application of law in the legal process.
Yet at the same time, and through these cases, LGBTI voices were brought before
the law and the courts, through for example the giving of expert testimony on the
embodied experiences of sexual and gender discrimination, thus serving to draw
these material realities more firmly into the legal frame.

(c) Reproducing homophobia
In each of the cases, the manner in which the litigation unfolded exposed how law,
the legal system, and those who enforce it (such as court officials), are implicated
in the exercise of discriminatory power. This relates to the gendered, heteronorma-
tive and racialised dynamics that are embedded in the production and practice of
law, and in relation to which, in complex ways, LGBTI people are both regulated
and resistant.[34] As a result, the law and its apparatuses (including the systems and
subjects that keep it in place) constitutively re-enact the sexual, gendered and
racial marginalisations that LGBTI people face. An example of this is how, in
response to the litigation in *Mazibuko*, *Qwelane* and *Semugoma*, the kinds of
homophobic behaviour that the litigation was attempting to challenge, were
reproduced during the legal proceedings.

This reproduction of homophobia was most notable in *Mazibuko* where one of
the accused arrived in court wearing a t-shirt displaying the words 'Dip me in

---

[31] *Psychological Society of South Africa v Dubula Jonathan Qwelane and others* [2016] ZACC 48;
2017 (8) BCLR 1039 (CC).

[32] Ibid para 30.

[33] Ibid para 39.

[34] See Ruthann Robson *Lesbian Out Law: Survival Under the Rule of Law* (1992); Catherine
MacKinnon 'Difference and dominance: On sex discrimination' in Will Kymlicka (ed) *Critiques and
Alternatives* (1992); Kimberlé Crenshaw 'Race, gender, and sexual harassment' (1992) 65 *S Cal L
Rev* 1467–76.

chocolate and throw me to the lesbians'. This can be read as a brazen expression of the accused's non-repentance, a sentiment similarly expressed by Qwelane, who wrote in the article that was the subject of the case against him, '[B]y the way, please tell the Human Rights Commission that I totally refuse to withdraw or apologise for my views'. The presence of the t-shirt in court in *Mazibuko* can also be interpreted as a direct provocation toward gays and lesbians through a mocking display that, metaphorically, pushes the accused back onto 'the lesbians' in the form of a sexual threat. Astoundingly, the magistrate conducted the court proceedings making no mention of the t-shirt. This reflects the normalisation and a tacit legitimation of the exercise of hetero-patriarchy in the courtroom, the very kind of power that fuels violence against LGBTI people in the first instance.[35] The court was therefore complicit in exposing gays and lesbians to a renewed threat and provocation by the accused's wearing of the t-shirt, allowing its words to be publicly directed at the LGBTI bodies and interests in the courtroom. Fortunately, the complainant himself was not in court that day. However, a clear message was sent to his attorneys, and to everyone in court, that the legal system would not, in the course of justice, protect the complainant from revictimisation. The conduct of the accused and the magistrate on that day confirmed that the welfare of LGBTI people was overlooked in legal proceedings. In the sentencing phase of the trial, the *amicus* argued that the wearing of the t-shirt had demonstrated a clear lack of remorse and that this should be taken into account in sentencing the accused.[36] This argument was disregarded, reflecting the court's inability, perhaps unwillingness, to recognise and respond to its own perpetuation of prejudice. The magistrate handed down a sentence which was unduly lenient, and which included imposing an obligation on '*the LGBT group*' (who remained unnamed and unspecified) to

---

[35] See Nonhlanhla Mkhize et al *The Country We Want to Live in: Hate Crimes and Homophobia in the Lives of Black Lesbians* (2010); Andrew Martin et al 'Hate crimes: The rise of "corrective" rape in South Africa' *ActionAid* (2009).

[36] Advocate Kate Hofmeyr, representing Mazibuko, argued as follows: 'We submit that the wearing of that T-shirt represents a number of things, it represents a disdain for this process and a refusal to be remorseful about the conduct that accused 3 and indeed the other accused perpetrated. We submit that it is deeply offensive to wear such a T-shirt in this public setting where the purpose for us all gathering together is to assess the guilt of three men accused of brutally attacking a man because he was gay. It is also, we submit, a confirmation of the very prejudice that motivated that attack, it is a confirmation that those were not just words that crept into accused 3's mouth when he said, he is gay he does not deserve to live, those words were representative of a view that certain people are less worthy than others and that certain people do not deserve as much respect as others and the T-shirt simply confirmed that prejudice. We also submit that that representation of that prejudice was not confined to accused 3, none of his co-accused convinced him not to wear it or told him it was inappropriate, they acquiesced by their silence in the message that was sent to everyone in that courtroom and that was a message of intolerance' (pages 103–4 of the transcript of the trial on 27 January 2012).

provide '*awareness programmes*' to the accused.[37] This is, symbolically speaking, yet another act of 'throwing' the accused back to the gays and lesbians. Moreover, the magistrate had made no contact with said 'LGBT groups' (presumed to be the *amicus* organisation itself) before formulating her order to consider if it was indeed implementable. Underlying the order was the dangerous and endangering assumption that it is appropriate for LGBTI organisations—established for the benefit of LGBTI people—to use their limited resources for the benefit and rehabilitation of homophobic criminals. This court-sanctioned directive, given effect to without the consent of the 'LGBT groups', does violence to them. It also absolves the state from its mandated responsibilities to punish and prevent violence in ways that work against, rather than in support of, secondary victimisation. Worse still, the accused never attended the so-called awareness programmes (read rehabilitative programmes) that had been fancifully imagined by the court as readily available to homophobic criminals from the very people towards whom their violent prejudice was directed in the first instance.[38]

Another feature of *Mazibuko* and *Qwelane* was the extraordinarily long duration of the matters: it took just over four years for the accused in *Mazibuko* to be convicted and sentenced and in *Qwelane* it took approximately nine years before the trial commenced in the High Court, his article having been published in 2008, the SAHRC having instituted its claim in December 2009, and the trial finally proceeding in 2017.[39] The inordinate length of both matters can primarily be attributed to the offending parties and their respective attorneys having used

---

[37] The three accused were required to participate in 'awareness programmes of gays and lesbians' or 'awareness programmes of the LGBT group' for between two and three years, and to submit a certificate of attendance to the clerk of the Germiston Magistrates Court.

[38] The clerk of the Germiston Regional Magistrates Court confirmed that the accused did not place a certificate of attendance in the court file proving their attendance of the 'awareness programmes of gays and lesbians' (written correspondence between Webber Wentzel and the clerk of the Court, dated 19 October 2016, on file with authors).

[39] Some of the delay may be attributed to procedural complications arising out of Qwelane's decision to challenge the constitutionality of the Equality Act. In June 2012, while the matter was running in the Magistrates Court, he applied to the High Court for an order declaring s 10 of the Equality Act constitutionally invalid and requesting the Equality Court proceedings in the Magistrates Court be stayed pending the determination of his constitutional challenge in the High Court. In response the parties agreed that the Equality Court proceedings be transferred to the High Court and they jointly filed an application for transfer (the Magistrates Court then transferred the matter on 11 September 2012). However, Qwelane withdrew his constitutional challenge and then, 15 months later, changed course again. On 27 September 2013 he thus reinstituted his constitutional challenge, applying for an order declaring ss 10(1) and 11 of the Equality Act inconsistent with s 16 of the Constitution and sought a stay of the Equality Court proceedings (see, *Psychological Society of South Africa v Qwelane and Others* [2016] ZACC 48; 2017 (8) BCLR 1039 (CC) paras 6–8, which explains this history of the matter). As a result of the transfer of the Equality Court proceedings and Qwelane's constitutional challenge to the Equality Act, before the matter was able to proceed, the High Court was called upon to decide if it could hear both matters simultaneously (because there is no statutory provision enabling a High Court judge to hear Equality Court proceedings and High Court proceedings, in one consolidated case). The High Court on 21 November 2014 decided that it had inherent jurisdiction to hear both cases and ordered the cases be consolidated and be heard by a

procedural tactics to delay matters, taking advantage of a lethargic legal system that does not function optimally at the best of times, and that systematically fails those who are socially vulnerable.[40] Additionally, in *Mazibuko* the prosecuting arm of the state initially refused to prosecute, and, when it finally did, it failed to pursue the matter with the type of vigour one might reasonably expect.[41] As previously mentioned, in *Qwelane* the SAHRC failed to pursue the matter with a sense of due importance. It appeared that internal to the organisation the case had been handled by numerous people over the years, without anyone owning the case or its issues. Regardless of the reasons for the delays, it sent a strong social message that LGBTI discrimination is neither taken seriously nor treated with the urgency and importance it demands. When *Qwelane* did not proceed[42] in the High Court on the allocated trial dates in 2016, the distinction between how the courts address homophobic hate speech in comparison to racist hate speech became starkly apparent. As Juan Nel,[43] PsySSA's President (as he then was) stated at the time:

> Recent cases of racist hate speech,[44] for example statements that have likened black people to animals, have been dealt with far more swiftly by our courts, and rightfully so. Failure to actively condemn harmful insult sends a strong social message that it is in fact acceptable to dehumanise gays and lesbians and to liken them to animals, as Qwelane wrote in his article.

---

single judge of the High Court who was also an Equality Court judge (*Qwelane v Minister of Justice and Constitutional Development and Others* [2014] ZAGPHC 334; 2015 (2) SA 493 (GJ) para 11).

[40] See Lisa Vetten et al 'Tracking justice: The attrition of rape cases through the criminal justice system in Gauteng' *Tshwaranang Women's Legal Centre, Medical Research Council and the Centre for the Study of Violence and Reconciliation* (July 2008) last accessed on 13 March 2018 from <https://www.csvr.org.za/docs/tracking_justice.pdf>; Civil Society Prison Reform Initiative, Just Detention International & Lawyers for Human Rights 'Thematic alternate report on criminal justice and human rights in South Africa: Submitted to the African Commission on Human and Peoples' Rights in response to South Africa's Second Periodic Report under the African Charter on Human and Peoples' Rights, to be reviewed at the 58th Ordinary Session of the African Commission on Human and Peoples' Rights' (March 2016), last accessed from <http://southafrica.justdetention.org/wp-content/uploads/2016/05/ACHPR-shadow-report-criminal-justice-FINAL.pdf> on 9 November 2016.

[41] The role that OUT played in reviewing the prosecutor's initial decision not to prosecute is described at note 29 above.

[42] On the eve of the court hearing, Qwelane presented himself in person at a police station to commission an affidavit applying for a postponement, arguing that, due to a progressively degenerative medical condition, he was unable to present himself in person in court.

[43] Juan Nel was also one of the expert witnesses in *Mazibuko* who gave expert testimony on the effects of homophobic hate crimes. In *Qwelane* he spearheaded PsySSA's application to intervene as *amicus curiae* and gave expert testimony on the effects of homophobic hate speech.

[44] Less than three months before the date set for the commencement of the *Qwelane* trial, a woman who had uttered hurtful words about black people, was found to have breached s 10 of the Equality Act. Within eight months of her public utterances, which drew unprecedented public attention to racist hate speech, the woman was fined R150 000 and ordered to issue a public apology, with which she complied. See *ANC v Sparrow* [2016] ZAEQC 1.

The symbolic violence[45] of state lethargy in regard to homophobic crimes and speech reinforces the social and legal conditions in which such crimes and speech continue, largely undisturbed.

The unintended and ironic consequence of this litigation was that the attempt at *remedying* homophobia had given rise to *reproducing* it instead. This is a difficult dynamic to navigate and requires that the attorneys working for LGBTI litigants take extra measures to protect their clients from further violence, be that physical, psychological or state-driven.

(d)   A state of contradiction
A further feature of LGBTI PIL has been managing the contradictions of the state, which take various forms. Mention has already been made of the role of the prosecutor in *Mazibuko* and the SAHRC in *Qwelane*, pointing to: in the former, the support of the *amicus curiae* intervention with the simultaneous abdication of responsibility for pursuing the homophobic dimension of the crime; and in the latter, an inconsistent commitment to the case which contributed to the delayed hearing in the High Court. The High Court judgment in *Qwelane*[46] also displayed some contradictions. It was a stunning victory for the SAHRC, PsySSA and the LGBTI community in that it acknowledged, unequivocally, the context in which Qwelane's statements were made as well as the harm and hurt that they caused.[47] However, the judge opted for an overly narrow interpretation of s 10 of the Equality Act suggesting that to establish hate speech an applicant would have to show that the speech was hurtful, harmful (or incites harm) *and* promotes or

---

[45] Symbolic violence refers to the processes by which existing relations of domination are produced and maintained through the exercise of symbolic power—Pierre Bourdieu 'Social space and symbolic power' (1989) 7 *Sociological Theory* 14–25. For how symbolic power operates in relation to gender-based violence see, Karen Morgan & Suruchi Thapar Björkert ' "I'd rather you'd lay me on the floor and start kicking me": Understanding symbolic violence in everyday life' (2006) 29 *Women's Studies International Forum* 441–52.

[46] *South African Human Rights Commission v Qwelane* [2017] ZAGPJHC 218; 2018 (2) SA 149 (GJ) [FXI and Psychological Society of South Africa were admitted as *amici curiae*].

[47] At para 46 Moshidi J finds as follows: 'The offending statements uttered by the applicant, when evaluated objectively, in content and context, speaks ill of the gay and lesbian community, and went further by suggesting that the next step for South Africa will be allowing people to marry animals. It can never be acceptable, in the context and content of the legislation, and our democratic society, to equate human beings to bestiality or animals or suggest to them that they are "other" or "unnatural". It severely undermines their ability to feel that they belong and have support, which is essential to psychological health and well-being of all humans. . . . It is common knowledge from the evidence of Nel [PsySSA's expert witness] and the other witnesses of the [Human Rights] Commission that gay and lesbian people, who constitute a vulnerable group in society, and have been subject to societal discrimination purely on the ground of sexual orientation. They are a permanent minority in society and have suffered in the past from various patterns of disadvantage. . . . The evidence, in particular that of Mokoena and MN, showed convincingly that the offending statements were deeply hurtful and harmful to the victims and targeted group.' (para 49)

propagates hatred[48] (a bar that limits the utility of the provision and undermines its potential to promote equality and dignity).[49]

Another striking contradiction is illustrated in encounters with the Department of Home Affairs' (the DHA) in responding to LGBTI-related litigation. The DHA is intimately involved in LGBTI lives: amongst other things, it registers births and regulates adoptions (and hence must acknowledge same-sex parents), it issues marriage certificates (and hence must acknowledge same-sex marriages or civil unions), it controls entry to and exit from South Africa (and its recognition of same-sex relationships is essential for this function), and it issues new identity documents for transgender people (and is therefore required to recognise sex and gender re-assignment).

In its response to LGBTI PIL, the DHA has adopted a variety of inconsistent positions.[50] In *Semugoma* particularly, the DHA's disregard for the rule of law demands scrutiny. Semugoma was detained by DHA officials on 17 February 2014 on the basis that his work permit had expired and that the official document the DHA had issued (allowing travel while work permits were being renewed), was not valid.[51] The DHA indicated that they intended deporting Semugoma to Uganda despite the very real threat of his prosecution under the Anti-Homosexuality Bill,[52] the passing of which was imminent at that time. As a result, an urgent application was launched on the day of Semugoma's detention, in response to

---

[48] Ibid para 60.

[49] PsySSA argued that 'the prohibition in section 10(1) is aimed at combating three different and distinguishable effects hate speech may have. It may be "hurtful"; it may be "harmful or . . . incite harm" or it may "promote or propagate hatred". All three of these have subtly different meanings and engage different negative effects. We therefore support a disjunctive reading of s 10(1). If it is not read disjunctively, the prohibition would not address the variety of ways in which "hate speech" can and does impact a target group, including by way of (individual or communal) psychological or mental harm; societal marginalisation or rupture of the body politic' (Heads of argument in the Constitutional challenge, para 47).

[50] First, in *National Coalition II* (note 3 above) para 27 the DHA argued that it had an absolute discretion to exclude foreign nationals which meant that it could exclude foreign nationals who were in same-sex partnerships with South Africans without regard to the Constitution and its right to equality and dignity. Then in *J and Another* (note 4 above) para 11 the DHA decided not to argue that the statutory provisions, which denied recognition of same-sex parents who conceived by artificial insemination, constituted a justifiable limitation of constitutional rights. And finally, in *Fourie* (note 3 above) para 35, the DHA suggested that it was fair to exclude same-sex couples from being allowed to marry.

[51] The DHA officials who detained Semugoma and who corresponded with Webber Wentzel indicated there was a policy in place explaining that this document did not allow travel. They were, however, never able to produce the policy or explain why they issued the document in the first place with the explanation that it allowed travel.

[52] The Bill was enacted as the Anti-Homosexuality Act, 2014. The Act creates the criminal offences of 'homosexuality', 'aggravated homosexuality' and 'attempt to commit homosexuality' (amongst others) and makes offenders liable on conviction to life imprisonment.

which the High Court ordered his immediate release.[53] The DHA refused to comply with the court order and, instead, held Semugoma overnight at an unknown location, applied for leave to appeal the order, and continued threatening to deport him the following day. Finally, on the third day of Semugoma's detention, and when the application for leave to appeal was about to be heard, the DHA offered to settle. Even though a settlement offer was made, Semugoma's attorney was met with antagonism as the DHA's senior counsel suggested she should 'wipe the smirk off [her] face'. In another show of state resistance, when Semugoma's partner and his legal team went to collect him from the airport, they were initially refused access and only later able to secure his release.

The DHA, and more particularly its officials, has been similarly obstructionist in instances when transgender people have attempted to have their sex changed in terms of the Alteration of Sex Description and Sex Status Act 49 of 2003 (Sex Status Act).[54] South African law allows for transgender people to change their sex description both on birth registers and on identity documents.[55] However, the experience of submitting an application to the DHA is more often than not a humiliating affair characterised by bureaucratic obstacles designed to frustrate transgender and intersex people from accessing legal entitlements and thus constituting a violation of their rights.[56] Nadia Swanepoel, for example, went on a hunger strike in 2014 in order to try to force the DHA to comply with its own laws by issuing an identity document reflecting her sex as female. She had been waiting for an identity document for three years, and had faced consistent rejections, including suggestions that her application had been lost, and then finally a refusal to consider the application until she had genital surgery.[57]

---

[53] The urgency of the matter was such that Webber Wentzel and counsel did not have time to draft papers and approached a judge in chambers.

[54] The Act enables intersex persons to change their legal sex without having to undergo surgical or medical treatment.

[55] Section 2(1) of the Sex Status Act.

[56] The lack of proper administration of the Act has been attributed to a misreading of the legislation as requiring proof of genital surgery from applicants who wish to change their sex designation; the absence of national directives for the Act's implementation resulting in lengthy delays; no reasons being furnished when applications are denied; and the absence of measures to protect the marriages of transgender or intersex persons who change their sex descriptor after getting married. See Robert Hamblin & Mzikazi Nduna 'Alteration of Sex Description and Sex Status Act and access to services for transgender people in South Africa' (2013) 9 *New Voices in Psychology* 50–62; Legal Resources Centre, Iranti-Org & Gender Dynamix 'Report on the civil, political and socio-economic rights of transgender and intersex persons in South Africa under the African Charter on Human and Peoples' Rights in response to the Second Combined Periodic Report of the Government of South Africa and the initial report under the Protocol to the African Charter on the Rights of Women in Africa' (April 2016), last accessed from <http://lrc.org.za/art_external/pdf/2016%2004%20ACHPR-Trans-gender-and-Intersex-Shadow-Report.pdf> on 12 March 2018.

[57] Sipho Kings 'Transgender woman goes on hunger strike over ID application' *Mail & Guardian* 9 October 2014, last accessed on 9 November 2016 from <http://mg.co.za/article/2014-10-09-transgender-goes-on-hunger-strike-over-id-application>.

Such disregard for court orders and the rule of law from a state department is condemnable, particularly given the recent public stance of senior DHA officials on LGBTI-related discriminations whereby constitutional commitments to equality were publicly endorsed and enforced.[58] These contradictions can be understood in a number of ways: first, the officials responsible for implementing laws have personal views and values that do not accord with the Constitution or the law.[59] Second, the DHA is engaged in both domestic and international politics, which means that positions for or against trans/homophobia are also pressure points for political manoeuvres. The paradoxical positions taken on LGBTI rights also reflect geopolitical dynamics in which contradictions between domestic and international stances reflect the state's double-game on sexual orientation and gender identity issues.[60]

9.3 CONCLUSION

The litigation experiences in the three cases discussed in this chapter illustrate the difficulties of using the law in promoting, defending and advancing equality and dignity for LGBTI people post the legalisation of same-sex marriage. Importantly, for the purpose of progressing LGBTI PIL, the constraints in the practice and application of law prompt the need for unconventional tactics when litigating with—and in some ways against—these realities. The cases also demonstrate the pernicious ways in which social discrimination and exclusion feature not only in the merits of a particular matter around which litigation is fashioned, but also in the very legal processes by which that litigation is then pursued. In this sense, the legal system is a contested terrain where LGBTI people use law to resist social injustices, yet are confronted, and at times defeated, by the injustices of law in practice. This raises various conundrums for litigation strategies related to the

---

[58] In refusing Pastor Anderson, a renowned homophobe, entry into South Africa on the grounds that the Immigration Act 13 of 2002 prohibits admission of foreigners likely to promote hate speech or advocate social violence, the Minister of the DHA stated that, '[I]t is a constitutional imperative for organs of state and society at large to protect and jealously defend the rights of all people'. He also went on to concede that 'Home Affairs has also had instances in the past wherein our own officials had treated LGBTI persons in a manner that is inconsistent with our laws'. 'Minister Gigaba's statement at the media briefing on the decision on Pastor Anderson's visit to South Africa' *Department of Home Affairs* 13 September 2016, last accessed on 9 November 2016 from <http://www.dha.gov.za/index.php/statements-speeches/853-minister-gigaba-s-statement-at-the-media-briefing-on-the-decision-on-pastor-anderson-s-visit-to-south-africa>.

[59] Worryingly, the legalisation of same-sex marriage included a legislative sanction for officials holding personal views about homosexuality which entitles them to escape the obligation to solemnise same-sex civil unions. Section 6 of the Civil Union Act 17 of 2006 allows a marriage officer to object to solemnising a civil union between same-sex partners on the grounds of 'conscience, religion and belief' and to write to the Minister to inform him or her of this objection so as not to be required to effect same-sex civil marriages.

[60] Melanie Judge 'SA's abstinence on UN sexual and gender rights vote is reckless' *Mail & Guardian* 6 July 2016, last accessed on 9 November 2016 from <http://mg.co.za/article/2016-07-06-00-sa-reckless-on-un-gender-and-sexual-rights-vote/>.

pursuit of social justice. For one, the realisation of equality stretches far beyond the remit of law, and, in some instances, as we have argued, the practice of law might thwart its realisation. Also, when LGBTI people and the organisations that support them come before the legal system, prevailing prejudices frequently come into play. The experiences in the three cases suggest that LGBTI *amici* or applicants should plan for the systemic injustices and violence of the law in practice and develop principled approaches to guide appropriate litigious and political responses.

Moreover, PIL for LGBTI equality has largely been left over (or handed over) to LGBTI people and communities themselves. This reflects a broader context in which identity-based equality claims are dependent on specific claimants firmly defined by the very identities that are the basis of their claims. While this has been highly productive in furthering the rights of marginalised social groups (for example, people living with HIV and AIDS, refugees, the disabled), it can restrict rights-based legal struggles to singularised identities[61] amongst and between which, frequently, there is limited political solidarity. Identity-driven litigation can also be divisive as it appears to only protect the particular category of applicant around which the legal case is constructed. Viewing experiences of discrimination as intersectional[62]—as encompassing, for example, race, class, gender and sexual oppressions that are mutually reinforcing—requires legal strategies that take cognisance of how sexuality-based discrimination does *not* occur in isolation to other forms of discrimination. Consequently, litigation tactics ought to consider how multiple and intersecting forms of marginalisation produce uneven vulnerabilities to violence and injustice, and what the implications of this might be for litigation. For one, it might require the untangling of the discreet identity categories (that is, of sexuality and gender identity) on which many LGBTI equality cases have been so reliant. It might also require that LGBTI public interest cases be underpinned by facts that illustrate the diversity of LGBTI experiences across class, race, and health statuses, amongst other differentials, which may in turn invite the intervention of additional parties or *amici*. Future PIL will benefit from situating LGBTI experiences firmly in a social context, so that the sexual and gender dimensions of discrimination are but two of multiple dimensions to be pursued when litigating.

It might also mean that statutory bodies should be urged to play a more active role in PIL. Alongside the ongoing and necessary PIL spearheaded by non-

---

[61] This refers to how a legal case against discrimination might be based on a person's sexual orientation, gender, nationality or health status as singular and unconnected identities, but rarely in combination, even though the discrimination they face might be as a result of more than one identity factor. For example, a black lesbian, who might also be a refugee, could be subject to prejudice linked to her race, sexual orientation and refugee status.

[62] Kimberlé Crenshaw 'Mapping the margins: Intersectionality, identity politics, and violence against women of color' (1991) 43 *Stanf Law Rev* 1241–99.

governmental organisations and LGBTI individuals, perhaps it is time to 'throw the gays and lesbians' to the Chapter 9 institutions, which despite a constitutional mandate, have, in recent years, done little to systematically pursue litigation that gives succour to the defence of formal rights and the promotion of substantive equality. This is particularly concerning given the significant powers of these statutory bodies to institute special investigations, public hearings, commissions of enquiry, and to litigate directly on constitutional rights.

Finally, the three cases demonstrate the weakness of relying on the common law or the Equality Act to bring the full weight of constitutional protections to bear on LGBTI-related claims in the post same-sex marriage period. It may well be necessary for strategic litigators to i) revisit the right to dignity and consider how to develop the jurisprudence underpinning this right; and ii) reconsider how to develop the jurisprudence underpinning the right to equality so that the protections offered by the Equality Act's prohibition of unfair discrimination may be expanded to address the multiple forms of violence, exclusion and discrimination faced by LGBTI people. In this regard, the focus of inequality or unfair discrimination claims in future should move away from an analysis of differential or discriminatory treatment and towards a demand for social and legal systems that accommodate and advance difference[63] and that are attuned to intersectional forms of oppression. The reflections provided in this chapter also call for critical engagements with the constraints of the law, and how to address these in the pursuit of justice within the legal system. This requires lawyers and activists to develop new tactics that are directed both at winning cases and at building legal processes that promote rather than undermine dignity and equality. Whatever form future litigation in the public interest might take, it is vital that the practice and application of law affirms LGBTI people as full and equal citizens within the legal system itself.

---

[63] Sachs J in *Fourie* (note 3 above) para 60 planted the seeds of this idea when he explained in a section entitled '*A right to be different*' as follows:

Equality means equal concern and respect across difference. It does not presuppose the elimination or suppression of difference. Respect for human rights requires the affirmation of self, not the denial of self. Equality therefore does not imply a levelling or homogenisation of behaviour or extolling one form as supreme, and another as inferior, but an acknowledgement and acceptance of difference. At the very least, it affirms that difference should not be the basis for exclusion, marginalisation and stigma. At best, it celebrates the vitality that difference brings to any society.

Chapter 10

CHILDREN'S RIGHTS

Ann Skelton

10.1 INTRODUCTION

When the children's rights section in the Bill of Rights was first debated, opposition leader Tony Leon was quoted as saying that it was unobjectionable because, like chicken soup, it could do no harm.[1] This chapter demonstrates that the South African courts' treatment of children's rights has been far more piquant than the bland potage that was apparently expected. If the legislature thought they would never be directed to refry their legislation pertaining to children (or have it recooked for them by the Constitutional Court), they were wrong, as some of the successful constitutional challenges described in this chapter show. After taking a while to warm up, children's rights issues got on the boil during 2007, and the case law amounts to a rich mélange that constitutionally imagines children who are human rights holders separate from their parents. The jurisprudence furthermore recognises both the protection and autonomy of children and has largely upheld children's dignity and other civil rights. Following a tentative start, the case law

---

[1] Julia Sloth-Nielsen 'Chicken soup and chain saws: Some implications of the constitutionalisation of children's rights in South Africa' 1996 *Acta Juridica* 6.

has set a reasonably sound basis for ongoing development of children's socio-economic rights.

The chapter examines the reasons for the slow start in strategic public interest litigation (PIL) on children's issues and identifies the factors behind the upsurge around 2007. Case law is analysed according to prominent themes that have emerged, while also attempting to be chronological. The chapter reveals some of the 'behind the scenes' strategic decision-making in the sector and describes the consultative approach that the children's rights sector has utilised to bring, support or find alternatives to litigation.

10.2 CHILDREN'S RIGHTS MOVEMENT

South Africa boasts a strong children's rights movement, which predates the constitutional era.[2] The struggle against apartheid had involved children themselves,[3] which led to the establishment of the Detainees Support Committee, the Children's Institute at UCT and the National Children's Rights Committee. The Community Law Centre (University of the Western Cape)[4] and Lawyers for Human Rights (LHR) were also active children's rights lobbyists during the final years of apartheid. In addition, the sector benefited from a century-old tradition of 'charitable organisations' such as Child Welfare South Africa and the National Institute for Crime Prevention and Reintegration of Offenders (NICRO) that had delivered services to children and also undertook important advocacy work. In the lead up to South Africa's negotiated solution, there was much 'rights talk' about children. The Bill of Rights in the interim Constitution contained a special section for children, s 30.[5] It was not as expansive as s 28 of the Constitution turned out to be. The improvements were largely due to the very active children's rights movement in South Africa. During the Constitutional Assembly process that culminated in the Constitution there were calls for written and oral submissions on all aspects of the Bill of Rights. Children's rights organisations made excellent use of these opportunities, and this resulted in the broader reach of s 28 of the Constitution. South Africa's ratification of the Convention on the Rights of the

---

[2] In fact, in the 1930s there was also a children's rights movement in which Leila Reitz, Charlotte Maxeke and Alan Paton played important roles. See Ann Skelton *The Theory and Practice of Restorative Justice in South Africa with Special Reference to Child Justice* (unpublished LLD thesis, University of Pretoria, 2005).

[3] Francis Wilson & Mamphela Ramphele *Children on the Frontline: The Impact of Apartheid, Destabilization and Warfare on Children in Southern and South Africa* (1998) 67.

[4] Now the Dullah Omar Institute.

[5] The interim Constitution commenced on 27 April 1994. During the negotiations to establish a new constitutional state in South Africa, it had been agreed that there would be an interim Constitution, and that a process would begin immediately to draft a final constitution through a participative process driven by the Constitutional Assembly.

Child (CRC) in 1995 was an important backdrop, and the influence of this instrument on the drafting of the constitutional provisions is evident.[6]

Skelton and Proudlock[7] have discussed the expansion of the children's rights clause in the Constitution. They pointed out some of the important changes that were made, such as 'the right to parental care' being amended to read 'every child has the right to family care or parental care, or to appropriate alternative care when removed from the family environment'.[8] In addition, the word 'shelter' was added to s 28(1)*(c)*. Protection from abuse and neglect was expanded to provide protection from 'maltreatment, neglect, abuse or degradation'.[9] Furthermore, the inclusion of a child's right 'not to be detained except as a measure of last resort' and 'only for the shortest appropriate period of time', as well as 'to be kept separately from detained persons over the age of 18 years'[10] significantly improved the provisions relating to child offenders. The right of a child to have a legal practitioner assigned to him or her in civil proceedings was also an addition introduced into the Constitution.[11]

10.3 SLOW TO TAKE OFF

Sloth-Nielsen wrote a series of three articles, the latter two with co-authors, which have tracked the development of children's rights litigation since 1994.[12] In her first article, published in 2002, she bemoaned the fact that the majority of cases that came before the courts were brought by adults opportunistically using children's rights to bolster their own claims.[13] She was concerned about the 'invisibility' of the children in the cases brought during the early years, particularly in the field of private law. She found it surprising, considering the strength of the children's rights movement, that children's rights organisations were not getting actively involved in the cases. She concluded that this was partly because the first few years of the new democracy created obligations and opportunities for

---

[6] The constitutional drafting committees relied directly on the wording of the CRC. See further Lourens M du Plessis & Hugh Corder *Understanding South Africa's Transitional Bill of Rights* (1994).

[7] Ann Skelton & Paula Proudlock 'Interpretation, objects, application and implementation of the Act' in CJ Davel & AM Skelton (eds) *Commentary on the Children's Act* (2012) 1–8.

[8] Section 28(1)*(b)* of the Constitution.

[9] Section 28(1)*(d)*.

[10] Section 28(1)*(g)*.

[11] Section 28(1)*(h)*.

[12] Julia Sloth-Nielsen 'Children's rights in the South African courts: An overview since ratification of the UN Convention on the Rights of the Child' (2002) 10 *Int'l J Children's Rts* 136–56; Julia Sloth-Nielsen & Benyam Mezmur '2+2=5? Exploring the domestication of the CRC in the South African courts (2002–2006)' (2008) 16 *Int'l J Children's Rts* 1–28; Julia Sloth-Nielsen & Helen Kruuse 'A maturing manifesto: The constitutionalisation of children's right in South African jurisprudence 2007–2012' (2013) 21 *Int'l J Children's Rts* 646–78.

[13] Sloth-Nielsen (note 12 above) 136–56.

policy and law making in the children's rights sphere, and that many child rights activists were deeply involved in those processes.

Sloth-Nielsen highlights adoption cases that illustrate the invisibility of the child. The first was the *Fraser* case,[14] which was essentially about equality and established the right of unmarried fathers to consent to their children's adoptions. The court applied the child's best interests standard in a sequel to the main case when Fraser was refused leave to appeal because the child had settled in his new adoptive family.[15]

The second adoption case was that of *Fitzpatrick*.[16] This matter concerned a foreign family that was barred by a provision of the Child Care Act 74 of 1983, from being able to adopt a child whom they had fostered for two years, due to the fact that they were not citizens. The adoptive parents argued that it was in the child's best interests to be adopted by them. The court appointed a curator *ad litem* to look after the interests of the child.

The court also appointed a curator *ad litem* to protect the interests of two teenage children in *Du Toit*,[17] another case about gender equality, which resulted in same-sex partners being able to adopt jointly. Although Sloth-Nielsen's critique that these early cases were not being brought by children's rights organisations or even on behalf of individual children is true, the children in these cases were never invisible to the court, as is evidenced by the appointment of curators to safeguard their interests.

In the field of public law, the judgments focused more directly on children themselves, although again it was the courts, rather than the litigants, that brought the focus. The first big children's right case heard by the Constitutional Court was that of *Williams*.[18] It was a magistrate, rather than a legal representative, who caused this matter to proceed to the Constitutional Court by sending a number of sentences requiring the administration of corporal punishment on review, in light of the possible unconstitutionality of the sentence. An *amicus curiae* was appointed to represent the interests of the accused in the High Court and continued to play the same role in the Constitutional Court hearing.[19] In a profound judgment that drew on international and foreign law, especially that of neighbouring

---

[14] *Fraser v Children's Court, Pretoria North and Others* [1997] ZACC 1; 1997 (2) SA 261 (CC). *Fraser v Naude and Another* [1998] ZACC 13; 1999 (1) SA 1 (CC). [CALS and LRH were admitted as *amici curiae*]

[15] Ibid.

[16] *Minister of Welfare and Population Development v Fitzpatrick and Others* [2000] ZACC 6; 2000 (3) SA 422 (CC) [CALS was admitted as *amicus curiae*].

[17] *Du Toit and Another v Minister of Welfare and Population Development and Others* [2002] ZACC 20; 2003 (2) SA 198 (CC) [Gay and Lesbian Equality Project was admitted as *amicus curiae*].

[18] *S v Williams and Others* [1995] ZACC 6; 1995 (3) SA 632 (CC) [LRC acted as *amicus curiae* for the accused].

[19] Mr Bozalek (with Mr Hathorn) appeared as *amicus curiae* for the accused, assisted by the LRC.

jurisdictions, Langa J (as he then was) struck down juvenile whipping as being cruel, inhuman and degrading treatment. Although a children's rights argument based on s 28 had been raised, the court found it unnecessary to pronounce on that because it located its finding of unconstitutionality in s 10 (dignity) and s 11(2) (freedom and security of person) of the interim Constitution. This did not mean that the court did not consider the plight of children—Langa J roundly rejected an argument that because children's characters were still in formation, they would be more susceptible to learning by being whipped. The court's response was clear: it was precisely because children were more impressionable that they should not be subjected to treatment that coarsened them.[20]

A few years later, in 2000, another case concerning corporal punishment came before the Constitutional Court.[21] A group of 196 independent Christian schools challenged the ban on corporal punishment in schools which had been introduced by the South African Schools Act 84 of 1996. They claimed that the provision infringed their individual, parental and community rights to practice their religion freely. The court found that, although their freedom of religion was *prima facie* infringed, it was reasonable and justifiable due to the need to protect children from degrading treatment. In this case Sachs J called for the voices of children to be more directly heard by the courts. In his postscript to the judgment, he regretted that no curator *ad litem* had been appointed to present the children's views to the court:

> Their actual experiences and opinions would not necessarily have been decisive, but they would have enriched the dialogue, and the factual and experiential foundations for the balancing exercise in this difficult matter would have been more secure.[22]

Chief Justice Langa in *Pillay*[23] picked up this theme again in 2008,—where he observed that legal matters involving children often exclude children, and the matter is left to adults to argue and decide on their behalf. He said that the court would have preferred to hear directly from the child at the centre of the 'nose stud' dispute.

The next year the court dealt with children's socio-economic rights for the first time in *Grootboom*.[24] The applicants were adults and children who lived in an informal settlement and needed housing. It was argued that children, in terms of s 28(1)*(c)*, have a right to shelter which, unlike the right to housing in s 26, is

---

[20] *Williams* (note 18 above) para 47. For an in-depth discussion of this case see Ann Skelton '*S v Williams*: A springboard for further debate about corporal punishment' 2015 *Acta Juridica* 240–63.

[21] *Christian Education South Africa v Minister of Education* [2000] ZACC 11; 2000 (4) SA 757 (CC).

[22] Ibid para 53.

[23] *MEC for Education: KwaZulu-Natal and Others v Pillay* [2007] ZACC 21; 2008 (1) SA 474 (CC) para 56 [LHR acted for the respondents and FXI was admitted as *amicus curiae*].

[24] *Government of the Republic of South Africa and Others v Grootboom and Others* [2000] ZACC 19; 2001 (1) SA 46 (CC) [LRC was admitted as *amicus curiae*].

unqualified. It does not contain terms such as 'progressive realisation' or 'within available resources' and is therefore immediately realisable.

The Constitutional Court began its examination of the question of whether children had a direct and immediately enforceable right by considering the CRC. The court found that the obligation to provide shelter falls primarily on the parents. The state's obligations regarding children living with their families are limited to providing the legal framework to prevent abuse and neglect, and, more broadly, to providing families with access to housing and other services. The full obligation rests on the state only where parental care is 'lacking'. The court found that all the families had a right to housing, a right to be realised progressively when sufficient funds became available, and that the government's plan was unreasonable. However, it declined to prioritise families with children, as it was of the view that children should not be used as 'stepping stones' in realising the socio-economic rights of their parents.

The children's rights sector was disappointed with this rationale, and this aspect of the judgment was subjected to critique.[25] Some writers viewed the judgment as ignoring children as rights bearers, seeing them as mere subservient extensions of adults.[26] However, the *Grootboom* judgment left space to explore the possibility that children's socio-economic rights would be directly and immediately enforceable (and not subject to progressive realisation) if they were 'lacking parental care'.[27] The *TAC* case[28] dealt with access to treatment to avoid mother-to-child transmission of HIV/AIDS. The court held that the state is obliged to ensure the protection of children's s 28 rights when the implementation of the right to parental or family care is lacking—and the *TAC* case dealt with children born in public hospitals to indigent mothers. So, while *Grootboom* had ruled that children living with their parents would have to look to their parents rather than the state for the fulfilment of their right to shelter, in the *TAC* case the court found that, although these children were living with their mothers, the latter were not able to provide medical treatment for them, and that it was the state's responsibility to do so.

10.4 PUBLIC INTEREST CHILDREN'S RIGHTS LITIGATION GETS OFF THE GROUND

Since approximately 2007 strategic impact litigation on children's rights picked up pace and increased in impact. The subtle change for this era was that there were

---

[25] Julia Sloth-Nielsen 'Children' in Dennis Davis et al (eds) S*outh African Constitutional Law: The Bill of Rights* (2002) 421; Kirsty McLean 'Housing' in Stuart Woolman et al (eds) *Constitutional Law of South Africa* (2005) 55-52; Murray Wesson '*Grootboom* and beyond: Reassessing the socio-economic jurisprudence of the South African Constitutional Court' (2004) 20 *SAJHR* 284, 304.

[26] Elsje Bonthuys 'The South African Bill of Rights and the development of family law' (2002) 119 *SALJ* 748; Marius Pieterse 'Reconstructing the private/public dichotomy? The enforcement of children's constitutional social rights and care entitlements' (2003) 1 *TSAR* 1.

[27] Sandra Liebenberg 'Taking stock: The jurisprudence on children's socio-economic rights and its implications for government policy' (2004) 5 *ESR Review* 2.

[28] *Minister of Health and Others v Treatment Action Campaign and Others No.2* [2002] ZACC 16; 2002 (5) SA 703 (CC) [LRC acted for the respondents] (*TAC*).

now cases being brought by or on behalf of children, or by children's rights organisations. The law-making phase was now drawing to a close and the courts became a new terrain for children's rights lawyers to do the work of promoting children's rights. The University of Pretoria's Centre for Child Law (CCL) litigation project[29] was launched in 2004, and it had some early successes in the High Courts. Two applications dealing with socio-economic rights of children living separately from their parents were brought. This seemed a safe way to try to advance children's socio-economic rights in the space created by *Grootboom*.

(a) Socio-economic rights

The first case, brought by the CCL and LHR, dealt with unaccompanied foreign children who had travelled alone to South Africa from neighbouring countries.[30] The case determined that, being without parents, they were immediately entitled to social services. The second case dealt with children in the care system who had been placed in a school of industries, a secure residential care centre where they were physically and psychologically neglected and abused.[31] The court made a series of orders to ensure their safety and protection. Although the state argued that it had insufficient funds, the court was adamant that children who are wards of the state have an immediately enforceable right to social services.

Support for the 'immediately enforceable' interpretation of s 28(1)*(c)* came a few years later from the Constitutional Court, in the case of *Juma Musjid*,[32] where the court pointed out that the right to a basic education in s 29(1)*(a)* is immediately realisable because it lacks internal limitations such as being 'progressively realised' within 'available resources' subject to 'reasonable legislative measures'. Although education cases are dealt with elsewhere in the book, this case is included here because the structure of s 29(1)*(a)* is the same as s 28(1)*(c)*, bolstering the view that the rights in s 28(1)*(c)* are immediately realisable.

(b) Best interests of the child principle

In 2007 in *S v M*[33] the Constitutional Court gave its most comprehensive explanation of the all-important 'best interests of the child' principle contained in s 28(2). This was not the first time that the court had discussed 'best interests'. In

---

[29] Annual Report of the Centre for Child Law (2004), available at <http://www.centreforchildlaw.co.za/images/files/annualreports/newsletter_july_2004.pdf>.

[30] *Centre for Child Law and Another v Minister of Home Affairs and Others* 2005 (6) SA 50 (T) [CCL was institutional applicant on behalf of a group of unaccompanied minors and was represented by LHR].

[31] *Centre for Child Law and Others v MEC for Education, Gauteng and Others* 2008 (1) SA 223 (T) [CCL acted for the applicant].

[32] *Governing Body of the Juma Musjid Primary School and Others v Essay NO and Others* [2011] ZACC 13; 2011 (8) BCLR 761 (CC) [CCL and SERI were admitted as *amici curiae*].

[33] *S v M* [2007] ZACC 18; 2008 (3) SA 232 (CC) [CCL was admitted as *amicus curiae*].

Fitzpatrick[34] the court made it clear that s 28(2) does not only refer to the rights enumerated in s 28(1), but also that s 28(2) is a right in itself, and not merely a guiding principle. In addition to being a self-standing right, it strengthens other rights. The court also indicated in *De Reuck* that the emphatic words 'paramount importance' contained in s 28(2), do not serve as a trump to automatically override other rights. As a right in a non-hierarchical system, the right to have best interests considered is itself capable of being limited.[35]

S v M not only built on the court's previous jurisprudence, but also explained the concept of best interests more fully and pronounced on the meaning of the paramountcy principle. The factual matrix from which the case arose was a criminal matter in which a single mother of three children was facing a short term of imprisonment for fraud. She appealed, claiming that when sentencing primary caregivers, the courts should consider the effects of imprisonment on the caregivers' children.

In *Strange Alchemy of Life and Law*,[36] Albie Sachs provides the back-story to the case, which he says, almost did not make it to hearing in the Constitutional Court—the initial impression being that Ms M was an opportunist 'using' her children to lighten her sentence. It was one of the female justices who pointed out that the case did raise important constitutional issues if viewed from the perspective of children's rights. The court decided to hear the case, and Sachs J ended up writing the eloquent judgment for the majority of the court. The judgment developed the law of sentencing to say that from then on, a sentencing court must consider children's best interests when sentencing a primary caregiver, that this should weigh in favour of a non-custodial sentence, and that a court must always be sure about what the effects of a sentence of a primary caregiver will be on the children concerned.

His poetic paragraph from the *S v M* judgment about how children should be 'constitutionally imagined' is often quoted:

> Every child has his or her own dignity. If a child is to be constitutionally imagined as an individual with a distinctive personality, and not merely as a miniature adult waiting to reach full size, he or she cannot be treated as a mere extension of his or her parents, umbilically destined to sink or swim with them. The unusually comprehensive and emancipatory character of section 28 presupposes that in our new dispensation the sins and traumas of fathers and mothers should not be visited on their children.[37]

He acknowledged the 'problem' of the indeterminacy of the best interests right, but he found that it is precisely the contextual nature and inherent flexibility of

---

[34] *Fitzpatrick* (note 16 above).

[35] *De Reuck v Director of Public Prosecutions (Witwatersrand Local Division)* [2003] ZACC 19; 2004 (1) SA 406 (CC) para 55.

[36] Albie Sachs *Strange Alchemy of Life and Law* (2009).

[37] *S v M* (note 33 above) para 18.

s 28(2) that provides its strength. The determination of best interests will require an in-depth consideration of the child's 'precise real-life situation.'[38] He cautioned that to apply a predetermined formula for the sake of certainty would in fact be contrary to the best interests of the child. This contextual approach has been faithfully followed by the Constitutional Court in several other cases in which they have appointed either curators or social workers to ensure that the children's precise circumstances are understood.[39]

The paramountcy principle was described by Sachs J as appearing to promise everything but delivering little in particular, and he went on to explore what he described as 'an operational thrust for the paramountcy principle'. Although *S v M* went further than any previous judgment in explaining paramountcy, it still defined the principle more by stating what it is not rather than what it is.[40]   It is not an 'overbearing and unrealistic trump', and it cannot be interpreted 'to mean that the direct or indirect impact of a measure or action on children must in all cases oust or override all other considerations'. Sachs J concluded that 'the fact that the best interests of the child are paramount does not mean that they are absolute'.[41] Acknowledging these realities is important because if the 'best interests' principle is spread 'too thin', it risks becoming devoid of meaning instead of promoting the rights of children, as it was intended to do.[42]

The *S v M* case has attracted worldwide attention.[43]   In 2011, the United Nations (UN) Committee on the Rights of the Child held a special theme day on 'children of imprisoned parents', at which *S v M* was featured.[44] The issue of children in prison with their mothers and the importance of policies to avoid imprisonment were subsequently included in two UN resolutions[45] and in the UN Rules for the Treatment of Women Prisoners and Non-custodial Measures for

---

[38] *S v M* (note 33 above) para 24.

[39] *AD and Another v DW and Others* [2007] ZACC 27; 2008 (3) SA 183 (CC) [CCL was admitted as *amicus curiae*]; *S v S* [2011] ZACC 7; 2011 (2) SACR 88 (CC) [CCL was admitted as *amicus curiae*]; *Van der Burg and Another v National Director of Public Prosecutions* [2012] ZACC 12; 2012 (2) SACR 331 (CC) [CCL was admitted as *amicus curiae*].

[40] Ann Skelton 'Case note: *S v M (Centre for Child Law as amicus curiae)*' (2008) 1 *CCR* 351–68.

[41] *S v M* (note 33 above) para 26.

[42] Ibid para 42.

[43] Ann Skelton & Lynne Mansfield-Barry 'Developments in South African law regarding the sentencing of primary caregivers' 2015 *European Journal of Parental Imprisonment* 14.

[44] Oliver Robertson *Collateral Convicts: Children of Incarcerated Parents: Recommendation and Good Practice from the UN Committee on the Rights of the Child Day of General Discussion* (2012). According to Oliver Robertson, '[t]his was the first time that any part of the UN system had looked in any detail at the issue of children affected by parental involvement in the criminal justice system, and it attracted unprecedented interest and engagement'.

[45] UNGA United Nations Rules for the Treatment of Women Prisoners and Non-custodial Measures for Women Offenders (the Bangkok Rules) (16 March 2011) UN Doc A/RES/63/241, and a resolution adopted by the Human Rights Council at its nineteenth session 'Rights of the child' (19 April 2012) A/HRC/RES/19/37.

Women Offenders (the Bangkok Rules).[46] On the African continent, the *S v M* case has inspired the first General Comment of the African Committee of Experts on the Rights and Welfare of the Child.[47] Several references are made to the judgment in the general comment, which also expressly draws its 'model' from *S v M* for how to deal with the sentencing of primary caregivers.

In a similar case heard in 2011,[48] the Constitutional Court narrowed the scope of the judgment to single primary caregivers in a case where a mother still living with the children's father was facing imprisonment. The court nevertheless saw fit to appoint a curator *ad litem* to investigate and report on the children's circumstances. The change in approach likely happened as the case was heard shortly after the departure of the four Constitutional Court justices who had all signed on to the majority judgment in *S v M*.[49] It was also brought by an individual and concerned by the risk that it might weaken *S v M*, the CCL decided to enter as *amicus curiae* in order to shore up the gains previously made. The minority judgment by Khampepe J resembles the *S v M* thinking most closely. She was evidently selected to write the judgment, as it is set out first and comprehensively describes the legal frameworks. However, she ended up writing a lengthy sole minority judgment which was overridden by a terse majority judgment written by Cameron J.[50] Nevertheless, the impact of *S v M* remains significant. Back at home, *S v M* has been followed in South African law in a range of criminal matters relating to sentencing and bail decisions,[51] including in a 2015 Supreme Court of Appeal (SCA) case.[52]

The Constitutional Court's analysis of best interests and paramountcy has been applied in a wide array of cases across the public law/private law spectrum. The idea that children's rights must be considered before the state makes a decision that interferes with the enjoyment of the child's right to family care has subse-

---

[46] UNGA Resolution adopted by the General Assembly on 21 December 2010 (16 March 2011) UN Doc A/RES/65/229.

[47] General Comment no 1: (Article 30 of the African Charter on the Rights and Welfare of the Child) on 'Children of Incarcerated and Imprisoned Parents and Primary Caregivers', available at <www.acerwc.org/general-comments>.

[48] *S v S* (note 39 above).

[49] The four justices were Chief Justice Langa and Justices Sachs, Mokgoro and O'Regan.

[50] Another judgment that characterised this phase was *Mpofu v Minister for Justice and Constitutional Development* [2013] ZACC 15; 2013 (2) SACR 407 (CC) [CCL was admitted as *amicus curiae*]. This case dealt with a young offender sentenced to life imprisonment who was claiming that he had been below the age of 18 years at the time of sentencing. The appeal was dismissed, with a lengthy dissent written by Van der Westhuizen J (Kampepe J and Nkabinde J concurring). Nevertheless, the majority of the court still endorsed the principles of child sentencing previously articulated by the court—they just did not give this offender the benefit of the doubt relating to his age at the time of the offence.

[51] Ann Skelton & Morgan Courtenay 'The impact of children's rights on criminal justice: Recent cases' (2012) 25 *South African Journal of Criminal Law* 180–93.

[52] *De Villiers v S* [2015] ZASCA 119; 2016 (1) SACR 148 (SCA) [CCL was admitted as *amicus curiae*].

quently been extended by the court to situations beyond imprisonment of a caregiver. Notably, in *Van der Burg*,[53] the court was faced with an appeal from a High Court order to forfeit the assets arising from the crime of running an illegal shebeen[54] (which also happened to be the family home of the couple and their three children). The CCL entered as *amicus curiae*, with the express purpose of extending the thrust of *S v M* beyond the ambit of sentencing. It argued that the state was making a decision which interfered with the children's rights to family or parental care and to shelter, and that their best interests had to be carefully considered before such a decision is made. Counsel for the National Director of Public Prosecutions (NDPP) argued that this case could be distinguished from *S v M*, because the right to parental care is a discreet right—whereas children's right to shelter was indistinguishable from their parents' right to housing—this much had been said by the court in *Grootboom*. In *Van der Burg* the court disagreed with this argument, finding that, while there may be overlap between the parents and children's interests, children's rights must be viewed separately—thus applying a *S v M* approach rather than the 'stepping stones' approach in *Grootboom*. The court found that the NDPP had a duty to consider the best interests of the child before making a decision. The court declined the *amicus curiae's* request to appoint a curator to investigate the real-life circumstances of the child—claiming that there was sufficient information on the record—but did not rule it out as a useful possibility in future cases. In the end, the forfeiture was upheld, and the court directed that a social worker should be appointed to investigate, and to protect the children's interests.

In 2015, children's right to be heard received a boost in a case that also relied on *S v M*. The matter of *Hoërskool Fochville*[55] concerned 37 black English-speaking learners who the Department of Basic Education placed in a single-medium Afrikaans school. The CCL and the Legal Resources Centre (LRC), in assisting the learners, got them to complete questionnaires, and on making an application to intervene on their behalf, mentioned the questionnaires and summarised them in an affidavit. When ordered by the High Court to hand over the questionnaires to the Governing Body, the CCL refused and took the matter on appeal. The appeal was upheld, and the court made it clear that, in striking the appropriate balance in a case of this nature, adequate weight must be accorded to the interests of the children. The right of children to representation, separate from their parents, flows from their right to participate in all matters that affect them. Section 28(1)(*h*) of the Constitution affords every child a right to legal representation in civil proceedings affecting such child, if a substantial injustice would otherwise result. This right is triggered not only when the child is a party to the proceedings but also whenever

---

[53] *Van der Burg* (note 39 above).

[54] The forfeiture was in terms of the Prevention of Organised Crime Act 121 of 1998.

[55] *Centre for Child Law v The Governing Body of Hoërskool Fochville* [2015] ZASCA 155; 2016 (2) SA 121 (SCA) [CCL was the appellant, represented by LRC].

he or she is affected by litigation. The SCA also referred to s 28(2) and indicated that whenever competing rights and interests must be weighed, considerable weight must be attached to the best interests of children. The SCA concluded that the High Court did not attach sufficient weight to the rights of the children. On a proper balancing of the competing rights and interests, the correct decision should have been in favour of protecting the children.

S v M is the post-constitutional *locus classicus* on the best interests' principle—it has been cited in almost every major children's rights case since 2007. Although the case was about the rights of children whose caregivers were facing imprisonment, subsequent strategic litigation has expanded the ambit of the principles to other areas of law.

(c) Criminal matters

The court considered the situation of child victims and witnesses in *Director of Public Prosecutions, Gauteng*[56] where it stopped short of declaring certain provisions of the Criminal Procedure Act 51 of 1977, unconstitutional. The court found that courts hearing matters involving child witnesses often did not fully protect children's best interests, despite an adequate legal framework. Relying heavily on the UN Guidelines for the Protection of Child Victims and Witnesses, the court set out detailed guidance for the lower courts, and gave a supervisory order aimed at improving the provision of assistance to child witnesses through intermediaries, CCTV cameras and special waiting rooms.

Section 28(1)(*g*) contains specific provisions for the protection of child offenders, notably the injunction that children must not be detained, except as a measure of last resort, and for the shortest appropriate period of time. Parliament passed an amendment that applied minimum sentences to 16 and 17-year olds. In response, the CCL challenged the constitutionality of the minimum sentences law insofar as it applied to 16 and 17-year olds.[57] The Constitutional Court held that the minimum sentencing legislation should not apply to children aged 16 and 17 years old. The court confirmed the order of constitutional invalidity handed down by the High Court[58] declaring sections of the Criminal Law Amendment Act 105 of 1997 (as amended) invalid. The majority of the Constitutional Court found that the minimum sentencing legislation limited the discretion of sentencing officers by

---

[56] *Director of Public Prosecutions, Transvaal v Minister of Justice and Constitutional Development* [2009] ZACC 8; 2009 (2) SACR 130 (CC) [CCL, Child Line South Africa, RAPCAN, Children First, Operation Bobbi Bear, POWA and Cape Mental Health Society were admitted as *amici curiae*; CCL acted for first and second *amici*; the LRC acted for third to seventh *amici* and WLC acted for the sixth *amicus curiae*].

[57] *Centre for Child Law v Minister of Justice and Constitutional Development* [2009] ZACC 18; 2009 (6) SA 632 (CC) [CCL was the applicant; NICRO, was admitted as *amicus curiae* represented by the LRC].

[58] The Minister of Justice originally raised a question about the Centre's standing but abandoned this argument by the time the case reached the Constitutional Court.

directing them to hand down long sentences (including life imprisonment) as a first resort. Furthermore, the legislation discouraged the use of non-custodial options, it prevented courts from individualising sentences, and was likely to cause longer prison sentences. All of these features of the law amounted to an infringement of child offenders' rights in terms of s 28(1)*(g)*, and the court found that no adequate justification had been provided for the limitation. The court found further that children should be treated differently from adults not for sentimental reasons, but because of their greater physical and psychological vulnerability and the fact that they were more open to influence and pressure from others. The court found it to be vitally important that child offenders are generally more capable of rehabilitation than adults. These are the premises on which the Constitution requires the courts and Parliament to differentiate child offenders from adults. The court went on to explain:

> We distinguish them because we recognise that children's crimes may stem from immature judgment, from as yet unformed character, from youthful vulnerability to error, to impulse, and to influence. We recognise that exacting full moral accountability for a misdeed might be too harsh because they are not yet adults. Hence we afford children some leeway of hope and possibility.[59]

The court went on to acknowledge that children can and do commit very serious crimes, and that the legislator has legitimate concerns about violent crimes committed by under 18s. The court pointed out that the Constitution does not prohibit Parliament from dealing effectively with such offenders—the fact that detention must be used only as a last resort in itself implies that imprisonment is sometimes necessary. However, the Bill of Rights mitigates the circumstances in which such imprisonment can happen. It must be a last (not first or intermediate) resort, and it must be for the shortest appropriate period. If there is an appropriate option other than imprisonment, the Bill of Rights requires that it be chosen. In this sense, incarceration must be the sole appropriate option. However, if incarceration is unavoidable, its form and duration must also be tempered, so as to ensure detention for the shortest possible period of time.[60] The order declared s 51(1) and (2) invalid to the extent that it refers to 16 and 17-year olds.[61]

In 2016, the Constitutional Court extended the application of 'detention as a measure of last resort' to the pre-trial detention of children and found that the best interests principle must be applied when considering and effecting their arrest.[62]

---

[59] *Centre for Child Law* (note 57 above) paras 26–8.

[60] Ibid para 31.

[61] To remedy the defect, the court declared that s 51(6) of the Criminal Law Amendment Act, as amended by the Criminal Law (Sentencing) Amendment Act 38 of 2007, is to read as though it provides as follows: 'This section does not apply in respect of an accused person who was under the age of 18 years at the time of the commission of an offence contemplated in subsection (1) or (2).'

[62] *Raduvha v Minister of Safety and Security and Another* [2016] ZACC 24; 2016 (2) SACR 540 (CC) [CCL was admitted as *amicus curiae*].

The court's jurisprudence, when it comes to children facing criminal charges, has not wavered. The narrative has consistently recognised that child offenders are different from adults, and that their culpability is affected by their lack of maturity. The court has displayed a consistent commitment to the idea that child offenders deserve individual attention and that they must be given chances to redeem themselves.

The court has grasped the nettle of difficult cases—from a public perception perspective—pertaining to sexual offences. The Criminal Law (Sexual Offences and Related Matters) Amendment Act 32 of 2007 was in many ways a progressive piece of legislation which expanded the sexual offences definition to make them gender neutral and to cover a range of different offences that had previously evaded prosecution. However, in its zeal to protect children and other vulnerable persons from sexual offences, the legislature over-reached in certain areas—in particular, the effects of the law on child offenders was not well thought through. The Constitutional Court has dealt with two examples of the negative effects of the Act on adolescents.

The first of these is the *Teddy Bear Clinic* case[63] where South Africa's new sexual offences legislation went too far by criminalising all consensual sexual activity, from kissing through to intercourse between adolescents aged 12 to 16 years. This was linked to a mandatory reporting provision, so parents, teachers and counsellors who knew about such activities needed to inform the police. The law exposed adolescents to the risk of prosecution, and if convicted, their names would be placed on the sex offenders register. Two children's rights organisations, Teddy Bear Clinic for Abused Children and Resources Aimed at the Prevention of Child Abuse and Neglect (RAPCAN), legally represented by the CCL, challenged this law on the basis that it unjustifiably infringed the rights of children to dignity, privacy, sexual autonomy and to have their best interests considered paramount. The Constitutional Court handed down a judgment in October 2013, declaring the law unconstitutional and therefore effectively decriminalising consensual sex between adolescents. The court found that the impugned provisions infringed adolescents' rights of dignity and privacy and further violated the best interests principle. The court relied on expert evidence adduced by the applicants and concluded that the impugned provisions criminalised developmentally normative conduct for adolescents and negatively affected the very children the law sought to protect. Thus, the law was not rationally connected to its purpose. Khampepe J, who wrote the judgment, said that it was important to stress what the case was *not* about: It was not about whether children should engage in sexual conduct, nor was it about setting a lower age of consent. The case was about the narrow issue of

---

[63] *Teddy Bear Clinic for Abused Children and Another v Minister of Justice and Constitutional Development and Another* [2013] ZACC 35; 2014 (2) SA 168 (CC) [CCL acted for the applicants; JASA, Women's Legal Trust Centre and Tshwaranang Legal Advocacy Centre were admitted as *amici curiae*].

whether it was constitutionally permissible to use criminal law in order to deter children from early sexual intimacy and combat the associated risks.

Khampepe J underlined the dignity of children, describing the law as having placed youthful transgressors in a state of disgrace. She clearly recognised that sexual intimacy and sexual choices are part of the innermost sanctity of a person's dignity, and she included children's intimacy within that constitutionally protected ambit. She also clearly stated that by prohibiting consensual intimate relationships, the impugned provisions intruded into the core of adolescents' privacy. Furthermore, in discussing children's best interests she found that the impugned provisions ran contrary to the best interests principle because they harmed children. An interesting feature about this case is the fact that it also attracted 'counter-mobilisation' by a conservative Christian organisation called the Justice Alliance of South Africa (JASA). Professor NeJaime described this as an external effect of strategic litigation, which those seeking social change through litigation have little control over.[64] This trend towards counter-mobilisation has been observed by South African writers Budlender et al who have noted a recent 'backlash' or resistance to the social change sought to be achieved by progressive public interest litigation in South Africa, and the rise of more conservative role players in the field—JASA's involvement in the *Teddy Bear Clinic* case is one such example.[65]

A second case that highlights the over-reach of the Sexual Offences Act is the *J* case.[66] The Act established a National Register for Sex Offenders (NRSO), which primarily aims to prevent persons who have been convicted of sexual offences against children from working with children. Once a person is convicted of any sexual offence, his or her name *must* be placed on the register. The presiding officer has no discretion in this regard. As the section applied to all offenders, the constitutionality of its application to child offenders was challenged. Teddy Bear Clinic, Childline and NICRO, represented by the CCL, made joint *amici curiae* submissions which were influential in the outcome of the case. The Constitutional Court found that the best interests of the child principle, was the correct point of departure in evaluating the matter. The court found that '[t]he contemporary foundations of children's rights and the best-interests principle encapsulate the idea that the child is a developing human being, capable of change and in need of appropriate nurturing to enable her to determine herself to the fullest extent and

---

[64] Douglas NeJaime 'Winning through losing' (2001) 96 *Iowa L Rev* 941.

[65] Steven Budlender, Gilbert Marcus & Nick Ferreira 'Public interest litigation and social change in South Africa: Strategies, tactics and lessons' (2014) *Atlantic Philanthropies*, last accessed on 17 March 2018 from <https://www.atlanticphilanthropies.org/app/uploads/2015/12/Public-interest-litigation-and-social-change-in-South-Africa.pdf >.

[66] *J v National Director of Public Prosecutions and Another* [2014] ZACC 13; 2014 (2) SACR 1 (CC) [Child Line South Africa, Teddy Bear Clinic for Abused Children and NICRO were admitted as *amici curiae*].

develop her moral compass'.[67] The court found that the law should generally distinguish between adults and children, in that the law should allow for an individuated approach to child offenders and that children should be given an opportunity to make submissions before a decision to place them on the register is made—in keeping with the principle of children's participation. The court found further that there were less restrictive means to achieve the aims of the register, such as allowing a discretion. The court declared the impugned provisions to be unconstitutional and suspended the order of invalidity, allowing Parliament a period of 15 months to bring the legislation in line with the Constitution. In this regard, the Sexual Offences Amendment Bill 5 of 2015 introduced significant amendments to the Sexual Offences Act, in line with the *Teddy Bear Clinic* and *J* cases.

10.5 STRATEGIC DECISIONS

The strategic decision-making behind some of the cases is often absent from a thematic discussion of jurisprudence. This chapter aims to remedy that by telling some of the behind-the-scenes stories about strategising and decision-making. An interesting example relates to the CCL case on minimum sentences. In deciding the legal strategy of the case, the CCL's legal team had to decide whether or not to base its case on neuroscientific evidence. Such evidence, which showed that adolescent brains continue to develop well past the age of 18 years, had been very effectively used by American litigators in *Roper*,[68] which struck down the death penalty for juvenile offenders. The CCL's legal team considered that, on the one hand, neuroscience could strengthen the case by reinforcing the claims that would be made about the rationale for a different sentencing approach for offenders below the age of 18 years. On the other hand, the litigators foresaw that a win based on such evidence would affect other areas of the law for children, and in particular another case that the CCL was in the early stages of developing, namely the *Teddy Bear Clinic* case mentioned above,[69] dealing with consensual sexual decision-making among adolescents. The team already knew that an important argument in that case would be based on children's autonomy. The concern was that if the minimum sentences case was won on the basis of neuroscientific evidence that showed diminished decision-making capacity, it would be more difficult to argue in the *Teddy Bear Clinic* case that children's decisions about whether to engage in sexual conduct should be respected as belonging to a private sphere of their lives.

The legal team's final strategy was that the case could be won without reliance on neuroscience, due to the fact that South African courts had always shown an

---

[67] *J v NDPP* (note 86 above) para 36.

[68] *Roper v Simmons* 540 US 1160 (2004).

[69] *Teddy Bear Clinic* (note 63 above).

instinctive understanding of the fact that child offenders were less culpable. Furthermore, the constitutional injunction that child offenders must be detained only as a measure of last resort and for the shortest appropriate period of time already provided strong protection. By avoiding reliance on the neuroscientific evidence, the flexibility of the 'evolving capacity' of children approach would be conserved, allowing arguments to be made about adolescent decision-making in the context of consensual sexual activity on another day.[70] However, the *Roper* judgment was referred to in the Heads of Argument, as it was a highly significant precedent on the world stage, and the majority judgment had much to offer in terms of its reasoning about why children were less culpable than adults. The plan to avoid reliance on neuroscience was nearly scuppered when NICRO decided to enter as *amicus*, and indicated in their letter requesting permission, that they intended to file papers containing precisely such evidence. The applicants' legal team engaged NICRO, represented by the LRC, and amicable discussions resulted in their submissions focusing on the value of rehabilitation instead.

Sometimes strategic decisions result in a case not coming to court at all. That is what happened in relation to a planned case on corporal punishment in the home. South Africa had done away with corporal punishment as a sentence in *Williams*[71] and in schools via the South African Schools Act in 1996, which, in *Christian Education*,[72] was found to be applicable to private schools too. Following these cases, leading players in the children's right movement lobbied around abolishing corporal punishment in the home. When efforts to have this included in the Children's Act 38 of 2005 failed, the advocates for abolition of corporal punishment[73] turned to the idea of using strategic litigation.[74] The strategy was to challenge the common-law defence of 'reasonable chastisement'. The plans were quite advanced—a legal opinion had been drafted, an expert opinion had been commissioned, and an individual as well as institutional client had been found. At the crucial moment, however, there was a major change at the Constitutional Court, with four experienced justices leaving the court at the same time.[75] At least three of these were known to be 'child rights sympathetic' judges. Their sudden absence, and the uncertainty about who would replace them, caused the legal team to pull back from filing the application. Although on paper the argument appeared to be strongly in favour of abolishing the defence of reasonable chastisement,

---

[70] For a full discussion of the reasons why the CCL team decided not to rely on neuroscience—and for proof that the decision was a correct one—see Ann Skelton 'Balancing autonomy and protection in children's rights: A South African account' (2016) 88 *Temp L Rev* 887.

[71] *Williams* (note 18 above).

[72] *Christian Education* (note 21 above).

[73] This was led by a coalition entitled 'the Positive Discipline Working Group'.

[74] The Positive Discipline Working Group approached the CCL to take a case to challenge the constitutionality of corporal punishment in the home.

[75] Justices Langa, Sachs, Mokgoro and O'Regan.

there was always a sense that the case could go the wrong way.[76] Given the fact that so many other African countries would be looking to South Africa to provide a lead on this issue, a loss was not to be contemplated. Consequently, the application was never filed.

Subsequently, in 2017, an appeal arising from a criminal conviction of a father for assaulting his son came before the South Gauteng High Court.[77] The court *mero motu* questioned the constitutionality of the defence of reasonable chastisement and invited *amici curiae* to make submissions. The CCL represented one set of *amici curiae* namely, Children's Institute, Quaker Peace Foundation and Sonke Gender Justice, who argued that the common law should be developed by abolishing the defence. Freedom of Religion South Africa (FORSA) weighed in on the other side, arguing that doing away with the defence would cause some parents to go against their religious teachings and would expose them to criminal punishment. The Minister of Social Development filed submissions stating her view that the defence was incompatible with the Constitution and pointed out that the Children's Act contains several non-punitive measures for ensuring positive parenting. The court declared the common-law defence of reasonable chastisement to be unconstitutional and no longer applicable in our law. At the time of writing, although no party is planning to appeal, FORSA has filed an application for leave to appeal—and the CCL's clients are planning to oppose that application.[78]

10.6 CHILDREN'S RIGHTS IN THE STRANGEST OF PLACES

One of the frustrating aspects of specialising in child law is that people, including other lawyers, tend to see it as a subset of family law. This is not the case, as child law straddles private law and public law, and includes all facets of constitutional law, procedural law, as well as aspects of international law. Child rights lawyers have even found themselves arguing cases in company law. An interesting example was an attempt by the CCL to enter as *amicus curiae* in a dispute about a planned coalmine at a heritage site called Mapungubwe. The Centre's objective was to argue that environmental rights of children were special, as the Constitution provides protection of the environment for future generations. In addition, arguments on children's right to know their heritage were planned. The respondents, Coal of Africa, fought to keep the Centre out of the fray by objecting to the *amicus* application, but in the end the main matter settled and so the arguments were never run.

---

[76] For a full discussion of the arguments for and against a hypothetical challenge, see Skelton (note 20 above) 336.

[77] *YG v S* [2017] ZAGPJHC 290; 2018 (1) SACR 64 (GJ).

[78] Although it is unusual for non-parties to appeal, it has been permitted previously in *Campus Law Clinic (University of KwaZulu Natal Durban) v Standard Bank of South Africa Ltd and Another* [2006] ZACC 5; 2006 (6) SA 103 (CC) and *Sidumo and Another v Rustenburg Platinum Mines Ltd and Others* [2007] ZACC 22; 2008 (2) SA 24 (CC).

Three cases that did reach the courts concerned disputed tender procedures. The aim of the CCL, represented by the LRC, in all three of these cases was to establish that when goods and services are intended for child beneficiaries, then the general procurement remedies such as setting aside the tender and re-starting it from the beginning or from a certain stage of the process can be altered so as to allow for the delivery of goods or services, to protect the child beneficiaries' interests. This was argued in a case about school stationery, and in another about school furniture—but the outcomes were disappointing, as in both cases the tenders were set aside. However, in the case of *All Pay Consolidated*,[79] in which the entire system of social grant payments was at risk of being set aside, the argument met with some success. The court observed that:

> [T]he Centre for Child Law made submissions in relation to the appropriate remedy in order to protect the rights of child grant beneficiaries. Part of the submissions dealt with the constitutional obligation that Cash Paymaster may have to continue with the current system even if the tender award is set aside, until a new system is in place. These considerations raise difficult factual and legal issues. The information currently before us is outdated and inadequate.[80]

As a result, the court asked for more information to be placed before it, and the final order clearly reflected an attempt to ensure that there would be no interruption of grant payments.

10.7 SETTLEMENTS TO 'SAVE' SYSTEMS

The CCL has brought cases to shore up failing systems, and because the departments concerned could see the extent of the problem, the cases settled with an order by agreement. The first of these related to a clause in the Children's Act that required every prospective temporary safe carer, foster carer or adoptive parent to be checked against the new NRSO. However, when the relevant section came into operation, the NRSO was not yet up and running, rendering the requirement impossible to fulfil. This led to a logjam of cases regarding children needing alternative care. Child Welfare South Africa was the applicant in the case, giving examples of many children whose cases were 'stuck'. Their application resulted in an order by agreement with the Minister of Justice, which suspended the operation of the section until such time that the NRSO was functioning. The order included a requirement to publish the order itself in the *Government Gazette*, (which was done),[81] and also to publish a notice in the *Government Gazette* putting the section back into operation, which has never happened.

---

[79] *All Pay Consolidated Investment Holdings (Pty) Ltd and Others v Chief Executive Officer of the South African Social Security Agency and Others* [2014] ZACC 12; 2014 (4) SA 179 (CC) [Corruption Watch and CCL were admitted as *amici curiae*, the latter represented by the LRC].

[80] Ibid para 96.

[81] GN 1670 *GG* 32850 of 29 December 2009.

A second application of a similar nature was a case about the foster care system. A foster care crisis developed in South Africa as a growing number of orphans living in the care of extended family members who sought foster care orders which gave them access to a foster child grant which was considerably more in value than the child support grant. Eventually the system, which required social work investigations, reports and court orders, collapsed. Over the period April 2009 to March 2011, approximately 120 000 foster child grants (FCGs) lapsed because the court orders were not renewed. The reason was that the Children's Court orders, which were required for their continued payment, had not been extended in time. The Social Assistance Act 13 of 2004 authorises the South African Social Assistance Agency (SASSA) to pay FCGs only in the case of a valid court order. In terms of the Children's Act, most foster care orders need to be extended by the court on a two-yearly basis to remain valid. Due to the shortage of social workers and the high demand for FCGs, many foster care court orders had expired and had not been renewed in time. More were likely to lapse if a solution was not found. In May 2011, the CCL and Minister of Social Development reached a court ordered settlement to prevent further lapsing of FCGs due to expired court orders. The May 2011 settlement order placed a temporary moratorium on lapsing, ordered the Department to reinstate the FCGs that had already lapsed, and granted the Department temporary authority to extend the majority of foster care court orders administratively rather than by a court order. This temporary authority was in direct conflict with the requirements of the Children's Act, therefore there was a time limit set by which the temporary authority would end: 31 December 2014. By this date, the Department was required to have designed a comprehensive legal solution to the foster care crisis by amending the Children's Act.[82] However, by early December 2014 the Department had not designed a comprehensive legal solution and they were still facing a significant backlog of expired foster care court orders—estimated at 300 000 at that time. They applied to court on 12 December 2014 on an urgent basis asking for the May 2011 court order to be varied and extended for a further three years—this time the order required them to report to the court and to the CCL every six months.

The in-house legal team at the CCL handled these two cases. The remedies were fashioned out of pragmatic necessity. Only later, after discussing the court orders with counsel, did it become apparent that the orders were very far-reaching in terms of separation of powers, and that it may not have been correct for the courts to suspend the operation of laws without a finding that the law or its operation was in conflict with the Constitution. The reason that they were granted was probably due to the fact that they were by agreement with the state departments concerned. This shortcoming was subsequently corrected when the CCL obtained an order by agreement with the Minister of Social Development in November 2017, declaring

---

[82] *Centre for Child Law v Minister of Social Development and Others* (North Gauteng High Court) unreported case 21726/11 of 10 May 2011.

that her conduct in failing to put in place a comprehensive legal solution was unconstitutional. The court order directed the Minister to initiate and table a Bill that will bring about a comprehensive legal solution to the foster care crisis, to be concluded within a period of two years.

10.8 NETWORKING AMONG CHILDREN'S RIGHTS ORGANISATIONS

The children's rights sector has been empowered by the use of litigation, and there has been a substantial degree of cooperation in developing coherent litigation strategies and in doing the necessary follow-up work after the fact, too. This was less noticeable in the early years but has been stronger since 2012. In particular, the two cases about the Sexual Offences Act were marked by a high degree of cooperation and participation by child rights non-governmental organisations (NGOs) across the spectrum. Those who work with child victims found considerable synergy with those who work with child offenders. There were workshops to discuss the strategy of the cases and there were post-judgment briefings to discuss the decision and next steps. Notably, the coalition drafted submissions to the Department of Justice and later, Parliament, on what should go into the Sexual Offences Amendment Bill. These efforts paid off, and the Amendment Act achieved all of what the cases set out to do, and in some respects, went further. There was considerable public debate about the cases and the changes to the law, so the NGOs played an important role in explaining the cases to the media. Generally, the children's rights sector has warmed to the idea of litigation to solve its problems, but due to the dependent relationship that many of them have with the Department of Social Development, litigation against that department is definitely a last resort. The foster care crisis is another area where cooperation between a range of organisations has seen a significant push towards policy changes, using a combination of litigation and advocacy.

10.9 USE OF INTERNATIONAL AND REGIONAL INSTRUMENTS

A full discussion of the use of international and regional instruments is beyond the scope of this chapter.[83] Suffice it to say, the courts (often prompted by strategic litigators) have drawn substantially on international and regional law. Sloth-Nielsen and Kruuse argue that, although South Africa has a dualist tradition, the courts have incorporated the CRC to the point where South Africa has 'crossed the

---

[83] See further, Ann Skelton 'The development of a fledgling child rights jurisprudence in Eastern and Southern Africa based on international and regional instruments' (2009) 9 *AHRLJ* 482; Karabo Ngidi 'The role of international law in the development of children's rights in South Africa: A children's rights litigator's perspective' in Magnus Killander (ed) *International Law and Domestic Human Rights Litigation in Africa* (2010); Ann Skelton 'South Africa' in Ton Liefaard & Jaap E Doek (eds) *Litigating the Rights of the Child: The UN Convention on the Rights of the Child in Domestic and International Jurisprudence* (2015).

line from dualism to monism'.[84] The Constitutional Court also favoured the African Charter on the Rights and Welfare of the Child (ACRWC), sometimes preferring its clauses over those of the CRC. In *S v M*,[85] the court relied on art 30 of the ACRWC which deals with imprisonment of caregivers, which does not have a counterpart in the CRC. Soft law has also been referred to in numerous judgments, especially in relation to criminal justice matters, where the UN Rules for the Administration of Juvenile Justice[86] and the UN Guidelines on Justice for Child Victims and Witnesses have been highlighted.[87]

10.10 WHAT IS NEXT ON THE MENU?

Children's socio-economic rights have not yet been fully expounded by the Constitutional Court. Section 28(1)*(c)* guarantees children the right to 'basic nutrition, shelter, basic health care services and social services'. Notably, the clause does not contain any internal qualifiers. In light of the court's interpretation of the s 29(1)*(a)* right to basic education as immediately realisable, it is likely that they will also interpret s 28(1)*(c)* in the same way. So, there is scope for litigation in relation to these socio-economic rights—which may come in the form of testing what is included in the term 'basic health care services' for example, or in the prioritisation of children's social services through improved funding.

Registration of births is another area that is likely to see increasing number of cases being brought before the courts. This is a gateway right that links to many other services and provisions, such as the payment of social grants, health care and education. Although South Africa has done well in rapidly increasing the number of births being registered, the Births and Deaths Registration Act 51 of 1992 is outdated, and recent amendments to it and to its regulations are at odds with the Children's Act.

Another area that is increasingly attracting the efforts of litigators is that of unaccompanied, separated or accompanied migrant children, be they asylum seekers, refugees or undocumented migrants. Problems with birth registration, statelessness, care and protection, adoption and procedures for repatriation continue to arise and are increasingly being brought to court. The possible introduction of stricter immigration and refugee laws make it likely that further litigation will ensue.

10.11 CONCLUSION

Children's rights litigation has developed in South Africa from tentative appetisers and entrees during the first decade of democracy, to some substantial main courses

---

[84] Sloth-Nielsen & Kruuse (note 12 above) 646.

[85] *S v M* (note 33 above).

[86] These rules, adopted by the UN in 1986, are also known as the Beijing Rules. The Constitutional Court referred to them in *Centre for Child Law v Minister of Justice and Constitutional Development and Others* (note 57 above).

[87] *Director of Public Prosecutions* (note 56 above).

during the second. The first decade of cases on children's rights were mostly about parents' rights, with the court stepping in to raise the child rights issues and asking to hear more from child litigators. Children's rights organisations started actively litigating from about 2007, and one of the first of this phase of cases was *S v M* which has the status of a modern *locus classicus* on the best interests principle and has had an international impact. The field of criminal law has seen some robust litigation regarding child offenders and child victims, including important work on sexual offences. The judgments in these cases are widely recognised as being profound.[88] Socio-economic rights cases concerning children got off to an uncertain start with *Grootboom* but improved with the *TAC* case and some High Court matters that at least established the rights of children living separately from their parents. This area of the law holds promise for future litigation to clarify the meaning and content of s 28(1)*(c)*. Other predictions of likely future litigation include birth registrations and migrant children's issues.

The chapter has revealed a high level of strategic intention behind the cases that were brought to court—and those that were not. International and regional law has been well utilised. Furthermore, activity in the courts, supported by the co-operative work of the children's rights sector in planning, executing and following up on litigation, has ensured that the cases have optimal impact.

---

[88] See the website case database of Children's Rights International Network (CRIN), where these cases are described as good examples of strategic litigation, last accessed on 6 December 2017 from <https://www.crin.org/en/home/law/strategic-litigation>.

Chapter 11

LITIGATING THE RIGHT TO BASIC EDUCATION

Cameron McConnachie and Samantha Brener[1]

---

[1] With thanks to Elizabeth Lathlean and Katie Joh for initial research and comments.

11.1 INTRODUCTION

(a) Context

Between 1948 and 1990, as an important part of its policy of apartheid, the Nationalist government put in place the Bantu Education Act of 1953 which, together with other legislation, created a system of completely segregated education.[2] Schools for white learners enjoyed substantial financial support from the state, while schools for their black counterparts received only a fraction of this. For most of South Africa's children, this resulted in a lack of access to schooling and shockingly inferior conditions for those black learners with access. Writing during the height of apartheid, photojournalist Ernest Cole described the conditions of schooling for black children as follows:

> Some of the school buildings are new but all are bursting at the seam . . . Some, for which there just is no room, do their lessons outdoors, following the shade around the school as the hot sun advances through the sky. There is a perpetual shortage of furniture. . . . In the winter, the scholars at empty schools bring strips of cardboard to sit on to ward off the chill of the concrete-slab floor.[3]

Many important gains have been made in the first 20 years of democracy, but tragically South Africa's current education system still exhibits a legacy of persistent devastating inequality and terrible conditions. This is the context in which public interest litigation (PIL) on education must take place and is crucial for understanding the systemic problems faced in this sector.

Provinces which, under the Nationalist government were 'homelands,'[4] bear the brunt of this inequality. Limpopo, (including former homelands such as Venda, Gazankulu and Lebowa), and the Eastern Cape, (including the former homelands of Transkei and Ciskei) face extreme poverty[5] and bureaucracies that are failing to meet the requirements of effective governance.[6] As a consequence, these two

---

[2] See J Brickhill & Y van Leeve 'From the classroom to the courtroom—Litigating education rights in South Africa' in S Fredman, M Campbell & H Taylor (eds) *Human Rights and Equality in Education* (2018) 148.

[3] Ernest Cole *House of Bondage* (1967) 94.

[4] Homelands were the areas established by the apartheid government, where the non-white population were forcibly moved in order to separate them from white South Africans.

[5] The poorest provinces in South Africa between 2006 and 2015 have consistently been Limpopo, the Eastern Cape and KZN. In 2015, 72,9% of the Eastern Cape population and 72,4% of the Limpopo population did not have the ability to purchase adequate levels of food and non-food items. This implies that food must be sacrificed in order to purchase essential non-food items. See Stats SA's *Poverty Trends in South Africa: An Examination of Absolute Poverty between 2006 and 2015* (2017) 7 and 65.

[6] In terms of sch 4 of the Constitution, education is a concurrent competence of both the national and provincial levels of government. In practice, the national government is responsible for standard-setting and oversight, and the province does the bulk of decision-making and implementation. Effectively, education policy implementation 'happens' in the provinces, unless the national government intervenes in terms of s 100 of the Constitution.

provinces have become the focal points for education strategic litigation campaigns—they are the provinces most in need of assistance.

By March 2011, approximately 17 years since South Africa entered a democratic goverment, 1 096 schools in the Eastern Cape had no water supply and 322 had an unreliable water supply; 3 160 schools were using pit latrines instead of toilets, 551 had no ablution facilities at all, and 1 152 had no electricity supply. At the same time, Limpopo had 260 schools with no water supply, 634 with an unreliable water supply, 2 857 schools were using pit latrines, 36 had no ablution facilities, and 226 had no electricity supply.[7] This disastrous state of affairs prompted much of the litigation that is discussed in this chapter.[8]

Due to maladministration, mismanagement, and very little progress in addressing the above-mentioned conditions, the provincial education departments of Limpopo and the Eastern Cape were placed under national administration in 2011, in terms of s 100 of the Constitution.[9] However, the nature, extent and impact of these interventions have been unclear. Litigation sought to clarify the powers and competencies of officials in national and provincial departments,[10] but this failed to improve the efficacy of the interventions. Push-back from provinces wanting to maintain financial authority has led to power-plays and the rapid turnover of heads of department. To mitigate the resulting confusion, litigation campaigns have been waged against both the provincial and national education departments.[11]

Other important role players in strategic litigation campaigns have included the Minister of Basic Education, the Members of the Executive Councils for education in the provinces (effectively provincial ministers), and school governing bodies (SGBs)—the representative bodies for individual schools. Learners themselves

---

[7] Department of Basic Education 'National Education Infrastructure Management Systems (NEIMS) Report' 2011, last accessed on 30 May 2018 from <http://www.thutong.doe.gov.za/administration/ Administration/GeneralInformation/Statistics/tabid/3338/Default.aspx>.

[8] It should be noted that by January 2018 (and according to the state's own statistics) in the Eastern Cape, no schools were entirely without water supply, statistics on unreliable water supply were not provided, 1945 schools were using pit latrines instead of toilets, 37 schools had no ablution facilities at all, and 154 schools had no electricity supply. In Limpopo, no schools were entirely without water supply, statistics on unreliable water supply were not provided, 2 524 schools were using pit latrines instead of toilets, and no schools were without ablution facilities or electricity supply. See 'National Education Infrastructure Management Standard Reports' *Department of Basic Education* January 2018, last accessed on 30 May 2018 from <https://www.education.gov.za/Portals/0/Documents/ Reports/NEIMS%20Report%20%2020172018.pdf?ver=2018-01-30-120305-787>.

[9] F Veriava *The 2012 Limpopo Textbook Crisis* (2013) 6.

[10] See *Save our Schools and Community and Another v President of the Republic of South Africa and Others* unreported case no 50/12 [LRC acted for the applicants]. The matter was settled on 20 March 2012.

[11] In *Head of Department of Education and Another v South African Democratic Teachers Union and Others* unreported case nos 3760/2016 and 3791/2016 of 8 September 2016, Lowe J held that the national administration of the ECDOE had lapsed after three years from its institution in May 2011 (paras 45–52).

and local communities have also played an important role as litigants.[12] The media has been crucial for campaign-building (discussed in part 11.3 below). Teacher unions, and in particular the South African Democratic Teachers' Union (SADTU), have also been an important force. SADTU plays a powerful role in the broader political landscape of South Africa and impacts directly on issues (and therefore cases) related to the employment of teachers at public schools.

As a final introductory point, there has been extensive interest in the right to education from civil society in South Africa. SECTION27, Equal Education (EE) and the Equal Education Law Centre (EELC), the Centre for Child Law (CCL) and the Legal Resources Centre (LRC) have all launched major campaigns to enforce the right to basic education.

(b) The education right

Education is seen as an 'empowerment right'—if fulfilled, it can lay the groundwork for the enjoyment of other crucial rights in our Constitution.[13] In recognition of this, the right to education in the South African Constitution bears some unique features. The right captured in s 29 of the Constitution provides that (emphasis added):

(1) Everyone has the right—

(a) to a basic education, including adult basic education; and

(b) to further education, which the state, through reasonable measures, must make progressively available and accessible.

(2) Everyone has the right to receive education in the official language or languages of their choice in public educational institutions where that education is reasonably practicable. In order to ensure the effective access to, and implementation of, this right, the state must consider all reasonable educational alternatives, including single medium institutions, taking into account—

(a) equity;

(b) practicability; and

(c) the need to redress the results of past racially discriminatory laws and practices.

(3) Everyone has the right to establish and maintain, at their own expense, independent educational institutions that—

(a) do not discriminate on the basis of race;

(b) are registered with the state; and

(c) maintain standards that are not inferior to standards at comparable public educational institutions.

---

[12] Veriava (note 9 above) 30–1.

[13] Article 13 of the International Covenant on Economic, Social and Cultural Rights, 993 UNTS 3, adopted 16 December 1966, entered into force 23 March 1976, provides that 'education shall be directed to the full development of the human personality and the sense of its dignity, and shall strengthen the respect for human rights and fundamental freedoms' and 'education shall enable all persons to participate effectively in a free society, promote understanding, tolerance and friendship among all nations and all racial, ethnic or religious groups . . .'. Although South Africa signed the Covenant in 1994, it only ratified it in 2015.

(4) Subsection (3) does not preclude state subsidies for independent educational institutions.

Section 29(1) of the Constitution deals separately with basic education and further education.[14] Litigation relating to s 29 of the Constitution has thus far focused almost exclusively on the right to basic education in s 29(1)*(a)*. The remainder of this chapter will therefore deal with basic education, understood to include primary and secondary schooling.

A crucial characteristic of the right to basic education is that it is, at least in theory, 'immediately realisable'.[15] This is in contrast to a number of other socio-economic rights in the Bill of Rights, such as the rights to housing,[16] food, water, health care (other than emergency health care) and social assistance,[17] in respect of which the state has the obligation to take reasonable steps to progressively realise the right within its available resources. These qualifications—reasonable steps, progressive realisation, and within available resources—do not apply when courts interpret the right to basic education. This means that the jurisprudence on this right is unique.

11.2 DEVELOPING THE CONTENT OF THE RIGHT TO BASIC EDUCATION

Litigation around the right to basic education can be understood as having developed in streams.

(a) A slow start

The Constitutional Court in the 1995 case of *In re: Gauteng School Education Bill* took the first step in defining the right to education in South Africa.[18] The court held that the right to basic education 'creates a positive right that basic education be provided for every person and not merely a negative right that such a person should not be obstructed in pursuing his or her basic education'.[19] While this decision confirmed an obligation on the state to take positive steps, the courts were not presented with opportunities to further define the right in relation to resources

---

[14] While there is some debate about the meaning of 'basic' education (see Cameron McConnachie & Chris McConnachie 'Concretising the right to a basic education' (2012) 129 *SALJ* 554 at 565–8), practically, the right to a basic education is accepted to include both primary education and secondary education, that is, schooling from the start of formal education in Grade R, to the completion of Grade 12.

[15] *Governing Body of the Juma Musjid Primary School and Others v Essay NO and Others* [2011] ZACC 13; 2011 (8) BCLR 761 (CC) para 37 [LRC acted for the applicants and CCL and SERI were admitted as *amicus curiae*].

[16] Section 26.

[17] Section 27.

[18] *Gauteng Provincial Legislature In re: Gauteng School Education Bill of 1995* [1996] ZACC 4; 1996 (3) SA 165 (CC).

[19] Ibid para 9.

for some time. It was not until 15 years later in *Juma Musjid* that some conceptual clarity was provided regarding the nature of the right.[20] The case concerned an appeal against an eviction order obtained by a private landowner, the Juma Musjid Trust, for the removal of a public school from its property. Crucially, the Constitutional Court confirmed that the right to basic education is *immediately realisable*:

> Unlike some of the other socio-economic rights, this right is immediately realisable. There is no internal limitation requiring that the right be 'progressively realised' within 'available resources' subject to 'reasonable legislative measures'. The right to basic education in section 29(1)(a) may be limited only in terms of a law of general application which is 'reasonable and justifiable in an open and democratic society based on human dignity, equality and freedom'.[21]

Section 29(1)(a) does not require merely 'reasonable measures' to provide a basic education; it creates the right to an *actual* basic education. *Juma Musjid* and *In re: Gauteng School Education Bill,* combined, established the unique nature of the right to basic education among South Africa's socio-economic rights—that it is immediately realisable and that at least the negative obligations arising from the right apply horizontally as against private persons.

(b) Struggles for power

Three cases were heard in the Constitutional Court between 2009 and 2013 which considered the powers of SGBs. The cases considered the extent to which heads of provincial education departments may intervene in respect of, or override, policies of SGBs in the areas of language, pregnancy, and admissions.[22]

Hoërskool Ermelo[23] dealt with a school whose language policy stipulated that Afrikaans was the only medium of instruction. The effect of the policy was that black learners from the nearby township were excluded from attending the school. The provincial head of department (HOD) purported to revoke the power of the SGB to set language policy and instead appointed a committee to decide the policy. The Constitutional Court ruled that the HOD had acted unlawfully. However, the power of the school to determine its language policy had to be exercised in accordance with the Constitution—the court consequently ordered the school to review its policy.[24]

---

[20] *Juma Musjid* (note 15 above).

[21] Ibid para 37 (footnotes omitted). The latter part of the quotation refers to s 36 of the Constitution, the limitations clause.

[22] See Brickhill & Van Leeve (note 2 above) and Y van Leeve 'Executive heavy handedness and the right to basic education: A reply to Sandra Fredman' (2016) 6 *CCR* 199.

[23] *Head of Department, Mpumalanga Department of Education and Another v Hoërskool Ermelo and Another* [2009] ZACC 32; 2010 (2) SA 415 (CC).

[24] See discussion in Brickhill & Van Leeve (note 2 above) 12.

In *Welkom High School,*[25] school pregnancy policies provided that women who fell pregnant would automatically be excluded. The provincial HOD intervened, instructing the schools to ignore the policies and readmit the learners. The SGBs looked to the court, seeking an order preventing the intervention. Again, the conduct of the HOD was found to be invalid and the schools were ordered to review their pregnancy policies in line with the Constitution.[26]

In *Rivonia Primary School,*[27] a primary school refused to admit a child on the basis that the school had reached its capacity. The provincial HOD considered the school to have sufficient capacity and overturned its decision to refuse the learner's admission. The principal's admissions function was withdrawn, and the child was physically placed at the school. The Constitutional Court affirmed the role of the provincial department to overturn a principal's admission decision, but set aside the conduct of the HOD for it being procedurally unfair when revoking the principal's functions.[28]

The tension between these authorities raised its head again in *Federation of Governing Bodies*[29] where FEDSAS, the representative body for SGBs, unsuccessfully challenged the validity of regulations that limited the ability of SGBs to participate in determining school feeder zones,[30] and allowed a department official to place learners in a school despite the contents of the SGB's school admissions policy.[31]

These cases are important for understanding the power dynamics amongst stakeholders in school governance. They consider the various ways in which SGBs may attempt to control access to public schools, and the extent to which provincial education departments may intervene in the face of such conduct.[32]

---

[25] *Head of Department, Department of Education, Free State Province v Welkom High School and Others* [2013] ZACC 25; 2014 (2) SA 228 (CC) [EE and CCL were admitted as *amicus curiae*].

[26] See discussion in Brickhill & Van Leeve (note 2 above) 5.

[27] *MEC for Education, Gauteng Province, and Others v Governing Body, Rivonia Primary School and Others* [2013] ZACC 34; 2013 (6) SA 582 (CC) [EE and CCL were admitted as *amicus curiae*, represented by LRC].

[28] See discussion in Brickhill & Van Leeve (note 2 above) 14. The question of school admissions has raised its head subsequently in the case of *Governing Body Hoërskool Overvaal & Another v Head of Department of Education, Gauteng & Others* Case no 83667/7 (15 January 2018). Appeal papers in this matter are, at the time of writing, before the Constitutional Court.

[29] *Federation of Governing Bodies for South African Schools v MEC for Education, Gauteng and Another* [2016] ZACC 14; 2016 (4) SA 546 (CC) [EE was admitted as *amicus curiae*].

[30] Ibid paras 34–9.

[31] Ibid para 40.

[32] For a more extensive discussion of this, see Brickhill & Van Leeve (note 2 above). Academic commentary has been critical of the approach of the Constitutional Court as focusing too much on procedural issues and therefore missing opportunities to develop the substantive content of the right to basic education in these cases. See S Fredman 'Procedure or principle: The role of adjudication in achieving the right to education' (2016) 6 *CCR* 165. And see the response of Van Leeve (note 22 above).

(c) Developing the content of the right

The third stream of education rights litigation began to develop substantive content. These cases focused on the provision of facilities, resources and teachers to schools.

(i) *Mud schools*

In his 2004 State of the Nation address, President Mbeki committed the national government to ensuring that there would be 'no learner and student learning under a tree, mud-school or any dangerous conditions that expose learners and teachers to the elements' by the end of that financial year.[33] Yet, by 2010 hundreds of schools in the Eastern Cape still comprised inappropriate classrooms made of mud, corrugated iron or crumbling bricks. Collapsing classrooms and roofs being blown away were common occurrences. Teaching and learning were severely compromised and those districts with the highest number of mud structures consistently fared worst in national assessments.

The LRC launched an application against the state in 2010 to eradicate mud schools in the province.[34] The applicants included the CCL and seven of the worst mud schools in the worst performing district of the province. The matter was ultimately settled by agreement,[35] whereby the state undertook to immediately replace the seven schools with temporary structures, and then spend more than R8.2 billion over three years to rebuild inadequate structures at schools across the country.[36] The roll-out of this infrastructure spend became the Accelerated Schools Infrastructure Development Initiative (ASIDI). While the case was largely successful, inadequate planning and underspending hampered the ASIDI programme which has resulted in funds being 'rolled over' to subsequent years and scores of mud schools still requiring attention.

Following continued failures by the state to deliver on their promise to eradicate mud schools, in 2014 a further application was launched in the High Court—'*Mud Schools 2*'. The case was an attempt to compel the state to plan better and improve

---

[33] Thabo Mbeki 'State of the Nation Address' *SA History* 21 May 2004, last accessed on 28 July 2017 from <http://www.sahistory.org.za/archive/2004-president-mbeki-state-nation-address-21-may-2004-after-national-elections#sthash.4s3uCuic.dpuf>.

[34] 'Mud schools', also referred to as 'inappropriate structures', are generally constructed by the community using traditional methods. Classrooms are made of mud bricks with a wooden frame, plastered with mud mixed with cow dung. Roofs are usually made of thatch or corrugated iron. The vast majority of schools constructed in this manner are in a poor condition, exposing students and teachers to serious health and safety risks.

[35] The state respondents in the matter tried hard to avoid filing answering papers. They took technical points and repeatedly called for settlement discussions. The applicants opted to insist that an answering affidavit be filed before considering settlement negotiations. This proved to be a strategically important moment since the answering affidavit showed that the respondents had no defence of substance. See S Budlender, G Marcus & N Ferreira 'Public interest litigation and social change in South Africa: Strategies, tactics and lessons' (2014) *The Atlantic Philanthropies* 81 for more detail on how this sequence of events transpired.

[36] Ibid 81.

its ability to spend its budget and provide safe and adequate infrastructure for learners. This second round of litigation resulted in another court order by agreement. The order established time frames for the implementation of the ASIDI programme and required that the department receive submissions from schools left off the ASIDI list but seeking inclusion, and that it provide clear time frames for the replacement or refurbishment of schools.[37]

Since neither of these cases resulted in court judgments, they do not technically form part of the body of jurisprudence developing the right to basic education. Nevertheless, the state's willingness to conclude massive, systemic settlements in these cases reflects an acknowledgment that it had, until that point, been failing in its duties to provide adequate school infrastructure. Ultimately, the fight to eradicate mud schools was subsumed in the subsequent campaign to improve all aspects of inadequate infrastructure through binding norms and standards.

(ii) *Norms and standards for school infrastructure*

In 2012, following the successful settlements that occurred in *Mud Schools 1* and *Mud Schools 2*, EE and two Eastern Cape public schools[38] embarked on an ambitious legal challenge in an attempt to remedy infrastructure conditions at schools. An order was sought directing the Minister of Basic Education to set binding minimum norms and standards to regulate adequate school conditions throughout the country. Until this point, no enforceable minimum standards had existed in either law or policy.

Before approaching the court, EE launched an extensive mobilisation campaign.[39] When the litigation was launched, the public campaign intensified.[40] This aspect of the case is discussed further below.

On the eve of the hearing of the case, a settlement was reached.[41] The Minister of Education undertook to publish draft regulations and adopt binding norms and standards by set dates.[42] While the draft was published on time, it was weak and elicited many comments through the public participation process.[43] When the final publication deadline was missed, the court was approached again, and the Minister was ordered to issue a revised draft of the norms and standards and publish a final

---

[37] While an improved database of needs was produced together with timeframes for many schools, many others had such low enrolments that they were earmarked for closure or merger. This process is ongoing, and some schools continue to operate with some or all of their classrooms being constructed of mud.

[38] Represented by the LRC.

[39] Budlender et al (note 35 above) 82.

[40] Ibid 83.

[41] Ibid.

[42] Ibid.

[43] Ibid.

version by 30 November 2013.[44] The public pressure campaign continued, and the Minister eventually complied.[45]

The Norms and Standards[46] require, amongst other things, the staged provision of various resources (or eradication of unacceptable conditions): within three years no school should be made from inappropriate material (including mud) and every school should have a source of water, electricity, and working toilets;[47] within seven years there must be security fencing around schools, safe classrooms with a maximum of 40 learners, Internet connectivity, and the broader provision of electricity, water and sanitation;[48] within ten years all schools must have access to libraries and laboratories;[49] and other aspects such as universal access[50] and sports facilities must be achieved within 17 years.[51] The Norms and Standards also included important provisions requiring provincial departments to plan and report to the Minister.

The Norms and Standards litigation powerfully illustrated the effectiveness of campaigns by social movements paired with legal interventions. The Norms and Standards are a useful benchmark for provincial education departments to measure their performance, and a standard against which local communities can hold them accountable.

The implementation of the regulations has met many familiar challenges. The first deadline (November 2016) was missed, schools made of mud still exist, and many schools still operate without access to any water or toilets.[52] Equal Education has approached the Bisho High Court in order to challenge a number of loopholes in the Norms and Standards. In a judgment handed down on 19 July 2018 the court held in their favour in respect of all aspects of the challenge.

The next section looks at the Limpopo textbooks litigation, which also made effective use of the media and social movements to complement legal strategies in addressing state failure to provide basic education.

---

[44] Ibid 84.

[45] Ibid.

[46] Regulations Relating to Minimum Uniform Norms and Standards for Public School Infrastructure to the South African Schools Act 84 of 1996 in GN R920 *GG* 37081 of 29 November 2013.

[47] Ibid regs 4(1)(*b*)(i) and 4(3)(*a*) and (*b*).

[48] Ibid regs 4(1)(*b*)(ii) and 4(3)(*c*).

[49] Ibid regs 4(1)(*b*)(iii) and 4(3)(*d*).

[50] School buildings must adhere to the principles of universal design: they must be usable by all people, to address the diversity of learners and teachers with functional limitations.

[51] Ibid regs 4(1)(*b*)(iv) and 15.

[52] Further, the required provincial plans for implementing the norms are often submitted late and are incomplete. Some staggered implementation of the norms has also meant that schools have had to hold back from launching cases seeking relief related to poor infrastructure until such time as the relevant regulation deadline has passed.

(iii) *Textbooks*

In 2010, the Limpopo Department of Education (LDE) appointed EduSolutions to provide Learner Teacher Support Materials (a large proportion of which are textbooks) in Limpopo. The contract was valued at R320 million.[53] Allegations of irregularities and financial mismanagement in respect of the award were made.[54] In 2012, SECTION27 began investigating reports in the media that textbooks had not been delivered to schools in the Limpopo Province.[55] Shortly thereafter, the National Department of Basic Education (DBE) cancelled the contract with EduSolutions.[56]

After several attempts were made to remedy textbook non-delivery through contacting the LDE and the DBE, an urgent application was launched. It asked the court to order delivery of textbooks to learners that had just begun the new standardised school curriculum and for the implementation of a catch-up plan for Grade 10 learners who had been prejudiced by the non-delivery of their learning materials.[57] The application succeeded; Kollapen J confirmed that learner support material in the form of textbooks is an essential component of the right to basic education.[58]

Compliance was sporadic, and many learners remained without textbooks even though the DBE claimed it had achieved 99% delivery of Grade 10 textbooks, and 100% delivery of textbooks to other grades.[59] An independent education expert, Mary Metcalfe, was appointed to verify these reports. The verification report uncovered that very few books had actually reached schools. The discrepancy arose because the DBE had claimed that compliance with the court order required only delivery to warehouses, not to schools.[60]

Further litigation ensued, some issues were settled, and further court orders were made.[61] By March 2014, 39 schools had not received their books for the 2014 school year. This meant that teachers had to borrow books to write notes on a board, photocopy content and use outdated books from a redundant curriculum.[62]

In court, Tuchten J affirmed that the provision of textbooks is a component of

---

[53] *Veriava* (note 9 above) 7.

[54] Ibid 8.

[55] Ibid 2.

[56] Ibid 8.

[57] Ibid 15.

[58] *SECTION27 and Others v Minister of Education and Another* [2012] ZAGPPHC 114; 2013 (2) SA 40 (GNP) para 25 [CALS acted for the applicants].

[59] Veriava (note 9 above) 20.

[60] Ibid 21.

[61] Ibid 23–4.

[62] *Minister of Basic Education and Others v Basic Education for All and Others* [2015] ZASCA 198; 2016 (4) SA 63 (SCA) para 19 [SECTION27 acted for the first to twenty-third respondents].

the right to a basic education.[63] However, he declined to order a structural interdict to monitor implementation of the respondents' commitment to deliver the 2014 textbooks.[64]

During this time, SECTION27 made highly effective use of the media to maintain pressure on the state to comply with court orders (discussed further in part 11.3 below). The litigation also gave rise to two important reports dealing with systemic failures in Limpopo—the Metcalf verification report and the report of a Presidential Task Team set up by President Jacob Zuma.

The Tuchten judgment was appealed to the Supreme Court of Appeal (SCA). The appeal court declared emphatically that the DBE had failed to properly plan and manage the process of procurement and distribution and thus had violated the learners' rights to a basic education:

> The truth is that the DBE's management plan was inadequate and its logistical ability woeful. One would expect proper planning before the implementation of the new curriculum. This does not appear to have occurred. The DBE also had a three-year implementation period during which it could have conducted proper budgetary planning, perfected its database, and ensured accuracy in procurement and efficiency in delivery. It achieved exactly the opposite and blamed all and sundry. It lacked introspection and diligence.[65]

Significantly, the SCA affirmed that the right to a basic education requires *every learner* to be provided with *every prescribed textbook*:

> It is declared that it is the duty of the State, in terms of s 7(2) of the Constitution, to fulfil the s 29(1)*(a)* right of every learner by providing him or her with every textbook prescribed for his or her grade before commencement of the teaching of the course for which the textbook is prescribed.[66]

Although there has not been full compliance, the litigation and accompanying public outcry have resulted in vastly improved textbook delivery in Limpopo and other provinces facing similar challenges, such as the Eastern Cape.

(iv) *Desks and chairs*
Of the failures that gave rise to the national intervention in the Eastern Cape in 2011, the shortage of furniture was arguably the most severe.

Similar to the textbooks debacle in Limpopo, the Eastern Cape Department of Education (ECDOE) simply did not know what the furniture needs were on the ground. Media reports, complaints from schools, and school visits confirmed that the shortages were often debilitating for schools and were felt widely across rural and urban no-fee schools.

---

[63] *Basic Education for All and Others v Minister of Basic Education and Others* [2014] ZAGPPHC 251; 2014 (4) SA 274 (GP) paras 46 and 51–2 and 82 [SECTION27 acted for the applicants].

[64] Ibid para 80.

[65] Ibid para 43.

[66] Ibid para 53.

The judgment in *Madzodzo*[67] was an important development of the jurisprudence, but only one stage of a lengthy process. The first application in the series of court cases asked that the High Court order the ECDOE to undertake a comprehensive audit of school furniture needs in the province and deliver the required furniture. Following non-compliance with court orders (or partial compliance at best) the applicants (the CCL and a group of individual schools that changed with each successive application, represented by the LRC) were forced to return to the court several times. This was eventually resulted in the *Madzodzo* judgment that required that all schools identified in the audit receive age- and grade-appropriate furniture before 31 May 2014.

Implementation has not been problem-free. The ECDOE has approached the court twice for extensions of time. November 2017 was the deadline for delivery of all furniture. While the process is not complete, more than 370 000 desks and 240 000 chairs have been procured and delivered since the case commenced. The litigation has also sought to address systemic planning problems within the ECDOE—discussed further in part 11.4 below.

In terms of legal developments, *Madzodzo* has confirmed that budgetary constraints cannot operate as a defence for the state's failure to comply with their constitutional obligations, when it had been aware of the shortages and consequent budgetary requirements for more than two years.[68] Most importantly, Goosen J confirmed that appropriate furniture in public schools is an element of the right to basic education.[69]

(v) Teachers

Each year in South Africa, provinces have their 'teacher post establishment' determined by the Member of the Executive Council.[70] This is a declaration of the number and provincial allocation of teacher posts. Teacher posts are then allocated to individual schools and teachers are appointed.[71]

The geographic circumstances of the Eastern Cape and rapid depopulation of rural areas has meant that enrolment figures at rural schools have dropped but they have risen in urban township schools. Some areas have too few teachers and other areas have far too many. The ECDOE has had immense trouble moving teachers from where they are teaching to where they are needed. Teachers, supported by powerful teacher unions, are resistant to being moved.[72] While this is an under-

---

[67] *Madzodzo v Minister of Basic Education* [2014] ZAECMHC 5; 2014 (3) SA 441 (ECM) [CCL was the fourth applicant and LRC acted for the applicants].

[68] Ibid para 35.

[69] Ibid para 36.

[70] Employment of Educators Act 76 of 1998 s 5(1)(*b*) and F Veriava, A Thom & T Hodgson *Basic Education Rights Handbook: Education Rights in South Africa* (2017) 251.

[71] Ibid 252.

[72] Ibid 259.

standable response, it serves to undermine the fulfilment of the right to basic education for learners across the province. By 2012, there were 4 000 vacant teacher posts in the Eastern Cape, at the same time as the ECDOE employed 7 000 'teachers in excess'—that is, teachers employed at the wrong schools.

The ECDOE's failure to deal with 'teachers in excess' places a huge burden on the fiscus—the additional teachers are paid government salaries but are not teaching where they are needed.[73] This has resulted in the appointment of temporary teachers to fill vacancies and left the ECDOE reluctant to fill more vacant posts.[74] In 2012, the need to appoint temporary teachers to fill vacant posts meant that over 90% of the Eastern Cape's education budget was spent on personnel. The alternative for the state is to neglect to fill these vacant posts at all. Failure by the department to fill posts forces schools to employ temporary teachers using funding raised by the school governing body (SGB) (despite very limited available funds), or in poorer schools to leave teaching posts vacant and learners without teachers.[75]

In 2012, several schools in the Eastern Cape complained of teacher shortages. The LRC initially brought a series of cases on behalf of small groups of teachers. These cases were successful but increasing numbers of schools came forward to seek assistance.

In *Centre for Child Law*,[76] the High Court was asked to order that the department declare the teacher post establishment, fill vacant posts with temporary teachers in the short term (and that these teachers be paid), and permanent appointments be made in the longer term. The case was settled, and the settlement was made an order of court.[77] Except for the appointment and payment of temporary teachers in 2012, the ECDOE failed to comply with the order.[78] Consistent non-compliance with the order meant that the court had to be approached twice more for enforcement. However, post-provisioning remained a serious problem in the Eastern Cape.

A further case, *Linkside*, was launched in the High Court. This time, the case was brought in two parts. Both dealt with similar claims. *Linkside Part 1* was brought on behalf of Linkside High School and 35 other schools in the Eastern Cape. The application sought to (1) have teachers appointed to vacant positions at schools; (2) have the schools reimbursed for the cost of paying for teachers to fill

---

[73] *Basic Education Rights Handbook* (note 70 above) 259.

[74] Ibid.

[75] Budlender et al (note 35 above) 87.

[76] *Centre for Child Law and Others v Minister of Basic Education* [2012] ZAECGHC 60; 2013 (3) SA 183 (ECG) [CCL as the first applicant and LRC acted for the first applicant and the *amicus curiae*].

[77] For the full order, see ibid para 35.

[78] *Basic Education Rights Handbook* (note 70 above) 256.

vacant posts[79] in the preceding three years; and (3) certify an opt-in class of similarly situated schools across the province.

An opt-in class action was chosen in this matter after full enforcement of the court order in *Centre for Child Law* was found to be extremely challenging. While the CCL had acted in the public interest in that case, the schools represented were nameless in the matter, which rendered follow-up very difficult.[80] In contrast, an opt-in class action would provide a named list of class members in an enforceable court order that each school could later use to claim its rights.[81]

The order was granted, and with the assistance of some litigation innovations to force compliance (discussed further in part 11.4 below), a reimbursement of R28 million was made to schools, a number of teachers were appointed, and the class action was certified.

The successful certification of the class resulted in approximately 80 schools opting in as applicants in *Linkside Part 2*, with the matter running as South Africa's first certified, opt-in class action following the development of court-created class action rules. *Linkside Part 2* was a resounding victory for the schools involved. The order handed down by the Grahamstown High Court required the state to pay over R81 million to the applicant schools as reimbursement for teacher salaries.[82] A number of teachers were deemed to be appointed in terms of the order.[83] The order also required that all vacant positions at schools should be properly advertised and filled.[84] Only this aspect of the case was not complied with until 'contempt of court' proceedings were instituted to force compliance.

Whilst the relief sought in *Linkside Part 1* and *Linkside Part 2* has been criticised for benefiting wealthier public schools, it represents an important step in ensuring that there are in fact teachers in classrooms and that schools are not faced with the choice of either funding vacant posts themselves or allowing their learners to go without a teacher. The model adopted in this litigation has added substantially to the jurisprudence and may be replicated by others to ensure the further realisation of the right to education.

(vi) *Scholar transport*
In the 2014 academic year, the Eastern Cape Department of Transport provided transport for only 60% of the 94 938 learners identified as eligible for state-funded

---

[79] These were teacher positions that the department deemed were required at the school and for which the department had an obligation to appoint and pay teachers.

[80] *Basic Education Rights Handbook* (note 70 above) 256.

[81] Budlender et al (note 35 above) 133–4.

[82] *Linkside and Others v Minister of Basic Education* [2015] ZAECGHC 36; 2015 JDR 0032 (ECG) para 1 [LRC acted for the applicants].

[83] Ibid para 2.

[84] Ibid para 4.

scholar transport.[85] The remaining 37 762 learners were forced to traverse distances as long as 10 km, or to pay for private transport in unsafe, overcrowded vehicles not legally permitted to transport scholars to and from school.[86]

Although the ECDOE had a policy for the provision of scholar transport dating back to 2003, in many instances, the necessary transport had not been provided. Media reports and complaints from schools seeking legal assistance resulted in an urgent application being filed in the Grahamstown High Court, on behalf of four schools in the Eastern Cape.[87]

The founding affidavit in *Tripartite Steering Committee* paints a dire picture. At the time of the application—mid-way through 2015—thousands of learners in the Eastern Cape were walking 10 km to and from school due to a lack of scholar transport.[88] The children worst affected were inevitably black and poor and came from the rural areas and townships of the Eastern Cape.[89] Children had been placed in very real physical danger as a result of a lack of scholar transport. The affidavits revealed incidents in which children forced to walk to and from school had been raped, robbed at knifepoint and gunpoint, and hit by cars.[90]

In the urgent application, the court was asked to order (1) that scholar transport be provided to individually identified learners and (2) that other learners' applications for transport be assessed in accordance with an appropriately flexible approach.[91] The applicants also asked for the publication of the criteria used to determine which learners qualified and the creation of a database of such learners.[92]

The court ordered that scholar transport be provided to learners who had already been evaluated and had qualified in terms of the policy,[93] but where learners' applications for transport had been refused, the decision was set aside and sent back to the ECDOE for reconsideration.[94] The court was unwilling to replace the

---

[85] Auditor-General of South Africa 'A performance audit of the learner transport scheme at the Eastern Cape Department of Transport' *AGSA* February 2016, last accessed on 31 July 2017 from <https://www.agsa.co.za/Portals/0/PA_Audit/A%20performance%20audit%20of%20the%20learner% 20transport%20scheme%20at%20the%20Eastern%20Cape%20Department%20of%20Transport. pdf> 12 The LRC is seeking certification of another class action where, if successful, all appropriately qualified teachers who were not paid by schools or were paid nominal amounts when teaching in fully-funded vacant post, will be paid the salaries they should have received.

[86] Ibid 12 and 27.

[87] The schools brought the case both in their own interest and in the public interest—on behalf of all learners in the Eastern Cape in a similar position. See *Tripartite Steering Committee and Another v Minister of Basic Education and Others* [2015] ZAECGHC; 2015 (5) SA 107 (ECG) para 4 [LRC acted for the applicants].

[88] *Tripartite Steering Committee* Founding Affidavit para 20.

[89] Ibid para 21.

[90] Ibid para 50.

[91] *Tripartite Steering Committee* (note 87 above) para 9.

[92] Ibid para 10.

[93] Ibid para 66.

[94] Ibid para 66.

ECDOE's decision with its own stating that it was not in as good a position as the original administrator to make the decision.[95] Finally, the court ordered that the ECDOE report on its progress in the adoption of the new scholar transport policy. It refused to order the creation of a database of qualifying learners.

Even though the applicants did not receive all of the relief that they sought, Plasket J's judgment developed the law, confirming that the right to a basic education includes scholar transport. Where distance and the inability to afford the costs of transport hinder access to schools, the state is obliged to provide such transport.[96]

11.3 A SOCIAL MOVEMENT IN PARALLEL

Much of the progress in fulfilling the right to basic education through strategic litigation has occurred alongside parallel strategies of social movements. The first, and arguably most successful, use of litigation in parallel with social mobilisation occurred in the norms and standards campaign. Later campaigns have used similar, if not as far-reaching, mobilisation techniques.

The most successful education social movement, EE, was formed in 2008. It is a grassroots community- and membership-based organisation, achieving its goals through analysis and community activism. Fairly early on in its operation, it launched its norms and standards campaign, which included a 20 000-person protest to Parliament in early 2011.[97]

Although EE's primary mode of operation was community organising, represented by the LRC, it instituted the litigation to compel the Minister of Basic Education to publish binding regulations on school infrastructure. In conjunction with the litigation, it continued its advocacy campaign. It used a number of methods—marches (including camping outside the High Court for the duration of the hearing), posters, pamphlets, radio and television advertisements.[98] When a settlement agreement was entered into, and a draft set of regulations was published for comment, EE arranged workshops in five provinces to encourage the public's participation in the comment process.[99] When the Minister missed the final deadline for publication of the regulations, EE further intensified its campaign. It created YouTube videos[100] and organised mass marches. The sustained pressure

---

[95] Ibid paras 52–4. The ECDOE's revised decision resulted in all 180 of the learners being granted scholar transport.

[96] *Tripartite Steering Committee* (note 87 above) paras 18–9.

[97] Budlender et al (note 35 above) 83.

[98] Ibid.

[99] Ibid.

[100] See, eg 'Build the Future' YouTube, last accessed on 13 August 2017 from <https://www.youtube-.com/watch?v=zJ1Xxg0kghg>; Equal Education '#FixOurSchools: Norms and Standards for School Infrastructure Now!' *YouTube* 30 May 2013, last accessed on 13 August 2017 from <https://www.youtube.com/watch?v=wqpUJaQHKT4>.

created by this advocacy and mobilisation campaign undoubtedly contributed directly to the victory achieved when the regulations were ultimately published in November 2013.[101]

The Limpopo textbooks case (discussed in part 11.2 above) is the second example of successful litigation being employed as part of a broader advocacy campaign. SECTION27 made extensive use of the media to draw public attention to the ongoing crisis in textbook delivery, as well as the consistent failure of the state to fulfil promises and abide by court orders. It relied on press statements, press conferences, publication of opinion pieces and posting updates on the case through social media.[102] Press conferences were well attended, and at one of these the Director General of Basic Education was subjected to a grilling by the media.[103]

The public outrage generated by the media coverage led President Zuma to appoint a task team to investigate delays in textbook delivery.[104] The idea of the 'education crisis in Limpopo' permeated public consciousness. As the case progressed, Basic Education For All—a community-based organisation similar to EE—was formed to promote the right to basic education in Limpopo.

The use of litigation and mobilisation in parallel has been mutually reinforcing.[105] The mud schools litigation was the first large case dealing with school infrastructure and served as a catalyst for the later framework-setting norms and standards litigation. The settlements achieved in the mud-schools litigation were indicative of the results that could be achieved, despite the fact that no enforceable precedent had yet been created. The case spurred on the harnessing of synergies between the newly formed EE and the LRC. EE supported the mud schools case with protests outside Parliament in solidarity with those in court for the case, while the LRC provided support in identifying clients and drafting court papers in the subsequent norms and standards case.

Emboldened by the extensive media coverage of the Limpopo textbooks crisis and the SCA judgment, schools in other provinces have sought legal assistance for textbook non-delivery.[106] Thus far, these issues have been settled without reaching the courts. The extensive mobilisation and campaigning done in the Limpopo textbooks matter may in future be the catalyst for further strategic litigation.

---

[101] Another useful mobilisation technique used by EE is the social audit, where communities evaluate or 'audit' the progress in delivery of infrastructure, sanitation and safety (see *Basic Education Rights Handbook* (note 70 above) 378).

[102] Veriava (note 9 above) 31.

[103] Ibid.

[104] Budlender et al (note 35 above) 86.

[105] Ann Skelton 'Strategic litigation impacts: Equal access to quality education' (2017) *Open Society Foundations* 51.

[106] Since the end of 2015, the LRC has received several complaints of textbook non-delivery in the Eastern Cape.

The use of a combination of litigation and advocacy campaigns (including social mobilisation) has undoubtedly advanced the fight for fulfilment of the right to basic education.

11.4 LESSONS LEARNED

(a) Innovative remedies

The most important lessons learned while litigating for the right to basic education have been related to the need for creative remedies for rights enforcement and effective implementation after judgment. The need to develop innovative remedies arose for several reasons, including the state's non-compliance with court orders, its failure to plan effectively and the need to monitor implementation. We discuss each in turn, highlighting some of the innovative remedies developed to address these challenges.

(i) *Anticipating and responding to non-compliance*

The challenge that arises most frequently in this area of rights litigation is non-compliance with court orders. This has forced litigants to adapt. Particularly effective responses have included the use of deeming provisions and having claims declared debts against the state and attaching state property.

In the string of cases for the appointment and payment of teachers, the LRC experienced precisely this problem—despite court orders, the ECDOE was simply not appointing teachers (which required the provision of a formal letter of appointment). Thus, the LRC opted to amend the relief being sought in later cases to include deeming provisions: if a teacher complied with statutory and policy requirements in terms of the qualification and hiring process, that teacher would be *deemed* to have been formally appointed.[107] These deeming provisions greatly assisted in circumventing departmental intransigence or tardiness.

In the same matter, where the ECDOE had failed, despite a court order, to reimburse schools for payment of teacher salaries, the relief was restructured in subsequent cases. The court was asked to declare that salaries owed to teachers were debts in terms of the State Liability Act 20 of 1957. Once this was ordered, attorneys could immediately take steps to attach state property and have it sold at sales in execution to realise money owed. For example, steps were taken to attach the motor vehicle of the Minister of Basic Education and the debt for teachers' salaries was immediately paid.

(ii) *The state's failure to plan effectively*

A major challenge at the heart of much of the litigation discussed here is the state's failure to engage in proper planning. This has had a bearing on how the litigation is conducted and how remedies have been designed. In the furniture case it became clear that the ECDOE had failed to plan for the provision of furniture so they did

---

[107] *Linkside* (note 82 above) paras 22–9.

not have a sense of what the needs were on the ground, and hence had no sense of what was required to ensure proper provision, nor what the cost would be.[108] This failure to plan drove much of the relief sought in this case.

The litigation attempted to address numerous systemic problems. The failure to accurately identify and record furniture needs resulted in the applicants asking the court to order that data be recorded in a way that could be integrated into existing information management systems and updated regularly.[109] The ECDOE's poor handling of the data that was constantly being generated as orders were placed, deliveries were made and the needs of schools changed, resulted in the applicants themselves hiring an IT specialist to help the ECDOE develop a programme to record the changes and train ECDOE staff to use it. Corrupt procurement processes and the resulting debilitating tender disputes that delayed delivery in the ECDOE saw the litigants approach the National Treasury, which agreed to oversee a 'transversal contract' whereby manufacturers were pre-selected and tender disputes were ended. The provincial department lacked a policy for furniture management, so the applicants insisted that a school furniture management policy be developed to guide schools on best practices to ensure the longevity of furniture usage and audit management.

Similarly, the failures in textbook delivery in Limpopo revealed a weakness in the province's ability to plan for and respond appropriately to a textbook delivery crisis. Aside from the failure to deliver, inadequate mitigation measures were in place for schools who did not receive textbooks when they were needed. This directly impacted on the quality of learning, since curriculum requirements are closely tied to the content of textbooks.

Thus, the failure of the LDE to deliver textbooks for an extended period of time meant that an entire cohort of learners was unable to cover the school curriculum effectively. In order to ensure that these learners were not casualties of the department's conduct, the applicants included in their prayers for relief that the LDE be ordered to draft and implement an extensive catch-up plan for learners.[110] This unprecedented request for relief attempted to remedy some of the damage done.

(iii) *Monitoring implementation*

Considering the problems with compliance with court orders discussed above, many litigants elected to build implementation monitoring mechanisms into the

---

[108] A similar factual scenario presented itself in the textbooks case. Before the textbooks crisis had become public knowledge, the LDE had outsourced textbook provision entirely to a company called EduSolutions. When this tender was cancelled, the DBE no longer had access to its database regarding textbook requirements. Lack of data proved to be one of the major obstacles to textbook delivery (see Veriava (note 9 above) 34).

[109] The data will now be included in the DBE's information management system, SA-SAMS.

[110] Veriava (note 9 above) 16.

relief sought. These have included the use of special masters or claims administrators, verification mechanisms and class action procedures.

During the early, smaller cases for payment of teachers, the ECDOE was found to be taking an exceedingly long time to make payments, and often lost relevant paperwork along the way. To address this, the applicants persuaded the court to appoint a claims administrator to manage all of the paperwork, verify the claims, and submit the amounts to the department, which were then paid to the claims administrator who then paid these out to the school.[111] The idea was conceived of drawing on the experience of the United States of America, Australia and Canada who had all made use of claims administrators in class actions. The purpose of the claims administrator is to assist the court in notifying members of the class and assisting with dispersal of amounts.

After a string of broken promises and inconsistencies in reporting, the parties to the textbooks matter came to an agreement that an independent person would be required to verify the contents of delivery progress reports provided by the DBE.[112] A verification report recommending large systemic changes to improve textbook delivery was provided. In a later iteration of the Limpopo textbooks case, the Human Rights Commission was required, in terms of a court order, to perform a similar monitoring role.[113] The use of an independent verifier and the Human Rights Commission to ensure court orders are complied with is another innovative step which has been necessitated by non-compliance with court orders.

The attorneys in the post-provisioning cases faced substantial difficulty in monitoring the implementation of orders. Extensive resources had to be used to monitor whether posts were being filled and teachers reimbursed in terms of multiple court orders. Using the 'opt-in' class action assisted in avoiding this difficulty.[114] The class comprised all schools with vacant posts that had themselves paid for teachers to fill the posts. Ninety schools paying approximately 200 teachers came forward. The presence of a class of named schools, who had voluntarily opted in and provided their details made the administration and follow up in respect of the case far easier.

(b) Securing systemic relief through orders and settlements
Litigators have found that it is most effective to bring cases in the name of both individual and institutional applicants. This ensures that individual and public interest concerns are captured, and the state's ability to settle matters, having addressed only a small fraction of the problem (that is, just the individual claimants), is minimised.

---

[111] *Linkside* (note 82 above) paras 19–21.
[112] Ibid 20.
[113] *Basic Education for All* (note 62 above) para 18.
[114] *Linkside* (note 82 above) para 2.

Many litigators have also found that upon being served with court papers, the state often attempts to draw litigants into protracted settlement negotiations. When negotiations break down, it is often difficult for the applicants to get the court process back on track. There appears to be merit in avoiding entering into settlement negotiations until the respondents have committed to a version in writing. This way, the respondents often make concessions, and the applicant's bargaining position is strengthened.

Finally, crafting remedies requires cognisance of the broader impacts of the relief sought as well as its unintended consequences. In the mud schools, textbooks and furniture litigation, the departmental action taken in response to a court order meant that such action was rushed and delivery less than fully effective due to the underlying systems being unable to cope with the urgency. This highlights the danger of compelling delivery through the courts (on pain of contempt) when the planning systems of the state are inadequate. The DBE has also complained that litigation often results in a 'drop everything else' response from the provincial education department in order to address the matter being litigated. This is often to the detriment of many other important departmental functions.

11.5 THE NEXT FRONTIER

Litigation on the right to education has thus far focussed almost exclusively on attacking the failure of the state to provide education inputs—infrastructure, textbooks, furniture, scholar transport and teachers. The logic is that improved inputs produce better outcomes—outcomes are a second order goal.

It is tempting to suggest that the next phase of education rights litigation and advocacy will shift to a focus on driving education outputs. However, we do not believe that this will happen. We speculate briefly below on what is on the horizon.

(a) The challenge of outputs cases

The litigation process lends itself to focusing on education inputs. It has been most successful when concrete claims can be formulated into court-ordered relief, and—in the context of socio-economic rights—where judges can be convinced that they will not be inappropriately encroaching on executive terrain. For this reason, education litigation will likely be slow to move into the realms of output-oriented relief. Outputs such as better trained teachers, more diligent administrators, learners with skill sets at particular levels, improved pass rates and better empowered parent bodies are all outcomes that may be too complex to be translated into specific relief in court papers. An example of PIL which unsuccessfully sought to secure wide-ranging 'output-oriented' relief was *Pease*.[115] The litigants challenged the issue of service delivery to schools broadly across the

---

[115] *Pease and Another v Government of the Republic of South Africa and Others* (HC) unreported case 18904/13 of 18 September 2015.

country, not seeking specific remedies. The applicants argued that the DBE was failing to equip the majority of South African learners with sufficient numeracy and literacy skills, failing to deliver textbooks and teaching materials on time, and were unable to provide teachers with adequate training. The court dismissed the claim.[116]

(b) Follow up and monitoring

Many of the cases discussed in this chapter still require substantial monitoring to ensure proper implementation. Many of the systemic failures uncovered run so deep that it is necessary to keep paying attention—one round of litigation will, in all likelihood, not produce the desired results.

However, finding the appropriate mechanism for monitoring the implementation of court decisions is challenging. Community-based organisations (community advice centres) could play an important role in ensuring that legal victories translate to change on the ground, however since the end of apartheid the numbers of such organisations in South Africa have dwindled.[117] Despite efforts to improve the situation,[118] our experience is that very few such organisations are involved in monitoring and implementation efforts.

The use of technology is a possible avenue for improved monitoring of implementation of court orders. In *Madzodzo*, the LRC attempted to use a smartphone app called Juggle (formerly Bambisa) to gather data from principals and other stakeholders on the status of furniture delivery after the judgment.[119] However, due to issues such as insufficient phone data, bad network coverage and glitches with the app, there was little to no uptake of the app.[120]

(c) Procurement challenges and budget cuts

The furniture cases forced the ECDOE to procure hundreds of millions of rands worth of desks and chairs over a short period. The ECDOE used the court orders as a reason to deviate from normal tender procedures which resulted in numerous tender disputes. Applicants in the furniture cases then intervened as *amici* in time-

---

[116] The court held that: (1) the applicants had not provided comparative legal precedent for their conception of what an adequate education is, leaving the court without a standard to gauge whether the required quality of education had been achieved (para 141); (2) the courts' role was to establish whether measures implemented by the government to fulfil a constitutional right were reasonable, not to put plans in place to give content to the right (para 146); and (3) due to the separation of powers doctrine, the court could not encroach on the field of another arm of the state. In this instance the court held that Parliament had fulfilled the state's obligation to give content to the right to education, a task that was not primarily that of the courts (paras 158 and 160).

[117] Budlender et al (note 35 above) 99–100.

[118] For example, the launch in 2007 of the National Alliance for the Development of Community Advice Offices. See Budlender et al (note 35 above) 100.

[119] Allison Corkery 'Opera in practice: Monitoring implementation of judgments in South Africa' *Centre for Economic and Social Rights* 8.

[120] Ibid 9.

consuming and costly court processes in (ultimately unsuccessful) attempts to ensure that procurement processes were not delayed.

A recent procurement dispute saw a successful challenge to the award of a large tender to build several schools in the Eastern Cape.[121] This has delayed the completion of these schools. Competition between service providers for government contracts also led to chaos in the provision of school nutrition in KwaZulu-Natal (KZN).[122]

We expect that procurement challenges will increasingly come to the fore. Lawful and cost-effective procurement processes are obviously important in improving education delivery, but there is a tension between the immediate service-delivery needs of learners and ensuring lawful procurement processes.

On the flip side has also been some concern that state spending on basic education, per pupil, has declined consistently over the last seven years.[123] If this trend continues it will be increasingly necessary that civil society demands accountability for such budgetary decisions.

(d)   The role of private schools

This is an issue likely to receive much attention going forward. In *KZN Joint Liaison Committee*, an association of independent schools in KZN challenged the reduction of the state subsidy provided to its members.[124] Initially, the Department of Education in KZN had notified the schools of the subsidy they would receive. Later, after experiencing a cash crisis, the provincial department provided subsidies that were approximately 30% less. The KZN Joint Liaison Committee took the matter to court seeking payment of the shortfall. In the Constitutional Court, the CCL as *amicus curiae* (represented by the LRC) argued that the right to basic education in the Bill of Rights applies to learners at both public and independent schools.[125] The state-provided subsidies assist in the fulfilment of the right to education.[126] As such, they argued, the right to a basic education comes under threat when promised subsidies are reduced or not paid.[127] Writing for the

---

[121] See Adrienne Carlisle 'Court challenge to R1.5bn project: May delay delivery of EC schools' *Daily Dispatch* 29 April 2017, last accessed on 15 August 2017 from <http://www.dispatchlive.co.za/news/2017/04/29/court-challenge-r1-5bn-project-may-delay-delivery-ec-schools/>.

[122] See Nokuthula Khanyile 'School meals scheme chaos' *News24* 1 August 2017, last accessed on 15 August 2017 from <http://www.news24.com/SouthAfrica/News/school-meals-scheme-chaos-20170731>.

[123] See Nic Spaull 'Throwing Basic Education under the bus' *Nic Spaull* 16 April 2018, last accessed on 29 May 2018 from <https://nicspaull.com/2018/04/16/throwing-basic-education-under-the-bus-my-business-day-article/>.

[124] *KwaZulu-Natal Joint Liaison Committee v MEC for Education, KwaZulu-Natal and Others* [2013] ZACC 10; 2013 (4) SA 262 (CC) [CCL was admitted as *amicus curiae* represented by the LRC] (*KZN Joint Liaison Committee*).

[125] Ibid para 26.

[126] Ibid.

[127] Ibid.

majority, Cameron J held that when the state pays subsidies to independent schools:

> it is plainly acting in accordance with its duty under the Constitution in fulfilling the right to a basic education of the learners at the schools that benefit from the subsidy. And once government promises a subsidy, the negative rights of those learners—the right not to have their right to a basic education impaired—is implicated.

The case established that the right to a basic education applies to all learners, including those attending independent schools, at least in respect of the negative obligation on the state not to impinge on existing access to education.

The recent case of *Pridwin Preparatory School*[128] concerned the expulsion of two learners from a private school based on the disruptive behaviour of their father at school sports events.[129] The removal of the learners occurred through the cancellation of the contract that had been concluded between their parents and the school. The application sought to ensure that the learners could remain at the school. The judgment held that the school was entitled to insist that the learners end their enrolment.[130] It also held that an independent school does not have an obligation to provide education in terms of s 29(1) of the Constitution.[131] At the time of writing the applicants had lodged an appeal with the Supreme Court of Appeal.

In addition, challenges to low-cost private schooling may soon be on the agenda. Although this issue has not squarely raised its head in South Africa, countries such as Kenya and Uganda have seen legal battles to prevent the spread of profit-driven low-cost schools, which are not subjected to the same level of oversight and scrutiny, have sprung up in response to an underperforming public-school system.

(e) Religion in schools

In *Laerskool Randhart*,[132] religious practice in public schools was challenged. The applicant sought interdicts preventing a range of instances of conduct that it considered infringed the right to freedom of religion, belief and opinion in s 15 of the Constitution and the National Religion Policy.[133] It also sought declaratory relief. The conduct complained of included a school 'having a Christian charac-

---

[128] *AB and CB v Pridwin Preparatory School and Others* [2017] ZAGPJHC 186 [EE was admitted as *amicus curiae* represented by the EELC].

[129] Ibid para 4.

[130] Ibid para 163.

[131] Ibid para 32.

[132] *Organisasie vir Godsdienste-Onderrig en Demokrasie v Laerskool Randhart and Others* [2017] ZAGPJHC 160; 2017 (6) SA 129 (GJ) [CASAC was admitted as *amicus curiae*, represented by the LRC].

[133] Ibid para 11.

ter', recording that its school badge represents the Holy Trinity and teaching creationism.[134]

The court refused to grant the interdicts prohibiting the conduct, citing the principle of subsidiarity—the parties had not considered the SGB policies on religion, or provincial and national legislation when challenging the impugned conduct.[135] However, the court granted the requested declaratory relief, holding that it is inconsistent with the relevant provisions of the South African Schools Act 84 of 1996 for a public school 'to promote or allow its staff to promote that it, as a public school, adheres to only one or predominantly only one religion to the exclusion of others; and to hold out that it promotes the interest of any one religion in favour of others'.[136]

The denial of the interdicts relating to specific conduct, coupled with the affirmation of the right to religion in the declaratory relief, leaves it unclear what conduct would fall foul of the declarator. We anticipate that more litigation will follow to clarify what is acceptable religious practice in public schools.

---

[134] *Laerskool Randhart* (note 132 above) para 6.

[135] Ibid paras 55–70.

[136] Ibid para 102.

Chapter 12

FREEDOM OF EXPRESSION

Dario Milo and Avani Singh

12.1 WHAT IS PROTECTED UNDER SECTION 16 OF THE CONSTITUTION?

(a) The ambit of the right to freedom of expression

Our courts have repeatedly recognised the importance of the right to freedom of expression. The Constitutional Court has described it as 'a *sine qua non* for every person's right to realise her or his full potential as a human being'.[1] It is both a fundamental right in itself, as well as a crucial enabling right necessary to realise

---

[1] *Case and Another v Minister of Safety and Security and Others; Curtis v Minister of Safety and Others* [1996] ZACC 7; 1996 (3) SA 617 (CC) para 26 [People Opposing Women Abuse, NICRO Women's Support Centre, Advice Desk for Abused Women, Rape Crisis (Cape Town), NISAA Institute for Women's Development and Women against Women Abuse, represented jointly by Wits Law Clinic, and CALS, FXI and Christian Lawyers' Association were admitted as *amici curiae*].

an array of other rights and the founding values contained in the Constitution. In *SANDU*, the Constitutional Court held:[2]

> Freedom of expression lies at the heart of a democracy. It is valuable for many reasons, including its instrumental function as a guarantor of democracy, its implicit recognition and protection of the moral agency of individuals in our society and its facilitation of the search for truth by individuals and society generally. The Constitution recognises that individuals in our society need to be able to hear, form and express opinions and views freely on a wide range of matters.

The constitutional protection of freedom of expression is bifurcated under s 16 of the Constitution. In the first part, s 16(1) provides a general protection for the right, stating that:

> Everyone has the right to freedom of expression, which includes—
> *(a)* freedom of the press and other media;
> *(b)* freedom to receive or impart information or ideas;
> *(c)* freedom of artistic creativity;
> *(d)* academic freedom and freedom of scientific research.

The broad formulation contained in s 16(1) applies regardless of the medium through which the expression is conveyed. This includes the typical forms of communication, such as publishing and broadcasting, as well as newer forms, such as blogging and tweeting. It also covers certain forms of conduct, such as protests.[3] The Constitutional Court has further accepted that the right to receive or impact information or ideas is applicable 'not only to "information" or "ideas" that are favourably received or regarded as inoffensive or as a matter of indifference, but also to those that offend, shock or disturb'.[4]

Section 16(2) of the Constitution then goes on to identify those types of speech that do *not* enjoy constitutional protection: propaganda for war; incitement of imminent violence; or advocacy of hatred that is based on race, ethnicity, gender, or religion, and that constitutes incitement to cause harm. Given the importance of the right and the serious import of the lack of constitutional protection, s 16(2) should be narrowly construed. Unlike s 16(1), which provides a non-exhaustive

---

[2] *South African National Defence Union v Minister of Defence and Another* [1999] ZACC 7; 1999 (4) SA 469 (CC) (*SANDU*) para 7.

[3] See, for instance, *South African Transport and Allied Workers Union and Another v Garvas and Others* [2012] ZACC 13; 2013 (1) SA 83 (CC) paras 62–6 [FXI was admitted as *amicus curiae*].

[4] *De Reuck v Director of Public Prosecutions (Witwatersrand Local Division) and Others* [2003] ZACC 19; 2004 (1) SA 406 (CC) para 49 [CCL was admitted as *amicus curiae*]. The Constitutional Court has further explained that freedom of expression extends 'even where those views are controversial. The corollary of the freedom of expression and its related rights is tolerance by society of different views. Tolerance, of course, does not require approbation of a particular view. In essence, it requires the acceptance of the public airing of disagreements and the refusal to silence unpopular views'. See *SANDU* (note 2 above) para 8.

list of the types of speech that are protected, the types of unprotected speech listed in s 16(2) are limited to what is expressly stipulated.[5]

In sum, a three-part test can be distilled when assessing whether a limitation to the right to freedom of expression can pass constitutional muster:[6]

- *Step 1:* Is the expression excluded in terms of s 16(2) of the Constitution? If yes, that is the end of the enquiry. If not, then the expression is protected under s 16(1) and it is necessary to move on to the next step.
- *Step 2:* Is there a common-law rule or statutory provision that limits the protection of freedom of expression? If yes, then it is necessary to move on to the next step. If not, that is the end of the enquiry.
- *Step 3:* Is the limitation of freedom of expression reasonable and justifiable, as contemplated under the general limitations clause in s 36 of the Constitution? If yes, the law permissibly limits freedom of expression. If not, then the law is an impermissible limitation of freedom of expression.

(b) Media freedom

As indicated, s 16(1) of the Constitution expressly refers to freedom of the press and other media. While the media clearly has an indispensable role in fostering democracy and the free flow of information, the Constitutional Court has also emphasised the duty of the media to be 'scrupulous and reliable':[7]

> In a democratic society, then, the mass media play a role of undeniable importance. They bear an obligation to provide citizens both with information and with a platform for the exchange of ideas which is crucial to the development of a democratic culture. As primary agents of the dissemination of information and ideas, they are, inevitably, extremely powerful institutions in a democracy and they have a constitutional duty to act with vigour, courage, integrity and responsibility. The manner in which the media carry out their constitutional mandate will have a significant impact on the development of our democratic society. If the media are scrupulous and reliable in the performance of their constitutional obligations, they will invigorate and strengthen our fledgling democracy. If they vacillate in the performance of their duties, the

---

[5] In *Laugh It Off Promotions CC v SAB International (Finance) BV t/a Sabmark International* [2005] ZACC 7; 2006 (1) SA 144 (CC) para 47 [FXI was admitted as *amicus curiae*], the Constitutional Court explained the interplay between ss 16(1) and (2) as follows:

> We are obliged to delineate the bounds of the constitutional guarantee of free expression generously. Section 16 is in two parts: the first subsection sets out expression protected under the Constitution. It indeed has an expansive reach . . . The second part contains three categories of expression which are expressly excluded from constitutional protection. It follows clearly that unless an expressive act is excluded by section 16(2) it is protected expression. Plainly, the right to free expression in our Constitution is neither paramount over other guaranteed rights nor limitless . . . In appropriate circumstances authorised by the Constitution itself, a law of general application may limit freedom of expression.

[6] For a diagrammatic representation of the three-part test, see Dario Milo & Pamela Stein *A Practical Guide to Media Law* (2013) 2.

[7] *Khumalo and Others v Holomisa* [2002] ZACC 12; 2002 (5) SA 401 (CC) para 24 [Webber Wentzel (WW) acted for the appellant].

constitutional goals will be imperilled. The Constitution thus asserts and protects the media in the performance of their obligations to the broader society, principally through the provisions of section 16.

The media today faces numerous challenges, including funding constraints, attempts at state regulation, lawsuits which are designed to intimidate, and threats, harassment and surveillance by both state and private actors. It should be remembered that s 16 of the Constitution does not only impose negative obligations on the state to respect the right to freedom of the press and other media, but also positive obligations to protect, promote and fulfil this right.

There are two important aspects that have developed in our law, which enhance media freedom and bear mention: source protection; and reluctance by our Courts to permit prior restraints on publication. As to the first, the duty to protect confidential sources is regarded as sacrosanct amongst journalists. This was upheld in the High Court decision of *Bosasa Operations*.[8] Although journalists are not entitled to a blanket journalistic privilege to not reveal their sources,[9] the High Court took into consideration that the sources appeared to have acted in the public interest and for the public good, and found no basis to limit the right to freedom of expression.[10] In this regard, the High Court explained as follows:[11]

> [I]t is apparent that journalists, subject to certain limitations, are not expected to reveal the identity of their sources. If indeed freedom of the press is fundamental and *sine qua non* for democracy, it is essential that in carrying out this public duty for the public good, the identity of their sources should not be revealed, particularly, when the information so revealed, would not have been publicly known. This essential and critical role of the media, which is more pronounced in our nascent democracy, founded on openness, where corruption has become cancerous, needs to be fostered rather than denuded.

The second aspect pertaining to prior restraints on publication is similarly important to freedom of the press. The test to be applied before a ban on publication will be considered is for there to be 'a demonstrable relationship between the publication and the prejudice that it might cause to the administration of justice, substantial prejudice if it occurs, and a real risk that the prejudice will occur'.[12] As noted by the Constitutional Court in *Print Media*,[13] '[t]he case law recognises that

---

[8] *Bosasa Operations (Pty) Limited v Basson and Another* [2012] ZAGPJHC 71; 2013 (2) SA 570 (GSJ) [(WW) acted for the respondents].

[9] Ibid para 46.

[10] Ibid para 52.

[11] Ibid para 38.

[12] *Midi Television (Pty) Ltd v Director of Public Prosecutions (Western Cape)* [2007] ZASCA 56; [2007] 3 All SA 318 (SCA) para 16.

[13] *Print Media South Africa and Another v Minister of Home Affairs and Another* [2012] ZACC 22; 2012 (6) SA 443 (CC) [JASA and FXI were admitted as *amici curiae*, the latter represented by WW]. The case concerned the system of administrative prior classification imposed by the Films and Publications Act 65 of 1996.

an effective ban or restriction on a publication by a court order even before it has "seen the light of day" is something to be approached with circumspection and should be permitted in narrow circumstances only'.[14]

(c) The categories of unprotected speech in terms of section 16(2) of the Constitution

Expression is *prima facie* protected as a point of departure under s 16(1) of the Constitution, unless it is excluded under s 16(2). Restrictions on expression that fall within the categories listed under s 16(2) need not be tested against s 36 of the Constitution, and cannot be challenged as being an unconstitutional limitation on freedom of expression: it is an internal limitations provision.

The first category of unprotected speech refers to propaganda for war.[15] The terms 'propaganda' and 'war' are not clearly defined, and should be applied narrowly. This provision has not, however, received much attention to date.

The second category of unprotected speech refers to incitement of imminent violence.[16] In order not to unduly narrow the right to freedom of expression, the term 'incitement' should be understood as actually encouraging or pressuring others to commit a violent act, where in all the circumstances the violent act actually occurred or was likely to occur.[17] Incitement to public violence remains a criminal offence on our statute books under s 17 of the Riotous Assemblies Act 17 of 1965,[18] and includes the speaking or publication of words that might reasonably be expected to lead to public violence by members of the general public or persons in whose presence those words were spoken or published. At the time of writing, there is a pending constitutional challenge to s 17 by the leader of the political party, the Economic Freedom Fighters, who has been charged with inciting supporters to occupy land.[19]

---

[14] *Print Media* (note 13 above) para 44. Although *Print Media* concerned administrative prior restraints, in practice the decision has been invoked in resisting attempts to obtain judicial prior restraints on publication.

[15] Section 16(2)*(a)* of the Constitution.

[16] Section 16(2)*(b)*.

[17] Milo & Stein (note 6 above) 13.

[18] Section 17 reads as follows:
   A person shall be deemed to have committed the common law offence of incitement to public violence if, in any place whatever, he has acted or conducted himself in such a manner, or has spoken or published such words, that it might reasonably be expected that the natural and probable consequences of his act, conduct, speech or publication would, under the circumstances, be the commission of public violence by members of the public generally or by persons in whose presence the act or conduct took place or to whom the speech or publication was addressed.

[19] See, for instance, Ernest Mabuza 'EFF loses bid to have order prohibiting incitement rescinded' *Times Live* 16 February 2018, last accessed on 19 May 2018 from <https://www.timeslive.co.za/politics/2018-02-16-eff-loses-bid-to-have-order-prohibiting-incitement-rescinded/>.

The third category refers to advocacy of hatred that is based on race, ethnicity, gender, or religion, and that constitutes incitement to cause harm.[20] This is commonly referred to as hate speech. In *Afri-Forum*, the Equality Court noted that hate speech at a social level is prohibited for four main reasons: to prevent psychological harm to targeted groups that would effectively impair their ability to positively participate in the community and contribute to society; to prevent both visible exclusion of minority groups that would deny them equal opportunities and benefits of society, and invisibly exclude their acceptance as equals; to prevent disruption to public order and social peace stemming from retaliation by victims; and to prevent social conflagration and political disintegration.[21]

Hate speech has further been codified under s 10 of the Promotion of Equality and Prevention of Unfair Discrimination Act 4 of 2000 (PEPUDA). Section 10(1) of PEPUDA is broader than s 16(2)*(c)* of the Constitution, and provides as follows:

> (1) Subject to the proviso in section 12, no person may publish, propagate, advocate or communicate words based on one or more of the prohibited grounds, against any person, that could reasonably be construed to demonstrate a clear intention to—
>
> *(a)* be hurtful;
>
> *(b)* be harmful;
>
> *(c)* promote or propagate hatred.

There are two points to mention in respect of s 10(1) of PEPUDA. First, it should be noted that the provision refers expressly to words. It therefore does not appear from a plain reading of s 10(1) that it will extend to images, non-verbal communications or other forms of conduct,[22] although the Equality Court has held that the definition does not exclude the relevance of gestures that may accompany the words.[23] The second point to note is that paras *(a)* to *(c)* should be read disjunctively; in other words, it is not required that all three elements be present for a claim to succeed.

Included in PEPUDA is a proviso that the following will not be prohibited as hate speech: bona fide engagement in artistic creativity, academic and scientific enquiry, fair and accurate reporting in the public interest or publication of any information, advertisement or notice in accordance with s 16 of the Constitution.[24] In respect of the media, this makes it clear that journalists reporting on incidences of hate speech will not themselves be guilty of hate speech.[25]

---

[20] Section 16(2)*(c)* of the Constitution.

[21] *Afri-Forum and Another v Malema and Others* [2011] ZAEQC 2; 2011 (6) SA 240 (EqC) para 29.

[22] See *Manamela and Others v Shapiro* GP/2008/1037/E (SAHRC) 12 May 2010 para 3.

[23] *Afri-Forum* (note 21 above) para 39.

[24] Section 12 of PEPUDA.

[25] This is consonant with the decision of the European Court of Human Rights in *Jersild v Denmark* (1995) 19 EHRR 1. In that case, the European Court of Human Rights overturned the conviction of a

The constitutionality of s 10 of PEPUDA, amongst other provisions was unsuccessfully challenged in *Qwelane*.[26] Mr Qwelane argued that this provision infringed his right to freedom of expression and was vague and overbroad. In assessing the alleged vagueness of the provision, the Equality Court explained as follows:[27]

> The first words in s 10(1) of [PEPUDA] are clear that the section imposes an objective test in order to determine whether the words in question reflect the requisite intention. Furthermore, the proviso in s 12 is not susceptible to any uncertainty. It is plain that speech that falls within the proviso is not prohibited by s 10, more so that no case has been made out to place the offending statements in the proviso. Furthermore, the words hurtful and harmful are capable of easy and intelligible meaning. Hurt connotes hurt to feelings and harmful relates to physical harm of whatever nature.

With regard to the second leg of the argument on overbreadth, the Equality Court held that s 10(1) did not suffer from overbreadth or fail to meet the requirements of the limitations clause under s 36 of the Constitution merely because it prohibited more speech than s 16(2) of the Constitution.[28] Instead, the Equality Court held that s 10(1)—

> [constitutes] a reasonable and justifiable limitation of the right to freedom of expression . . . because the hate speech of and extent of the harm that could be caused by speech of the kind prohibited by s 10(1) of [PEPUDA], by far outweighs the limited interests of speakers in nevertheless communicating such speech.[29]

The Equality Court therefore reached the conclusion that the constitutional challenge to s 10(1) of PEPUDA must fail.

Section 10(2) of PEPUDA goes further to provide that, notwithstanding any civil remedies for hate speech, a court may also refer the matter to the Director of Public Prosecutions to institute criminal proceedings in terms of the common law or relevant legislation. As such, civil proceedings may be brought in parallel with criminal proceedings, typically taking the form of a charge of *crimen iniuria*,

---

Danish journalist, who had been convicted under Danish law for aiding and abetting the dissemination of racist speech by including interviews with members of a racist organisation, the Greenjackets, in a documentary that he had made. As stated by the European Court of Human Rights (para 33):

> Taken as a whole, the feature could not objectively have appeared to have as its purpose the propagation of racist views and ideas. On the contrary, it clearly sought—by means of an interview—to expose, analyse and explain this particular group of youths, limited and frustrated by their social situation, with criminal records and violent attitudes, thus dealing with specific aspects of a matter that already then was of great public concern.

[26] *South African Human Rights Commission v Qwelane; Qwelane v Minister for Justice and Correctional Services* [2017] ZAGPJHC 218; 2018 (2) SA 149 (GJ) [SAHRC was the applicant; FXI and the Psychological Society of South Africa were admitted as *amici curiae*, the latter represented by WW].

[27] Ibid para 58.

[28] Ibid para 64.

[29] Ibid.

which is a common-law crime for the impairment of another's dignity. In March 2018, the Randburg Magistrate's Court sentenced Vicki Momberg to three years' imprisonment, with one year suspended, following a guilty verdict of *crimen iniuria* for racist speech, including the repeated use of the deeply offensive racial slur '*kaffir*' towards police officers.[30] This was the first time that a sentence of imprisonment has been handed down for *crimen iniuria* in the post-apartheid era in South Africa.

At the time of writing, new proposed legislation—the Prevention and Combating of Hate Crimes and Hate Speech Bill—has been approved by the South African Cabinet and submitted to Parliament.[31] The Bill, inter alia, proposes the creation of a new statutory offence of hate speech, which has not previously been found in South African law.

12.2   RESTRICTIONS ON THE RIGHT TO FREEDOM OF EXPRESSION

Any restriction on the right to freedom of expression—other than the limitations expressly provided under s 16(2)—must be tested against the general limitations clause in s 36 of the Constitution. As with all rights, the right to freedom of expression is not absolute, and is not elevated above other competing rights under South African law. As stated by the Constitutional Court: '[T]he right to freedom of expression cannot be said automatically to trump [other rights such as] the right to human dignity . . . [F]reedom of expression does not enjoy superior status in our law.'[32] It is therefore necessary to balance competing rights and interests when assessing a restriction on the right to freedom of expression. As a result, public interest litigation involving the right to freedom of expression may see contestation between different constitutional concerns that may be in tension, with litigants invoking the public interest on both sides of such matters. In this section, we discuss some of the significant areas of contestation involving balancing expression with other constitutional rights and values, including civil and criminal defamation, statutory restrictions on expression, and matters pitting expression against privacy.

---

[30] See, for instance, Iavan Pijoos 'Vicki Momberg sentenced to an effective 2 years in prison for racist rant' *News24* 28 March 2018, last accessed on 19 May 2018 from <https://www.news24.com/SouthAfrica/News/vicki-momberg-sentenced-to-an-effective-2-years-in-prison-for-racist-rant-20180328>. For a discussion on the genesis of the use of the word '*kaffir*', see *South African Revenue Service v Commission for Conciliation, Mediation and Arbitration and Others* [2016] ZACC 38; 2017 (1) SA 549 (CC) paras 1–14. Further, see *Rustenburg Platinum Mine v SAEWA obo Bester and Others* [2018] ZACC 13 for a broader discussion on the unacceptability of racist speech.

[31] B9-2018, last accessed on 25 May 2018 from <https://pmg.org.za/bill/779/>.

[32] *S v Mamabolo* [2001] ZACC 17; 2001 (3) SA 409 (CC) para 41 [FXI was admitted as *amicus* [E-TV, Business Day and FXI were admitted as *amici curiae*]. See also, *Johncom Media Investment Limited v M and Others* [2009] ZACC 5; 2009 (4) SA 7 (CC) paras 24, 27, 29 and 31 [Media Monitoring Project was admitted as *amicus curiae*, represented by the CCL].

(a) Civil defamation

Central to the law of defamation is the presumption that every individual has the right to an unimpaired reputation, and the need to balance this with the right to freedom of expression. Civil defamation enables one person to sue another to seek damages and other recourse for the impairment suffered. The Constitutional Court has held that it should not be considered an actionably injurious slight to offend someone's feelings by merely classing them in a condition that the Constitution protects—be it religious, racial, age, birth or sexual.[33] In other words, for instance, to simply call someone Muslim, Christian, gay, black, white, lesbian, female, male, an old-age pensioner, atheist, Venda or Afrikaans is not actionably injurious.[34] Something more is needed.

The elements of a claim of defamation, which the plaintiff must prove, are three-fold: there must be publication; the matter published must have a defamatory meaning; and the defamatory matter must refer to the plaintiff.[35] Once a plaintiff is able to establish these elements, it is then presumed that the publication is unlawful and that the defendant acted with the intention to defame. In order to avoid liability and rebut the presumption of unlawfulness, there are certain defences that can be raised, namely that the statement was true and published for the public benefit or in the public interest; that the statement was protected comment (previously known as 'fair comment'), being made upon true facts on matters of public interest; that the statement was protected by qualified privilege, because it was made in the course of a fair and accurate report of the proceedings of a court, Parliament or a public body; or that in all the circumstances in which the statements were published, it was reasonable for the media to have published them (referred to as the 'reasonableness defence').[36]

In defamation cases brought against the media, it is possible for claims to be lodged against all participants in the publication process, including the journalist, the editor and the publisher. While the media is not absolved from defamation claims, in general a wider berth is allowed. For instance, in *McBride*,[37] despite the view taken in the judgment that the contents of the articles may be 'vengeful', 'distasteful' and 'unrelentingly harsh and unforgiving',[38] the Constitutional Court nevertheless held that the commentary qualified as 'an honest, genuine (though possibly exaggerated or prejudiced) expression of opinion relevant to the facts

---

[33] *Le Roux and Others v Dey* [2011] ZACC 4; 2011 (3) SA 274 (CC) para 182 [WW acted for the appellants; FXI and Restorative Justice Centre were admitted as *amici curiae*].

[34] Ibid.

[35] For a fuller discussion of these elements, see Milo & Stein (note 6 above) 20–9.

[36] Ibid 29–43.

[37] *The Citizen 1978 (Pty) Ltd and Others v McBride* [2011] ZACC 11; 2011 (4) SA 191 (CC) [Lara Johnstone, FXI, South African National Editors' Forum (SANEF), Joyce Mbizana and Mbasa Mxenge were admitted as *amici curiae*, with all except Johnstone represented by WW].

[38] Ibid paras 102 and 111.

upon which it was based, and not disclosing malice'.[39] Accordingly, it held that the bulk of the statements fell within the bounds of constitutionally protected comment.[40]

Distinguishing between comment and fact is not always straightforward. Although not a defamation case, an interesting judgment that explores this distinction in the context of political speech is the Constitutional Court decision in *DA v ANC*.[41] The case concerned a text message that was sent to over 1.5 million voters by the national opposition party, the Democratic Alliance, regarding former President Jacob Zuma. The text message (SMS) referred to a report on an investigation into security upgrades at President Zuma's private home (referred to as the 'Nkandla report'), and read: 'The Nkandla report shows how Zuma stole your money to build his R246m home. Vote DA on 7 May to beat corruption. Together for change.'

The majority of the Constitutional Court (per Cameron J, Froneman J and Khampepe J) reached the conclusion that the text message constituted an expression of opinion interpreting the findings of the Nkandla report, rather than a statement of fact. In this regard, the majority held as follows:[42]

> The SMS indicated that the [Nkandla] Report would show 'how' the money was stolen. In other words the method or modality of how a misappropriation of the public's money occurred. And crucially, 'shows how' must not be understood literally to mean that the [Nkandla] Report actually says, in as many words, that the President is guilty of theft. It may also mean 'demonstrate[s] or prove[s]'. In other words, the SMS tendered to its recipients an interpretation of the [Nkandla] Report. A reasonable reader of the SMS would have understood this.
>
> The SMS therefore was not intended to be, and did not hold itself out as being, authoritative. It rather based its conclusion, and was a comment, on the [Nkandla] Report.

The minority judgment (per Zondo J) disagreed. In reaching the conclusion that the message meant, and would ordinarily have been understood by a reasonable reader to mean, that the Nkandla report finds that President Zuma stole taxpayers' money to build his home,[43] the minority judgment explained as follows:

> An ordinary reasonable reader who read the statement in the SMS would not think that the Nkandla Report could give an exposition of how Mr Zuma stole the taxpayers' money without making a finding that he had stolen taxpayers' money to build his home. Accordingly, an ordinary reader would have understood the SMS as saying that the Nkandla Report was to the effect that Mr Zuma stole 'your money to

---

[39] Ibid para 103.

[40] Ibid para 112.

[41] *Democratic Alliance v African National Congress* [2015] ZACC 1; 2015 (2) SA 232 (CC) (*DA v ANC*).

[42] Ibid paras 152–3.

[43] Ibid para 62.

build his R246m home'. The meaning of the SMS that the applicant contends for would only apply if the SMS read: 'An analysis of the Nkandla Report shows how Zuma stole your money to build his R246m home'. In other words, this meaning would indicate that how Mr Zuma stole 'your money' was not a conclusion of the Nkandla Report but a conclusion resulting from an analysis of the Nkandla Report.

To underscore the complexity that can arise when distinguishing between comment and fact, the further minority judgment (per van der Westhuizen J) noted that:

> [O]n closer consideration, one finds that this clear-cut boundary between a factual statement and an opinion may well be something of a fiction. Whereas extremes on both ends of the fact/opinion continuum are easily identifiable, in reality there is no clear line somewhere in the middle that makes this a binary inquiry.[44]

In the event that a plaintiff is able to establish the required elements of defamation, and the defendant is not able successfully to raise a defence, the next consideration is that of remedy. In civil claims, an award of damages is the typical remedy ordered by courts. Factors that may be taken into account when assessing the quantum of damages include the seriousness of the defamation, the extent of the publication, the nature of the publication, and the reputation, character and conduct of the plaintiff. A prominent and prompt bona fide apology and retraction by a defendant may mitigate the quantum of damages awarded.

Although an interdict may also be a competent remedy in appropriate circumstances, it should be noted that where the defamatory matter is already in the public domain, a plaintiff cannot easily bring an interdict against a publication and must instead seek damages. Notably, any attempt to restrain publication must be approached with caution, particularly where the media is involved.[45]

An important development has been the recognition of awarding an apology as a competent form of remedy in defamation law, at least against non-media defendants. This was developed by the Constitutional Court in *Le Roux*. The case involved a defamation claim brought by a deputy principal of a high school against learners for an image that transposed the heads of the principal and the deputy principal onto the bodies of two naked men sitting next to each other in a sexually suggestive manner.[46] Developing the common law on this issue was informed by

---

[44] *DA v ANC* (note 41 above) para 182.

[45] *Midi Television* (note 12 above) paras 15–20. As explained in that judgment (para 19):
> [A] publication will be unlawful, and thus susceptible to being prohibited, only if the prejudice that the publication might cause to the administration of justice is demonstrable and substantial and there is a real risk that the prejudice will occur if publication takes place. Mere conjecture or speculation that prejudice might occur will not be enough. Even then publication will not be unlawful unless a court is satisfied that the disadvantage of curtailing the free flow of information outweighs its advantage. In making that evaluation it is not only the interests of those who are associated with the publication that need to be brought to account but, more important, the interests of every person in having access to information.

[46] *Le Roux* (note 33 above) para 14.

the value of restorative justice and fairness.[47] Accordingly, the learners were ordered to tender an unconditional apology, in addition to paying damages as compensation.[48]

It remains to be decided whether such a remedy would be competent for a court to award against a media defendant where issues of media freedom are involved, although this is a remedy that can be—and frequently is—awarded by the Press Ombudsman for those members of the media that subscribe to the Code of Ethics and Conduct for South African Print and Online Media (Press Code).[49]

(b) Criminal defamation

In *S v Hoho*,[50] the Supreme Court of Appeal (SCA) confirmed that the common law crime of defamation exists in South African law. It is defined as the unlawful and intentional publication of matter concerning another, which tends to injure his or her reputation.[51] In distinction to civil defamation, the state enforces criminal defamation, and the state is required to prove each element beyond reasonable doubt. Although a person charged with criminal defamation can raise all of the same defences as in a civil case, there is no onus on the accused to disprove his or her guilt.[52]

In the subsequent High Court decision of *Motsepe v S*,[53] the court was faced with an appeal against a conviction of criminal defamation against a journalist, based on an article that he wrote in which he incorrectly alleged that a particular magistrate imposed a heavier sentence on a black male than he did on a white female for the same offence.[54] The court noted further that while a criminal sanction is indeed a more drastic remedy than a civil sanction, 'this disparity is counterbalanced by the fact that the requirements for succeeding in a criminal

---

[47] Ibid para 197. As explained by the Constitutional Court (para 202):
Respect for the dignity of others lies at the heart of the Constitution and the society we aspire to. That respect breeds tolerance for one another in the diverse society we live in. Without that respect for each other's dignity our aim to create a better society may come to naught. It is the foundation of our young democracy. And reconciliation between people who opposed each other in the past is something which was, and remains, central and crucial to our constitutional endeavour. Part of reconciliation, at all different levels, consists of recantation of past wrongs and apology for them. That experience has become part of the fabric of our society. The law cannot enforce reconciliation but it should create the best conditions for making it possible. We can see no reason why the creation of those conditions should not extend to personal relationships where the actionable dignity of one has been impaired by another.

[48] Ibid paras 203 and 206.

[49] Para 1.11 of the Press Code.

[50] *S v Hoho* [2008] ZASCA 98; 2009 (1) SACR 276 (SCA) [Adv G Marcus SC and Adv S Budlender were admitted as *amici curiae* at the court's request].

[51] Ibid para 23.

[52] Ibid paras 25 and 33.

[53] *Motsepe v S* [2014] ZAGPPHC 1016; 2015 (5) SA 126 (GP) [WW acted for the appellant].

[54] Ibid para 3.

defamation matter are much more onerous than in a civil matter'.[55] In balancing the right to freedom of expression with other rights, such as the right to dignity, the court concluded that criminal defamation insofar as it pertains to the media is consistent with the Constitution.[56]

There have been more positive developments at the regional level. In *Konaté*,[57] the African Court of Human and Peoples' Rights (African Court) found that the imposition of a custodial sentence for criminal defamation violated the right to freedom of expression under art 9 of the African Charter on Human and Peoples' Rights (although non-custodial sentences did not constitute a violation).[58] On the facts of the particular case, the African Court held further that the sentence imposed on Mr Konaté was excessive, and therefore also constituted a violation of art 9 of the African Charter. Accordingly, the respondent state was ordered to amend its legislation by repealing custodial sentences for defamation and to adapt its legislation to ensure that other sanctions for defamation meet the test of necessity and proportionality, in accordance with its obligations under international law.[59]

Several other African states have also since amended their laws to decriminalise defamation.[60] However, in South Africa, despite the Minister in the Presidency having announced in 2015 that the African National Congress would spearhead legislation to decriminalise defamation,[61] this has regrettably not yet been brought to fruition.

(c) Statutory restrictions
There are a number of statutes that contain restrictions on reporting. These statutes are based on various rationales, including the protection of national security and

---

[55] Ibid para 46.

[56] Ibid para 51.

[57] *Konaté v Republic of Burkina Faso* Application No 004/2013, 5 December 2014.

[58] Ibid 48.

[59] Ibid para 49.

[60] For instance, in 2016, *Misa-Zimbabwe and Others v Minister of Justice and Others*, Case No CCZ/07/15, the Constitutional Court of Zimbabwe declared the offence of criminal defamation unconstitutional and inconsistent with the right to freedom of expression as protected under the Zimbabwean constitution. The following year, in 2017, in *Okuta v Attorney-General* [2017] eKLR (Petition No 397 of 2016), the High Court of Kenya similarly declared the offence of criminal defamation under the Penal Code unconstitutional, finding it too disproportionate and excessive for the purpose of protecting personal reputation, and that there existed an alternative civil remedy for defamation. In May 2018, in *Peta v Minister of Law, Constitutional Affairs and Human Rights and Others*, Case No CC 11/2016, the Constitutional Court of Lesotho also declared the offence of criminal defamation inconsistent with the right to freedom of expression and therefore unconstitutional.

[61] Dario Milo 'The timely demise of criminal defamation law' *Webber Wentzel* 4 October 2015, last accessed on 17 May 2018 from <http://blogs.webberwentzel.com/2015/10/the-timely-demise-of-criminal-defamation-law/>.

law enforcement. Any restriction on reporting must be assessed in light of s 36 of the Constitution to determine whether it is a reasonable and justifiable limitation of the right to freedom of expression. As explained in *Print Media*:[62]

> Because freedom of expression, unlike some other rights, does not require regulation to give it effect, regulating the right amounts to limiting it. The upper limit of regulation may be set at an absolute ban, which extinguishes the right totally. Regulation to a lesser degree constitutes infringement to a smaller extent, but infringement nonetheless.

For instance, in *Maharaj*,[63] the SCA considered the reporting restrictions contained in s 28 read with s 41(6) of the National Prosecuting Authority Act 32 of 1998 (NPA Act). In that case, the *Mail & Guardian* newspaper had sought to publish an excerpt of an enquiry conducted by the National Prosecuting Authority (NPA) in terms of s 28(1) of the NPA Act.[64] However, s 41(6) of the NPA Act provides that, subject to certain exceptions, no person may disclose the record of any evidence given at a s 28(1) enquiry without the permission of the National Director of Public Prosecutions (NDPP).

On threat of legal action, it decided to delay publication in order to seek permission in terms of s 41(6) of the NPA Act.[65] The acting NDPP however refused permission.[66] Before the SCA, in ultimately reaching the conclusion that the acting NDPP had failed to exercise her discretion properly, several factors were taken into consideration. This included that the acting NDPP had not considered the s 28 record itself in arriving at her decision;[67] that the case concerned a matter of public interest relating to the probity of a senior public office-bearer and raised allegations of corruption and mismanagement of public funds;[68] and that the information was already in the public domain following prior publications—notwithstanding the fact that those had also not been authorised by the NDPP—on the basis that information cannot be protected once it loses its secrecy.[69]

Maharaj is important in particular for its clear acceptance of public interest and public domain considerations when assessing the permissibility of restrictions on reporting. These considerations have repeatedly been emphasised as much-needed defences that should be contained in other legislation, most notably the Protection

---

[62] *Print Media* (note 13 above) para 51.

[63] *Maharaj and Others v M&G Centre for Investigative Journalism and Others* [2017] ZASCA 138; 2018 (1) SA 471 (SCA) [WW acted for the respondents].

[64] Section 28(1) of the NPA Act authorises a Director of Public Prosecutions to conduct an investigation if he or she has reason to suspect that a specified offence has been or is being committed. Section 28(6) of the NPA Act provides for the proceedings to take place in camera.

[65] *Maharaj* (note 63 above) paras 6–7.

[66] Ibid para 10.

[67] Ibid paras 24–5.

[68] Ibid paras 27–9.

[69] Ibid paras 34–7.

of State Information Bill (POSIB).[70] POSIB has arguably been one of the most controversial bills to be tabled in post-apartheid South Africa, and was criticised for creating space for corrupt government officials to conceal information from the public and stifle investigative reporting through the harsh criminal penalties that it would impose. While these concerns would, to some extent, have been allayed by the inclusion of public interest and public domain defences, the drafters did not adopt these submissions (though there was a concession in relation to the proposed crime of disclosing classified information if the disclosure was done to 'reveal criminal activity'). However, POSIB is nevertheless a good example of the role that civil society, the media and members of the public can play in resisting draconian legislation. At the time of writing, POSIB has still not been signed into law, some five years after having been passed by the National Assembly.

(d) The flipside: Balancing freedom of expression with the right to privacy

The balance between freedom of expression and privacy is of particular concern to the media which may want to publish private facts, in circumstances where the person to whom those facts relate may wish to exclude them from the knowledge of outsiders. In assessing the extent of privacy rights, the Constitutional Court has developed the doctrine of 'reasonable expectation of privacy', which requires there to be a subjective expectation of privacy that society recognise as reasonable.[71]

In the *Johncom* decision, the Constitutional Court had to consider whether the prohibition of reporting contained in s 12 of the Divorce Act 70 of 1979 (Divorce Act) struck the appropriate balance between the right to privacy and the right to freedom of expression. The impugned provision sought to protect the privacy and dignity rights of divorcing parties and their children by prohibiting publication of information that comes to light during a divorce action.[72] The Constitutional Court accepted that while the objective of s 12 was clear, the chosen method went too far and was not particularly effective in achieving the purpose.[73] Accordingly, it held that the purpose could be achieved by less restrictive means—such as to prohibit the publication of the identities of the parties and the children, rather than prohibiting the publication of any evidence— and declared s 12 of the Divorce Act to be inconsistent with the Constitution.[74]

---

[70] B6D–2010, last accessed on 25 May 2018 from <https://pmg.org.za/bill/278/>.

[71] *Bernstein and Others v Bester NO and Others* [1996] ZACC 2; 1996 (2) SA 751 (CC) para 76.

[72] *Johncom* (note 31 above) para 2. See also *NM v Smith and Others* [2007] ZACC 6; 2007 (5) SA 250 (CC) [ALP acted for the applicants; FXI was admitted as *amicus curiae*] concerning a claim for damages by three HIV positive women whose names were disclosed without their consent. See further the recent decision reviewing the classification of the film 'Inxeba' in *Indigenous Film Distribution (Pty) Ltd v Film and Publication Appeal Tribunal and Others* [2018] ZAGPPHC 438 [WW acted for the applicants].

[73] *Johncom* (note 72 above) para 30.

[74] Ibid.

Both domestically and globally, the right to privacy is garnering particular attention, with a significant number of countries promulgating data protection laws. In South Africa, although the Protection of Personal Information Act 4 of 2013 (POPIA) is not yet fully in force, this will, going forward, also give rise to important considerations of the appropriate balance between the right to freedom of expression and the right to privacy.[75]

12.3 THE RIGHT TO OPEN JUSTICE

The right to open justice is by now well entrenched under South African law.[76] This entails the right of the public to access proceedings of courts and tribunals and is implicit in the constitutional rights to freedom of expression, access to courts, the right of every accused person to a public trial, and the foundational values of openness, transparency and accountability.

While openness and access is the general principle, and provided for in terms of

---

[75] Section 7 of POPIA provides for certain exclusions in the interests of freedom of expression and journalistic activity. In this regard, it states as follows:

(1) This Act does not apply to the processing of personal information solely for the purpose of journalistic, literary or artistic expression to the extent that such an exclusion is necessary to reconcile, as a matter of public interest, the right to privacy with the right to freedom of expression.

(2) Where a responsible party who processes personal information for exclusively journalistic purposes is, by virtue of office, employment or profession, subject to a code of ethics that provides adequate safeguards for the protection of personal information, such code will apply to the processing concerned to the exclusion of this Act and any alleged interference with the protection of the personal information of a data subject that may arise as a result of such processing must be adjudicated as provided for in terms of that code.

(3) In the event that a dispute may arise in respect of whether adequate safeguards have been provided for in a code as required in terms of subsection (2) or not, regard may be had to—

(a) the special importance of the public interest in freedom of expression;

(b) domestic and international standards balancing the—

(i) public interest in allowing for the free flow of information to the public through the media in recognition of the right of the public to be informed; and

(ii) public interest in safeguarding the protection of personal information of data subjects;

(c) the need to secure the integrity of personal information;

(d) domestic and international standards of professional integrity for journalists; and

(e) the nature and ambit of self-regulatory forms of supervision provided by the profession.

[76] In *S v Mamabolo* (note 32 above) para 29 [E-TV, Business Day and FXI were admitted as *amici curiae*], the Constitutional Court noted that:

Since time immemorial and in many divergent cultures it has been accepted that the business of adjudication concerns not only the immediate litigants but is a matter of public concern which, for its credibility, is done in the open where all can see. Of course this openness seeks to ensure that the citizenry know what is happening, such knowledge in turn being a means towards the next objective: so that the people can discuss, endorse, criticise, applaud or castigate the conduct of their courts. And, ultimately, such free and frank debate about judicial proceedings serves more than one vital public purpose. Self-evidently such informed and vocal public scrutiny promotes impartiality, accessibility and effectiveness, three of the important aspirational attributes prescribed for the judiciary by the Constitution.

legislation,[77] there are also stipulated exceptions to this.[78] For instance, in terms of s 153(1) of the Criminal Procedure Act 51 of 1977 (Criminal Procedure Act), a judge or magistrate has a discretion to exclude the public or any class of the public from attending proceedings 'in the interests of the security of the State or of good order or of public morals or of the administration of justice'. Moreover, certain courts and court proceedings are closed as the default position, with access being allowed in exceptional cases subject to the discretion of the presiding officers, such as child justice courts,[79] children's courts,[80] and the tax court.[81]

In *M&G v Chipu*,[82] the Constitutional Court had to consider whether s 21(5) of the Refugees Act 130 of 1998 (Refugees Act) was inconsistent with the right to freedom of expression to the extent that it precluded the Refugee Appeal Board (RAB) from allowing members of the public and the media from attending and reporting on proceedings of the RAB in appropriate cases. The impugned provision did not admit any exception to the requirement of confidentiality, and the RAB had no discretion. The Constitutional Court held that absolute confidentiality of such proceedings was not essential, and that s 21(5) was not a reasonable and justifiable limitation of the right to freedom of expression.[83]

The Constitutional Court suspended the order of invalidity for a period of two years to allow Parliament to amend the Refugees Act appropriately.[84] As an interim measure pending the defect being remedied, the Constitutional Court read into s 21 exceptions to the confidentiality of the RAB proceedings, namely where the asylum seeker gives consent or where it is in the public interest to allow any person or the media to attend or report on its hearing.[85]

The right to report on and broadcast court and tribunal proceedings has now concretised in both law and practice. This applies to all media, including Internet

---

[77] See, for instance, s 32 of the Superior Courts Act 10 of 2013; s 5 of the Magistrates' Court Act 32 of 1944; and s 152 of the Criminal Procedure Act.

[78] See Milo & Stein (note 6 above) 89–92.

[79] Section 63(5) of the Child Justice Act 75 of 2008.

[80] Section 56 of the Children's Act 38 of 2005.

[81] Section 124 of the Tax Administration Act 28 of 2011.

[82] *Mail & Guardian Media Limited and Others v Chipu NO and Others* [2013] ZACC 32; 2013 (6) SA 367 (CC) [the applicants were represented by WW; SALC (represented by Wits Law Clinic) and LHR were admitted as *amici curiae*] (*M&G v Chipu*).

[83] Ibid paras 93–4.

[84] Ibid para 115.

[85] Ibid. The Constitutional Court identified the following factors to consider when determining whether it would be in the public interest to allow a member of the public or the media to attend or report on RAB hearings: the interests of the asylum seeker in retaining confidentiality; the need to protect the integrity of the asylum process; the need to protect the identity and dignity of the asylum seeker; whether the information is already in the public domain; the likely impact of the disclosure on the fairness of the proceedings and the rights of the asylum seeker; and whether allowing any person or the media access to its proceedings or allowing the media to report on them would pose a credible risk to the life or safety of the asylum seeker or of his or her family, friends or associates.

publishers and social media users.[86] In a matter pertaining to the broadcast of Olympic athlete Oscar Pistorius' criminal trial, the High Court considered whether permitting media access for print and broadcast journalists would violate Mr Pistorius' right to a fair trial.[87] In granting media access, the High Court crafted the order to expressly allow the broadcast of opening and closing arguments, inter-locutory applications, the evidence of experts called by the state, the evidence of police officers regarding the crime scene, the evidence of all other witnesses for the state unless the witness did not consent, and the delivery of judgment on the merits and the sentence.[88] However, in respect of the testimony of Mr Pistorius and the witnesses called by him, the High Court held that while audio coverage was permissible, audio-visual coverage may have an inhibitory effect on the testimony being given and thereby deprive Mr Pistorius of his right to a fair trial.[89]

In the *Van Breda* decision,[90] the SCA recently took one step further than the High Court in the *Pistorius* matter. Ponnan JA upheld the general default rule that court proceedings should be broadcast as a matter of course. The SCA did so on the basis of both the right to freedom of expression as well as the principle of open justice: 'freedom of the press and the principle of open justice are closely interrelated. The media, reporting accurately and fairly on legal proceedings and judgements, make an invaluable contribution to public confidence in the judiciary and, thus, to the rule of law itself'.[91] The task of the court was to harmonise as far as possible freedom of expression and the fair administration of justice (in particular the right to a fair trial).[92] As noted by the SCA, there was no logic in permitting journalists to use the reporting techniques of the print media but not permitting a television journalist to 'utilise his or her technology and method of communication'; televised proceedings aid the public in its oversight of the judiciary, and enable proceedings to be meaningfully accessible to the public.[93] The SCA also rejected the traditional justifications for resisting broadcasting of court cases. For instance, privacy concerns have to give way when disputes are

---

[86] The Constitutional Court has noted that audio-visual broadcasts (such as for the purposes of television or live-streaming the broadcasts) raise particular considerations in light of the intense impact that this can have and the potential to distort the character of the proceedings. See *South African Broadcasting Corporation Limited v National Director of Public Prosecutions* [2006] ZACC 15; 2007 (1) SA 523 (CC) para 68.

[87] *Multichoice (Proprietary) Limited and Others v National Prosecuting Authority and Another, In Re; S v Pistorius, In Re; Media 24 Limited and Others v Director of Public Prosecutions North Gauteng and Others* [2014] ZAGPPHC 37; 2014 (1) SACR 589 (GP) para 12 [Multichoice and Primedia were represented by WW].

[88] Ibid para 30.

[89] Ibid paras 25–6.

[90] *Van Breda v Media 24 Limited and Others* [2017] ZASCA 97; 2017 (2) SACR 491 (SCA) [Media Monitoring Africa was admitted as *amicus curiae*, represented by WW].

[91] Ibid para 16.

[92] Ibid para 42.

[93] Ibid para 44.

being resolved in public forums.[94] Moreover, while there is a risk of precognition of witnesses who have not yet given evidence (by them being able to watch other evidence on television), 'the adversarial nature of criminal proceedings . . . should enable the judge to safely make findings as to whether or not a witness' testimony has been tainted by the exposure'.[95]

Integral to the right to open justice is the right to access court records relating to the proceedings being reported on. In this regard, the Constitutional Court has confirmed that 'the default position is one of openness'.[96] As has been noted,

> from the right to open justice flows the media's right to gain access to, observe and report on, the administration of justice and the right to have access to papers and written arguments which are an integral part of court proceedings subject to such limitations as may be warranted on a case-by-case basis in order to ensure a fair trial.[97]

The SCA expanded hereon in *South African National Roads Authority*,[98] which stated, after quoting the above passage, as follows:[99]

> Accordingly, court proceedings should be open unless a court orders otherwise. The logical corollary must therefore be that departures should be permissible when the dangers of openness outweigh the benefits. And by extension, the right of open justice must include the right to have access to papers and written arguments which are an integral part of court proceedings . . . That must follow axiomatically, it seems to me, because the public would hardly be in a position to properly assess the legitimacy or fairness of the proceedings if they could observe the proceedings in open court but were denied access to the documents that provide the basis for the court's decision.

12.4 FREEDOM OF EXPRESSION IN THE DIGITAL AGE

The United Nations and the African Commission on Human and Peoples' Rights have both recognised that the same rights that people have offline must also be protected online, in particular the right to freedom of expression.[100] The advent of the Internet and other communications technologies has significantly enhanced the

---

[94] *Van Breda* (note 90 above) para 57.

[95] Ibid para 55.

[96] *Independent Newspapers (Pty) Ltd v Minister for Intelligence Services, In Re: Masetlha v President of the Republic of South Africa and Another* [2008] ZACC 6; 2008 (5) SA 31 (CC) para 43 [WW acted for the applicant; FXI was admitted as *amicus curiae*].

[97] Ibid para 41.

[98] *City of Cape Town v South African National Roads Authority Limited and Others* [2015] ZASCA 58; 2015 (3) SA 386 (SCA) [Right2Know Campaign, Section16, Open Democracy Advice Centre, M&G Centre for Investigative Journalism, SANEF, SECTION27, Socio-Economic Rights Institute of South Africa, Corruption Watch, Democratic Governance and Rights Institute, South African History Archive were admitted as *amici curiae*, all represented by the LRC].

[99] Ibid para 19.

[100] United Nations Human Rights Council, Resolution on the promotion, protection and enjoyment of human rights on the internet, A/HRC/32/L.20, 27 June 2016; African Commission, Resolution on

way in which we exercise and enjoy the right to freedom of expression, and the extent to which this facilitates the enjoyment of various other rights. It enables the borderless enjoyment of the right and the ability to engage, mobilise and support people all around the world.

However, there is a marked digital divide that tends to deepen existing socio-economic disparities and inequality. While various initiatives at both the public and private levels are in place, this divide nevertheless persists. Although an express right to the Internet has not yet been recognised, it is certainly arguable that the Internet is an indispensable tool to fully realise a myriad of fundamental rights.

The Internet also presents unique challenges. These include, for instance, the proliferation of cybercrimes, the ease with which disinformation and false news can be spread, and the sharing of 'revenge pornography' on websites and social media platforms. Online perpetrators are often difficult to identify, and there are further challenges in respect of jurisdiction as the perpetrator and the victim may be in different countries. Moreover, in light of the immediacy of publication and the amplified audience that the Internet provides, it is often difficult practically to limit the spread of impermissible information and the harm that this may cause.

There have been several High Court decisions in South Africa pertaining to social media platforms. The High Court has indicated that the posting on a Facebook wall, for instance, is akin to a person who has 'attached a scrappy piece of paper to a felt notice board in a passage with a pin or a stub of prestik'.[101] In the *Sooknunan* decision, the High Court noted that Mr Sooknunan, to whom the Facebook profile belonged, had 'created and made available this noticeboard in a public passage . . . [and] then has an obligation to take down those scrappy pieces of paper which are shown to be unlawful in content or impact'.[102] Significantly, the High Court likened Mr Sooknunan to a newspaper publisher, holding that '[h]e has made available the opportunity for such unlawful content and is, in effect, the publisher thereof—much as a newspaper takes responsibility for the content of its pages.'[103]

In both the *Sooknunan* and *Herholdt* decisions, the courts granted interdicts in favour of the applicants in respect of statements posted on social media plat-forms.[104] In the latter decision, the High Court reflected that:[105]

---

the right to freedom of information and expression on the internet in Africa, ACHPR/Res.362(LIX), 4 November 2016.

[101] *Vergesig Johannesburg Congregation and Another v Rayan Sooknunan t/a Glory Divine World Ministries* [2012] ZAGPJHC 97; 2012 (6) SA 201 (GSJ) para 48.

[102] Ibid para 49.

[103] Ibid.

[104] Ibid para 114; *Herholdt v Wills* [2014] JOL 31479 (GSJ) para 47.

[105] *Herholdt* ibid para 43.

Those who make postings about others on the social media would be well advised to remove such postings immediately upon the request of an offended party. It will seldom be worth contesting one's obligation to do so. After all, the social media is about building friendships around the world, rather than offending fellow human beings. Affirming bonds of affinity is what being 'social' is all about.

This, however, should depend on the circumstances of the particular case and the need to strike an appropriate balance with the right to freedom of expression. A blanket deference to acting on demands to remove content would be inimical to the right to freedom of expression online.

Damages have also been awarded for content posted on a social media platform. In *Isparta*,[106] the High Court awarded damages in the sum of R40 000 against both defendants jointly and severally, despite the fact that the second defendant was not the author of the post.[107] However, as indicated by the High Court, the second defendant knew about the posts from being tagged in them and allowed his name to be coupled with that of the first defendant, and was therefore as liable as the first defendant.[108] In determining the quantum of damages, the High Court took into consideration that the defendants had not apologised or retracted their statements, noting that '[a]n apology in the same medium (Facebook) would have gone a long way towards mitigating the plaintiff's damages'.[109]

The Internet presents both opportunities and challenges for the realisation of freedom of expression and other rights. To a large extent, the ordinary principles of law may be applied both offline and online, with the necessary adaptations applied in a reasonable manner that is duly cognisant of the changing digital landscape. A general trend that is being seen is a desire to regulate the Internet, with efforts often being impractical and likely to lead to a chilling effect on the right to freedom of expression. There is an urgent need for improved digital literacy and technology training across all sectors, including for lawmakers, judicial officers, in schools and for members of the public.

12.5 PROTEST AS A FORM OF EXPRESSION

The right to freedom of assembly is an essential element of freedom of expression, as the right would be severely curtailed if it did not also allow views to be made publicly known. As explained by the Constitutional Court:

> The right to freedom of assembly is central to our constitutional democracy. It exists primarily to give a voice to the powerless. This includes groups that do not have political or economic power, and other vulnerable persons. It provides an outlet for

---

[106] *Isparta v Richter and Another* [2013] ZAGPPHC 243; 2013 (6) SA 529 (GNP).

[107] Ibid para 35.

[108] Ibid.

[109] Ibid paras 40–1.

their frustrations. This right will, in many cases, be the only mechanism available to them to express their legitimate concerns.[110]

In South Africa, this is guaranteed in terms of ss 17 and 18 of the Constitution.[111] While the only express restriction imposed in terms of the Constitution is that it must be exercised peacefully and unarmed, the Regulation of Gatherings Act 205 of 1993 (RGA) puts in place a number of further restrictions, including a system of prior notification.[112]

Although prior notification can serve a useful purpose to enable public officials to facilitate an assembly, it is important to note that this is not tantamount to seeking authorisation from the state.[113] Indeed, assemblies are often by their very nature geared towards criticising or challenging the status quo, and are permissible even in circumstances where they may give offence, be provocative, or criticise the state or state officials.[114] In this regard, the European Court of Human Rights has stated 'that public events related to political life should be given particular deference . . . and that those expressing opinions which are critical of important public figures should be shown greater tolerance'.[115] Even to the extent that protests may cause some disruption, authorities should nevertheless show a certain degree of lenience, in particular to accommodate an organiser's legitimate interests in assembling within sight and sound of the target audience.[116]

Notably, in *Mlungwana and Others v S and Another*,[117] the applicants successfully challenged the constitutionality of s 12(1)*(a)* of the RGA in the Western Cape High Court. The case concerned whether it was permissible for a person to be found guilty of a criminal offence for convening a gathering without giving notice as contemplated in the RGA. The High Court concluded that 'because of the disastrous impact of a criminal conviction and the lifelong impact it has on the

---

[110] *Garvas* (note 3 above) para 61.

[111] Section 17 of the Constitution guarantees that: 'Everyone has the right, peacefully and unarmed, to assemble, to demonstrate, to picket and to present petitions.' Further, s 18 of the Constitution states: 'Everyone has the right to freedom of association.'

[112] Section 3 of the RGA.

[113] African Commission, Guidelines on freedom of association and assembly in Africa, 2017 para 71. At paras 71–2, it provides that prior notification regimes should be non-burdensome and require a presumption in favour of holding assemblies, with a failure to notify not resulting in an automatic penalisation or rendering the assembly illegal. Further, at para 75, it provides that: 'No notification need be submitted for small assemblies, assemblies unlikely to generate disturbance or spontaneous assemblies.'

[114] Ibid paras 77–2. However, expression that would fall within the ambit of s 16(2) of the Constitution, such as propaganda for war or incitement of imminent violence, would not enjoy constitutional protection.

[115] *Chumak v Ukraine* Application No 44529/09, 6 March 2018 (ECtHR) para 55.

[116] Ibid para 53.

[117] [2018] ZAWCHC3; 2018 (1) SACR 538 (WCC) [the appellants, all of whom were members of the Social Justice Coalition, were represented by the LRC; the Open Society Justice Initiative (represented by WW), the United Nations Special Rapporteur on the Rights to Peaceful Assembly and of Association, and Equal Education were admitted as *amici curiae*].

lives of those convicted of contravening s 12(1)*(a)*, the criminal sanction is disproportionate to the offence of merely failing to comply with the notice requirement.'[118] At the time of writing, the declaration of constitutional invalidity has been referred to the Constitutional Court for confirmation proceedings.

South Africa has a long-standing protest culture.[119] In recent years, this has included the striking mineworkers in Marikana, the students during the #Rhodes-MustFall and #FeesMustFall protests, and an array of service delivery protests, to name a few. A hallmark of recent protests in South Africa—and globally—has been the important role that social media has played in organising and sharing real-time information on the protests, and the use of mobile technology to record videos and other information as evidence.

In this regard, a final aspect to note in the context of the interplay between freedom of expression and assembly is the right to record during an assembly. Standing Order 156 on media communication in the South African Police Service provides the general position that the police may not prohibit a media representative from taking photographs or making visual recordings.[120] The broader right to freedom of expression would arguably extend this to all persons, including citizen journalists and members of the public, who wish to record police conduct during an assembly and ensure that authorities are held accountable for their conduct.

12.6 STRATEGIES FOR REALISING THE RIGHT TO FREEDOM OF EXPRESSION

The right to freedom of expression, including media freedom, has been healthily developed in our law through strategic litigation and advocacy campaigns. South African jurisprudence on freedom of expression and media freedom is the envy of many countries, as our courts have consistently been willing to serve as bastions against attempts to impermissibly encroach on the right. In seeking to pursue such outcomes, particularly as the next frontier of digital rights litigation emerges we

---

[118] Ibid para 93. The High Court went further to note that: '[I]t cannot be seriously contested that in the context of the South African society, those most likely to fall foul of s 12(1)*(a)* are the very previously disadvantaged communities as they, to a certain extent, remain the voiceless. Although this is quite inadvertent, it also flies in the face of the foundational values of our Constitution, namely, freedom, dignity and equality.'

[119] See *Garvas* (note 3 above) paras 62–63.

[120] Standing Order (General) 156, Media communication in the South African Police Service, 2003. In *Butkevich v Russia*, Application No 5865/07, 13 February 2018 (ECtHR) para 116, regarding a journalist who was arrested during a demonstration, the European Court of Human Rights noted 'the crucial role of the media in providing information on the authorities' handling of public demonstrations and the containment of disorder' and that 'the 'watchdog' role of the media assumed particular importance in such contexts, since their presence was a guarantee that the authorities could be held to account for their conduct vis-à-vis demonstrators and the public at large when it came to the policing of large gatherings, including the methods used to control or disperse protesters'. As such, the court held that 'any attempt to remove journalists from the scene of demonstrations must therefore be subject to strict scrutiny'.

set out several key strategies and considerations that have been effective in realising the right to freedom of expression in previous cases:

*   *Media and NGO coalitions:* There is manifest benefit to media organisations and NGOs, particularly those NGOs focused on the public's right to know, working together and collaborating in litigation when pursuing aligned outcomes. This can ensure that there is mutual support and that no individual organisation is targeted or risks retribution. It can also lead to cost sharing and reduce the burden on the court. In matters pertaining to broadcasts, for example, it is typically helpful for media applicants to agree in advance to share the feed to limit any disturbance that may be caused in the courtroom by the setting up of cameras.

*   *Pre-litigation negotiation:* Reaching consensus where possible prior to litigation can often avoid unnecessary time and money being wasted. For instance, prior to the application to broadcast the Oscar Pistorius criminal trial, the discussions that took place during the pre-litigation negotiation led to the prosecution withdrawing its opposition to the broadcast. Similarly, negotiations with the liquidators prior to the enquiry into Aurora Empowerment Systems played a significant role in the media being granted access, including by reaching agreement that the broadcast would only take place once the enquiry was complete.

*   *The role of amici curiae:* The important role that *amici curiae* play in court proceedings has repeatedly been emphasised. In freedom of expression matters, typical *amici curiae* roles have included providing international and comparative foreign law experience, highlighting the broader social context that a matter may have, and placing evidence before the court. In the *Print Media* decision, the Constitutional Court's order went beyond the relief sought by the applicant, with the order ultimately more closely resembling that sought by the *amicus curiae*.

*   *Explaining the impact and implications of technology:* In *Herholdt*, the High Court noted:

    > [I]t is the duty of the courts harmoniously to develop the common law in accordance with the principles enshrined in our Constitution. The pace of the march of technological progress has quickened to the extent that the social changes that result therefrom require high levels of skill not only from the courts, which must respond appropriately, but also from the lawyers who prepare cases such as this for adjudication.[121]

As digital rights litigation is likely to increase, litigants should be conscious of ensuring that the judicial officers hearing the matter understand the more complex, technical aspects of the technology being considered, and the

---

[121] *Herholdt* (note 104 above) para 8.

impact and implications that this may have. *Amici curiae* can play an important role in explaining these aspects to the court.

- *Media regulatory bodies:* Courts are not the only recourse when seeking relief. Many members of the media also subscribe to media regulatory bodies, such as the Press Council of South Africa and the Broadcasting Complaints Committee of South Africa (BCCSA). In addition, the Complaints and Compliance Committee of the Independent Communications Authority of South Africa (CCC) also regulates those media whose content is not regulated by the BCCSA and polices adherence to the broadcasting statutes and licence conditions. For instance, in June 2016, the CCC held that the Policy Statement of the South African Broadcasting Corporation, to the effect that it would no longer broadcast footage of destruction of public property during protests, was in conflict with its duties as a public broadcaster and thus invalid.[122]

- *Public support and the importance of counter-narratives:* The media has a unique and important platform at its disposal that can be used to express support for worthy causes and to raise counter-narratives. While this should not be used as a self-serving tool, it is a component of the role of the media in informing and educating the public. Airing a plurality of views, highlighting important issues that are matters of public interest in an accessible manner, and offering the opportunity for diverse counter-narratives to be expressed (for instance, in response to instances of hate speech) have a crucial role to play in strengthening democracy and supporting the work being done by civil society and other members of the public.

---

[122] *The Trustees for the Time Being of the Media Monitoring Project Benefit Trust and Others v South African Broadcasting Corporation SOC Limited*, CCC Case No. 195/2016 [WW acted for the complainants].

Chapter 13

ACCESS TO INFORMATION

Dario Milo and Avani Singh

13.1 INTRODUCTION: THE SAGA OF *M&G MEDIA LTD v PRESIDENT OF THE REPUBLIC OF SOUTH AFRICA*

South Africa has seen a substantial body of public interest litigation concerning access to information, driven largely by the print media and non-governmental organisations. The landmark decision regarding access to a report about the 2002 Zimbabwean presidential election is one of the most important decisions of our courts to date in various respects, and is particularly illustrative of the intricate mechanism created under the Promotion of Access to Information Act 2 of 2000 (PAIA), the challenges in litigating such cases, and the persistence and resilience that can sometimes be needed to see such cases to fruition.

The report at the centre of this litigation had been prepared at the request of former President Thabo Mbeki by Justice Sisi Khamepe and former Deputy Chief Justice Dikgang Moseneke on the legal and constitutional dimensions of the Zimbabwean election. M&G Media Limited (M&G Media), the publisher of the *Mail & Guardian* newspaper, only learnt of the existence of this report in 2008. In that year, M&G Media lodged a request for access to the report in terms of s 18(1) of PAIA. The Presidency refused the request and dismissed the internal appeal.

This was done based on two grounds for exemption from disclosure under PAIA, namely: (i) the report contained information provided in confidence by the Zimbabwean government, as contemplated in s 41(1)*(b)*(i) of PAIA; and (ii) the report had been prepared for the purpose of formulating executive policy on Zimbabwe, as contemplated in s 44(1)*(a)* of PAIA.

In 2009, M&G Media applied to the North Gauteng High Court (as it then was), seeking an order granting access to the report. In its 2010 judgment, the High Court held that the Presidency had not established that the report fell within the exemptions relied upon, as the Presidency had only presented affidavits from officials who had no personal knowledge of why the judges were sent to Zimbabwe, or what information the judges received while in Zimbabwe.[1] Accordingly, the High Court ordered that the report be made available to M&G Media in its entirety.

The Presidency appealed to the Supreme Court of Appeal (SCA), arguing that it could not provide a fuller justification for refusing the request as to do so would reveal the contents of the report. The SCA was unpersuaded, and unanimously upheld the High Court's order.[2] The SCA decided not to use its power to take a 'judicial peek' at the report, on the basis that this power was not a substitute for the Presidency's failure to justify its refusal.[3]

The matter came before the Constitutional Court in 2011, culminating in the narrowly split decision in *M&G Media Ltd*.[4] The majority, per Ngcobo CJ, held that, although the Presidency had not justified the grounds of refusal on the papers, it would have been in the interests of justice for the High Court to invoke its power to take a judicial peek under s 80 of PAIA,[5] and that the merits of the exemptions claimed, the legality of the refusal to disclose the report, and the procedural matters regarding the judicial peek still needed to be decided by the High Court.[6] As such, the Constitutional Court remitted the matter to the High Court to examine the record in terms of s 80 of PAIA, in light of the Constitutional Court's judgment.[7]

In June 2012, the parties returned to the High Court for the next instalment of this matter. In line with the Constitutional Court's order, the respondents were

---

[1] *M&G Limited and Another v President of the Republic of South Africa and Others* [2010] ZAGPPHC 43.

[2] *President of the Republic of South Africa and Others v M&G Media Ltd* [2010] ZASCA 177; 2011 (2) SA 1 (SCA) para 55.

[3] This is provided for in s 80 of PAIA, which permits a court to examine the contents of a record in order to assess, for instance, whether the grounds of refusal relied upon are justified by the contents of the record.

[4] *President of the Republic of South Africa and Others v M&G Media Ltd* [2011] ZACC 32; 2012 (2) SA 50 (CC) (*M&G Media*) [Webber Wentzel (WW) acted for the respondent].

[5] Ibid para 64.

[6] Ibid para 68.

[7] Ibid para 72.

required to produce the report for the High Court to take a judicial peek at its contents. The High Court invited the parties to make ex parte representations, which it shared between the parties, although M&G Media's legal team was not granted access to the report itself for the purpose of making the submissions. Following the judicial peek, the High Court found that the contents of the report did not support the grounds of refusal relied upon by the Presidency,[8] and that the public interest in disclosure would in any event supersede any harm that may ensue if the report were to be released.[9] The High Court therefore ordered the respondents to make a copy of the report available to M&G Media within ten days of the order.[10]

The Presidency again appealed to the SCA, which heard the appeal in September 2014. After taking a judicial peek, the SCA agreed with the High Court and dismissed the appeal—for a second time.[11] The case finally came to end in November 2014, when the Constitutional Court dismissed the Presidency's further application for leave to appeal, ultimately resulting in the Presidency being compelled to disclose the report to M&G Media. This came after six years of litigation, eight sets of court proceedings,[12] and four court orders ordering disclosure of the report.

The Constitutional Court's reasoning in *M&G Media* is discussed in more detail below. However, for present purposes, this saga illustrates the persistent challenges that have been a hallmark of access to information litigation under PAIA: that it is lengthy and time-consuming; that it is costly; that it is of little assistance where the information sought is time-sensitive in nature; and that there is a serious and urgent need to review whether the existing mechanisms meaningfully give effect to the right of access to information when assessed in practice and context.[13] It is against this backdrop that we turn to explore the mechanisms provided under the South African law for accessing information.

13.2 THE CONSTITUTIONAL GUARANTEE OF A RIGHT OF ACCESS TO INFORMATION

The right of access to information is important both in itself, as well as in order to enable the realisation of other rights. As such, much access to information

---

[8] *M&G Media Ltd v President of the Republic of South Africa & Others* [2013] ZAGPPHC 35; 2013 (3) SA 591 (GNP) para 59.

[9] Ibid para 67.

[10] Ibid para 69.

[11] Ibid para 32.

[12] This relates to the first set of proceedings before the High Court decision; the first application for leave to appeal to the High Court; the first appeal to the SCA; the first appeal to the Constitutional Court; the second set of proceedings before the High Court; the second application for leave to appeal to the High Court; the second appeal to the SCA; and finally the application to the Constitution Court. [WW acted for M&G Media throughout the litigation].

[13] See also, Okyerebea Ampofo-Anti & Ben Winks 'There and back again: The long road to access to information in *M&G Media v President of the Republic of South Africa*' (2015) 5 *CCR* 466.

litigation is often about accessing relevant information for the benefit of pursuing a further aim or outcome based on that information. Through the exercise of the right of access to information, it is made possible, for instance, to influence policy and budgetary decisions, expose truths, guarantee meaningful political participation, and ensure transparency and accountability. As stated in *Brümmer*:[14]

> The importance of this right too, in a country which is founded on values of accountability, responsiveness and openness, cannot be gainsaid. To give effect to these founding values, the public must have access to information held by the State. Indeed one of the basic values and principles governing public administration is transparency. And the Constitution demands that transparency 'must be fostered by providing the public with timely, accessible and accurate information'.

The constitutional guarantee of the right of access to information is contained in s 32 of the Constitution, which provides:

> (1) Everyone has the right of access to—
> *(a)* any information held by the state; and
> *(b)* any information that is held by another person and that is required for the exercise or protection of any rights.
> (2) National legislation must be enacted to give effect to this right, and may provide for reasonable measures to alleviate the administrative and financial burden on the state.

The enactment of PAIA was therefore a direct response to the directive from s 32(2) of the Constitution to give effect to the right. PAIA supersedes any other legislation that prohibits or restricts the disclosure of a record, and that is materially inconsistent with the objects or provisions of PAIA.[15] As the Constitutional Court has explained:[16]

> PAIA is the national legislation contemplated in section 32(2) of the Constitution. In accordance with the obligation imposed by this provision, PAIA was enacted to give effect to the right of access to information, regardless of whether that information is in the hands of a public body or a private person. Ordinarily, and according to the principle of constitutional subsidiarity, claims for enforcing the right of access to information must be based on PAIA.

Central to the application of PAIA is that it applies to all records of both public and private bodies. This relates to any recorded information, regardless of its form or medium, which is in the possession or under the control of that public or private body.[17] It is irrelevant whether or not that body created the record, or when it came

---

[14] *Brümmer v Minister of Social Development and Others* [2009] ZACC 21; 2009 (6) SA 323 (CC) paras 62–3 [SAHRC was admitted as *amicus curiae*, represented by WW].

[15] Section 5 of PAIA.

[16] *PFE International Inc (BVI) and Others v Industrial Development Corporation of South Africa Ltd* [2012] ZACC 21; 2013 (1) SA 1 (CC) para 4.

[17] Section 1 of PAIA.

into existence.[18] As discussed below, PAIA provides a complex and intricate mechanism through which information can be accessed or refused.[19] We focus here on the following important features of PAIA: (i) the distinction between public and private bodies; (ii) the grounds for refusal of access; (iii) the public interest override; and (iv) internal appeals and the role of the new Information Regulator.

(a) Distinguishing between public and private bodies

The distinction between public and private bodies is important to the application of PAIA. This is because, when it concerns information held by a public body[20] (typically the state or an organ of state), the default position is mandatory disclosure, and there is no need for requesters to justify why the information is sought or why they would be entitled to it. Records of public bodies must be provided as a matter of right, unless a valid ground of refusal exists. Public bodies are dealt with under Part II of PAIA, and requests to public bodies must be completed on Form A.

On the other hand, in relation to information held by a private body,[21] requesters must show that the information is required for the exercise or protection of a right. Given the extra hurdle for requesters when it comes to private body requests, it is therefore strategically advantageous to request information from a public body where the information is held by both a public and a private body. Private bodies are dealt with under Part III of PAIA, and requests to private bodies must be completed on Form C.

With regard to requests to private bodies, s 53(2)(d) of PAIA provides that the request must identify the right that the requester seeks to exercise or protect, and

---

[18] See ss 1 and 3 of PAIA. A record is defined in s 1 as being any recorded information, regardless of the form or medium, that is in the possession or under the control of the public or private body, whether or not it was created by that body.

[19] For an overview of the step-by-step mechanism created under PAIA, see Dario Milo & Pamela Stein *A Practical Guide to Media Law* (2013) 64. Furthermore, for guidance on how to submit a request for information under PAIA, see 'PAIA resource kit: A guide to requesting information in terms of the Promotion of Access to Information Act 2 of 2000 (PAIA)', last accessed on 19 May 2018 from <http://foip.saha.org.za/uploads/images/PAIA_Resource_Kit%20(3).pdf>.

[20] A public body is defined in s 1 of PAIA as:
  (a) any department of state or administration in the national or provincial sphere of government or any municipality in the local sphere of government; or
  (b) any other functionary or institution when—
      (i) exercising a power or performing a duty in terms of the Constitution or a provincial constitution; or
      (ii) exercising a public power or performing a public function in terms of any legislation.

[21] A private body is defined in s 1 of PAIA as:
  (a) a natural person who carries or has carried on any trade, business or profession, but only in such capacity;
  (b) a partnership which carries or has carried on any trade, business or profession; or
  (c) any former or existing juristic person, but excludes a public body.

provide an explanation of why the requested record is required for the exercise or protection of that right. The right in question may be a contractual, statutory, delictual or constitutional right. The Constitutional Court has interpreted 'required' in this context to mean 'reasonably required'; in other words, the requester needs to establish a 'substantial advantage or element of need', but does not need to show absolute necessity.[22] Whether the record is required for the exercise or protection of a right will depend on the facts of each case.[23]

In *Clutchco*, the SCA warned that, in considering private body requests for information, the protection of private bodies should not be lightly disregarded:[24]

> The machinery established by legislation and the common law for the protection of shareholders is in my opinion not lightly to be disregarded. In enacting PAIA Parliament could not have intended that the books of a company, great or small, should be thrown open to members on a whiff of impropriety or on the ground that relatively minor errors or irregularities have occurred. A far more substantial foundation would be required.

This, however, should not in itself necessary be a deterrent to requesters seeking information from private bodies: all will depend on the facts. For instance, in the later decision of *Arcelormittal*[25] – in which various information was sought from the mining company relying on the right in s 24(a) of the Constitution that everyone has a right 'to an environment that is not harmful to their health or well-being'—the SCA stated as follows:[26]

> I am mindful of the caveat in *Clutchco* that one must guard against forcing corporates to throw open their books on claims of alleged minor errors or irregularities. The basis provided by [the Vaal Environmental Justice Alliance] for its application does not fall into the category of trivial or frivolous. It concerns us all.

As was noted in the *Arcelormittal* judgment, in determining whether the threshold requirement has been met, a court is entitled to consider both the basis provided in Form C on making the request, as well as the evidence adduced by the parties, including the affidavits filed in support of or resisting the application.[27] As such, while it is certainly desirable to provide as much information as possible in the initial request, it is possible to supplement the basis for requiring the information later.

Although the definitions of public bodies and private bodies are designed to be mutually exclusive—with the definition of a private body stating expressly that it

---

[22] *My Vote Counts NPC v Speaker of the National Assembly and Others* [2015] ZACC 31; 2016 (1) SA 132 (CC) para 31 [WW acted for the applicant]. The court went on to describe the standard as one that is 'accommodating, flexible and in its application fact-bound'.

[23] *Unitas Hospital v Van Wyk and Another* [2006] ZASCA 34; 2006 (4) SA 436 (SCA) para 6.

[24] *Clutchco (Pty) Ltd v Davis* [2005] ZASCA 16; 2005 (3) SA 486 (SCA) para 17.

[25] *Arcelormittal South Africa and Another v Vaal Environmental Justice Alliance* [2014] ZASCA 184; 2015 (1) SA 515 (SCA) [CER acted for Vaal Environmental Justice Alliance].

[26] Ibid para 80.

[27] Ibid para 51.

excludes a public body—it is not always so easy to determine whether a body is in fact public or private. Indeed, as noted in s 8(1)*(b)* of PAIA, a body may in one instance be a public body, and in another instance be a private body, depending on whether the record relates to the exercise of a power or performance of a function as a public body or as a private body.

In *Mittalsteel*,[28] the SCA endorsed both the 'control' and the 'function' test.[29] The court observed that, '[i]n an era in which privat[is]ation of public services and utilities has become commonplace, bodies may perform what is traditionally a government function without being subject to control by any of the spheres of government and may therefore, despite their independence from control, properly be classified as public bodies'.[30]

Also relevant in this regard is the High Court decision regarding the PAIA application made by M&G Media to the 2010 FIFA World Cup Local Organising Committee (LOC), regarding the tenders that had been advertised and awarded by the LOC.[31] The first PAIA request had been submitted on the basis that the LOC was a public body, which the LOC denied. The applicants then submitted a private body request in the alternative, while still maintaining that the LOC was a public body. The LOC refused this request as well.

The LOC was the body responsible for the operational matters pertaining to the 2010 soccer world cup. It had been registered as a public company in terms of s 21 of the Companies Act 61 of 1973, but was not listed on any exchange. Considering the *Mittalsteel* decision mentioned above, the court reiterated that:[32]

> [t]he case law therefore establishes that whether an institution qualifies as a 'public body' under PAIA will depend on the nature of the powers and functions it performs. Although the level of state control of these powers and functions may be relevant to the question of classification, it is not decisive.

In reaching its conclusion that the LOC was a public body, the court relied on the following criteria to determine the nature of the LOC: the relationship of coercion or power that the actor has in its capacity as a public institution; its impact on the

---

[28] *Mittalsteel South Africa Limited (previously known as Iscor Limited) v Hlatshwayo* [2006] ZASCA 93; 2007 (1) SA 66 (SCA) para 18, citing *Greater Johannesburg Transitional Metropolitan Council v Eskom* [1999] ZASCA 95; 2000 (1) SA 866 (SCA) para 12.

[29] Ibid para 19 where the SCA stated: 'The control test is useful in a situation when it is necessary to determine whether functions, which by their nature might as well be private functions, are performed under the control of the State and are thereby turned into public functions instead. This converts a body like a trading entity, normally a private body, into a public body for the time and to the extent that it carries out public functions.'

[30] Ibid para 22.

[31] *M&G Media Ltd and Others v 2010 FIFA World Cup Organising Committee South Africa Ltd and Another* [2010] ZAGPJHC 43; 2011 (5) SA 163 (GSJ) [WW acted for the applicants].

[32] Ibid para 158.

public; the source of the power; and whether there is a public interest need.[33] The court held *obiter* that, in any event, even if the LOC was a private body, M&G Media was still entitled to the records as the right to freedom of expression and the media qualified under the threshold test on the facts of the case and the records were required for the exercise and protection of these rights.[34]

The strategic approach adopted by the applicants in this litigation was to maintain the line of argument that the LOC was a public body, but to argue in the alternative that even if it was not, a case had been established that the information was required for the exercise or protection of a right. Such an approach may similarly work in other cases where there is uncertainty as to whether the body is a public body or a private body.

(b) Grounds for refusing to grant access to information

Once the procedural requirements have been met for submitting an access to information request—and, in the case of private bodies, the threshold requirement that the record is required for the exercise or protection of a right has been met as well—the record must be released unless there is a valid basis under PAIA to refuse to do so. PAIA stipulates the time periods within which a requester must be notified of a request being refused, which differs for public and private bodies. Where no response is provided within the prescribed time period, it is deemed to be a refusal.[35]

In broad terms, there are four general bases on which a request for information can be denied under PAIA. In terms of the first basis, PAIA expressly excludes certain records of particular public bodies or officials from its application. For instance, PAIA cannot be used to request a record for the purpose of criminal or civil proceedings after those proceedings have commenced,[36] or to obtain a record of Cabinet or its committees.[37]

Second, PAIA gives guidance on what is required when the record cannot be found or it does not exist.[38] In this regard, PAIA provides that in circumstances where all reasonable steps have been taken to find the requested record, and there

---

[33] *M&G* (note 31 above) para 187. These criteria were based on the minority judgment of Langa CJ in *Chirwa v Transnet Limited and Others* [2007] ZACC 23; 2008 (4) SA 367 (CC) para 186, in the context of determining whether a body was an organ of state as contemplated in the Promotion of Administrative Justice Act 4 of 2000 (PAJA).

[34] *M&G v FIFA World Cup Organising Committee* (note 31 above) para 389.

[35] Section 27 of PAIA in respect of public bodies; s 58 of PAIA in respect of private bodies.

[36] Section 7 of PAIA.

[37] In terms of s 12, PAIA does not apply to the following records: a record of Cabinet and its committees; a record relating to the judicial functions of a court or special tribunal or a judicial officer of such court or tribunal; a record of a member of Parliament or provincial legislature in that capacity; or a record relating to a decision under PAJA regarding the nomination, selection or appointment of a judicial officer or any other person by the Judicial Service Commission.

[38] Section 23 of PAIA in respect of public bodies; s 55 of PAIA in respect of private bodies.

are reasonable grounds to believe that the record either does not exist or that it is in the possession of the public or private body but cannot be found, the information officer must notify the requester by way of an affidavit or affirmation. It is not sufficient to merely state that the record does not exist or cannot be found; rather, the affidavit or affirmation must give a full account of all steps taken to find the record or determine whether it exists, including all communications with every person who conducted the search on behalf of the information officer. The requirement that the response must be provided under oath is an important one, and offers an important strategic lever if the matter proceeds to litigation. In particular, if there is reason to doubt the deponent and a consequent dispute of fact arises as to whether the record does indeed exist or can be found, litigants may seek a referral to oral evidence in terms of the Uniform Rules of Court to test the veracity of the deponent's version.

The third basis for denying access to information is contained in s 45 of PAIA. This provides that a public body is permitted to deny a request if it is either manifestly frivolous or vexatious, or if the work involved in processing the request would substantially and unreasonably divert the resources of the public body.[39]

The fourth basis for denying access to information is by far the most comprehensively dealt with in PAIA, and likely the most commonly encountered: the stipulated grounds for refusal listed under PAIA.[40] PAIA purports to distinguish between mandatory grounds of refusal—for which requests *must* be refused—and discretionary grounds of refusal—for which requests *may* be refused. However, as dealt with below, in practice there is a discretionary element to all of the listed grounds of refusal with the exception of SARS records as they are all still subject to the public interest override contained in ss 46 and 70 of PAIA that may favour disclosure.

The person refusing a request for information bears the burden of proving that the refusal is justified.[41] As the Constitutional Court explained in the *M&G Media* decision, '[e]xemptions are construed narrowly, and neither the mere *ipse dixit* of

---

[39] See, for instance, *South African History Archive Trust v South African Reserve Bank and Another*, Case No 5598/16 (19 March 2018).

[40] Sections 34–44 of PAIA in respect of public bodies; ss 64–9 in respect of private bodies. Some grounds of refusal apply to both public bodies and private bodies (although the wording of the respective sections is not necessarily identical), such as the grounds of refusal pertaining to the mandatory protection of the privacy of a third party who is a natural person; the mandatory protection of the safety of individuals and the protection of property; and the mandatory protection of privileged records in legal proceedings. Other grounds of refusal are only available to public bodies, such as the grounds of refusal pertaining to the mandatory protection of certain records of the South African Revenue Service; the defence, security and international relations or the economic interest and welfare of South Africa; and the commercial activities of public bodies.

[41] Section 81(3) of PAIA.

the information officer nor his or her recitation of the words of the statute is sufficient to discharge the burden borne by the state.'[42] The court further stated that:[43]

> The agency claiming the exemption can discharge its burden only by presenting the court with evidence that the information withheld falls within the exemption claimed, and such evidence should not be controverted by either contrary evidence on the record or evidence of bad faith on the part of the agency.
>
> The state may not rely on affidavits that are conclusory, merely repeat the language of the statute, or are founded upon sweeping and vague claims. Affidavits must describe the justification for nondisclosure with reasonably specific detail for the requester of information to be able to mount an effective case against the agency's claim for exemption.

For instance, in *Right2Know Campaign*,[44] the applicants wanted to know which places and areas were listed as national key points in terms of the National Key Points Act 102 of 1980. In response, the respondents sought to argue that beyond disclosing the number of national key points and certain general information pertaining to them, no further information could be appropriately disclosed because to do so would prejudice the security of the national key points and the country.[45] The court held that the respondents' articulation of their reasons did not pass the test set by Ngcobo CJ in the *M&G Media* decision, and that there had been no evidence disclosed in the papers to support the refusal.[46] As such, the court ordered the respondents to disclose the records.

(c) The public interest and the public domain
A crucial provision contained in PAIA is the public interest override.[47] This is triggered in circumstances where a ground of refusal has been established, but there are still prevailing considerations in the public interest that militate in favour of the information being disclosed. In terms of the public interest override, an information officer must grant a request for access to information if:

• the disclosure of the record would reveal evidence of either a substantial contravention of or failure to comply with the law, or an imminent and serious public safety or environmental risk; and
• the public interest in the disclosure of the record clearly outweighs the harm contemplated in the ground of refusal.

---

[42] *M&G Media* (note 4 above) para 22.

[43] Ibid paras 17–8.

[44] *Right2Know Campaign and Another v Minister of Police and Another* [2014] ZAGPJHC 343; [2015] 1 All SA 367 (GJ) [*M&G Media* was admitted as *amicus curiae*].

[45] Ibid paras 6–7.

[46] Ibid paras 16–17.

[47] Section 46 of PAIA in respect of public bodies; s 70 of PAIA in respect of private bodies.

There have only been a handful of cases that have grappled with the ambit and threshold set by the public interest override. In *Qoboshiyane*,[48] the SCA stated that 'the exercise that an information officer must undertake under s 46 is a careful balancing, on the facts of the particular case, of the harm that would accrue from permitting disclosure of the record and the public interest in its disclosure. In other words the enquiry in every case is a fact-sensitive one, the outcome of which will vary from case to case depending on the particular facts'.

Information that is already in the public domain is a further relevant consideration favouring disclosure. In *BHP Billiton*,[49] Billiton argued that the requested information contained pricing formulae, and therefore relied on the mandatory protection of commercial information of a third party as its grounds for refusal.[50] The argument by Billiton was that the pricing information requested was ordinarily unavailable to competitors, and that disclosure would harm its financial and commercial interests.[51] However, it later transpired that a significant amount of the information sought was already publicly available to Billiton's competitors.[52] Accordingly, in ultimately ordering disclosure, the SCA held: 'In the circumstances, if the information of the kind described above is already in the public domain . . . I do not see how giving access to it would result in the perceived harm to Billiton. The harm relied on by Billiton is not of the kind that would be "likely" to occur or "reasonably" be expected to occur.'[53]

(d) Internal appeals and the new role of the Information Regulator

The Protection of Personal Information Act 4 of 2013 (POPIA) creates a new statutory body: the Information Regulator, which has duties and functions in terms of both PAIA and POPIA.[54] The schedule of amendments in POPIA provides for extensive changes to PAIA, including an amendment to the definition of 'personal information' to align PAIA and POPIA with each other. The Information Regulator also replaces the South African Human Rights Commission (SAHRC) as the body responsible for the oversight and implementation of PAIA, although the SAHRC retains its mandate to promote access to information.

One of the most important amendments is that the Information Regulator will have jurisdiction to adjudicate a complaint regarding a refusal of a request for information. In terms of the new s 77A of PAIA, a requester may submit a

---

[48] *Qoboshiyane NO and Others v Avusa Publishing Eastern Cape (Pty) Ltd and Others* [2012] ZASCA 166; 2013 (3) SA 315 (SCA).

[49] *BHP Billiton PLC Inc and Another v De Lange and Others* [2013] ZASCA 11; 2013 (3) SA 571 (SCA).

[50] Sections 36(1)*(b)*, 36(1)*(c)* and 37(1)*(a)* of PAIA.

[51] *BHP Billiton* (note 49 above) para 27.

[52] Ibid.

[53] Ibid para 28.

[54] Section 39*(c)* of POPIA.

complaint to the Information Regulator only once the internal appeal procedure of a public body has been exhausted. In respect of private bodies, where there is no internal appeal procedure, the Information Regulator may be approached once the decision from the information officer of the private body has been received.[55] Requesters have 180 days from the date of the decision to lodge a complaint with the Information Regulator.

On receipt of a complaint, the Information Regulator may investigate the complaint in the prescribed manner; refer the complaint to the Enforcement Committee established in terms of s 50 of POPIA; or decide to take no action or require no further action.[56]

The amended s 78 of PAIA provides that a requester or third party may only apply to a court for relief after the internal appeal procedure referred to in s 74 has been exhausted, or after the requester or third party has exhausted the complaints procedure referred to in s 77A. A requester or third party that is aggrieved by a decision of the Information Regulator has 180 days to apply to court for relief against that decision.

At the time of writing, these amendments have not yet come into force. However, the role of the Information Regulator provides a new opportunity for disputes regarding PAIA requests to be settled without resorting to litigation, which can be time-consuming and costly, as discussed in the next section. On the other hand, if the Information Regulator process is not efficient, it will add an additional layer to PAIA litigation, which will further exacerbate the delays in being provided with information which ought to be released to requesters.

13.3 LITIGATING ACCESS TO INFORMATION REQUESTS

(a) Burden of proof

Proceedings under PAIA are civil proceedings made on application,[57] and the rules of evidence in civil procedure—including resolving disputes of fact on a balance

---

[55] In this regard, s 77A(2) of PAIA (as amended by POPIA) states as follows:

A requester—

(*a*) that has been unsuccessful in an internal appeal to the relevant authority of a public body;

(*b*) aggrieved by a decision of the relevant authority of a public body to disallow the late lodging of an internal appeal in terms of section 75(2);

(*c*) aggrieved by a decision of the information officer of a public body referred to in paragraph (*b*) of the definition of 'public body' in section 1—

(i) to refuse a request for access; or

(ii) taken in terms of section 22, 26(1) or 29(3); or

(*d*) aggrieved by a decision of the head of a private body—

(i) to refuse a request for access; or

(ii) taken in terms of section 54, 57(1) or 60,

may within 180 days of the decision, submit a complaint, alleging that the decision was not in compliance with [PAIA], to the Information Regulator in the prescribed manner and form for appropriate relief.

[56] Section 77C(1) of PAIA (as amended by POPIA).

[57] Section 81(1) of PAIA.

of probabilities—apply.[58] However, the Constitutional Court has emphasised that proceedings under PAIA differ from ordinary civil proceedings in certain key aspects, including that such disputes involve a constitutional right of access to information; that access to information disputes are generally not purely private disputes, as requesters often act in the public interest; and that parties to access to information disputes may be constrained by factors beyond their control in presenting and challenging evidence.[59]

In proceedings under PAIA, a court is not limited to reviewing the decisions of the information officer or the officer who undertook the internal appeal; it decides the claim of exemption from disclosure afresh, and is required to engage in a reconsideration of the merits.[60] The Constitutional Court has held that the question of whether the information put forward is sufficient to place the record within the exemption claimed will be determined by the nature of the exemption; as stated by the Constitutional Court: 'The question is not whether the best evidence to justify refusal has been provided. If the information provided is sufficient for the court to conclude, on the probabilities, that the record falls within the exemption claimed, then the state has discharged its burden under section 81(3).'[61]

The burden of proof for a refusal of a request rests with the party refusing the request.[62] PAIA applications create a tension that needs to be manoeuvred. On the one hand, PAIA requires that a refusal of a request for information must exclude any reference to the content of the record from the reasons.[63] However, in certain circumstances, it is conceivable that this may lead to a bare denial, which is normally not sufficient to raise a genuine dispute of fact. Accordingly, as the Constitutional Court has noted, courts should approach such disputes mindful of both the disadvantage that the requester is at in challenging the evidence, and the restraints placed on the party holding the information.[64] As discussed next, one way in which the courts are able to manage this tension is through the exercise of a judicial peek.

(b) Judicial peeks
A judicial peek is a particular procedure created under s 80 of PAIA, in terms of which a court hearing an application may independently review the record to

---

[58] Section 81(2) of PAIA.

[59] *M&G Media* (note 4 above) para 33.

[60] Ibid para 14.

[61] Ibid para 25.

[62] Section 81(3)*(a)* of PAIA.

[63] Sections 25(3)*(b)* and 77(5)*(b)* of PAIA.

[64] *M&G Media* (note 4 above) para 36.

assess whether the ground of refusal claimed is a valid basis to deny access.[65] While s 80 does not in itself entitle the requester to have sight of the record, it does empower a court to receive ex parte representations and conduct its hearings in camera.

The Constitutional Court has cautioned that the discretionary power under s 80 was drafted as an override provision—one that may be applied despite the other provisions of PAIA and any other law—and as such should be used sparingly.[66] A court should not use its power under s 80 as a substitute for the holder of the information laying a proper basis for its refusal.[67]

As set out above, at the crux of the *M&G Media* decision before the Constitutional Court was whether the High Court should have taken a judicial peek at the record before ordering the disclosure. The majority concluded that it would indeed have been in the interests of justice for s 80 to have been invoked, and accordingly remitted the matter. Several considerations led the majority to this conclusion.[68] First, the majority was cognisant of the SCA's finding that refusal of the record might have been justified, but that this had not been established by acceptable evidence. Second, the Presidency had alleged that it could not provide more detailed reasons because of the requirement under PAIA that a refusal must exclude any reference to the content of the record from its reasons. Third, the Presidency had asserted that the report was not severable, and the validity of this assertion could not be assessed without having regard to the content of the report.

The minority, per Cameron J, disagreed. According to the minority, the Presidency had failed to justify its refusal of the record or to provide a plausible basis

---

[65] Section 80 of PAIA provides as follows:

(1) Despite this Act and any other law, any court hearing an application, or an appeal against a decision on that application, may examine any record of a public or private body to which this Act applies, and no such record may be withheld from the court on any grounds.

(2) Any court contemplated in subsection (1) may not disclose to any person, including the parties to the proceedings concerned, other than the public or private body referred to in subsection (1)—

(a) any record of a public or private body which, on a request for access, may or must be refused in terms of this Act; or

(b) if the information officer of a public body, or the relevant authority of that body on internal appeal, in refusing to grant access to a record in terms of section 39(3) or 41(4), refuses to confirm or deny the existence or non-existence of the record, any information as to whether the record exists.

(3) Any court contemplated in subsection (1) may—

(a) receive representations ex parte;

(b) conduct hearings in camera; and

(c) prohibit the publication of such information in relation to the proceedings as the court determines, including information in relation to the parties to the proceedings and the contents of orders made by the court in the proceedings.

[66] *M&G Media* (note 4 above) paras 39 and 42.

[67] Ibid para 49.

[68] Ibid paras 54–66; see also *Right2Know Campaign* (note 46 above) para 14.

that PAIA made it impossible to provide adequate reasons for the refusal.[69] The minority opined that the s 80 power should only be invoked where the government had laid a plausible foundation for its hands being tied, or where it had laid such a basis but the court determining the matter doubted the validity of this claim.[70]

In *Right2Know Campaign*, heard subsequently, the High Court had cause to apply the test laid down by the Constitutional Court to determine whether it should invoke its s 80 powers to look at the list of national key points before determining whether or not to grant disclosure. As noted in the judgment, counsel for the state respondents had conceded in argument that there was no evidential material disclosed in the papers to support the refusal. The respondents nevertheless invited the court to take a judicial peek at the record, without providing any substantiation for why the court should do so. This, the court stated, 'veered towards the peek being used merely to perform the very exercise which the respondents were obliged to undertake . . . That expectation is inappropriate.'[71]

As such, in declining to take a judicial peek, the High Court held that[72]

[T]he idea of a peek in this particular case is inapposite because no case is attempted to justify its need, and it is plain that because of the grave policy considerations that attend upon its use, it is never available for the asking, but must be seriously motivated as the only appropriate mechanism to avert a failure of justice.

As explained by the court, appropriate circumstances in favour of a judicial peek would include, for instance, where the holder of the information has indicated that it was prevented from discharging its burden under s 81(3) of PAIA because of the provisions of PAIA; or where the probabilities are evenly balanced and the doubt as to the validity of the exemptions claimed are due to the limitation placed on the parties to adduce evidence.[73]

(c) *Amici curiae*

While the important role of *amici curiae* generally has been dealt with in chapter 4 of this volume, it nevertheless bears mention that *amici curiae* have been shown to be of significant benefit in access to information litigation. This can include through providing context or comparative positions; highlighting the impact that the matter has on a particular grouping of persons, such as members of the media where the main parties are not journalists or media houses; or assisting the court in assessing how competing interests may be balanced. For instance, in *M&G Centre v Minister of Public Works*—a case involving a request for information about the security upgrades that were made to former President Jacob Zuma's private home

---

[69] *M&G Media* (note 4 above) para 79.

[70] Ibid.

[71] *Right2Know Campaign* (note 46 above) para 20.

[72] Ibid para 21.

[73] Ibid para 13.

in Nkandla—the South African History Archive was admitted as *amicus curiae* to, as described in the judgment, 'provide statistics on research conducted by it on requests for information and to assist the court in appreciating the developing trend, the pervasive culture of secrecy which impacts on the implementation of PAIA and the enjoyment of the [c]onstitutional right of access to information'.[74] Such interventions can be of great assistance to the court and to the main parties seeking to give meaningful effect to the right of access to information.

(d) Challenges in litigating access to information requests
Two of the key challenges in litigating access to information requests are that there can be lengthy delays and it can be costly. Often, the time-value of the information is lost through delays caused by the non-responsiveness of the holders of the information and through the duration of the litigation. Indeed, even where the matter ultimately results in a victory for the requester, the impact can be significantly restricted when this victory only arises several years later, after it has been through the gauntlet of appeal processes. This can impede the public interest impact where the objective of the litigation was to publicise the requested information or to vindicate rights.

Section 195(1)*(f)* of the Constitution provides that '[t]ransparency must be fostered by providing the public with timely, accessible and accurate information'.[75] Undue delays occasioned by the mechanism created under PAIA are inimical to this requirement, and do not serve either the right of access to information or the public interest. In this regard, to truly give effect to this stipulation, both public and private bodies should be encouraged—and, in appropriate circumstances, required—to promote access to information through voluntary disclosures and by making certain records automatically available.[76]

Aligned to this are the significant legal and other costs that a requester can accumulate during the litigation proceedings. Under the ordinary prescribed tariffs, even where a successful litigant is awarded costs as part of the court order, this will not be sufficient to cover the full total of the costs incurred. However, as a mark of displeasure, it is now well established for courts to award punitive costs orders against holders of information who have acted 'obdurately and unreasonably' in refusing to furnish information.[77] There is also the potential for a *de bonis propriis* costs order to be issued in specific circumstances.

---

[74] *M&G Centre for Investigative Journalism and Another v Minister of Public Works and Another* [2014] ZAGPPHC 226 para 19 [WW acted for the applicants].

[75] See the application of this provision to PAIA in *Brümmer* (note 14 above) para 62; *AVUSA Publishing Eastern Cape (Pty) Ltd v Qoboshiyane NO and Others* [2011] ZAECPEHC 42; 2012 (1) SA 158 (ECP) para 46.

[76] This is already contemplated to some extent under PAIA: s 15 of PAIA for public bodies; s 52 of PAIA for private bodies.

[77] *Claase v Information Officer, South African Airways (Pty) Ltd* [2006] ZASCA 163; 2007 (5) 469 (SCA) para 11; *M&G Centre for Investigative Journalism NPC and Another v Minister of Defence and Military Veterans and Another* [2017] ZAGPPHC 195 [WW acted for the applicants].

It is hoped that the Information Regulator will play a key role in ensuring more effective and efficient access to information to requesters and alleviate some of the burden that PAIA has placed on requesters thus far.

13.4 OTHER MEANS OF ACCESSING INFORMATION

In some instances, PAIA may not be the quickest or most effective way to access information. Notably, various pieces of legislation contain provisions granting rights of access to particular types of information. These include, for instance, s 26 of the Companies Act 71 of 2008 (2008 Companies Act); s 110 of the Labour Relations Act 66 of 1995; ss 142 and 145 of the National Water Act 36 of 1998; and ss 21, 28 and 30 of the Mineral and Petroleum Resources Development Act 28 of 2002.

In *Nova Property Group Holdings v Cobbett*,[78] the SCA was called on to adjudicate a request for a securities register sought in terms of s 26 of the 2008 Companies Act, and in particular, on the interplay between s 26 of the 2008 Companies Act and PAIA. The SCA confirmed that the right of access contained in s 26(2) of the 2008 Companies Act is additional to the rights conferred by PAIA, and need not be exercised in accordance with PAIA.[79] Furthermore, with reference to s 26(4)(*c*) of the 2008 Companies Act, the SCA noted that a requester has the option of choosing between the procedural alternatives of relying on s 26 or relying on PAIA to request the information sought.[80] As noted by the SCA:[81]

> The approach of Parliament, in this regard, was eminently sensible. PAIA is a general statute. It regulates access to innumerable types of information held by a wide range of bodies, with various different types of interests at stake. Parliament, therefore, had to lay down general rules to balance the competing interests at stake by means of threshold requirements, grounds of refusal and public interest overrides. By contrast, s 26(2) confers a specific right in respect of one type of information only—securities registers and directors registers. Parliament justifiably took the view that, in respect of this narrow category of information, it was unnecessary to build in the PAIA balances and counter balances with all the complexity and delay that might entail. Instead, it conferred an unqualified right that is capable of prompt vindication.

Court proceedings are another key mechanism that can be used to access information. Section 32 of the Superior Courts Act 10 of 2013 provides that court proceedings are generally carried out in open court (although there are certain exceptions to this). Furthermore, while PAIA does not apply to a record requested for the purpose of criminal or civil proceedings or where the request is made after such proceedings have commenced, the Uniform Rules of Court do provide for

---

[78] *Nova Property Group Holdings v Cobbett* [2016] ZASCA 63; 2016 (4) SA 317 (SCA) [M&G Centre for Investigative Journalism was admitted as *amicus curiae*, represented by WW].

[79] Ibid para 19.

[80] Ibid para 20.

[81] Ibid para 21.

such disclosure. For instance, rule 35 of the Uniform Rules of Court provides for the discovery, inspection and production of documents during litigation; and rule 53 of the Uniform Rules of Court provides for the record of a decision to be made available in judicial review applications. The SCA has confirmed that the right of open justice must include the right to have access to papers and written arguments, on the basis that these are an integral part of court proceedings and that the public would not be in a position to properly assess the legitimacy or fairness of proceedings if they were denied access to the documents that provide the basis for the court's decision.[82]

13.5 DOES THE CURRENT FRAMEWORK GIVE EFFECT TO THE RIGHT OF ACCESS TO INFORMATION?

The question of the disclosure of sources of political party funding has brought the effectiveness and adequacy of PAIA directly to the fore. In *My Vote Counts*,[83] the applicant's argument before the Constitutional Court was that PAIA failed to require the disclosure of party funding, and that in failing to do so, Parliament had in turn failed to fulfil its obligation in terms of s 32 of the Constitution when enacting PAIA.[84] However, relying on the doctrine of separation of powers and the principle of subsidiarity, the majority of the court held that the applicant's failure to challenge the constitutional validity of PAIA was fatal to the application, and accordingly dismissed the application.

This resulted in a fresh iteration of the case before the High Court in Cape Town. In these proceedings, the applicant sought a declaration that information about the private funding of political parties and independent candidates registered for elections was reasonably required for the effective exercise of the political rights contained in s 19 of the Constitution. The applicant further argued that PAIA was inconsistent with the Constitution and invalid insofar as it did not allow for the continuous and systematic recordal and disclosure of private funding information.

The High Court agreed with the applicant that the information sought was indeed required for the exercise of the right to vote.[85] The High Court noted that, while s 32(1) of the Constitution gives a right of access to information, the ambit of PAIA is restricted to recorded information, and therefore information can be

---

[82] *City of Cape Town v South African National Roads Authority Limited and Others* [2015] ZASCA 58; 2015 (3) SA 386 (SCA) para 19 [12 organisations, including Right2Know Campaign, Section 16, Open Democracy Advice Centre, M&G Centre for Investigative Journalism, South African National Editors' Forum, Legal Resources Centre (LRC), Section27, Socio-Economic Rights Institute of South Africa, Corruption Watch, Democratic Governance and Rights Institute and South African History Archive, were admitted as *amici curiae*, represented by LRC].

[83] *My Vote Counts* (note 22 above).

[84] Ibid para 19.

[85] *My Vote Counts NPC v President of the Republic of South Africa and Others* [2017] ZAWCHC 105; 2017 (6) SA 501 (WCC) para 30 [WW acted for the applicant].

deleted, destroyed or never recorded without falling foul of PAIA.[86] Furthermore, political parties may rely on an exemption under PAIA, giving voters the arduous task of meeting the test for the public interest override.[87]

Accordingly, the High Court concluded that PAIA's limitation of ss 19 and 32 of the Constitution was unjustifiable, therefore rendering PAIA unconstitutional and invalid insofar as it did not allow for the disclosure of information about private funding of political parties.[88] However, while the High Court concluded that it could order disclosure, it stopped short of ordering the disclosure to be 'continuous and systematic', finding that to be in the remit of Parliament to determine.[89]

The order was referred to the Constitutional Court for confirmation in terms of s 172(2) of the Constitution. In an important judgment—one that will have significant implications for the right of access to information during elections and regarding private body access more broadly—the Constitutional Court unanimously confirmed the declaration of invalidity, declaring that: (i) information on the private funding of political parties and independent candidates is essential for the effective exercise of the right to make political choices and to participate in the elections; (ii) information on private funding of political parties and independent candidates must be recorded, preserved and made reasonably accessible; and (iii) PAIA is invalid to the extent of its inconsistency with the Constitution by failing to provide for the recordal, preservation and reasonable disclosure of information on the private funding of political parties and independent candidates. [90]

As noted by the Constitutional Court, '[b]y its very nature, the proper exercise of the right to vote is largely dependent on information',[91] and that '[a]ll information necessary to enlighten the electorate about the capabilities and dependability or otherwise of those seeking public office must not only be compulsorily captured and preserved but also made reasonably accessible.'[92]

Although the majority judgment declined to expressly declare that the recordal of information must be 'continuous and systematic'—opting instead to leave this to be determined by Parliament[93]—the separate concurrence (per Froneman J) took a different view. In this regard, Froneman J noted that while he agreed that there was no necessity for the order to explicitly record the constitutional obligation as being systematic and continuous, this was not borne out of concerns regarding separation of powers; rather, it was because '[i]t would simply be

---

[86] *My Vote Counts v President* (note 85 above) paras 58–9.

[87] Ibid paras 61–2.

[88] Ibid para 69.

[89] Ibid para 70.

[90] *My Vote Counts NPC v Minister of Justice and Correctional Services and Another* [2018] ZACC 17 para 91 [WW acted for the applicant].

[91] Ibid para37.

[92] Ibid para 39.

[93] Ibid para 80.

irrational not to do it systematically and on a continuous basis.'[94] Notably, political party funding is just one facet of the broader access to information considerations during elections, with the other aspects likely to garner similar attention in due course; it is undeniable that access to accurate, credible and reliable information about a wide range of issues prior, during and after elections is indispensable for citizens to meaningfully exercise the right to vote and for elections to be free and fair.[95]

Furthermore, in addition to these matters, there remain a number of under-litigated provisions under PAIA. Two issues that are in need of further guidance—either from the legislature or the courts—include issues pertaining to voluntary disclosures, and the threshold required by the public interest override. Private sector accountability for non-disclosure also remains a key issue. And, in the digital age with increasing amounts of information being placed online, for instance in databases, it is unclear whether PAIA is equipped to appropriately address such requests, either in terms of access or in terms of the information itself.

PAIA is certainly both comprehensive and important. Access to information is a crucial site of public interest lawyering, be it in cases to secure the release of information in the public interest for its own sake or in matters where access to information serves to vindicate other rights or the rule of law. However, requesters may also find PAIA to be draconian in its complexity, resulting in delays that hinder rather than foster the right of access to information. That said, in the absence of PAIA being reformed, much of the difficulty being experienced currently can be alleviated by holders of information more readily embracing the spirit in which PAIA was intended, and displaying a willingness to realise the right of access to information through better and quicker disclosures.

---

[94] Ibid para 94.

[95] See African Commission on Human and Peoples' Rights, Guidelines on access to information and elections in Africa, 2017, last accessed on 25 May 2018 from <http://www.achpr.org/files/special-mechanisms/freedom-of-expression/guidelines_on_access_to_informa-tion_and_elections_in_africa_eng.pdf>.

Chapter 14

PUBLIC INTEREST LITIGATION AND PRISONERS' RIGHTS

Clare Ballard and Frances Hobden

14.1 INTRODUCTION

Despite the robust and comprehensive standard of protection introduced by the Bill of Rights and constitutional legislation, the South African corrections system falters in the face of prison overcrowding, mismanagement, ill treatment of inmates, and its inability timeously to process applications for release on parole. The Department of Correctional Services (DCS) strives—but frequently fails—to achieve effective and humane incarceration of inmates, rehabilitation, and the social reintegration of offenders. The first democratic administration inherited overcrowded prisons with aging infrastructure and a correctional system structurally unequipped to fulfil the new range of prisoner rights. Since then, an increasing population, inadequate human resource capacity and a lack of prompt maintenance of facilities have prevented the full realisation of prisoner rights for inmates in South African prisons.

The plight of prisoners has not enjoyed the groundswell of popular support within civil society seen in other areas over the last 20 years. The lack of public will and the absence of a focused and strategic public interest litigation (PIL) strategy, resulted in sporadic litigation brought by and on behalf of inmates that has expanded and given practical content to legislated prisoner rights and compelled performance of the state's positive constitutional obligations.

In this chapter, we examine the role of litigation in the protection, promotion, and fulfilment of prisoners' rights through a discussion of the following subjects:

(i) the constitutional rights of prisoners;
(ii) litigation relating to prison conditions consistent with human dignity, including in relation to accommodation, amenities and sanitation, health and medical treatment, and education;
(iii) litigation relating to the protection and fulfilment of other prisoners' rights, such as voting, privacy, just administrative action and parole; and
(iv) challenges within the penal reform and criminal justice sector.

14.2 THE CONSTITUTIONAL RIGHTS OF PRISONERS

The Constitution assumes the power of the state to impose punishment as part of the criminal justice system[1] but limits this power in three ways. The first limitation concerns the lawful basis for punishment; the second, the extent to which incarceration may limit rights of prisoners; and the third concerns the rights of all detained persons. We discuss each of these constitutional limitations in turn.

First, punishment can only be imposed pursuant to courts imposing a sentence and following a fair criminal trial.[2] It follows, for example, that punishment may not be imposed for breach of a law that does not constitute a crime, such as breach of certain immigration regulations.

Second, in respect of custodial sentences, the Constitution reinforces the common-law *residuum* principle that imprisonment should limit only those rights necessary to secure incarceration.[3] Prisoners 'are entitled to all their personal rights not temporally taken away by law or necessarily inconsistent with the

---

[1] Section 12(1)*(e)* of the Constitution, for example, confers an expansive power on the state to punish, save that which results in individuals being tortured or 'treated or punished in a cruel, inhuman or degrading way'. This sets a relatively high threshold for restrictions on the state's power to punish. (See also the reference to sentenced prisoners in s 35(2)*(e)* and 35(3)).

[2] Section 35.

[3] *Whittaker v Roos & Bateman; Morant v Roos & Bateman* 1912 AD 92 (*Bateman*); and *Minister of Justice v Hofmeyr* [1993] ZASCA 40; 1993 (3) SA 131 (A).This dictum, known as the *residuum* principle, has been endorsed in subsequent decisions of the Constitutional Court and SCA. In *S v Makwanyane* [1995] ZACC 3; 1995 (3) SA 391 (CC) [LRC acted for the applicants; LHR, CALS and the Society for the Abolition of the Death Penalty were admitted as *amici curiae*], Chaskalson P affirmed the application of the *residuum* principle in the constitutional context. At para 142, he said:

circumstances in which they had been placed'.[4] Any limitation of prisoners' rights arising from the imposition of punishment must be imposed by legislation, either expressly or by necessary implication,[5] and must meet the requirements of the limitations clause of the Constitution.[6] This is echoed in the Correctional Services Act 111 of 1998 (Correctional Services Act), which empowers and requires the DCS to take the necessary steps to ensure the safe custody of every inmate and to maintain security and good order in every correctional centre. The Correctional Services Act seeks to balance the rights of inmates with the steps necessary to achieve these goals through a number of careful restrictions. Any limitation on the rights of personal integrity and privacy must be 'reasonably necessary'[7] and the application of duties and restrictions must conform to their purpose and must not affect the inmates to a greater degree, or for a longer period than necessary.[8] Rights may not be limited for disciplinary or other purposes.[9]

Third, the Constitution and the Correctional Services Act make specific provision for the rights of detained people. Section 35(2)(a) to (d) of the Constitution ensures that a detained person can obtain the necessary information and advice to challenge the lawfulness of his or her detention. Every detainee has the right to be informed promptly of the reason for being detained, to have access to a legal representative of his or her choice, or to be assigned a legal representative at state expense in certain circumstances, and to challenge his or her detention in court.

A person, once detained, has the right to be held in 'conditions . . . that are consistent with human dignity, including at least exercise and the provision, at state expense, of adequate accommodation, nutrition, reading material and medical treatment'.[10] This includes access to their spouse, next of kin, religious counsellor, or doctor.[11] Chapter 3 of the Correctional Services Act, coupled with

---

'Dignity is inevitably impaired by imprisonment or any other punishment, and the undoubted power of the state to impose punishment as part of the criminal justice system, necessarily involves the power to encroach upon a prisoner's dignity. But a prisoner does not lose all his or her rights on entering prison. Imprisonment is a severe punishment, but prisoners retain all the rights to which every person is entitled under Chapter 3 subject only to limitations imposed by the prison regime that are justifiable under section 33.' See also *Minister of Correctional Services and Others v Kwakwa and Another* [2002] ZASCA 17; 2002 (1) SACR 705 (SCA) para 36.

[4] *Whittaker* (note 3 above) 123.

[5] *Thukwane v Minister of Correctional Services and Others* 2003 (1) SA 51 (T) para 22.

[6] Section 36 of the Constitution.

[7] Section 26 provides that these rights are 'subject to the limitations reasonably necessary to ensure the security of the community, the safety of correctional officials and the safe custody of all inmates'.

[8] Section 4(2)(b). Section 22(1) provides: 'Discipline and order must be maintained with firmness but in no greater measure than is necessary for security purposes and good order in correctional centre.'

[9] Section 4(2)(c).

[10] Section 35(2)(e).

[11] Section 35(2) provides:
'Everyone who is detained, including every sentenced prisoner, has the right—

the Correctional Services Regulations,[12] gives further detail to this right and sets the minimum standards for accommodation, exercise, nutrition, contact with the community, health care and recreation.[13] Detention is also regulated by internal policy documents, 'B Orders,' issued by the National Commissioner in terms of s 134(2) of the Correctional Services Act.

In addition to these domestic rights and obligations, inmates in South African prisons are protected by the provisions of the United Nations Convention Against Torture and Other Cruel, Inhuman or Degrading Treatment or Punishment (UNCAT)[14] as well as several guideline documents setting out standards for treatment of people in custody.[15] In *Kwakwa*, the court summed up the correct approach to prisoner rights as follows:

> In section 35 of the Bill of Rights the rights of all detained persons are spelt out in detail. The manner in which we treat our prisoners should not be out of line with the values on which the Constitution is based. Human dignity and the advancement of human rights and freedom and respect for the rule of law are not just hollow phrases. They must be made real.[16]

   (a) to be informed promptly of the reason for being detained;
   (b) to choose, and to consult with, a legal practitioner, and to be informed of this right promptly;
   (c) to have a legal practitioner assigned to the detained person by the state and at state expense, if substantial injustice would otherwise result, and to be informed of this right promptly;
   (d) to challenge the lawfulness of the detention in person before a court and, if the detention is unlawful, to be released;
   (e) to conditions of detention that are consistent with human dignity, including at least exercise and the provision, at state expense, of adequate accommodation, nutrition, reading material and medical treatment; and
   (f) to communicate with, and be visited by, that person's—
       (i) spouse or partner;
       (ii) next of kin;
       (iii) chosen religious counsellor; and
       (iv) chosen medical practitioner.'
       Correctional Services Regulations GN R914 in *GG* 22626 of 30 July 2004 (Correctional Services Regulations).

[13] Chapter 2 of the Correctional Services Regulations and ss 3–7 of the Correctional Services Regulations. Detained children have additional rights, which include but also go beyond those enjoyed by all detained persons. Section 19 provides specifically that children are entitled to educational and recreational programmes, social and psychological services, religious care and, where practicable, additional visitation opportunities. In addition, their specific accommodation and nutritional requirements must be met. (See, s 7 of the Correctional Services Act and s 4(1)*(c)* of the Correctional Services Regulations.

[14] United Nations Convention against Torture and Other Cruel, Inhuman or Degrading Treatment or Punishment 1465 UNTS 85, adopted 10 December 1984, entered into force 26 June 1987. South Africa ratified the UNCAT on 10 December 1998.

[15] United Nations *Standard Minimum Rules for the Treatment of Prisoners*, adopted on 30 August 1955, UN Doc A/Conf/611, annex I, ESC res 663C (*Standard Minimum Rules for the Treatment of Prisoners*); ICRC *International Red Cross Handbook* (2012).

[16] *Kwakwa* (note 3 above) para 33.

14.3 LITIGATION RELATING TO PRISON CONDITIONS CONSISTENT WITH HUMAN DIGNITY

Prisoner rights litigation most commonly seeks to secure conditions of dignity for prisoners in fulfilment of s 35(2)*(e)* of the Constitution.[17] In many cases, these rights are protected and advanced through delictual actions or challenges to the administrative decisions of prison authorities. In this section we discuss the public interest cases that have relied directly on s 35(2)*(e)* of the Constitution to challenge prison conditions.

(a) Accommodation, access to amenities and sanitation

The recent case of *Sonke Gender Justice*[18] is a prominent example of a direct challenge to the conditions of incarceration of inmates in terms of s 35(2)*(e)*. The applicants provided the Western Cape High Court with extensive evidence of severe overcrowding and inhuman prison conditions at Pollsmoor Remand Facility in Cape Town. The court declared that the state had failed to provide the inmates with exercise, nutrition, accommodation, ablution facilities and health care services to the standard required by the Correctional Services Act and that the failure was inconsistent with the Constitution. The court handed down supervisory directions requiring the state to compile a comprehensive plan addressing the constitutional violations identified in the judgment and reduce dramatically the level of overcrowding within six months.[19]

In *Strydom*,[20] the court considered whether a prisoner's right to access electricity for the purposes of enjoying privileges that need electricity (such as television) was required in order for the conditions of detention to be consistent with human dignity. The court found that, although '[a]ccess to electricity can never be said to be a necessity of life', for prisoners who faced the long-term reality of spending 18 and a half hours each day in what was, in effect, 'solitary confinement . . . it could be an amenity of life that makes the difference between mental stability and derangement'.[21] The court also found that denying access to electricity in this context could furthermore materially affect the applicant's prospects of rehabilita-

---

[17] See generally, Pierre de Vos 'Prisoners' rights litigation in South Africa since 1994: A critical evaluation.' (2005) 16 *LDD* 89 and Rudolph Jansen & Emily Tendayi Achiume 'Prison conditions in South Africa and the role of public interest litigation since 1994' (2011) 27 *SAJHR* 183.

[18] *Sonke Gender Justice v Government of the Republic of South Africa and Another* (HC) unreported case 24087/15 of 23 February 2017 [LHR acted for the applicant].

[19] Another unreported matter of relevance is *Centre for Child Law v Minister of Correctional Services and Others* (HC) unreported case 15269/2010 [CCL was the applicant]. The court was approached on an urgent basis and presented with evidence of breaches of the Correctional Services Act as well as the Child Justice Act 75 of 2008 in relation to the treatment of children at Westville Prison. The interim order, although not a declaration of constitutional breach, directed that the prison comply immediately with certain conditions. These conditions mirror the statutory requirements in respect of visitation, meals, and access to amenities.

[20] *Strydom v Minister of Correctional Services and Others* 1999 (3) BCLR 342 (W).

[21] Ibid para 15.

tion and concluded that 'to deprive them entirely and in perpetuity of this prospect could also result in their being "treated and punished in a cruel or degrading manner" or their being detained in conditions that are inconsistent with human dignity.'[22]

In *Kwakwa*, the Supreme Court of Appeal (SCA) drew on s 35(2)(*e*) of the Constitution and the *residuum* principle in determining that a privilege system established by the National Commissioner that involved removing the use of certain amenities and facilities, such as the use of radio equipment, contact visits, access to library facilities and the use of musical instruments, was inconsistent with the core values of the Constitution and, accordingly, the statutory regime from which he derived his powers.[23]

(b) Health and medical treatment

In the *Sonke Gender Justice* matter the High Court declared that insufficient medical staffing (leading to delayed treatment), the poor turnaround of medication dispensing and conditions of detention conducive to the spreading of disease were, indeed, a violation of s 35(2)(*e*).

In *Van Biljon*,[24] the central issue was whether the applicants (and other HIV-infected prisoners) who had reached the 'symptomatic stage' of HIV/AIDS were entitled to antiretroviral treatment in prison at the state's expense. Brand J rejected the idea that prisoners were not entitled to better medical treatment than ordinary citizens under s 35(2)(*e*) of the Constitution. On the contrary, the court pointed out that s 35(2)(*e*) provides greater protection to detainees than it does to the general population. Moreover, the fact that prisoners are kept in conditions that render them more susceptible to infection meant that the state must provide them with treatment 'better able to improve their immune systems than that which the state provided for HIV patients outside'.[25] The court held that once the content of 'adequate medical treatment' had been established, a claim that it was unaffordable was not a defence to the applicant's assertion of the right.[26] Thus, noting that the DCS had failed to establish that it could not afford to provide the combination anti-viral therapy, the court held that the failure to provide this treatment to the first and second applicants infringed their s 35(2)(*e*) right to 'adequate medical

---

[22] Ibid.

[23] *Kwakwa* (note 3 above) para 35.

[24] *Van Biljon and Others v Minister of Correctional Services* 1997 (4) SA 441 (C) [LRC acted for the applicants].

[25] Ibid para 54.

[26] Ibid para 49. Brand J held, however, that financial conditions or budgetary constraints were not irrelevant and that they might reasonably preclude access to 'the best available treatment', a prisoner only being entitled to the 'adequate medical treatment'.

treatment'. The court ordered that the applicants be provided with the prescribed anti-viral therapy.[27]

The High Court has made it clear, that, where a national policy on HIV treatment fails to accommodate the urgent needs of HIV positive prisoners, such policy cannot be relied upon. In *EN and Others v Government of South Africa*,[28] Pillay J ordered the government to attend to the specific needs of certain HIV-positive prisoners by immediately providing them with antiretroviral treatment. The court noted that the government's national plan to realise progressively the needs of the 'less fortunate' HIV-positive people in the country was simply insufficient when it came to the needs of certain prisoners.[29] Accordingly, the respondents had 'fallen short of their constitutional and legislative obligations to the applicants'.[30]

Vitally important jurisprudence concerning prisoner health arose from the delictual claim against the state in *Lee*.[31] Mr Lee contracted tuberculosis (TB) after four and a half years awaiting trial at Pollsmoor Prison. He instituted an action for delictual damages against the Minister for Correctional Services, on the basis that the negligent or intentional failure of the prison authorities to meet their constitutional obligations in ss 12(1) and 35(2)*(e)* and ensure reasonably adequate systems to manage the disease, caused his active TB infection. The High Court found that the DCS was aware of the overcrowding and poor ventilation in Pollsmoor Prison but had failed to take measures to prevent the spread of TB. The court declared the Minister for Correctional Services liable to Mr Lee in delict and ordered her to pay costs.[32] The Minister successfully appealed to the SCA who held that on the pleaded facts and evidence Mr Lee had failed to show the necessary causation. The SCA noted, however, that Mr Lee had met all the other elements of a delictual action. The matter proceeded to the Constitutional Court for determination of the factual issue of causation. The Constitutional Court confirmed:

> That there is a duty on Correctional Services authorities to provide adequate health care services, as part of the constitutional right of all prisoners to 'conditions of detention that are consistent with human dignity', *is beyond dispute.*[33]

---

[27] See also *B and Others v Minister of Correctional Services and Others* 1997 (6) BCLR 789 (C).

[28] *EN and Others v Government of South Africa* 2007 (1) BCLR 84 (D) [TAC was an applicant].

[29] Ibid paras 29–31. Albertus makes a convincing argument in favour of the right to palliative care in Chesne Albertus 'Palliative care for terminally ill inmates: Does the State have a legal obligation?' 2012 *SACJ* 67.

[30] *EN* (note 28 above) para 31.

[31] *Lee v Minister of Correctional Services* [2012] ZACC 30; 2013 (2) SA 144 (CC) [TAC, Wits Justice Project and CALS were admitted as *amici curiae*; SECTION 27 acted for the *amici curiae*].

[32] The parties had agreed to a separation of the issues relating to liability from those relating to the quantum of damages. The High Court remitted the matter for a determination on the issue of quantum.

[33] *Lee* (note 31 above) para 56.

The court described the extent of the state's obligations to provide health care services as those required for 'every inmate to lead a healthy life'.[34] There have also been numerous instances of the state being held delictually liable for damages arising from prisoners suffering injuries as a result of being assaulted by other prisoners. State officials owe a duty of care to prisoners, which duty, courts have held, is breached when officials fail to search and disarm prisoners regularly, resulting in injury;[35] fail to separate certain prisoners from others following altercations;[36] fail to take steps to prevent known violent prisoners from attacking others;[37] and fail to take steps to protect vulnerable prisoners.[38]

(c) Education

In *Hennie*,[39] the Pretoria High Court considered whether the DCS' prohibition of prisoners' use of laptops for study purposes within single cells would breach the right to education[40] and a detainee's right to reading material.[41] The court, recognising that 'personal computers [had] in many ways replaced conventional textbooks', held that access to a personal computer by students was a 'necessity and not a privilege'.[42] The respondents' concerns regarding security, the court noted, could easily be assuaged by imposing certain restrictions on the use of personal computers. Accordingly, the court held that the applicants were indeed permitted to use their personal computers for study purposes on the condition that they make such computers available for inspection at any time and that the use of computers exclude the use of a modem.[43]

14.4 LITIGATION TO ENFORCE OTHER RIGHTS OF PRISONERS

In addition to litigation relating to conditions of detention under s 35(2)*(e)*, there have been attempts to enforce other constitutional rights of prisoners through the courts. Four important areas of litigation in this regard concern the right to vote,

---

[34] Ibid para 70.

[35] *Tyatya v Minister of Correctional Services* [2014] ZAECPEHC 8; [2015] JOL 32718 (ECP); *Spence v Minister of Correctional Services* [2017] ZAECPEHC 46.

[36] *Jaftha v Minister of Correctional Services* [2012] ZAECPEHC 15; [2012] 2 All SA 286 (ECP).

[37] *Mxolisi v Minister of Correctional Services* [2008] ZAGPHC 107; [2008] JOL 21669 (W).

[38] *Spence* (note 35 above).

[39] *Hennie and Others v Minister of Correctional Services and Others* [2015] ZAGPPHC 311.

[40] Section 29 of the Constitution.

[41] Section 35(2)*(e)*.

[42] *Hennie* (note 39 above) para 28.

[43] Several years earlier the High Court considered a prisoner's right to education in *Thukwane* (note 5 above). The DCS had prohibited the applicant from accessing the Internet and from using study facilities outside the prison for the purposes of furthering his education. The court held that the prison authorities were entitled to place restrictions on any subject/course study field prejudicial to the security, good order or administration of the prison or which is contrary to the objectives of the Correctional Services Act and the aim of imprisonment.

privacy rights, the right to just administrative action and rights relating to parole. We briefly discuss some of the most important cases in each of these areas.

(a) Voting
One particularly controversial question that has come before the Constitutional Court is the right of prisoners to vote. In *NICRO*,[44] the provisions of the Electoral Act 73 of 1998 were challenged on the basis that they excluded from voting prisoners who were serving terms of imprisonment without the option of a fine.[45] The court dismissed the state's argument that prohibiting certain categories of prisoners from voting was necessary for both logistical reasons and in order to be seen as being 'tough on crime,' finding that the right to vote, 'which must be vigilantly respected and protected,' had been unjustifiably infringed.[46]

(b) Privacy
The High Court has considered the right to privacy of trial awaiting prisoners in *Pretorius*.[47] The applicants complained of the noise generated by centrally controlled speakers in their cells broadcasting a radio channel at a 'considerable' decibel level for more than 12 hours per day. The court made it clear that as trial awaiting prisoners, the applicants were entitled to the full measure of their constitutional rights that are not lawfully restricted as a result of their incarceration.[48] This, the court reasoned, meant that the applicants were entitled to as much of their right to privacy as possible in the circumstances. The right to privacy, the court found, includes the right of choice of radio and television channels as well as the right not to have one's personal space invaded by a broadcast to which he or she has not consented.[49]

(c) Just administrative action
Prisoners have also sought to rely on their rights to fair and just administrative action in challenging the decisions of the DCS.

---

[44] *Minister of Home Affairs v National Institute for Crime Prevention and the Re-integration of Offenders and Others* [2004] ZACC 10; 2005 (3) SA 280 (CC) [LRC acted for the first to third respondents] (*NICRO*).

[45] The court had previously recognised the fundamental constitutional importance of the right to vote in *August and Another v Electoral Commission and Others* [1999] ZACC 3; 1999 (3) SA 1 (CC) [LRC acted for the applicants; CALS was admitted as *amicus curiae*]. In that matter the court declared unconstitutional administrative action that would have deprived prisoners of the right to vote. However, the court carefully left open the question whether legislation disqualifying prisoners or categories of prisoners from voting could be justified in terms of the limitations clause.

[46] *NICRO* (note 44 above) para 47. The court referred to the renowned Canadian case, *Sauvé v Canada (Chief Electoral Officer)* [2002] 3 SCR 519.

[47] *Pretorius and Others v Minister of Correctional Services and Others* 2004 (2) SA 658 (T).

[48] Ibid para 38.

[49] Ibid.

In *Ehrlich*,[50] the applicant challenged the Head of Prison's decision to prohibit medium-category offenders from accessing the prison gymnasium located at the maximum-security section of the prison, a decision that had been based on the ground that it was necessary to segregate the different categories of prisoners. The court found that the decision had been based on an error of law, for the Correctional Services Act requires strict separation in respect of sleeping accommodation only, and specifically provides for the mixing of categories for the purpose of 'providing development services'.[51] The court held, accordingly, that the applicant's right to just administrative action had been infringed and set aside the decision.

In *Nortjé*,[52] the SCA made it clear that legitimate expectations should also embrace the requirement of procedurally fair hearings when decisions are taken that will result in a substantial limitation of privileges. In this case, the process of transferring a prisoner from a medium-security section of a prison to a maximum-security area, where no prior notice was given to the appellants, was found to have been taken unlawfully for having failed to comply with the *audi alteram partem* rule. The case of *Tshikane* also concerned the transfer of a prisoner without notice.[53] In this case, the court stated:

> [T]he conduct of the respondents . . . was not only not in accordance with rights in sec 35(2) of the Constitution [or the Act and its regulations. . . . and], but was equally in violation of the principles of natural justice, particularly the *audi alteram partem* rule.[54]

(d) Parole

The most frequently litigated subject in the South African penal field is parole. The backlogs in processing inmates' parole applications, particularly in relation to offenders serving sentences of life imprisonment,[55] result in many inmates waiting for years for a decision on whether they will be released from prison.[56] There has also been considerable litigation regarding the refusal of release on parole. Courts

---

[50] *Ehrlich v Minister of Correctional Services and Another* [2008] ZAECHC 33; 2009 (2) SA 373 (E).

[51] Ibid para 40.

[52] *Nortjé en 'n ander v Minister van Korrektiewe Dienste* [2001] ZASCA 20; 2001 (3) SA 472 (SCA).

[53] *Tshikane v Minister of Correctional Services and Others* [2014] ZAGPJHC 261; [2015] 1 All SA 384 (GJ).

[54] Ibid para 11.

[55] Offenders serving sentences of life imprisonment are subject to a more rigorous and lengthy parole determination process. The Act requires that, in addition to the parole board, the National Council for Correctional Services as well as the Minister are required to consider whether an offender is eligible for release on parole.

[56] See, eg, *Gwebu v Minister of Correctional Services and Others* [2013] ZAGPPHC 205; 2014 (1) SACR 191 (GNP); *Groenewald v Minister of Correctional Services and Others* [2010] ZAGPPHC 6; 2011 (1) SACR 231 (GNP); *Derby-Lewis v Minister of Correctional Services and Others* [2009]

have found the following actions on the part of the DCS and the Minister of Justice and Correctional Services to be unlawful, unreasonable and procedurally unfair:

1. The Minister's refusal to give reasons when refusing parole.[57]
2. The Minister's insistence on a second medical opinion, when the applicant's application for release on medical parole contained a medical opinion confirming his suitability for release.[58]
3. The Minister's misinterpretation of a medical report and the failure to consider the rights to dignity and to be detained in conditions consistent with human dignity, in considering an application for release on medical parole.[59]
4. The Parole Board's insistence that parole could be delayed on account of a 'restorative justice aspect'—something on which the Correctional Services Act is wholly silent—not having been concluded prior to the parole application.[60]
5. The Parole Board's insistence that an inmate's parole application must be delayed on account of certain reports being outstanding. This approach, the court stated, did not take into account the applicant's right to liberty.[61]
6. The Minister's failure to consider the various instances of the applicant's displays of remorse.[62]

14.5 CHALLENGES AND POTENTIAL REFORM IN THE ADVANCEMENT OF PRISONERS' RIGHTS THROUGH PUBLIC INTEREST LITIGATION

(a) The nature of prisons and the problems associated with incarceration

There is an obvious and extreme gap between the legally required standards of treatment in the Bill of Rights and the reality experienced by inmates of prisons in South Africa. Moreover, the problems associated with prisons are systemic in nature and, accordingly, tend to be ongoing. This also means that a vast number of inmates are affected on a daily basis, but most are not able to access individual legal assistance to remedy the violation of their rights. Redress can therefore only be effective from a PIL point of view if it can address any offending legislation and the existing (but faulty) frameworks—be it legislation or policy—that govern the prisons setting.

ZAGPPHC 7; 2009 (2) SACR 522 (GNP); *Mbonani v Minister of Correctional Services* 2011 JDR 1290 (GNP).

[57] *Du Plooy v Minister of Correctional Services and Others* 2004 (3) All SA 613 (T).

[58] *Mazibuko v Minister of Correctional Services and Others* 2007 (2) SACR 303 (T).

[59] *Stanfield v Minister of Correctional Services and Others* [2003] ZAWCHC 46; 2003 4 All SA 282 (C).

[60] *Gwebu* (note 56 above).

[61] *Groenewald* (note 56 above).

[62] *Derby-Lewis* (note 56 above).

In this section we describe some of the fundamental obstacles in relation to strategic litigation that beset the penal environment. We also examine, briefly, the most pressing concerns within this environment and suggest how strategic litigation might address these.

(b) Lack of a dedicated lobby

Over the last 20 years, South Africa's public interest sector has failed to establish a dedicated and persistent lobby to engage in strategic litigation on prisoner rights.[63] Among the public interest organisations operating in South Africa, only LHR has a dedicated penal reform programme,[64] with other organisations such as the LRC and SERI taking on these cases only on a limited and ad hoc basis. No clear reason for this is apparent, but certainly, the general retributive feeling amongst South Africans in the face of extremely high levels of violent crime is an important factor.[65] So too are the practical difficulties and resources required to represent prisoners incarcerated in prisons and the obvious constraints inmates themselves face in organising their own advocacy campaigns.

The lack of a specialist organisation to monitor and coordinate this litigation means that that litigation has taken place on an ad hoc and piecemeal basis with no overarching strategy. Few test cases are identified and prosecuted. Where public interest organisations have the capacity and interest to intervene, they have, in the past, mostly represented other specific interest groups or the general public.[66] There are, therefore, some unique complexities when it comes to cases involving inmates. In many cases, inmates launch urgent motion proceedings in the High Court without legal representation and with the intention of appearing in person at the hearing. These applications are often poorly pleaded and no evidence is adduced to substantiate the serious allegations of rights violations or to provide the court with sufficient information to fully comprehend the inmate's complaint. In addition, the application may not be properly served on the relevant parties. Recently, Moshidi J highlighted the range of difficulties the courts face when dealing with these applications, and noted that they compound to hinder the fair

---

[63] Pierre de Vos 'Prisoners' rights litigation in South Africa since 1994: A critical evaluation' (2003) CSPRI Research Paper No 3 ss 6.1 and 6.2.

[64] See LHR website at <www.lhr.org.za/programme/penal-reform-programme>, last accessed on 20 April 2018. One of the current authors, Clare Ballard, is the Programme Head: Penal Reform Programme at LHR. The programme, based in Cape Town, was established in July 2014 amid concerns for the protection of the rights of prisoners and detainees and constitutional compliance in relation to the imposition of punishment, sentencing, independent oversight and conditions of detention. Particular areas of interest include prison overcrowding, independent oversight and sentencing reform.

[65] Clare Ballard & Ram Subramanian 'Lessons from the past: Remand detention and pre-trial services' (2013) 44 *SA Crime Quarterly*.

[66] For example, in *Lee* (note 31 above), it was the TAC, Wits Justice Project and Centre for Applied Legal Studies that acted as *amicus curiae*, represented by SECTION27. In *EN* (note 28 above) the ALP represented the prisoners.

adjudication of the merits of the applications.[67] Even once an inmate has done enough to have his or her application heard, in many cases DCS, as the respondent in the matter, is unable or unwilling to properly respond to litigation, or to comply with court orders.[68] In some cases, DCS appears to actively frustrate the litigation by raising technical points in limine on locus standi or joinder, objecting to evidence, or putting the applicants to the proof in respect of issues where DCS clearly has knowledge of the true facts. Individual prisoners will also be induced to settle cases with DCS in order to obtain certain and speedy redress. This leaves the legal questions unresolved and does not assist the many other inmates affected by the conduct.

(c) Poor jurisprudence

A further constraint is that the courts are reluctant to quantify constitutional minimum standards.[69] In other areas of PIL, test cases guide the development of

---

[67] *Tshikane* (note 53 above) para 2:
'[A]pplications are launched in the motion court, and mostly in the urgent court with increasing frequency. Common in the features of the applications, is the relief for transfer to another prison; resistance against transfer . . . parole; copies of transcripts of trial records; and access to certain facilities. In all the applications, the applicants appear in person, and without legal representation. The result is that the papers [are] often prepared in a defective manner, in several respects. In several instances, the founding affidavits were not commissioned at all. The more recent reason advanced for this deficiency is that the prison officials detest the litigation which leads to their refusal to attest the affidavits. It was also not unusual for the applicants to contend that they are lay litigants. In other instances, the applications are not served on the respondents timeously or at all. Where service was effected, the State Attorney sometimes failed to respond until at the hearing. As a result, the proper adjudication of the merits of the matter became compounded. In addition, these kind of applications quite often have to be dealt with on a priority basis, namely the first day of the motion court. The obvious reason for this was that the applicants are escorted by prison warders, and have to return to prison in time. There are therefore, not only security issues involved, but also administrative and cost factors. In many applications of this nature, the applicants often either omitted to provide full details of their transgressions and circumstances, or supply scanty information. This resulted in the court finding it difficult to comprehend fully their plight . . .'

[68] De Vos (note 63 above) s 5.

[69] See, eg, *Mazibuko and Others v City of Johannesburg and Others* [2009] ZACC 28; 2010 (4) SA 1 (CC) [CALS/Wits Law Project and the FXI acted for the applicants; COHRE was admitted as *amicus curiae*, represented by the LRC]. There is, however, international precedent for this approach. As Steinberg notes in J Steinberg 'Prison overcrowding and the constitutional right to adequate accommodation in South Africa' (2005) CSVR Paper 19:
'The Council of Europe's CPT has established four square metres per prisoner as a minimum in a communal cell, six square metres in single cells. In the United States, both the American Correctional Association and the American Public Health Association have set standards requiring a minimum of 60 square feet (18.18 square metres) per prisoner. These latter standards have found their way into United States federal regulations; the Bureau of Prisons has used them to establish the rated capacity of its prisons. (In the United States, rated capacity reflects the number of inmates that can be housed safely in a facility.) Courts have used these standards to establish judicially enforceable minima. In the state of Florida, for instance, it is illegal for a prison to exceed its rated capacity. A similar situation prevails in Norway and Holland. In these jurisdictions, the size of the prison population is directly determined by available space.'

the jurisprudence to determine the scope and practical implications of specific rights in the Bill of Rights. However, prisoner rights litigation often arises from judicial review or delictual actions where no formal declaration of the violation of constitutional standards is required. The lack of properly pleaded and conceptualised test cases contributes to this dearth of jurisprudence. The courts have, however, in a number of cases, imposed reporting obligations on the Department by way of interdicts.[70]

(d) Key areas for reform

(i) *Overcrowding and its knock-on effects*

The Judicial Inspectorate for Correctional Services' (JICS) 2016/2017 Annual Report makes it clear that many of the country's prisons are overcrowded and that 'it remains the norm that some centres are grossly overcrowded'. Overcrowding results in 'the poor quality of treatment and the appalling conditions under which inmates are living. . . . [S]uch conditions remain below the acceptable standard when measured against the Bill of Rights and international Human Rights standards'.[71]

Prison overcrowding is a multifaceted issue, the causes of which are linked to a vast array of factors including sentencing, arrest, prosecution policy and prison management. Most of these factors are linked to the stages between arrest and the imposition of punishment, that is, the functioning of the entire criminal justice system, as opposed to the role of a single department, Correctional Services.

The rate of overcrowding has hovered between 130% and 137% capacity over the last decade.[72] It is important to note, however, that an increase in sentenced admissions is not the cause of overcrowding. In fact, South Africa is sending fewer people to prison today than it was just over 20 years ago.[73] The more fundamental shift has been in the profile of the prison population. In 1995 there were 443

---

[70] See, eg *Strydom* (note 20 above) where the court imposed an obligation on the Department to report to court with a timetable within which the electrical upgrades would take place. In *S v Z en vier ander sake* 1999 (1) SACR 427 (E) the Department of Education was ordered to plan and present to the court the building of a reform school. In *EN* (note 28 above) para 4 of the order, the court imposed an obligation to report on steps taken to provide treatment to affected inmates.

[71] Judicial Inspectorate for Correctional Services *Annual Report 2016/2017* (2017) 76.

[72] The prison population figures are recorded annually in the annual reports for the DCS and the JICS. Averages can be misleading, however. The occupancy rates of individual prisons paint a far clearer picture of the conditions of detention to which inmates are subjected. The JICS acknowledges this in its 2011/2012 report when it stated:

'although overcrowding on a national level is reflected in an occupancy level of 133 per cent, there is a vast difference between overcrowding in individual centres, with some centres extremely overcrowded and some operating below capacity.'

It is therefore unsurprising that the provinces with the highest occupancy rates have the country's most overcrowded prisons, which range between 200 and 290% capacity (statistics sourced from JICS Annual Reports).

[73] In 1995, people were being sentenced to terms of imprisonment at a rate of almost 290 people per 100 000. In 2015 that figure was 210. Statistics are sourced from DCS and JICS annual reports.

offenders serving sentences of life imprisonment, less than 0.5% of the total sentenced population.[74] In 2016, there were more than 18 000.[75] That is an increase of around 4 400%. We think that these figures explain why the prison population, despite the reduction in sentenced admissions, has increased by 24% during the same period. Although fewer people are being sent to prison, those sentenced are spending much longer there than ever before. Undoubtedly, the most important contributing factor to the change in the sentenced population was the establishment of mandatory minimum sentencing legislation—the Criminal Law Amendment Act 105 of 1997 (CLAA), which drastically reduced sentencing courts' discretion to depart from long-term sentences for a variety of serious crimes. The constitutionality of the CLAA was challenged, unsuccessfully, in *S v Dodo*,[76] rendering the scope for a future challenge much narrower. Nevertheless, such a challenge is not entirely off the cards since a body of evidence has been amassed in respect of the CLAA's inability to carry out one of its primary objectives—the deterrence of crime—as well as its adverse effects on inmates and the prison system as a whole.[77]

Another driving factor behind overcrowding is remand detention. The JICS has lamented the plight of remand detainees in every one of its annual reports since 2000. The JICS' 2011/2012 Annual Report indicated that in prisons where overcrowding has reached a 'critical' level, remand detainees accounted for 52% of the inmate population. On 31 March 2016 the awaiting trial population was 45 257, approximately 30% of the total inmate population and almost double the Department's benchmark of 25 000. This is particularly worrying, given the likelihood that approximately half of those in remand detention will be released due to acquittal or have the charges against them withdrawn.[78]

To the extent that overcrowding is a consequence of an accused being refused bail on account of the seriousness of the crime, the current bail regime as established by the Criminal Procedure Act 51 of 1977 (CPA) is partly to blame. The controversial 'reverse onus' provision in the CPA makes it extremely difficult for an accused charged of certain offences to be released on bail.[79] A constitutional

---

[74] Department of Correctional Services *Annual Report* 1995/1996.

[75] Comment from DCS spokesperson during 2017.

[76] *S v Dodo* [2001] ZACC 16; 2001 (3) SA 382 (CC).

[77] See, eg, L Muntingh & C Giffard 'The effect of sentencing on the size of the prison population' (2006) CSPRI and OSF Occasional Paper; M O'Donovan & J Redpath 'Reaching a verdict: The impact of minimum sentencing' (2007) 19 *South African Crime Quarterly*; J Sloth-Nielsen & L Ehlers 'Mandatory and minimum sentences in SA' (2005) ISS Paper.

[78] Vanja Karth 'Between a rock and a hard place: Bail decisions in three South African courts' (2008) Research paper prepared for the Open Society Foundation for South Africa, Cape Town.

[79] Section 60(11) of the CPA states:
'Notwithstanding any provision of this Act, where an accused is charged with an offence referred to—

challenge to these provisions failed.[80] However, in our view there is scope to revisit the bail regime, given the lengthy period of time many accused are compelled to spend behind bars awaiting trial.[81] It has been argued that this practice may infringe the liberty provision of the Constitution requiring detention to be imposed with just cause and not arbitrarily.[82] The burden on the state to justify the continued detention of trial awaiting prisoners becomes greater with the passage of time. Put differently, the reasons that initially justified remand detention will at a certain point no longer constitute sufficient justification for continued remand detention.[83] The current legislative framework does not require that bail decisions be brought before courts repeatedly and at regular intervals. A legislative amendment requiring automatic review would not only promote the robust jurisprudential protection of the right to liberty but also remedy the current failure of the CPA to protect a remand detainee's right not to be detained arbitrarily or without just cause adequately. A PIL strategy targeting key cases at High Court level could also target the incremental development of jurisprudence whereby courts are required to interrogate the state's progress more robustly.

(e) Human rights violations

Because inmates are wholly dependent on the state, it is not surprising that the complaints emanating from the prison population are extremely varied. Indeed, the complaints recorded annually range from the quality and quantity of food, delays in the parole process and prison transfers, access to amenities, poor health care and inadequate access to education. We have chosen to highlight prison

---

    (a) in Schedule 6, the court shall order that the accused be detained in custody until he or she is dealt with in accordance with the law, unless the accused, having been given a reasonable opportunity to do so, adduces evidence which satisfies the court that exceptional circumstances exist which in the interests of justice permit his or her release;

    (b) in Schedule 5, but not in Schedule 6, the court shall order that the accused be detained in custody until he or she is dealt with in accordance with the law, unless the accused, having been given a reasonable opportunity to do so, adduces evidence which satisfies the court that the interests of justice permit his or her release.'

  See generally MG Cowling 'The incidence and nature of an onus in bail application' 2002 *SACJ* 176.

[80] *S v Dlamini*; *S v Dladla and Others*; *S v Joubert*; *S v Schietekat* [1999] ZACC 8; 1999 (4) SA 623 (CC).

[81] On 31 March 2010, more than one third of remand detainees had spent 2 to 6 months in custody; approximately 5 000 had spent 6 to 9 months in custody; almost 3 000 had spent 12 to 15 months in custody; and just less than 2 000 had been in remand detention for more than 2 years. Department of Correctional Services *2009/2010 Annual Report* (2010) 30.

[82] Although haphazard, there is South African case law supporting the position that the longer a remand detainee is kept in custody pending trial, the greater the infringement on his or her right to liberty will be. See, eg *S v Yanta* 2000 (1) SACR 237 (Tk); *S v Mpofana* 1998 (1) SACR 40 (Tk); *S v Kok* 2003 (2) SACR 5 (SCA). See also the Zimbabwean case of *S v Hitschmann* 2007 (2) SACR 110 (ZH).

[83] See Clare Ballard 'A statute of liberty? The right to bail and a case for legislative reform' 2012 *SACJ* 24.

violence in this section as a priority issue for future PIL. Not only do the assault and torture of inmates amount to criminal offences, but the state also has a clear international treaty obligation to combat and prevent such crimes.[84] Moreover, insofar as our ideas for reform to combat prison violence relate to the restructuring of the existing complaints mechanisms, such recommendations are equally applicable to all inmate concerns and complaints.

The consistently high number of complaints of assaults recorded by the DCS over several years indicates that violence is a 'normal' feature of the South African prison system.[85]

Table illustrating the number of inmates injured as a result of assaults[86]

YEAR	TOTAL NUMBER OF ASSAULTS
2011–2012	5 284
2012–2013	6 884
2013–2014	7 370
2014–2015	7 850
2015–2016	8 801
2016–2017	7 338

The number of complaints relating to official-on-inmate assaults is also alarmingly high. Importantly, the JICS does not identify which assaults amount to torture. Given that the definition of torture adopted by the South African legislature mirrors that of the UNCAT,[87] it is difficult to imagine a scenario where assaults within this category that do not amount to the justified use of force, would *not* amount to torture.

---

[84] Torture was, however, only legislated to be a domestic offence in 2013. See the Combating and Prevention of Torture of Persons Act 13 of 2013 (Prevention of Torture Act).

[85] L Muntingh 'Reducing prison violence: Implications from the literature for South Africa' (2009) CSPRI Research Report No. 17 15.

[86] Statistics are sourced from the DCS' Annual Reports. The Department does not delineate between official-on-inmate and inmate-on-inmate assaults.

[87] Section 3 of the Prevention of Torture Act states:
'torture' means any act by which severe pain or suffering, whether physical or mental, is intentionally inflicted on a person—
(a) for such purposes as to—
   (i) obtain information or a confession from him or her or any other person;
   (ii) punish him or her for an act he or she or any other person has committed, is suspected of having committed or is planning to commit; or
   (iii) intimidate or coerce him or her or any other person to do, or to refrain from doing, anything; or
(b) for any reason based on discrimination of any kind,
when such pain or suffering is inflicted by or at the instigation of, or with the consent or acquiescence of a public official or other person acting in an official capacity, but does not include pain or suffering arising only from, inherent in or incidental to lawful sanctions.'

Table illustrating the number of inmates injured as a result of official-on-inmate assaults

YEAR	OFFICIAL-ON-INMATE ASSAULTS
2011–2012	3 940
2012–2013	6 144
2013–2014	9 145
2014–2015	6 606

The fact that inmates are entirely dependent on the state for protection and care means that there is a positive obligation on the state to take appropriate steps to protect inmates against violations of their constitutional rights.[88] Furthermore, the obligation on the state to 'respect, protect, promote and fulfil' the rights in the Bill of Rights gives rise to a duty to establish and maintain an efficient prison oversight mechanism in order to secure accountability of the DCS for the treatment of inmates and prevent the violation of their human rights. Institutions charged with such duties must be 'sufficiently detached from the authority alleged to have perpetrated the ill-treatment to be deemed impartial'.[89] It would appear that, at the very least, institutional independence requires both financial and administrative independence.[90]

The JICS, an 'independent office under the control of the Inspecting Judge', is the institution tasked with the inspection of correctional centres for the purpose of reporting on the treatment of inmates.[91] It is also tasked with investigating the complaints of inmates, which it does primarily by deploying a lay visitor to each prison to record and follow up on inmate complaints. The JICS lacks both financial and administrative independence, and, thus, over the years has come under scrutiny for not having full independence from the Department on which it is mandated to report.[92] Although the Correctional Services Act guarantees the

---

[88] Section 2(1)(*b*) of the Correctional Services Act states that inmates must be detained 'in safe custody whilst ensuring their human dignity'.

[89] Interim Report of the Special Rapporteur on Torture and Other Cruel, Inhuman or Degrading Treatment or Punishment (a/68/295), 19 August 2013 para 76. See also the following 'soft law' principles: United Nations Body of Principles for the Protection of All Persons Under Any Form of Detention or Imprisonment, Principle 29.1; arts 17–43 of the Robben Island Guidelines for the Prohibition and Prevention of Torture in Africa; arts 57(3), 71(1)–(2) and 83(1)–(2) of the United Nations *Standard Minimum Rules for the Treatment of Prisoners*; and art 18 of the UNGA *Optional Protocol to the Convention Against Torture and other Cruel, Inhuman and Degrading Treatment or Punishment*, entered into force 9 January 2003, UN Doc A/RES/57/199 .

[90] See the Constitutional Court decisions of *New National Party of South Africa v Government of the Republic of South Africa and Others* [1999] ZACC 5; 1999 (3) SA 191 (CC) and *Glenister v President of the Republic of South Africa and Others* [2011] ZACC 6; 2011 (3) SA 347 (CC) [HSF was admitted as *amicus curiae*, represented by WW].

[91] Section 85 of the Correctional Services Act.

[92] Both the Independent Police Investigative Directorate and the Public Protector draw their funding from their own respective parliamentary budget votes. See the Public Protector Act 23 of 1994 and Independent Police Investigative Directorate Act 1 of 2011.

independence of the JICS, the same act also states that the Department is responsible for all the expenses of the JICS.[93] The effects of the JICS' dependence on the Department are not only theoretical. It has impacted negatively on the ability of the JICS to function effectively by rendering the JICS under-capacitated due to a lack of funds required to fill essential posts, which, in turn, limits its effectiveness in carrying out its inspection and investigative mandates.[94] A 2015 research report, 'Human rights violations and South Africa's law enforcement— assessing investigation processes by oversight mechanisms',[95] noted the following in respect of the 2013/2014 financial year:

> Out of the 21 investigations [the JICS] conducted . . . nine related to official-on- inmate assaults (43% of all JICS investigations but only 8% of the total number of assaults reported to JICS during that financial year). The number of investigations conducted is much lower than the number of incidents reported to JICS, reportedly due to limited human resources.

It is perhaps unsurprising then that there have been very few prosecutions for the assault of inmates and not one for the offence of torture.[96]

The unique complexities of litigating for prisoner rights mean that progress is slow. Moreover, given the range, complexity, and degree of prisoners' needs, and the scarcity of litigious resources, a strategy that can assist only a small number of affected inmates is somewhat futile. PIL could in future successfully assist the broad range of inmates' needs by challenging the failures of the existing oversight mechanisms established to monitor the fulfilment of prisoners' rights. Effective oversight of prisons, the experience of inmates and the Department will be an important first step in the fulfilment of prisoner rights.

---

[93] Sections 85 and 91 of the Correctional Services Act.

[94] Over the years, the JICS's annual reports have consistently and repeatedly described and lamented its lack of resources and the effects thereof. See in particular its annual reports for the years 2011/2012, 2012/2013 (Foreword and pages 13–15, 20). 2013/2014 (23–5), 2014/2015 (15, 22), 2015/2016 (p 33, 40).

[95] CSPRI and APCOF (2015) 37–8.

[96] In late October 2014, Parliament put forward a question to the Minister of Justice and Correc- tional Services regarding assaults on prisoners by prison officials and subsequent convictions. The response illustrated a large disparity. In the 2011–2012 financial year, officials assaulted 609 prisoners, while 6 officials were convicted. The 2012–2013 financial year saw 943 such assaults, but only 10 convictions. In 2013–2014, there were 1 298 officer assaults on prisoners, and 19 convictions (with 2 of these convictions in the form of suspended sentences). Finally, from 1 March 2014 up until the date of the Minister's response, there were 590 assaults by prison officials on prisoners, and 5 convictions. In total during this time period, therefore, 3 440 prisoners were assaulted by correctional officials while only 40 such assaults resulted in a conviction of the official.

INDEX